Business Analytics and Cyber Security Management in Organizations

Rajagopal
*EGADE Business School, Tecnologico de Monterrey, Mexico City, Mexico &
Boston University, USA*

Ramesh Behl
International Management Institute, Bhubaneswar, India

A volume in the Advances in Business Information
Systems and Analytics (ABISA) Book Series

www.igi-global.com

Published in the United States of America by
    IGI Global
    Business Science Reference (an imprint of IGI Global)
    701 E. Chocolate Avenue
    Hershey PA, USA 17033
    Tel: 717-533-8845
    Fax: 717-533-8661
    E-mail: cust@igi-global.com
    Web site: http://www.igi-global.com

Library of Congress Cataloging-in-Publication Data

Names: Rajagopal, 1957- editor. | Behl, Ramesh, editor.
Title: Business analytics and cyber security management in organizations /
  Rajagopal and Ramesh Behl, editors.
Description: Hershey : Business Science Reference, 2016. | Series: Advances
  in business information systems and analytic | Includes bibliographical
  references and index.
Identifiers: LCCN 2016028048| ISBN 9781522509028 (hardcover) | ISBN
  9781522509035 (ebook)
Subjects: LCSH: Business intelligence. | Electronic commerce. |
  Cyberspace--Security measures.
Classification: LCC HD38.7 .B866 2016 | DDC 658/.05--dc23 LC record available at https://lccn.loc.gov/2016028048

This book is published in the IGI Global book series Advances in Business Information Systems and Analytics (ABISA) (ISSN: 2327-3275; eISSN: 2327-3283)

For electronic access to this publication, please contact: eresources@igi-global.com.

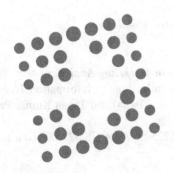

Advances in Business Information Systems and Analytics (ABISA) Book Series

Madjid Tavana
La Salle University, USA

ISSN:2327-3275
EISSN:2327-3283

MISSION

The successful development and management of information systems and business analytics is crucial to the success of an organization. New technological developments and methods for data analysis have allowed organizations to not only improve their processes and allow for greater productivity, but have also provided businesses with a venue through which to cut costs, plan for the future, and maintain competitive advantage in the information age.

The **Advances in Business Information Systems and Analytics (ABISA) Book Series** aims to present diverse and timely research in the development, deployment, and management of business information systems and business analytics for continued organizational development and improved business value.

COVERAGE

- Information Logistics
- Business Models
- Forecasting
- Data Strategy
- Decision Support Systems
- Business Decision Making
- Business Process Management
- Legal information systems
- Geo-BIS
- Statistics

IGI Global is currently accepting manuscripts for publication within this series. To submit a proposal for a volume in this series, please contact our Acquisition Editors at Acquisitions@igi-global.com or visit: http://www.igi-global.com/publish/.

Titles in this Series

For a list of additional titles in this series, please visit: www.igi-global.com

Handbook of Research on Intelligent Techniques and Modeling Applications in Marketing Analytics
Anil Kumar (BML Munjal University, India) Manoj Kumar Dash (ABV-Indian Institute of Information Technology and Management, India) Shrawan Kumar Trivedi (BML Munjal University, India) and Tapan Kumar Panda (BML Munjal University, India)
Business Science Reference • copyright 2017 • 428pp • H/C (ISBN: 9781522509974) • US $275.00 (our price)

Applied Big Data Analytics in Operations Management
Manish Kumar (Indian Institute of Information Technology, Allahabad, India)
Business Science Reference • copyright 2017 • 251pp • H/C (ISBN: 9781522508861) • US $160.00 (our price)

Eye-Tracking Technology Applications in Educational Research
Christopher Was (Kent State University, USA) Frank Sansosti (Kent State University, USA) and Bradley Morris (Kent State University, USA)
Information Science Reference • copyright 2017 • 370pp • H/C (ISBN: 9781522510055) • US $205.00 (our price)

Strategic IT Governance and Alignment in Business Settings
Steven De Haes (Antwerp Management School, University of Antwerp, Belgium) and Wim Van Grembergen (Antwerp Management School, University of Antwerp, Belgium)
Business Science Reference • copyright 2017 • 298pp • H/C (ISBN: 9781522508618) • US $195.00 (our price)

Organizational Productivity and Performance Measurements Using Predictive Modeling and Analytics
Madjid Tavana (La Salle University, USA) Kathryn Szabat (La Salle University, USA) and Kartikeya Puranam (La Salle University, USA)
Business Science Reference • copyright 2017 • 400pp • H/C (ISBN: 9781522506546) • US $205.00 (our price)

Data Envelopment Analysis and Effective Performance Assessment
Farhad Hossein Zadeh Lotfi (Islamic Azad University, Iran) Seyed Esmaeil Najafi (Islamic Azad University, Iran) and Hamed Nozari (Islamic Azad University, Iran)
Business Science Reference • copyright 2017 • 365pp • H/C (ISBN: 9781522505969) • US $160.00 (our price)

Enterprise Big Data Engineering, Analytics, and Management
Martin Atzmueller (University of Kassel, Germany) Samia Oussena (University of West London, UK) and Thomas Roth-Berghofer (University of West London, UK)
Business Science Reference • copyright 2016 • 272pp • H/C (ISBN: 9781522502937) • US $205.00 (our price)

www.igi-global.com

701 E. Chocolate Ave., Hershey, PA 17033
Order online at www.igi-global.com or call 717-533-8845 x100
To place a standing order for titles released in this series, contact: cust@igi-global.com
Mon-Fri 8:00 am - 5:00 pm (est) or fax 24 hours a day 717-533-8661

List of Reviewers

Tom Breur, *Cengage Learning Inc., USA*
Raquel M. Castaño, *EGADE Business School, Mexico*
Bindu Chhabra, *Management Institute, India*
Meeta Dasgupta, *Management Development Institute, India*
James Dong, *University of Auckland, New Zealand*
Geeta Dupatti, *Waikato University, New Zealand*
Kamal Ghose, *Management Consultant, New Zealand*
D. P. Goyal, *Management Development Institute, India*
Angappa Gunasekaran, *University of Massachusetts – Dartmouth, USA*
M. P. Jaiswal, *Management Development Institute, India*
Padmini Jindal, *Management Institute, India*
Suresh Kalathur, *Boston University, USA*
Arpita Khare, *Indian Institute of Management Rohtak, India*
Evzen Kocenda, *Charles University (CERGE), Czech Republic*
Bala Krishnamoorthy, *School of Management, India*
Andree Marie Lopez-Fernandez, *Pan American University, Mexico*
Gianpiero Lugli, *Parma University, Italy*
Sabita Mahapatra, *Indian Institute of Management Indore, India*
Jorge Vera Martinez, *ITESM, Mexico*
Jack McCann, *Tusculum College, USA*
Pavel Reyes Mercado, *Anahuac University, Mexico*
Manit Mishra, *Management Institute, India*
Ram Kumar Mishra, *Institute of Public Enterprise, India*
Hiranya Nath, *Sam Houston University, USA*
Gopal Nayak, *IIIT Bhubaneswar, India*
Aparajita Ojha, *Indian Institute of Information, Technology, Design, and Management, India*
S. P. Parashar, *Aarsh Management Consultancy, India*
Narender Rao, *North Eastern Illinois University, USA*
A. M. Rawani, *National Institute of Technology Raipur, India*
Kamal Ghosh Ray, *Vigyan Jyoti Institute of Management, India*
Ravi Seethamraju, *University of Sydney, Australia*

Table of Contents

Section 3
Financial Management

Section 4
Corporate Performance, Marketing, and Socio-Economic Indicators

Detailed Table of Contents

Section 1
Business Analytics and Cyber Security Management

Chapter 1

Globalization has triggered many new ways for companies to improve their business performance and stay competitive in the marketplace. Initially most companies strengthen their capability and competence towards developing competitive differentiation through continuous innovation to stay competitive and build sustainable brand image for their products and services. Over the mid-twentieth century, the information technology has made manifold advance proving scope for the companies to access the market information, carry out data analytics to meet their corporate requirements, and to derive right business decision for developing right competitive strategies. Accordingly, the new approaches of decision support systems have emerged and companies are interestingly adapting to the new environment of information analysis. The Big Data, business analytics, and business intelligence approaches have enveloped the business-to-business and business-to-customer industries as a strong decision making tool of the twenty-first century. This chapter discusses the state-of-art approaches and their impact on market competitiveness of the companies.

Chapter 2

Information and Communications Technologies (ICTs), particular the Internet, have been an increasingly important aspect of global social, political and economic life, and are the backbone of the global information society today. Their evolution and development has brought many benefits along with the threat of serious cyber-attacks that had been demonstrated over the past few years. Due to cybercrime business world drains huge money each year and incurs a large amount in resolving a single attack. It also damages organization's reputation and brand image, loss of intellectual property and sensitive data, loss of customer trust etc. Addressing major threats and challenges begins with setting up information security policy to ensure confidentiality, integrity and availability of company information and communication. Since telecom Sector is on its boom, a technological solution can solve the immediate challenges of identifying, investigating, and prosecuting computer- related crimes and changes required for long-term problem solving.

Chapter 3

This study aims to investigate youth consumer's perception and intention towards online shopping through integration of technological acceptance model (TAM). Data were collected from 263 young people residing in Bhubaneswar city of Odisha, a state in the eastern region of India through a structured questionnaire during May/June 2015. The structural Equation modeling was employed to analyze the data and validate the research model. The results of this study indicated that different perception variables have different relationships with behavioral intention of youths towards online shopping. The results from this study will be useful for e-commerce companies in formulating appropriate marketing strategies, as well as developing appropriate applications that will attract more consumers by increasing their benefit perception. This study is confined to the response of 263 young people residing in Bhubaneswar city of Odisha. In future of similar types of study may be conducted in either part of the state as well as country with a relatively larger sample size including customers from different age groups. Although past literatures have focused on technological aspects of online shopping, few studies have examined the perception and intention of youth towards online shopping. Furthermore, most studies on online shopping perception have focused on the relationships between technology adoption factors and perception of users. This study provides a basis for further refinement of TAM model to predict behavioral intentions of consumers towards online shopping.

Chapter 4

The marketing analytics function has received increasing attention from managers as information processing has permeated all marketing domain. However, value is realized once data is properly processed and firms develop and activate consumers and customers' insights to make decisions, that is, during the implementation stage of the marketing analytics function. This study aims to propose a research model to analyse how ready are organizations to reap the benefits of implementing the marketing analytics function and understand its impact on the overall marketing performance. The model is derived from the Resource-Based view of the firm, a research perspective that argues that for a firm to reach a sustainable competitive advantage, its key assets –the marketing function– has to be: valuable, rare, inimitable, and the organisation has to be capable of exploit such assets. Managerial and research implications are discussed and further research avenues are offered.

Section 2
Globalization and International Trade

Globalization has brought innovation to center stage of marketing activities. This can be related to opportunities as well as scope for consumer proficiency. Initial years of this decade have found that over dependence on innovation has made it consistent, compulsive and converging. With this impetuous innovation, certain aspect of critical thought process brings technology to the spot-light. Marketing philosophy that recognizes technology as the rationale of foundation of globalization and innovation must retrospect and further critically assess that how far technology has dissociated both the terms. Globalization by nature has been divergent, yet struggling to ensure marketing success because innovation is converging with the help of technology. Global Marketing is in a precarious juncture where every alternate day new technology is wiping out the old and with this new market is superimposing the old one. This transition is threatening concepts like segmentation, targeting and branding. This chapter is a critical assessment of role of technology in redefining the relationship between globalization, innovation and marketing. Secondary data of 51 Indian business sectors, consisting some of the leading market players have been analyzed to explore the relationship and propose a conceptual model.

Global trade in services has increased significantly over last three decades. Earlier, the growth was confined primarily to trade among advanced economies. In more recent times, even developing countries – especially, the emerging market economies (EMEs) – have experienced substantial increase in services trade. Services trade still accounts for only a small share of national income in most EMEs. However, one important trend has been the rapid growth of information-intensive services (IISs). This chapter examines the growth and patterns of services exports and imports from and to a number of EMEs. The analysis indicates that the importance of services trade has been growing for most EMEs. Further, among the EMEs, China, India, and Korea are the most dominant players in services exports and imports. For China, both export and import shares have been rising while for India the export share has been consistently rising. This chapter further discusses some of the intuitively plausible explanations for the growth of trade in services in general and in IISs in particular. It also discusses some of the challenges associated with the growth of IISs trade.

Existing research on impulsive buying focuses mainly on goods displayed in physical spaces and services delivered face to face. This paper aims to present a novel approach to analyze the impulsiveness on purchase through mobile devices by the development of a reliable and valid scale of impulsiveness in the context of mobile commerce, also known as m-commerce. To achieve the aforementioned research purpose, this paper views impulsiveness in m-commerce as a holistic process encompassing personal traits, stimulus level, and, product attributes to understand the motivational, emotional, and cognitive factors underlying the impulse buying journey and purchase decision on the basis of a scale to measure the construct. The paper concludes with a discussion on its conceptual and managerial contributions and interesting directions for future research.

Chapter 8

Alexander Schülke, Boston University, USA
Pierre Haddad, Boston University, USA
Saerom Jang, Boston University, USA
Melissa Renneckendorf, Boston University, USA

The automobile industry is the single largest industry in Germany. Demand for German car brands in foreign countries, including China, is strong as German car manufacturers enjoy reputation of high quality products. In recent years, several factors showed an effect on Germany's external trade development through a shift in the automobile sector. Globalization had an effect on external trade as developing countries try to push many exporting countries, including Germany, to manufacture locally. This is an ongoing trend that is supported by lower labor costs in developing countries. Boosting other sectors is one strategy to be less dependent on these developments and the focus on electric vehicles could ensure further exports. Economic growth in foreign countries remains one of the big opportunities for Germany's external trade development. However, it is important to take potential challenges and barriers into consideration, including environmentalism, strong competition, and new trends and business models that lead to less car ownership.

Section 3
Financial Management

Chapter 9

Gazal Punyani, Mody University, India
Sourabh Sharma, International Management Institute (IMI), India

Technology is entwined in almost every part of one's lives. Today's students are using more technology than ever before. Information technology has revolutionized every industry and especially the banking industry. Tremendous improvements in technology have taken place in the Indian banking sector. Among all, Mobile Banking (m-banking) is the recent phenomenon that changed country's banking system. Students, being considered as most technically knowledgeable make most use of mobile banking services among all the banking customers. Therefore, the focus is particularly towards the young students engaging in m-banking services and to evaluate the factors that influence them to adopt m-banking. The study considers extended Technology Adoption Model (TAM) to measure the impact of the factors on adoption of m-banking. For the study, data was collected through questionnaire from 217 students of Western Rajasthan. The result of this research would provide valuable information to service providers in order to improve their m-banking services.

Regardless of the success of e-banking services in India, a sizeable fraction of the customers still do not use online banking primarily because of security issues. Rising cybercrimes have further heightened these security concerns. This necessitates the adoption of faster and more reliable ways of user identification and authentication. Banks are ready to adopt biometric enabled systems to offer secure and seamless transactions but we need to find out if the customers are ready to adopt this technology. This paper attempts to evaluate the customer's perception about biometric enabled e banking services in India and their intention to use biometric enabled e-banking services. The study also tries to identify the factors which influence usage of biometrics by these customers. A survey has been carried out among customers to gather primary data and the Technology Acceptance Model has been applied. The value of the paper lies in the understanding of customer perceptions about biometrics enabled banking services which can help banks formulate strategies to encourage customers to use e-banking services.

This chapter attempts to critically examine the available literature on the subject, discuss a model that provides a framework for analyzing the variables associated with customer value, and to identify potential research areas. The chapter argues through a set of linear equations that maximizing customer value which is interdependent factor for technology adoption and profit optimization in the banks need to be backed with appropriate economic parameters for attaining competitive efficiency and optimizing profit. The framework of the construct is laid on the theory of competitive advantage and customer lifetime value, so as to maximize the potential of the organization and all its subsystems to create and sustain satisfied customers. The theoretical impetus from new technologies in banking services such as mobile banking in the North American region and discusses the technology led marketing process towards optimizing profit have been discussed in this chapter. The discussion in the paper also analyzes the main criteria for successful internet-banking strategy and brings out benefits of e-banking from the point of view of banks, their technology and customer values and tentatively concludes that there is increasing returns to scale in the bank services in relation to the banking products, new technology and customer value.

Section 4
Corporate Performance, Marketing, and Socio-Economic Indicators

Corporate Social Responsibility (CSR) and corporate governance are two distinct concepts that may seem to be isolated in practice. However, there are many parallels to the extent that the latter may define the engagement of the former. As such, it may be argued that corporate governance is essential to the implementation of CSR. Thus, a question arises, are firms' governance policies conducive to the engagement in corporate social responsibility? This study aims to evaluate the dynamics between corporate social responsibility and corporate governance of multinational firms operating in Mexico. Findings indicate that the practice of disclosing corporate social responsibility is more common than the transparent communication of corporate governance; however, the compliance with corporate governance is consistent with that of corporate social responsibility within the analysed firms.

Chapter 13

One of the most important goals of brand managers is to build strong, long-lasting brands. The meaning consumers give to brands comes from a dynamic process of interpretation formed in terms of the context in which they are used, the socio-psychological nature of their consumers, and the cultures to which these costumers belong. By acknowledging the importance of understanding how brands can be built in emerging economies, this paper analyzes the case of three brands in three different emerging economies. We highlight how successful firms develop their marketing strategies based on their understanding of the local consumer market they are serving. Ultimately, this paper is intended to provide managerial guidance on the basis of the analysis of brands and consumers in emerging economies.

Chapter 14

HR practitioners time and again busy in finding the worth of their training programs. Outputs of training/ Training Effectiveness/ROI of training programs are taking a huge attention of any HR department in any organization. Often attention was paid to the training program itself, the training environment, the trainer and the organizational climate and culture to apply the same into work. But many a times the very important part i.e. trainees were left aside. Present research is an attempt to address this gap. Trainees though found to be an important factor in success of any training program often this factor is limited to theoretical analysis. Rarely organizations and particularly the training department dare to ponder this. The type of trainee or in other way the characteristic of a trainee is found to be influential in many of the researches earlier. Here the attempt is to measure the link between the level of engagement and the perception of training effectiveness of the same trainees. This will help the training department to be more cautious while choosing their trainees to deliver an effective training program to fetch a dream achieved.

Chapter 15

This study is carried out in Mexico with an objective to analyse empirically the role of education in a transforming services marketing strategies of the firms. The study is carried on in Mexico through pragmatic investigation among the consumers subscribing to the communication and entertainment services. The analysis of primary data is developed around the theory of action that demonstrates the skills and confidence of individuals or groups towards making decision in acquiring or hiring services to improve their quality of life. The results of the study reveal that knowledge acquired on the services and value perceived by the consumers play key role in determining the intentions to purchases services. This study meticulously rows several arguments on how consumers with high level of education scrutinize the benefits offered by the firms marketing their communication and entertainment services, and build their value propositions on the services bought or contracted.

Section 5
Organizational Culture, Consumerism and Green Economics

Chapter 16
Bindu Chhabra, International Management Institute, India

The purpose of the present study was to explore the direct effect of work role stressors and Demands-Abilities (D-A) fit on the employee outcomes of job satisfaction, organizational citizenship behavior (OCB) and turnover intentions. The study further aimed to investigate the moderating role of D-A fit in the relationship between work role stressors and the above mentioned employee outcomes. The study was conducted using structured questionnaires for measuring the above mentioned variables. The sample of the study was 317professionals from five sectors. Hierarchical multiple regression was used to analyze the data. Hierarchical multiple regression results showed that the work role stressors were negatively related to job satisfaction and OCB and positively related to turnover intentions. D-A fit was seen to be positively related to job satisfaction and OCB and negatively related to turnover intentions. The analysis also found some support for the stress buffering effect of high D-A fit in the prediction of job satisfaction, OCB and turnover intentions. This study contributes to the organizational behavior literature by focusing on the fact that the negative effects of work role stressors on employee outcomes can be mitigated by identifying the variables which act as a buffer to weaken this effect. The results of the study provide support for the fact that matching employees to their job can help in the mitigation of employees' stress resulting in positive employee outcomes, hence benefiting the organization in the long run.

Chapter 17
Manit Mishra, International Management Institute, Bhubaneswar, India

The present study aims at attaining a better understanding of the hedonic consumer value of materialism and non-hedonic values of happiness, life-satisfaction and religiosity. As a conceptual paper, the study refers to literature and prior empirical research with the objective of linking a significant body of literature on these apparently diverse constructs into a unifying theoretical framework. The study offers new research directions in the form of propositions for further empirical investigation.

Chapter 18

Rajwinder Singh, International Management Institute, India

Ajit Pal Singh, Defense University, Ethiopia

Bhimaraya A. Metri, International Management Institute, India

The Non-livestock products include Horticulture products (flowers, fruits, nuts, vegetables and medicinal plants) and Agriculture products (Crops like; rice, cotton, wheat). These items share the maximum sale of the farm products. Unfortunately, the farm production in India has witnessed a huge wastage. It has attracted the attention of many practitioners and policy makers. Witnessing the opportunity many organized retail players have entered the arena to sell farm products. However, the supply chain (SC) performance measurement has remained the major challenge as "No measurement no improvement". Many organizations are searching for an efficient SC performance measurement system. Our study recommends that the SC performance shall be improved by developing a SC strategy based on a limited set of key performance indicators (KPI). Otherwise, managers shall waste time and resources on the undesirable performance indicators. We have identified and classified the KPI for non-livestock retailing SC management into five groups. These are 1) Customer Attraction Metrics (product quality, product personality, process quality); 2) Inventory Metrics (fill rate, customer response time, return adjustment, spoilage adjustment, and Vendor managed inventory); 3) Attractiveness Metrics (inventory cost, distribution cost, Return on investment, stakeholder value, sales profit and channel flexibility); 4) Transportation Metrics (shipping errors, and volume flexibility); and 5) Customer Metrics (lead time, delivery flexibility, and backorder flexibility). This grouping shall help the practitioners to focus on a limited set of KPI for better management of supply chains.

Chapter 19

Ramakrushna Panigrahi, International Management Institute, Bhubaneswar, India

The traditional growth theories and neoclassical economic development models have dominated the economic policies in both developed and developing economies over last decades. As a result, the global output has increased manifold due to inherent cost competitiveness ingrained in neoclassical model that heavily relies on optimization of output and resources based on the marginality principle. However, income growth has resulted in environmental degradation and depletion of natural resources as the framework of SNA does not treat these resources as fixed capital and hence, the depreciation of such resources are not treated aptly in the framework of income accounting. The environmental degradation and the recent phenomenon in global warming and the debate of climate change have taken centre-stage in the political discourse. This prompts for an urgent need for an institutionalized market oriented framework to treat environmental costs and depletion of natural resources. This paper makes an attempt to provide a framework to estimate green income from Mining and Quarrying sector by incorporating depreciation factor and examines its implications for export competitiveness of the sectors which use the output of Mining sector as inputs.

The purpose of the current research is to examine moderating role of demographics on attitude towards organic food purchase behavior. Environmental attitude components were classified as actual, verbal, and affect commitment. Data was collected through survey technique in six cities across India. The findings revealed that consumers' attitude towards organic food purchase was influenced by attitude components of Actual and Verbal commitment and moderated by demographic factors of income, gender and age. The findings can be of use to firms marketing organic food brands in India. Environmental attitude factors and demographic factors like income, age, and gender can be used for profiling consumers. With increased growth of organic food market in the country, green marketing and organic food products are upcoming research areas. There is limited research on Indian consumers' attitude towards organic food products. The findings can provide valuable insights to companies marketing these products in the country.

Preface

The growing importance of Internet in improving business performance and competitiveness in the global marketplace in the twenty-first century has drastically changed the strategies of companies towards manufacturing and marketing. As many conventional marketing approaches have become outdated today and have been completely transformed in view of the present needs of the companies to survive in the competitive marketplace, the new digital marketing approaches are being architected and continuously improved across the geo-demographic regions. The emerging digital focus on doing business is principally based on the philosophy of information analytics to develop right business decisions in the right destination market at an appropriate time. The information technology today provides the companies access to vast amounts of information about products, firms, and consumer behavior to use business analytics and make suitable decisions for quality business performance. The Internet is now anchoring decision making process in core business activities such as new product design, advertising, marketing and sales, consumer psychodynamics as information spreads through the word-of-mouth, new start-up funding, and customer service. Business analytics has been adopted by most companies as a significant tool for driving improved decision-making and increased returns on investments across the markets and industries. Growing advancements in information technology and cost effective data storage infrastructures have made the access of market information easier for the companies to process and store it in required quantities for managing data analysis to support dynamic decision making. The remarkable growth of social media, sensor and data capture technologies, mobile spatial information analysis across the markets, commercial online activities, and increasing interconnectivity across the market players involved in the business has evolved the concept of 'Big Data' to the business world. 'Big Data' offers great opportunities for the companies to apply information analysis strategically to harness the best decisions to improve business performance. The small and medium size companies are also using business analytics today as a business decision making tool not only to enhance business operations and managerial efficiencies but also to improve the customer experience in the competitive marketplace.

In every aspect of business, from the C-Suit to marketplace, customer relations, and social media, the process is generating as well as consuming voluminous information. Hence, inflow and outflow of information has become a dynamic hub in managing businesses today. More often the common business activities and consumer interactions create a trail of digitized data that can be stored, mined, and analyzed by companies to generate valuable business intelligence. With perennial advancements in the information technological and streamlined customer databases, companies have access to vast data warehouses of high-quality data that allows them to analyze the data clusters, understand market and customer behavior, and customize business strategies to stay sustainable in the marketplace. However, the major challenge in managing data mining, business analytics and data-driven policies is towards analyzing the right information clusters and developing actionable policies. This book is an outgrowth of selected papers of the International Conference on Business Analytics Strategies and Cyber Security Management, co-hosted by International Management Institute, Bhubaneswar, India and EGADE Business School, Tecnologico de Monterrey, Mexico during December 11-12, 2015 at Bhubaneswar, India. The chapters in this book addresses information analysis related topics that are used for business decisions in the global marketplace. This book addresses the fact that business analytics is not a statistics or mathematics course but a logical process of decision making.

In the age of data-centric decision sciences, the advanced analytics approaches permit companies to derive inferences from the generic data bases. Right and valid inferences transform data into knowledge for a company, which drives business process transparency, improvements, and competitiveness of the company. While evaluating the need to institute analytics as part of data strategy of the company, it is necessary to develop skills on managing actionable knowledge. Information technologists play an indispensable role in business management today as a bridge between the executives to run analytics and make the decisions based on the results. Management of Big Data analytics projects needs a strong business background and operational competencies in the C-Suit to lead model analytics centers. In order to succeed in managing the business analytics, information technologists of the company should blend their experience with the innovation platforms and pre-defined initiatives to achieve business results. A forward-thinking analytics strategy thus needs to take place right at the bottom of the company engaging each employee in information analysis. Companies should also set the management priorities to reinforce functional goals at various operational levels with targets and metrics compatible to the information resources.

As business houses, governments, and individuals generate massive raw data as a byproduct of their activity, decision-makers and systems are increasing relying on information technology to analyze market information and other related socio-economic datasets systematically to improve decision-making and business performance. Some companies have automatized analytical and decision-making processes of the pre-determined information. Some chapters in this book examine real-world examples and cases to place data-mining techniques in context, to develop data-analytic thinking, and to illustrate that business analytics is both an art and science. Most companies today are engaged in carrying out the business analytics approaches to improve their international trade performance through developing awareness among managers on the key concepts in international trade, finance, marketing, strategy, and logistics and supply chains. The business analytics tools are applied to the context of cross-border businesses towards managing their international businesses better. Companies are experiencing the power of business analytics in re-shaping their business to make sustainable in the rapid growing complex global business environment. Employing high performance data visualization with the computing technologies like big data and cloud, companies are able to analyze the market competitiveness across hundreds of trading partners and develop market trends for large number of commodities by analyzing their performance in the across the markets historically.

Furtiveness in marketing among existing and emerging companies in the global market place has increased in the twenty-first century and has driven tactical thinking among firms to manage the market competition. Due to increasing competition, shifting market trends, and rapid emergence of consumption patterns, multinational companies are finding it difficult to manage their markets through conventional strategies. Unlocking the hidden insight in data presents companies with a viable alternative to determine their source of competitive advantage. This means that graduates with business analytics skills are in high demand across the globe. Multinational companies are employing covert market strategies to gain first mover advantages and stay sustainable in the market against the growing competition. Most companies are inviting their resources in analyzing the market data through statistical and operations analysis to understand the market dynamics and guide formation of predictive models by application of optimization techniques and communication. These techniques are integrated in business analytics, which have emerged as a powerful tool to measure the market transformations and suggest the right ways of developing marketing strategies for sustaining against market competition. Companies play around both marketing strategies and tactics in an integrated mode to gain competitive advantage.

Besides the applications of business analytics in assessing the market trends and forecasting, use of Internet in business has enhanced the cyber threats despite the opportunity of being omnipresent on the global platform. Hackers frequently use the global network to steal vital business information and compel companies to compromise on various businesses issues. Thus, organizations today have to rethink their defenses and move from reaction to anticipation. Managing information security is a more complex issue than the technical challenges. The information management is built on the critical infrastructures, organization, and technology. Although critical infrastructures are beyond the direct control of the organization, balancing them is a critical component of corporate governance. Security lapses are management failures more than technical failures.

This anthology contributed by several authors on the business analytics and cyber security management aims at providing an international forum for rich discussion on reviewing and learning lessons from contemporary and innovative strategies in managing business analytics as well as the cyber security issues in the global markets. This book discusses new taxonomy of business analytical strategies for emerging markets and provides suggestions as how firms can improve cyber security in their business for securing against the data theft. Contrary to conventional wisdom, the contributions in this book would also contemplate on developing new visions on business analytics and cyber protection strategies for emerging markets.

We hope that this book would provide general and research based information on the subject and successfully drive new insights among the practicing managers, researchers, and students working on business analytics and cyber security management.

Rajagopal
EGADE Business School, Tecnologico de Monterrey, Mexico City, Mexico & Boston University, USA

Ramesh Behl
International Management Institute, Bhubaneswar, India
April 15, 2016

Section 1
Business Analytics and Cyber Security Management

Chapter 1
Competing on Performance on the Global Marketplace:
Applying Business Analytics as a Robust Decision Tool

Rajagopal
EGADE Business School, Tecnologico de Monterrey, Mexico City, Mexico & Boston University, USA

ABSTRACT

Globalization has triggered many new ways for companies to improve their business performance and stay competitive in the marketplace. Initially most companies strengthen their capability and competence towards developing competitive differentiation through continuous innovation to stay competitive and build sustainable brand image for their products and services. Over the mid-twentieth century, the information technology has made manifold advance proving scope for the companies to access the market information, carry out data analytics to meet their corporate requirements, and to derive right business decision for developing right competitive strategies. Accordingly, the new approaches of decision support systems have emerged and companies are interestingly adapting to the new environment of information analysis. The Big Data, business analytics, and business intelligence approaches have enveloped the business-to-business and business-to-customer industries as a strong decision making tool of the twenty-first century. This chapter discusses the state-of-art approaches and their impact on market competitiveness of the companies.

INTRODUCTION

Globalization has driven tremendous entrepreneurial dynamism in the marketplace down-to the bottom-of-the-pyramid of the market strata causing bi-directional movements of business forces. Most multinational companies are aiming at expanding their business activities in the local markets, while the enterprises operating at the niche are trying to go beyond territorial boundaries. Consequently, the marketplace today has been congested with the overflowing brands, corporate interventions, instability in demand, and chaos in making business decisions. Every company, irrespective of its operational size and investment,

DOI: 10.4018/978-1-5225-0902-8.ch001

is competing today for improving its performance and stay competitive in the marketplace. Decision making has turned complicated for the companies as the uncertainties in the market increased discretely across the destination in the world. The term *decision making* has become more stakeholder oriented among the firms since the mid-twentieth century. Indeed decision terminology was imported from public administration into the business world as it was needed to treat decision making more bureaucratically to manage the result oriented strategies of the companies to gain the competitive lead. Further decision making incorporated the terms like resource allocation and policy making, shifting the managerial thought process, and the role toward a series of interlinked actions that envelopes any decision in a company. Yet, decision making in business emerges out of a conventional process to a broad competitive market pursuit, putting the managers of a company on pretest to implement the decision in a controlled situation, measure the results, and take the business decisions at the macro level across the markets and consumer segments. All business decision needs to be calculated meticulously for the potential risks along with an indulging human behavior. The advances in technology that support the cognitive processes have improved the decision making in complex business situations. The business decisions today are largely supported by scientific data analytics than subjective judgments. The data based decision support systems are reliable provided the quality of data is acceptable and has passed through the reliability tests. Such information analysis could lead executives to make well-enough decisions and test the decision-response matrices before implementing the decisions at macro level (Buchanan and O'Connell, 2006)

Making appropriate decision in the changing market environment is an up-hill challenge for most companies especially when there is paucity of information and the available data is not of adequate quality. Market information analysis for decision making is subject to the quality of the data and when it comes to support business decisions, it is difficult to build the value of managers' experience and intuition around the business analytics process as they are based on qualitative parameters. Internet has given the sporadic access to the market information system in small quantities, which attracts most researchers and managers to use the information for making arbitrary decisions. However, it would be reckless to make a business decision based on isolated information without attempting to draw some meaningful inferences from the larger data sets spread across the temporal and spatial parameters. As the intensive use of cross-company spatial and temporal data in decision-making is growing among the companies since the last decade of twentieth century, this process leads to better decisions and improved business performance. One academic study cited in this report found that, controlling for other variables, firms that emphasize decision-making based on data and analytics have performed 5-6 percent above the average performance. However, still many regional and small firms rely on conventional measures, managerial intuitions, and experience for decision-making. Though there is a direct connection between data-driven decision-making and firm performance, the quality of decisions largely depends on the size of the data-sets and its reliability indicators. The approach to Big Data has provided the companies, opportunity to analyze and interpret the segments of information for decision-making. The Big Data is distinguished by its large volume, reliability, and availability across the information channels. The current trend in the global marketplace shows that companies have growing preferences for data analytics and data-driven decisions despite the problems of data accessibility and choosing the right analytics process. Some companies believe that management decisions based purely on intuition or experience are increasingly regarded as suspicious, while most companies consider that management decisions are increasingly based on hard analytic information to derive competitive strategies. A large number of managers feel that the decisions they have made in the recent past would have been better if they would had all the relevant data in hand as it would have helped to derive sustainable and strategic decisions in business focusing on a long-term business growth (Economist, 2012).

MANAGING BUSINESS ANALYTICS

The dependency on the data driven decision making among the companies has increased over the past decade (2001-10) and they have used business analytics a tool to learn the competitor strategies. Business Analytics has helped the companies to make competitive and sustainable decisions through statistical and operations analysis, developing predictive models, and application for optimization techniques, using the large data bases of corporate information over spatial and temporal dimensions. The business analytics results qualify companies on taking various high value decisions like innovation and technology and to see that business is moving in the right direction in the competitive marketplace. However, it is always a mounting question among the companies that which best practices the managers involved in business analytics projects should employ, how they would advise their less experienced peers, and how they would be able to convince the top management of the company about a right decision emerging out of the business analytics. The use of business analytics in the corporate decisions has the following positive impact on the companies:

- Delivers clarity towards decision making,
- Reduces biases towards execution,
- Provides value in learning competitor moves and market dynamics,
- Creates working abilities among managers to gain commitment,
- Builds managerial orientation towards intelligent experimentation, and
- Promotes smart use of information technology.

Most business analytics project managers offer opportunities to the strategic managers and explain market scenarios in conjunction with the information technology (IT) department. In good companies IT department acts proactively in the business analytics and decision process by pursuing opportunities to deliver faster implementation cycles, maintaining just enough process, and designing the business decisions process maps to ensure quality and professional support (Viaene & Van den Bunder, 2011).

Business analytics in the twenty-first century has rose into the prominence as it offers solutions that benefit a variety of disciplines in business like marketing, new product development, innovation, and customer services. Interestingly, business analytics is not just primarily an extension of information technology or business intelligence or a business function, but a convergence of IT capabilities and competencies, and business performance measures in a company. Business analytics demands an increased collaboration across organizations on issues relating to information selection and screening the data-sets, as well as to warn managers about the data intricacies, risks, and teams for the information oversights. The software tools that companies consider as a part of business analytics span across various areas, including analytics, data integration, querying and reporting and managing information technology projects. As business analytics is designed to enable fact-based real time decision-making, it might be one of the expensive tools to work with for the companies that have paucity of resources. The key benefits of business analytics functions are currently derived from using business analytics software encompassing various areas of business analytics, with the he following benefits related to improving and speeding up the decision-making process:

- Aligning market information and corporate resources with strategic decision process
- Managing cost effective and real time business decisions
- Enabling customer-centric decisions to be implemented by the companies
- Improving the market competitiveness and business performance of the companies
- Producing a unified enterprise-wide business information
- Synchronizing financial and operational strategies, and
- Supporting corporate decision to increase revenue and reduce financial risk

In reference to the changing scenarios of market economy and information technology, most companies are leaning towards reaching the cost efficiencies, improving market competitiveness, and increasing revenues as the principal objectives of their companies. Driving through the business analytics experiences every organization gets different outcomes as the appropriateness of the decisions taken and implemented varies by companies towards realizing the benefits. The major challenges observed in acquiring and analyzing market information include data integration with multiple systems or information channels, data quality, and finally building integration with other enterprise applications. Data integration components provide business organizations with market and enterprise data access and processing across systems and platforms, as well as integrated data quality, which is critical to providing accurate and consistent information. In the global marketplace, companies tend to invest in business analytics to access the right information at the right time in order to empower fact-based real-time decisions at every level of the enterprise, to achieve key objectives and to gain maximum return using the IT tools appropriately. Business analytics is generally both historical and predictive, helping the companies take more proactive, fact-based decisions for building market competitiveness (Computerworld, 2009).

As the data flow continues to plunge the companies with the market information, more companies are under increasing pressure to develop systems that create both business value and competitive advantage by using the business analytics approached effectively. It has been observed that companies gain competitive value from analytics provided they have the right tools, technology and people, and organizational factors. The management support for analytics is essentially needed from top-down directions and engaging managers in using analytics to identify and address strategic threats and opportunities. In order to inculcate data-oriented organizational cultures companies should determine that:

- Business analytics is used as an effective IT tool and a strategic asset for supporting business decisions,
- Business analytics approaches are used as integrated tools in the decision making process, and
- Employees of the company exhibit involvement in business analytics approaches and disseminate new insights within the company and to those who need them.

In addition, organizations that excel at using analytics attain proficiency in information management and real-time decision making, and possess real analytics expertise though the path to developing these competencies are time consuming and challenging (Ward et al, 2014).

Managing the large data sets of market information in a company needs a new organizational culture, which should be able to shift the decision making and performance reporting culture from top-down to bottom-up formats based on analyzing the real time market situations rather than deriving decisions on the perceptional, emotional, or cognitive biases. In companies that compete through market information based decisions, managers are made aware that business analytics stays as the central to strategy. Such companies launch multiple initiatives involving complex data and statistical analysis, and manage quantitative approaches at the enterprise level. Shifting from conventional to business analytics based decision making culture in business organizations requires a significant investment in technology, the accumulation of massive stores of data, and the formulation of companywide strategies for managing the data. However, transforming the decision making culture in the companies also requires commitment and willingness to change to the analytics based thinking. A new breed of organizations like Amazon, Harrah's, Capital One, and General Electric Company have all dominated their fields by deploying industrial-strength analytics across a wide variety of activities. However, among companies that offer competing products and services and use comparable technologies, business processes used in decision making serve as points of differentiation. Companies engaged in using business analytics hire talented employees and offer intensive training in analytics to improve their performance on managing quantitative tools and techniques for advising managers to take appropriate business decisions in marketing, logistics and operations, investments, and customer services. Consequently, business analytics appears to be the most contemporary tool for making the real time business decisions (Davenport, 2006). Advances in data analytics as decision marking tool encompasses the following attributes that convincingly drive companies to invest in the data analytics projects (Chester eta al, 2016):

- **In-Company Models:** Companies interested in getting engaged with the business analytics process for decision making develop customized models required for their business profile that demonstrate how analytics can add new insights and deliver clear added value. However, as such business analytics models are often developed in isolation with limited volume of information and connecting through specific information channels, the companies often struggle with the full adoption of their business analytics models. For instance, financial institutions like banks and insurance companies work with business analytics models limiting to their products and services but in the longer run they face difficulty in analyzing the industry data to make decisions to improve market competitiveness.
- **Capturing Value:** As companies continue to work with the business analytics function and gain maturity, they work closely with the business analytics models and engage frontline staff who become involved with the business analytics model of the company. Over the period, conceptualizing the role of business analytics companies should shift their focus from developing models to their adoption and measure the impact of business analytics on decision making.
- **Achieving Scale:** Right decision strategies would enhance the market competitiveness and revenues of the companies. A sustainable analytics leadership could drive the companies to achieve economies of scale in manufacturing, logistics, inventory, and marketing over the period.

Most companies are engaged in exploring the opportunities of using business analytics to raise productivity, improve decision making, and gain competitive advantage. As stated in the pre-text business analytics will provide scope for the companies to win the competition in the marketplace in a scientific way by analyzing the information. Emerging companies initially undertake mapping out an analytics plan to determine the investment and its return across the business areas and the time span. However, the investment on business analytics helps the companies increase their market competitiveness in the selected business portfolios that have higher competition such as consumer products manufacturing and marketing, personal care products, automobiles, consumer electronics, and healthcare products and consumer services. The business analytics in the high capital oriented business portfolios like aeronautics, research and development, and ship building might not be very encouraging in improving the business performance of the companies. Companies need to set a strategy, draw a detailed road map for investing in assets such as information channels, data banks, technology, analytical tools, and decision support system platforms as well as manage the intrinsic challenges of organizational commitment, change management, and reinventing processes. Business Analytics is used through statistical and operations analysis to determine predictive models and application of optimization techniques to improve the business performance of the companies.

The business decision process (BDP) focused on decision making to solve problems is exhibited in Figure 1, which could also be applied to finding opportunities in data and deciding what is the best course of action to take advantage of them. The process of BDP using business analytics approaches should be understood in reference to the conventional perception of decision disequilibrium. This situation develops in companies in reference to the perception of existing problems and decision required to resolve them for sustainable growth- a long term perspective. In this process, the first step is to recognize the databases that may contain information fit for analysis to both solve problems and find opportunities, and improve business performance of the company. In the following step of the business analytics, focus is laid on exploring the problem to determine its size, impact, and other factors to diagnose the core attributes of the problem. The descriptive analytic analysis explores factors that might prove useful in solving problems and offering opportunities for decision making. Finally, the last step of business analytics concludes in

Figure 1. Business analytics process in a company

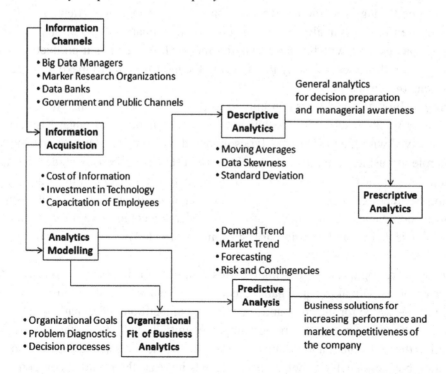

the strategy selection and implementation of the decisions towards manufacturing, logistics, inventory, marketing, innovation, technology, new product development, and customer (Schniederjans et al, 2014).

Descriptive analytics explores the 'what' and 'why' issues concerned with a business situation. This approach also evaluates past performances by using historical data to find the causes and effects associated with the success or failure of business decisions. Descriptive analytics are used in quality management techniques and other methods of statistical process control. Predictive analytics includes a variety of statistical techniques such as modeling, machine learning, and data mining that analyze chronological facts to make estimates about future business strategies. Business analytics indicates relationships among various factors and assesses the embedded and potential risk associated with a particular set of conditions. This attributes of business analytics guide companies to take interrelated decisions in reference to the affecting factors such as decision to change pricing strategies also to be considered in reference to the new product development strategies of the company. Data mining is also a part of the business analytics and used by the companies to identify patterns that can then be identified as opportunities or risks. Predictive analytics help decision makers to predict the outcome(s) of a decision before it is implemented. Using the probabilities, decision makers can calculate the expected value of alternatives once risks and benefits are taken into account. Predictive analytics are particularly useful when there is a high degree of uncertainty. Forecasting consumer behavior in response to a new product or marketing initiative are practical examples of the use of predictive analytics.

Large multinational companies tend to exploit the tremendous amounts of data available through internal and external sources. These companies are likely to steer the information using business analytics approach with all their IT projects. They focus informational analysis results on building and deploying technology on time and to take appropriate business decisions within budget. Business analytics works for projects designed to improve business processes and increase efficiency by extracting valuable insights from data and using information to make better decisions. Managers need a different approach and mind-set. Companies can opt for a big data or analytics project, which is likely to be smaller in size than conventional IT initiatives such as installing an ERP system for business divisions. The data driven decision making projects are commissioned not only to address a problem but also to explore the business or market opportunities for the companies to gain competitive advantages. The business analytics projects enable the companies to frame questions, develop hypotheses, and then carry-out experiments to gain knowledge and understanding. Companies using the business analytics projects, tools, and techniques engage employees who can make the initiatives close to the requirement of the company, use the IT constituents develop analytics projects to address their business problems, and equip teams with cognitive and behavioral scientists, who understand how people perceive problems and analyze data (Marchand & Peppard, 2013).

Big Data as Decision Tool

To understand the challenges and opportunities associated with the use of business analytics companies should take business executives, managers and analysts from data mining organizations and build a consortium for managing the Big Data projects. Accordingly, companies can capitalize on market information and apply analytics for knowing the market situation today as well as developing right spatial and temporal business decisions in the future. Most multinational companies including, General Electric Company, General Motors, Toyota, Samsung, Apple, and many pharmaceutical companies are developing such consortiums as there is a clear connection between performance and the competitive value of analytics. They have found that the use of business information and analytics differentiate them from other companies in the marketplace to become top performers. The Big Data projects are developed around aspiration, experience and transformation objectives of the company and enable organizations to identify the path to fall in the continuum of business performance in the rapidly changing business scenarios in the global marketplace. It has been experienced by many companies that using the business analytics approaches through churning of market information offers them the best entry points and decision opportunities at various geo-demographic, spatially spanned competitive markets, and the measures to avoid the most common pitfalls. Based on data analytics insights companies may be able to arrive at a convergent methodology for successfully implementing analytics-driven management and rapidly creating value for stakeholders of the company by setting high performance goals. Accordingly, companies in the twenty-first century are focusing on the biggest and highest data priorities and within their priorities they start analyzing the available data. The results of the continuous analysis of business information allows the companies to embed insights into their business processes to make them more actionable and sustainable in the marketplace by keeping the existing capabilities and tools while adding new ones appropriately. Big Data led companies develop an overarching information agenda that enables decision making and strategy for the future (LaValle et al, 2011).

The combination of big data and advanced analytics offers retail and consumer packaged goods (CPG) companies numerous opportunities across the value chain. Companies get a better understanding of consumer needs, purchase intentions, and value for money experience precisely to identify consumer segments, and improve their ability to target the highest-value opportunities in developing their portfolio strategy and product development. The returns on investment for each unit of resource spent on marketing spend across both traditional and innovative products and services can be measured using the data analytics parameters. The informational analysis and appropriate market decisions would help the companies move through newer marketing vehicles such as social media that could drive the company's decisions towards building online portfolios and virtual markets at low cost to serve across the geo-demographic consumer segments. The Big Data projects provide a perennial analysis opportunity to companies on the dynamic market information ranging from detailed hourly analysis of in-stock rates by store to daily and other temporal intervals. Based on the analytics results of the market information marketing organizations can reduce stock-outs, provide a value for money experience for consumers, and boost sales and customer value for gaining the comparative advantage in the marketplace. Big Data and advanced analytics allow companies to make better and faster decisions in their day-to-day business, and deliver improved performance. Many consumer retail companies in the North America and Europe have revolutionized retailer-specific assortments and plans by applying advanced analytics to consumer data. The decisions of the retail companies are also supported by various other technologies like Radio Frequency Identification to determine which SKUs are selling well and where the inventories need to be replenished to make the products always available in the shelves of the retail store and meet the consumer satisfaction to the optimum level (Breuer et al, 2013).

General Electric (GE) Company has rebuilt its performance with the business-to-consumer (B2C) sectors by opening a new software center in California in 1991. GE has employed a huge number of software engineers to complement the company's existing IT software workers who are focused on developing applications for power plants, aviation, medical systems and electric vehicle charging stations. The company has installed more and more sensors on all the equipment as technology revolution to seek the performance information and to remotely monitor and diagnose each device. It represents a huge productivity gain to the company to keep information updated on the performance of various resources. Consequently, the company is now able to sell a gas turbine and remotely monitor its operating state and help to optimize it. Similarly, *Trip Optimizer* is a fuel-saving system that GE has developed for freight trains. It takes into account a wealth of data, including track conditions, weather, the speed of the train, geographic position system data and train dynamics, and makes decisions about how and when the train should brake as well as the freight loading status at different yards. In tests, the *Trip Optimizer* increased fuel efficiency and train companies could manage the biggest overheads for freight trains operations and enhance their profit. Besides using the new technology, the data analytics also helped the company analyze the comparative freight and train operation scenarios across the destinations and other freight operating companies in the rail industries (Economist, 2012).

Though Big Data projects have been thought as a contemporary development in the business houses, it is still to catch fire in various industrial segments. The Big Data is far more powerful than the analytics of the past hence, companies can measure and manage more precisely the information analysis than ever before. Companies using the Big Data projects can make better predictions and smarter decisions, and target more effective interventions in the marketplaces that have high competition and are dominated by the data and rigor. The differences between Big Data and analytics are a matter of volume, velocity, and variety, which can be realized by the fact that now more data is shelved and continuously modified on Internet every second than on any physical systems. The Big Data encompassing nearly real-time information makes it possible for a company to be much more sustainable than its competitors. Market information can also come from social networks, images, sensors, the web, or other unstructured sources. However, such information needs to be filtered for reliability before putting it to the analytics for decision making. The managerial challenges in managing Big Data and business analytics however, are very real and complex. Management teams engaged in decision making should learn to set right key information indicators and analytical tools to embrace information-based decision making using the real time data. Companies must hire information analysts who can find patterns in very large data sets and translate them into useful business information. The IT departments of the companies have to work hard to integrate all the relevant internal and external sources of data (McAfee & Brynjolfsson, 2012).

Information Technology

It has been discussed over the corporate debates that Big Data will give companies new capabilities and value as a revolution in the information technology. But exponentially increasing amount of data and much of it in forms that are impossible to manage by traditional analytics is posing a major challenge to the companies. Big Data includes information such as call center voice data, social media content and video entertainment, as well as clickstream data from the web. Most organizations that are learning to take advantage of Big Data understand their business environments and are creating new products and services complying with the current trend and need of adapting to the analytics for right decision making. These companies gain distinct experience from those organizations using traditional data analysis environment for making competitive business decisions in reference to the following differentiations:

- Most companies today work on analyzing the real time or most recent data bases identifying occurrences in the business in a given marketplace rather than making decisions on the basis of antecedents,

- The Big Data driven companies make business analytics as a principal platform for making business decisions considering data in dynamic terms of flows and processes across the companies in the industry and for stakeholders to make decisions quickly and watch their implementation consequences,
- In addition, the companies that are already involved with Big Data projects tend to take a lead on hiring and training data analysis experts and data mining software engineers along with the product and process developers to support the corporate decision making, and
- Large multinational companies that have gained expertise in the real time informational analytics are moving the decision resources from IT into their core business and operational functions.

The Big Data projects are evolving along with a new information ecosystem that may be explained as a network that is continuously sharing information, optimizing decisions, communicating results and generating new insights for businesses (Davenport et al, 2012).

The technology companies today sweep up huge amounts of customer data of their clients that are engaged in the information analysis projects as core resource for carrying out the business decisions. But they tend to be impervious about the information they collect and often resell, which often makes their clients uncertain about the data usage. Though firms with such practice can edge revenues in the short term; however, in the long run it undermines consumers' trust which might jeopardize the competitiveness of the client companies over the longer run. As the social media is turning transparent with more rush of users, companies, market players, and the stakeholders would assess the information trails that are left online by the users, competitors, and business grate-keepers. Accordingly, it can be clearly monitored and understood on which organizations consumers expressed their trust with the data they shared and vice-versa. The information analysis also shows which data consumers valued the most. The value consumers place on different types of information is based on its relevance and use. However, the perceived value of users rises as the breadth and sensitivity of information increases from basic, voluntarily shared information to comprehensive and predictive profiles. For example, firms create a thorough dashboard of information using analytics for review of investors and publish in the Initial Public Offer (IPO) for attracting investments in the public equity of the company. Thus, the information analytics which is an integral part of the Big Data projects also benefits the stakeholders of the company towards understanding the performance, risk, and growth opportunities of the company in a competitive marketplace. If information analytics is used to improve a product, consumers generally feel the enhancement of knowledge and get a comparative profile of the company and its portfolios. However, the Big Data processing companies need to play ethical in the process of information analysis and adhere to the terms of confidentiality. Some companies void such ethical norms in informational acquisition, analysis, and sharing process and expect more in return for data used to target marketing, sell the data base to third parties. To build trust on handling market information, which is an intangible asset, companies must lay standards on acquiring, analyzing, and sharing the information, be transparent about the data they gather, and offer consumers appropriate value in exchange for it. Simple legal disclosures do not provide enough protection to the data but they need to work actively educating the industry partners, information agencies, and their customers by incorporating fairness and legal support in the usage of information. Such arrangements towards the Big Data projects would develop goodwill and continued access to their data in the mutual interest of the companies (Morey et al, 2015).

Business Intelligence

Business Intelligence (BI) is often confused as business analytics. Though the business intelligence has the same origin of the information technology, it focuses on the particular field of data processing and consolidation to retrieve information for decision making. The business analytics is the outgrowth of business intelligence, which offers decision support solutions on the basis of information filtered through the business intelligence. The overarching objectives of the business intelligence can be stated to provide the right information acquired thorough various sources to the right people at the right time for steering results to make right decisions. Carrying out business intelligence projects successfully in a company requires the right mix of IT systems, architectures, data structures, data collection processes, and responsibilities for providing meaningful information. Business intelligence has a been observed as a proven impact on key performance indicators, which is evident from the experience of most managers that business intelligence is an essential resource of the company and can be the used as a performance management tool. Business intelligence enables the company to exhibit right market information and the performance of the company that creates positive impact on shareholder value. The return on equity stays high in companies that widely use performance management tools as compared to those not in the same industry. Streamlining the BI information is necessary of the company and it should be used as a tool to create recurring, standard, information reports in an efficient and user-friendly manner. Reports should be predefined and static by nature, generated by the demand raised by the decision makers of the company periodically.

Business intelligence reports presented through dashboards contain high-level, aggregated strategic company data on various functional and key performance indicators, inclusive of comparable statistics within and outside the industry players while the business analytics reports are presented in reference to the consolidated performance indicators, and action oriented managerial points are discussed in the presentations. The BI dashboard includes both static and interactive reports with data translated into graphics, charts, gauges and illustrations to simplify the communication of complex topics. Dashboards allow basic interactions such as drill down, slice-and-dice operations, and provide various levels of detail to achieve deeper insights. However, the explanatory power of dashboards relies mostly on the interpretations of corporate managers. At the analysis level, BI systems provide not only consolidated information that users can detail and filter, but also forecasts and trend analyses to develop new insights based on the raw data. With the use of information technology, companies upgrade continuously the BI system and most companies use the automated intelligent data analyses based on sophisticated fuzzy logic and neuro-fuzzy systems. Based on user-friendly and powerful functions, companies can draw sensible inferences and retrieve meaningful insights through the BI system. What-if scenarios and simulation functionality provide advanced, tailored decision-making support. The basic business intelligence systems focus on corporate financial data only, while advanced systems interconnect internal and external sources with qualitative and quantitative data. Advanced BI systems that process the comprehensive data sets are tailored to the requirements of the company and filter information for strategic decisions by selecting right indicators to make the right judgments. BI offers the following benefits for proper decision making:

- Access to the required information and KPIs
- Consistency of data across organizational units
- Easy analysis of information based on the functionality parameters of the company, and
- Reports can be presented in a manager desired format

The process of analyzing information through a business intelligence solution needs to consider the business benefits, including improved overall decision making and increased efficiency for business reporting and analysis. A well-designed business intelligence solution brings the information across the organizations in a consistent and reliable way. Figures can be combined and compared in different business units, assuring the validity of symmetric data comparisons for operations and decision managers for better decision making. Essentially, BI improves efficiency on both the information technology and business decision sides. On the IT front business intelligence projects appear to be a recurring task of creating new data analysis plans and developing data reports following the market dynamics trend while on the business side, it saves time in carrying out the data analysis and doing preparation to deliver management reports directly from the BI dashboards. The business intelligence operations in a company can be successfully carried out by streamlining the various stages as detailed below:

- Developing dashboard of activities
- Creating design of information analysis
- Implementation of BI system

Business intelligence is a systems approach and it is necessary to define the key activities in reference to the key performance indicators. The BI reports and KPIs need to be congruent and managed objectively to serve the corporate goals, which often mean eliminating unnecessary information and cleaning data filters regularly. Companies working with the BI project should meticulously plan for mapping the data sources, and the spatial and temporal span of the information to calculate the defined KPIs and develop a sound data base forming and implementing the business decisions. However, external sources connecting to existing data warehouses and additional calculations should be rationally planned and the junk and intervening information need to be avoided. Also, companies should evaluate the various layers of a BI system to define the sensitive decision areas and link the KPIs to various functional sectors like manufacturing, production, logistics, marketing, and finance to gain competence in performance and develop sector-wise appropriate decision trees. Companies should take due precautions in defining KPIs as they vary by business models and market requirements. If companies deploy the long-term strategy to analyze operational KPIs, this should be addressed at the beginning of the project (Martin et al, 2011).

CONCLUSION

In view of the discussions in this chapter it can be stated that new trends in the business decision making are largely driven by the information technology based tools and techniques. The concepts of Big Data, business analytics, and business intelligence have emerged in the twentieth-century and became popular in the later decade among the large multinational companies as trusted tools for decision making to competitive in the global marketplace. There are many start-up companies such as *hiQ* engaged collecting public information and analyzing, *Sumall* helping businesses optimize their social-marketing campaigns, and *Duetto*, a start-up company, that makes it easier for companies in leisure and tourism industries to personalize data to individuals searching online for hotels. The trend of business analytics is growing along with the new start-ups and supporting large companies in appropriate decision making for augmenting their business performance.

REFERENCES

Breuer, P., Moulton, J., & Turtle, R. (2013). *Applying advanced analytics in consumer companies.* New York: McKinsey & Co.

Buchanan, L., & O'Connell, A. (2006). Brief History of Decision Making. *Harvard Business Review, 84*(1), 32–41. PMID:16447367

Chester, A., Clarke, A., & Libarikian, A. (2016). *Transforming into an analytics-driven insurance carrier.* New York: McKinsey & Co.

Computerworld. (2009). *Defining Business Analytics and Its Impact on Organizational Decision-Making.* Author.

Davenport, T. H. (2006). Competing on Analytics. *Harvard Business Review, 84*(1), 98–107. PMID:16447373

Davenport, T. H., Barth, P., & Bean, R. (2012). How Big Data Is Different, *MIT. Sloan Management Review, 54*(1), 22–24.

Economist. (2012). *The Deciding Factor: Big Data and Decision Making.* The Economist Intelligence Unit.

LaValle, S., Lesser, E., Shockley, R., Hopkins, M. S., & Kruschwitz, N. (2011). Big Data, Analytics and the Path from Insights to Value. *MIT Sloan Management Review, 52*(2), 21–31.

Marchand, D. A., & Peppard, J. (2013). Why IT Fumbles Analytics. *Harvard Business Review, 91*(1), 104–112.

Martin, A., Jekel, R., & Simons, E. (2011). *Better Decision Making with Proper Business Intelligence.* Chicago, IL: A.T. Kearney.

McAfee, A., & Brynjolfsson, E. (2012). Big Data: The Management Revolution. *Harvard Business Review, 90*(10), 60–68. PMID:23074865

Morey, T., Forbath, T., & Schoop, A. (2015). Customer Data: Designing for Transparency and Trust. *Harvard Business Review, 93*(5), 97–105.

Schniederjans, M. J., Schniederjans, D. G., & Starkey, C. M. (2014). *Business Analytics Principles, Concepts, and Applications: What, Why, and How?* Upper Saddle River, NJ: Pearson Education.

Viaene, S., & Van den Bunder, A. (2011). The Secrets to Managing Business Analytics Projects, *MIT. Sloan Management Review, 53*(1), 64–70.

Ward, M. J., Marsolo, K. A., & Froehle, C. M. (2014). Applications of business analytics in healthcare. *Business Horizons, 57*(5), 571–582. doi:10.1016/j.bushor.2014.06.003 PMID:25429161

Chapter 2
Cyber Security and Business Growth

Akanksha Sharma
Symbiosis Institute of Telecom Management, India

Prashant Tandekar
Symbiosis Institute of Telecom Management, India

ABSTRACT

Information and Communications Technologies (ICTs), particular the Internet, have been an increasingly important aspect of global social, political and economic life, and are the backbone of the global information society today. Their evolution and development has brought many benefits along with the threat of serious cyber-attacks that had been demonstrated over the past few years. Due to cybercrime business world drains huge money each year and incurs a large amount in resolving a single attack. It also damages organization's reputation and brand image, loss of intellectual property and sensitive data, loss of customer trust etc. Addressing major threats and challenges begins with setting up information security policy to ensure confidentiality, integrity and availability of company information and communication. Since telecom Sector is on its boom, a technological solution can solve the immediate challenges of identifying, investigating, and prosecuting computer- related crimes and changes required for long-term problem solving.

INTRODUCTION

In today's era when everything is going digital, reliance on computers and internet have deeply integrated in everyday life. Be it political, social, economic, or political interaction, the web provides a platform for a whole range of sector and services like healthcare, finance, information and communication technology, manufacturing, transportation, defence etc. In such environment, in organizations, more valuable data is being stored and processed on a large scale; information is shared, combined and linked with other information with greater frequency. In parallel to all such developments, it has given rise to cybercrime where criminals or hackers use computer technology to access personal information, business financial data, etc to cause damage and loss to organizations. Cybercrime has become a fastest growing area of

DOI: 10.4018/978-1-5225-0902-8.ch002

crime, even the defence sector has come under the cyber-attack. Statistics also showed that cybercrime has risen to around 3, 00,000 in India only in 2015 which is almost double the level last year. Many cases have come into the picture which tells about the seriousness of cyber security. Last year hackers had dumped 5 million username and passwords of Gmail to a Russian bitcoin forum, Sony suffered the loss of $200 million on account of cyber-attack on movie 'the interview'. Since it has reached to such alarming stage, it becomes necessary to explore the challenges and possible security measure available to the organizations.

Cybercrime includes wide range of activities. Crime that targets computer network or devices includes denial of service attack and viruses and crime that uses computer network to advance other criminal activities includes hacking, phishing, identity theft, cyberstalking etc. Some of the cybercrimes are explained below:

- **Hacking:** It is a type of crime where a person's personal and sensitive information can be accessed without even the person knowing that his computer is being accessed from remote location.
- **Theft:** As the name suggest, this is a type of crime where person rejects the copyrights and downloads music, games etc.
- **Cyber Stalking:** This is a kind of online harassment where instead of offline stalking criminals use internet to stalk through online messages and emails.
- **Phishing:** It is a cyber-attack where criminal sends a legitimate email to gain personal and sensitive information like username, password and other details for malicious reasons.
- **Denial of Service Attack:** The type of cyber-attack where attacker sends high volume of useless traffic to a host device which is connected to internet which leads to network overloading.
- **Viruses:** This is oldest type of cyber-attack where they infect the computer by attacking to programmes or files.

Due to cybercrime a business drains almost $445 billion each year. Also average cost to resolve a single attack totaled more than $1 million. It also causes damage to the organization's reputation and brand image, loss of intellectual property and sensitive data, & loss of customer trust (see Figure 1).

Figure 1. Attacks contributing to largest losses

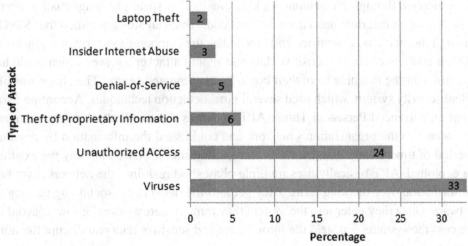

Today cybercrime has become a serious crime as it doesn't really need the physical presence of the attacker and can be committed from the remote location due to which it is increasing and causing potential losses as shown in the graph above. Due to such potential threat and losses when it is necessary for the businesses and organizations to set cyber security as their priority and where 98% of respondents cite cyber security as their priority, only 48% respondents actually follow cyber security practises. With the increasing use of information technology and smart phones, threats are moving to mobile sphere also. While downloading apps users do not check security certificates and when using services like online banking, online shopping, business transactions etc. important credentials like password, pin, account no get saved and thus increases the chances of threat. Hence, data should be encrypted on the device for transmitting it to third party for processing. Further security software which not only scan computers for virus but also stop it from entering into the systems should be employed into the systems. Use of a good firewall will add to security strength. In organizations, BYOD practise is being promoted which allow employees to access company's information and applications, increases the risk of data breaches. To protect, employees should not be able to put in flash drives or their own internet dongles into the USB. Telecom Sector being on its boom, need to manage network traffic intelligently and identify fraudulent behaviour, denial of service attack etc. As such threats tend to disrupt the working of an organization it is necessary to have a backup plan so that businesses or organizations can continue its operations and functions. In order to do this, it need to establish cyber security as an intelligent cyber security management that links information from variety of data source and analyse it in real time.

GETTING REAL ABOUT SECURITY THREATS: WHERE ARE WE HEADING & WHAT IS EXPECTED

Criminals can launch critical attack against the critical infrastructure in various fields like defence, Information technology, banking and finance, telecom infrastructure, and many more. With growing use of technology and dependence on internet cybercrime has reached to every sphere, even to defence department which are known to be itself protectors have become vulnerable to cybercrime.

Since the military networks are becoming more complex and more intertwined daily, department of defence has the fear of being at more risk. Recently, In October 2014, there was an attempt to steal the sensitive data from defence metallurgical research laboratory(DMRL), the research lab of DRDO, where the attack was directed through the genuine looking email. This spear phishing email when opened, it opened a fake document that download the malicious code. Such an attack is called the 'SINON CAMPAIGN'. Though the attack was identified and blocked by the computer's security system, but had it not been detected, it could have copied sensitive data and sent to attacker's server which could have given them full control over the machine from their control and command centre. The attack was blocked by the Quick Heal security system, which used several virus detection techniques. According to quick heal the attack was an Advanced Persistent Threat(APT) which is a network attack where an unauthorized person gains access to the organization's network and could steal the information by remaining there for a long period of time. It says that there was no special technique used and only the existing vulnerabilities are exploited. APT basically uses multiple phases to break into the network, avoid detection, & harvest information over the long term. They get into the network by social engineering to deliver targeted malware. Once they enter into the system they remain there as slow or low to avoid detection. They then access the systems and steal the information and sensitive data and disrupt the information.

This information is then sent to attacker's home base for further analysis and exploitation. The best way to resolve such attack is to make the network visible through the corners without any restriction to ports, devices or type of traffic. With effective network monitoring tool each packet passing or moving in the network can be examined i.e. source IP address, destination IP address, protocol that the packet is using and the information of the packet which includes whether it is a continuation of the traffic or the acknowledgement of the receipt of the packet. Along with this it will also help to monitor if there is any unwanted packet being sent or received from the computer. Sometimes the attacker introduction into the systems slow down the speed, network monitoring also helps in tracking the programme which is taking up all the network traffic and thus slows down the network. Some other solutions include the identification of early signs where the malware components of targeted attack should be identified early, which includes malicious URLs, C&C servers etc. With such malicious threats it becomes necessary to protect countries' protection.

From past some years there has been marked increase in the frequency of cyber-attack on Indian assets with government and private infrastructure equally affected. According to the research report there is an alarming 136 percent increase in cyber-attack against Indian government organization and 126 percent increase in attack against financial services organization. According to Symantec, sophisticated cyber-attacks cost Indian companies US $ 3.8 billion each year. With the fast pacing technology and changing information technology (IT) needs cyber-attacks are getting bolder and are bringing forth the concerns of IT security across industries. Hacking has become the place of origin of attacks and is increasingly becoming difficult to trace.

In 2014, the most prominent industry Apple, hackers broke into the iCloud accounts of the number of Hollywood celebrities and made off with nude photos. Hackers have broken almost 500 iCloud accounts, to which the internet security experts say that it happened due to the weak passwords. Such attack is named as 'Brute Force Attack'. In Brute Force Attack, hackers try to gain information like user password or PIN by error and trial method through software. Automated software generates a large number of consecutive guesses as to the value of desired data and thus cracks the encrypted data. Here hackers were supposed to use the iCloud password reset functions to gain access to accounts which allowed the user to enter the username and correctly answering the two security questions. iCloud secures the data by encrypting it when it is sent over the web and use secure tokens for authenticating. Hackers thus obtain the credentials of the account and pretend to be the user to bypass the encryption. The basic preventive measure in order to be protected from this attack is to set the passwords strong enough. In order to make password strong it should be long enough and avoid making use of dictionary words. Multiple characters and symbols should be used to enhance the password strength as it has different character has different encryption process or key to decrypt the passwords. In fact in order to get secured from brute force attack, encryption system must be strong enough. This can be in turn done by increasing the key length. Thus the brute force attack can be made less effective by using AES encryption algorithm where the key size is increased to 128 bits or 192 bits or 256 bits and is designed on the principle of substitution-permutation. Here the key specifies the large number of repetitions of rounds of transformation that convert the plain text into the cipher text, where each round contains multiple processing steps each containing four similar but different stages. Also reverse steps are used to convert the cipher text into plain text with the same key. And thus to breaking of 128 or 192 or 256 bit key by brute force attack will be requiring high computational power which will require large time to exhaust the 256 bit key. Second approach could be by limiting the failed login attempts. In this feature, it block outs user once they have reached to the pre-configured number of failed attempts thus blocking the user for some period of time. This can be done by number of plugins already available. Two-Factor- Authentication is another solution to such an attack. Almost all the sites had made use of it with help of smart phone where along with username and password they ask for the OTP (one Time Password) sent on their smartphones. This is effective because such passwords cannot be used later and is valid only for short period of time. The Gmail account has made use of captcha to mitigate the attack where after few login attempts, it will show you image of captcha to affirm that it is not a computer automatically attempting passwords. Captcha is a program or system intended to distinguish human from machine input, typically as a way of thwarting spam and automated extraction of data from websites.

Brute force attacks are sometimes to be concerned about protecting the data, choosing encryption algorithm and selecting passwords. They also form the reason for development of secure cryptographic algorithms. Apple suffered with the cyber-attack where hackers embedded malicious software in large number of iPhones and iPad apps. The malicious programme was XcodeGhost which allows the hackers to collect data and confidential information from the devices. The hackers have embedded the malicious program by winning over developers of legalize software to use a counterfeit version of apple software i.e. XCode for creating iOS and MAC. The code can trick developers to use apple's genuine software to develop counterfeit versions. XcodeGhost is a harmful and dangerous malware that can gain access to credentials, infect apps, hijack URL, steal iCloud passwords from the device and upload them to the attackers control and command servers without the user being known. After receiving the information it will decrypt the content. XcodeGhost used http code for uploading the information and then used the DES encryption method which is bit easy due to short key length. To mitigate the potential attacks Two step authentication process should be used.

Such attacks are harmful for the organization as organizations and employees does their most of the work via mobile apps. With this the work is more convenient and productive. But the problem lies that the companies are struggling as they are not properly equipped to be developing the secure apps. The app developers don't consider security as their priority while developing an app and thus leave behind the holes which are exploited by the hackers. According to a study, 73% respondents said that they lack training and understanding of secure code with mobile apps. Also, for an IT professional, user experience was at the top priority that counts for 44% followed by ease of development(24%) then performance(15%) and lastly security (which forms only 11%). Also 50% of the companies do not include security in their mobile development budget. In order to prevent insecure apps being downloaded from untrusted sources and preventing unsecured networks, business have started the BYOD practises and mobile device management policies. But such practices and policies are not enough in order to be protected from the attack; it must have visibility of devices connecting to their network along with the visibility of installed app to know malicious capabilities and vulnerabilities to the mobile devices. Thus there need to be the balance between the development and deployment on one hand and security on the other hand in order to help in business grows in every area considering all aspects.

Cyber-attacks against financial services institutions are getting more frequent, more sophisticated and more widespread. In recent years major financial institutions, credit unions, money transmitters, regional and community banks and third-party service providers (such as credit card) have received attempted breaches. Banks find themselves having to adapt to relying on third party systems that are outside their control in order to provide many of their digital services like external data feeds, customer and staff devices or cloud services. This interconnectedness of financial institutions leaves them defenceless to disruption ultimately threatening national security and the stability of the international financial system.

Cyber security is growingly vital threat to global financial institutions and the broader financial system, yet it is not well understood. Some biggest cyber fears the financial industries are as discussed below:

A Consistent Attack on the Whole Markets

If customer data leaks leading to fraud, either the bank or the customers will figure it out finally when the user accounts do not align. For such case frauds detecting systems and advanced control systems have been used for many years by the financial services industry. However, Attackers in this scenario were very much conversant with financial services network and software and depicted typical computer processes to process fraudulent transactions using internal commands.

Criminals have stolen up to $1 billion from banks worldwide and attempted to breach out NASDAQ in year 2014. U.S. officials successfully disrupted the attack and inspected other banks and exchanges that could have been aimed, but detected little proof of a broader attack. What they did find were systematic security failures diffusing some most important U.S. financial institutions. It turned out that many on the list were defenceless to quiet the same type of attack that struck NASDAQ. They were actually spared only because the hackers had not bothered to try.

Handling of Product Data

The plan of attack on an exchange could be disastrous to the economy. An equally unsettling condition would be if hackers got a way to interfere with specific stocks prices to wreak havoc on individual companies. Todd Morris, founder and CEO of New York-based Brick House Security suggested "It would be easy for someone to manipulate the stock market and it would blend in the background noise and somebody could already be doing it", whose clients include about half of the Fortune 500 companies.

Losing Customer Data to the Extent of Losing Customer Confidence

Privacy is the key for customers and most of the companies regard it as topmost priority. It is of high risk to trade or lose customers data. Banks manage massive amounts of data, which makes their technology requirements quite complex. Trying to ensure information is protected from hackers can make it so it is not usable by others. You need to be able to protect data, but also be able to press a button in order to respond to regulators. You need to think about security upfront when collecting data. You need a real-time system that allows for the processing of data at the point of collection.

Employees Becoming the Weakest Links

The 2014 J P Morgan Chase data breach was a cyber-attack against American bank JPMorgan Chase. It is considered to have endangered data associated with over 83 million accounts -76 million households and 7 million small businesses. The data breach is considered as one of the largest data breaches in history and the most serious violation into an American corporation's information system. In the case of data breach at J.P. Morgan, hackers supposedly gained entry into the bank's network via personal computer of employees. Employees can also fall victim to phishing attacks by clicking on malicious attachments in emails. One of the Kaspersky report says "Despite increased awareness of cybercrime within the financial institutions, it seems that phishing attacks remain effective against larger companies,"

Increasing Attacks on Financial Institutions Using Different Techniques.

"Zeus Trojan" which is used by one of the criminal group successfully stole up $70 million from US banks and 6 million from UK accounts. This Trojan can be bought for few thousand dollars and other plug-ins being bought for as little as hundreds of dollars each,. Such a low cost purchase has yielded a huge pay back for the cyber criminals, except for the reality that they got caught eventually. Zeus is only the most recent example of a successful Trojan targeting user banking accounts. The firm said the hackers had broken into banks' virtual networks before spending months installing programs and collecting data in order to quietly withdraw money. To get into victims bank accounts and to steal money, Hackers are increasingly targeting Smartphone users. Near about 60 percent of the malware aiming Android devices was designed to steal money or banking details as reported by Kaspersky.

The large number of cyber-attacks came from the Trojan-SMS malware family, a malicious program which grant access to hackers for user passwords, user names and user bank card data for online banking services. Cloning of credit/debit cards and Phishing attacks of online banking accounts are common occurrences. The increasing use of Smartphone/ mobile/tablets for online financial transactions has also enhanced the vulnerabilities to a great extent. These attacks have been discovered to be initiating from the cyber space of a number of countries including the US, of Europe, Brazil, Turkey, China, Pakistan, Bangladesh, Algeria and the UAE.

Growing penetration of an internet and popularity of online banking have made India a favourite country among the cybercriminals, who mainly target online banking transactions using different types of malware and after Japan and US India ranks third in the tally of countries that are most affected by online financial malware during the year of 2014. Publication of obscene contents, hacking, banking and credit card frauds among other cyber-crimes have registered an annual increase of more than 40% in the country in the past two years till year 2015. Malwares that targets mobile phones and tablets will continue to be a substantial threat in 2014. When it comes to mobile, there are a various methods that banks need to adopt to protect their mobile applications. But to protect these mobile applications efficiently most of the banking institutions don't have necessary resources. The most serious issue that banks and all of us face in trying to protect assets and data is open architecture. Actually there are so many different channels users can come in from. We're pretty much an open society: The Web code is there to be deciphered and the mobile apps are there to be downloaded.

The leak of classified documents by Edward Snowden's about the National Security Agency's surveillance programs was the major insider threats in 2013. There is major impact on security in all industries and is focused on insider privacy, threats, trust and responsibility. Ultimately not only just customers who need secure authentication but also employees who have access to important data need to be inspected as well. There are more opportunities for the employees, who are dissatisfied to commit fraud with outside parties. So companies need to pay attention to whom to continuously authenticate those individuals and who to hire. The average number of threats against banking services institutions is nearly four times higher than that of companies in other industries, according to report from Web sense Security Labs. Criminals using banks as way to reach other victims so they are not just going after the money. For example, a hacked email account at a bank could allow hackers to minimize the satisfaction and trust that customers have in respective financial institutes and to reach out to their retail and business customers.

The widespread use of mobile phones and online banking has exposed weaknesses in banks armour. A cyber-attack on a banking institution not only results in the loss of important data, but can have a hazardous effect on the reputation of the firm and it will require large amounts of money and time to restore lost trust. These financial instructions are prone to disruption as they are interconnected hence threatening stability and security of the international financial system.

Risk vs. Opportunity: New Technologies, New Threats

The financial services industry needs to balance the protection of the banks information and assets against the needs of employees, partners and customers to access information at preferred times and locations. Banks have to innovate to be competitive and expose themselves to risk, without jeopardizing reputation and financial assets.

- **Social Media:** Is an emerging customer channel, a point of contact and a potential point of sale. Nearly 75% of banking employees are making use of social media, yet only 20% of banks have used technical controlling systems to block institutional usage. This opens up a new window of opportunity for criminals to use social engineering to target victims or spread infected links.

- **Mobile Devices:** Offer productivity and improve the quality of services but they also increase exposure to risk. Although malware is not prevalent, the risk comes from phishing and fraud through unprotected mobile devices. In fact, mobile computing was identified as a primary risk in a Symantec report released in February 2012.

- **Mobile Banking:** Is growing rapidly and becoming the primary access point for most of the customers. The frequently used out-of-band authentication through mobile devices, where the mobile is used to add multi-factor authentication, could emerge as a target for attacks if adoption increases. Mobile banking, payments, services and employee mobility represent the major risks for a financial institution as per the Symantec report.

- **Bring Your Own Device (BYOD):** BYOD has major implications. These devices are less secure and firms don't effectively control them. The challenge is banks can't really use the typical defenses on employees' devices.

- **Cloud:** Enables IT departments to distribute costs, deliver new services more rapidly, scale capacity and outsource applications and systems. However, it also brings potential risks. Transactional data and customer information need to be protected according to regulations and policies, and the security officer needs to understand potential exposure to cyber-attacks. Much of the finance industry has already implemented or purchased cloud computing services, and there is a consensus that the benefits outweigh the security risks. Nevertheless, cloud services must be integrated into the overall security infrastructure. The movement of services or data to the cloud is a major concern as firms don't have control of that data.

- **Improved Real-Time Tracking and Business Intelligence:** Will alert companies to any security breach. The ability to monitor every transaction across global operations will be the key to protecting against internal and external threats. Managed security services, or a security operations center, will help detect real-time external or internal security breaches.

- **Big Data for Detection of Fraud:** Are enhanced by the banking institutions for prevention and fraud detection capabilities. Enhancements will revolve around big data and Analytics technology is getting efficient at pointing out activities that are of high risk. The process and systems of the most of the financial institutions are not equipped to handle the large amount of data that is available. Organizations are learning to get used to data in real time and these institutions are starting to make more connections between cross-channel fraud trends. To efficiently deal with attacks and cybercrime, financial institutions should use a strategical approach demanding collaboration and wider communication across the international banking industry.

Steps People Can Take to Better Protect Their Accounts Against Cyber-Attacks

- Using passwords for devices and using password managers which store passwords in encrypted vaults or behind biometric security can help people keep track of complex pass codes.
- Turning on two-factor authentication so that website will email or text you a passcode when you try to log in to verify that you are the real account holder.
- Signing up to receive alerts from the bank each time a transaction is made using your account.
- Checking your accounts daily, monitoring transactions to ensure that you actually made all the purchases.
- Credit cards offer more protections than debit cards. Credit card holders are liable for up to limited amount in unauthorized transactions and can simply report a purchase as fraudulent. Debit swipes pull money from the account immediately, so owners must wait to be reimbursed by their bank, and account holders are liable for large amount depending on when they reported the fraud

Implementing Best Practices Against Targeted Attacks

There are a number of key issues that financial institutions should consider in order to move beyond a one-size-fits-all approach and begin to successfully fight targeted attacks.

1. Predictive Threat Analysis

Threat intelligence is a key starting point for any enhanced security strategy. Before selecting an information security tool, institutions should identify their core business processes, classify the information they handle, understand how data flows, comprehend the legal and regulatory landscape they exist within, and then adopt a risk-based approach to setting priorities. By identifying assets, threats and vulnerabilities, this approach allows the qualification and quantification of probable occurrence and impact.

2. Employee Training

Due to the extensive list of information security domains some organizations focus mainly on initiatives around governance in reference to risk and compliance, identity management and access control, data loss prevention, network and information security, and penetration testing. While these five domains set the foundation for information security, organizations should not forget that security processes, tools and infrastructure are defined and supported by people, not machines. Thus, effective awareness programs and well-trained staff are crucial to cyber security solutions. An internal security task team should work with a trusted security vendor to perform a detailed analysis of risk management. As cybercriminals shift their focus to bank employees and mobile banking gains momentum, the only constant in this game is change. Security strategies and infrastructures need to become more agile and predictive as no technology can rule out the human factor completely, so security awareness will remain critical.

Education of employees is the best defense against many threats. However, this is most effective when organizations break away from traditional security awareness models to employ creative and immersive techniques and deploy technologies that can influence user behaviors.

3.   Identity Management

The key to protecting customer information is establishing a stringent identity management program that implements multi-factor authentication; strong data encryption mechanisms to protect data storage and transmission; and fraud detection and monitoring mechanisms. In addition, when mobile devices are part of the strategy, all associated threats must be identified before granting consumer access to sensitive functions and data.

4.   Test your Plan

Test your plan before a breach happens. Security intelligence should enable breaches to be discovered rapidly and stopped at an early stage. Processes and tools, such as backup and data loss prevention, should also be available to recover and restore information.

5.   Developing a Framework for Thinking About the Risk

The first step in addressing this threat is changing the way most people think about it: What you need to do is analyze the problem from an enterprise perspective and need to start with the assumption that something is going to get through few truly understand the nature of the cyber threat and hence how to manage it properly.

The travel and hospitality industries are the main target for cyber-attacks. As these industries and its loyalty programs continue to be digitalized with heavy dependence on mobile devices, the chance of attacks remains high. How the industry collects, uses, transmits and operates the large amount of sensitive data is revolutionized by technology. But travel and hospitality industries need to understand how to manage these risks to meet the security and privacy law requirements of state and global laws. These industries also need to know where vulnerabilities exist from to point-of-sale software used at restaurants, bars, and gift shops to reservation systems and loyalty databases.From enterprise-wide platforms to personal medical devices, various systems are being targeted maliciously. As healthcare services moves outside hospital walls and into the communities and homes using consumer-based technologies, patient trust in providers extends to the data and new devices used for monitoring and treatment.

Security and privacy of the patient must be managed in a cost effective way by health organizations and many times healthcare organizations don't understand risks related to security and privacy or don't know how improve their security. It is important to drive effective health outcomes at a lower cost while remaining compliant. It requires a comprehensive understanding of the risks involved in staying connected to health consumers, dealing with them, and ensuring their sensitive data is kept secure and private. Retailers always need to amass huge amounts of data, information about employees, business partners, customers and competitors. With threats given forth from data thieves, regulators, insurers, lawyers, hackers and cyber security and privacy of credit card companies are massive challenges for retail companies.

The latest cyber-attack was on large US-based retailer The Home Depot, where Data from about 56 million payment cards of customers been used at US and Canadian Home Depot self-checkout registers over a period of six months were at risk of being compromised. Also, the hackers stole 53 million customer email addresses to use in email scams that plumb for sensitive personal information. It was particularly frustrating because Home Depot was in the process of enhancing the encryption of customer payment data for internal audit and corporate compliance at Home Depot.

Retailers that are most advanced to cyber security and most aware of the impact of outsourced parties on their own security, are those who have moved responsibility for the issue to the top. Retailers and their security teams should be used of doing more checks on more vendors, establishing relationships with vendors including communication about security regularly, and, in some cases, that means site visits. With the increase in cybercriminals and increasing sophisticated methods of attack, retailers need to be armed with advance leading solutions to fight cyber-crimes to prevent the loss of customer data.

The frequency and the impact of cyber incidents have increased with financial and reputational damage as their main effects. Collaborative cyber security is the business-to-business cyber security related exchange of knowledge and information. To mitigate the growing amount of cyber risks in the retail sector, retail organizations can collaborate with each other in the field of cyber security which can in turn be done by the exchange of information and knowledge between the organizations. Exchanging information will lead to better detection of threats and more accurate analyses on one hand, exchanging knowledge leads to the development of higher quality solutions and saving organizations from developing the same solutions by identifying cyber threats to the retail sector. This Collaboration is possible in retail organizations regardless of size, degree of cyber security risk or cyber security maturity. It will help them to integrate collaboration into their cyber security program which will reduce the related cyber risks. So, collaborative cyber security is beneficial and directly applicable to the retail and hospitality sector.

CONCLUSION

India being host of some of the biggest IT companies is vulnerable to cyber-crime on account of its growing economic progress. Increasing use of smartphones, online transactions and government initiative of Digital India open the opportunities in the industries globally on one hand, on the other side the success of such projects depends upon the greater connectivity with the limited cyber security firms since India has the poor cyber security track record. A rough estimate shows that the rate at which the number of cases is rising is 107 percent and is expected to reach 300000 by 2015 which is almost the double next year. Further as per findings, mobiles are the big area of concerns as 35-40% financial transactions are done through the mobile devices which are expected to grow to 55-60%and more in coming years. Cyber-attack has increased tremendously in world and in India and thus is required to be protected. From past many years steps and measures have been taken in this aspect. The Centre of Excellence for Cyber Security Research and Developments in India (CECSRDI) has also been discussing the techno legal issues of cyber security in India and globally. As per them some recent developments that took place are:

1. **Policy and Legal Framework:** India again missed an opportunity to formulate proper policies and laws regarding the cyber security. Despite a positive step of government in forming the National Cyber Security policy of India, it doesn't answer all questions of cyber-attacks.

2. **NCCC of India:** National cyber coordination centre of India which is approved by the government of India will screen the online threats and co-ordinate with the intelligence industry to handle national security issues.

3. **Bitcoins Exchanges:** These are the frequently targeted area of cyber-criminal which has forced many of them to shut down.

4. **Director's Cyber Security Obligations:** The companies act has increased the cyber security obligation of Directors of many companies. Along with it, law firms' cyber security obligations are also increasing over the world including India.

5. **Tri Service Cyber Command:** A suggestion of the Indian Government for armed forces that will create three new tri services commands that will handle space, cyber, and Special Forces.

6. **Critical Infrastructure Protection:** Setting up and protection of an infrastructure is a real challenge that lies for security. Telecom Commission has provided internet connectivity and free wireless but the wireless security is the question which it still raises.

7. **International Legal Issues of Cyber-Attack:** This is something which has started gaining importance as the countries around worldwide has realized that the international cooperation is necessary to deal with cross border cyber crime and cyber-attack.

Despite many steps and actions, India fell short of the reasonable effort in this regard and thus require more skills to be developed to improve cyber security capabilities. Some of the prone areas where it still need to thrust upon are

- **E-Commerce Websites:** Many E-commerce websites are gaining importance due to ease and comfortability and this is increasing their risk of being targeted by the attackers to steal the data and username and passwords of the users. This further raises questions on them of following cyber security due diligence.

- **Crisis Management Plan:** India lacks a proper management plan which makes the infrastructure vulnerable to sophisticate cyber attacks

- **Rise of Malware:** Cyber security breaches are increasing and hence India has been exposed to malware infection and the cyber-attacks as computers and mobile phones forms the essential part of the daily life and hence no firm or organization can afford to take risk.

- **Telecom Security Policy of India:** Absence of such policies and regulations are not balanced and not compliance with the constitutional requirements. And hence will create problem for both the government and the telecom companies.

- **Setting up of Cyber Forensic Training and Investigation Labs:** As to provide training and generate awareness among the employees and staff and as an individual about the security issues and the cyber-attack. Also there are very less cyber security research and educational centres in India and this is why here is an urgent need to draw the attention towards it.

The danger of cyber-attacks and crimes against computers and the information on computers, on governmental and non-government organizations r proprietary firms calls for a special attention from countries around the world. Since the existing laws and policies are lacking in one or the other aspect and are unsatisfactory in providing security, business and government will rely on technical measures for protecting themselves and making the environment safe to work on. Since telecom companies have a critical infrastructure and stores the personal information, they play a major role in providing and assuring the security. Telecom businesses are taking actions to enhance the level of protection by enhancing the intelligence into the vulnerabilities and the potential threat. The measures that have been taken by the telecom industries in such directions include:

1. **Intrusion Detection Tool:** The type of security software that will inform the administrator when someone tries to get into or compromise information systems through malicious activities. It monitors the system and conduct analysis on patterns based on known threats. Along with this it also searches the internet for any new threat that could harm the systems in future terms. It has three components-
   a. Network Intrusion detection system which monitors the traffic on whole subnet,
   b. Network Node Intrusion Detection System which also watches the traffic but only on a host and not on whole subnet
   c. Host Intrusion Detection System which take the picture of the system and compare sit with the original one to know the discrepancies. If there are any then it informs the administrator.
2. **Assets Management Tool:** This oversees both the software and hardware that deals with an organizations computers and networks. It controls the software by restricting what and by whom particular software can be run.
3. **Patch Management Tool:** They help in assuring that computers are up to date and that they meet the applicable security and efficiency standards by
4. **Centralized user Data Storage:** It is the central database which keeps record of the users and is located, stored and maintained in a single location. Users can access the centralized database through the computer network which give them access to central CPU.

With some of these measures, the battle has yet not ended as there still lays a long road ahead to be travelled. As telecom is going more digital there will be more risks involved with the data, application and the networks. There is a demand of not only high quality of services but also for the enhanced capacity along with fresh content without increasing the rates to customers. Going more digital require some changes in the delivery and managing of product and services like cloud computing, big data, Internet of things which has its own risks and so need to be addressed. Also mobile devices gaining popularity has given the attackers a chance to take advantage of it by deploying malware in the games and the apps. Thus there is a need to deploy the technology that could address the solution in such a manner which could manage the traffic and also look into the fraudulent behaviour. This in turn could be done by deep packet inspection technology along with packet processing solution can be employed which ensures that malicious traffic is eliminated and will also provide high speed to legitimate users. Also this helps in zero packet lost that may be carrying important information. But addressing threats and challenges begins with setting up information security policy to ensure confidentiality, integrity and availability of company information and communication, thus credentials should be made password protected.

Apart from above threats that have increased the risk, several miles still need to be walked in order to combat the cyber-crime like deference to successful public private partnership, necessity of international standards, a critical framework to protect crime. There is a need to play smart and employ risk management tools, big data paradox and other techniques and solutions in order to secure the information and overcome the losses it incurs.

REFERENCES

Federal Bureau of Investigation. (2014). Annual Report, Internet Crime Compliant Center (IC3). New York: Author.

Kaushik, R. K. (2015). Smart Cities Cyber Security in India: The Problems and Solutions. *Cyber Security in India Blogspot*. Retrieved on November 10, 2015, from http://cybersecurityforindia.blogspot.mx/2015/11/smart-cities-cyber-security-in-india.html

Morgan Lewis. (2014). *IT Governance blog, List of Data Breaches and Cyber Attacks*. Retrieved on November 15, 2015, from http://www.itgovernance.co.uk/blog/list-of-data-breaches-and-cyber-attacks-in-july/

Morgan Lewis. (2016). *Privacy and Cyber Security, Corporate information available publicly on Internet*. Retrieved from www.morganlewis.com

Nassbaum, B. (2016). *Smart Cities – The Cyber Security and Privacy Implications of Ubiquitous Urban Computing*. The Center for Internet and Society. Retrieved on March 20, 2016, from http://cyberlaw.stanford.edu/blog/2016/02/smart-cities

PricewaterhouseCoopers. (2016). Turnaround and Transformation in Cyber Security. In The Global State of Information Security. PwC.

Singh, M. (2014). *10 biggest cyber-attacks of 2014*. BGR India. Retrieved on November 15, 2015, from http://www.bgr.in/news/10-biggest-cyber-attacks-of-2014/

Verghees, B. J. (2014). *Cyber Security, A Growing CIO Priority*. Bangaluru, India: Wipro Ltd.

Chapter 3
Perception and Intention of Youth's Towards Online Shopping:
An Empirical Assessment

Ajitabh Dash
Regional College of Management, India

ABSTRACT

This study aims to investigate youth consumer's perception and intention towards online shopping through integration of technological acceptance model (TAM). Data were collected from 263 young people residing in Bhubaneswar city of Odisha, a state in the eastern region of India through a structured questionnaire during May/June 2015. The structural Equation modeling was employed to analyze the data and validate the research model. The results of this study indicated that different perception variables have different relationships with behavioral intention of youths towards online shopping. The results from this study will be useful for e-commerce companies in formulating appropriate marketing strategies, as well as developing appropriate applications that will attract more consumers by increasing their benefit perception. This study is confined to the response of 263 young people residing in Bhubaneswar city of Odisha. In future of similar types of study may be conducted in either part of the state as well as country with a relatively larger sample size including customers from different age groups. Although past literatures have focused on technological aspects of online shopping, few studies have examined the perception and intention of youth towards online shopping. Furthermore, most studies on online shopping perception have focused on the relationships between technology adoption factors and perception of users. This study provides a basis for further refinement of TAM model to predict behavioral intentions of consumers towards online shopping.

DOI: 10.4018/978-1-5225-0902-8.ch003

INTRODUCTION

With the advancement in information and communication technology, online shopping has emerged as one of the growing business models and has attracted the attention of both business and researchers. Its role is turning very significant as it allows consumers to access shopping facilities 24 hours a day, while allowing the vendors to reduce their cost. Online shopping sites are also valuable retail outlets due to their wide domestic and global reach, low cost, innovation on continuous basis, and order taking and customer feedback facilities (Eroglu et al., 2001). However, unlike the traditional rock & brick retail stores, inability to interact with a salesman and the goods, as well as the confidence on electronic payment methods increase perceived risk with regard to online shopping (Casaló et al., 2007). Thus, despite of its advantages, the online shopping has not spread in fact as it was expected. The traditional retail stores are still the leading channels in retail industry representing an improper diffusion of online shopping in the society.

In the last decade plethora of research has been conducted to explore the adoption of online shopping, testing a series of factors considered to be essential for improved diffusion. Some studies have analysed technological characteristics such as usefulness, ease of use and security (Davis, 1989; Yu et al., 2005), others focus on the emotions and experiences of users (Agarwal and Prasad, 2000; Fiore and Kim, 2007). The technology acceptance model (TAM) (Davis, 1989) is widely used to explain individuals' intentions and actual use of information technology (IT). The primary interface for customers to purchase products and services online is the web site, a form of IT. Accordingly, online shopping behaviour can be partially explained by the TAM.

This study aims to investigate the consumer's perception and intention towards online shopping through integration of technological acceptance model (TAM). Youth are of particular interest, because it has been noted that these typically early adopter of innovative products, which eventually filters through to older age groups.

Conceptual Background

Online Shopping

Online shopping is defined as a channel whereby the consumers interact with a retailer through internet using a laptop or Personal computer. In that sense it can be seen as a subset of e-commerce with its own unique characteristics. In the literature there are several recent studies focused on online shopping adoption. As per the study conducted by Tonita et al. (2004) useing the constructs of the Technology Acceptance Model (TAM) as a basis revealed that attitudes toward online shopping and intention to shop online are not only affected by ease of use, usefulness, and enjoyment, but also by perceived risk in online shopping. Jayawardhena et al., (2007) conducted a study to examine the purchase intentions of online retail consumers and findings of this study indicates that consumer purchase orientations in both the traditional world and on the Internet are largely similar.

Koufaris et. al (2001) studied Consumer Behavior in Web-Based Commerce with an objective to design electronic systems and interactions that retain customers and increase sales. Findings of this study indicate that perceived control and shopping enjoyment can increase the intention customers. This study also revealed that a Web store that utilizes value-added search mechanisms and presents a positively challenging experience can increase customers' shopping enjoyment. Rezaei et al (2010) studied consumers' perception of the Internet trade, general perceptions of privacy and security of the Web, perceptions of the risks and benefits of online shopping in the Iran and also examined the effect of individual characteristics on consumers' decision to buy online. This study revealed that the perceived risks have the strongest predictive value in terms of the formation of consumers trust in online shopping.

Shashikala et. al (2011) attempted to investigate the factors influencing customer perceived risk of online shopping in Indian context. This study generated 6 major factors: Monetary, Performance, Time, Source, Social, and Psychological. Monetary and performance risks have highest mean scores and social and psychological risks being the lowest. Further T test confirmed that all of these factors had significant impact on perceived risk with online shopping.

Technology Acceptance Model

The TAM (Davis, 1989; Davis et al., 1989) was originally developed to predict users' initial adoption or use of a new IT in the workplace. It suggests that user acceptance of IT can be explained by two salient beliefs: perceived usefulness and perceived ease of use. Perceived usefulness is defined as "the degree to which a person believes that using a particular system would enhance his or her job performance" and perceived ease of use is defined as "the degree to which a person believes that using a particular system would be free of effort" (Davis, 1989, p. 320). Perceived usefulness and perceived ease of use are considered instrumental in achieving valued outcomes, and thus reflect the utilitarian or extrinsic aspects of IT usage. Explicitly to model the role of intrinsic motivation in the TAM, Davis et al. (1992) introduced a third belief called perceived enjoyment. Perceived enjoyment is defined as "the extent to which the activity of using the computer is perceived to be enjoyable in its own right, apart from any performance consequences that may be anticipated" (Davis et al., 1992, p. 1113). Enjoyment reflects the hedonic or intrinsic aspects of IT usage.

In the model, perceived usefulness, perceived ease of use and Perceived enjoyment predict attitude, defined as the user's evaluation of the desirability to use the technology. The individual's behavioral intention is directly influenced by the attitude and perceived usefulness. TAM is found as able to provide a reasonable description of a user's intention to use technology (Legris et al., 2003) and it has been widely utilized in research to determine the probability of adopting an online system and user perceptions of system use (Moon and Kim, 2001). On this basis, it was hypothesized that:

H1: Perceived usefulness positively affects the attitude towards using online shopping.
H2: Perceived enjoyment positively affects the attitude towards using online shopping.
H3: Perceived ease of use positively affects the perceived usefulness of online shopping.
H4: Perceived ease of use positively affects the attitude towards using online shopping.
H5: Perceived usefulness positively affects the purchase intention to use online shopping.
H6: Attitude towards using online shopping positively affects the purchase intention to use online shopping.

Perceived Risk

Perceived risk, introduced by Bauer (1960), refers to the nature and amount of risk perceived by a consumer in contemplating a particular purchase decision. Lim (2003) argued that the consumers' perceived risk is technology-related and includes issues such as download delays, limitations in the interface, search problems, inadequate measurement of web application success, security weakness and a lack of internet standards. Consumers appreciate simplicity or clear design in e-commerce web sites because they reduce the perceived risks of wasted time, deception and frustration, and because customers may get annoyed when they see the interface design and format of interface elements varying among the different pages of a web site Presumably a consumer is motivated to make a purchase in order to attain some set of buying goals. The element of risk is often present because prior to making a purchase the consumer cannot always be certain the planned purchase will allow them to achieve their buying goals.

H7: Perceived risk is negatively affects the attitude towards using online shopping.

Proposed Research Model

Based on the above literature and hypothesis, the research model is presented in figure no-1. The dependent variable – purchase intention– is posited as the primary construct to determine customers' purchase behaviour. Purchase intention refers to the subjective probability that an individual will purchase products from the online vendor or store in the future. The TAM initially focused on the adoption or use of a new IT in the workplace. Therefore, the proposed model integrates additional variables that are important for buyer-seller relationship maintainability, such as perceived risk and perceived enjoyment. The practical utility of considering the TAM stems from the fact that it contains variables that are critical to purchase intention. Perceived risk is considered because of the uncertainty and information asymmetry of the online shopping environment. Enjoyment is considered because not considering the hedonic aspects of online shopping is a major omission (Bart et al., 2005).

Figure 1. Proposed model

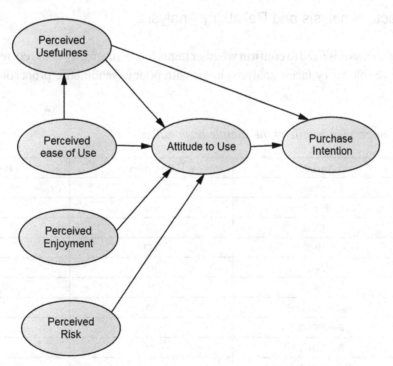

Methodology

The aim of this study was to improve the predictive ability of established models for forecasting uptake of new technological services like online shopping; therefore the methodology adopted for this study is like that used by previous models-mainly quantitative. A survey instrument was used to collect data including multi-item measure using a five point Likert scale. To discover and eliminate probable problems in this study, a pretest of the questionnaire was also done. Reverse translation was also adopted for little modification in words used in the questionnaire.

Scale Development

Perceived risk was assessed by six item measures modified from Corbittet al. (2003). Purchase intention was assessed by three item measures modified from Pavlou (2003). Perceived Usefulness, perceived ease of use and attitude towards online shopping was assessed by item measures modified from Davis (1989), Davis et al. (1989), Taylor and Todd (1995), Yu et al. (2005). Finally Enjoyment was measured by items adapted from Moon and Kim (2001). The questionnaire is provided in the Appendix.

Data Collection

The hypotheses were tested upon the young consumers aged between 15 to 35 years. The data were gathered through face to face interview with 263 students residing in Bhubaneswar city of Odisha in the month of May/June 2015. The socio demographic profile of the sample respondents are presented in Table-1.

Exploratory Factor Analysis and Reliability Analysis

Exploratory factor analysis is used to confirm whether items loaded correctly to the corresponding factors as identified. With exploratory factor analysis, items with poor psychometric properties were removed.

Table 1. Socio-demographic profile of the sample respondent

	Variable	Frequency	Percentage
Gender	Male	80	30.4
	Female	183	69.6
Age	15-18	20	7.7
	19-23	133	50.5
	24-28	65	24.7
	29-35	45	17.1
Monthly expenditure	Rs.2000 and below	12	4.7
	Rs. 2001-3000	64	24.3
	Rs. 3001-4000	136	51.7
	Rs. 4001 and above	51	19.3

The results of Exploratory factor analysis the results of Cronbach's alpha are displayed are displayed in Table-2. As all Cronbach's alpha values are greater than 0.70, all factors are acceptedas being reliable (Nunnaly,1978).

Structural Equation Modeling

In order to test the proposed model, Structural equation modeling (SEM) was conducted to test the relationship between independent and dependent variables. Table-3 shows the results from the SEM analysis. The overall indicators shows that model is good fit with each comparative fit index, goodness fit index and normal fit index above the 0.9 level.

Table 2. Factor loading and reliability test

	Scales	Factor Loading	Cronbach's α
Perceived risk (PR)	online purchases are risky because theproducts/services delivered may fail to meet my expectations.	0.689	0.867
	online purchases are risky because theproducts/services delivered may be inferior.	0.787	
	online purchases are risky because they may lead to financial loss for me.	0.756	
	online purchases are risky because they may causeothers to think less highly of me.	0.827	
	online purchases are risky because the products/services delivered may fail to fit well with my personal image or self-concept	0.734	
	online purchases are risky because they may lead to a time loss for me .	0.809	
Perceived usefulness (PU)	Using the online shopping to acquire a product would allow me to shop more efficiently	0.836	0.831
	Using the online shopping to acquire a product would allow me to do my shopping more quickly	0.821	
	Using the online shopping to acquire a product would be useful to do my shopping	0.790	
Perceived Ease of Use (PEOU)	Learning to use the online shopping to buy a product would be easy for me, even for the first time	0.836	0.798
	Using the online shopping to buy a product would be easy to do for me	0.828	
	The online shopping would be easy to be use to do my shopping	0.790	
Perceived Enjoyment (PE)	I will have fun when interacting with the online shopping site	0.689	0.713
	Using the online shopping site to purchase products will provide me with a lot of enjoyment	0.751	
	I think that purchasing products from the online shopping site will be interesting	0.796	
Attitude towards online shopping (AT)	Using the online shopping site to do my shopping is a good idea	0.846	0.771
	My general opinion of online shopping is positive	0.830	
	Using the online shopping to purchase a product seems an intelligent idea to me	0.808	
Purchase intention (PI)	I intend to use online shopping to conduct product purchases.	0.860	0.796
	I expect to purchase through online shopping in the future.	0.855	
	It is likely that I will transact with online shopping in the near future	0.818	

Results and Analysis

The structural equation modeling approach (SEM) approach was applied as it tests hypothesized causal relationship among multiple variables simultaneously and estimates the strength of interrelationship among latent constructs. The data were analysed using AMOS version 20 with maximum likelihood estimation. We have followed two step procedure of SEM by first, examining scale validity from the measurement model by using Confirmatory Factor Analysis (CFA), and second, focusing on testing the proposed hypotheses using the SEM. Measurement reliability and validity of the model containing multi-item constructs were assessed using CFA, Table-3 displays the chi-squared degree of freedom ratio as well as the good ness fit indicators.

The χ^2/df ratio for the proposed model was 1.82 and thus within the recommended range of 1 to 3. Again, the values of CFI, GFI and IFI values were all above the recommended value of 0.9 indicating a good model fit. Furthermore, the RMSEA value was computed to be below 0.01 indicating an acceptable fit. Thus based on these findings, the proposed model found to be fit with the data collected. Table-4 as exhibited below presents a summary of hypotheses tests. All the hypothesized paths of the structural model are highly significant as $\alpha=0.01$.

Table 3. Model Fit Indices

Model fit Indices	Computed value	Recommended Value
Chi-square (χ^2)	107.142	
Degrees of Freedom (df)	59	
χ^2/df	1.816	1-3
Probability level	0.000	
Comparative fit index(CFI)	0.969	>0.9
Goodness Fit Index(GFI)	0.912	>0.9
Incremental Fit Index(IFI)	0.970	>0.9
Root mean squared error of Approximation (RMSEA)	0.073	<0.1

Table 4. Hypothesis tests

Hypothesis	Path	Estimate	P-Value	Remark
H1	PU AT	0.373	0.000	Supported
H2	PE AT	0.434	0.000	Supported
H3	PEOU PU	0.616	0.000	Supported
H4	PEOU AT	0.025	0.973	Not Supported
H5	PU PI	0.066	0.295	Not Supported
H6	AT PI	0.855	0.000	Supported
H7	PR AT	-0.131	0.009	Supported

R^2 PU=0.323; R^2 AT=0.684; R^2 PI=0.529

The squared multiple correlations (R^2) for the dependent variables obtained from the proposed model were 0.323 for perceived usefulness, 0.684 for attitude towards online shopping and 0.529 for purchase intention. It represents that perceived ease of use explains 32.3 percent variance in perceived usefulness. Similarly perceived usefulness, perceived ease of use, perceived enjoyment and perceived risk are responsible for 68.4 percent variance in attitude towards online shopping. Likewise attitude towards online shopping explains 52.9 percent variance in purchase intention using online shopping.

Furthermore it is also revealed that perceived usefulness, perceived enjoyment and perceived risk had a significant impact on attitude towards online shopping as the p-value is less than 0.01 whereas perceived ease of use had no significant impact on attitude towards online shopping($p>0.01$). It was also found that attitude towards online shopping has a significant impact on purchase intention with p-value less than 0.01. But perceived usefulness has no significant impact on purchase intention as the computed p-value is 0.235 (<0.01). Similarly perceived ease of use has a statistically significant impact on perceived usefulness.

FINDINGS AND CONCLUSION

The results of this study extends an empirically based argument that the online shopping intentions of the consumers are significantly influenced by their attitude towards online shopping which in turn gets affected by perceived usefulness, perceived enjoyment and perceived risk. Perceived enjoyment is closely related to the attitude towards online shopping, followed by perceived usefulness which sought to validate previous researches. Perceived ease of use is not having any significant impact on attitude towards online shopping but has the strongest influence on perceived usefulness. However, it had been expected that perceived usefulness will have an effect on Purchase intention, but not supported in this study. It has an indirect effect on purchase intention mediated through attitude. Perceived risk with online shopping had a significant negative effect on attitude towards online shopping, that's why online vendors must seek to reduce this.

Thus we can conclude that, this study have a wide range of managerial as well as research implications. For researcher community, this study extends a basis for further refinement of models of consumer behavior as well as adoption in the context of online shopping. From managerial perspective, the proposed research model is useful to design and implement online shopping services that yield higher consumer acceptance.

Limitations and Scope for Further Research

This study has been operationalized according to the generally accepted research guidelines. However, it is important to bear in mind some of its limitations while generalizing its results. First the results of this study are restricted to the view of 263 sample respondents residing in Bhubaneswar city of Odisha only. Secondly this study has focused only on young consumers aged between 15-35, because people in this age group tended to be early adopters of new products in general and over time products adopted by this group are likely to be adopted by older groups. Finally response corresponding to any specific online vendor has not been dictated for this study. In future the same type of study may be done through carrying out a survey on larger number of customers of different online vendors. As this study is confined to youth only, future studies may ensure data collection from the other customers of older age groups, which will help the researcher to avoid the selection bias.

REFERENCES

Agarwal, R., & Prasad, J. (1998). The antecedents and consequents of user perceptions in information technology adoption. *Decision Support Systems*, *22*(1), 15–29. doi:10.1016/S0167-9236(97)00006-7

Agarwal, R., & Prasad, J. (2000). A field study of the adoption of software process innovations by information systems professionals. *IEEE Transactions on Engineering Management*, *47*(1), 295–308. doi:10.1109/17.865899

Bart, Y., Shankar, V., Sultan, F., & Urban, G. L. (2005). Are the drivers and role of online trust the same for all web sites and consumers? A large-scale exploratory empirical study. *Journal of Marketing*, *69*(4), 133–152. doi:10.1509/jmkg.2005.69.4.133

Bauer, R. A. (1960). Consumer behaviour as risk taking. In D. F. Cox (Ed.), *Risk Taking and Information Handling in Consumer Behaviour* (pp. 22–23). Cambridge, MA: Harvard University Press.

Casalo´, L. V., Flavian, C., & Guinalıu, M. (2007). The role of security, privacy, usability and reputation in the development of online banking. *Online Information Review*, *31*(5), 583–603. doi:10.1108/14684520710832315

Corbitt, B. J., Thanasankit, T., & Yi, H. (2003). Trust and e-commerce: A study of consumer perceptions. *Electronic Commerce Research and Applications*, *2*(3), 203–215. doi:10.1016/S1567-4223(03)00024-3

Davis, F. D., Bagozzi, R. P., & Warshaw, P. R. (1989). User acceptance of computer technology: A comparison of two theoretical models. *Management Science*, *35*(8), 982–1003. doi:10.1287/mnsc.35.8.982

Davis, F. D., Bagozzi, R. P., & Warshaw, P. R. (1989). User acceptance of computer technology: Acomparison of two theoretical models. *Management Science*, *35*(8), 982–1002. doi:10.1287/mnsc.35.8.982

Davis, F. D., Bagozzi, R. P., & Warshaw, P. R. (1992). Extrinsic and intrinsic motivation to use computers in the workplace. *Journal of Applied Social Psychology*, *22*(14), 1111–1132. doi:10.1111/j.1559-1816.1992.tb00945.x

Eroglu, S. A., Machleit, K. A., & Davis, L. M. (2001). Atmospheric qualities of online retailing: A conceptual model and implications. *Journal of Business Research*, *54*(2), 177–184. doi:10.1016/S0148-2963(99)00087-9

Fiore, A. M., & Kim, J. (2007). An integrative framework capturing experiential and utilitarian shopping experience. *International Journal of Retail & Distribution Management*, *35*(6), 421–442. doi:10.1108/09590550710750313

Jayawardhena, C., Wright, L. T., & Dennis, C. (2007). —Consumers Online: Intentions, Orientations and Segmentation. *International Journal of Retail & Distribution Management*, *35*(6), 515–526. doi:10.1108/09590550710750377

Koufaris, Kambil, & LaBarbera. (2001). Consumer Behavior in Web-Based Commerce: An Empirical Study. *International Journal of Electronic Commerce, 6*(2).

Lim, N. (2003). Consumers perceived risk: Sources versus consequences. *Electronic Commerce Research and Applications, 2*(3), 216–228. doi:10.1016/S1567-4223(03)00025-5

Moon, J. W., & Kim, Y. G. (2001). Extending the TAM for a world-wide-web context. *Information & Management, 38*(4), 217–230. doi:10.1016/S0378-7206(00)00061-6

Pavlou, P. A. (2003). Consumer acceptance of electronic commerce: Integrating trust and risk with the technology acceptance model. *International Journal of Electronic Commerce, 7*(3), 101–134.

Perea y Monsuwé, T., Dellaert, B. G. C., & de Ruyter, K. (2004). What drives consumers to shop online? A literature review. *International Journal of Service Industry Management, 15*(1), 102–121. doi:10.1108/09564230410523358

Rezaei Dolatabadi, H., & Ebrahimi, H. (2010). ―Factors Influencing Iranian Consumers' Trust in Internet Shopping‖. *European Journal of Soil Science, 16*(2).

Suresh, M., & Shashikala, R. (2011). Identifying Factors of consumer Perceived Risk towards Online Shopping in India. *3rd International Conference on Information and Financial Engineering*. IPEDR.

Taylor, S., & Todd, P. A. (1995). Assessing IT usage: The role of prior experience. *Management Information Systems Quarterly, 19*(4), 561–570. doi:10.2307/249633

Venkatesh, V., & Davis, F. D. (2000). A theoretical extension of the technology acceptance model: Four longitudinal field studies. *Management Science, 46*(2), 186–204. doi:10.1287/mnsc.46.2.186.11926

Yu, J., Ha, I., Choi, M., & Rho, J. (2005). Extending the TAM for a t-commerce. *Information & Management, 42*(77), 965–976. doi:10.1016/j.im.2004.11.001

Chapter 4
A Readiness Index for Marketing Analytics:
A Resource–Based View Conceptualization for the Implementation Stage

Pável Reyes-Mercado
Anahuac University, Mexico

ABSTRACT

The marketing analytics function has received increasing attention from managers as information processing has permeated all marketing domain. However, value is realized once data is properly processed and firms develop and activate consumers and customers' insights to make decisions, that is, during the implementation stage of the marketing analytics function. This study aims to propose a research model to analyse how ready are organizations to reap the benefits of implementing the marketing analytics function and understand its impact on the overall marketing performance. The model is derived from the Resource-Based view of the firm, a research perspective that argues that for a firm to reach a sustainable competitive advantage, its key assets –the marketing function– has to be: valuable, rare, inimitable, and the organisation has to be capable of exploit such assets. Managerial and research implications are discussed and further research avenues are offered.

INTRODUCTION

The marketing analytics function has received increasing attention from managers as digital marketing has expanded to become a wide marketing domain. Despite such expansion, only few organizations are able to act on competitive and timely insights from the data they collect, that is, during the marketing analytics implementation stage.

The complexity of the marketing landscape has evolved and managers need to trust in sound frameworks that enable them to assess their key assets, how to exploit them, and how to allocate resources into the overall marketing dimension. A readiness index comes in handy to provide answers to such managerial needs.

DOI: 10.4018/978-1-5225-0902-8.ch004

When analysing the implementation stage, market orientation, which is a construct focused on specific activities instead of philosophical concepts in order to facilitate the implementation of the marketing function (Kohli & Jaworski, 1990), can shed light on how to align organisational resources. From market orientation, marketing intelligence –"customers' verbalized needs and preferences" involving also exogenous influences, its dissemination, and organisational responses to it, have been considered moderators of the organizational performance (Kohli & Jaworski, 1990). Moreover, organisations with higher marketing orientation largely determine business profitability along with other business-specific and market-level influences. Particularly, customer orientation, competitor orientation, and the capability to organise the firm's resources to create more value play a role in building marketing orientation (Narver & Slater, 1990).

Marketing technology has evolved from basic applications of data base marketing (Kahan, 1998) to better understand the cognitive and behavioural patterns of consumers to novel applications of market research as automated online review analysis (Lee & Bradlow, 2011). Furthermore, Customer Relationship Management CRM has been one of the marketing technology domains more focused on cumulative data acquired form transactional interchanges between a customer and a supplier along time.

While there is a plethora of definitions to explain what are the reach and scope of marketing analytics, this paper defines all kinds of data analytics, involving consumers and customers, gathered from primary and secondary sources that comes from market research and transactional activity at customer level.

This study proposes a readiness index model to measure how ready are organizations to realize the benefits from implementing the marketing analytics function and understand its relationship with the overall marketing performance. From the perspective of the Resource-Based View (RBV) of the firm, this paper firstly attempts to answer if the marketing analytics function is a resource that generates sustained competitive advantage (SCA) to the firm. To achieve this first objective, this paper uses the VRIO framework proposed by the resource based view of the firm. Specifically, the VRIO framework analyses how valuable, rare, and organization-related are a resource in order to provide sustained competitive advantage. As the marketing analytics function is regarded as a resource that provides SCA, this paper then proposes a readiness index to implement such function. To achieve this second objective, this paper develops a literature review to bring the relevant conceptualizations on implementing and exploiting VRIO resources. Such review includes studies that analyses factors which are considered to influence implementation of the marketing analytics function. The comprehensive literature review indicates that RBV provides a sound theoretical model to frame the implementation stage of marketing analytics.

In summary, drawing from to RBV of the firm, this paper aims to:

1. Analyse the marketing analytics function in reference to the VRIO attributes, and
2. Develop a conceptual model to measure how ready organisation is to implement the marketing analytics function.

This paper is structured as follows: Section 2 reviews existing literature, conceptualizes marketing analytics implementation, and develops a set of research propositions interlinked in a conceptual framework. Next, Section 3 discusses the implications of the research framework ranging from model measurement and testing to implications for researchers. Some implications from marketing practitioners are discussed in Section 4. Finally, the paper concludes with some potential limitations and interesting research directions in Section 5.

Literature Review and Conceptual Model

Resource-based View

Firm performance has long been studied in the marketing and strategic management fields in order to understand what are the endogenous and exogenous variables that generate a differentiated level of profits. The Resource-Based Theory (RBT) of the firm was developed under the assumption that internal resources and capabilities explain profits (Wernerfelt, 1984). One the first postulates indicate of this theory is that firms can identify key resources that leads to higher average profits. Alongside, a firm can use rare resources to increase resources barriers (a similitude with Porter's product barriers), which in turn, increase the resource returns. Later, Barney (1991) supported that valuable, rare, imperfectly imitable, and difficult to substitute resources, which are heterogeneously distributed across firms in an industry, leads not only to a competitive advantages (CA, a strategy only implemented by an incumbent) but also to a sustained competitive advantage (SCA) –one that competitors are unable to imitate (Barney, 1991).

Marketing Resources

Barney (1991) made the case on the relationship between information processing systems and sustained relative advantage. In his assertion, hardware per se is not considered a single source of SCA but a complementary part of internal decision-making routines of the firm. The interaction between management and information processing systems is clearly the source of SCA as it is rare, socially complex, hard to imitate, in spite of availability of substitutes. This suggests that marketing function is an information processing unit along with decision-making routines can be conceptualised as a marketing resource.

Antecedent: Marketing Strategy

In implementing the marketing concept, the market orientation serves as a departing point for organisations who want to align efforts and resources to reach competitive advantages in the market. Outcomes of marketing orientation include customer focus, coordinated efforts of marketing, and profitability (Kohli & Jarowsky, 1990) which are reached through intelligence generation, intelligence dissemination, and responsiveness. The first instance is intelligence generation which refers to present and future customer needs gathered by organisations through primary and secondary information sources in such a way the products may be enhanced with no sole responsibility for the marketing function. The second instance related to intelligence dissemination, a concept that encompasses activities focused on sharing information to internal stakeholders so they can develop aligned initiatives. Third instance refer to responsiveness which refers to act according to intelligence that has been generated and shared. The previous involve defining value proposals, product development, as well as pricing, distribution and promotion activities (Kohli and Jarowsky, 1990). From the previous discussion, given that market orientation serves as aligning instrument of organizational effort, it becomes an antecedent of the VRIO framework. Therefore, we propose:

RP1: A higher level of market orientation of the firm is related to higher marketing analytics as VRIO resource.

Focal Construct: Marketing Analytics and its Implementation

From the perspective of RBT, resources are tangible and intangible assets that firms use to implement their strategies (Barney and Arikan, 2001). In line with this definition, this paper propose that the marketing analytics function relates to how an organization draws relevant, timely, and actionable consumer-related insights from internal and external information repositories, and market research studies. This conceptual view corresponds with RBT that emphasizes the implementation of particular resources to reach a CA.

Marketing Analytics as a Marketing Resource

The VRIO (valuable, rare, imperfect imitability, organization) framework (Barney and Hesterly, 2012) analyses how valuable (enables the firm to develop and implement strategies based on lower costs or increasing revenues), rare (implemented by a small number of competitors in a given market), imperfectly imitability (costly to implement or imitate by competitors), and organization (how organizational, policies, procedures, skills, and capabilities enable an efficient exploitation of the resource) is an organizational resource to generate a sustained competitive advantage (SCA).

Marketing Analytics Implementation

Taking into consideration that deploying strategic assets to pursue a specific strategy, assumes that the firm is able to exploit such assets with in suitable combination (Makadok, 2001), RBT defined capabilities as specific and organizationally embedded resources which improve productivity of other resources owned by the firm. Capabilities may affect information-based tangible and intangible processes that enable the firm to deploy other resources more efficiently. (Makadok, 2001). CA is achieved through combining physical and capital assets with the proper firm's capacity to deploy organizational resources (Amit and Schoemaker, 1993). Technology resources for marketing analytics comprise valuable physical resources as: computer networks, telephony, web platforms for information storage and retrieval. Hence, organizational resources and capabilities are inseparably bundled together in achieving CA.

In the marketing domain, the capabilities approach has been linked to market sensing and customer linking capabilities. They include diagnosis of current capabilities, anticipation of future needs and capabilities, redesign of underlying processes, top-down commitment, creative use of information technology, and continuous monitoring of progress (Day, 1994). Day (2011) further refined marketing capabilities according to their orientation and function. According to Day's classification, RBV of the firm would be an inside-out oriented marketing capability focused on exploiting internal resources. This paper aims to analyse not only marketing analytics as an isolated resource or capability but to include the concept of marketing analytics implementation as a bundled concept on the valuable, rare, and imperfectly imitable organisational resource.

Marketing Analytics as a Valuable Resource

Marketing analytics can be considered a valuable resource that may help the firm decrease costs or increase revenues (Barney and Akiran, 2001) which could be impossible to reach without the use of such valuable resource. Moreover, valuable resources help the firm to cope with external threats and opportunities (Barney, 1991). For example, by using marketing analytics, firms can find profitable market segments to which increase its price margin, and hence to reap a higher margin. Similarly, firms can increase revenues by knowing accurate consumers' willingness to pay premium prices and also by detecting loyal customers which add more customer value. In contrast, as marketing analytics involve process-specific information technology resources -which may be easy to acquire in the market- and taking only the valuable feature of marketing analytics is not sufficient for achieving CA (Powell and Dent-Micallef, 1997) because other competitors may have such resources too. Hence, the following research proposal is framed:

RP2: Value of marketing analytics implementation is positively related to its competitive advantage.

Marketing Analytics as a Rare Resource

Marketing analytics may be praised as a rare resource as long is only possessed by only a handful of firms in a given industry and show a varying degree of heterogeneity. Cost to develop CRM projects involve hardware –which is now easily accessible-, and software which includes the capabilities to perform analytical tasks through hardware, a feature that is cost-prohibitive. The process of developing suitable information processing solutions require long commitments as well as tact and explicit knowledge routines embedded in the form of a marketing analytics product. Therefore:

RP3: Rareness of marketing analytics implementation is positively related to its competitive advantage.

Marketing Analytics as an Imperfectly Imitable Resource

Industry players may be unable to imitate a specific feature of marketing analytics so its effect continues through a wider time span for the firm. Imperfectly imitable resources refer to socially complex assets as trademarks, relational interchanges among many parties, and tacit knowledge components in such interchanges. For example, a long relational interchange between a brand and customers are likely to develop tacit knowledge routines to build upon, making difficult to replicate them by competitors. Hence:

RP4: Imperfect imitability of marketing analytics implementation is positively related to its competitive advantage.

Marketing Analytics and Organization

The organizational perspective of marketing analytics implementation refers to the capabilities, routines, and commitments made by the top management to implement new systems of marketing management, which in turn lead so SCA. The organizational perspective in the VRIO framework includes visualizing management as an enabler of products and processes focused on the marketing analytics function. Moreover, the organizational component also includes training, learning techniques, marketing analytics deliverables design, management teams, and management systems. A culture of marketing orientation affects CRM since it involves both tacit and explicit knowledge between the brand and the customer. Therefore:

RP5: Organisation dimension of marketing analytics implementation is positively related to its competitive advantage.

Consequence: Firm Performance

The desired consequence of implementing the marketing analytics function is to reach a SCA. Consistent with RBV, the readiness index model proposed in this paper considers SCA as a function of the VRIO resources, and this paper extends the applicability of RBV to the marketing analytics function (a VRIO resource) and its implementation. Therefore, it is reasonable to assume that the consequences of implementing the marketing analytics function are positively associated with SCA. This can be framed in the following research proposal:

RP6: Marketing analytics implementation is positively related to a higher firm performance.

Noteworthy, implementing the marketing analytics function involves a long-term marketing orientation and strategy. Firms can engage in the acquisition of any hardware and software and in developing processes and products for the marketing analytics function which not necessarily indicates that a specific marketing strategy is being implemented. Such measure has to be taken only as an antecedent of implementing the marketing analytics function. To conclude, the literature review reveal that marketing analytics implementation can be conceptualized as a firm's aligned set of internal and external actions initiated by the organization. The main goal of deploying such actions is perform a specific marketing project that involves the organization, product, and process dimensions of the marketing analytics function.

The previous discussed research proposals can be depicted in a nomological network in which marketing strategy becomes an antecedent of the VRIO variables. RBV of the firm is a valuable framework to analyse firm performance by considering the marketing analytics function a key asset. Firm performance is the outcome of exploiting marketing analytics as a key marketing asset. The interrelationships between the research proposals are showed in Figure 1.

General Discussion

Prospects for Measurement and Empirical Testing

The empirical testing of the proposed theoretical framework and the relationships between variables involves a methodological decisions and analytical techniques to derive solid conclusions. Measurement items related to the constructs detailed in the previous sections can be seen as discrete or continuous variables —discrete if respondents mark a number in a specific scale and continuous if the respondent marks a place into a broader subjective scale. Consistent with this notion, data analysis techniques as linear regression to test individual influences in the research frameworks and structural equations to assess the complete set of direct and moderating effect of variables on others. Importantly, as the purpose of this RBV-derived model is to become a predictive tool that helps managers to understand how ready their company is to embrace analytics function, survey measurement item should be developed from a formative perspective. Data can be collected using online and paper-and-pen questionnaires with a standard 5-7-points Likert scale. Questionnaire items can be derived from existing literature in which previously scales have been validated in terms of constructs reliability and validity. An important aspect for theory

Figure 1. Readiness index model to analyse implementation stage of marketing analytics

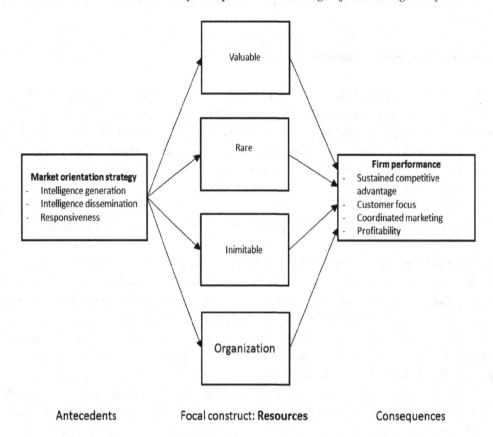

testing is to consider RBV constructs as higher order construct with resources attributes: valuable, rare, imperfect, imitable, and organization, as lower-order components. This methodological approach has the advantage to express why resources in general have a significant effect on firm performance rather than explaining every component of these resources. Including resources attributes as a higher-order construct would also reduce the sample size requirement. This methodological approach is presented in Figure 2.

Implications for Theory Development

This study has implications for theory development. Existing literature focused on RBV is summarized in reviews; see for example Kozlenkova (2014). This paper contributes to the existing literature on RBV

Figure 2. Readiness index model to analyse implementation stage of marketing analytics with VRIO variables modelled as second order variable

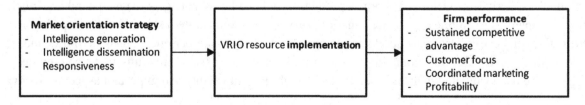

from the perspective of marketing by including the core aspects of the theory and develops a specific framework to assess the features of the analytics function as a strategic resource that impacts firm performance. The research framework also proposes that the strength of links between resources attributes and firm performance are moderated by contextual influences as industry maturity, and managerial tenure.

Managerial Implications

The current concern on how to realize value from the existing data that is created by firms and consumers is addressed in this paper by providing a conceptual view on the factors related to implementing the marketing analytics function. The framework offers a view of the marketing analytics function as a VRIO resource for the firm. Afterwards it presents a comprehensive perspective of marketing analytics in the form of organization, process, and product dimensions. Marketing managers can benefit from using this framework in a number of ways. Managers can generate a roadmap to plan the implementation of the marketing analytics function; this would bring the benefit of knowing in advance which dimension requires the allocation of different levels of organizational resources. Managers may also want to utilise the proposed framework to vary the emphasis and sequences of the different dimensions of the implementation stage of marketing analytics functions.

CONCLUSION

This paper has only considered VRIO variables into the research model for parsimony purposes. For researchers, this conceptual readiness index may serve as a basis upon which research can be advanced. Interesting future research may include a qualitative stage focused on refining the readiness index variables and proposing a data collection instrument complementary to the literature survey. Additionally, another research opportunity relates to collecting data from marketing managers to test the validity and reliability of the proposed index. A limitation of this study is that the readiness index follows the streamline of RBT while there are other theories aimed at explaining how resources –and its utilization, influence firm's performance (see for example market-based assets or resource advantage theory of competition, to mention a couple). Future research may derive instruments from such theoretical perspectives.

REFERENCES

Amit, R., & Schoemaker, P. (1993). Strategic assets and organizational rents. *Strategic Management Journal*, 4(1), 33–46. doi:10.1002/smj.4250140105

Barney, J. B. (1991). Firm resources and sustained competitive advantage. *Journal of Management*, 17(1), 99–120. doi:10.1177/014920639101700108

Barney, J. B., & Arikan, A. M. (2001). The resource-based view: origins and implications. In The Blackwell handbook of Strategic Management. Blackwell.

Barney, J. B., & Hesterly, W. S. (2012). *Strategic Management and Competitive Advantage*. New Jersey: Pearson.

Day, G. S. (1994). The capabilities of market-driven organizations. *Journal of Marketing*, *58*(4), 37–52. doi:10.2307/1251915

Day, G. S. (2011). Closing the marketing capabilities gap. *Journal of Marketing*, *75*(4), 183–195. doi:10.1509/jmkg.75.4.183

Kahan, R. (1998). Using database marketing techniques to enhance your one-to-one marketing initiatives. *Journal of Consumer Marketing*, *15*(5), 491–493. doi:10.1108/07363769810235965

Kohli, A. K., & Jaworski, B. J. (1990). Market orientation: The construct, research propositions, and managerial implications. *Journal of Marketing*, *54*(2), 1–18. doi:10.2307/1251866

Kozlenkova, I. V., Samaha, S. A., & Palmatier, R. W. (2014). Resource-based theory in marketing. *Journal of the Academy of Marketing Science*, *42*(1), 1–21. doi:10.1007/s11747-013-0336-7

Lee, T. Y., & Bradlow, E. T. (2011). Automated marketing research using online customer reviews. *JMR, Journal of Marketing Research*, *4*(5), 881–894. doi:10.1509/jmkr.48.5.881

Narver, J. C. & Slater, S. F. (1990). The effect of a market orientation on business profitability. *Journal of Marketing*, *54*, 20-35.

Powell, T. C., & Dent-Micallef, A. (1997). Information technology as competitive advantage: The role of human, business, and technology resources. *Strategic Management Journal*, *18*(5), 375-405.

Wernerfelt, B. (1984). A resource-based view of the firm. *Strategic Management Journal*, *5*(2), 171–180. doi:10.1002/smj.4250050207

Wernerfelt, B. (2014). On the role of the RBV in marketing. *Journal of the Academy of Marketing Science*, *42*(1), 22–23. doi:10.1007/s11747-013-0335-8

Section 2
Globalization and International Trade

Chapter 5

Globalization, Innovation, and Marketing Philosophy:
A Critical Assessment of Role of Technology in Defining New Dimensions

Sandeep Kumar Mohanty
Birla Global University, India

ABSTRACT

Globalization has brought innovation to center stage of marketing activities. This can be related to opportunities as well as scope for consumer proficiency. Initial years of this decade have found that over dependence on innovation has made it consistent, compulsive and converging. With this impetuous innovation, certain aspect of critical thought process brings technology to the spot-light. Marketing philosophy that recognizes technology as the rationale of foundation of globalization and innovation must retrospect and further critically assess that how far technology has dissociated both the terms. Globalization by nature has been divergent, yet struggling to ensure marketing success because innovation is converging with the help of technology. Global Marketing is in a precarious juncture where every alternate day new technology is wiping out the old and with this new market is superimposing the old one. This transition is threatening concepts like segmentation, targeting and branding. This chapter is a critical assessment of role of technology in redefining the relationship between globalization, innovation and marketing. Secondary data of 51 Indian business sectors, consisting some of the leading market players have been analyzed to explore the relationship and propose a conceptual model.

INTRODUCTION

The new age marketing is dependent on innovation. The reasons are many but the concern is genuine. Organizations want to survive and in this process only innovation can guide them to find a new place to operate without stiff competition and complex marketing problems. Yet, the theory of innovation is subject to prominence because of another major force called technology. Technology has brought another concept, globalization to center stage. Eventually globalization brings marketing thought process to be

DOI: 10.4018/978-1-5225-0902-8.ch005

challenging and constantly self-critical. This paper tries to find out whether the concepts of innovation, globalization and marketing can have any significant change or shift with the presence of technology. The research has considered varied sectors consisting both manufacturing as well as services where technology has been a driving force and due to technological change and alteration innovation, globalization and marketing approach have been relatively affected. This paper has covered the initial results of a lengthy research process and subject to theory generation and radical introspection.

LITERATURE REVIEW

The literature pertaining to this research paper has been intermingled with three major concepts of innovation, globalization and marketing philosophy. These concepts have been crystalized by technology. During the literature review the researcher has taken care of both theoretical (fundamentals) and practical aspect of these terms so that less confusion would be there to introspect and consent.

Innovation

Christensen (2013) has been very critical in declaring the disturbing nature of innovation and he had suggested that any dilution in innovative thought process will fall without any further analysis. Managing innovation must take care of creative destruction (Bhat and Bowonder, 2001). New age innovation and technological variations have been deeply involved in social dislocation, uncertainty and indecision (Wolfe, 2000). Innovation has been resulted in excessive complexity and uncontrollable organizational dealings (Gerybadze and Reger, 1999). National innovation systems are missing vertical links as well as misplacing the national and global actor. This process of exclusion of vital partners ending in resulting confusion in global innovation networks (Hotz-Hart, 2000). Globalization requires more attention to innovate. Technological innovation energies globalization, and take along collaborations to global business scenario (Rycroft, 2003). Technological innovation affects globalization and this brings challenges in organizations in different shapes especially in R&D capabilities (Miao *et al.*, 2007). Organizations capable enough of high level of innovation, learning and internationalization achieve competitiveness through globalization (Baffour and Amal, 2011). Knowledge intensive and sensitive industries are concentrated and cluttered in one place. This defies the concept of true globalization (Dunning, 2002). Organization's R&D (innovation) and marketing activities are increasingly surpassing national boundaries and becoming more of international activities (Ready, 2002). Considering this internationally dispersed innovation activities, Bartlett and Ghoshal (1991) has pointed out four different kind of administrative and organizational structure. This confirms that managing innovation in global set up requires managerial adjustments. Organizations in an ever changing technological set up follow imitation to transform. They are following joint ventures to move from low to high level of innovation (Fan, 2011). Technology is making innovation converging and this is helping global adaptation of innovation process meaningful (Dekimpe *et al.*, 2000). There is a positive relationship between global competition and innovation. This relationship does not change across different industries and service sectors (Gorodnichenko *et al.* 2010).

Globalization

Technological changes and innovation are deliberated as the determining factors of globalization (Narula, 2014). In a borderless economy organizations must create new subsidiaries to facilitate added values with the help of technology and R & D efforts (Nakahara, 1997). Globally catered products and services affect the marketing and sales network of the organization (Chell, 2001). Similarly organizations are facing challenges of monitoring innovation and globalization, further this is affecting marketing (Griffiths *et al.*, 2000). Globalization has several implications for marketing theory expansion and managerial performances. This shows that marketing resources and marketing performances have been affected by globalization. Under these circumstances researches must study the role of globalization and marketing (Luo *et al.*, 2005). Global marketing is notional and in a managerial context difficult to apply (Svensson, 2002). Globalization is more of a "cultural concept" and has the capability to drive mind of marketing practitioners (Applbaum, 2006). Globalization depends on the behavior of the actors in the distribution channel and nature of marketing followed in the industry. Global marketing is advocating for strong support for standardization (Wind, 1998). Globalization and standardization of products are not mere coincidence, but marketing mix elements must not be standardized in a global business context (Lascu, 1994). Globalization has given new challenges to marketing functions and new technology has been the real threat to marketing activities (Brady and Davis, 1993). Technology carries players to market and progressively create segmentations (Dedrick and Kraemer, 2008). Globalization has influenced major disciplines. It has transformed itself as an unavoidable and determined social actor (Drori *et al.*, 2006). It has brought changes and propelled innovation in a major sector like pharma (Abrol *et al.*, 2011).

Marketing Philosophy

Marketing orientation is affected by entrepreneurial behavior (Sun and Pan, 2011). "Entrepreneurial abilities, skills, competencies and perspectives" are the distinguished preconditions for new global approach to marketing (Passaris, 2006). Innovation has a role in restructuring marketing orientations specifically in market segments like rural areas (Dinis, 2006). Interaction of innovation and marketing capabilities considerably impact organizations market place performance. This also affects the organization's marketing orientation (O'Cass and Ngo, 2011). Upsurge of integrated set of information technologies in the form of computers, telecommunication and media have influenced production process and distribution channels (Wolfe, 2000). Opposing this view, Ozer and Cebeci (2010)have found that in an international set up product development is of financial implications and not of marketing complications. In this connection FDI (Foreign Direct Investment) has been an indicator of global business growth, competition and marketing excellence (Chesnais and Simonetti, 2000).

Literature review has tried to explore the relationship between innovation, globalization and marketing philosophy in a situation where dominance factor is technology. This part of the paper has raised the concern for finding out new relationship dimensions between these three major players. Literature review has considered a generalist view without constraining to any product, industry or regulation. There are industry specific literatures that maintain equal distance between these three players, but in an extremely dominant global business scenario such narrow and polarized view are not recommended.

RESEARCH QUESTIONS

After analyzing the existing literature few research questions can be framed here. Technology has been the connection between these three elements, yet how organization are dealing with technology remains to be reexamined. Has the thrust to technology dissociating globalization and innovation? Has innovation decided the marketing fortune of MNCSs last decade and still maintaining this? Has globalization really address the marketing thought process in long term and short term business perspectives? What extent innovation has integrated the globalization of technology? What extent global marketing has been a hope for innovation? With these questions in mind, research has been conducted to integrate the three major terms and find a relationship.

Conceptual Model

Here the conceptual model has three components (factors). Innovation and Globalization are independent factors while Marketing Philosophy has been the dependent factor. Globalization is also dependent when Innovation is expected to propel this as an independent factor. So the conceptual model is given below in Figure 1. The context of this research is technology.

Objectives

The study has been guided by two major objectives. These objectives are aimed at finding the relationship between three major components like globalization, innovation and marketing philosophy while dealing with technology. This study has considered different sectors while dealing with these components. So the objectives of this study can be

1. To study the role of technology in defining the relationship between globalization, innovation and marketing philosophy.
2. To assess whether sector variations affects the above mentioned relationship or not.

While dealing with these objectives the researcher has redefined the three major concepts and that has been another facet of this research. This extension of recapturing these major concept has been research specific and makes specific adjustments keeping technology in mind.

Figure 1. Conceptual model

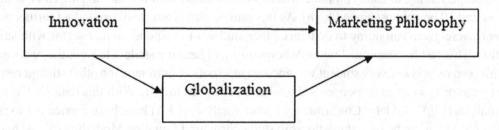

Hypotheses

The study has six hypotheses. The first three of them are directional and the other three are non-directional.

Hypothesis 1: There is positive relationship between globalization and innovation.
Hypothesis 2: There is positive relationship between globalization and marketing philosophy.
Hypothesis 3: There is positive relationship between innovation and marketing philosophy.
Hypothesis 4: There is no relationship between sector and innovation.
Hypothesis 5: There is no relationship between sector and globalization.
Hypothesis 6: There is no relationship between sector and marketing philosophy.

Methodology

The study has followed a step-wise approach to achieve its objectives. The first phase has defined the concepts like globalization, innovation and marketing philosophy. Here two experts were contacted to select relevant components acknowledged by the researcher. These experts have more than two decades of marketing and new product development experience and they belong to a R&D lab of a reputed Public Sector Undertaking (PSU). The selected components are considered as items and a comprehensive questionnaire was prepared to get the response.

Sampling

It is difficult to get the responses from different sectors and it is equally difficult to get competent authority related to specific sectors who can provide their valuable response. So the researcher has selected fifty one sectors where the students of a major B-School has done their class assignment covering the majority of secondary data related to globalization, innovation and marketing philosophy. So each students represented as company experts and they could respond the questionnaire. This is an expert oriented research and may be from an academic point of view more relevant. Here the researcher has ensured that the knowledge level or understanding of sector wise information by each student is sufficient and can be considered as research reference. With help of this technique the study has certified that from technology perspective, customers and stakeholders view on these three concepts can be captured and studied.

Survey

Initially fifty-one students' responses have been collected with the help of a structure questionnaire. The response pertaining to each component/item was collected with a scale of 1 to 10 (1 being least agreed/low and 10 being most agreed/high). As this sample size is too small to conduct further tests, the respondents were given autonomy to convince other students to respond on that sector with sufficient information. This test has generated multiple responses and here the student has got the opportunity to validate his own response. Every student was encourage to collect minimum ten other student responses. Now every sector has eleven responses and total response goes to 561. With this data set Exploratory Factor Analysis (EFA) and later Confirmatory Factor Analysis (CFA) have been carried out to confirm the final items which can be part of relationship study. Structural Equation Modelling (SEM) have been used to study the relationship between different components.

Data Collection

Data has been collected with help of a structured questionnaire. After getting responses from the experts a detail item wise analysis was done. Here the major components like Globalization, Innovation and Marketing Philosophy has been defined by twelve items each. The questionnaire contains thirty six items and every item has been answered in a lower to higher order of agreement or score. Here the items are conceptual and respondents have been gives proper orientation to understand the concepts before filling the questionnaire. The relevance of these items are high and can be linked to literature review where most of the conceptual issues are raised by researchers found across the globe and industry. The items are provided in the Table 1 below.

Table 1. Variable and items

Variable	Code	Items
Globalization	Item1	Concentration towards standardization
	Item 2	Easy market segmentation
	Item 3	Easy entrance to a foreign market
	Item 4	Scope of online trading
	Item 5	Scope for FDI
	Item 6	Foreign technology availability and collaboration
	Item 7	Outward movement of resources
	Item 8	Globally situated R&D labs
	Item 9	Global brand preference and choices
	Item 10	Global vision
	Item 11	Negative cross cultural issues
	Item 12	Timeless approach
Innovation	Item13	Concentration towards customization
	Item 14	Role of IT and web based programs
	Item 15	Reduction of resource utilization
	Item 16	Up gradation and centralization of business units
	Item 17	Increase of R&D budget and related resources
	Item 18	Integration of business strategy
	Item 19	Emphasizing local preference and choices
	Item 20	Diffusion of innovation
	Item 21	Patents and IPR
	Item 22	Competition based innovation
	Item 23	Imitation friendly innovation
	Item 24	Short term innovation
Marketing Philosophy	Item25	Customer life cycle
	Item 26	Brand loyalty
	Item 27	Interaction with company
	Item 28	Demand of a new product
	Item 29	Value products
	Item 30	Quest for quality
	Item 31	Quest for product functionality
	Item 32	Experimentation habit of customers
	Item 33	Customer expectations
	Item 34	Evoked set
	Item 35	Peripheral issues
	Item 36	Scope of relationship marketing

Data Analysis

Responses were collected from 561 respondents. Every respondent has given his response pertaining to eleven sectors. In this process the collected data can be considered as valid and uniform. All the responses were considered for EFA and CFA and further SEM. Only fifty-one responses were considered for proving the fourth hypothesis (Average values of eleven responses were considered here).

EFA (Exploratory Factor Analysis)

Before conducting an exploratory factor analysis, it was assessed that the number of items are too many, and to reduce the numbers of items a pilot study was conducted. The initial fifty one responses were analyzed by doing a descriptive statistics analysis and based on the results sixteen items were excluded from the questionnaire. The final questionnaire (see Appendix-1) was having twenty items. In this way the sampling criteria were also justified. EFA was conducted with 280 valid responses. The researcher has followed Principal Component Analysis with Varimax Rotation. The KMO measure of sample adequacy and Bartlett's test of sphericity was as per specification. The results of the initial analysis has been provided below in Table 2.

After this purification study, three factors namely innovation, globalization and marketing philosophy have come out with three items each. The factor loadings obtained from the EFA were further analyzed to remove the items that perform poorly. Tabachnik and Fidell (2001) have suggested a factor loading of 0.4 as a good rule of thumb for lowest loading of an item. However, the study has measured a minimum loading of 0.5. Further, a cross-loading item is an item that loads at 0.4 or higher on two or more than two factors. However, there were no cross-loading that were identified. The three factors that were extracted and the factor loadings are provided in Table 3 below.

Measurement Model Evaluation

In order to assess the convergent and discriminant validity of the model, the measurement model was evaluated using AMOS 18. The convergent validity and Discriminant validity test results were acceptable.

Table 2. Results of the purification study

Latent Variables	Items	Item- to- total correlation	Alpha if item deleted	Coeff. Alpha
Innovation	-Concentration towards customization	.559	.559	.667
	-Reduction of resource utilization	.404	.628	
	-Upgradation and centralization of business units	.429	.612	
Marketing Philosophy	-Customer life cycle	.593	.686	.761
	-Customer Expectation	.595	.687	
	-Quest for product functionality	.533	.720	
Globalization	-Outward movement of resources	.525	.634	.713
	-Scope for online trading	.483	.660	
	-Global brand preference and choices	.506	.648	

Table 3. Factor loadings in the EFA

Factor 1 Innovation	Factor2 Marketing Philosophy	Factor3 Globalization
.740	.853	.767
.731	.647	.690
.645	.625	.634

CFA (Confirmatory Factor Analysis)

Confirmatory factor analysis was conducted to validate the factors. The model showed measures CMIN/DF as 15.708, CFI as .733, IFI as .736, TLI as .600, and RMSEA as .162. These model indicators are not in a very positive side but considering the varieties of industries and data complexity involved in this research, it is moderately adaptable. Modification indices do not suggest any major changes in the model. The final model after CFA has been expressed in the Figure 2 below.

Figure 2. Factor Structure after CFA

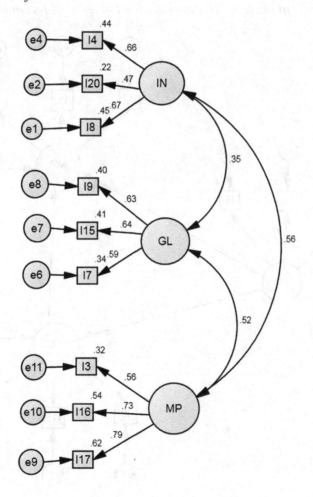

SEM (Structural Equation Modeling)

After conducting EFA and CFA it is found that the three major components of this study are expressed by three items each. To study the conceptual model and to find out the strength of the relationship SEM with the help of AMOS 18 was conducted. As the conceptual model has indicated Innovation as independent component while affecting both globalization and marketing philosophy and again globalization becomes an independent entity to affect marketing philosophy. Taking innovation as an independent component gives the research a thrust towards the concern for innovation and change in overall approach to innovation. The relationship model has been provided below in Figure 3. This shows the strength of the relationships between these three factors under the influence of technology.

Results of SEM

The model fit indices are moderately acceptable range and approve the relationships between the factors. The standardized regression weights (IN-MP= 0.43, IN-GL=0.35 and GL-MP=0.37)are considered for further analysis and it shows that innovation and globalization both positively affect the marketing phi-

Figure 3. SEM of Relationship between Factors under the Influence of Technology

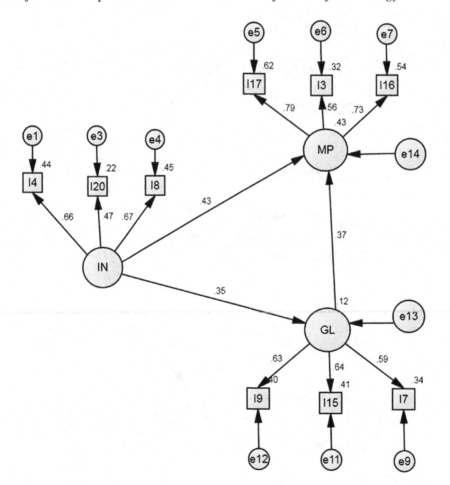

losophy. Between Innovation and globalization, marketing relationship is more affected by innovation. It shows that all the three are positively associated with each other. Among these three relationships, innovation and globalization has a low value, which indicates lesser integration.

Analyzing Sectors and Factors Relationship

The differentiation of sectors were done base on high technology and low technology sectors as per the classification by Oakey and Cooper (1989). So it is very easy to analyze all the three factors and find out whether sector wise there any different view exists or not. A one way ANOVA was conducted and it was found in all the three cases there is no relationship between sectors and factors. So the claim by Gorodnichenko *et al.* (2010) on similar ground is justified. The MNCs score card on three different elements have been provided in Appendix-2. The ANOVA results are provided below in Figure 4.

OVERALL RESULTS AND FINDINGS

The study had two objective and these two objective have been achieved by carefully analyzing the need of research structure. Initially EFA and further CFA captured the three factors with three items each. It is found that the concept of innovation is affecting marketing philosophy of the organization more than the concept of globalization affecting Marketing Philosophy. This show that marketers are more concern for innovation. Concept of innovation and globalization are positively affecting each other. Marketing philosophy has been positively affected by both the concepts of Innovation and Globalization. Irrespective of having a classification of high or low technology sectors the study found that the concern for the three factors remains same. There is no sector that has a major inclination for any factor. It means all the sectors are equally sensitive to Innovation, Globalization and Marketing Philosophy.

MANAGERIAL IMPLICATIONS

The paper has major managerial implications as it sensitizes the managers to form a Marketing thought process from the Innovation and Globalization aspects while dealing with intricacies of technology. Marketing Philosophy has realized the importance of Innovation to globalization. Globalization might have brought innovation to center stage but today Innovation has the upper hand in defining marketing. So the managers must look how the innovation must make a collaborative association with Globalization. Mangers must look beyond the nature of the concept of Innovation which is by default converging and Globalization that has been diverging. So in the context of marketing, innovation is defining technology

Table 4. ANOVA results

Factors	F Value	Sig.	Interpretation
Innovation	.355	.554	No relationship between Sectors and Innovation
Globalization	.760	.387	No relationship between Sectors and Globalization
Marketing Philosophy	2.895	.095	No relationship between Sectors and Marketing Philosophy

more than Globalization. Today marketing managers have less concern for market expansion rather they are more focus for integration of technologies and innovative approach to need satisfaction. The study fundamentally admits that the Marketing Philosophy remains the identical irrespective of high or low technological dependence in business concept.

LIMITATION AND CONCLUSION

This is a collective approach to research as business management students those who understand the concept of marketing took initiative to do secondary research and made their assessments on three important concepts. Their personal understanding with all the theoretical inputs have made this paper possible. But we can accept that this is a passive view as majority have no experience of managing marketing processes in MNC. Apart from this the study has relevance as it tries to define technology from three major components of industrial policies. So the study has the potential to explore new dimensions in understanding the nexus of innovation, globalization and marketing philosophy. The scope of this study may cover further technological variations to examine the found relationship. Future research may take any other component of technology or may include other factors to study dynamic nature of Innovation, Globalization and Marketing.

REFERENCES

Abrol, D., Prajapati, P., & Singh, N. (2011). Globalization of the Indian pharmaceutical industry: Implications for innovation. *Institutions, Etc., 3*(2), 327–365.

Applbaum, K. (2000). Crossing borders: Globalization as myth and charter in American transnational consumer marketing. *American Ethnologist, 27*(2), 257–282. doi:10.1525/ae.2000.27.2.257

Baffour Awuah, G., & Amal, M. (2011). Impact of globalization: The ability of less developed countries(LDCs) firms to cope with opportunities and challenges. *European Business Review, 23*(1), 120–132. doi:10.1108/09555341111098026

Bhat, B., & Bowonder, B. (2001). Innovation as an enhancer of brand personality: Globalization experience of titan industries. *Creativity and Innovation Management, 10*(1), 26–39. doi:10.1111/1467-8691.00188

Brady, J., & Davis, I. (1993). Marketing's mid-life crisis. *The McKinsey Quarterly,* (2): 17.

Chell, E. (2001). *Entrepreneurship: Globalization, Innovation and Development.* Cengage Learning EMEA.

Chesnais, F., & Simonetti, R. (2000). Globalization, Foreign Direct Investment and Innovation. *European Integration and Global Corporate Strategies, 17*, 1.

Christensen, C. (2013). *The innovator's dilemma: when new technologies cause great firms to fail.* Harvard Business Review Press.

Dedrick, J., & Kraemer, K. L. (2008, April). Globalization of innovation: the personal computing industry. In *2008 Industry Studies Conference Paper.* doi:10.2139/ssrn.1125025

Dekimpe, M. G., Parker, P. M., & Sarvary, M. (2000). Globalization: Modeling technology adoption timing across countries. *Technological Forecasting and Social Change*, *63*(1), 25–42. doi:10.1016/S0040-1625(99)00086-4

Dinis, A. (2006). Marketing and innovation: Useful tools for competitiveness in rural and peripheral areas. *European Planning Studies*, *14*(1), 9–22. doi:10.1080/09654310500339083

Drori, G. S., Meyer, J. W., & Hwang, H. (2006). *Globalization and organization: World society and organizational change*. Oxford University Press.

Dunning, J. H. (2002). *Regions, Globalization, and the Knowledge-based Economy*. Oxford University Press. doi:10.1093/0199250014.001.0001

Fan, P. (2011). Innovation, Globalization, and Catch-up of Latecomers: Cases of Chinese telecom firms. *Environment and Planning-Part A*, *43*(4), 830–849. doi:10.1068/a43152

Gerybadze, A., & Reger, G. (1999). Globalization of R&D: Recent Changes in the Management of Innovation in Transnational Corporations. *Research Policy*, *28*(2), 251–274. doi:10.1016/S0048-7333(98)00111-5

Gorodnichenko, Y., Svejnar, J., & Terrell, K. (2008). *Globalization and Innovation in Emerging Markets (No. w14481)*. National Bureau of Economic Research. doi:10.3386/w14481

Gorodnichenko, Y., Svejnar, J., & Terrell, K. (2010). Globalization and Innovation in Emerging Markets. *American Economic Journal. Macroeconomics*, *2*(2), 194–226. doi:10.1257/mac.2.2.194

Griffiths, P., Sedefov, R., Gallegos, A. N. A., & Lopez, D. (2010). How Globalization and Market innovation Challenge,How We Think about and Respond to Drug Use: 'SpiceaCase Study. *Addiction (Abingdon, England)*, *105*(6), 951–953. doi:10.1111/j.1360-0443.2009.02874.x PMID:20659053

Hotz-Hart, B. (2000). Innovation Networks, Regions, and Globalization. The Oxford Handbook of Economic Geography, 432-450.

Lascu, D. N., & Yip, G. S. (1994). Total Global Strategy: Managing for Worldwide Competitive Advantage. *Journal of Marketing*, *58*(3), 121. doi:10.2307/1252318

Luo, X., Sivakumar, K., & Liu, S. S. (2005). Globalization, Marketing Resources, and Performance: Evidence from China. *Journal of the Academy of Marketing Science*, *33*(1), 50–65. doi:10.1177/0092070304265050

Miao, C. H., Wei, Y. D., & Ma, H. (2007). Technological Learning and Innovation in China in the Context of Globalization. *Eurasian Geography and Economics*, *48*(6), 713–732. doi:10.2747/1539-7216.48.6.713

Nakahara, T. (1997). Innovation in a Borderless World Economy. *Research Technology Management*, *40*(3), 7.

Narula, R. (2014). *Globalization and Technology: Interdependence, Innovation Systems and Industrial Policy*. John Wiley & Sons.

Oakey, R. P., & Cooper, S. Y. (1989). High technology industry, agglomeration and the potential for peripherally sited small firms. *Regional Studies*, *23*(4), 347–360. doi:10.1080/00343408912331345542

OCass, A., & Ngo, L. V. (2011). Winning through Innovation and Marketing: Lessons from Australia and Vietnam. *Industrial Marketing Management*, *40*(8), 1319–1329. doi:10.1016/j.indmarman.2011.10.004

Ozer, M., & Cebeci, U. (2010). The Role of Globalization in New Product Development. *Engineering Management. IEEE Transactions on*, *57*(2), 168–180.

Passaris, C. E. (2006). The Business of Globalization and the Globalization of Business. *Journal of Comparative International Management*, *9*(1).

Reddy, P. (2002). *The Globalization of Corporate R & D: Implications for Innovation Systems in Host Countries*. Routledge.

Rycroft, R. W. (2003). Technology-based Globalization Indicators: The Centrality of Innovation Network Data. *Technology in Society*, *25*(3), 299–317. doi:10.1016/S0160-791X(03)00047-2

Sun, L. Y., & Pan, W. (2011). Market Orientation, Intrapreneurship Behavior, and Organizational Performance: Test of a Structural Contingency Model. *Journal of Leadership & Organizational Studies*, *18*(2), 274–285. doi:10.1177/1548051809334189

Svensson, G. (2002). Beyond Global Marketing and the Globalization of Marketing Activities. *Management Decision*, *40*(6), 574–583. doi:10.1108/00251740210433963

Tabachnick, B. G., & Fidell, L. S. (2001). *Using multivariate statistics*. Academic Press.

Wind, Y. (1986). The Myth of Globalization. *Journal of Consumer Marketing*, *3*(2), 23–26. doi:10.1108/eb008160

Wolfe, D. A. (2000). Globalization, Information and Communication Technologies and Local and Regional Systems of Innovation. In Transition to the knowledge society: Public policies and private strategies. Vancouver: UBC Press.

APPENDIX 1

Questionnaire

Name: _____

Organization: _____

Technology Orientation of the organization: High_____ Low_____

(Kindly fill the blank place after the sentence with a number between 1 (lowest /highly disagree/Low) and 10 (highest /highly agree/high) as a form of agreement.)

In this organization or in relation to this organization I find…

1.   Upgradation and centralization of business units ____
2.   Scope for online trading ____
3.   Customer life cycle ____
4.   Customer Expectation ____
5.   Concentration towards customization ____
6.   Quest for product functionality ____
7.   Reduction of resource utilization ____
8.   Demand of a new product____
9.   Increase of R&D budget and related resources____
10.   Interaction with company____
11.   Experimentation habit of customers____
12.   Foreign technology availability and collaboration____
13.   Negative cross cultural issues____
14.   Patents and IPR____
15.   Quest for quality____
16.   Easy entrance to a foreign market____
17.   Timeless approach____
18.   Role of IT and web based programs____
19.   Outward movement of resources ____
20.   Global brand preference and choices ____

APPENDIX 2

Table 5. MNCs Score Card on Three Elements

Sl No	Sector	MNCs	Code	Innovation	Globalization	Marketing Philosophy
1	Video Games	Sony Play Station	1	16	23	21
2	Two Wheelers	Hero Moto Corp.	1	14	20	29
3	Tractor	Mahindra Tractors	1	21	23	27
4	Tyre	MRF	1	21	22	27
5	Chocolate	Cadbury	0	18	21	25
6	Banking	State Bank of India	1	17	25	23
7	Silk	EISL	0	20	19	22
8	Leather	Bata	0	20	25	23
9	E-tailing	Flifkart	1	22	14	24
10	Toy	Lego	1	23	20	28
11	Retailing	Future Group	0	21	17	26
12	Aviation	Indi Go	1	21	16	27
13	Biscuits	Parle	0	14	15	25
14	Laptop	Lenovo	1	18	27	25
15	Packaged Water	Bisleri	0	26	25	26
16	Automobile	Maruti Suzuki	1	19	17	23
17	Mutual Funds	Birla Sun Life	0	21	23	24
18	Aluminum	Hindalco	1	19	15	25
19	Furniture	Godrej interio	0	22	15	25
20	Power	NTPC	1	21	21	24
21	Media	COMCAST	0	19	17	24
22	Photography	Canon	1	21	24	15
23	Paper Industry	Ballarpur Industries	1	14	17	22
24	Cosmetics	L'Oréal	0	24	22	22
25	Washing Machine	IFB	1	23	24	24
26	Hotel	The Leela	0	19	26	22
27	Eye Glass	Lenskart	1	19	17	24
28	Men's Garment	Levis Strauss	0	15	18	19
29	Telecom	Airtel	1	24	24	26
30	Wine	United Spirits	0	13	16	20
31	IT sector	IBM	1	23	25	29
32	Health Care	Apollo Hospitals	0	25	21	22

continued on following page

Table 5. Continued

Sl No	Sector	MNCs	Code	Innovation	Globalization	Marketing Philosophy
33	Detergent	Ghari (RSPL)	0	13	13	19
34	Print Media	TOI Group	0	20	22	24
35	Music	T-series	0	17	18	20
36	Health Drinks	Horlicks	0	14	19	17
37	Gold Jewelry	Tanisq	0	20	21	21
38	Paint	Asian Paints	1	23	18	26
39	Pharmacy	Sun Pharmacy	1	20	18	19
40	Advertisement	O & M	0	27	24	21
41	Real-estate	DLF	1	20	17	29
42	Pen drive	Sandisk	1	22	29	26
43	Television	Samsung	1	15	22	23
44	Tobacco	ITC	0	9	16	22
45	Fast Food	McDonalds	0	19	23	24
46	Film Distribution	Warner Bros.	1	14	19	17
47	Gas	ONGC	1	16	20	20
48	Bath soap	Lux	0	19	20	22
49	Mobile phone	Apple	1	21	20	21
50	Insurance	LIC	0	21	21	22
51	Refrigerator	LG	1	23	24	20

1= High Technology Sector
0=Low Technology Sector

Chapter 6
Services Trade in Emerging Market Economies

Raju Mandal
Assam University, India

Hiranya K. Nath
Sam Houston State University, USA

ABSTRACT

Global trade in services has increased significantly over last three decades. Earlier, the growth was confined primarily to trade among advanced economies. In more recent times, even developing countries – especially, the emerging market economies (EMEs) – have experienced substantial increase in services trade. Services trade still accounts for only a small share of national income in most EMEs. However, one important trend has been the rapid growth of information-intensive services (IISs). This chapter examines the growth and patterns of services exports and imports from and to a number of EMEs. The analysis indicates that the importance of services trade has been growing for most EMEs. Further, among the EMEs, China, India, and Korea are the most dominant players in services exports and imports. For China, both export and import shares have been rising while for India the export share has been consistently rising. This chapter further discusses some of the intuitively plausible explanations for the growth of trade in services in general and in IISs in particular. It also discusses some of the challenges associated with the growth of IISs trade.

INTRODUCTION

In recent decades, the world has experienced a significant increase in services trade. One of the most important aspects of this growth is the manifold increase in the share of emerging market economies (EMEs) in services trade. There are two parallel developments that have contributed to this trend. *First*, as these economies conduct market-oriented reforms and adopt economic liberalization policies, there is an increase in the demand for traditional services such as transportation and travel. *Second*, the unprecedented advances in information and communication technologies (ICT) have not only made certain service items tradable but also, through rapid proliferation, created an opportunity for the developing

DOI: 10.4018/978-1-5225-0902-8.ch006

countries to trade those services. In particular, these technological advances have enhanced tradability of information-intensive services (IISs). These are the services that involve creating, processing, and communicating information. Because of ICT, these services do not require physical presence of producers and consumers in the same location, a trait that traditionally characterizes services. The low cost of these technologies seems to be a major driver of the increase in both demand and supply of IISs in developing countries.

The main objective of this paper is to examine the major trends and patterns of services trade in EMEs. A secondary objective is to investigate the importance and growth of trade in IISs in these economies. Although growth of services trade in EMEs could be necessary and beneficial for the overall growth of those countries, it may also create formidable challenges. It is of utmost concerns that the institutional framework to handle some of the challenges associated with services trade is in its nascent state even in the developed countries. As countries increasingly trade in IISs, cybersecurity enters into the realm of national security. The policies and measures to promote trade in these services should recognize this and work towards building a comprehensive framework to address these challenges. This paper discusses some of the challenges created by services trade, particularly IISs trade in EMEs.

Although there has been an emerging literature on services trade, the focus has been primarily on the developed countries. Only a handful of studies examine services trade in EMEs. A lack of reliable data has been a formidable constraint. This, in turn, is related to the issues on how to measure services and what constitute trade in services. However, as international organizations, such as World Trade Organization (WTO) and United Nations Conference on Trade and Development (UNCTAD), have started publishing detailed data on services trade, researchers have also embarked on studying trade in services using empirical data. Thus, a number of articles on this topic have appeared in last two decades or so.

There are several strands of this literature. There are some studies that examine the determinants of international trade and investment in services (e.g., Polese and Verreault 1989; Freund and Weinhold 2002; Grunfeld and Moxnes 2003; Kimura and Lee 2006; Co 2007; Mann and Civril 2008). There are others that focus on gains from trade in services in terms of productivity and growth (e.g. Mattoo et al. 2006; Hoekman and Mattoo 2008; Amity and Wei 2009). Further, some other studies discuss policy issues related to services trade (e.g. Bhagwati 1987; Hoekman 1996; Deardorff 2001; Hoekman et al. 2007; Deardorff and Stern 2008). Francois and Hoekman (2010) give a comprehensive review of these different strands of the literature. To the best of our knowledge, none of these studies provides a comprehensive account of growth and patterns of EMEs trade in services in general and EME trade in IISs in particular.

The rest of the paper is organized as follows. Section 2 presents an overview of trade in services. This section is divided into two subsections. In Subsection 2.1, we discuss the definitional framework for trade in services, as adopted by the General Agreement on Trade in Services (GATS). Subsection 2.2 includes a brief discussion on current trends and patterns of world trade in services. In Section 3, we focus on the EME trade in services in general and IISs in particular. It discusses in details the composition and growth of various IISs. Section 4 discusses some theoretically plausible intuitions behind the rapid growth of trade in services in EMEs. In Section 5, we discuss some of the challenges the EMEs face as the services trade grows. In particular, we discuss certain issues related to cyber security and trade negotiations. Our concluding remarks are included in Section 6.

AN OVERVIEW OF TRADE IN SERVICES

A New Framework for Services Trade

Historically, services that accompany movements of goods and people across borders were perhaps the earliest to be traded across borders. In the past it was almost inconceivable that services could be traded as the production of most services required physical presence of both producers and consumers in the same location.[1] Thus, services were largely considered as non-tradable. Furthermore, in an era when agriculture and then manufacturing were the predominant sectors of the economy, many services were just activities auxiliary to the production of goods and many others were simply not marketed. Consequently, even the General Agreement on Trade and Tariff (GATT), which was the forum for multilateral trade negotiations, was almost silent about services trade.

Several developments in recent decades made countries aware of the importance of services trade. The deregulation of the US airline industry in the late 1970s, increasing presence of American banks and entertainment industries overseas, the formation of the European Common Market (ECM), and, most importantly, ICT advances that made a number of services tradable across borders are some of these developments that contributed to the rise of services trade.[2] The recognition of the importance and viability of services trade among nations led to the General Agreement on Trade in Services (GATS) - a treaty of the World Trade Organization (WTO) negotiated under the Uruguay Round of negotiations - that came into effect on January 1, 1995. In view of the wide array of international transactions that services trade encompass (unlike merchandise trade), the GATS takes a broad view of trade in services. Thus, GATS defines services trade to include four categories of transactions:

1. **Cross-Border Trade:** This category includes services supplied across borders. Examples include electricity, telecommunications, and transportation.
2. **Consumption Abroad:** It includes services supplied in a country to the foreigners. Tourism and education abroad are two examples.
3. **Commercial Presence:** The services supplied in a country by foreign business establishments are included in this category. Examples include restaurant chains, hotel chains etc.
4. **Presence of Natural Persons:** This category includes services supplied in a country by foreign nationals. For example, services provided by visiting entertainers are included in this category.

Recently, the statistical agencies across the world have tried to be consistent with this definition while collecting data on services trade.[3] Note that the range of transactions that this definitional framework classifies into services trade may not be very useful in thinking of services in terms of a unified theoretical model.

Current Trends in Global Services Trade

In this subsection, we discuss the major trends in services trade across the globe as well as in the EMEs. The main sources of data for our analysis are: the *Trade in Commercial Services Trade* database of the World Trade Organization (WTO) and the *World Development Indicators* (WDI) database of the World Bank. The data are publicly available from the websites of these two organizations: http://www.wto. org/ and http://www.worldbank.org/ respectively. We use annual data between 1980 and 2013, mainly due to the fact that services trade gained some prominence only in the 1980s.[4] Note that the trade data are available more consistently for the EMEs only since the mid-1990s.

Table 1. shows that the share of total private commercial services trade in world GDP was about 3 per cent in 1980 and this ratio increased to about 6 per cent in 2013. In contrast, merchandise trade as a share of world GDP increased from about 19 per cent in 1980 to 25 per cent in 2013. Services trade as a percentage of total trade increased from about 17 per cent to about 20 per cent during this period. It implies that trade in services grew faster than that in goods. While the value of merchandize trade increased about 9 times, the value of services trade increased almost 13 times during this period of over three decades.

A list of 10 leading exporters and 10 leading importers of services in 2013 is presented in Panel A of Table 2. Note that the U.S. is the leader in both exports and imports of services, accounting for about 14 and 10 percent of services exports and imports respectively. Among the EMEs, China and India made it to the list of top 10 exporters of commercial services. These two countries, together account for about 8 per cent of total commercial services trade in the world. The list of 10 leading importers also includes Russia in addition to these two EMEs. One interesting observation about these three EMEs is that while China and Russia are net importers of commercial services, India is a net exporter. As some studies (e.g. Liu et al 2015) show, India gained comparative advantage in information-intensive services vis-à-vis the U.S. and other developed nations around the turn of the twenty-first century. In China and Russia, as the manufacturing sector grew, it created substantial demand for services that seems to have been reflected in large imports of services by these countries.

To highlight the contrasts with services trade, we list 10 leading exporters and 10 leading importers of goods in 2013 in Panel B of Table 2. While China is the largest exporter accounting for about 12 per cent of total exports of goods, the United States is the largest importer accounting for about 12 per cent of total imports in the world. Besides China, Republic of Korea and Russia – two other EMEs – are also in the list of leading exporters of goods. Further, both China and the Republic of Korea appear in the list of leading importers.

TRENDS AND PATTERNS OF SERVICES TRADE IN EMES

We compile a list of 21 EMEs from five different sources: Morgan Stanley Capital International (MSCI), the FTSE Group, Standard and Poor-Dow Jones (S&P-DJ), Banco Bilbao Vizcaya Argentaria (BBVA) Research, and Russell Investments. We use the most recent lists of EMEs prepared by these agencies and

Table 1. World trade in goods and services and GDP, 1980 and 2013

	1980		2013		Average annual growth rate (1980-2013)
	Value in billions of current USD	As percentage of world GDP	Vale in billions of current USD	As percentage of world GDP	
	(1)	(2)	(3)	(4)	(5)
Trade in goods	2,034	18.2%	18,954	24.9%	6.8%
Trade in commercial services	367	3.3%	4,644	6.1%	7.7%
GDP	11,156	100.0%	76,124	100.0%	5.8%

Table 2. Leading exporters and importers of services and goods, 2013

Rank	Exporters	Value in billions of current USD	% share in total world exports	Rank	Importers	Value in billions of current USD	% share in total world imports
Panel A: Trade in Services							
1	United States	662	14.3	1	United States	432	9.8
2	United Kingdom	293	6.3	2	China	329	7.5
3	Germany	286	6.2	3	Germany	317	7.2
4	France	236	5.1	4	France	189	4.3
5	China	205	4.4	5	United Kingdom	174	4.0
6	India	151	3.2	6	Japan	162	3.7
7	Netherlands	147	3.2	7	Singapore	128	2.9
8	Japan	145	3.1	8	Netherlands	127	2.9
9	Spain	145	3.1	9	India	125	2.8
10	Hong Kong, China	133	2.9	10	Russian Federation	123	2.8
Panel B: Trade in Goods							
1	China	2209	11.7	1	United States	2329	12.2
2	United States	1580	8.3	2	China	1950	10.2
3	Germany	1452	7.7	3	Germany	1192	6.3
4	Japan	715	3.8	4	Japan	833	4.4
5	Netherlands	672	3.5	5	France	681	3.6
6	France	581	3.1	6	United Kingdom	656	3.4
7	Korea, Republic of	560	3.0	7	Hong Kong, China	621	3.3
8	United Kingdom	541	2.9	8	Netherlands	590	3.1
9	Hong Kong, China	535	2.8	9	Korea, Republic of	516	2.7
10	Russian Federation	523	2.8	10	Italy	479	2.5

select those countries that appear in multiple lists and for which data are consistently available. These EMEs include: Brazil, Chile, China, Colombia, Czech Republic, Egypt, Hungary, India, Indonesia, Republic of Korea, Malaysia, Mexico, Peru, Philippines, Poland, Qatar, Russian Federation, South Africa, Thailand, Turkey, and United Arab Emirates (UAE). In this section, we will analyze service trade data for these 21 EMEs.

Overall Trends and Shares

Table 3 presents the merchandize and services trade shares for these 21 EMEs. In 1980, these EMEs accounted for about 11% of the world merchandize trade (exports *plus* imports). This ratio steadily increased to about 33 per cent or the one-third of the world goods trade by 2013. Thus, the EME share tripled during this period of over three decades. In case of services trade, the share of the EMEs in total trade increased from about 8 per cent in 1980 to about 24 per cent in 2013 that implies a three-fold

Table 3. Goods and services trade shares in EMEs

Description	1980			2000			2013		
	Exports	Imports	Total trade	Exports	Imports	Total trade	Exports	Imports	Total trade
	(1)	(2)	(3)	(4)	(5)	(6)	(7)	(8)	(9)
EMEs share in									
World goods trade	11.1	10.9	11.0	20.3	18.3	19.3	33.6	31.4	32.5
World services trade	7.6	8.6	8.1	14.2	16.8	15.5	20.2	27.0	23.5
EMEs GDP share of									
Goods trade	16.8	16.9	33.7	24.1	22.6	46.8	26.5	24.8	51.3
Services trade	2.2	2.8	5.1	4.0	4.7	8.7	4.0	5.1	9.0

increase. If we examine exports and imports separately, imports by the EMEs increased more than did exports. This seems to indicate that as these economies grew the demand for certain services imports increased at a faster pace. Intuitively, as a country experiences growth in manufacturing sector it creates demand for a number of high-end support services as we will see below. These services are usually produced in developed countries. In terms of GDP share, goods trade was about 34 per cent of total GDP for these EMEs in 1980. This increased to more than 51 per cent in 2013. Increased trade liberalization and growth could be responsible for a large part of this increase in merchandize trade. In contrast, services trade increased from about 5 percent of total GDP of these countries to more than 9 per cent in 2013. The share of services trade is still small relative to the size of these economies. However, there are variations across these countries.

Figure 1 depicts the evolution of GDP shares of exports for both goods and services in all 21 EMEs in 5-yearly intervals from 1980 to 2010 and 2013. In Czech Republic, Hungary, Malaysia, Qatar, Thailand, and UAE, goods exports accounted for more than 50% in most recent years. The share grew and reached the maximum in 2013 in a number of countries: Czech Republic, Hungary, India, Korea, Mexico, Poland, and the UAE. In contrast, Chile, China, Egypt, Thailand achieved their maximum in 2005. Furthermore, the GDP share of goods exports has been falling for Indonesia, Malaysia, Philippines, and Russia since 2000. Overall, the GDP share of merchandize exports has been increasing globally. In contrast, overall merchandize exports share in total GDP for these EMEs reached the peak in 2005 and it has decreased since then. GDP share of services exports has been rising in the most recent decade in Hungary, India, Republic of Korea, Poland, and Thailand. In others including China, the share of services exports has declined during the period of recent global and financial crisis. Note that the GDP share of services exports is much smaller relative to merchandize exports for each of these countries. It exceeded 10% only in Czech Republic, Egypt, Hungary, Malaysia, and Thailand. The merchandize services exports share for the entire world has been persistently increasing since the early 1990s.

In Figure 2, we present the GDP shares of goods and services imports. For five EMEs, namely Czech Republic, Hungary, Malaysia, Thailand, and UAE, the share of goods imports exceeded 50% in most recent years. In contrast, services imports shares are relatively smaller and exceeded 10% for one or more years only in Egypt, Hungary, Malaysia, Qatar, Thailand, and UAE. Chile, Czech Republic, Hungary, India, Republic of Korea, Mexico, Peru, Poland, South Africa, Thailand, Turkey and UAE have witnessed increases in GDP share of goods imports. Similarly, Hungary, India, Korea, Poland, Turkey, and UAE

Figure 1. Merchandize and services exports as % of GDP in the EMEs: 1980 - 2013

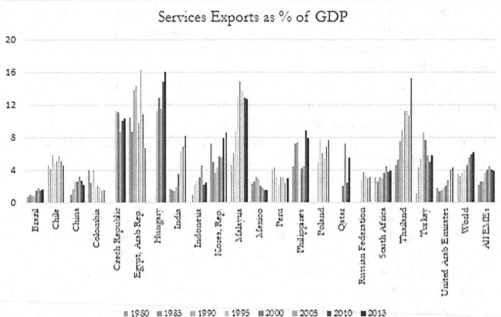

have seen sustained increase in GDP share of services imports. Overall, although the GDP share of services imports has been constantly rising for the world, it has changed little for the EMEs since 2000.

We further examine how the country shares of services exports and imports in total for the EMEs have evolved over time. Figure 3 presents these shares at 5-yearly intervals from 1980 to 2010 and 2013. While the export share has been consistently increasing for China since the mid-1980s, it has been ris-

Figure 2. Merchandize and services imports as % of GDP in the EMEs: 1980 - 2013

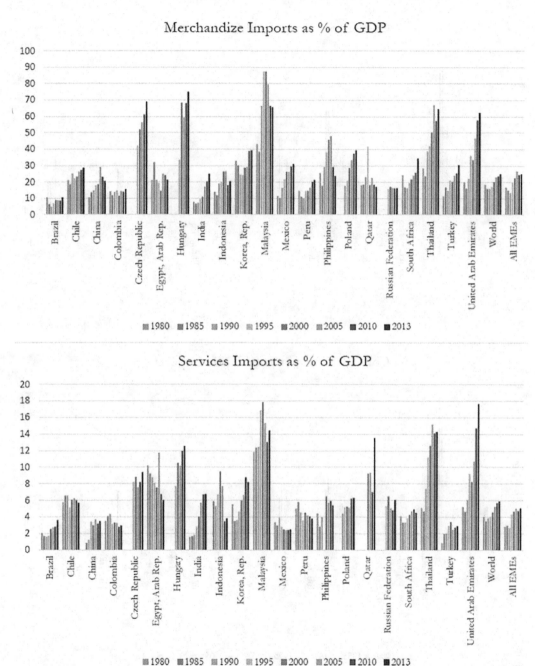

ing for India since the mid-1990s. These two countries together accounted for more than 37 per cent of total services exports from the EMEs in 2013. Although, with about 12 per cent of total EMEs exports, Korea is a relatively large exporter, its share has been declining. For most other EMEs, the shares are relatively small and have been either declining or fluctuating. With more than 25 per cent of total EME service imports, China is the largest importer in 2013 followed by India at the distant second with about

Figure 3. Country shares in total EME exports and imports of services: 1980 – 2013

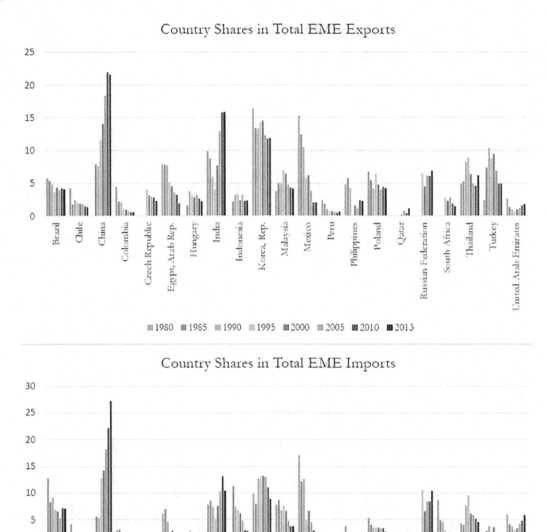

10 per cent. For some EMEs, such as Chile, Colombia, Czech Republic, Hungary, Peru, and Qatar, both services exports and imports accounted for less than 5 per cent of total EME exports and imports during this time period.

Overall, we can draw a few conclusions about goods and services trade in EMEs. *First*, there has been a steady growth of goods and services trade in EMEs. *Second*, a few of these EMEs (e. g. Czech Republic, Hungary, Malaysia, Thailand, and UAE) are heavily dependent on merchandize trade as their total trade (exports plus imports) shares in respective GDPs exceeding 100 per cent. However, services trade does not play such a role although its importance has grown for most EMEs. Services trade accounted for more than 25 per cent of GDP only in Hungary, Malaysia, and Thailand. *Third*, among the EMEs, China, India, and Korea are the most dominant players in services exports and imports. For China, both export and import shares have been rising while for India the export share has been consistently rising. However, the fact that the shares of other EMEs have been declining does not necessarily mean that the services exports and imports have been decreasing in those countries. In fact, they have been growing although the growth has been relatively slower than the leading EMEs.

Share and Growth of Information Intensive Services (IISs)

As we discuss above, the unprecedented advances in ICT have contributed to the growth of trade in goods as well as in services. Previous studies (Liu and Nath 2016) show that there has been a disproportionately larger growth of trade in IISs. IISs involve creating, processing, and transmitting information. In the past, transportation and travel – two non-IISs – were the primary service trade items. Some of the IIS categories were either non-existent or were traded in such negligible amounts that the trade values were not reported separately and were clubbed together as other commercial services. However, with the proliferation of ICT, trade in communication (telecommunications) services, financial and insurance services, computer and information services, professional, business, and technical services grew in volume and value. Therefore, in most recent years, data have been reported separately for these categories. However, for some EMEs, these services still account for a negligible share of total services trade.

Table 4. reports the percentage share of IISs in total services exports, imports, and total trade (exports *plus* imports) for five leading EMEs in 2000 and 2013. Exports and imports data on IISs for 2000 are obtained by subtracting corresponding data for 'construction' and 'personal, cultural and recreational services' from 'other commercial services'.[5] As the table indicates, in all five countries, the share of IISs increased for exports and total trade. However, the import shares have slightly declined for China and India. As the service industries grow in these two economies and foreign direct investments (FDI) take place in service producing sectors these declines may be explained by substitution of imports by domestic production of those services. For Brazil and India, IISs accounted for more than half of services

Table 4. Share of information-intensive services in five leading traders of IISs among EMEs: 2000 and 2013

Country	2000			2013		
	Export	Import	Total trade	Export	Import	Total trade
	(1)	(2)	(3)	(4)	(5)	(6)
Brazil	57.4	42.1	47.6	64.5	47.9	53.1
China	31.6	31.4	31.5	50.8	30.8	38.5
India	60.5	38.4	48.7	73.4	37.5	57.1
Republic of Korea	28.7	43.5	36.3	35.6	47.1	41.2
Russian Federation	24.7	27.6	26.5	39.1	33.0	35.1

trade in 2000 and they were joined by China in 2013. Imports of IISs were less than half of total services imports for all five EMEs in 2000 as well as 2013 although these shares increased for three countries: Brazil, Korea, and Russia.

To shed some lights on the exact nature of these IISs, we can take a look at the distribution of services trade by various disaggregate categories for the most recent year. Data are not available by this level of disaggregation for earlier years and therefore we present the export and import shares for each of the five countries for 2013 in Table 5. Other businesses that include a wide range of IISs such as legal, accounting, management consulting, public relations services, advertising, market research and public opinion polling, research and development services, architectural, engineering, and other technical services, accounted for the largest shares in both exports and imports for all five leading EMEs. However, there are variations across countries For example, it accounted for more than 80 percent of exports of IISs in Brazil while it is about 46 per cent in India. In contrast, computer and information services accounted for about 44 per cent of total IISs exports from India. Imports of royalties and license fees account for about one-fifth of IISs imports in China, Korea, and Russia. These are the payments these countries have to make for using trademarks, industrial processes, and software to their trading partner countries. Exports of financial services from Brazil and imports of insurance and financial services to India have large shares in their respective IISs trade.

Overall, EME trade in IISs has been increasing, particularly among the leading nations. Going by the relative importance of various IIS items for different countries, we may infer that these EMEs have comparative advantages in different IISs. In fact, there is some evidence of that in the literature (e.g. see Liu et al 2015). Furthermore, as previous studies (Freund and Weinhold 2002, Liu and Nath 2013 & 2016) indicate, this growth in IISs trade may have been facilitated by increased use of ICT. As countries use ICT as a vehicle of international trade in services, it has substantial implications for cyber security.

Explaining the Rise in Information-Intensive Services Trade in EMEs

We will now present some of the intuitively plausible explanations for the growth of cross-border trade in services in general and IISs in particular in the EMEs. However, we will neither develop any formal theory nor will we empirically confirm or refute any plausible hypothesis.

Table 5. Distribution of IIS exports and imports by component items in five leading EMEs in 2013

Component Service Items	Brazil		China		India		Korea		Russia	
	Exports	Imports	Exports	Imports	Exports	Imports	Exports	Imports	Exports	Imports
	(1)	(2)	(3)	(4)	(5)	(6)	(7)	(8)	(9)	(10)
Telecommunication services	1.0	0.7	NA	NA	2.0	2.3	1.5	2.1	6.0	6.6
Insurance services	1.9	3.6	3.9	21.9	1.9	12.6	1.6	1.6	2.2	3.5
Financial services	11.5	4.2	3.1	3.7	5.3	11.7	9.0	1.9	6.6	6.2
Computer and information services	1.8	11.5	15.0	5.9	44.4	5.6	2.3	1.3	10.1	7.8
Royalties and license fees	2.4	8.6	0.9	20.8	0.4	8.3	10.2	19.2	2.9	19.8
Other business services	81.3	68.4	77.0	47.1	45.6	59.2	74.4	73.3	71.1	54.1
Audio-visual and related services	0.1	2.9	0.2	0.7	0.5	0.4	1.0	0.7	1.1	2.0

First, the ICT advances since the 1990s – particularly the development and proliferation of the internet mobile phones - have played (and will play) a key role in the growth and expansion of trade in IISs. A growing number of studies have provided evidence of a positive relationship between ICT advances and the growth of trade in goods as well as in services.[6] ICT advances can stimulate trade in IISs through both direct and indirect channels. For example, by lowering the cost of communicating information or transferring data this technology provides a direct channel of influencing such trade. The low cost not only helps with the actual delivery of the service but also with the entry into the market in another country. In contrast, ICT-enabled service innovations such as geographically dispersed production of service components (of which service outsourcing is an example) and assembly provide indirect channels for ICT to affect services trade.[7] Using data for forty EMEs from 1995 to 2010 Liu and Nath (2013) show that Internet subscriptions and Internet hosts have significant positive effects on both exports and imports in EMEs. Although they do not identify the specific channels through which these ICT variables affect trade, the evidence of significant effects itself highlights the importance of ICT for trade. In a follow-up study (Liu & Nath 2016) using cross-country disaggregated data on various services trade items, they show that ICT development has significant positive impacts on exports of other business services and transportation services and the imports of 'insurance services', 'telecommunications services', and 'travel services'. This study also shows that ICT development is more important for growth of services trade in EMEs than in advanced economies.

Second, as the economies grow there is higher demand for services in general and IISs in particular. Besides the growth in demand from consumers with higher per capita income, the range and complexity of economic activities in those economies also create vast demand for a number of IISs. For example, the diagrammatic illustration of Quinn (1992) shows how the size and growth of manufacturing can create demand for a host of services. As Figure 4 shows, manufacturing needs direct support of value-added services like financing, leasing, and insurance; business services like consulting, auditing, and

Figure 4. Interactive role of services (Quinn 1992)

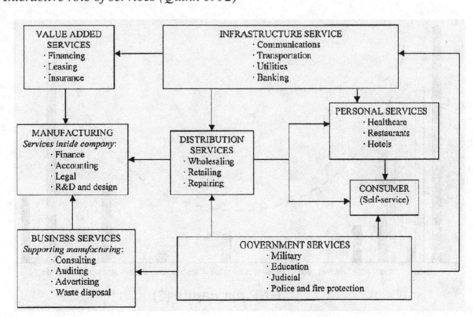

advertising; and distribution services like wholesaling, retailing, and repairing. Then, there is an additional layer of infrastructure services, government services, and personal services behind these support services. Many of these support services, particularly the IISs, can be produced at lower costs in EMEs and traded across borders.

Third, the decades since the early 1990s have witnessed deregulation of service industries and liberalization of foreign trade and investment regimes in many EMEs around the world. Since service industries are heavily regulated, it is often very difficult to attract foreign investment and trade. However, due to the technology-driven enhanced tradability of services, many governments around the world have deregulated a number of IISs primarily to increase competition and gain efficiency. Similarly, bilateral trade agreements and policies to encourage FDI in services also help increase trade in services primarily through affiliated trade.[8] Thus, regulatory reforms and liberalization policies adopted by countries across the world provided further impetus for growth in services trade.

Finally, unlike in merchandise trade, language and culture play an important role in services trade. Apte and Karmarkar (2007) argue that the topography of services trade and outsourcing will be strongly colored by language, culture, and colonial history. In particular, language barriers will essentially direct and define this topography for most consumer services that will be traded across borders. Figure 5 shows the distribution of world population for five major languages by different income groups, measured by GNP per capita. It is clear from the figure that the world English market for services is unique in its size,

Figure 5. Distribution of different language speaking population by income (Modified from Apte and Karmarkar 2007)

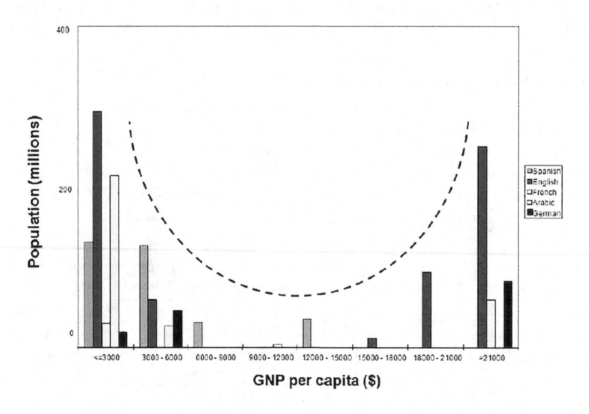

geographic distribution and, most importantly, in potential for trade. It also happens to be one of the most open market. Although the distribution of Spanish-speaking population has some similarities, it is less extreme and therefore offers less opportunity for those in poorer countries. Since other major language groups are concentrated in one or a few countries, the potential for offshoring and international trade is rather limited. This might well prove to be a boon for those engaged in services in those countries, since they will not be subject to the intense competition seen due to outsourcing and offshoring in the English and perhaps the Spanish worlds.

There could be additional factors that affect and determine services trade in EMEs. However, the above discussion provides only a partial list of factors that have been suggested in the literature.

CHALLENGES

As trade in services grows in EMEs, these countries also face challenges. If services trade were to become a welfare enhancing economic activity, recognizing these challenges and formulating and implementing appropriate policies are extremely important. These challenges may come from the impediments that get along the way of promoting IISs trade or may come arise due to rapid growth of trade in these services.

First, in order to take full advantage of IISs trade, a country must have well-developed ICT infrastructure and ICT capabilities. However, the EMEs in our sample are at different stages and states of ICT development. Table 6 shows the ranking of these countries in terms of ICT development. Among these 21 countries, while Korea ranks second globally, India ranks 129 in 2013. The ranking is based on a composite ICT development index measured by the International Telecommunication Union (ITU). This index includes three aspects of ICT development: ICT readiness (infrastructure, access), ICT use, and ICT capability. Due to this inequality, all countries may not have been able to realize the full potential of IISs trade. Thus, the countries that are falling behind must invest in all three aspects of ICT development.

Second, increased trade in IIS may make countries vulnerable to cyber-attacks. Thus, issues related to cyber security become extremely important. In particular, trade in certain types of IISs such as financial services, insurance services, are extremely vulnerable to cyber-attacks exposing a large number of consumers in different countries to the risks of identity theft and other associated risks. Many firms in the U.S. and other advanced countries offshore a part of their operations to third-party vendors in EMEs giving access to critical information about the businesses and consumers. This may create a cyber security risk that may well be considered in the realm of national security. Since cyber-crimes are new, some countries do not have the legal and technical framework to handle those crimes. Besides, if there is no uniformity in laws and regulations across countries, it may lead to additional problems.

Third, GATS mandates WTO member governments to progressively liberalize trade in services through successive rounds of negotiations. The negotiations in the Doha Round are being conducted on both bilateral and multilateral tracks. There are four major areas of services negotiations: market access; domestic regulations; GATS rules on emergency safeguard measures, government procurement and subsidies; and implementation of least-developed countries (LDC) modalities. These are all very relevant areas for the growth services trade in EMEs. The GATS preamble includes the aim of increasing the participation of developing countries in services trade. At the Eighth Ministerial Conference in 2011, WTO members adopted a waiver to allow preferential treatment for services and service suppli-

Table 6. Global ranks of the EMEs according to ICT development in 2013

Sl. No.	Country	IDI Rank
1	Brazil	65
2	Chile	56
3	China	86
4	Colombia	77
5	Czech Republic	41
6	Egypt, Arab Republic of	89
7	Hungary	46
8	India	129
9	Indonesia	106
10	Korea, Republic of	2
11	Malaysia	71
12	Mexico	95
13	Peru	105
14	Philippines	103
15	Poland	44
16	Qatar	34
17	Russian Federation	42
18	South Africa	90
19	Thailand	81
20	Turkey	68
21	United Arab Emirates	32

ers from least-developed countries. The 2013 Bali Ministerial Decision has established various steps to encourage WTO members to make use of this waiver. Although the negotiations have made some progress, there are more sticking issues that need to be addressed. The relative underdevelopment of the service sector, presence of heavy regulations or no regulation, obsolete legal framework are some of these issues in developing countries.

Fourth, as we discuss above, services trade is not entirely independent of the cultural contexts of the countries that are involved in trade. With the increase in services trade, there may be an apprehension of cultural invasion and as such certain societies may be resistant to what could be economically viable and profitable opportunities. In particular, since language is such an important factor in services trade that there may be concerns about marginalization of the regional and/or local languages. These concerns may create formidable challenges to the growth of services trade, particularly in developing countries.

In this section, we have discussed only a few challenges. As service trade grows, there will be new problems and challenges. In particular, ICT-enabled service innovations and trade are growing very rapidly posing new challenges and concerns.

CONCLUSION

Global trade in services has increased significantly over last three decades. Earlier, the growth was confined primarily to trade among advanced economies. In more recent times, even developing countries – especially, the emerging market economies (EMEs) – have experienced substantial increase in services trade. Services trade still accounts for only a small share of national income in most EMEs. However, one important trend has been the rapid growth of information-intensive services (IISs). This paper examines the growth and patterns of services exports and imports from and to a number of EMEs. The analysis indicates that the importance of services trade has been growing for most EMEs. Further, among the EMEs, China, India, and Korea are the most dominant players in services exports and imports. For China, both export and import shares have been rising while for India the export share has been consistently rising. This paper further discusses some of the intuitively plausible explanations for the growth of trade in services in general and in IISs in particular. It also discusses some of the challenges associated with the growth of IISs trade.

REFERENCES

Amity, M., & Wei, S.-J. (2009). Service Offshoring and Productivity: Evidence from the US. *World Economy*, *32*(2), 203–220. doi:10.1111/j.1467-9701.2008.01149.x

Apte, U. M., & Karmarkar, U. S. (2007). Business Process Outsourcing (BPO) and Globalization of Information Intensive Services. In U. M. Apte & U. S. Karmarkar (Eds.), *Managing in the Information Economy: Current Research Issues* (pp. 59–81). doi:10.1007/978-0-387-36892-4_3

Apte, U. M., Karmarkar, U. S., & Nath, H. K. (2008). Information Services in the U.S. Economy: Value, Jobs, and Management Implications. *California Management Review*, *50*(3), 12–30. doi:10.2307/41166443

Apte, U. M., & Nath, H. K. (2012). U.S. Trade in Information-Intensive Services. In U. S. Karmarkar & V. Mangal (Eds.), *The UCLA Anderson Business and Information Technologies (BIT) Project: A Global Study of Business Practice*. Singapore: World Scientific Books. doi:10.1142/9789814390880_0006

Bhagwati, J. N. (1987). Trade in Services and the Multilateral Trade Negotiations. *The World Bank Economic Review*, *1*(4), 549–569. doi:10.1093/wber/1.4.549

Clarke, G. R. G., & Wallsten, S. J. (2006). Has the Internet increased trade? Developed and developing country evidence. *Economic Inquiry*, *44*(3), 465–484. doi:10.1093/ei/cbj026

Co, C. Y. (2007). US Exports of Knowledge-intensive Services and Importing-country Characteristics. *Review of International Economics*, *15*(5), 890–904. doi:10.1111/j.1467-9396.2007.00703.x

Deardorff, A. V. (2001). International Provision of Trade Services, Trade, and Fragmentation. *Review of International Economics*, *9*(2), 233–248. doi:10.1111/1467-9396.00276

Deardorff, A. V., & Stern, R. M. (2008). Empirical Analysis of Barriers to International Services Transactions and the Consequences of Liberalization. In A. Mattoo, R. M. Stern, & G. Zanini (Eds.), *A Handbook of International Trade in Services*. Oxford, UK: Oxford University Press.

Francois, J., & Hoekman, B. (2010). Services Trade and Policy. *Journal of Economic Literature*, *48*(3), 642–692. doi:10.1257/jel.48.3.642

Freund, C., & Weinhold, D. (2002). The Internet and International Trade in Services. *The American Economic Review*, *92*(2), 236–240. doi:10.1257/000282802320189320

Freund, C., & Weinhold, D. (2004). The effect of the Internet on international trade. *Journal of International Economics*, *62*(1), 171–189. doi:10.1016/S0022-1996(03)00059-X

Grunfeld, L. A., & Moxnes, A. (2003). *The Intangible Globalization: Explaining the Patterns of International Trade in Services*. Norwegian Institute of International Affairs Working Paper 657.

Hoekman, B. (1996). Asssessing the General Agreement on Trade in Services. In The Uruguay Round and the Developing Countries. Cambridge, UK: Cambridge University Press.

Hoekman, B., & Mattoo, A. (2008). Services Trade and Growth. In J. A. Marchetti & M. Roy (Eds.), *Opening Markets for Trade in Services: Countries and Sectors in Bilateral and WTO Negotiations*. Cambridge, UK: Cambridge University Press. doi:10.1596/1813-9450-4461

Hoekman, B., Mattoo, A., & Sapir, A. (2007). The Political Economy of Services Trade Liberalization: A Case for International Regulatory Cooperation? *Oxford Review of Economic Policy*, *23*(3), 367–391. doi:10.1093/oxrep/grm024

Karmarkar, U. S. (2010). The Industrialization of Information Services. In *Handbook of Service Science*. Springer. doi:10.1007/978-1-4419-1628-0_18

Kimura, F., & Lee, H. (n.d.). The Gravity Equation in International Trade in Services. *Review of World Economics, 142*(1), 92-121.

Koncz-Bruner, J., & Flatness. (2010, October). U.S. International Services Cross-Border Trade in 2009 and Services Supplied Through Affiliates in 2008. *Survey of Current Business*, 18-35.

Lennon, C. (2009). *Trade in Services and Trade in Goods: Differences and Complementarities*. The Vienna Institute for International Economic Studies Working Papers 53.

Liu, L., & Nath, H. (2013). Information and Communications Technology (ICT) and Trade in Emerging Market Economies. *Emerging Markets Finance and Trade*, *49*(6), 67–87. doi:10.2753/REE1540-496X490605

Liu, L., & Nath, H. (2016). *Information and Communications Technology (ICT) and Services Trade*. SHSU Economics and International Business Working Paper No. 1601.

Liu, L., Nath, H., & Tochkov, K. (2015). Comparative Advantages in U.S. Bilateral Services Trade with China and India. *Journal of Asian Economics*, *38*, 79–92. doi:10.1016/j.asieco.2015.04.002

Mann, C. L., & Civril, D. (2008). *U.S. International Trade in Other Private Services: Do Arm's Length and Intra-Company Trade Differ?*. Brandeis Business School, Brandeis University.

Mattoo, A., Rathindran, R., & Subramanian, A. (2006). Measuring Services Trade Liberalization and Its Impact on Economic Growth: An Illustration. *Journal of Economic Integration*, *21*(1), 64–98. doi:10.11130/jei.2006.21.1.64

Mattoo, A., Stern, R. M., & Zanini, G. (2008). *A Handbook of International Trade in Services*. Oxford, UK: Oxford University Press.

Polese, M., & Verreault, R. (1989). Trade in Information-Intensive Services: How and Why Regions Develop Export Advantages. *Canadian Public Policy*, *XV*, 4, 376–386.

Quinn, J. B. (1992). *Intelligent Enterprise: A Knowledge and Service Based Paradigm for Industry*. The Free Press.

World Bank (WB). (n.d.). *World Development Indicators*. Retrieved from http://data.worldbank.org/data-catalog/world-development-indicators

World Trade Organization (WTO). (n.d.). *Trade in Commercial Services Trade*. Retrieved from http://www.wto.org/

World Trade Organization (WTO). (2011). *Composition, definitions & methodology*. Available at: https://www.wto.org/english/res_e/statis_e/its2011_e/its11_metadata_e.pdf

ENDNOTES

[1] For a discussion on the defining characteristics of services vis-à-vis goods, see Apte et al. (2008). Also, for a discussion on the characteristics of services that affect their tradability, see Lennon (2009)

[2] See Apte and Nath (2013) for a brief but comprehensive discussion of these developments

[3] For a discussion on the efforts made by the Bureau of Economic Analysis (BEA), see Koncz-Bruner and Flatness (2010).

[4] For some detailed analysis in the following section, we use shorter sample periods, depending on the data availability.

[5] For detailed description of various service trade items, see Appendix 1.

[6] Freund and Weinhold (2002) use bilateral trade data between the U.S. and 31 other countries to show that the Internet penetration in foreign countries has a positive impact on services trade. Freund and Weinhold (2004) further show that use of the Internet also contributes positively to the growth of merchandise trade. They argue that the Internet stimulates exports by lowering the costs of entering the market. However, using data for a sample of 98 countries that include both developed and developing countries, Clarke and Wallsten (2006) find that Internet penetration has a significant positive effect only on exports from developing to the developed countries and not on exports to developing or from developed to other developed and developing countries.

[7] These innovations are a major part of the fundamental changes in services, collectively known as service industrialization. For a discussion, see Karmarkar (2010)

[8] Mann and Civril (2008) provide evidence in support of this.

APPENDIX

Definitions and Coverage of Services Trade

Transportation services covers sea, air and other including land, internal waterway, space and pipeline transport services that are performed by residents of one economy for those of another, and that involve the carriage of passengers, the movement of goods (freight), rentals (charters) of carriers with crew, and related supporting and auxiliary services

Travel includes goods and services acquired by personal travelers, for health, education or other purposes, and by business travelers. Unlike other services, travel is not a specific type of service, but an assortment of goods and services consumed by travelers. The most common goods and services covered are lodging, food and beverages, entertainment and transportation (within the economy visited), gifts and souvenirs.

Other commercial services correspond to the following components defined in' Balance of Payments Manual 5 (BPM5):

(i) *communications services* includes telecommunications, postal and courier services. Telecommunications services encompasses the transmission of sound, images or other information by telephone, telex, telegram, radio and television cable and broadcasting, satellite, electronic mail, facsimile services etc., including business network services, teleconferencing and support services. It does not include the value of the information transported. Also included are cellular telephone services, Internet backbone services and on-line access services, including provision of access to the Internet;

(ii) *construction* covers work performed on construction projects and installation by employees of an enterprise in locations outside the territory of the enterprise (the one- year rule to determine residency is to be applied flexibly). In addition goods used by construction companies for their projects are included which implies that the "true" services component tends to be overestimated;

(iii) *insurance services* covers the provision of various types of insurance to non-residents by resident insurance enterprises, and vice versa, for example, freight insurance, direct insurance (e.g. life) and reinsurance;

(iv) *financial services* covers financial intermediation and auxiliary services provided by banks, stock exchanges, factoring enterprises, credit card enterprises, and other enterprises;

(v) *computer and information services* is subdivided into computer services (hardware and software related services and data processing services), news agency services (provision of news, photographs, and feature articles to the media), and other information provision services (database services and web search portals);

(vi) *royalties and license fees,* covering payments and receipts for the use of intangible non-financial assets and proprietary rights, such as patents, copyrights, trademarks, industrial processes, and franchises;

(vii) *other business services*, comprising trade-related services, operational leasing (rentals), and miscellaneous business, professional and technical services such as legal, accounting, management consulting, public relations services, advertising, market research and public opinion polling, research and development services, architectural, engineering, and other technical services, agricultural, mining and on-site processing; and

(viii) *personal, cultural,* and *recreational services* is subdivided into two categories, (i) audiovisual services and (ii) other cultural and recreational services. The first component includes services and fees related to the production of motion pictures, radio and television programs, and musical recordings. Other personal, cultural, and recreational services includes services such as those associated with museums, libraries, archives, and other cultural, sporting, and recreational activities.

Chapter 7
Consumer Impetuosity in M–Commerce:
Designing Scale to Measure the Shopping Behavior

Natasha Patricia Bojorges Moctezuma
EGADE Business School, Tecnologico de Monterrey, Mexico

ABSTRACT

Existing research on impulsive buying focuses mainly on goods displayed in physical spaces and services delivered face to face. This paper aims to present a novel approach to analyze the impulsiveness on purchase through mobile devices by the development of a reliable and valid scale of impulsiveness in the context of mobile commerce, also known as m-commerce. To achieve the aforementioned research purpose, this paper views impulsiveness in m-commerce as a holistic process encompassing personal traits, stimulus level, and, product attributes to understand the motivational, emotional, and cognitive factors underlying the impulse buying journey and purchase decision on the basis of a scale to measure the construct. The paper concludes with a discussion on its conceptual and managerial contributions and interesting directions for future research.

INTRODUCTION

Impulse buying permeates every dimension of marketing. In branding, the inception of Nike's campaign ´Just do it' in 1988 (Conlon, 2015) that played with the concept of doing things without thinking, thus prompting impulsivity, helped the brand to foster their sales in the time span of a decade. In retailing, Costco has been displaying only the most popular items on the shelves and create a sense of urgency by rotating the products on a seasonal basis in order to increase product consumption and to generate among their customers the need to buy suddenly before the season is over (Virgin, 2011). The convergence of marketing strategies and tactics along with the advent of Internet-based retailing channels have made feasible the appearance of novel sales contexts which unique features have received little

DOI: 10.4018/978-1-5225-0902-8.ch007

attention. This is the case of mobile commerce or m-commerce, as the ability to perform transactions using any wireless device connected to Internet practically with no time or space constraints on the consumer's preferences (Balasubramanian et al., 2002). The increasing use of mobile devices among consumers together with other current digital trends such as the use of live streaming applications and content sharing in real time, has strengthened the implementation of new digital marketing strategies and empowered consumers, communities and societies in whole (OECD, 2014). Actually, Worldwide Internet penetration reached 38.1% of global population in 2013 (Internet Society, 2015). Furthermore, according to the Organization for Economic Co-operation and Development (OECD), in less than two years, the number of pages viewed from mobile devices, on a sample of 3 million websites monitored, rose from 11.7% to 24.3% worldwide, and from about 15% to more than 30% when tablets are included. Together businesses and consumers have benefited from mobile commerce's main advantages such as efficiency, convenience, competitive prices and variety; however, its use also poses new challenges. Therefore, since traditional marketing strategies have become obsolete and more emphasis on latent needs is required, the exponential growth of mobile devices usage has captured the attention from both scholars and practitioners. For instance, the increasing preference for social networks through mobiles has unleashed new business opportunities that must be addressed in order to succeed in the new digital arena. The evidence for consumers' mobile preference can be perceived through statistical data generated by the most popular social network around the world, Facebook. Active Facebook users connecting to the social network with a mobile passed from 28% of all users at the end of 2009 to over 75% at the end of 2013 while the revenue Facebook declared from mobile advertising rose from 13% of total revenues in 2012 to 40% in 2013 (OECD, 2014). In Latin America, about 60% of Internet transactions are carried out using mobile devices and it is expected to reach 100% by 2017 (Internet Society, 2015). Moreover, according to recent surveys, 81% of spontaneous shopping is associated to smartphones (Google, 2012).

In brief, even though current e-commerce and m-commerce developments combined with mobile devices' preference yield improvements in consumer welfare and offer several promising marketing activities, including viral marketing campaigns for mobiles, the use of influencer marketing and programmatic content management, the success of its application, which depends on the consumers' purchase, remains scarcely studied (Pescher *et al.,* 2014). Therefore, it is important to identify and understand the factors that influence consumer behavior via mobile devices. For the present study, the information obtained will lay the foundation for developing a reliable and valid scale of impulsiveness on m-purchases by analyzing what is the meaning of impulse buying in the context of mobile devices, in order to understand better the main factors involved in this process. In summary, this paper aims:

1. To analyze what are the main definitions and constructs associated to impulse buying in the context of m-commerce.
2. To analyze the motivations, emotions, and cognitions that lead consumers to purchase on impulse using mobile devices.
3. To develop a scale specifying the nature and level of consumer impulsiveness in m-commerce that is reliable and valid but also convenient to practitioners and researchers.
4. To examine the relationships between mood management and impulsiveness in m-purchase.

In order to establish a logical manner in which ideas are presented, the paper is structured as follows. In section 2 it is reviewed existing literature on impulse buying and its relevant drivers. Afterwards, in section 3 it is detailed the methodology used for the development of the scale. Results about the reliability and validity of the scale are analyzed and discussed in section 4. Finally, the paper closes with conclusions and future research in section 5.

BRIEF LITERATURE REVIEW

As every complex phenomenon, impulsivity can be addressed from different perspectives; in this case it can be evaluated from a trait or state perspective. In the trait perspective, impulsiveness is a predisposition relatively stable over time, but not always perceptible by behavior. For this research, impulsivity will be evaluated from a state perspective, in which environmental or biological conditions generate transitory disparities on impulsivity levels (Iribarren, 2011).

Consumer behavior research has arrived to the development of an information processing model (Bettman, 1979), which evolved from an initial stage of rational choice and subsequently, logical flow (Howard & Sheth, 1969), assuming that decision-making processes are centered on cognition. However, researchers have realized that the information processing perspective has ignored interesting consumption phenomena to marketing research (Olshavsky & Granbois 1979; Sheth 1979). Relegated phenomena include the higher order psychological process of affect, which can be summarized as hedonic, giving emphasis on symbolic meanings and impulsivity rather than rationality and information. Holbrook and Hirschman (1982) termed this affective perspective as "the experiential view", which focuses on the emotional, desire and primitive aspect of fulfilling these hedonic needs. By exploring a deeper understanding of consumer behavior, researchers acknowledged that consumers' decision to purchase was affected by both long-term rational processes and by short-term emotional processes (Hirschman, 1985; Hoch & Loewenstein, 1991) that culminate in the purchase behavior. As it is well known, most of the people are much less rational in their buying behavior since their purchases often seem to be driven by mood or emotion. Such irrational purchase styles have become known as impulsiveness on purchase (Verplanken & Herabadi, 2001). Academics have studied impulsiveness on purchase for more than 50 years (Harmancioglu et al., 2009) and studies in the field are still growing. Since then, a plethora of researchers have analyzed a broad number of impulsiveness on purchase dimensions ranging from consumer psychographic traits as Impulse Buying Tendency (IBT) (Rook, 1987; Weun et al., 1998; Dittmar, 2001; Crawford & Melewar, 2003), emotional intelligence and self-esteem (Peter & Krishnakumar, 2010), subjective norms and purchase intention (Xiaoni et al. 2007), store environment and category (Crawford & Melewar, 2003; Zhou and Wong, 2003), marketing mix: well-known brands, search for deals with big discounts and confidence in receiving the product, product attributes (Jones et al., 2003; Zhou and Wong, 2003), and situational factors (Dholakia, 2000; Mai et al., 2003). Regarding online consumer behavior, Koufaris (2002) present one of the first studies to include variables as Web skills and value-added search mechanisms to analyze channel-related behaviors and Adelaar (2003) studies how different media formats influence consumer's response and impulsive buying intents. In all, existing above functional literature and meta-analysis (Xiao & Nicholson, 2011; Amos et al., 2014) lack including mobile devices in the scope of Marketing strategy as a new distribution channel and crucial feature for brand building and value-creation in order to attract consumers and associate it with the impulse buying phenomena.

Consumer Impulsiveness Traits

Impulse buying is influenced by consumer-related variables inner to personality traits and individual's demographic, socioeconomic and psychographic differences such as educational experience (e.g. Wood, 1998), gender (e.g. Dittmar and Drury, 2000; Verplanken and Herabadi, 2001; Xiaoni, et al., 2007), personal income (e.g. Beatty and Ferrell, 1998) and actual or perceived time availability (e.g. Beatty and Ferrell, 1998). Furthermore, it can be suggested that temporary motives elicited by positive or negative events in an individual's personal life, might encourage impulse buying behavior as a means to relieve an uneasy or depressed mood (Verplanken and Herabadi, 2001). Previous research developed by Dittmar et al. (1995) employed an identity approach, which might also explain some group differences, since it implies that impulse purchases might symbolize an expression of self-identity. Moreover, Verplanken and Herabadi (2001) suggest that personality-related individual difference measures, including the Big Five, are deeply rooted to the tendency to buy on impulse and serves as expression of broader personality patterns of which particularly extraversion was found to be positively related to impulsive buying behavior.

Impulsiveness in Purchasing Decisions

Impulsiveness in purchasing decisions has been defined as the "tendency to buy spontaneously, unreflectively, immediately and kinetically" (Rook and Fisher 1995, p. 306). Although early studies indicated that impulse purchases represent a substantial proportion of all unplanned purchases made in-store (Kollat and Willett 1967), recent measures focus on an alternative operational approach in favor of personal trait measures that estimated the psychological factors beneath purchase decisions (Rook and Fisher 1995). This trait conceptualization is rooted in psychology and is strongly associated with the development of scales to measure general impulsiveness, such as the Barratt Impulsiveness Scale or the Plutchik Impulsivity Scale (Patton *et al.* 1995). Arens and Rust (2012) demonstrate in a series of experiments that satisfaction and impulsiveness metrics make different but strong predictions of consumer decisions or in this context, their purchase choices. On the one hand, they argue that impulsiveness relates to choice directly, while on the other, the satisfaction-choice path is mediated by loyalty intention. Likewise, a neuroscience theory describes buying behavior as the outcome of "liking" (a hedonic reaction of enjoyment) and "wanting" something (a motivational force to obtain it) (Berridge, 2004). These notions suggest that consumer decision-making involve two distinct processes, so customer satisfaction metrics reflect how much customers "like" or prefer a product rather than others and the reflective, overt decision process. In contrast, impulsiveness metrics reflect the immediate, unconscious process (Strack et al. 2006) and the purely motivational "wanting" for the product (Depue & Collins 1999). Therefore, impulsiveness metrics, basically reveal how much customers "want" a product (Ramanathan & Menon 2006; Vohs & Faber 2007).

Impulsiveness in M-Commerce and Its Dimensions

This analysis is grounded on the conceptual framework of impulsiveness in consumer behavior as a function of two main psychological processes for decision-making: cognitive and affective; and their six sub-dimensions or sub-components defined by Coley (2002), which are classified below.

For the affective component, these are:

- Irresistible urge to buy
- Positive buying emotions
- Mood management

And for the cognitive component:

- Cognitive deliberation
- Unplanned buying
- Disregard for the future

The overall power of each higher order psychological process and the degree of influence between them represents the ultimate outcome of whether or not an impulse buy emerges. Hence, as the emotional irresistible desire to buy competes and takes over the cognitive control of willpower, impulse buying takes place (Youn, 2000). Nevertheless, for classifying a buying behavior as impulsive it is required more than just an involuntary and unplanned purchase, that is to say, not all unplanned purchases are impulsive (Iyer, 1989; Kollat & Willet, 1967; Piron, 1993; Rook, 1987; Rook & Fisher, 1995; Weun, Jones, & Beatty, 1998). According to Weinberg and Gottwald (1982), the extent of impulsive behavior is not ruled by cognition itself but it is also influenced by the individual personality, his intention to behave in certain way and his decision process. Therefore, an impulse buying was defined as a purchase with high levels of emotion and low levels of rational control during the buying decision, which essentially involves an automatic reaction activated by a particular stimulus (Iyer, 1989). When impulsive buying decisions or acts are produced, cognitive control is minimal and it is accompanied by strong emotions. Hirschman (1985) suggested that self-generated or autistic stimuli, which refers to wishes, desires, cravings, fantasies, daydreams and other internal thoughts that are related to emotion and sensitivity (Piron, 1991), were also responsible of impulse buying since they trigger unanticipated purchases as an illogical answer to prohibited or unreachable goals. Later, Piron (1991) recognized internal thinking as a primary process of impulse buying, which functions accordingly to the pleasure principle and shapes consumer motives that are centered on hedonic features (Youn, 2000). In their study of impulse buying Rook and Hoch (1985), outlined the construct by identifying the internal psychological conditions that impact on impulse buying behavior. They focused on cognitive and emotional components that consumers experienced when purchasing by impulse and they identified five key elements:

1. A sudden and spontaneous desire to act, that is urge to consume;
2. A state of psychological disequilibrium;
3. The onset of psychological conflict and struggle, considered as the inner dialogue;
4. A reduction in cognitive evaluation; and
5. Lack of regard for the consequences of impulse buying (Rook & Hoch, 1985).

Consequently, Rook (1987) defined impulse buying as following: "Impulse buying occurs when a consumer experiences a sudden, and often powerful and persistent urge
to buy something immediately. The impulse to buy is hedonically complex and may stimulate emotional conflict. Also, impulse buying is prone to occur with diminished regard for its consequences" (p. 191). Later, Hoch and Lowenstein (1991) revealed a struggle between the two psychological processes of affect, the emotional component, and cognition, the rational or logical component, in the impulse buy-

ing process. On the one hand, the affective process generates a strong hedonic feeling of desire causing impulsivity, and on the other, the cognitive process enables willpower or self-control. Even though in previous research they are examined individually, these two psychological processes that characterize impulsive buying are not considered independent, since neither one alone can explain the complete decision making process (Hoch & Lowenstein, 1991). Therefore, their integration is an important feature of impulse buying (Burroughs, 1996; Gardner & Rook, 1988; Hoch & Loewenstein, 1991; Rook & Gardner, 1993). Hoch and Lowenstein (1991) described impulse buying as: "A struggle between the psychological forces of desire and willpower. Two psychological processes of emotional factors which are reflected in the reference-point model of deprivation and desire and cognitive factors which are reflected in the deliberation and self-control strategies that consumers utilize. The two are by no means independent of one another. A change in either desire or willpower can cause the consumer to shift over the buy line, resulting in a purchase. Emotions influence cognitive factors (e.g., desire motivating a rationalization of the negative consequences of a purchase) and vice versa (e.g., cost analysis reducing a desire)" (p.504).

In summary, all impulse buying definitions described include reference to the sudden overwhelming urge to consume and to the speed of the decision making process. Each relates impulsivity to an out of control state of feeling and a conflict between emotional and cognitive aspects. Many of these definitions evolve to develop comparisons between psychological cognitive and affective processes. Nevertheless, since Hoch and Lowenstein's (1991) definition provides the best general explanation of impulsive buying, their definition will be used in this paper. However, after the review of previous literature on impulsiveness measures and analyzing the items proposed by different impulsivity scales, it was perceptible that an additional dimension was latent; this dimension corresponds to a behavioral component, which according to the attitudinal theory is important part of the consumer behavior. The dimension comprises two sub-dimensions or lower order components studied by Coley (2002), unplanned behavior and irresistible urge to buy, since the representative items of this sub-dimensions suggest that the individual actually performed or use to perform certain behaviors associated to impulse buying.

Hence, according to the previous literature review, three dimensions will compose the construct of impulsiveness in m-purchase or purchasing decisions via mobile devices: the cognitive, the affective and the behavioral components. Affect and cognition are rather different types of psychological responses consumers can have in any purchase situation, that lead to the third psychological response, the buying behavior itself. Although the affective and cognitive processes are different, they are deeply connected, and each process can influence and be influenced by the other. Affect refers to feeling responses, whereas cognition consists of mental (thinking) responses, and finally, behavioral refers to mechanic responses or actually performing a purchase by impulse (Youn, 2000).

METHODOLOGY

Sample and Data Collection

A scale was developed based on different scales for measuring the impulsiveness on buying behavior, adapting particularly the Rook and Fisher's (1995) buying impulsiveness scale (see Appendix 1), Verplanken and Herabadi's (2001) impulse buying tendency scale (see Appendix 2), and Coley (2002) impulse buying scale (See Appendix 3).

Given that previous literature has shown that the income is a relevant variable for impulsive buying and since the instrument measures impulsiveness buying behavior for 'on-the-go shoppers' the more feasible subjects for this study are young people who's acquisitive power is relatively high and that form part of the economically active population, that means men and women between 20 and 33 years old.

In order to create the initial scale to be self-applied (see Appendix 4), a structural survey was created with items selected by five Marketing experts of the aforementioned scales and additional proposed items adapted to the Mexican culture, as well as for the m-commerce context. For the initial phase, it was elaborated the first instrument with 25 items: 12 for the affective dimension, 6 for the cognitive dimension and 10 for the behavioral dimension. After developing a pilot test was applied to 10 people from the target in order to receive feedback about the instrument (items redaction and correct understanding). The scale's construct and validity was statistically examined afterwards with the data of 50 people from the target population of the study. In order to obtain better results and representation of the dimensions, the scale was refined and a second application of the instrument and its analysis of reliability and validity were performed. The final scale reduced to 12 items, 4 for each dimension was applied through an online structured survey to 50 people of the target in order to be analyzed.

Results and Analysis

The analysis of the scale is summarized as follows:

1. Exploratory analysis
   a. Reliability Analysis
   b. Validity Analysis
   c. Content Validity
2. Confirmatory analysis
   a. Validity analysis
      i. Construct validity: convergent and discriminant
      ii. Concurrent and Predictive Validity

EXPLORATORY ANALYSIS

Reliability by Consistency

In order to examine the initial scale's reliability, a series of statistical tests were obtained. The first test to examine the internal consistency of the scale conformed by 25 items is Cronbach's Alpha.

Cronbach's Alpha

The consistence of the initial scale is high with a Cronbach's Alpha of 0.945 (Gliem & Gliem, 2003), both normal and standardized, which means that the measurement instrument is *apparently* reliable. Nevertheless, due to the number of items, and thus the degrees of freedom that increase by multiple variables, dimensionality and sample size, this reliability might be artificial (Peterson, 1994). Since the developed scale has multiple dimensions, Cronbach's Alpha is not the most appropriate statistic for analyzing reliability. Therefore, in order to assure the scale's reliability and internal consistency, further statistical tests are presented.

After the purification of the scale, it was run a reliability test by each dimension in order to obtain Cronbach's Alpha by dimension. The results showed high consistence of the scale given that the Alphas were 0.814 for the cognitive component, 0.863 for the affective component and again 0.863 for the behavioral component. Also the Cronbach's Alpha for the overall scale comprising 12 items was 0.874.

Guttmann Coefficient

Reliability lambdas between 0.88 and 0.98 were obtained for the initial scale. The fact that the lambdas obtained are better can be attributed to the multidimensionality (supported in the previous literature review) and number of items of the initial scale (25 items). This reveals high reliability, that is, internal consistency of these items (Heinemann *et al.*, 1994).

Relating to the final scale the lambdas obtained were between 0.801 and 0.933, which indicates that the final scale was also highly reliable (Heinemann *et al.*, 1994).

Reliability by Stability

The stability of the instrument is simulated with the method of split-halves and the test results support the initial scale's reliability and stability with a Cronbach's Alpha of 0.914 for the first half and 0.899 for the second in the case of the initial scale. However, for the case of the 12-item final scale the Cronbach's Alpha for the first half was 0.794 and 0.880 for the second, which might be a bit lower than the initial scale but it still acceptable for explaining the stability of the instrument. Relative to Guttmann's split-half coefficient it is 0.880, which is acceptable to argument in favor of the scale's stability (Heinemann *et al.*, 1994). In the case of the final scale it was also developed a test for the scale's goodness of fit, and the outputs were favorable with a significant Chi-Square value of 222.949, reinforcing therefore the scale's reliability.

Content Validity

By being developed based on previous valid and reliable scales such as the buying impulsiveness scale (Rook and Fisher, 1995), the impulse buying tendency scale (Verplanken and Herabadi, 2001) and the impulse buying scale (Coley, 2002), the scale is grounded in solid foundations. Additionally, 5 marketing experts and the opinion of 15 surveyed individuals helped to refine the initial scale. However, additional tests were performed to show the validity content of the scale. The KMO and Bartlett's test barely confirm that the items actually form factors with content. Nevertheless, the KMO coefficient of 0.756 is acceptable and significant. In other words, the resulting factors as a matter of fact, reflect the content of the items, although this coefficient could and is expected to be after the purification process, substantially improved.

Exploratory Factor Analysis

In order to test the scale's validity, a Factor Analysis was performed. The higher the variability of each item, the better it is represented in the scale to measure the construct. The imp9 variable is better represented than the variable imp2, which is the worst represented variable. All other variables considered being poorly represented, are imp2, imp10, imp14, imp15 and imp25. In this case only eigenvalues greater than 1 are considered being significant. It is revealed as Coley (2002) suggests that only 6 eigenvalues or principal components are significant, in other words, the scale has 6 dimensions representing 72.4% of the scale's variability. Likewise, in order to corroborate the validity of the theory about the inter-dependence of the dimensions comprising the scale, the rotated component matrix was obtained with a Varimax orthogonal rotation method. The results show that not all the items fit in one dimension, thus proving that the scale's dimensions are not independent from each other. Additionally, to prove scale's validity and support the inter-dependence of the dimensions suggested by theory (i.e. Hoch and Lowenstein, 1991) a non-orthogonal rotation method was performed, the direct oblimin rotation. The outputs and inter-dependence are demonstrated (see Appendix 5), since all the items fit in only one dimension represented as a principal component. Nevertheless, it took 31 iterations to do so.

In conclusion, the results in the rotated component matrix with an Oblimin method show that some factorial loadings of the items (in bold) are not relevant, this coupled with the number of interactions it took to obtain the results, indicates that the scale needs further purification and that some of the items of the scale could be eliminated in order to obtain a scale with better reliability and validity.

CONFIRMATORY ANALYSIS

Construct Validity

In order to confirm the validity of the purified final scale composed by 12 items a Confirmatory Factor Analysis with an Oblimin rotation with Kaiser Normalization was performed. The convergent validity is confirmed with the observation that all factor loadings fit in their respective dimension and these were greater than 0.5 (Bentler, 2007). On the other hand, the discriminant validity is shown with the distinction between the items conformed by the three proposed dimensions and the fact that they don't blend into other dimensions (Bentler, 2007). Table 1, shows the items used in the final scale and their factor loadings. It is important to remember that the dimensions are not independent, reason why a non-orthogonal rotation method was applied.

As it is evident, the items 4 and 11 (before 3 and 12) where modified form the original scale, obtaining better results in the convergent and discriminant validity analysis.

Concurrent and Predictive Validity

To examine our final scale's validity, it was performed a predictive validity test. According to some authors such as Coley (2002) and Hoch & Lowenstein (1991), self-control or as the first author refers, mood management, is associated with the impulsiveness on purchase behavior. Therefore, a simple scale of mood management was developed and analyzed, in order to perform a linear regression in which the mood management is the dependent variable and the impulsiveness in m-purchase is the independent variable. To do so, the three dimensions of the impulsiveness in m-purchase were reduced to one factor. On the other hand, the three items comprising the mood management scale were reviewed before to examine its reliability and validity, afterwards there were reduced to one factor to represent mood management.

Table 1. Final scale

FINAL SCALE			
	Component		
	Cognitive	Affective	Behavioral
1. I feel excited while purchasing through mobile devices	.911		
2. It is fun to shop spontaneously through mobile devices	.845		
3. I feel a sensation of excitement when I am shopping something new through mobile devices	.788		
4. When I see something in the web that I love, I want to buy it immediately through my mobile	.613		
5. It is not my style to buy things through mobile devices just because		.906	
6. I use to think carefully before I buy something through mobile devices		.826	
7. I am a person that plans carefully my purchases through mobile devices		.783	
8. I never buy through mobile devices impulsively		.677	
9. When I surf the Internet through some of my mobile devices I shop things that I had not intended to purchase			-.918
10. "Just do it" describes the way I buy things through mobile devices			-.901
11. I always take advantage of the exclusive promotions for online purchases			-.642
12. Sometimes I'm a bit reckless about what I buy through mobile devices			-.637

Source: Proposed by the author

The results obtained were the following, for each unit mood management decreases the impulsivity raises in 0.624. The relationship coefficient, R Square explains 39% of the dependent variable, of impulsiveness in m-purchase. The coefficient of multiple determination, or Adjusted R Square explains 37.7% of the impulsiveness in m-purchase.

In the ANOVA test, the F- Fisher's coefficient of 30.669 compares what the model is explaining against the error. In this case, the model explains 31 times more the involved variables than the residuals. It is statistically significant given, therefore explains a good percentage of the reliability (normally 95% or more). In conclusion, the model explains significantly the dependent variable (Mood Management) that should be explained.

Therefore, the relationship between mood management and impulsiveness in m-purchase could be explained as follows: $Y = a + b_1X_1$; where $a = -3.524$ E^{-17} $b_1 = 0.624$

Hence, mood management is influenced by impulsiveness in m-purchase by 0.624. The following can be represented arithmetically as:

$$Y = -3.524 \ E^{-17} + 0.624X_1$$

or

Mood Management $= -3.524 \ E^{-17} + 0.624$ (Impulsiveness in m-purchase).

However, this only shows a relationship between these two variables, since the regression was performed in the opposite direction and the results were the same, this means, with the mood management component as the independent variable and impulsiveness in m-purchase as a dependent variable. Consequently further examination should be developed in order to state a causal relationship. Finally, the results explained, suggest that the scale's predictive validity is acceptable. The original outputs are further exhibited in Appendix 6.

CONCLUSION AND FUTURE RESEARCH

By purifying the scale and reducing the number of items within it, despite increasing convergence and discrimination validity (since the factor loadings for item within three relevant dimensions were greater) part of the reliability of the scale was sacrificed, which was reflected in a decline in the Cronbach's Alpha coefficients and Guttmann's Lambdas. So it was decided to keep a scale with a larger number of items to remain valid and reliable.

Although it started as a 25-item scale, comprehensive purification process allowed scaling a total number of 12 items, 4 for each dimension.

It was interesting to note how the items of the subdimensios unplanned buying and irresistible urge to buy studied by Coley (2002) as part of the affective dimension mingled among them. Therefore, it can be concluded that the proposed dimensions were appropriate, since despite being classified as affective, items of these two subdomains converged between them in one dimension not previously explored in the field of online shopping, and yet they differed from the items of the affective dimension. Thus, one can say that what these items have in common is that they all make mention if not explicitly, implicitly, to the completion of a purchase.

Likewise, it is important to emphasize the importance of external factors that encourage impulsivity in purchases such as marketing activities, as well as internal factors such as subjective norms and personality characteristics, which have direct influence impulsiveness in consumer purchasing. Since according to the analysis of predictive validity, we can see a connection between those internal factors and impulsiveness in purchasing. Future research on consumer behavior could benefit from the results of this research and explore further the relationship between management and impulsiveness mood in m-commerce, including establishing a causal relationship between these constructs.

It is also important to mention that buying impulsiveness may increase in the context of m-commerce, as consumers may feel more comfortable when making such purchases without judgments about their "irrational" behavior issue. This represents a good opportunity for both practitioners and academics to study such an interesting phenomenon that gives guidelines to develop new digital marketing strategies that enable marketers exploit a neglected stream, as is the insatiable hedonic aspect of human being.

I conclude by emphasizing that such purchases involve a cognitive and emotional process, which may differ greatly from everyday purchase process quickly and unmanaged emotions involved. However, it is equally important for the development of new products, and in a larger scale, of new business models focused on the consumer that are impressive in emerging markets such as Mexico.

REFERENCES

Adelaar, T., Chang, S., Lancendorfer, K. M., Lee, B., & Morimoto, M. (2003). Effects of media formats on emotions and impulse buying intent. *Journal of Information Technology*, *18*(4), 247–266. doi:10.1080/0268396032000150799

Amos, C., Holmes, G. R., & Keneson, W. C. (2014). A meta-analysis of consumer impulse buying. *Journal of Retailing and Consumer Services*, *21*(2), 86–97. doi:10.1016/j.jretconser.2013.11.004

Arens, Z. G., & Rust, R. T. (2012). The duality of decisions and the case for impulsiveness metrics. *Journal of the Academy of Marketing Science*, *40*(3), 468–479. doi:10.1007/s11747-011-0256-3

Balasubramanian, S., Peterson, R. A., & Jarvenpaa, S. L. (2002). Exploring the implications of m-commerce for markets and marketing. *Journal of the Academy of Marketing Science*, *30*(4), 348–361. doi:10.1177/009207002236910

Beatty, S. E., & Ferrell, M. E. (1998). Impulse buying: Modeling its precursors. *Journal of Retailing*, *74*(2), 169–191. doi:10.1016/S0022-4359(99)80092-X

Bentler, P. M. (2007). Can scientifically useful hypotheses be tested with correlations? *The American Psychologist*, *62*(8), 772–782. doi:10.1037/0003-066X.62.8.772 PMID:18020745

Berridge, K. C. (2004). Motivation concepts in behavioral neuroscience. *Physiology & Behavior*, *81*(2), 179–209. doi:10.1016/j.physbeh.2004.02.004 PMID:15159167

Bettman, J. R. (1979). An information processing theory of consumer choice. *Journal of Marketing*, *43*(1), 37–53. doi:10.2307/1250740

Burroughs, J. E. (1996). Product symbolism, self meaning, and holistic matching: The role of information processing in impulsive buying. *Advances in Consumer Research. Association for Consumer Research (U. S.)*, *23*, 463–469.

Coley, A. L. (2002). Affective and cognitive processes involved in impulse buying. *MSc Study*, 1-91.

Conlon, J. (2015). *The Brand Brief Behind Nike's Just Do It Campaign*. Branding Strategy Insider Website. Retrieved from: http://www.brandingstrategyinsider.com/2015/08/behind-nikes-campaign.html

Crawford, G., & Melewar, T. C. (2003). The importance of impulse purchasing behavior in the international airport environment. *Journal of Consumer Behaviour*, *3*(1), 85–98. doi:10.1002/cb.124

Depue, R. A., & Collins, P. F. (1999). Neurobiology of the Structure of Personality: Dopamine Facilitation of Incentive Motivation and Extraversion. *Behavioral and Brain Sciences*, *22*(3), 491–569. doi:10.1017/S0140525X99002046 PMID:11301519

Dholakia, U. M. (2000). Temptation and resistance: An integrated model of consumption impulse formation and enactment. *Psychology and Marketing*, *17*(11), 955–982. doi:10.1002/1520-6793(200011)17:11<955::AID-MAR3>3.0.CO;2-J

Dittmar, H. (2001). Impulse buying in ordinary and "compulsive" consumers. In E. U. Weber, J. Baron, & G. Loomes (Eds.), *Conflicts and Tradeoffs in Decision Making* (pp. 110–135). Cambridge, UK: University of Cambridge.

Dittmar, H., Beattie, J., & Friese, S. (1995). Gender identity and material symbols: Objects and decision considerations in impulse purchases. *Journal of Economic Psychology, 16*(3), 491–511. doi:10.1016/0167-4870(95)00023-H

Dittmar, H., & Drury, J. (2000). Self-image–is it in the bag? A qualitative comparison between ordinary and excessive consumers. *Journal of Economic Psychology, 21*(2), 109–142. doi:10.1016/S0167-4870(99)00039-2

Gardner, M. P., & Rook, D. W. (1988). Effects of impulse purchases on consumers' affective states. *Advances in Consumer Research. Association for Consumer Research (U. S.), 15*, 127–130.

Gliem, J. A., & Gliem, R. R. (2003). *Calculating, interpreting, and reporting Cronbach's alpha reliability coefficient for Likert-type scales*. Midwest Research-to-Practice Conference in Adult, Continuing, and Community Education.

Google. (2012). *The New multi-screen world: Understanding cross-platform consumer behavior*. Retrieved from https://think.withgoogle.com/databoard/media/pdfs/the-new-multi-screen-world-study_research-studies.pdf

Harmancioglu, N., Zachary Finney, R., & Joseph, M. (2009). Impulse purchases of new products: An empirical analysis. *Journal of Product and Brand Management, 18*(1), 27–37. doi:10.1108/10610420910933344

Heinemann, A. W., Linacre, J. M., Wright, B. D., Hamilton, B. B., & Granger, C. (1994). Prediction of rehabilitation outcomes with disability measures. *Archives of Physical Medicine and Rehabilitation, 75*(2), 133–143. PMID:8311668

Hirschman, E. C. (1985). Cognitive processes in experimental consumer behavior. *Research on Consumer Behavior, 1*, 67–102.

Hoch, S. J., & Loewenstein, G. F. (1991). Time-inconsistent preferences and consumer self-control. *The Journal of Consumer Research, 17*(4), 492–508. doi:10.1086/208573

Holbrook, M. B., & Hirschman, E. C. (1982). The experiential aspects of consumption: Consumer fantasies, feelings, and fun. *The Journal of Consumer Research, 9*(2), 132–140. doi:10.1086/208906

Howard, J. A., & Sheth, J. N. (1969). *The theory of buyer behavior* (Vol. 14). New York: Wiley.

Internet Society. (2015). *Global Internet Report 2015. Mobile evolution and development of the Internet*. Internet Society Website. Retrieved from: http://www.internetsociety.org/globalinternetreport/section/2

Iribarren, M. M., Jiménez-Giménez, M., García-de Cecilia, J. M., & Rubio-Valladolid, G. (2011). Validación y propiedades psicométricas de la escala de impulsividad estado (EIE). *Actas Españolas de Psiquiatría, 39*(1), 49–60. PMID:21274822

Iyer, E. S. (1989). Unplanned purchases: Knowledge of shopping environment and time pressure. *Journal of Retailing, 65*(1), 40–57.

Jones, M. A., Reynolds, K. E., Weun, S., & Beatty, S. E. (2003). The product-specific nature of impulse buying tendency. *Journal of Business Research*, *56*(7), 505–511. doi:10.1016/S0148-2963(01)00250-8

Kerlinger, F. N., & Lee, H. B. (2002). *Investigación del comportamiento*. México City, Mexico: McGraw-Hill.

Kollat, D. T., & Willett, R. P. (1967). Customer impulse purchasing behavior. *JMR, Journal of Marketing Research*, *6*(1), 21–31. doi:10.2307/3150160

Koufaris, M. (2002). Applying the technology acceptance model and flow theory to online consumer behavior. *Information Systems Research*, *13*(2), 205–223. doi:10.1287/isre.13.2.205.83

Mai, N. T. T., Jung, K., Lantz, G., & Loeb, S. G. (2003). An exploratory investigation into impulse buying behavior in a transitional economy: A study of urban consumers in Vietnam. *Journal of International Marketing*, *11*(2), 13–35. doi:10.1509/jimk.11.2.13.20162

OECD. (2014). The digital economy today. In *Measuring the Digital Economy: A New Perspective*. Paris: OECD Publishing; doi:10.1787/9789264221796-5-en

Olshavsky, R. W., & Granbois, D. H. (1979). Consumer decision making-fact or fiction? *The Journal of Consumer Research*, *6*(2), 93–100. doi:10.1086/208753

Patton, J. H., Stanford, M. S., & Barratt, E. S. (1995). Factor structure of the barratt impulsiveness scale. *Journal of Clinical Psychology*, *51*(6), 768–774. doi:10.1002/1097-4679(199511)51:6<768::AID-JCLP2270510607>3.0.CO;2-1 PMID:8778124

Pescher, C., Reichhart, P., & Spann, M. (2014). Consumer decision-making processes in mobile viral marketing campaigns. *Journal of Interactive Marketing*, *28*(1), 43–54. doi:10.1016/j.intmar.2013.08.001

Peter, P., & Krishnakumar, S. (2010). Emotional Intelligence, Impulse Buying and Self-Esteem: The Predictive Validity of Two Ability Measures of Emotional Intelligence. *Advances in Consumer Research. Association for Consumer Research (U. S.)*, 37877–37878.

Peterson, R. A. (1994). A meta-analysis of Cronbachs coefficient alpha. *The Journal of Consumer Research*, *21*(2), 381–391. doi:10.1086/209405

Piron, F. (1991). Defining impulse purchasing. *Advances in Consumer Research. Association for Consumer Research (U. S.)*, *18*, 509–514.

Piron, F. (1993). A comparison of emotional reactions experienced by planned, unplanned and impulse purchasers. *Advances in Consumer Research. Association for Consumer Research (U. S.)*, *20*, 341–344.

Ramanathan, S., & Menon, G. (2006). Time-varying effects of chronic hedonic goals on impulsive behavior. *JMR, Journal of Marketing Research*, *43*(4), 628–641. doi:10.1509/jmkr.43.4.628

Rook, D. W. (1987). The buying impulse. *The Journal of Consumer Research*, *14*(2), 189–199. doi:10.1086/209105

Rook, D. W., & Fisher, R. J. (1995). Normative influences on impulsive buying behavior. *The Journal of Consumer Research*, *22*(3), 305–313. doi:10.1086/209452

Rook, D. W., & Gardner, M. P. (1993). In the mood: Impulse buying's affective antecedents. *Research in Consumer Behavior, 6*(7), 1-28.

Rook, D. W., & Gardner, M. P. (1993). In the mood: Impulse buying's affective antecedents. *Research in Consumer Behavior, 6*, 1–28.

Rook, D. W., & Hoch, S. J. (1985). Consuming impulse. *Advances in Consumer Research. Association for Consumer Research (U. S.), 12*, 23–27.

Sheth, J. N. (1979). The surpluses and shortages in consumer behavior theory and research. *Journal of the Academy of Marketing Science, 7*(4), 414–427. doi:10.1007/BF02729689

Stern, H. (1962). The significance of impulse buying today. *Journal of Marketing, 26*(2), 59–62. doi:10.2307/1248439

Strack, F., & Deutsch, R. (2006). Reflective and impulsive determinants of consumer behavior. *Journal of Consumer Psychology, 16*(3), 205–216. doi:10.1207/s15327663jcp1603_2

Verplanken, B., & Herabadi, A. (2001). Individual differences in impulse buying tendency: Feeling and no thinking. *European Journal of Personality, 15*(1), 71–83. doi:10.1002/per.423

Virgin. (2011). *The psychology of impulse purchase*. Retrieved from http://www.virgin.com/entrepreneur/psychology-impulse-purchase

Vohs, K. D., & Faber, R. J. (2007). Spent resources: Self-regulatory resource availability affects impulse buying. *The Journal of Consumer Research, 33*(4), 537–547. doi:10.1086/510228

Weinberg, P., & Gottwald, W. (1982). Impulsive consumer buying as a result of emotions. *Journal of Business Research, 10*(1), 43–57. doi:10.1016/0148-2963(82)90016-9

Weun, S., Jones, M. A., & Beatty, S. E. (1998). Development and validation of the impulse buying tendency scale. *Psychological Reports, 82*(3c), 1123–1133. doi:10.2466/pr0.1998.82.3c.1123 PMID:9709520

Wood, M. (1998). Socio-economic status, delay of gratification, and impulse buying. *Journal of Economic Psychology, 19*(3), 295–320. doi:10.1016/S0167-4870(98)00009-9

Xiao, S. H., & Nicholson, M. (2011). Mapping impulse buying: A behaviour analysis framework for services marketing and consumer research. *Service Industries Journal, 31*(15), 2515–2528. doi:10.1080/02642069.2011.531123

Xiaoni, Z., Prybutok, V. R., & Strutton, D. (2007). Modelling influences on impulse purchasing behaviours during the online marketing transactions. *Journal of Marketing Theory and Practice, 15*(1), 79–89. doi:10.2753/MTP1069-6679150106

Youn, S. H. (2000). *The Dimensional Structure of Consumer Buying Impulsivity: Measurement and Validation* (Doctoral Dissertation). The Graduate School of The University of Minnesota.

Zhou, L., & Wong, A. (2003). Consumer impulse buying and in-store stimuli in Chinese supermarkets. *Journal of International Consumer Marketing, 16*(2), 37–53. doi:10.1300/J046v16n02_03

APPENDIX 1

Table 2. Rook and Fisher's Buying Impulsiveness Scale

Item	Factor loading	Mean	SD
1. I often buy things spontaneously.	.81	3.08	1.1.8
2. "Just do it" describes the way I buy things.	.75	2.65	1.17
3. I often buy things without thinking.	.73	2.33	1.19
4. "I see it, I buy it" describes me.	.71	2.36	1.15
5. "Buy now, think about it later" describes me.	.65	2.25	1.20
6. Sometimes I feel like buying things on the spur-of-the-moment.	.64	3.40	1.04
7. I buy things according to how I feel at the moment.	.63	3.17	1.19
8. I carefully plan most of my purchases*	.62	2.81	1.16
9. Sometimes I am a bit reckless about what I buy.	.60	2.99	1.08

Source: Rook and Fisher (1995)

APPENDIX 2

Table 3. Verplanken and Herabadi's Impulse Buying Tendency Scale (2001)

Item	TOTAL	Cognitive	Affective
Cognitive items			
1. I usually think carefully before I buy something*	0.63	0.83	-0.18
2. I usually only buy things that I intended to buy*	0.84	0.79	0.19
3. If I buy something, I usually do that spontaneously.	0.75	0.78	0.07
4. Most of my purchases are planned in advance*	0.69	0.78	-0.02
5. I only buy things that I really need*	0.77	0.74	0.16
6. It is not my style to just buy things*	0.81	0.74	0.21
7. I like to compare different brands before I buy one*	0.45	0.67	-0.23
8. Before I buy something I always carefully consider whether I need it*	0.56	0.66	-0.04
9. I am used to buying things 'on the spot'	0.65	0.65	0.09
10. I often buy things without thinking.	0.67	0.65	0.12
Affective items			
11. It is a struggle to leave nice things I see in a shop.	0.56	0.02	0.81
12. I sometimes cannot suppress the feeling of wanting to buy something.	0.61	0.02	0.79
13. I sometimes feel guilty after having bought something.	0.32	-0.15	0.66
14. I'm not the kind of person who 'falls in love at first sight' with things I see in shops*	0.25	-0.20	0.65
15. I can become very excited if I see something I would like to buy.	0.42	-0.09	0.63
16. I always see something nice whenever I pass by shops.	0.44	0.08	0.54
17. I find it difficult to pass up a bargain.	0.61	0.32	0.48
18. If I see something new, I want to buy it.	0.42	0.12	0.47
19. I am a bit reckless in buying things.	0.71	0.44	0.47
20. I sometimes buy things because I like buying things, rather than because I need them.	0.44	0.15	0.45

Source: Verplanken and Herabadi (2001)

APPENDIX 3

Table 4. Coley's Impulse Buying Scale (2002)

Question Number	Empirical Support
Affective Components *Irresistible Urge to Buy*	
1. When I shop I tend to decide what I want to buy while I am looking around a store.	Han, 1987
2. I always buy if I really like it.	
Positive Buying Emotions	
3. I feel a sense of thrill when I am buying something new.	Youn, 2000
10. I feel excited when making a purchase.	Beatty, 1998
Mood Management	Youn, 2000
5. Buying is a way of reducing stress in my daily life.	
6. Sometimes, I buy something in order to make myself feel better.	
7. Sometimes I regret buying new things.	
8. I experience mixed feelings of pleasure and guilt from buying something on impulse.	
Cognitive Components *Cognitive Deliberation*	
4. I make a list when I go shopping and buy only what is on the list.	Han, 1987; Rook & Fisher, 1995
15. I rarely ever buy impulsively.	Youn, 2000
16. When you think about your buying behavior in general, do you consider yourself to be an impulse buyer?	
17. Would people who know you consider you to be an impulse buyer?	
Unplanned Buying	
11. When I go shopping, I buy things that I had not intended to purchase.	Beatty, 1998; Youn, 2000
12. If I see something that I think I need, I buy it even though I went shopping for other purposes.	Han, 1987; Rook & Hoch, 1985; Martin, Weun & Beatty, 1993; Youn 2000
Disregard for the Future	
13. I tend to spend money as soon as I earn it.	Youn, 2000.

Source: Coley (2002)

APPENDIX 4

Original Measurement Instrument (Adapted to Spanish Speakers)

No. _____

Buenas tardes, mi nombre es Natasha Bojorges, soy estudiante de Doctorado del Tec de Monterrey y me encuentro realizando una investigación sobre compras electrónicas a través de dispositivos móviles. Su opinión es muy importante, por lo que le agradecería me contestara unas breves preguntas.

1. ¿Realiza compras en línea a través de su dispositivo móvil (Laptop, Smartphone o Tablet) al menos 1 vez por mes? _____ Sí _____ No

Indique con una X la respuesta que considere representa mejor su opinión con respecto a las siguientes afirmaciones, donde 1 significa Totalmente de acuerdo y 7 Totalmente en desacuerdo, como se muestra a continuación:

**RECUERDE: Queremos conocer su opinión *única y exclusivamente* cuando realiza compras en línea a través de dispositivos móviles (Laptop, Smartphone y/o Tablet).

Datos

Sexo: _____F _____M Edad: _____ Edo. Civil: _____Soltero _____Casado

Colonia: _____

Delegación: _____

Ocupación:_____

Table 5. Original measurement instrument (adapted to Spanish speakers)

Totalmente de acuerdo	De acuerdo	Algo de acuerdo	Ni de acuerdo ni en desacuerdo	Algo en desacuerdo	En desacuerdo	Totalmente en desacuerdo
7	6	5	4	3	2	1

(Si su respuesta fue NO a la pregunta anterior, le agradezco mucho su participación)

Table 6. Totalmente Totalmente de acuerdo en desacuerdo

1. Siempre que me gusta mucho algo, lo compro a través de dispositivos móviles	7	6	5	4	3	2	1
2. Suelo gastar el dinero tan pronto como lo gano	7	6	5	4	3	2	1
3. Cuando veo algo en la red que me encanta, siento la necesidad de comprarlo a través de alguno de mis dispositivos móviles inmediatamente.	7	6	5	4	3	2	1
4. A menudo compro cosas a través de dispositivos móviles manera espontánea	7	6	5	4	3	2	1
5. Suelo pensar con cuidado antes de comprar algo a través de dispositivos móviles	7	6	5	4	3	2	1
6. A veces no puedo suprimir el sentimiento de querer comprar algo a través de dispositivos móviles	7	6	5	4	3	2	1

continued on following page

Table 6. Continued

7. Cuando navego a través de alguno de mis dispositivos móviles, compro cosas que no tenía intención de comprar	7	6	5	4	3	2	1
8. Experimento sentimientos encontrados de placer y culpa al comprar algo a través de dispositivos móviles por impulso	7	6	5	4	3	2	1
9. La frase "Simplemente hazlo" describe la forma en que compro a través de dispositivos móviles	7	6	5	4	3	2	1
10. Cuando veo en la red algo que realmente me interesa, lo compro a través de alguno de mis dispositivos móviles sin considerar las consecuencias	7	6	5	4	3	2	1
11. Es una lucha interna evitar comprar a través de dispositivos móviles cosas buenas que veo en la red	7	6	5	4	3	2	1
12. Me resulta difícil dejar pasar una ganga exclusiva para compras en línea	7	6	5	4	3	2	1
13. A veces me siento con ganas de comprar cosas a través de dispositivos móviles en el calor del momento	7	6	5	4	3	2	1
14. Yo casi nunca compro a través de dispositivos móviles impulsivamente*	7	6	5	4	3	2	1
15. Yo sólo compro a través de dispositivos móviles cosas que realmente necesito*	7	6	5	4	3	2	1
16. A veces soy un poco alocad@ al comprar a través de dispositivos móviles	7	6	5	4	3	2	1
17. He comprado al instante cosas en Internet que no necesito, por miedo a que se agoten	7	6	5	4	3	2	1
18. Siento una sensación de emoción cuando estoy comprando a través de dispositivos móviles algo nuevo	7	6	5	4	3	2	1
19. Estoy acostumbrad@ a comprar cosas a través de dispositivos móviles al momento	7	6	5	4	3	2	1
20. Me olvido de mis problemas cuando compro algo a través de dispositivos móviles	7	6	5	4	3	2	1
21. Soy una persona que planea cuidadosamente las compras que realiza a través de dispositivos móviles*	7	6	5	4	3	2	1
22. A veces compro a través de dispositivos móviles para sentirme mejor	7	6	5	4	3	2	1
23. La siguiente frase me describe: "Lo veo en línea, lo pongo en mi carrito de compra"	7	6	5	4	3	2	1
24. Es divertido comprar a través de dispositivos móviles espontáneamente	7	6	5	4	3	2	1
25. La gente que me conoce me considera un comprador en línea impulsivo	7	6	5	4	3	2	1
26. No es mi estilo comprar cosas a través de dispositivos móviles sólo por comprarlas*	7	6	5	4	3	2	1
27. La siguiente frase me describe: "Cómpralo ahora, piénsalo después"	7	6	5	4	3	2	1
28. Me siento emocionad@ al hacer una compra a través de dispositivos móviles	7	6	5	4	3	2	1

APPENDIX 5

Table 7. Exploratory factor analysis

	Principal Component Analysis with Oblimin Rotation					
	Component					
	1	2	3	4	5	6
imp11	.861					
imp8	.841					
imp9	.668					
imp13	.654					
imp7	.562					
imp6	.529					
imp12						
imp26		.903				
imp5		.844				
imp14		.706				
imp21		.696				
imp15		.533				
imp22			-.740			
imp23			-.619			
imp20			-.604			
imp27						
imp28				.886		
imp18				.810		
imp24				.674		
imp3				.557		
imp2						
imp4						
imp17					-.663	
imp16					-.576	
imp25					-.564	
imp1						.928
imp10						
imp19						

Source: Generated by the author with SPSS 24

APPENDIX 6

Table 8. Predictive validity analysis outputs

Model Summary						
Model	R	R Square		Adjusted R Square		Std. Error of the Estimate
1	.624[a]	.390		.377		.78921549
ANOVA[a]						
	Model	Sum of Squares	df	Mean Square	F	Sig.
1	Regression	19.103	1	19.103	30.669	.000[b]
	Residual	29.897	48	.623		
	Total	49.000	49			
Coefficients[a]						
	Model	Unstandardized Coefficients		Standardized Coefficients	t	Sig.
		B	Std. Error	Beta		
1	(Constant)	-3.524E-17	.112		.000	1.000
	Impulsiveness in M-purchase	.624	.113	.624	5.538	.000
a. Dependent Variable: Mood management						
b. Predictors: (Constant), Impulsiveness in M-purchase						

Source: Generated by the author with SPSS 24

Chapter 8
Germany's External Trade Development:
A Case of the German Automotive Industry

Alexander Schülke
Boston University, USA

Saerom Jang
Boston University, USA

Pierre Haddad
Boston University, USA

Melissa Renneckendorf
Boston University, USA

ABSTRACT

The automobile industry is the single largest industry in Germany. Demand for German car brands in foreign countries, including China, is strong as German car manufacturers enjoy reputation of high quality products. In recent years, several factors showed an effect on Germany's external trade development through a shift in the automobile sector. Globalization had an effect on external trade as developing countries try to push many exporting countries, including Germany, to manufacture locally. This is an ongoing trend that is supported by lower labor costs in developing countries. Boosting other sectors is one strategy to be less dependent on these developments and the focus on electric vehicles could ensure further exports. Economic growth in foreign countries remains one of the big opportunities for Germany's external trade development. However, it is important to take potential challenges and barriers into consideration, including environmentalism, strong competition, and new trends and business models that lead to less car ownership.

INTRODUCTION

Germany is known for its strong economy. One of the reasons for that is the *German Mittelstand*, small and medium-sized enterprises that make up for 99 percent of German firms and contribute to 52 percent of total economic output (BMWi, 2013). However, the single largest industry in Germany is the automotive industry (GTAI, 2015). With sales of EUR 384 billion in 2014, which account for around 20 percent of German industry revenue, and a workforce of 775,000 employers in the same year, automotive companies are important for the country. A great amount of the production in the automobile industry

DOI: 10.4018/978-1-5225-0902-8.ch008

is exported to other countries. While EUR 133 billion was generated in the domestic market in 2014, EUR 251 billion of German passenger car and light commercial vehicle revenue was generated in foreign markets. For both the domestic and foreign market, revenue increased in 2014 over 2013 by seven and five percent, respectively. In a global perspective, every fifth car was made by a German original equipment manufacturer (OEM). One reason why German cars are so strong in the global market could be related to German car manufacturers' research and development (R&D) focus. With EUR 17.6 billion in 2014, R&D expenditure of German OEMs account for over 30 percent in the worldwide automotive industry. Automotive is Germany's most innovative sector and is at the same time responsible for over half of Europe's R&D growth.

Even though Germany's automobile industry is in a strong global position, a focus on continuous innovative activity is especially important now as the overall automotive ecosystem is expected to change. Consumers look for comprehensive mobility experience, new technologies will offer more safety and convenience and vehicles will become more intelligent. Further globalization, integration, and collaboration will increase the complexity that automobile companies have to face (IBM, 2008).

To stay competitive on a worldwide perspective, companies and governments have to work together to set the basis for policies that support, not hinder, innovative business activities. Even further, as exports are so important for Germany's economy, automobile brands have to stay innovative and defend their leading position in global markets to remain competitive against new competitors that might enter the automobile industry.

ANALYSIS

The following paper is going to analyze Germany's external trade development and current trade posture in the automotive sector. The approach is the following: at first, the effects of globalization on the German automotive industry and how the strategies of German car manufacturers changed in response will be analyzed. Such strategies are also known as internationalization strategies. Afterwards, the development of German car brands and their expansion to other countries is explored in greater detail. What follows is a comprehensive breakdown of the existing problems that the German automotive industry is currently facing with regard to exports. This will then be complemented by a description of trade policies that Germany goes by and how the German government has intervened in the market in the past. Such interventions can also stem from foreign countries. Lastly, the opportunities, challenges and barriers of German exports will be evaluated and finally a conclusion summarizes the findings and provides an outlook.

Globalization Philosophy

Based on the fact, automotive industry has enormously changed during the past two decades due to globalization, especially the organization of its production. To be specific, the globalization allows the automotive industry not only to be the fragmentation of international production in its industry, but also to be associated with an increase of trade in intermediate goods. Consequently, automotive firms are able to organize their activities in global value chains to have the best profit and outcome, as well as production to reduce the production cost through emerging countries across the world. As a result, the industry is currently regarded as one of the most globalized industries in the manufacturing segment (Chiappini, 2012).

After the automotive industry has become an assembly industry which allows to relocate its assembly line to other emerging or developing countries to have some benefits such as acquiring lower labor cost and restructuring of domestic production lines to cut the unnecessary costs, many countries including Germany have had a significant impact on increasing in the trade of automotive parts and components (Chiappini, 2012; Kwon, 2004). Particularly, Germany has been suitable for this globalization circumstance because of the following reasons: First reason is that German automotive industries concentrate on in-house mass production instead of hierarchical integration. Second, German automotive industries are very good at adopting a new and flexible production system due to a cross-functional team structure. Third, German automotive industries are closely interactive contractual relations within dependent suppliers for a long term (Kwon, 2004). Those patterns of national production and globalized market system have dedicated German automotive industries to have competitiveness in the global market.

In 2013, more than 8.6 million cars have been manufactured by German automotive firms abroad. This impressive number is 133.7 percent higher than what has been accomplished in 2000. Manufacturing in developing countries is often seen as low quality work, but nowadays the infrastructures and machines used to make these cars are getting better with the quality of work. This is why the qualitative growth is also increasing. In contrast, the car companies in Germany are making around 5 million cars a year. So they are manufacturing more abroad than in their domestic plants. In this way, the foreign manufacturers are boosting car production. As a consequence, the amount of direct investment of automotive industries has increased to 130 billion euros. This number represents 43 percent of the total FDI of the entire German manufacturing sector (Heymann, 2014). Volkswagen is a good example of this situation where the car production in Germany has decreased by 13 percent from 2000 to 2013, and at the meantime it skyrocketed by 27 percent in China. This example is summarized in the graph below, comparing the country shares of the Volkswagen production between 2000 and 2013 (Figure 1) (Quest Trend Magazine, 2015a).

Internationalization

For the past fourteen years the market and the automobile industry have dramatically changed. It is actually at the end of the 1990s that the main automobile manufacturers started to change their strategy to international relocation of their production. This move has been made according to the attractiveness of the countries where the plants are now located with the low costs of the labor, low taxes etc. (Quest Trend Magazine, 2015b).

The internationalization strategy of German automotive companies has been a key element of their success. This strategy turned out to be particularly effective. It not only helped massively exporting its products in many foreign countries around the world but has also begun to diversify its purchases. Indeed, the German automotive sector is much supplied in terms of parts abroad. In addition to its car exports and its imports of foreign parts, the German automotive industry established production facilities in foreign countries. As depicted in the graph below, the production of most of the industrialized countries in the automotive industry is shifting to developing countries. Consequently, German brands of car production grew increasingly in recent years. In addition, they relocated their research and development (Figure 2) (R&D) (Heymann, 2014).

Figure 1. Volkswagen – Internationalization of production 2013 to 2000
(*Quest Trend Magazine, 2015a*)

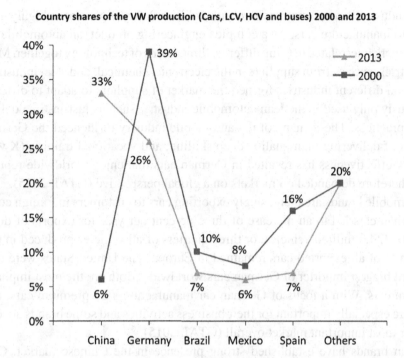

Country shares of the VW production (Cars, LCV, HCV and buses) 2000 and 2013

Figure 2. Worldwide auto production shifting away from industrialized countries
(*Quest Trend Magazine, 2015a*)

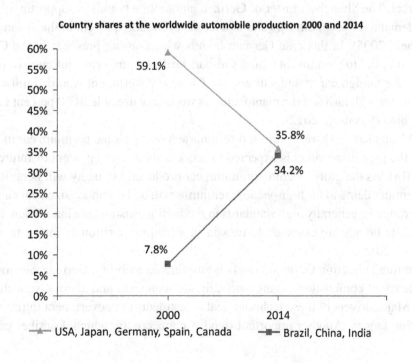

Country shares at the worldwide automobile production 2000 and 2014

Market Development for German Brands

The automobile industry, in any country where automobile industry is present, is highly interrelated with other industries to manufacture cars. As a complex engineering product, an automobile contains about 20,000 parts that work interrelated to bring different dimensions of technology together. Many parts come from other industries, such as from suppliers in the electronic, chemical, and steel industry. In Germany, this dependency on different industries formed the market of suppliers to adapt to different techniques that were previously only used in the lean automobile industry, such as just-in-time delivery and other new production practices. The demand of the automobile industry influenced the German industry of supplier in terms of delivering high quality, deep skilling, and vocational training (Kwon, 2004). The resulting industry effectiveness has resulted in German cars that enjoy worldwide reputation for high quality and are therefore demanded on markets on a global perspective (GTAI, 2015).

German automobile brands are increasingly exporting cars to customers in foreign countries. Strong demand for German cars led to an increase of three percent per year for exports of domestic vehicle production. In 2014, 4.3 million vehicles, or three quarters of all vehicles produced in Germany, were exported. Over half of all exported cars remained in Europe. The United States were the second, and Asia was the third biggest importer of German cars worldwide. Both are the most important buyers for German premium cars. With a focus of German car manufacturers on premium cars, this means that these countries are especially important for their business activities and some brands are even dependent on China as their most important market overall (GTAI, 2015).

Some German brands have established strong presence in the Chinese market. One example is Volkswagen, which established an automobile industry cluster in Shanghai. Volkswagen was supported by local and national policy makers and could therefore implement and extend production systems and market reach in China. As part of the process to establish business in Shanghai, Volkswagen required many other German car manufacturers to be present in Shanghai and to strengthen their interests in the Chinese market. The Shanghai cluster of German automobile brands is supporting their position to fulfill Chinese demand for premium cars and to become even more present in the Asian market overall (Depner & Bathelt, 2005). In this case German brands with a strong presence in the Chinese market would also have it easier to circumvent China's import tariffs on imported automotive parts. Aware of its attractiveness for foreign car manufacturers, the Chinese government would significantly decrease the brands' profits through tariffs if the manufacturers would not use at least 60 percent Chinese content in cars sold in China (Swenson, 2012).

German OEM cars have a share of almost three quarters of the global premium car market. This will be beneficial as the premium market is expected to account for over 50 percent of future profit growth (Mohr, et al., 2013). As the global leading premium car producer, Germany will benefit from growing international premium demand for high-value, premium small and compact-sized cars and also for premium SUVs. Through its generally high standards in production, sustainable innovation, and know-how, German automobile brands are expected to remain in a leading position in international automobile production (GTAI, 2015).

An important trend affecting German brands is sustainable mobility. German car brands are focusing on the efficiency of combustion engines, new, lighter materials, and alternative technologies, such as electric cars. Major drivers of these technological investments are government initiatives and carbon emission reduction targets. Another important trend is connectivity, which describes cars that will be connected to the Internet. These trends are increasing German car manufacturers R&D focus. Around 25 percent of researchers in Germany's private economy are working in automotive (GTAI, 2015).

Existing Problems

In order to access some existing and new markets, export is fundamental for German automotive companies. Moreover, there is a growing demand in Asia, Eastern Europe and Latin America. However, this demand results in a change in the policy of different countries. Some of them now want to have a plant directly in their country with the intention to benefit of all advantages from it, for example increased employment. Consequently, these countries are implementing new regulations that are barriers for exporting countries such as high import duties. India is imposing a high duty for German cars. In order to avoid this duty, the car manufacturer has to establish a plant locally, even if it is just a small one. German automotive manufacturers are facing the same problem when it comes to export cars in Brazil (VDA, n.d.).

As a reaction, the EU Commission, for whom it goes against the trade liberalization, requested a consultation of the WTO. We can find the same case in Russia, consequently, the exportations from Germany, concerning car manufacturer have decreased. Those regulations are usually based on high duties but they can also be technical. Therefore, there has been a restriction on all German exports. This is mainly done in developing countries in order to protect their domestic industry and it is clearly an issue for European countries (VDA, n.d.).

The German automotive industry and other relative industries are supporting a removal of these barriers that complicate the export of their products. They talk in favor of trade agreements in order to promote exchanges between countries. The Doha Round, which began in November 2001 and aims to reduce or eliminate barriers to international trade, has not yet yielded concrete results. However, a breakthrough was made during the 9th WTO ministerial conference in Bali in December 2013, which resulted in a trade facilitation thanks to treaties (VDA, n.d.).

The Ukraine crisis specifically harmed the German automotive exports. The sanctions against Moscow resulted in a reduction of exports by 24.4 percent (EUR 3.1 billion) in 2014. The Russian automobile market had long been a bearer of hope for Europe. Now, European and therefore German manufacturers have to fear losing their lucrative business opportunities to Asian suppliers (Reuters, 2014).

One of the main sectors in which Germany is exporting is the automobile industry. This sector is a major component of the German economy and is central to it. It is known for its quality and durability, this has shaped an international reputation to car makers like BMW, Audi, etc. These car brands are exporting all around the world in developed countries as well as in developing countries. This contributes to the good health of the German economy. So the more they export, the more their profit will increase. However, it could be seen as a weakness or a potential future emerging problem. These exportations create a dependency to other countries. Therefore, if there were any problem in the partner country (e.g., political problem, war etc.), it would badly impact the German economy. This can be pointed out by an info-graph below that is showing the importance of exports for the country (Figure 3). Consequently, exports are a real asset for Germany but it shows also that they cannot only rely on it (Rattner, 2011). In addition to that, Germany mainly exports machines and chemical products besides automobiles. If there is a global shift in demand towards other products, such as those related to IT, pharmaceuticals, or electronics, Germany would at the moment not be able to cater to these new needs and subsequently suffer from a structural problem.

Figure 3. Germany is the World's No. 1 Automobile Exporter by Far
(McCarthy, 2013)

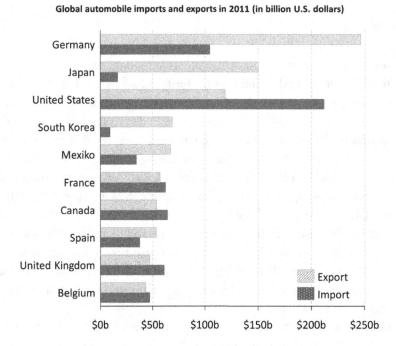

Trade Policies and Government Interventions in the Automobile Industry

German government has a high interest in supporting its automotive industry, since it plays a crucial role in its external trade development and its economic performance. Consequently, it takes an active role in the framing of new European trading policies and objectives that deal with this specific sector. Since the European automotive industry is facing several pressures, such as its market decline and structural overcapacities, the European Commission responded with an action plan for the EU automotive industry for 2020 in 2012 (European Commission, 2012a).

This plan consists of four pillars:

1. Investing in advanced technologies and financing innovation through a range of regulatory initiatives and support to research and innovation,
2. Improving market conditions through a stronger internal market and the consistent implementation of smart regulation,
3. Enhancing competitiveness on global markets through an effective trade policy and the international harmonization of vehicle regulations, and
4. Anticipating adaptation by investing in human capital and skills and softening the social impacts of restructuring. With regard to Germany's external trade development the third pillar provides the necessary framework to shape a playing field that grants access to markets and harmonizes regulations (European Commission, 2012b).

For one, in order to facilitate the market access in developing countries Free Trade Agreements (FTA) are strongly considered, both multilateral and bilateral. The goal is to further remove tariff and non-tariff barriers. In addition to that, bilateral regulatory cooperation with new key players and countries like the United States and Japan under the UNECE (United Nations Economic Commission for Europe) framework will be nurtured (European Commission, 2012b).

Next, harmonizing vehicle regulations on an international level will remain one of the main priorities of the Commission. This ensures that compliance costs are minimized, economies of scale achieved and technical barriers to trade reduced. The principle to be followed is "tested once, admitted everywhere" (European Commission, 2012b, p. 18). The instrument to be applied for this purpose is the UNECE 1958 Agreement which targets the technical harmonization in the motor vehicle sector. Besides the European Union's member states, Japan, Australia, New Zealand and South Africa joined the set of countries that seek harmonization within the industry. This Agreement will be further modernized and the adoption of more third markets will be encouraged.

Besides the negotiation of free trade agreements and driving mutual recognition of technical standards worldwide, the German government has also taken concrete actions to intervene in the automotive industry in the past. After the automobile crisis in 2008/2009 it introduced a scrappage program to stimulate the industry and to create demand. For every car that was older than nine years EUR 2,500 were paid out to applicants that wanted to buy a new car (Focus, 2009). While it did benefit automotive manufacturers in Germany, it also had another side effect: used cars that were handed out to German scrap dealers were subsequently exported to Africa and Eastern Europe instead of being wrecked. Hence, the government's market intervention to help boost the industry resulted in illegal exports (Dougherty, 2009).

Yet, also the market interventions of other countries are harming German automobile exports. When Russia joined the WTO in 2012 the expectations were high among European member states that this would help their local businesses to increase sales and exports. However, even though joining the WTO aims at abolishing tariffs and reducing trade barriers, the Russian government imposed new kinds of tariffs, taxes and fees in a creative way so that exports from Germany to Russia were even lower after Russia's WTO accession than before. This specifically harmed the automotive industry. While Russia did indeed reduce the import tariffs for new vehicles, it also levied a new recycling fee for imported cars as a form of protectionism to give local manufacturers an advantage and to offset the unavailable earnings from import tariffs (Kaiser & Steiner, 2013). Another example would be Brazil, which introduced fiscal regulations that favor domestic automobile manufacturers. Hence, besides tariffs or bureaucratic chicanery the protectionist measures of foreign countries are increasingly harming German auto export firms (Rossbach, 2013).

Future Prospects Related to Opportunities

Since automobile industry has enormous impact on Germany's economy, it is significantly important to identify market opportunities. Based upon our analysis, so far, German automotive industry has dominated global market well and there are more promising opportunities that would bring a huge benefits for the German automotive industry.

Specifically, one of the most important opportunities is the economic growth, as well as growing demand in Asia, especially in China. According to The World Bank (2015), China has reformed its market structure from a centrally planned to a market based economy in 1978 and experienced rapid economic and social developments. The average GDP has grown about 10 percent a year, and it allows

Chinese to overcome their poverty. Furthermore, China recently became the second largest economy with enormous population which is about 1.3 billion and plays a lucrative role in the global economy. Based upon the fact, it is clear that China has a huge amount of possibility which means China is one of the biggest and most potential market for the German automotive industries.

Moreover, investing more money to build German automotive firms' own factories into Mexico would make the firms to curb unnecessary spending and have some benefits as well. In fact, according to Althaus and Boston (2015), some German automotive firms such as Volkswagen and Audi are currently operating its factories in Mexico. The companies have obtained advantages, not only unrivaled trade relationship in the global market but also low labor cost with improved logistics through Mexico factories. Specifically, Mexico has more than 40 free-trade agreements. Therefore, pacts play a lucrative role attracting foreign companies which require many numbers of trade like automotive industry because exporters are able to get duty-free access from Mexico to markets that particularly contain 60 percent of the world's economic output. Consequently, more concentrating on Mexico for its assembly plants or factories would cause beneficial profits to German automotive industry.

Lastly, Transatlantic Trade and Investment Partnership (TTIP) between the United States and European Union would be one of the most significant and important events to the automotive industry, as well as to car enthusiasts if it adopted. The purposes of TTIP are abolishing tariffs on imported cars and finally aligning U.S. and European automotive safety and environmental standards as well. Specifically, the current standard tariff for importing cars to the U.S. is 2.5 percent of its value, and for pickup trucks and commercial vans, it is a whopping 25 percent. Conversely, individual European countries don't charge import duties, but they charge a flat rate of 10 percent on imported automobiles (Berkowitz, 2013). The Transatlantic Trade and Investment Partnership (TTIP) would be amazing point for German automotive industry because they could get the price competitiveness through the partnership.

Future Challenges, Barriers, and Recommendation

To sustain and enhance its current status for the German automotive industry, it is important not only to look at the current business and market circumstances, but also to predict potential challenges and barriers that might encounter during its future business. Based upon our analysis, it is clear that the German automotive industry well continues to dominate the performance parts of the luxury market and has striking opportunities for its future business. However, German automotive firms still have several challenges and barriers to overcome.

Among the many challenges, environmentalism would be one of the most significant challenges for German automotive firms. In other word, they need to focus on the environmentally friendly cars such as electric or hybrid cars to meet customers' demands. According to The Economist (2007), currently consumers' tastes are changing and they have qualms feelings about the environment. Moreover, there is possibility that some governments require intensive tax to buyers who buy emissions-heavy cars. Therefore, Germany's luxury car brands such as Mercedes Benz and BMW need to focus on developing environmental friendly cars.

Another challenge related to environmentalism would be a late release date and strong competition. Geuss (2014) explained that even though German automotive firms such as Porsche, Mercedes Benz, and Audi have plan to provide better electric cars for its customers, the release date would be between 2017 and 2021. Furthermore, in automotive industry, Toyota, Nissan, and Tesla already have dominated the environmentally friendly car market. Consequently, even though the German automotive industry has strong brands in its market, it will be hard to acquire the electric car market due to late response to customers' needs and strong competitors. Therefore, German automotive firms need to adjust releasing day and have competitive advantages to attract potential customers. Also, having strategic alliance with its strong competitors to release environmental friendly cars would be great strategy for German automotive industry.

To enter different market such as other area or countries, German automotive firms should have flexibility in diverse aspects, such as organizational structure of the firms in terms of business model and strategies because each country has different political issues, customer preferences, and attitudes to new products. According to the Tang (2009), China's automobile industry has consistently expanded its market. Specifically, from January to October 2009, more than 10 million vehicles were sold in China. As opposed to South Korea and Japan, China's automotive industry has developed through foreign direct investment such as alliances and joint ventures between international automotive manufacturers and Chinese partners. Based on this fact, German automotive firms need to realize that they should adjust its business model to enter different countries. Also, Cheyipai (2015) indicates that currently, China's used-car e-commerce is drastically rising. Consequently, German automotive firms need to look at the market's circumstance and reflect it for its future businesses. In addition, the German automotive industry should examine, analyze, and reflect customers' preferences as well. For instance, in China or the United States, especially west side, most people drive long distance every day for commute or their daily lives which means the people who live in that area tend to consider fuel efficiency as the most important factors when they buy a car. Therefore, depending on countries or areas, German automotive firms should research the market in order to forecast what customers want and need, as well as political aspects to acquire new markets.

Another challenge affecting automobile manufacturers in general might be a trend to less car ownership. In Germany, especially young people show high amounts of driver's license ownership but less car ownership compared to earlier years. This change can partly be explained due to structural changes such as an increasing amount of enrolled students, who therefore start their professional career later and are therefore are less likely to have an income to afford car ownership in their early twenties. Other reasons might include increased gasoline prices compared to a less strong increase of public transportation prices, information and communication technology that changes consumer behavior, and psychological factors, such as environmental awareness (Kuhnimhof, Buehler, Wirtz, & Kalinowska, 2012). Even in the United States, car usage could decrease. Especially gasoline prices influence Americans in their car travel demands. When gasoline prices are currently not considered a big problem, future gasoline price increases could significantly hurt German car exports to North America (Buehler, 2010).

CONCLUSION

The German automobile industry has demonstrated to be very successful over the years. It is recognized all over the world to be a synonym for quality. It rapidly became one of the main pillars of the German economy. Their strategy turned out to be triumphant with an internationalization of their production. This means that they started to relocate some of their factories in foreign countries in order to lower their costs while keeping their high quality products. They also imported car parts from other countries.

However, some developing countries would like to develop their own industry and their own market, therefore they established trade barriers in order to push the exporting country, such as Germany, to manufacture locally. These are issues faced by many European countries. Consequently, they are trying to remove them by consulting with the World Trade Organization.

Germany has been very proactive to their exporting problems. That is why they found an alternative: they are trying to boost other industries in order to not be dependent of only one sector. Fortunately, it enjoys the benefit and power of influence of being part of the European Union. Europe as a whole is interested in setting a specific framework that favors the support of the German automobile exports.

German car brands have also embraced the trend of electric vehicles, the market of the future, which is going to ensure that the demand of its exporting markets will be met. Leading the way in R&D it is taking all the necessary precautions to retain its position as a powerful exporter and to not lose it to one of the new emerging market players.

New trade agreements that are being negotiated, such as the Transatlantic Trade and Investment Partnership (TTIP), could have a great impact on German exports if they came into effect. The abolishment of tariffs and reduction of trade barriers are going to facilitate exports further. However, despite the new emerging concurrences it is going to continue facing restrictions from foreign countries as they are trying to foster their own economies and automotive industries by methods of protectionism.

REFERENCES

Althaus, D., & Boston, W. (2015, March 17). *Why Auto Makers Are Building New Factories in Mexico, not the U.S.* Retrieved from The Wall Street Journal: http://www.wsj.com/articles/why-auto-makers-are-building-new-factories-in-mexico-not-the-u-s-1426645802

Berkowitz, J. (2013, June). *Free-Trade Cars: Why a U.S.–Europe Free-Trade Agreement Is a Good Idea.* Retrieved from Car and Driver: http://www.caranddriver.com/features/free-trade-cars-why-a-useurope-free-trade-agreement-is-a-good-idea-feature

BMWi. (2013). *German Mittelstand: Engine of the German Economy.* Retrieved from Federal Ministry of Economics and Technology: https://www.bmwi.de/English/Redaktion/Pdf/factbook-german-mittelstand,property=pdf,bereich=bmwi2012,sprache=en,rwb=true.pdf

Buehler, R. (2010). Transport Policies, Automobile Use, and Sustainable Transport: A Comparison of Germany and the United States. *Journal of Planning Education and Research, 30*(1), 76–93. doi:10.1177/0739456X10366302

Cheyipai. (2015, July 30). *China's Used-Car E-commerce is Rising Rapidly.* Retrieved from Financial Content: http://markets.financialcontent.com/stocks/news/read?GUID=30362668

Chiappini, R. (2012, October). Offshoring and Export Performance in the European Automotive Industry. *Competition & Change, 16*(4), 323–342. doi:10.1179/1024529412Z.00000000020

Depner, H., & Bathelt, H. (2005). Exporting the German Model: The Establishment of a New Automobile Industry Cluster in Shanghai. *Economic Geography, 81*(1), 53–81. doi:10.1111/j.1944-8287.2005.tb00255.x

Dougherty, C. (2009, August 7). *Driving Out of Germany, to Pollute Another Day.* Retrieved from The New York Times: http://www.nytimes.com/2009/08/08/world/europe/08germany.html?hpw&_r=0

European Commission. (2012a, November 8). *Action plan for the EU automotive industry in 2020.* Retrieved from European Commission: http://europa.eu/rapid/press-release_MEMO-12-845_en.htm

European Commission. (2012b, November 8). *CARS 2020: Action Plan for a competitive and sustainable automotive industry in Europe.* Retrieved from European Commission: http://eur-lex.europa.eu/legal-content/EN/TXT/PDF/?uri=CELEX:52012DC0636&from=EN

Focus. (2009, January 25). *Abwrackprämie - 2500 Euro Kaufanreiz.* Retrieved from Focus Online: http://www.focus.de/auto/news/abwrackpraemie-2500-euro-kaufanreiz_aid_364939.html

Geuss, M. (2014, October 25). *Porsche, Mercedes building electric cars to challenge Tesla.* Retrieved from Ars Technica: http://arstechnica.com/cars/2014/10/porsche-mercedes-building-electric-cars-to-challenge-tesla/

GTAI. (2015). *Industry Overview - The Automotive Industry in Germany.* Retrieved from Germany Trade & Invest: http://www.gtai.de/GTAI/Content/EN/Invest/_SharedDocs/Downloads/GTAI/Industry-overviews/industry-overview-automotive-industry-en.pdf

Heymann, E. (2014, May 26). *The future of Germany as an automaking location.* Retrieved from Deutsche Bank Research: https://www.dbresearch.com/PROD/DBR_INTERNET_EN-PROD/PROD0000000000335484/The+future+of+Germany+as+an+automaking+location.pdf

IBM. (2008, August). *Automotive 2020 - Clarity beyond the chaos.* Retrieved from IBM Global Business Services: http://www-07.ibm.com/shared_downloads/6/IBM_Automotive_2020_Study_Clarity_beyond_the_Chaos.pdf

Kaiser, T., & Steiner, E. (2013, September 6). *Absurde russische Zölle nerven deutsche Exporteure.* Retrieved from Die Welt: http://www.welt.de/wirtschaft/article119765151/Absurde-russische-Zoelle-nerven-deutsche-Exporteure.html

Kuhnimhof, T., Buehler, R., Wirtz, M., & Kalinowska, D. (2012, September). Travel trends among young adults in Germany: Increasing multimodality and declining car use for men. *Journal of Transport Geography*, *24*, 443–450. doi:10.1016/j.jtrangeo.2012.04.018

Kwon, H.-K. (2004, February). Markets, Institutions, and Politics under Globalization. Industrial Adjustments in the United States and in Germany in the 1990s. *Comparative Political Studies*, *37*(1), 88–113. doi:10.1177/0010414003260128

McCarthy, N. (2013, September 13). *Germany is the World's No. 1 Automobile Exporter By Far.* Retrieved from Statista: http://www.statista.com/chart/1451/germany-is-the-worlds-no-one-automobile-exporter-by-far/

Mohr, D., Müller, N., Krieg, A., Gao, P., Kaas, H.-W., Krieger, A., & Hensley, R. (2013, August). *The road to 2020 and beyond: What's driving the global automotive industry?* Retrieved from McKinsey & Company: http://www.mckinsey.com/~/media/mckinsey/dotcom/client_service/automotive%20and%20assembly/pdfs/mck_the_road_to_2020_and_beyond.ashx

Quest Trend Magazine. (2015a, June 11). *How the 10 largest automakers have internationalized their production.* Retrieved from Quest Trend Magazine: http://www.quest-trendmagazine.com/en/automobile-industry/economic-trends/internationalization/internationalization-of-production-by-the-automobile-manufacturers.html

Quest Trend Magazine. (2015b, June 15). *The dramatic internationalization of the locations of world-wide automobile production.* Retrieved from Quest Trend Magazine: http://www.quest-trendmagazine.com/en/automobile-industry/economic-trends/internationalization/internationalization-of-automobile-production.html

Rattner, S. (2011). The Secrets of Germany's Success: What Europe's Manufacturing Powerhouse Can Teach America. *Foreign Affairs, 90*(4), 7–11.

Reuters. (2014, August 20). *Stress für Exporteure nach Russland.* Retrieved from Handelsblatt: http://www.handelsblatt.com/politik/konjunktur/nachrichten/export-einbrueche-stress-fuer-exporteure-nach-russland/10358412.html

Rossbach, H. (2013, August 2). *Exporteure stoßen zunehmend auf Hindernisse.* Retrieved from Frankfurter Allgemeine: http://www.faz.net/aktuell/wirtschaft/wirtschaftspolitik/aussenhandel-exporteure-stossen-zunehmend-auf-hindernisse-12315836.html

Swenson, D. L. (2012). The influence of Chinese trade policy on automobile assembly and parts. *CESifo Economic Studies, 58*(4), 703-730.

Tang, R. (2009, November 16). *The Rise of China's Auto Industry and Its Impact on the U.S. Motor Vehicle Industry.* Retrieved from Federation Of American Scientists: http://fas.org/sgp/crs/row/R40924.pdf

The Economist. (2007, February 22). *The big-car problem.* Retrieved from The Economist: http://www.economist.com/node/8738865

The World Bank. (2015, March 25). *Overview.* Retrieved from The World Bank: http://www.worldbank.org/en/country/china/overview

VDA. (n.d.). *Importance of trade policy for industry and for Germany as an industrial location.* Retrieved from Verband der Automobilindustrie: https://www.vda.de/en/topics/economic-policy-and-infrastructure/trade/importance-of-trade-policy-for-industry-and-for-germany-as-an-industrial-location

Section 3
Financial Management

Chapter 9

Assessing the Determinants of Adoption of M–Banking by Students:
A Study Using an Extended TAM Model

Gazal Punyani
Mody University, India

Sourabh Sharma
International Management Institute (IMI), India

ABSTRACT

Technology is entwined in almost every part of one's lives. Today's students are using more technology than ever before. Information technology has revolutionized every industry and especially the banking industry. Tremendous improvements in technology have taken place in the Indian banking sector. Among all, Mobile Banking (m-banking) is the recent phenomenon that changed country's banking system. Students, being considered as most technically knowledgeable make most use of mobile banking services among all the banking customers. Therefore, the focus is particularly towards the young students engaging in m-banking services and to evaluate the factors that influence them to adopt m-banking. The study considers extended Technology Adoption Model (TAM) to measure the impact of the factors on adoption of m-banking. For the study, data was collected through questionnaire from 217 students of Western Rajasthan. The result of this research would provide valuable information to service providers in order to improve their m-banking services.

INTRODUCTION

Technology has become important part in almost everyone's lives. The innovations in technology have modernized our society as well as the way business is done. The Banking Industry is the one which is most significant in terms of information technology and various other innovations in transactions processing. These innovations have altered the way customers conduct their day to day operations. Among

DOI: 10.4018/978-1-5225-0902-8.ch009

all the revolutions, Mobile Banking (m-banking) is the latest development in electronic bank services, allowing customers to access banking facilities 24*7, while allowing banks to cut their costs and at the same time increase their revenues by attracting customers. Today mobile banking applications are considered as an emergent activity and one of the future payment tools (Ondrus & Pigneur, 2006). The term mobile banking (m-banking) has been widely used to describe a division of electronic banking and refers to the system that allows customers to conduct financial transactions via mobile devices. It is an open Internet technology which is not dependent on any specific service provider or mobile company. These mobile based services have made an immense effect on the banking sector, generating flexible payments methods and user-friendly banking services. It has led to an intense revolution because of its economic and social influence (Ghezzi et al., 2010).According to Cellular Operators Association of India, GSM telecom subscribers added 4.49 million in August 2015 (0.62% increased from previous month), taking all- India GSM subscriber base to 726.10 million. The Table 1 shows the increment/decrement of mobile subscribers in India in last 12 months.

According to a report published by Juniper Research (KPMG analysis), the number of global mobile subscribers is set to continue rising very rapidly from 0.8 billion in 2014 to 1.8 billion by 2019.

Adoption of M-Banking

The mobile based services are changing the face of banking, ensuring a more convenient, user friendly and low cost access to financial services. The m-banking transactions outlays about 2% of cost of branch banking, 10% of the ATM based transaction cost and 50% of the cost incurred on internet banking (Bhattacharya, 2015). Despite these benefits and large population of mobile users in India, it was found that usage of m-banking is very low & customers are reluctant to adopt this technology (Thakur & Srivastava, 2013). Mobile banking or m-banking "is the provision of banking services to customers for automated banking and other financial services on their mobile devices". It involves facilities to undertake bank transactions, to administer bank accounts and to access personalized information.

Table 1. Net Subscriber Additions in Last 12 months (in millions)

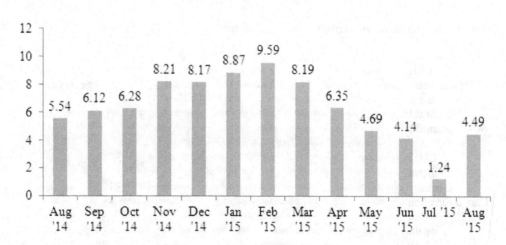

In a survey conducted by Forrester Research, India has the youngest population of m-banking users across the globe. Europe has a comparatively higher average age of m-banking customers with an average age of 39 years. Furthermore, m-banking is the channel of choice for younger generation among all the countries. The Table 2 illustrates the comparative average age of m-banking users across different geographies.

According to a report published by KPMG (May 2015), Worldwide mobile banking services CAGR is expected to be over 119 percent between 2014 and 2019. The scenario of mobile based banking services is favorable as evident from increasing user adoption numbers across all regions. Among all, China and India record the highest banking app users at 73 percent and 59 percent respectively.

In another survey data by UBS Evidence Lab, India stands number four globally in adoption of mobile banking. China, South Africa, South Korea and Singapore are the topmost countries in m-banking penetration.

According to a comparative survey by KPMG International (2009) in 19 countries, a slight majority (53 percent) are at least somewhat comfortable with using a mobile phone for financial transactions, while 47 percent are not at all comfortable. Looking regionally, respondents from Asia (64 percent) are at least somewhat comfortable, behind of 51 percent from Middle East and Africa, which were very or somewhat comfortable. Also, young generation is more inclined towards the adoption of mobile based banking services. The youngest users between the ages of 16-34 years old, were the most comfortable using m-banking, while 65+ age group (75 percent) were not at all comfortable. The study also explored two issues that impact the decision to use m-banking. Security (60 percent) or privacy (55 percent) and Ease of use (20 percent) are key consumer concerns. It is clear from the above that mobile transactions are increasing rapidly globally, but it has not yet reached maturity. Despite the inherent advantages, customers are reluctant to adopt new technologies to make financial transactions (Kim et al., 2009). Bank's branches still are the predominant mode of making financial services to the customers, as seen in Table 3.

From the above, it is clear that m-banking adoption across many countries is significantly low. Against this backdrop, there is a strong need to study the factors that are impeding customers to adopt m-banking in an emerging nation like India. Many researchers have used TAM to predict m-banking adoption, but TAM itself is insufficient to explain users' decision. Therefore, the aim of this study is to

Table 2. Average age of Mobile banking users, by country

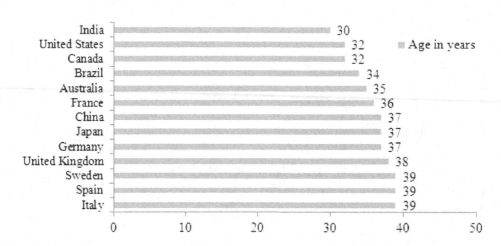

Table 3. Average daily number of requests serviced (%)

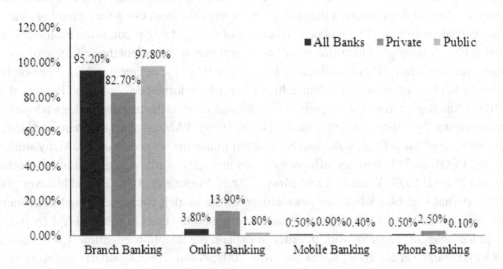

investigate the factors that influence young customers' intention to adopt m-banking service by adding external variables in the framework of technology acceptance model (TAM). The research focused on a specific segment of the m-banking services market- younger students, as the students are more likely to use new technologies and become more advanced in the future.

THEORETICAL BACKGROUND

Mobile Phones serve as a system for transmitting a variety of services like Voice, internet access, SMS, etc. The technological innovation of using mobile for conducting financial transactions is mobile banking, which allows customers to conduct their transactions without the constraints of place and time. Mobile banking is a subset of electronic banking and it can also be defined as an extension of internet banking (Ngai and Gunasekaran, 2007). Laukkanen and Passanen (2008) have defined mobile banking as "a channel whereby the consumer interacts with a bank via a mobile device". A numerous activities can be performed via mobile phones like transferring money, checking account balance, making bill payment, communicating with the banks, etc. In that sense it can be seen as adopting mobile terminals to conduct banking transactions.

Technology Acceptance Model (TAM)

The Technology Acceptance Model (TAM) was proposed by Fred Davis (1989), to explicate customers' acceptance of information technology. Based on theory of reason action (TRA) and theory of planned behavior (TPB), it has been validated as a dominant model for describing the factors influencing the adoption of IT by the users. TAM has been widely used to explain the factors influencing consumers' decision to adopt internet banking services (Suh and Han, 2002; Abbad, 2013; Bashir and Madhavaiah, 2014). During recent years, TAM has also been applied to predict mobile banking adoption (Davis, 1989; Luarn and Lin, 2005; Liao et al., 2007; Amin et al., 2008; Wei et al., 2009).

TAM proposed that the adoption of new information technology is determined by customers' intention to use it, which is further determined by the customers' perception about using the technology. According to TAM, perceived usefulness (PU) and perceived ease of use (PEOU); predicts the customers' attitude towards using new technology, which affects the behavioral intention to adopt the new technology (Davis, 1989). Perceived usefulness (PU) is defined by Davis (1989) as "the degree to which a person believes that using a particular system would enhance his or her job performance", whereas Perceived ease of use (PEOU) is "the degree to which the prospective adopter expects the new technology adopted to be a free effort regarding its transfer and utilization" (Davis, 1989). TAM assumes that perceived usefulness and perceived ease of use influence the user's intention to use the new technology. Many studies have predicted that PEOU and PU have an influence on user attitude towards acceptance of new technology (Agarwal and Prasad, 1999; Venkatesh and Morris, 2000; Venkatesh et al., 2003).However, there are some other external variables which are not included in the model, but are expected to influence the intentions to adopt the system. Several researchers have stated the need to extend TAM by incorporating external variables in the framework in order to explain the adoption intention (Chircu and Kauffman, 2000; Pikkarainen et al., 2004; Kamarulzaman, 2007; Amin, 2007; Gounaris and Koritos, 2008). Hence, an attempt is made in this study to examine the factors determining m-banking adoption using extended TAM by adding external variables such as trust, self-efficacy, facilitating conditions, personal innovativeness, etc.

Review of Literature on Mobile Banking Adoption

In the context of m-banking, numerous studies have been made from various perspectives by researchers. Some studies have analysed the advantages of m-banking, while others have examined the issues, growth and adoption of m-banking. Several studies have unfolded new insights about acceptance and use of m-banking technology; emerging theories of acceptance. Among all, TAM is one of the most widely used technology adoption model (Jeyaraj et al., 2006). There are several studies which extended TAM to determine the factors of adoption behavior. Lin and Chang (2011) investigated the factors and explored that perceived usefulness, perceived ease of use, compatibility and trust are the strong predictors of attitude and behavioral intention. Yao and Zhong (2011) reported perceived monetary risk constraining the customers' usage intention of m-banking services. One research worth citing is the study by Koenig-Lewis et al. (2010) concluded that perceived usefulness, perceived ease of use, compatibility and perceived risk are the strong indicators determining customers' intention to adopt m-banking services. In another similar study, Laukkanen and Kiviniemi (2010) found that the information and support offered by the bank are main key factors and play an important role in increasing use of m-banking services. Riquelme and Rios (2010) examined the factors influencing the use of m-banking among the existing users of internet banking and concluded that perceived usefulness, perceived case of use, perceived risk, and social norms are the strong indicators. Dimitriads and Kyrezis (2010) concluded perceived usefulness, trust, familiarity, customer information, innovativeness as important factors affecting customers' intention to adopt the technology-based service channels. Furthermore, Cruz et al. (2010) found that the reasons behind not using the system were perceived cost and risk, low perceived usefulness and complexity in the new technology. Kim et al. (2009) investigated the mechanisms related with the primary formation of customers' trust in m-banking, and their attitude to use the service. The results indicated that perceived usefulness, trust and structural assurance are major determinants of consumers' intention to use m-banking. Laforet and Li (2005) applied extended TAM to analyze adoption of online and mobile banking in China. Their results indicated that security, being the most important factor that motivated the adoption of online and mobile banking, while high perceived risk and low self-efficacy were the barriers to mobile banking adoption. In a similar study by Luran and Lin (2005) investigated the adoption of mobile banking by adding perceived credibility to the TAM. Their results confirmed that extended Technology Acceptance Model had a higher ability to predict the adoption behavior. Shih (2004) found security, being a major aspect in studying customers' intention. He concluded that customers have security concerns related to their bank information and other sensitive details. They tend to use it only provided their information is kept safe. Pikkarainen et al. (2004) also reported privacy risk perception as a major determinant for m-banking services. Kleijnen et al. (2004) indicated perceived usefulness as the strongest predictors, while perceived ease of use has quite little influence on adoption intentions. In another study, Lee et al. (2003) examined the factors supporting mobile banking adoption and confirmed that innovative qualities and consumers' perceived risk concerns are the major factors affecting intention to use mobile banking. Brown et al. (2003) in their study investigated the factors influencing the adoption of m-banking. They concluded that relative advantage, consumer banking needs, trial periods and perceived risk are major determinants influencing negative on the adoption of mobile banking by the users. Gerrard and Cunningham (2003) reported that the users are afraid to share their personal details. They worry that the bank may share the information with the other companies. Wang et al. (2003) confirmed that trust in the m-banking services is a crucial factor for the success of m-banking services. Also, they reported that customers feel that mobile banking is riskier than non-mobile banking. This is in accordance with the findings by Aladwani (2001) which says that transactions made online are considered more risky due to the absence of physical branch. A number of studies had been found to determine the intention to adopt m-banking, moreover to better understand customers' usage intention this study also targets to study the existence of variables if any.

RESEARCH MODEL AND HYPOTHESES

The research model of this study is displayed in Figure 1, which is intended to examine the factors that influence customers' intention of mobile banking. The proposed model is an extension of TAM, in which seven additional variables viz. trust, self-efficacy, social influence, perceived risk, facilitating conditions, perceived enjoyment, personal innovativeness are incorporated. Attitude construct has been excluded from the TAM framework in accordance with the previous study by Davis and Bagozzi (1989). In the proposed model, customers' acceptance of m-banking is determined by behavioral intention which, in turn, is expected to be affected by TAM variables (PU and PEOU), trust, self-efficacy, social influence, perceived risk, facilitating conditions, perceived enjoyment and personal innovativeness. The selection of additional variables is supported by the studies in the technology adoption literature.

Perceived Usefulness and Perceived Ease of Use

Perceived usefulness and perceived ease of use are two most studied and important variables in the technology adoption studies (Bashir and Madhavaiah, 2015).Perceived usefulness (PU) is, "the prospective users' subjective probability that using a specific application system will increase his or her job performance within an organizational context". Perceived ease of use (PEOU) refers to "the degree to which the prospective user expects the target system to be free of effort" (Davis et al., 1989).

Figure 1. Research model

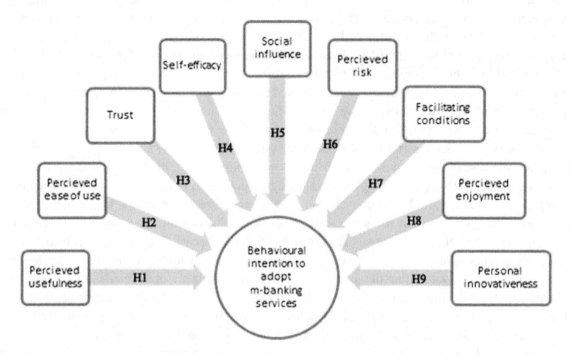

PU and PEOU had been found as major factor to predict customers' decision to use m-banking services (Davis and Bagozzi, 1989; Jackson et al., 1997; Agarwal and Prasad, 1999; Venkatesh, 1999; Pikkarainen et al., 2004; Venkatesh and Morris, 2000; Curran and Meuter, 2005; Eriksson et al., 2005; Cheong and Park, 2005; Cheng et al., 2006; Jahangir and Begum, 2008). It means that customer tends to use m-banking if they perceive that using m-banking services increases the productivity of their banking transactions and the system is easy to use, because if the system is useful and easier to use, it is likely to be accepted by the customers. Hence, it is hypothesized that:

H1: Perceived usefulness positively affects the users' behavioral intention to adopt m-banking services.
H2: Perceived ease of use positively affects the users' behavioral intention to adopt m-banking services.

Trust in M-Banking

Customers' trust in an online environment plays a significant role in developing and maintaining relationship (Yang et al., 2009). Trust is defined as, "the extent to which user believes that using the system is secured and has no privacy concerns". Thus it reflects that the low level of trust is the reason for the low level of adoption rate of m-banking. Several studies have confirmed that trust is very crucial factor affecting consumer behavior and included trust as predictor of intention to use m-banking (Ratnasingham, 1998; Kim et al., 2000; Aladwani, 2001; Wang et al., 2003; Mukherjee and Nath, 2003; Eriksson et al., 2004; Holsapple and Sasidharan, 2005;Lee, 2005; Kassi and Abdulla, 2006).Based on the above we hypothesize that:

H3: Trust positively affects the users' behavioral intention to adopt m-banking services.

Self-Efficacy

Dory et al. (2009) defined Self-efficacy as, "a user's understanding and beliefs in his or her own skills and capabilities to perform a task". Several studies have revealed that there is positive relationship between self-efficacy and usage intentions (Igbaria and Jivari, 1995; Venkatesh and Davis, 1996; Agarwal and Prasad, 1999; Agarwal and Karahanna, 2000, Venkatesh, 2000, Agarwal and Sambamurth, 2000), which means that stronger a persons' self-efficacy, more is he or she likely to adopt new technology. Hence, following hypothesis is propounded:

H4: Self-efficacy positively affects the users' behavioral intention to adopt m-banking services.

Social Influence

Venkatesh and Davis (2000) defined social influence as, "the degree to which an individual perceives that most people who are important to him think he or she should use the system". Before using new technology, there is some excitement about how to use it and their expected advantages in the mind of the users. The fear of uncertainty increases the chances that users tend to interact with his friends or family. Therefore, intention towards adoption of new technology is likely to be influenced by friends or family. There are various studies found which documented the relationship between social influence and behavioral intention(Venkatesh and Davis, 2000; Karjaluoto, 2002; Wang et al., 2003; Pikkarainen et al., 2004; Kleijnen et al., 2004; Nysveen, 2005; Wu and Chan, 2005; Amin, 2008; Venkatesh et al., 2012). Thus, in light of the above fact, it would be interesting to examine the effect of social influence on users' intention to adopt m-banking services. Hence, the following hypothesis is proposed:

H5: Social influence positively affects the users' behavioral intention to adopt m-banking services.

Perceived Risk

Bauer (1960) defined Perceived risk as, "the nature and amount of risk perceived by a consumer in contemplating a particular purchase decision". A consumer tends to consider all the uncertainties and risks associated with the use of new technology. There is a negative risk perception in the minds of the users that m-banking will lead to hinder their sensitive information to other companies. Some studies have shown the negative relationship of perceived risk with the intention to adopt new technology (Salisbury et al., 2001; Sylvie and Xiaoyan, 2005; Kesharwani and Bisht, 2012). On that basis, it is hypothesized that:

H6: Perceived risk negatively affects the users' behavioral intention to adopt m-banking services.

Facilitating Conditions

Facilitating conditions refers to the degree to which user believes that the proper resources and technical infrastructure exists to support the use of the new technology (Venkatesh et al., 2003). It is believed that customers who have all the resources available to use new technology and due knowledge about using the technology and services, are likely to have positive attitude towards using m-banking services (Deb and David, 2014).So from the above it can be hypothesize that:

H7: Facilitating conditions positively affects the users' behavioral intention to adopt m-banking services.

Perceived Enjoyment

According to Davis (1992), enhancing the enjoyment ability of using a new system definitely increases its acceptability, and therefore, enjoyment will motivate the users to use the new technology. Perceived enjoyment can be defined as the degree to which the activity of using m-banking is perceived to be enjoyable in its own rights (Davis and Bagozzi, 1992). A number of researches have included perceived enjoyment as motivator in the framework of TAM (Igbaria and Zinatelli, 1997; Agarwal and Sambamurth, 2000; Moon and Kim, 2001; Pikkarainen et al., 2004; Celik, 2008; Chan and Chong, 2013; Abbad, 2013). Based on the previous literature following hypothesis is proposed:

H8: Perceived enjoyment positively affects the users' behavioral intention to adopt m-banking services.

Personal Innovativeness

Agarwal and Prasad (1998) defined personal innovativeness as, "the willingness of an individual to try out any new information technology". Although the role of innovativeness is clearly represented, only few researchers have analyzed its influence for electronic channels (Lassar et al., 2005; Yi et al., 2006; Laukkanen et al., 2007, Thakur and Srivastava, 2014). Thus, the hypothesis is proposed:

H9: Personal innovativeness positively affects the users' behavioral intention to adopt m-banking services.

RESEARCH DESIGN AND METHODS

Research Instrument

A self-administered structured questionnaire was distributed to collect data from potential young customers of m-banking. The questionnaire contained two sections; the first section captured respondents' demographic characteristics, and the second section consists of 37 measurement items related to ten constructs developed based on extant literature on technology acceptance. These constructs were adopted for their previously confirmed reliability and validity as well as its relevance to the research model. The wording of measurement items was modified according to the present context only to change for m-banking context. All the items were measured on a Five-point Likert scale ranging from 1 (strongly disagree) to 5 (strongly agree) to ensure statistical variability among survey responses for all items measured. Before the questionnaires were sent out, the instrument was reviewed by an academician to avoid the inconsistency in meanings and some of the corrections were resolved thereafter. Also, the purpose of the study was presented at the top of the questionnaire to help the respondents having a better understanding of the research.

Data Collection and Sample Profile

Data was sourced from respondents who are familiar with m-banking. The sample of population of the study incorporated young students of the universities in Western Rajasthan. The sampling method used in this research is purposive sampling because this method is confined to specific types of people who can provide the desired information which are m-banking users. The questionnaire was distributed among 300 young students and the participation was made voluntary. The respondents were requested to complete the questionnaire based on their perception towards the usage of m-banking. Of the 300 questionnaires distributed, 217 questionnaires were returned and collected with valid data.

In terms of gender, the distribution of sample is 67 per cent for male and 33 percent for female. Considering the age groups, 61 percent of the respondents were aged 18-25 and 39 percent of the respondents were aged 26-35 years, showing the majority of the respondents were aged between 18-25 years old.

DATA ANALYSIS AND RESULTS

Exploratory Factor Analysis (EFA)

In this research, factor analysis was conducted to develop the constructs and to assess the factors that influence customers' behavioral intention to adopt m-banking services. An exploratory factor analysis was conducted by employing principal component analysis (PCA) to validate the structure of TAM variables using IBM SPSS package. The Kaiser-Meyer-Olkin (KMO) index for this data was 0.712 indicated the appropriateness of data for factor analysis (Table 4). Also, the associated significance level for Bartlett's test of sphericity was extremely small (0.000), signifying the correlation matrix contained sufficient co-variance for factoring. Results of the factor analysis indicated the existence of nine significant dimensions with eigen values greater than one, as shown in Table 6 with their factor loadings. The 9-factor instrument accounts for 68.443% of the total variance (Table 5).

All the factor loadings were greater than 0.5, reflecting an acceptable significance level of internal validity. According to the loadings of the factors on the nine dimensions, the dimensions were named Perceived Usefulness (PU), Perceived Ease of Use (PEOU), Trust (T), Self-efficacy (SE), Social Influence (SI), Perceived Risk (PR), Facilitating Conditions (FC), Perceived Enjoyment (PE), and Personal Innovativeness (PI). The result of principal component analysis is shown in Table 6.

Table 4. KMO and Bartlett's Test

Kaiser-Meyer-Olkin Measure of Sampling Adequacy.	.712
Approx. Chi-Square	2943.606
Bartlett's Test of Sphericity df	528
Sig.	.000

Table 5. Total variance explained

Component	Initial Eigen values			Extraction Sums of Squared Loadings		
	Total	% of Variance	Cumulative %	Total	% of Variance	Cumulative %
1	4.460	13.516	13.516	4.460	13.516	13.516
2	3.236	9.805	23.321	3.236	9.805	23.321
3	3.029	9.180	32.501	3.029	9.180	32.501
4	2.337	7.083	39.584	2.337	7.083	39.584
5	2.248	6.812	46.396	2.248	6.812	46.396
6	2.047	6.204	52.601	2.047	6.204	52.601
7	1.918	5.813	58.414	1.918	5.813	58.414
8	1.719	5.210	63.623	1.719	5.210	63.623
9	1.590	4.820	68.443	1.590	4.820	68.443

Reliability and Validity Measures

To evaluate the construct's reliability, The Cronbach's alpha (CA) was used. As shown in Table 7, The Cronbach's alpha for each construct ranges from 0.729 to 0.869; it is 0.716 for the whole scale. As, the Cronbach's alpha for each construct is above the expected threshold limit of 0.7, the scale was considered to possess adequate internal consistency and reliability among the items (Hair, 2013).

Multiple Regression Analysis

A multiple regression analysis was conducted to determine the relationship among the determinants of m-banking adoption and behavioral intention to adopt m-banking services. There were nine independent variables (namely: perceived usefulness, perceived ease of use, trust, self-efficacy, social influence, perceived risk, facilitating conditions, perceived enjoyment, and personal innovativeness), and one dependent variable (behavioral intention to adopt m-banking services). The independent variables are analysed against dependent variable, to measure the relationship between independent variables and dependent variable. The results of multiple regression analysis are shown in Table 8.

As results, the coefficient of determination (R-square) is 0. 563 and (Adjusted R-square) is 0.544. It is indicating that 56.3 percent of variance is explained by these nine independent variables. The result shows that these nine variables explain adequate amount of variance in behavioral intention to adopt m-banking services. Also, the F-value of 29.636 for the research model is appropriate at (p=0.000). Therefore, the overall research model was considered fit and statistically significant interferences can be drawn.

The results of the regression analysis further reveals that the two most important TAM variables; perceived usefulness, ($\beta = 0.143$, p<0.01) and perceived ease of use, ($\beta = 0.148$, p<0.01) positively affects the users' behavioral intention to adopt m-banking service. Therefore, H1 and H2 are both supported. It implies that perceived usefulness and perceived ease of use are the two dimensions that positively affect the behavioral intention of young students, as they perceive that it is useful in increasing the productivity of their banking transactions as well as it is easy to use.

Table 6. Rotated component matrix[a]

	1	2	3	4	5	6	7	8	9
PU1	.760								
PU2	.807								
PU3	.821								
PU4	.742								
PU5	.815								
PEOU1		.764							
PEOU2		.839							
PEOU3		.729							
PEOU4		.837							
T1			.833						
T2			.839						
T3			.813						
T4			.802						
SE1				.881					
SE2				.811					
SE3				.787					
SI1					.783				
SI2					.758				
SI3					.896				
PR1						.706			
PR2						.761			
PR3						.753			
PR4						.776			
PR5						.879			
FC1							.867		
FC2							.778		
FC3							.742		
PE1								.868	
PE2								.803	
PE3								.823	
PI1									.766
PI2									.808
PI3									.901

Note: Extraction method: Principal component analysis.
Rotation method: Varimax with Kaiser Normalization.
a. Rotation converged in 6 iterations.

Table 7. Cronbach's alpha of measurement scale

Dimension	Number of Items	Cronbach's alpha
Perceived Usefulness (PU)	5	.869
Perceived Ease of Use (PEOU)	4	.838
Trust (T)	4	.848
Self-efficacy (SE)	3	.777
Social Influence (SI)	3	.760
Perceived Risk (PR)	5	.826
Facilitating Conditions (FC)	3	.729
Perceived Enjoyment (PE)	3	.788
Personal Innovativeness (PI)	3	.785

Table 8. Multiple Regression Analysis

	Effect	β	t-value	Sig.	Result
	(Constant)	---	5.485	0.000	---
H1	Perceived usefulness → Behavioral Intention	0.143	2.767	0.006	*Supported*
H2	Perceived ease of use → Behavioral Intention	0.148	2.867	0.005	*Supported*
H3	Trust → Behavioral Intention	0.561	11.923	0.000	*Supported*
H4	Self-efficacy → Behavioral Intention	0.097	2.079	0.039	*Supported*
H5	Social influence → Behavioral Intention	0.139	2.980	0.003	*Supported*
H6	Perceived risk → Behavioral Intention	-0.183	-3.929	0.000	*Supported*
H7	Facilitating conditions → Behavioral Intention	0.136	2.923	0.004	*Supported*
H8	Perceived enjoyment → Behavioral Intention	0.128	2.752	0.006	*Supported*
H9	Personal innovativeness → Behavioral Intention	0.130	2.790	0.006	*Supported*

Note: Dependent variable: Behavioral Intention
β represent standardized regression coefficients.

On the other hand, H3 (Trust in m-banking) have attributed more importance than the two most important beliefs (PU and PEOU). The results show the β value of 0.561 for trust in m-banking, which is the highest among all the dimensions. Hence, hypothesis H3 is supported (β = 0.561, p<0.01), which reflects that trust in m-banking positively affects the users' behavioral intention to adopt m-banking service. It indicates that the young students are not considering trust as limiting factor for using m-banking; rather they trust their service providers.

Hypothesis H4 examined the effect of self-efficacy on behavioral intention to use m-banking services. It is found that the young students have given lesser importance to the effect of self-efficacy than other dimensions (β = 0.097, p<0.05). But, still it is statistically significant. Thus, hypothesis H4 is also supported. The lower β value may reflect that young students feel that they have the high level of confidence and they are able to use m-banking by their own. As they have given less importance, it can be concluded that self-efficacy has significantly low positive effect in understanding the students' responses.

Hypothesis H5 investigated the impression of social influence on behavioral intention to adopt m-banking services. The results show that social influence affects positively on students' behavioral intention ($\beta = 0.139$, p<0.01), which indicates that young students do influence by the other users in the society who are using m-banking services. Hence, hypothesis H5 is accepted.

Hypothesis H6 revealed that perceived risk has significantly negative impact on behavioral intention to adopt m-banking services ($\beta = -0.183$, p<0.01). The possible explanation of this can be that though they trust their service providers, but the fear of hacking and phishing among the other users somewhere create negative perception on their behavior. Therefore, H6 is also supported.

Hypotheses H7, H8 and H9 found out the effect of facilitating conditions, perceived enjoyment and personal innovativeness respectively. The results show that all three facilitating conditions ($\beta = 0.136$, p<0.01), perceived enjoyment ($\beta = 0.128$, p<0.01), and personal innovativeness ($\beta = 0.130$, p<0.01) have significant positive effect on behavioral intention to adopt m-banking services. Therefore, hypotheses H7, H8 and H9 are all accepted.

DISCUSSION AND IMPLICATIONS

The purpose of this paper is to evaluate the factors that are determining m-banking adoption. The study extended the TAM model with the inclusion of trust, self-efficacy, social influence, perceived risk, facilitating conditions, perceived enjoyment and personal innovativeness. The result of exploratory factor analysis and reliability test showed that all the dimensions are relevant and reliable. In addition, the results of the multiple regression analysis showed that all the hypothesized relationships were valid, explaining adequate proportion of the variance in usage of m-banking. There were nine independent variables and one dependent variable. It was found that eight among the nine factors (perceived usefulness, perceived ease of use, trust, self-efficacy, social influence, facilitating conditions, perceived enjoyment and personal innovativeness) have significant positive impact on students' behavioral intention to adopt m-banking services. On the other hand, perceived risk has significantly negative effect on the behavioral intention of the students. As perceived usefulness and perceived ease of use are the two most important beliefs, system developers should focus more on the features that are more frequently used with the clear instructions and simple navigation procedures. In the study, trust was considered having a high and positive impact on the students' intention to adopt m-banking. Thus, banks should build consumer confidence in m-banking by adopting various trust building strategies. Bankers should pay attention to security policies and measures as well. This will not only reduce the customer risk perception but will help in gaining the customers trust. Results have also revealed that perceived enjoyment has positive effect. Hence, the system developers should pay more attention on developing the system more enjoyable in order to gain new customer and retain existing ones. It is also been observed that influence of others have the positive effect, therefore, bankers should encourage the existing m-banking customers to communicate good word of mouth by providing incentives for referring a friend or family member. Taking all the factors together, the service developers and providers should develop and provide better system by focusing on the needs of the consumers.

The present study has contributed to an overall conceptual understanding of m-banking adoption by extending some additional intention factors. The extended model will be helping the further researches to measure adoption of new technology, as the dimensions have been proven reliable. Further, the study will help the banks in order to provide the insights of the students' behavioral intention or their potential customer's behavioral intention. This study will be very beneficial to the system developers in order to have the better understanding of the factors that contribute to the m-banking adoption and thereby improving the system efficiently by focusing on the key factors.

REFERENCES

Abbad, M. M. (2013). E-banking in Jordan. *Behaviour & Information Technology, 32*(7), 618–694. doi:10.1080/0144929X.2011.586725

Agarwal, R., & Prasad, J. (1998). A conceptual and operational definition of personal innovativeness in the domain of information technology. *Information Systems Research, 9*(2), 204–215. doi:10.1287/isre.9.2.204

Agarwal, R., & Prasad, J. (1999). Are individual differences germane to the acceptance of new information technologies? *Decision Sciences, 30*(2), 361–391. doi:10.1111/j.1540-5915.1999.tb01614.x

Aladwani, A. M. (2001). Online banking: A field study of drivers, development challenges, and expectations. *Internet J Informat Manag, 21*(3), 213–225. doi:10.1016/S0268-4012(01)00011-1

Amin, H. (2007). Internet banking adoption among young intellectuals. *Journal of Internet Banking and Commerce, 12*(3), 1–14.

Amin, H., Hamid, M. R. A., Lada, S., & Anis, Z. (2008). The adoption of mobile banking in Malaysia: The case of Bank Islam Malaysia Berhad. *International Journal of Business and Society, 9*(2), 43–53.

Bashir, I., & Madhavaiah, C. (2014). Determinants of Young Consumers' Intention to Use Internet Banking Services in India. *Vision: The Journal of Business Perspective, 18*(3), 1–11.

Bhattacharya, A. (2015). New Paradigms in Business Strategies of Banks. *Bank Quest, 86*(3), 10–16.

Chircu, A. M., & Kauffman, R. J. (2000). Limits to value in electronic commerce-related IT investments. *Journal of Management Information Systems, 17*(2), 59–80.

Davis, F. D. (1989). Perceived usefulness, perceived ease of use, and user acceptance of information technology. *Management Information Systems Quarterly, 13*(3), 319–340. doi:10.2307/249008

Ghezzi, A., Renga, F., Balocco, R., & Pescetto, P. (2010). Mobile payment applications: Offer state of the art in the Italian market. *Info, 12*(5), 3–22. doi:10.1108/14636691011071130

Gounaris, S., & Koritos, C. (2008). Investigating the drivers of internet banking adoption decision: A comparison of three alternative frameworks. *International Journal of Bank Marketing, 26*(5), 282–304. doi:10.1108/02652320810894370

Hair, J. F., Black, W. C., Babin, B. J., & Anderson, R. E. (2013). *Multivariate data analysis: a global perspective* (7th ed.). New Delhi: Pearson Education.

Jeyaraj, A., Rottman, J. W., & Lacity, M. C. (2006). A Review of the Predictors, Linkages, and Biases in IT Innovation Adoption Research. *Journal of Information Technology, 21*(1), 1–23. doi:10.1057/palgrave.jit.2000056

Kamarulzaman, Y. (2007). Adoption of travel e-shopping in the UK. *International Journal of Retail & Distribution Management, 35*(9), 703–719. doi:10.1108/09590550710773255

Kim, G., Shin, B., & Lee, H. G. (2009). Understanding dynamics between initial trust and usage intentions of mobile banking. *Information Systems Journal, 19*(3), 283–311. doi:10.1111/j.1365-2575.2007.00269.x

Koenig-Lewis, N., Palmer, A., & Moll, A. (2010). Predicting young consumers take up of mobile banking services. *International Journal of Bank Marketing, 28*(5), 410–432. doi:10.1108/02652321011064917

Laukkanen, T., & Kiviniemi, V. (2010). The role of information in mobile banking resistance. *International Journal of Bank Marketing, 28*(5), 372–388. doi:10.1108/02652321011064890

Laukkanen, T., & Pasanen, M. (2009). Mobile banking innovators and early adopters: How they differ from other online users. *Journal of Direct, Data and Digital Marketing Practice, 10*(3), 294–261.

Liao, C., Chen, J. L., & Yen, D. (2007). Theory of planning behavior (TPB) and customer satisfaction in the continued use of e-service: An integrated model. *Computers in Human Behavior, 23*(6), 2804–2822. doi:10.1016/j.chb.2006.05.006

Lin, J. S., & Chang, H. C. (2011). The role of technology readiness in self-service technology acceptance. *Managing Service Quality, 21*(4), 424–444. doi:10.1108/09604521111146289

Luarn, P., & Lin, H. H. (2005). Toward an understanding of the behavioural intention to use mobile banking. *Computers in Human Behavior, 21*(6), 873–891. doi:10.1016/j.chb.2004.03.003

Ngai, E. W. T., & Gunasekaran, A. (2007). A review for mobile commerce research and applications. *Decision Support Systems, 43*(1), 3–15. doi:10.1016/j.dss.2005.05.003

Ondrus, J., & Pigneur, Y. (2006). Towards A Holistic Analysis of Mobile Payments: A Multiple Perspectives Approach. *Electronic Commerce Research and Applications, 5*(3), 246–257. doi:10.1016/j.elerap.2005.09.003

Pikkarainen, T., Pikkarainen, K., Karjaluoto, H., & Pahnila, S. (2004). Consumer acceptance of online banking: An extension of the technology acceptance model. *Internet Research: Electronic Networking Applications and Policy, 14*(3), 224–235. doi:10.1108/10662240410542652

Riquelme, H. E., & Rios, R. E. (2010). The moderating effect of gender in the adoption of mobile banking. *International Journal of Bank Marketing, 28*(5), 328–341. doi:10.1108/02652321011064872

Suh, B., & Han, I. (2002). Effect of trust on customer acceptance of Internet banking. *Electronic Commerce Research and Applications, 1*(3-4), 247–263. doi:10.1016/S1567-4223(02)00017-0

Thakur, R., & Srivastava, M. (2013). Customer usage intention of mobile commerce in India: An empirical study. *Journal of Indian Business Research, 5*(1), 52–72. doi:10.1108/17554191311303385

Venkatesh, M., Morris, G., & Davis, F. D. (2003). User acceptance of information technology: Toward a unified view. *Management Information Systems Quarterly, 27*(3), 425–478.

Venkatesh, V. (2000). Determinants of perceived ease of use: Integrating control, intrinsic motivation, and emotion into the technology acceptance model. *Information Systems Research, 11*(4), 342–365. doi:10.1287/isre.11.4.342.11872

Venkatesh, V., & Davis, F. D. (1996). A model of antecedents of perceived ease of use: Development and test. *Decision Sciences, 27*(3), 451–481. doi:10.1111/j.1540-5915.1996.tb01822.x

Venkatesh, V., & Davis, F. D. (2000). A theoretical extension of the technology acceptance model: Four longitudinal field studies. *Management Science, 46*(2), 186–204. doi:10.1287/mnsc.46.2.186.11926

Venkatesh, V., & Morris, M. G. (2000). Why Dont Men Ever Stop to Ask for Directions? Gender, Social Influence, and Their Role in Technology Accptance and Usage Behavior. *Management Information Systems Quarterly, 24*(1), 115–139. doi:10.2307/3250981

Wei, T., Marthandan, G., Chong, A., Ooi, K., & Arumugam, S. (2009). What drives Malaysian m-commerce adoption? An empirical analysis. *Industrial Management & Data Systems, 109*(3), 370–388. doi:10.1108/02635570910939399

Yao, H., & Zhong, C. (2011). The analysis of influencing factors and promotion strategy for the use of mobile banking. *Canadian Social Science, 7*(2), 60–63.

Chapter 10
Customer Perception and Behavioral Intention to Use Biometric–Enabled e–Banking Services in India

Siddharth Varma
International Management Institute, India

Ruchika Gupta
Amity University, India

ABSTRACT

Regardless of the success of e-banking services in India, a sizeable fraction of the customers still do not use online banking primarily because of security issues. Rising cybercrimes have further heightened these security concerns. This necessitates the adoption of faster and more reliable ways of user identification and authentication. Banks are ready to adopt biometric enabled systems to offer secure and seamless transactions but we need to find out if the customers are ready to adopt this technology. This paper attempts to evaluate the customer's perception about biometric enabled e banking services in India and their intention to use biometric enabled e-banking services. The study also tries to identify the factors which influence usage of biometrics by these customers. A survey has been carried out among customers to gather primary data and the Technology Acceptance Model has been applied. The value of the paper lies in the understanding of customer perceptions about biometrics enabled banking services which can help banks formulate strategies to encourage customers to use e-banking services.

INTRODUCTION

India has one of the largest and rapidly growing populations of netizens i.e internet users in the world with over 190 million (June 2014) and expected to reach 500 million in the next 3 years. Different sectors of the economy have seized the benefits of this tech savvy population of the country however; the banking industry seems to have failed in utilizing this opportunity. As per the recent survey by IDC, out

DOI: 10.4018/978-1-5225-0902-8.ch010

of the 190 million internet users in the country barely 1 million uses internet banking which constitutes for only 0.096% of the total population and only just 15% of the internet users of the country. In comparison, western countries like UK, have probably 25 million internet banking users constituting nearly 70% of the online population of the country.

Despite the numerous benefits that internet banking has to offer to the banks in terms of increased efficiency, reduced cost, greater convenience or customer satisfaction; privacy and security are the two major issues which inhibit the growth of internet banking users. Furthermore, the increasing incidents of frauds aggravate such concerns. As per the Deloitte India Fraud Survey 2014, conducted by Audit & Consultancy Company Deloitte, the 44 banks surveyed unveil an increase of 10% in the number of fraud incidents in the last two years and that too with an average loss of Rs 10 lakhs per fraud with respect to retail banking and nearly 2 crores in case of corporate banking.

A similar report on cyber crime by NCRB states that out of the total 759 fraud cases of online crime reported to them, 248 relate to online banking fraud thus necessitating banks to provide higher security protection to their customers. Adding to this, investment in the development of e-banking systems worldwide is substantial and it is of paramount importance that online systems remain secure as the survival of e-banking is dependent on the bank's trustworthy reputation and ability to convince customers their services and assets are protected (Rana, 2012).

Consequently, banks need to look for more secure and reliable methods of user authentication & authorization. Three different types of methods, or a combination of these, are employed for authentication, viz, something the user possesses like a swipe card, something that user knows like a password and thirdly some unique feature of the user, either physical or behavioral. The last method of authentication is gaining momentum because of the increased security assurance associated with it. This recognition based on physical/ behavioral aspects of a person is what is commonly termed as "Biometrics". Since physical/ behavioral traits like handwriting, iris, voiceprints or fingerprints are unique for every individual, biometrics seems to be more reliable and secure authentication method in comparison to other methods of authentication. This is probably the reason that a number of banks worldwide including India are adopting biometric enabled authentication methods for secure and seamless transactions more specifically in e-banking.

Although technically biometric proves to be a good solution to all these security issues, still their implementation success largely depends on the customer's acceptance. Therefore, this paper attempts to evaluate the customer's perception about biometric enabled e banking services and their intention to use these services.

REVIEW OF LITERATURE

Security and privacy are the most common issues for e-banking users. The increasing number of security breaches and internet frauds call for a strong authentication method to replace the traditional methods of user authentication. Biometric based authentication and identification systems are the new solutions to address the issues of security and privacy as indicated by various researchers.

Using biometrics for identification restricts individuals from access to physical spaces and electronic services (Amtul Fatima, 2011). The study identifies the various security threats in e-banking, their possible biometric enabled solution and its acceptance by consumers using descriptive and exploratory research.

According to Normalini et al (2012), biometric enabled user authentication system in e-banking could remove password vulnerabilities and secure the log in process to the system. Additionally, it would be more convenient for the employees and the bank's customers as well. They emphasized on combining the three approaches of user authentication i.e using debit card, password and biometrics for enhanced security. Similarly, Hossienie et al (2012) review current biometric applications in banking industry in the world and more specifically the authentication systems used in Iran's banking system. The study provides valuable suggestions that banks could utilize for enabling secure transactions.

Das and Debbarma (2011) emphasized on replacing password based authentication through biometric enabled authentication. Their study focuses on vulnerabilities and the escalating wave of criminal activities occurring at Automated Teller Machines (ATMs) where quick cash is the prime target for criminals. They propose fingerprint based identification system at the ATMs using high resolution fingerprint scanner for preventing unauthorized access. A similar study conducted by Onyesolu and Ezeani (2012) also proposed an embedded fingerprint based authentication system for ATMs to ameliorate the security system.

Successful implementation of biometric enabled user authentication systems entails various issues. According to Fatima (2011) reliable performance, customer acceptance, interoperability with existing system and scalability to accommodate growth are the critical success factors for an effective authentication method. Venkatraman and Delpachitra (2008) conducted a study to analyze the impact of these biometric enabled security solutions in banks keeping in view various managerial, social, technological and ethical challenges. The key success factors proposed using a case study served as a guideline for a biometric enabled security project called BioSec, which is envisaged in a large banking organisation in New Zealand. This pilot study recommends that formulation of a viable security system to address user's security and privacy fears is more important than merely trying to cope up with embedding the biometrics in the existing information systems.

In order to understand customer's intention towards biometric enabled e-banking systems, Tassabehji et al. (2012) evaluated the potential user's perspective using System Usability Scale (SUS). The case exhibit that as a whole user's seems to be positive towards biometric enabled banking systems and findings suggest evaluation of such systems should focus on different individual components like technology and the process as well. Adewale et al. (2014) conducted a study to review the perception of customers and managers of Central Bank of Nigeria towards using biometric enabled banking system.

Customer's intention towards biometric enabled e-banking systems can be evaluated through various research tools developed and validated by eminent researchers. Technology Acceptance Model (TAM) proposed by Davis et al. (1989) is one of the most widely used models for the purpose. Many empirical studies have used technology acceptance model (TAM) to explain user's acceptance for different new technologies.

Tsai (2012) makes use of TAM to evaluate consumer's behavioral intention to use e-books. Using 3 cognitive factors- perceived ease of use, perceived usefulness and brand & service trust; an attempt was made to analyze the effect of these factors on customer's attitude towards using and behavioral intention to use. Zhu et al. (2012) applied TAM to identify external factors that affect user's acceptance of online games. Wangpipatwong et al. (2008) applied TAM to understand various factors affecting the citizen's continuance intention with regard to e-government's websites whereas Park (2009) used TAM to verify the e-learning process adoption and use by university students in Korea. In addition, several other researchers have investigated the user's behavioral intentions to use e-learning systems through TAM (Alharbi & Drew 2014; Williams et al. 2014; Nair & Das 2012; Lee, Hseib & Chen 2013; Punnoose 2012)

From the literature review, it is apparent that various studies have already been undertaken with respect to biometric enabled e-banking services as well as for understanding consumer's behavioral intention to use such services by implementing Technology Acceptance Model. However, it seems that no such study for understanding user perception about biometric enabled e-banking has been done for the Indian banking customer. The current study tries to fill in this gap.

Objectives of the Study

This study has the following objectives:

- To understand customer's perception about usefulness and ease of use of fingerprint based biometrics for authentication in e-banking services
- To evaluate customer's attitude and intention to use fingerprint based biometrics for authentication in e-banking services.
- To determine if any demographic factors influence usage of biometrics by these customers.

Methodology

This paper tries to understand users perception about biometric enabled e-banking based on the well known Technology Acceptance Model (Davis et. al., 1989). This is shown schematically in Figure 1. The terms used in TAM are explained as follows.

- *Perceived usefulness* is the extent to which customers believe biometrics is helpful in e-banking authentication.
- *Perceived ease of use* is the is extent to which customers believe biometrics is easy to use and does not require much effort.
- *Attitude towards using* is the evaluation of the customers on using biometrics for e-banking authentication.
- *Behavioral intention to use* is the willingness of the customer to use biometrics for e-banking authentication.

Figure 1. Technology acceptance model (Davis, Bagozzi and Warshaw, 1989)

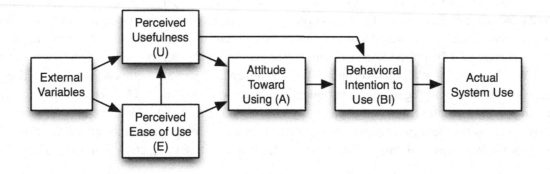

Research Hypotheses

This study has the following hypotheses.

H1: Education level has a significant effect on perceived usefulness of biometric enabled e-banking.
H2: Education level has a significant effect on perceived ease of use of biometric enabled e-banking.
H3: Education level has a significant effect on attitude of customer towards use of biometric enabled e-banking.
H4: Education level has a significant effect on intention of customer to use of biometric enabled e-banking.
H5: Occupation has a significant effect on perceived ease of use of biometric enabled e-banking.
H6: Occupation has a significant effect on the perceived usefulness of biometric enabled e-banking.
H7: Occupation has a significant effect on intention of customer to use biometric enabled e-banking.
H8: Occupation has a significant effect on attitude of customer towards use of biometric enabled e-banking.
H9: Income level has a significant effect on attitude of customer towards use of biometric enabled e-banking.
H10: Income level has a significant effect on perceived ease of use of biometric enabled e-banking.
H11: Income level has a significant effect on perceived usefulness of biometric enabled banking.
H12: Income level has a significant effect on intention of customer to use biometric enabled e-banking.
H13: Prior usage of internet banking has a significant effect on perceived ease of use for biometrics.
H14: Prior usage of internet banking has a significant effect on perceived usefulness of biometrics.
H15: Prior usage of internet banking has a significant effect on attitude towards use of biometrics.
H16: Prior usage of internet banking has a significant effect on the intention to use biometrics.

Questionnaire Design and Data Collection

The questionnaire is based on the TAM proposed by Davis et al. (1989). It tries to collect data on four constructs, ie, perceived usefulness, perceived ease of use, attitude towards use and intention of customer to use biometrics for authentication in e-banking. The data has been collected on a five point Likert scale with responses varying from "strongly disagree" to "strongly agree". A pilot study was carried out with 20 respondents using the pre-test questionnaire. A reliability analysis was carried out using the pre-test data collected. Cronbach Alpha values for three out of the four constructs as found to be greater than 0.7. For one construct the value was found to be less than 0.7. It was found that one particular question was causing value of Cronbach Alpha to drop. Hence, this question was dropped. Another question which respondents during pre test found to be repetitive was also dropped. Finally, value of Cronbach Alpha for all four constructs was more than the required value of 0.7

The final questionnaire had thirteen questions in all: five questions to assess perceived usefulness, four questions to assess perceived ease of use, and two questions each to assess customer attitude and intention to use biometrics for e-banking. The questionnaire also collected data on gender, age, education, income and whether respondents had used internet banking earlier.

The modified questionnaire was used for data collection and a questionnaire designed on Google Docs was mailed to prospective respondents. A total of 139 responses was received which have been used for the purpose of data analysis.

RESULTS

Data analysis was carried out using SPSS version 20.

Descriptive Statistics

The respondents consisted of 26.6% females and 73.4% males. Of the total respondents 53.2% were uptil 30 years of age, 38.8% were between 30 and 50 years and 7.9% were above 50 years of age. The respondents had 44.6% post graduates, 10.1% had Ph. Ds and rest had education less than or upto graduation. The survey had 47.5% students, 49.6% who were working with some organization and balance were self employed. The respondents had 85.6% people who were using internet banking and 14.4% who were not using internet banking.

Importance of the Indicator Variables

For each of the constructs, the values of means and standard deviations for each of the measured variables were determined to assess the customers perception regarding perceived usefulness, perceived ease of use, attitude to use and intention to use biometrics based authentication for e-banking. The mean and variances for the measured variables are given in Table 1.

The value of means for all the measured variables varies from a minimum of 3.62 to a maximum of 4.14 on a scale of 5. This shows that each of the variables was important to the respondents. For the item: "perceived usefulness" the highest recognition was for the statements: "biometric is useful because it provides a more reliable method for authentication" and "biometric is useful because it saves time for authentication". For "perceived ease of use", the highest recognition was for the statements: "biometric is easy to use because one does not have to remember any passwords for authentication" and "biometric is easy to use as it requires only placing your thumb or finger on the instrument". Attitude to use and intention to use scored somewhat lower than either perceived usefulness or perceived ease of use. Moreover, standard deviation varied from a minimum of 1.04 to a maximum of 1.19 which shows that there is fair amount of agreement among the respondents regarding all the measured variables.

Hypothesis Testing

For hypothesis testing, both independent sample t test as well as Anova were used. Independent sample t test was used for finding out if there was any significant difference for perceived usefulness, perceived ease of use, attitude to use and intention to use between respondents who were using internet banking and those who did not use internet banking. Anova was used to determine if there was any significant difference in the four constructs depending on occupation, income and education. The results of hypothesis testing are enumerated as follows.

1. **Effect of Education:** Anova results showed that there was no significant difference between mean values for respondents with different education levels. Three categories were used: graduates and below, post graduates and Ph. Ds. The p values were very high meaning that the mean values of the four constructs were virtually same across respondents with differing education levels. Thus, null hypotheses are accepted and hypotheses 1 to 4 are rejected.

Table 1. Mean and standard deviation for the indicator variables

Construct	Indicator variable	Mean	Std deviation
Perceived usefulness	I think that biometric is useful because it provides a more reliable method for authentication.	4.1	1.05
	I think biometric is useful because it saves time for authentication.	4.0	1.09
	I think biometric is useful because it can be made available at any location	3.65	1.07
	I think biometric is useful because it can be used anytime (24x7)	3.87	1.04
	I think biometric is useful as one cannot make mistakes entering wrong passwords for authentication	3.94	1.16
Perceived ease of use	Biometric is easy to use as it requires only placing your thumb or finger on the instrument.	4.04	1.11
	Learning to use biometric will be easy and will not take much time.	3.99	1.11
	Biometric is easy to use because one does not have to remember any passwords for authentication	4.14	1.11
	Overall, biometric is easier to use than other techniques for authentication.	3.82	1.07
Attitude towards use	I feel it is a good idea to use biometrics for authentication	3.75	1.18
	I want to use biometrics for authentication.	3.64	1.19
Intention to use	I will use biometrics for authentication.	3.62	1.18
	I will recommend to others to use biometrics for authentication.	3.62	1.16

2. **Effect of Occupation:** Three categories were used: students, working respondents and self employed ones. While analyzing effect of occupation on the perceived ease of use p value was found to be 0.05 which is significant at 95% confidence level. Null hypothesis is rejected and hypothesis 5 is accepted. This means that there is significant difference in the means for respondents across different occupations. The mean value was found to be highest for students. While analyzing effect of occupation on perceived usefulness, the p value was found to be 0.2. Though this means that there is no significant effect of occupation at 95% confidence levels it still shows some effect of occupation on perceived usefulness. Incidentally, the highest mean value was for respondents doing a job. This is different from the perceived ease of use which had a highest mean value for students. For attitude to use and intention to use the p values were very high meaning that the mean values of these two constructs were virtually same across respondents with different occupations. Hypotheses 7 and 8 are clearly rejected and null hypotheses are maintained (Table 2).

3. **Effect of Income:** Income had the most pronounced effect on all the four constructs. The classes of income used were: nil, upto 3 lacs, between 3 and 6 lacs, between 6 and 12 lacs and above 12 lacs per annum. The p values are shown in the Table 3. All p values are less than 0.05 and hence significant at 95% confidence level. Thus, we can say that there is a significant effect of income on perceived usefulness, perceived ease of use, attitude to use and intention to use. Null hypotheses are rejected and hypotheses 9 to 12 are accepted.

4. **Users and Non-Users of Internet Banking:** The p values were found to be very high indicating that there was no significant difference for the four constructs between respondents who used internet banking and who did not. This means that perceived usefulness, perceived ease of use, attitude to use and intention to use was similar for both users and non-users of internet banking. Hence, hypotheses 13 to 16 are rejected and null hypotheses are maintained.

Table 2. ANOVA for effect of occupation on perceived ease of use and perceived usefulness

Perceived ease of use	Degrees of freedom	P value
Between groups	2	0.05
Within groups	136	
Total	138	
Perceived usefulness	**Degrees of freedom**	**Significance**
Between groups	2	0.204
Within groups	136	
Total	138	

Table 3. ANOVA for effect of income on all four constructs

Perceived usefulness	Degrees of freedom	P value
Between groups	4	0.001
Within groups	134	
Total	138	
Perceived ease of use		
Between groups	4	0.01
Within groups	134	
Total	138	
Attitude to use		0.009
Between groups	4	
Within groups	134	
Intention to use		0.045
Between groups	4	
Within groups	134	

CONCLUSION

Based on the Technology Acceptance Model, this paper has tried to determine customer perception about use of biometrics for authentication in e-banking in India. Respondents strongly endorsed the variables and had consistent views about all the indicator variables used to measure the four constructs, viz, perceived usefulness, perceived ease of use, attitude to use and intention to use biometrics for e-banking. This paper also tried to determine if there was any significant effect of demographic variables like education, occupation, income and prior usage of internet banking on the four constructs of TAM. Occupation was found to have a significant effect on perceived ease of use of biometrics. Students perceived the highest ease of use for biometrics. The effect of occupation on perceived usefulness was less pronounced with a p value of 0.2. On the other constructs occupation had no significant effect. Income had the most pronounced effect on all the four constructs. Education had no significant effect on any of the four constructs. This paper has helped in understanding customer perception about biometrics for online banking in India

REFERENCES

Adewale, A. A., Ibidunni, A. S., Joke, B., & Tiwalade, O. (2014). Biometric Enabled E-Banking in Nigeria: Management and Customers' Perspectives. *Information and Knowledge Management*, *4*(11), 23–28.

Alharbi, S., & Drew, S. (2014). Using the Technology Acceptance Model in Understanding Academics Behavioural Intention to Use Learning Management Systems, (IJACSA). *International Journal of Advanced Computer Science and Applications*, *5*(1), 143–155. doi:10.14569/IJACSA.2014.050120

Ambak, K., Ismail, R., Abdullah, R. A., Latiff, A. A., & Sanik, M. E. (2013). Application of Technology Acceptance Model in Predicting Behavioral Intention to Use Safety Helmet Reminder System, *Research Journal of Applied Sciences. Engineering and Technology*, *5*(3), 881–888.

Crime in India. 2011-Compendium. (2012). National Crime Records Bureau, Ministry of Home Affairs, Government of India, New Delhi, India. Retrieved from reportwww.ncrb.gov

Das, S., & Jhunu, D. (2011). Designing a Biometric Strategy (Fingerprint) Measure for Enhancing ATM Security in Indian E-Banking System. *International Journal of Information and Communication Technology Research*, *1*(5), 197–203.

Davis, F. D. (1989). Perceived Usefulness, Perceived Ease of Use and User Acceptance of Information Technology. *Management Information Systems Quarterly*, *13*(3), 319–339. doi:10.2307/249008

Davis, F. D., Bagozzi, P. R., & Warshaw, P. (1989). User acceptance of computer technology: A comparison of two theoretical models. *Management Science*, *35*(8), 982–1003. doi:10.1287/mnsc.35.8.982

Deloitte India Fraud Survey Edition. (2014). Retrieved from http://www2.deloitte.com/content/dam/Deloitte/in/Documents/finance/in-finance-annual-fraud-survey-noexp.pdf

Fatima, A. (2011). E-Banking Security Issues – Is There A Solution in Biometrics? *Journal of Internet Banking and Commerce*, *16*(2), 1–9.

Hosseini, & Mohammadi. (2012). Review Banking on Biometric in the World's Banks and Introducing a Biometric Model for Iran's Banking System. *Journal of Basic and Applied Scientific Research*, *2*(9), 9152–9160.

International Data Corporation's (IDC)'s Business Strategy: 2014 U.S. Consumer Channel Preference Survey Results - Online and Internet Banking Is a Key Component of Omni-Channel Strategy. (n.d.). Retrieved from https://www.idc.com/getdoc.jsp?containerId=FI252651

Lee, Y.-H., Hsieb, Y.-C., & Chen, Y.-H. (2013). An investigation of employees use of e-learning systems: Applying the technology acceptance model. *Behaviour & Information Technology*, *32*(2), 173–189. doi:10.1080/0144929X.2011.577190

Michael, D. (2014). Consumer's intentions to use e-readers. *Journal of Computer Information Systems*, (Winter), 66–76.

Nair, I., & Mukunda Das, V. (2012). Using Technology Acceptance Model to assess teachers attitude towards use of technology as teaching tool: A SEM Approach. *International Journal of Computers and Applications*, *42*(2), 1–6. doi:10.5120/5661-7691

Normalini, M. K., & Ramayah, T. (2012), Biometrics Technologies Implementation in Internet Banking Reduce Security Issues? *Procedia- Social and Behavioral Sciences*, *65*, 364-369.

Okechukwu, O. M., & Majesty, E. I. (2012). ATM Security Using Fingerprint Biometric Identifer: An Investigative Study. *International Journal of Advanced Computer Science and Applications*, *3*(4), 68–72. doi:10.14569/IJACSA.2012.030412

Park, S. Y. (2009). An Analysis of the Technology Acceptance Model in Understanding University Students' Behavioral Intention to Use e-Learning. *Journal of Educational Technology & Society*, *12*(3), 150–162.

Punnoose, A. C. (2012). Determinants of Intention to Use eLearning Based on the Technology Acceptance Model. *Journal of Information Technology Education: Research*, *11*, 301–337.

Rana, T., & Kamala, M. A. (2012). Evaluating biometrics for online banking: The case for usability. *International Journal of Information Management*, *32*(5), 489–494. doi:10.1016/j.ijinfomgt.2012.07.001

Sitalakshmi, V., & Indika, D. (2008). Biometrics in banking security: A case study. *Information Management & Computer Security*, *16*(4), 415–430. doi:10.1108/09685220810908813

Wangpipatwong, S., Chutimaskul, W., & Papasratorn, B. (2008). Understanding Citizen's Continuance Intention to Use e-Government Website: A Composite View of Technology Acceptance Model and Computer Self-Efficacy. *The Electronic Journal of E-Government*, *6*(1), 55–64.

Wen-Chia, T. (2012). A study of consumer behavioral intention to use e-books: The Technology Acceptance Model perspective. *Innovative Marketing*, *8*(4), 55–66.

Yaghoubi & Bahmani. (2010). Factors Affecting the Adoption of Online Banking An Integration of Technology Acceptance Model and Theory of Planned Behavior. *International Journal of Business and Management*, *5*(9), 159–165.

Zhu, D.-S., Lin, T. C.-T., & Hsu, Y.-C. (2012). Using the technology acceptance model to evaluate user attitude and intention of use for online games. *Total Quality Management*, *23*(8), 965–980. doi:10.108 0/14783363.2012.704269

Chapter 11

Interplay of Technology and Customer Value Dynamics in Banking Industry:
Analytical Construct for Measuring Growth and Performance

Rajagopal
EGADE Business School, Tecnologico de Monterrey, Mexico City, Mexico & Boston University, USA

Ananya Rajagopal
HSBC Corporate Office, Mexico

ABSTRACT

This chapter attempts to critically examine the available literature on the subject, discuss a model that provides a framework for analyzing the variables associated with customer value, and to identify potential research areas. The chapter argues through a set of linear equations that maximizing customer value which is interdependent factor for technology adoption and profit optimization in the banks need to be backed with appropriate economic parameters for attaining competitive efficiency and optimizing profit. The framework of the construct is laid on the theory of competitive advantage and customer lifetime value, so as to maximize the potential of the organization and all its subsystems to create and sustain satisfied customers. The theoretical impetus from new technologies in banking services such as mobile banking in the North American region and discusses the technology led marketing process towards optimizing profit have been discussed in this chapter. The discussion in the paper also analyzes the main criteria for successful internet-banking strategy and brings out benefits of e-banking from the point of view of banks, their technology and customer values and tentatively concludes that there is increasing returns to scale in the bank services in relation to the banking products, new technology and customer value.

DOI: 10.4018/978-1-5225-0902-8.ch011

INTRODUCTION

The new information technology is becoming an important factor in the future development of financial services industry, and especially banking industry. The developments information and communication technology have significantly contributed to the exponential growth and profits of the financial institutions worldwide. This evolution had transformed the way banks deliver their services, using technologies such as automated teller machines, phones, the Internet, credit cards, and electronic cash. However, banks face a number of important questions on strategies for deriving full advantage of new technology opportunities and tracking electronic development changes affecting interactions with the customers.

In general terms, increasing convenience is a way of raising consumers' surplus provided new technology is adopted by the banks in order to offer convenience to the customers may be through an electronic transaction as a substitute for a trip to the branch. The technology based services imply different combinations of accessibility attributes (time, distance, and search costs), ease of use and price. Another factor in determining the magnitude of the surplus that the bank can seize is the relative importance of cross-selling. The bundle of services provided electronically is usually not the same as the one available at a branch. For this reason new technology based banking services with high customer value may offer better service conditions to harmonize the flow of information and services across the spatial and temporal dimensions.

The following sections of the paper will critically examine the available recent literature on this subject and present an analytical framework to measure the intrinsic contribution of various attributes related to technology and customer value in banking services. The construct of the measure is described through liner equations for technology, customer value and their symbiotic relationship followed by the general discussion on the sub-models. The locus of the model has been placed on the subsets of technology adoption and customer value as a profit driver in the banking industry.

REVIEW OF LITERATURE

Electronic Banking vs. Conventional Wisdom

The maxims of technology spread in the operations of financial institutes may have relational effect with the size and volume of operations of the organization. Whenever the innovation is initially introduced, large banks have an advantage to adopt it first and enjoy further growth of size. Over time, as the innovation diffuses into smaller banks, the aggregate bank size distribution increases stochastically towards a new steady state. Applying the theory to a panel study of internet banking diffusion across 50 US states, it has been observed that technological, economic and institutional factors largely govern the transaction process supported with technology. The empirical findings disentangle the interrelationship between internet banking adoption and growth of average bank size, and explain the variation of diffusion rates across geographic regions (Sullivan & Wang, 2005). Technology in banking industry also has cost implications which lead to slow down the adaptation process in many countries. The effect of technical change on the costs of banking firms operating in Central and Eastern European countries has been studied using Fourier - flexible cost function specification for the period 1995–2002. A common cost frontier with country-specific variables is employed in order to take into account the macroeconomic and regulatory conditions that vary over country and time. The findings of the study reveal that the rate of reduction in costs resulting from technical change increased during the sample period. Banks operating in Hungary, Czech Republic and Poland benefited more from technical change than their counterparts. In terms of cost reduction, large banks benefited more from technical progress which underpins that large banks are more able to change their optimal input mix in response to changes in technology (Adnan & Saadet, 2006).

The recent dotcom boom/bust cycle, as equilibrium industry dynamics triggered by technology innovation, has been analyzed in various studies. When a major technology innovation arrives, a wave of new firms enters the market implementing the innovation for profits. However, if the innovation complements existing technology, some new entrants will later be forced out as more and more incumbent firms succeed in adopting the innovation. Such situation has revealed that the diffusion of Internet technology among traditional brick-and-mortar firms is indeed the driving force behind the rise and fall of dotcoms as well as the sustained growth of e-commerce (Wang, 2005). However in reference to banking reforms in India, technology has been found to be the major input in driving competition which has been evidenced in a study revealing a positive relationship between the level of competition and banking efficiency. However, a negative relationship between the presence of foreign banks and banking efficiency is found, which attributes to a short-run increase in costs due to the introduction of new banking technology by foreign banks (Ali & Hang, 2006).

Many financial institutions have built websites to inform and attract customers. Financial aggregation presents an opportunity by which they can build stronger relationships with customers. Information technology affects banking in two main ways. First, it may reduce costs by replacing paper-based, labor intensive methods with automated processes. Second, it may modify the ways in which consumers have access to banks' services and products and, hence, may enhance the contestability of markets, especially in retail banking. Due to deregulation and technological advances, new opportunities become available, but the skill needed to exploit them effectively may be unknown. Early entry of financial institutions into the technology expanding activities may have learning benefits that are manifested in discovery of the skill needed to operate effectively. E-banking products and services are getting more and more advanced and increasing in variety by providing information at the early stage to providing transactional activities. The average e-banking penetration for developing countries by the end of 1999 was close to 5 percent. In Brazil, the number of e-banking users reached 8 million in 2000 while in Mexico, the number of e-banking users reached 1.25 million in 2000.

The e-banking services include e-remittances, e-payments, e-trades, and e-credit. However, many e-banking businesses have been forced out of market due to the low customer perception such as e-procurements supporting the banking transactions of large work tenders. Internet-based transactions require their own security measures for which private solutions may not be sufficient. For example, government actions are needed to set up a framework for digital signatures and to designate agencies or processes to authenticate public keys associated with transactions. Consequently, internet-only banks have been substantially less profitable. They generate lower business volumes and any savings generated by lower physical overheads appear to be offset by other types of non-interest expenditures, notably marketing to attract new customers. (de Young 2001). However, e-banking develops automated credit authorization system by developing appropriate credit scoring system and cash- flow scoring system to reduce operating costs, improve asset quality, and increase client profitability. One of the major benefits of credit scoring system is that lenders can make credit decisions without necessarily obtaining financial statement, credit reports, or other time-consuming and hard-to-get information.

There have been strings of research studies exploring the economic and relational issues on internet and advanced technology diffusion in the banking industry. The model developed for estimating the internet banking adoption at the early stages when there is considerable uncertainty about consumers' demand argues that relative bank size and demographic information predictive of future demand positively influence the process of internet banking adaptation (Courchane et al, 2002). Similarly, the Logit model estimates the determinants of internet banking adaptation, which reveals that larger banks are more likely to adapt to internet banking when they are younger, better performing, located in urban areas, and members of a bank holding company (Furst et al, 2001). However, other studies analyze the reverse effect of technology on bank performance but obtain mixed results in reference to characteristics, including costs and profitability, of early adopters of internet banking and find little difference from non-adopters (Sullivan, 2000) though many banks enjoyed rising profits during the 1990s, and attribute this to banks' increasing market power gained by adopting new technologies (Berger & Mester, 2003).

Advances in technologies have allowed service providers to incorporate many different technologies into the delivery of their services. These technologies have been implemented in the service encounter for the customer to use with varying degrees of success. The factors influencing consumer attitudes towards and adoption of self-service technologies (SSTs) across three different technologies used in the banking industry reveals that service attributes related to trust, quality and time are major attributes influence attitudes toward each of these technologies and offers an explanation of the varying degrees of acceptance found among consumers (Curren & Mueter, 2005). Further, on the issue of technology adaptation Lassar *et al* examine the relationships between consumer innovativeness, self-efficacy on the internet, internet attitudes and online banking adoption, while controlling for personal characteristics. While results confirm the positive relationship between internet related innovativeness and online banking they also surprisingly show that general innovativeness is negatively related to online banking (Lassar *et al*, 2005). Bank characteristics such as asset size, number of employees, number of full service locations, areas of lending, and return on assets largely influence the technology diffusion process and adaptation at the customer levels. It has been observed in a study that a number of bank composition and operations variables behaved statistically independent between size variables (assets, number of employees, and number of branches) and wide area network access. The survey data also indicate that return on assets and network system variables are independent. Therefore, networks systems have not had a direct impact on the bottom line (Zhu *et al*, 2004).

Customer Value Management

The customer values for banking services are shaped more by habits, reinforcement effects, and situational influences than strongly-held attitudes. However, the aggregate returns on the customer value towards the new product from the perspective financial institution may be manifesting in enhancing the market share, services coverage and augmenting profit in a competitive environment. The academics, consultants and business people speculated that marketing in the new century would be very different from the time when much of the pioneering work on customer loyalty was undertaken (Churchill 1942; Brown 1953; Cunningham, 1961; Tucker 1964; Frank 1967). Yet there exists the scope for improving the applied concepts as there have been many changes over conventional ideologies. It has been observed in one of the studies that the customer values are created through individual perceptions, and organizational and relational competence (Johanson *et.al.*, 2001). Management of business relationships is a key strategic success factor to fully utilize the market potential. The goal of relationship development has been defined as the ability to attract, maintain, and enhance new customer relations (Berry 1983). Contributions to this area have developed a number of models for relationship management (Zeithaml, Berry and Parasuraman 1988) and a common denominator of these models is that firms need to adjust to market conditions. This involves, for instance, narrowing perceptional gaps, to adjust workflows in the organization, or to activate the customer as a relationship partner.

The value concept in the above relationship governs the customer portfolio decision in terms of formulation of recursive utility over time. It shows that the optimal portfolio demand for products under competition varies strongly with the values associated with the brand, industry attractiveness, knowledge management and ethical issues of the organization. The extent of business values determines the relative risk aversion in terms of functional and logistical efficiency between the organization and supplier while the switching attitude may influence the customers if the organizational values are not strong and sustainable in the given competitive environment (Rajagopal, 2006[a]).

A study examines the success of product pricing practices and the conditions upon which success is contingent discussing three different pricing practices that refer to the use of information on customer value, competition, and costs respectively. The study argues that the success of these practices is contingent on relative product advantage and competitive intensity. The study reveals that there are no general "best" or "bad" practices, but that a contingency approach is appropriate (Ingenbleek *et.al.*, 2003). Value and pricing models have been developed for many different products, services and assets. Some of these are extensions and refinements of convention models value driven pricing theories (Gamrowski & Rachev, 1999; Pedersen, 2000). Also there have been some models that are developed and calibrated addressing specific issues such as model for household assets demand (Perraudin & Sorensen, 2000). The key marketing variables such as price, brand name, and product attributes affect customers' judgment processes and derive inference on its quality dimensions leading to customer satisfaction. The experimental study conducted indicates that customers use price and brand name differently to judge the quality dimensions and measure the degree of satisfaction (Brucks *et.al.*, 2000).

The value of corporate brand endorsement across different products and product lines, and at lower levels of the brand hierarchy also needs to be assessed as a customer value driver. Use of corporate brand endorsement either as a name identifier or logo identifies the product with the company, and provides reassurance for the customer (Rajagopal & Sanchez, 2004). A perspective from resource-advantage theory (Hunt & Morgan, 1995) is used to formulate expectations on the degree to which the use of information on customer value, competition, and costs contribute to the success of a price decision. It is argued that the success of these practices is contingent on the relative customer value the firm has created and the degree to which this position of relative value is sustainable in the competitive market place. These expectations are empirically tested on pricing decisions with respect to the introduction of new industrial capital goods.

The studies that advocate the models of building customer value through traditional relationship marketing discuss the long term value concepts to loyal customers. Most importantly, these are expected to raise their spending and association with the products and services of the company with increasing levels of satisfactions that attribute to values of customers (Reichheld & Sasser, 1990). In the most optimistic settings, such value creation is observed to generate new customers for new products in view of the customer relationship and value management strategies of the firm (Ganesh, *et.al.*, 2000). In the high customer value framework, the firm ensures diminished costs to serve (Knox, 1998) and exhibits reduced customer price sensitivities. A database-driven approach, customer tenure in reference to the length of a customer's relationship and values retention with a company has often been used to approximate the loyalty construct (Ganesh *et.al.*, 2000; Reinartz & Kumar, 2000; 2002). Hence the relationship marketing with a customer value orientation thrives on the concept that raises the length of the customer-company relationship which contributes in optimizing the profit for the firm (Reichheld & Sasser, 1990). However, the contributions of long-life customers were generally declining and in a non-contractual setting short-life but high-revenue customers accounted for a sizeable amount of profits (Reinartz & Kumar, 2000).

The role of customer value has been largely recognized over time by the financial institutions as an instrument towards stimulating market share and profit optimization. The customer values for a new product of financial institution in competitive markets are shaped more by habits, reinforcement effects, and situational influences than strongly-held attitudes. A strong and sustainable customer value associated with a new product launched by a financial institution may also lead to build the customer loyalty in the long run. An analysis of the new product-market structuring based on customer value may be developed well within the microeconomic framework of financial institutions. The aggregate returns on the customer value towards the baking services from the perspective of financial institution may be observed manifesting in enhancing the market share, services coverage and augmenting brand in a given market. The value of a customer may be defined in reference to a firm as the expected performance measures are based on key assumptions concerning retention rate and profit margin and the customer value also tracks market value of these firms over time. The value of all customers is determined by the acquisition rate and cost of acquiring new customers (Gupta *et al*, 2003).

In the process of enhancing the customer value for the new products, a financial institution may simultaneously use intensive customer value for technology based banking services and intensive customer relationship management (CRM) strategies to the competitive sales and marketing strategies. The integrated impact of CRM, sales and marketing strategies at different stages of service attractiveness would contribute to the customer value and influence the aggregate returns on the customer value derived at various stages of service attractiveness of the financial institutions. However, a financial institution may need to compute the trend of customer value for all the services in its product line, and measure the variability in the customer values perceived for its new services. The customer values are broadly reflected in the competitive gains, perceived values, and extent of association with the financial services and level of quintessence with the customer relationship management services of the organization.

Framework of Analytical Construct

Technology and Profit Optimization Equilibrium

Let us assume that banks with conventional wisdom, without access to improved services technology, function at a steady state. The operational equilibrium at the given prices using the existing technology for optimizing profit may be expressed for individual banks as:

$$z_0 = q_0^{\max 1-\infty} \left(p q_0 \right) - \alpha_c q_0^{\beta_c} \tag{1}$$

Wherein is profit of the banks, p is price, $\left(q_0 \right)$ denotes the financial performance of the bank which may also be determined as out of the organization, and $\left(\beta_c > 1 \right)$ represent the cost parameter in application of the existing technology. The profit optimization solution may be derived considering equation (1) as below:

$$q_0 = \left[\frac{p}{\alpha_c \beta_c} \right]^{\frac{1}{\beta_c - 1}} \tag{2}$$

When new technology with significant improvements over the conventional, at a given time t, an individual bank may optimize its profit and decide on adoption of innovative practices or otherwise. Hence,

$$z_1 = q_0^{\max 1 - \infty} \left(p q_1 \right) - \frac{\alpha_c}{\gamma} \left(q_1 \right)^{\beta_c} - c' \tag{3}$$

where $\left(z_1 \right)$ represents profit and $\left(q_1 \right)$ denotes the performance of the bank after adoption of new technology, the cost savings incurred by the adoption of new technology is indicated by $\left(\gamma \right)$ and $\left(c' \right)$ expresses the period cost of adoption of new technology by the banks. The performance optimization of an individual bank may be derived solving the above equation as:

$$q_1 = \left(\frac{\gamma p}{\alpha_c' \beta_c} \right)_t^{\frac{1}{\beta_c - 1}} \tag{4}$$

$$z_1 = p q_1 \left(\frac{\beta_c - 1}{\beta_c} \right) - c' \tag{5}$$

Thus, an individual bank will adopt new technology if $\left(z_1 \geq z_0 \right)$ with the threshold size of adoption $\left(q'' \right)$. This situation may be expressed as:

$$z_1 \geq z_0 \Rightarrow q'' = \frac{c'}{p \left(\frac{\beta_c - 1}{\beta_c} \right) \left(\gamma^{\frac{1}{\beta_c - 1}} - 1 \right)} \tag{6}$$

It may be observed from the above equation that the size of requirement for adoption suggests that large banks have an advantage in conceiving and implementing the new technology leading to further adding value. This process is induced in large banks through customer services and various value augmentation approaches pertaining to customer relations management. Assuming that bank size distribution as $\left(D_b \right)$ and threshold size of adoption as $\left(q'' \right)$, the role of aggregate adoption of new technology may be expressed as:

$$A_t = 1 - D_b \left(q'' \right) = \cfrac{1}{1 + \left(\cfrac{kq''}{Eq_0} \right)^{1/g}} \tag{7}$$

whereas $\left(A_t \right)$ represents rate of aggregate adoption of technology, $\left(Eq_0 \right)$ and g are mean and Gini Co-efficient respectively and k is the constant. Accordingly a proposition may be drawn for the above equation that the rate of technology adoption $\left(A_t \right)$ increases with the customer demand in reference to various satisfaction parameters, average bank productivity and cost savings factor $\left(\gamma \right)$. However $\left(A_t \right)$ decreases with the increase in the cost of adoption of new technology $\left(c' \right)$. Over time banks adopt the new technology, the average bank size keeps increasing and the aggregate rate of adoption augments stochastically to a new state of equilibrium. During transitional stage at a given time t financial institutions run into critical size requirement $\left(q'' \right)$ ripping the size into two parts- conventional and newfangled, which reveals $\left(q_{0t} \leq q_t'' \right)$.

Overtime $\left(q'' \right)$ may face stronger challenges than existing due to the internal and external environmental shifts in reference to change in customer demand, decrease in the cost of technology adoption, banking deregulation etc. Consequently the new technology becomes accessible to the smaller banks and overall technology-profit equation moves to a new state of equilibrium. Hence, future innovation in technology may be adopted by smaller banks at a probability of marginal change in the profit during the technology gestation period. Therefore, at each time $\left(t \geq 0 \right)$, the optimization behavior of a bank may imply:

$$q_t'' = \max \left(q_{0t}, q_{1t} \right) + \omega \left(q_{t-1}'' \right) \tag{8}$$

where $\left(q_t'' \right)$ represents maximum value of a bank with new technology and ω is a discount factor. It implies that in order to increase overall performance of the bank or a financial institution, a simple dynamic path at the initial time (0) works out to be a decision for technology adoption. Accordingly, the customer value associated with the performance of a bank using innovative technology may be expressed as:

$$V_t^\theta = \exp \left(c', \gamma, D_b \right)_t^{\lim 1 - \infty} + \max \left(q_0, q_1, q'', A_t \right) + \mu V_{t+1}^\theta \tag{9}$$

In the above equation $\left(V_t^\theta \right)$ denotes the customer value with adopted technology in a bank at tine t and $\left(\mu \right)$ represents the mean of the cognitive variables in reference to perceived values of the customers over the period of effective usage of new technology. As regards the value parameters for banking technology adoption and diffusion, a financial institution may attain many equilibrium paths over different time lags. However, the major determinants for technology adoption for banks include cost of technology adoption, profit impact of technology, operational area and size of the organization, cost saving probabilities and customer value. The technology and innovation keep rising from time $(t+1)$ to shift the equilibrium of profit and customer values to a new state leading to change in overall efficiency of the organization. Therefore, financial losses may emerge as a result of *ex ante* adoption of new technology with overestimation of the profit targets.

Measuring Customer Value

The customer values for goods and services are largely associated with the retail stores brands and customer services offered therein. The beginning of customer preferences is the basic discrete time that helps the customers in making a buying decision and maximizing the value of product. Ofek Elie (2002) discussed that the value of product and services are not always the same and are subject to value life cycle that governs the customer preferences in the long-run. If customers prefer the product and service for N periods with Q as value perceived by the customer, the value may be determined as Q>N, where Q and N both are exogenous variables. If every customer receives higher perceived values for each of his buying, the value added product q ≥ Q, where 'q' refers to the change in the quality brought by innovation or up-graded technology. The customer may refrain from buying the products if q ≤ Q, that does not influence his buying decisions. However, a strong referral 'R' may lead to influence the customer values, with an advantage factor β that may be explained by price or quality factor. In view of the above discussion it may be assumed that customer preferences have high variability that grows the value factors in customer decisions:

$$D'_{bn} = \sum_{t=1}^{N} \rho^t \left(C_t, \hat{Z} \right) + \rho^{N+1} Q_t \tag{10}$$

where, D_{bn} is expressed as initial buying decision of the customers, (ρ) is quality of services, C_t represents consumption, $\hat{Z}$ is a vector of customer attributes (*viz.* preferential variables) and Q_t is the value differences perceived by the customer with and without technology based services.

A customer value is a dynamic attribute that plays a key role in buying and is an intangible factor to be considered in all marketing and selling functions. The value equation for customer satisfaction may be expressed as a function of all value drivers wherein each driver contains the parameters that directly or indirectly offer competitive advantages to the customers and enhance the customer value.

$$V' = K_s, K_m, K_d, K_c \left[\prod \left\{ V \left(x, t, q, p \right) \right\} \right] \tag{11}$$

In the above equation V' is a specific customer value driver, K are constants for services (K_s), margins (K_m) retained by the banks for providing services (which is also commonly known as commission), services spread (K_d) in reference to inter- and intra-branch movements, and cost to customers (K_c); x is volume of operations, t is time, q is organizational quality and p denotes price. The perceived customer value (V) is a function of price (p) and non-price factors including organizational quality (q) and volume (x) in a given time t. Hence $\prod$ has been used as a multiplication operator in the above equation. The quality of the product and volume are closely associated with the customer values. The total utility for the conventional services goes up due to economy of scale as the quality is also increased simultaneously ($\partial_v/\partial_x > 0$). The ∂ customer value is enhanced by offering larger volume of product at a competitive price in a given time ($\partial_v/\partial_p > 0$) and ($\partial_v/\partial_t > 0$). The conventional products create lower values to the customers ($\partial_v/\partial_x < 0$) while the innovative products irrespective of price advantages, enhance the customer value ($\partial_v/\partial_x > 0$). The value addition in the conventional services deliver lower customer satisfaction as compared to the innovative products (Rajagopal, 2005). Such transition in the customer value, due to shift in the technology may be expressed as:

$$V'_{hj} = a \left[\sum \frac{T_p}{\left(1 + V_p\right)^{(1+j+i)}} \right] + b\left(X_j\right) \tag{12}$$

In this equation V'_{hj} represents enhancements in customer value over the transition from conventional to innovative products, a and b are constants, T_p denotes high-tech and high-value products, V_p represents value of product performance that leads to enhance the customer value, the volume is denoted by X, and j is the period during which customer value is measured (Rajagopal, 2006[b]).

Besides the high-tech and high-value products the customers and companies may also find scope of enhancing values with appropriate promotional strategies. The customer values often get enhanced by offering better buying opportunities that reflect on short- and long- term gains. Let us assume that the competitive advantage in existing products over time is G_x that offers j^{th} level of satisfaction through various sales promotion approaches adopted by the company. Such market situation may be explained as:

$$G_x = \left[r_1 m_1 ; r_2 m_2 ; r_3 m_3 ; \ldots\ldots ; r_j m_j \right] \tag{13}$$

where r_j denotes the jth level of satisfaction (j = 1,2,3,….,n) and m_j is the number of customers attracted towards buying the product. It may be stated that competitive advantage for the existing products of a firm over time is determined by the level of satisfaction derived by the customers and number of customers favoring the buying decisions for the products in a given market. The parameters of customer satisfaction may include product innovativeness, perceived use value, sales promotion, influence of referrals, price and non-price factors. The competitive advantage of a firm is also measurable from the perspective of product attractiveness to generate new customers. Given the scope of retail networks, a feasible value structure for customers may be reflected in repeat buying behavior ($\hat{R}\,\mathfrak{M}$) that explains the relationship of the customer value with the product and associated marketing strategies. The impact of such customer value attributes in a given situation may be described as:

$$\sum_{j=1}^{n} r_j m_j = \hat{R} \tag{14}$$

The repeat buying behavior of customers is largely determined by the values acquired on the product. The attributes, awareness, trial, availability and repeat (AATAR) factors influence the customers towards making re-buying decisions in reference to the marketing strategies of the firm. The decision of customers on repeat buying is also affected by the level of satisfaction derived on the products and number of customers attracted towards buying the same product, as a behavioral determinant.

Customer Value Enhancement Through Banking Technology

Let us assume that $(x_0, x_1, x_2, \ldots x_{n-1}, x_n)$ represents customer value at different stages of banking services attractiveness, increasing with reference to the derived advantage from the competing products in a given market at a given time (t). In the process of enhancing the customer value for the new products a firm may use intensive customer value for banking products; a financial institution may simultaneously use intensive customer relationship management (CRM) and the competitive strategies in reference to the new technology used in a bank. The integrated impact of CRM, sales and marketing strategies at different stages of product attractiveness would contribute to the customer value. Such an aggregated customer value represented by R_n, can be measured by a firm. Hence the R_n can be calculated with the following operation:

$$A\left(R_n\right) = f\left(x_0\right)\Delta x + f\left(x_1\right)\Delta x + f\left(x_2\right)\Delta x + \ldots + f\left(x_{n-1}\right)\Delta x \qquad (15)$$

Further simplifying and substituting the values of equations (9) and (12) in this equation, we get,

$$A\left(R\right) = A\left(R_n\right)_{\lim n \to \infty} + \sum_{km}^{jm}\left[\left(\Delta v' + \Delta b'\right)\left(\Delta s\right)\right]^t + V_t^{\theta} + V_{hj}' \qquad (16)$$

In the above equation A(R) represents the aggregate returns on the customer value derived at various stages of banking services attractiveness and quantitative changes in the volume of banking products positioned by a bank, repeat buying, and market coverage in terms of changes in the market shares of the financial institutions. The aggregate returns on the customer values may be measured by a firm for not only the existing products in the market but also for the new products in the potential markets $A\left(R_n\right)_{\lim n \to \infty}$. The number of customers attracted towards the new product promotion, influence of referrals and augmented perceived use values derived by the customers may be the major factors contributing in determining the potential markets for the new products. However a bank may identify the potential markets in reference to its banking products and branch expansion policies. Besides, a firm may need to compute the trend of customer value for all the products in its product line, and measure the variability in the customer values perceived for its banking products.

The model explains that the value based customer portfolios would enhance the customer value as the product efficiency viewed from the customer's perspective, i.e., as a ratio of outputs (*e.g.* resale value, reliability, safety, comfort) that the customers obtain from a product relative to inputs (price, running costs) that the customers have to deliver in exchange. The derived efficiency value can be understood as the return on the customer's investment. Products offering a maximum customer value relative to all other alternatives in the market are characterized as efficient. Market partitioning is achieved endogenously by clustering products in one segment that are benchmarked by the same efficient peer(s). This ensures that only the products with a similar output-input structure are partitioned into the same sub-market. As a result, a sub-market consists of highly substitutable products. The customer values are reflected in their competitive gains, perceived use values, volume of buying and level of quintessence with the customer relationship management services of the organization. If these variables do not measure significantly, there emerges the development of switching attitude among the customers. If the organizational values are low, the customer relationship may be risk averse due to weak dissemination of information and technology based values to the customers.

GENERAL DISCUSSION

Few contributions address the measurement of the customer value as an intangible asset of the financial institutions, though substantial literature is available discussing the customer relations and loyalty building perspectives. In view of growing customer demand for innovative technology with quality banking services to accelerate the information and transaction process, it may be observed that greater household access to the Internet drives a higher website adoption rate. There are many information and transaction access outlets in developed western countries and developing countries of Latin America and Caribbean which include phone banking, mobile services and internet banking portals. However, greater household access to the Internet and mobile devices in banking operations may be negatively related to local average bank assets. A possible explanation is that once the customers have access to the information and transactions on internet and mobile devices, they would form a relationship with bank outside of their region/country, which may have a negative impact on the size of banks in their region.

Over time, due to internal and external changes in the organizational environment in reference to customer demand, technology progress and improvements in banking regulation, the innovation diffuses into smaller banks. The major factors affecting technology adoption and augmenting include mean bank size, per capita income, household access to internet, average bank age, bank loan specialization, competitive advantages in banking products, product-mix of banks, self-service technologies, cost of adoption, level of customer satisfaction and customer density in the region availing banking services. The costs of accessing electronic banking services need to be reduced for wider coverage of customers on e-banking bay. Comprehensive knowledge dissemination and trust play pivotal role in creating customer value, in absence of which knowledge barriers may limit the size of the market to a subset of bank customers in the short term. Therefore, once a bank has taken the decision of adopting new technology for improving its services and optimizing profit, the bank will lean to depend on market-specific demand characteristics.

The common services such as brokerage and asset management services, personal banking services, checking accounts and services bills collections are standardized and homogeneous, hence self-service technologies can be considered as a substitute to a branch transaction regardless the issue of complementarity of the entire bundle of banking services. Exploring the synergy between online and offline channels in general reveals that a bank typically delivers standardized, low-value-added transactions such as bill payments, balance inquiries, account transfers and credit card lending through the inexpensive Internet channel, while delivering specialized, high-value-added transactions such as small business lending, personal trust services and investment banking through the more expensive branch channel. By providing more service options to its customers, an improved technology adoption will enable the bank to retain its most profitable customers and generate more revenue from cross-selling. Some banks, which operate on branchless concepts and depend only on internet, have lower asset returns than incumbent branching banks as well as new branching entrants. This is primarily due to their lower interest margins and fee income, lower levels of loan and deposit generation, fewer business loans, and higher non-interest expense for equipment and skilled labor. The financials of such banks turn robust after implementing stick surveillance measure to sustain future competition.

An augmented and sustainable customer value builds the loyalty towards the product and brand implying that bank managers should develop customer driven strategies so that relationship augmentations can be achieved. This is not simply a matter of segmenting customers, but also signals the need to manage the reciprocities of relationship. It has been argued that relationships are constituted by value creating transformations in which the customer may contribute in different ways. Relationship development is to improve these processes by capitalizing on an increasing customer involvement in adaptation of new technology used in the bank. However, acquiring new customers is the easiest way to develop enhanced customer-technology relations favoring the growth of the bank.

Systematically explored concepts in the field of customer value, and market driven approach towards new products would be beneficial for a company to derive long term profit optimization strategy over the period. Hence, a comprehensive framework for estimating both the value of a customer and profit optimization need to be developed. On a tactical level, managers need to consider the optimum spread of customers on a matrix of product attractiveness and market coverage. This needs careful attention and the application of managerial judgment and experience to measure the value driven performance of the product of the firm. It is necessary for the managers to understand that customer value is context dependent and there exists a whole value network to measure, not just a value chain. This value network will contain important entities far beyond the ones commonly taken into consideration in financial projections and business analyses.

REFERENCES

Ataullah, A., & Le, H. (2006). Economic reforms and bank efficiency in developing countries: The case of the Indian banking industry. *Applied Financial Economics*, *16*(9), 653–663. doi:10.1080/09603100500407440

Berger, A., & Mester, L. (2003). Explaining the Dramatic Changes of Performance of U.S. Banks: Technological Change, Deregulation and Dynamic Changes in Competition. *Journal of Financial Intermediation*, *12*(1), 57–95. doi:10.1016/S1042-9573(02)00006-2

Berry, L. (1983). Relationship Marketing. In L. Berry, L. Shostack, & G. Upah (Eds.), *Emerging Perspectives on Services Marketing* (pp. 25–28). Chicago, IL: American Marketing Association.

Churchill, H. (1942). How To Measure Brand Loyalty. *Advertising and Selling*, *35*, 24.

Courchane, M., Nickerson, D., & Sullivan, R. J. (2002). Investment in Internet Banking as a Real Option: Theory and Tests. *Journal of Multinational Financial Management*, *12*(4-5), 347–363. doi:10.1016/S1042-444X(02)00015-4

Cunningham, R. M. (1956). Brand Loyalty - What, Where, How Much? *Harvard Business Review*, *34*, 116–128.

Cunningham, R. M. (1961). Customer Loyalty to Store and Brand. *Harvard Business Review*, (November-December), 127–137.

Curran James, M., & Meuter Matthew, L. (2005). Self-service technology adoption: Comparing three technologies. *Journal of Services Marketing, 19*(2), 103–113. doi:10.1108/08876040510591411

de Young, R. (2001). *The financial progress of pure-play internet banks*. BIS Papers, No. 7.

Ofek, E. (2002). *Customer Profitability and Lifetime Value*. Harvard Business School (Publication reference 9-503-019).

Frank, R. E. (1967). Is Brand Loyalty a Useful Basis for Market Segmentation? *Journal of Advertising Research, 7*(2), 27–33.

Furst, K., Lang, W., & Nolle, D. (2001). Internet Banking in the U.S.: Landscape, Prospects, and Industry Implications. *Journal of Financial Transformation, 2*, 45–52.

Gamrowski, B., & Rachev, S. (1999). A Testable Version of the Pareto-Stable CAPM. *Mathematical and Computer Modelling, 29*(10-12), 61–81. doi:10.1016/S0895-7177(99)00093-X

Ganesh, J., Arnold, M. J., & Reynolds, K. E. (2000). Understanding the Customer Base of Service Providers: An Examination of the Difference between Switchers and Stayers. *Journal of Marketing, 64*(July), 65–87. doi:10.1509/jmkg.64.3.65.18028

Gupta, S., Lehmann, D. R., & Stuart, J. A. (2003). *Valuing Customer*. HBS Marketing Research Paper, No. 03-08.

Hunt, S. D., & Morgan, R. M. (1995). The Comparative Advantage Theory of Competition. *Journal of Marketing, 59*(April), 1–15. doi:10.2307/1252069

Kasman, A., & Kasman, S. K. (2006). Technical Change in Banking: Evidence from Transition Countries. *International Journal of the Economics of Business, 13*(1), 129–144. doi:10.1080/13571510500520044

Knox, S. (1998). Loyalty Brand Segmentation and the Customer Development Process. *European Management Journal, 16*(6), 729–737. doi:10.1016/S0263-2373(98)00049-8

Lassar, W. M., Chris, M., & Lassar, S. S. (2005). The relationship between consumer innovativeness, personal characteristics, and online banking adoption. *International Journal of Bank Marketing, 23*(2), 176–199. doi:10.1108/02652320510584403

Merrie, B. (2000). Price and Brand Name as Indicators of Quality Dimensions of Customer Durables. *Journal of the Academy of Marketing Science, 28*(3), 359–374. doi:10.1177/0092070300283005

Paul, I., & Marion, D. (2003). Successful New Product Pricing Practices: A Contingency Approach. *Marketing Letters, 14*(4), 289–305. doi:10.1023/B:MARK.0000012473.92160.3d

Pederson Christian, S. (2000). Sparsing Risk and Return in CAPM: A General Utility Based Model. *European Journal of Operational Research, 123*(3), 628–639. doi:10.1016/S0377-2217(99)00114-9

Perraudin William, R. M., & Sorensen, B. E. (2000). The Demand of Risky Assets: Sample Selection and Household Portfolios. *Journal of Econometrics, 97*(1), 117–144. doi:10.1016/S0304-4076(99)00069-X

Rajagopal, , & Sanchez, R. (2004). Conceptual Analysis of Brand Architecture and Relations within Product Categories. *The Journal of Brand Management, 11*(3), 233–247. doi:10.1057/palgrave.bm.2540169

Rajagopal. (2005). Measuring Variability Factors in Consumer Values for Profit Optimization in a Firm – A Framework for Analysis. *Journal of Economics and Management, 1*(1), 85-103.

Rajagopal. (2006a). Measuring Customer Value Gaps: An Empirical Analysis in the Mexican Retail Market. *Economic Issue, 10*(1), 19-40.

Rajagopal. (2006b). Measuring Customer Value and Market Dynamics for New Products of a Firm: An Analytical Construct for Gaining Competitive Advantage. *Global Business and Economics Review, 8*(3-4), 187-205.

Reichheld, F. F., & Sasser, W. E. (1990). Zero Defections: Quality Comes to Services. *Harvard Business Review, 68*, 105–111. PMID:10107082

Reinartz, W. J., & Kumar, V. (2000). On the Profitability of Long-Life Customers in a Non- contractual Setting: An Empirical investigation and implementation for Marketing. *Journal of Marketing, 64*(4), 17–35. doi:10.1509/jmkg.64.4.17.18077

Reinartz, W. J., & Kumar, V. (2002). The Mismanagement of Customer Loyalty. *Harvard Business Review*, (July), 4–12. PMID:12140857

Sullivan, R. J. (2000). *How Has the Adoption of Internet Banking Affected Performance and Risk in Banks? A Look at Internet Banking in the Tenth Federal Reserve District*. Financial Industry Perspective, Federal Reserve Bank of Kansas City, Occasional Papers.

Sullivan, R. J., & Zhu, W. (2005). *Internet Banking: An Exploration in Technology Diffusion and Impact*. Federal Reserve Bank of Kansas City, Payments System Research Working Paper # PSR-WP-05-05.

Tucker, W. T. (1964). The Development of Brand Loyalty. *JMR, Journal of Marketing Research, 1*(3), 32–35. doi:10.2307/3150053

Ulf, J., Maria, M., & Matti, S. (2001). Measuring to Understand intangible Performance Drivers. *European Accounting Review, 10*(3), 407–437. doi:10.1080/09638180126791

Zeithaml, V., Berry, L., & Parasuraman, A. (1988). Communication and Control Process the Delivery of Services Quality. *Journal of Marketing, 52*(2), 35–48. doi:10.2307/1251263

Zhiwei, Z., & Larry, S. (2004). Information network technology in the banking industry. *Industrial Management & Data Systems, 104*(5), 409–417. doi:10.1108/02635570410537499

Zhu, W. (2005). *Technology Innovation and Market Turbulence: A Dot com Example*. Federal Reserve Bank of Kansas City, Payments System Research Working Paper # PSR-WP-05-02.

Section 4
Corporate Performance, Marketing, and Socio-Economic Indicators

Chapter 12
Corporate Social Responsibility and Corporate Governance:
Analysis across Industries in Mexico

Andrée Marie López-Fernández
Universidad Panamericana, Mexico

ABSTRACT

Corporate Social Responsibility (CSR) and corporate governance are two distinct concepts that may seem to be isolated in practice. However, there are many parallels to the extent that the latter may define the engagement of the former. As such, it may be argued that corporate governance is essential to the implementation of CSR. Thus, a question arises, are firms' governance policies conducive to the engagement in corporate social responsibility? This study aims to evaluate the dynamics between corporate social responsibility and corporate governance of multinational firms operating in Mexico. Findings indicate that the practice of disclosing corporate social responsibility is more common than the transparent communication of corporate governance; however, the compliance with corporate governance is consistent with that of corporate social responsibility within the analysed firms.

INTRODUCTION

Corporate social responsibility (CSR) is an important element in business dynamics. It is a clear indicator that firms are not only concerned with the interests and needs of all current and potential stakeholders, but are also creative and proactive in tackling social issues that permeate society and the environment. The choice to actively engage in corporate social responsibility practices sends a distinct message to all current and potential interested parties that the firm's moral compass is aligned with that of its stakeholders, and that the organization is looking out for the best interests and wellbeing of the societal ambiance in which it operates.

One of the elements that first brought corporate governance to flourish was that organizational leaders found the need to prioritize shareholders' requirements and interests in the firms' operations. However, the mere compliance with shareholders' needs and wants resulted insufficient, as organizational leaders

DOI: 10.4018/978-1-5225-0902-8.ch012

came to understand that shareholders were not the only parties with stake in the organization; as such, stakeholders' objectives and interests became essential to the business dynamics of organizations, as well as the achievement of the organizations' desired performance. The engagement in corporate social responsibility, then, is indicative of the attributes and value of a firm's governance.

The concepts of corporate social responsibility and corporate governance have several elements in common. First, neither are new concepts, companies have always had, to some extent, social and environmental interests as well as policies, structures and norms that direct the organization and its dynamics. Second, there are no universal definitions for the concepts, rather there are as many as there are types of organizations. And, third, the approach to corporate social responsibility and corporate governance systems well depends on the type of organization, management and leadership styles, structure, among others.

In 1989, Belkaoui and Karpik argued that disclosing an organization's social information was voluntary; today, transparently communicating corporate social responsibility efforts and corporate governance policies still remains a voluntary practice. As such, it may seem that there has been little advancement on the matter; however, perhaps the most significant change has been in stakeholders' interest to know and understand organizations' business dynamics, their stance on social and environmental development, as well as financial performance.

The objective of the study is to understand the relationship between the engagement in corporate social responsibility and firms' corporate governance. That said, two questions arise, is corporate governance conducive to the engagement in corporate social responsibility? And, do the attributes of corporate governance lead to a sustainable engagement in corporate social responsibility? In order to address the general objective of the study and the research questions, content analysis was employed to evaluate the relationship between the governance and social responsibility of multinational firms operating in Mexico. The paper is sectioned as follows. Section two reviews previous literature on both corporate social responsibility and corporate governance, as well as their relationship. Section three includes the study design and section four encompasses a discussion on the study's findings. Section five includes concluding remarks, limitations of the study and directions for future research.

LITERATURE REVIEW

The existence of an organization significantly depends on stakeholders' acknowledgement of its legitimacy (Deegan, 2002), and accountability. Corporate social responsibility (CSR) is an important strategy carried out by organizations with the aim to address certain social and environmental issues. It is a concept that has many definitions; it is charged with different meanings for diverse organizations (Crowther & Rayman-Bacchus, 2004), determined by their context of operations and characteristics of business dynamics. CSR has been considered as organizations' concern for the impact of their efforts on their activities as well as on society (Bowman & Haire, 1976). CSR consists of organizations' clear communication of their policies and practices that reflect their responsibility towards the achievement of social wellbeing (Matten and Moon, 2008). And, according to Kotler and Lee (2005), corporate social responsibility is a "commitment to improve community well-being through discretionary business practices and contributions of corporate resources." Therefore, it is a firm's active use of its resources (financial and non-financial) to proactively engage in socially responsible practices with the purpose of positively contributing to society's wellbeing.

All firms have the potential to engage in corporate social responsibility; nonetheless, larger and older organizations have greater probabilities of undertaking corporate social responsibility practices because of their resources, strategic alliances, objectives, and experience (Stanwick & Stanwick, 1998). According to Chapple and Moon (2005a), firms operating in two or more countries, otherwise known as multinational companies, are more likely to engage in corporate social responsibility as well as be more sensitive to the corporate social responsibility agendas of the regions in which they operate. The firms that have achieved financial stability, which tend to be older and/or larger, also are more likely to be actively engaged in corporate social responsibility.

CSR Involvement Around the World

Firms' stance on social involvement seems to vary with the region in which they operate. Organizations in the United States have been widely known for their creation and adoption of norms and policies for the development and implementation of corporate social responsibility agendas; as such, American philosophies, ethics and values are the basis of the development of the engagement in corporate social responsibility (Fig, 2005; Chapple and Moon, 2005b). Furthermore, according to Haslam (2004), the engagement in corporate social responsibility in America may be classified in four degrees of activity; Canada and the United States are "running", developed countries in Latin America are "catching-up", South American countries are "walking" and Central American and Caribbean countries are "stalled".

In Europe, corporate social responsibility objectives and strategies are mainly carried out by larger organizations (Spence & Schmidpeter, 2003), and are mostly government driven (Matten & Moon, 2008); therefore, there are slight differences with organizations operating in the United States. For instance, Maignan and Ralston (2002) conducted a study of firms' description of corporate social responsibility on their official websites and found that over fifty percent of US firms clearly describe their engagement in CSR while less than thirty percent do so in European firms. Moreover, Brammer and Pavelin (2005) found that, in 2001, community contributions delivered by US organizations were ten times more than those delivered by British firms.

It is clear that there are various approaches to corporate social responsibility which wildly depend on the country in which organizations operate, that is, the local policies, norms, needs, and wants. A study conducted with Australian companies regarding their community involvement found that about seventy five percent of the firms consider that their sustainability based on community involvement is one of their goals (CCPA, 2000). Russian organizations have, for example, slowly begun to implement policies in transparency and accountability due to an increased participation in international operations (OECD, 2008). Therefore, there are contrasting approaches where in Australia organizations consider CSR to be part of their business dynamics and Russian organizations seem to be adopting corporate social responsibility initiatives as a way to participate in the market.

There are also examples where governments have begun to mobilize regulatory authorities to create legislature to successfully stimulate the engagement in corporate social responsibility in order to have a positive effect on societal development and growth. The Nigerian government has made significant efforts to promote that certain contributions related to corporate social responsibility are made mandatory for organizations to do businesses in the country (Forstater, Zadek, Guang, Yu, Hong & George, 2010). And, in 2013, the Indian government approved the Companies Act in which it is stated under Article 135 that organizations should tend to local areas and/or the communities surrounding (i.e. the areas in which they operate), when delegating expenses related to their corporate social responsibility practices (Rossow, 2015).

Interests in corporate social responsibility have continuously increased in developing countries (Ferre, Melgar & Rossi, 2010), however, corporate social responsibility agendas in Latin America and the Caribbean are still in beginning stages; the engagement in corporate social responsibility is still largely based on the countries' socioeconomic and political conditions (De Oliveira, 2006), and have traditionally been more focused on the countries' social issues (Schmidheiny, 2006). It was not until the 1990s when, in Latin America, corporate social responsibility became known as a significant element in business dynamics (Correa, Flynn, & Amit, 2004).

More developed countries in Latin America, such as Brazil, have shown a significant advancement as hundreds of organizations have begun to transparently communicate their corporate social responsibility endeavours by developing formal annual reports (Correa, Flynn, and Amit, 2004). Corporate social responsibility is not a new practice in Mexico (Logsdon, Thomas, and Van Buren III, 2006) as, in 1988, the civil association Mexican centre for philanthropy, *Centro Mexicano para la Filantropía (Cemefi)* to oversee recognitions to socially responsible organizations (Cemefi, 2013). Nonetheless, organizations operating in Mexico that engage in corporate social responsibility are usually large and multinational firms and non-profit organizations, therefore, the societal ambiance and other organizations do not tend to recognize their CSR involvement (Rosas, 2010).

Organizations operating in Latin America and the Caribbean that engage in corporate social responsibility are encouraged to design and execute strategies that allow them to work with the communities that are located in the areas in which such organizations operate (Casanova & Dumas, 2010). Community involvement is important not only for the organizations' achievement of strategic objectives, but also to nurture the relationship with stakeholders. According to Niello (2006), there is a long history of restrictions and abuse in the region on behalf of governmental and regulatory authorities which has created a sense of distrust amongst stakeholders towards most types of institutions, organizations, policy makers, and, in general, authority figures. Therefore, this difficult relationship requires special attention, that is, organizations need to do much more than just stating that they engage in corporate social responsibility practices, they have to make sufficient efforts to promote their actions through transparent and timely communication.

There are many reasons why organizations operating in Latin America and the Caribbean have shown to be falling behind in the development and execution of corporate social responsibility strategies and practices. The reasons include, the notion that profit is organizations only responsibility, lack of required compliance with CSR regulations, lack of civil society's active participation in business dynamics, and the notion that CSR is not a priority (López-Fernández & Rajagopal, 2013). Further, there are few or no local corporate social responsibility initiatives (Peinado-Vara, 2006); that is, most organizations that do engage in CSR do so by adhering to international guidelines and/or standards. Pratt and Fintel (2002) argue that such delay is mostly due to government's institutional capacity or lack thereof; that is, the lack of engagement in CSR is a reflection of government and regulatory authorities' procrastination on the issue at hand. And, according to Chong, Izquierdo, Micco and Panizza (2003) the deferment in corporate social responsibility engagement is due to the organizations' weak corporate governance; meaning that, organizations' formidable and efficient corporate governance is elemental to the effective engagement in corporate social responsibility.

Corporate social responsibility may aid in the development of public policy, control resources via strategic partnerships, and make other significant resources available (UN, 2007). Thus, there is great, or even greater, need for corporate social responsibility practices in developing countries because of existing lack of governance and societal requirements (Dobers & Halme, 2009) to achieve wellbeing. CSR is also a means by which firms determine the way that their stakeholders will be treated, furthermore, according to Hopkins (1998), "behaving socially responsibly will increase the human development of stakeholders both within and outside the corporation." Thus, corporate social responsibility speaks of organizations' managerial and leadership styles, strategic objectives, and tactics. CSR practices, therefore, reflect the organizations' belief system, one might say it reveals the essence of an organization and its direction, which is a lot like their corporate governance.

Corporate governance has been defined and explained through two main models; one model focuses on the relationship between various stakeholders, and the second model focuses on the maximization of shareholder value; further, Hilb (2012) has proposed a model of "new corporate governance" which incorporates elements from both models. Corporate governance is a set of processes and procedures that determine the manner in which an organization is directed and controlled (OECD, 2005), as well as made responsive to current and potential stakeholders' rights and requirements (Demb & Neubauer, 1992). According to the ASX Corporate Governance Council (2003), corporate governance is the organization's system that indicates the way it is managed. Furthermore, such system defines the way that the organization's objectives are determined, risk is assessed, and performance is improved. Its purpose is to fulfil effective decision making through policies, rules, procedures, and structures that allow an organization to control its activities (Baker and Anderson, 2010). Further, the effectivity of an organization's corporate governance leads to productivity, efficiency and positive effects on the societal ambiance (Solomon, 2007).

Most organizational leaders are concerned with the achievement of competitive advantage and added value, and corporate governance can, in fact, influence the organization's performance by addressing the interests of shareholders (Baker and Anderson, 2010), and stakeholders in general. The structure of corporate governance is particular to each firm and defines the rules for decision making, each stakeholder's rights and responsibilities (OECD, 2005) and, thus, their accountability. The efficiency of a firm's corporate governance has to do with its business dynamics, including its practices, compliance, disclosure or transparency, and enforcement (Berglöf & Claessens, 2006). Furthermore, it produces significant results when it is worked with other organizational structural measures (Capaul, 2003).

Disclosure of CSR and Corporate Governance

A strong, long-lasting relationship with current and potential stakeholders is elemental to the achievement of organizations' objectives and their desired performance. Therefore, firms need not only to engage in socially responsible practices and sustain an effective corporate governance system, but also need to effectively communicate their endeavours with current and potential stakeholders. Reporting or disclosure is the practice of an organization sharing its information (Solomon, 2007) via formal or informal communication; reporting on corporate social responsibility and corporate governance is usually carried out through formal annual reports (Patten, 1991; Solomon, 2007) and/or through their official websites (UNCTAD, 2008); however, there are many other platforms on which organizations may communicate their endeavours with current and potential stakeholders, such as, social media (Fernández & Rajagopal, 2014), product labels and advertising material (European Commission, 2013), among many others.

The practice of reporting or disclosure is principally accomplished voluntarily because, in the majority of cases, there is little or no regulation that deems such practice as obligatory. This also means that there are a vast number of organizations worldwide that lag behind in the process of transparently communicating their policies, actions and outcomes. This ultimately results in a disservice to the organization, as the lack of communication leads current and potential stakeholders to make misinformed decisions which may, potentially, negatively impact the organization's performance.

Voluntary disclosure, which is reporting above the minimum required (Core, 2001), enables organizational leaders to inform the public of their actions as well as encourage the acceptance of the organization's views (Zerban, 2013). The practice of disclosing significantly improves and organization's transparency (Solomon, 2007) which attracts potential investors (Kim and Verecchia, 1994), and increases their sense of ownership (Healy, Hutton and Palepu, 1999). Since reporting is a form of self-presentation which informs stakeholders of the organization's public behaviours, it is possible to uphold their satisfaction as interested parties (Snider, Hill, & Martin, 2003). Furthermore, effectively reporting stimulates a sense of trust towards the firm which is essential as stakeholders value organizations' honesty (O'Connor & Meister, 2008).

Elements of CSR and Corporate Governance

There are several attributes of corporate social responsibility and corporate governance which should be transparently communicated with current and potential stakeholders in order for them to be informed of the firm's practices. Furthermore, the prompt communication of said attributes may be a strong determinant in the satisfaction of the firm's stakeholders.

According to Rogerson (2004), there are six elements in corporate social responsibility, including the firm's "investment in community outreach, employee relations, creation and maintenance of employment, environmental responsibility, human rights, and financial performance." Dahlsrud (2008) argues that there are five dominant elements in corporate social responsibility, these being dimensions related to the firm's social, economic, environmental, stakeholder, and voluntary policies and actions. And, CSR Europe has stated that the CSR guidelines are focused on six elements, the firm's workplace, marketplace, its impact on the environment and the community, as well as the firm's stance on ethics and human rights (CSR Europe, 2000). That said, Carroll and Buchholtz (2008) posit that stakeholders want to be informed of firms' stance on sustainability and fair trade commerce, as well as their workplace conditions, community involvement, and social and environmental impacts.

In regards to corporate governance, Drew, Kelley and Kendrick (2006) state that there are five elements that organizations must consider for their corporate governance in order to manage risk, including, culture, systems, structure, leadership, and alignment. Black, Jang, and Kim (2006) argue that the elements of corporate governance include shareholder rights, board structure, board procedures, audit committees, and disclosure; and, Demb and Neubauer (1992) make reference to ownership, board structure, regulations or codes, and direct social pressure as the basic attributes of corporate governance. There are several international organizations that provide guidelines on what attributes should be included in organizations' reports. Table 1 incorporates a brief description of elements that international organizations state that should be included in formal reports on corporate social responsibility and corporate governance.

The decision to report on social information is explained by organizations' social performance and political visibility (Belkaoui & Karpik, 1989). The disclosure of corporate social responsibility is equally as important as that of corporate governance. Transparently disclosing CSR practices is significant as it improves organizational performance and enhances corporate image (Maguire, 2011); the latter leads stakeholders to acknowledge the organization's accountability (UNCTAD, 2008; Solomon, 2007),

Table 1. A brief description of international guidelines for reporting on corporate social responsibility and corporate governance

Corporate social responsibility				
Global Reporting Initiative (GRI, 2013)	Corporate governance	Commitment to external initiatives	Awards and recognitions	Financial indicators and performance
	Stakeholders	Environmental indicators and performance	Social indicators and performance, supply chain, training and human rights, among others	
United Nations Global Compact, (UN Global Compact, 2013)	Human rights	Anticorruption	Labour	Business and peace
	Environment	Financial markets	Supply chain sustainability	United Nations-business partnership
	Business for development			
Organization for Economic Co-operation and Development (OECD, 2011)	Policies	Communication	Human rights	Research and development
	Competition	Environment	Anticorruption	Stakeholder relationships
	Employees	Taxation		
The World Business Council for Sustainable Development (WBCSD, 2013)	Natural capital referring to ecosystems, forest and water solutions, energy and climate, electric utilities, and greenhouse gas protocols			
	Business applications related to cement sustainability, chemical use, efficient buildings, infrastructure, and others			
	Social capital involving inclusive growth and performance			
	Capacity building including value chain, education, stakeholders, among others			
	Financial capital referring to investments and formal reporting			
Corporate governance				
Ministry of Corporate Affairs. Government of India (MCA, 2009)	Board of directors	Auditors	Audit committee of board	Responsibilities of the board
	Secretarial audit	Institutional mechanism for whistleblowing		

it positively influences consumer behaviour, collaborators' motivation, and enhances brand loyalty, (European Commission, 2013), among others. Similarly, disclosing corporate governance principals provides stakeholders with a clear understanding of processes and procedures, decision making (TSX, 2006), the company's manoeuvres, and guarantees that the organization is acting in the best interest of its stakeholders (UN, 2006).

The communication of both CSR and corporate governance are essential to maintaining a long-term relationship with current and potential stakeholders. Nonetheless, although firms are gradually perfecting their reporting policies, in practice, the disclosure remains inconclusive (Chatterjee, 2011). Many organizations operating in developed countries and those in development alike are still merely informally communicating their intentions to be socially responsible; likewise, they only mention general statements regarding their corporate governance system. This type of communication reads as organizational initiatives, rather than standardized processes and procedures that guide an organization's business dynamics. Informal reporting is fruitful provided that the firm either also has a formal report or gradually steers its disclosure towards a full-blown, detailed and comprehensive formal report.

The elements that most determine a firm's reporting practice are size (Adams, Hill and Roberts, 1998; Gray, Javad, Power & Sinclair, 2001), age (Singh & Ahuja, 1983), capital structure (Cormier & Gordon, 2001), financial performance (Herremaus, Akathaporn, & McInnes, 1993; Stanwick & Stanwick, 1998), industry associates and membership (Baker & Naser, 2000), overseas' status, and number of independent board directors (Chatterjee, 2011). Therefore, there are many aspects that may lead organizations to be more proactive in their transparent communication of policies, actions and results. This also means that the practice of reporting is not limited to one type of organization. Furthermore, although there are many guidelines for proper disclosure and organizations are somewhat pressured to do so, the decision to report such information, both on corporate governance and CSR, remains a voluntary practice.

Gray, Owen and Maunders (1987) have stated that reporting on corporate social responsibility is carried out by an accountable organization in order to disclose information on their social accountability. Firms are improving their engagement in CSR by creating codes of conduct which are operationalized within the firm and throughout the supply chain. Further, firms are also collaborating with international organizations as to address their CSR on a global scale; the latter is done by aligning strategic objectives with the UN Global Compact's ten principals, the Eight Millennium Development Goals, the International Business Leaders Forum, and the Global Reporting Initiative, among others (Kolk, 2005; Moon, 2007).

There are many advantages to the engagement in corporate social responsibility, most of which are also advantages of corporate governance. Firms, then, may benefit from improved corporate image, competitive advantage, cost reduction, stakeholder added value and satisfaction (Porter and Kramer, 2006; Xueming and Bhattacharya, 2006; Utting, 2005; Rochlin et al; 2005). And effective disclosure informs current and potential stakeholders of the organizations' alignment with society's values, their principals, stance on social responsibility, enables them to assure investments, and is a solid tactic when facing pressure groups (O'Donovan, 2002). Furthermore, reporting also opens the doors to the achievement of stakeholder dialogue via firm-to-stakeholder proactive and transparent communication (López-Fernández & Rajagopal, 2015).

Study Design

The main objective of this study is to understand the relationship between firms' engagement in corporate social responsibility and their corporate governance guidelines. The nature of the analysis was qualitative; the corporate governance and corporate social responsibility reports of twenty five multinational companies operating in Mexico were evaluated with content analysis (Chatterjee, 2011; Nerantzidis et al; 2012). The twenty five firms were chosen from a purposively selected sample. There were three principal criteria taken into consideration for the selection of the studied firms: first, firms should have stated to be actively engaging in corporate social responsibility and have received a recognition for their social responsibility awarded by the *Centro Mexicano para la Filantropía*, Mexican Centre for philanthropy (Cemefi, 2013); second, all firms should have stated to have well-defined corporate governance; and third, all firms either should have had a corporate social responsibility and a corporate governance report, or a report that included both elements.

The information was collected over a period of two months; there was consistency throughout the period, meaning that, the firms in question did not alter or amend their CSR and/or corporate governance reports during such time. The sample included companies operating in various industries in order to obtain a panoramic view of firms' governance and engagement in corporate social responsibility in different contexts of business dynamics. In total, thirteen industries were incorporated in the analysis, these including, the beverage, pharmaceutical, banking, food, construction, electric, computer, digital and IT, retail, consumer goods, mining, automobile, and technology industries.

Findings and Discussion

There are many elements that may be incorporated into a corporate social responsibility report; for the purpose of this study, such elements were grouped into nine sections or domains including, governance, communication, regulation, industry membership, financial performance, environmental performance, operations, work environment, and social performance. Correspondingly, the elements encompassed in a corporate governance report were grouped into nine sections or domains including, management mission and leadership, board structure (policies, norms, and standards), ethics, disclosure and communication, stakeholder rights and relations, risk management, fair remuneration, regulatory framework, and performance evaluation.

The availability of reports is essential because disclosure is important for the firms' business dynamics as well as current and potential stakeholders' decision making. In reference to CSR, all evaluated firms share reports which are available on their official websites; however, only seven report in Spanish, thirteen in English and five in both languages. Twenty one out of the twenty five firms analysed report their corporate governance through their official website; from the latter, eight firms share information on their corporate governance at a global rather than on a local level (i.e. for Mexico). Three firms only provide statements on their website, that is, such firms do not have formal reports on their corporate governance but do briefly describe certain aspects of their governance, such as bylaws, management, and structure. Four firms report in Spanish and the rest in English. The latter is significant because being as though English is learned as a second language in Mexico the understanding of the content of the reports may be difficult, despite their availability, therefore, lowering potential influence on decision making.

The differences between the two types of reports are quite subtle, particular similarities and differences that were found during the study include stakeholder relations, governance, working conditions, disclosure, and performance indicators. In a CSR report domains regarding stakeholders might make reference to stakeholder dialogue whilst in corporate governance reports might reference their rights and relations. In corporate social responsibility reports the firm's governance generalities is required, and, in most cases, this domain includes the management mission and leadership and board structure which are relevant elements of a corporate governance report. A CSR report, in reference to the working environment, may include indicators of turnover, incidents, accidents, fair wages, equal payment, gender equality in top management, among others, while a corporate governance report may adhere to disclosing matters on remuneration or fair compensation.

Communication is essential for both types of reports, as well as regulations, labour conditions, execution monitoring and firms' stance on ethics. Further, while corporate social responsibility reports often hold specific information regarding the firms' financial, environmental and social performance, corporate governance reports tend to only incorporate the firms' undertakings of risk management. Therefore, there are many general aspects that overlap in both types of reports; it is the specific details of business dynamics that differentiate one from the other. Furthermore, this also means that compliance with both corporate social responsibility and corporate governance reports is important to the satisfaction of current and potential stakeholders.

Initially, it seems as though these analysed firms consider that corporate social responsibility is more mainstream than corporate governance. In the sense that CSR would seem to be of greater interest to stakeholders and, as such, firms are more particular in their communication of CSR practices with their current and potential stakeholders. This was also explained by the availability of the reports. Corporate social responsibility reports were found with more ease than corporate governance reports. Meaning that, locating corporate governance reports was more time-consuming as their whereabouts on the firms' official websites was not evident. This poses a problem for effective communication because it is fair to say that a significant number of stakeholders will, in all probability, not invest too much time searching for a firm's corporate governance report.

Findings indicate that, generally speaking, the firms that are more transparent with their governance are more likely to be compliant with the disclosure of their socially responsible policies, actions and results. The firms that are active in the practice of disclosure, then, tend to share information on both their CSR endeavours, as well as their corporate governance system. Nonetheless, upon further analysis, it was found that the firms in question that have a greater compliance with CSR related guidelines are more prone to comply with the standards for disclosing corporate governance attributes. Table 2 illustrates the relationship between the analysed firms' compliance within their corporate social responsibility report and their disclosure of corporate governance domains.

In regards to the corporate social responsibility reports, there was an overall compliance of roughly seventy four percent with the CSR domains considered for analysis. Only seven firms comply with each of the nine abovementioned sections. There was only one firm that did not disclose any information on its environmental performance, which makes such domain the most complied with. Regulations and industry membership account for a compliance of sixty four percent. And, results show that governance, communication and work environment each present eighty four percent compliance rate. However, the compliance with work environment was found to be the least detailed section of the reports. Meaning that, the firms merely refer to their workers' conditions on a superficial level.

Information on the firms' operations was the domain with least compliance (i.e. forty eight percent), followed by financial performance (i.e. fifty two percent). The latter would indicate that the firms consider that said domains are of little importance to their CSR or that stakeholders have little or no interest in the firms' operations and financial performance. However, stakeholders' preferences and tone and content of their word-of-mouth, especially accomplished via social media, regarding firms' operations would indicate the contrary. For instance, a number of companies worldwide have been targeted via Twitter with the hashtag *#boycott*, because of extreme dissatisfaction with the firms' actions including: manufacturing processes, workers' exploitation, animal cruelty, exploitation of local suppliers, tax evasion, among many others. This type of stakeholder-to-stakeholder communication clearly illustrates how stakeholders

Table 2. Firms' CSR and corporate governance compliance with domains

Corporate social responsibility	Firm Compliance	Corporate governance	Firm Compliance
Governance	84	Management mission and leadership	92
Communication	84	Board structure	88
Regulation	64	Ethics	72
Industry membership	64	Disclosure and communication	76
Financial performance	52	Stakeholder rights and relations	40
Environmental performance	96	Risk management	60
Operations	48	Fair remuneration	60
Work environment	84	Regulatory framework	68
Social performance	88	Performance evaluation	80

are, in fact, concerned with organizations' operations and performance. Therefore, not disclosing such information is detrimental to firms' reputation and, in turn, their business growth and development.

As stated above, twenty one firms address their corporate governance within their corporate social responsibility formal reports. This means that these firms consider their corporate governance to be a part of their CSR practices, that is, it is one of their social responsibilities. As such, these firms believe that their corporate governance should be adequately disclosed and communicated with current and potential stakeholders in alignment with their CSR endeavours. Further, within the corporate governance domain, only eighteen firms (i.e. seventy two percent) described the relevance of their social responsibility. This is interesting because, although the report is on corporate social responsibility, twenty eight percent of the firms failed in the simplest task of stating the significance of their engagement in CSR. In these cases, the firms' corporate governance system is not conducive to the proactive engagement in corporate social responsibility.

To no surprise, as it is a report on corporate social responsibility, the second domain most complied with was social performance. Interestingly enough, three firms do not report on their social performance. Said firms are those with overall least disclosure; the first firm only reports on its environmental performance, the second on communication, and the third on its environmental performance and working conditions. In these cases, having a corporate social responsibility report seems to be more of a trend as not disclosing results on social performance defeats the purpose of preparing such a report. Furthermore, these firms happen to be three of the four firms with less corporate governance compliance reported. Therefore, thus far, the greater firms' engagement and disclosure of CSR policies, actions and results, the greater their disclosure of corporate governance bylaws, structures, and standards.

In relation to the corporate governance reports, a compliance of approximately seventy one percent with the domains was found. Although all firms state that corporate governance is elemental to their operations and business dynamics, four firms do not offer a formal report; from the latter, the first firm only discloses information on management mission and leadership and board structure, the second on board structure, and the third and fourth do not communicate any of their corporate governance undertakings. It is clear that for these four firms, corporate governance is either not as important as they state it to be, or consider its disclosure to be inconsequential or that it does not add value. In other words, in the cases of these firms, stakeholders' knowledge of the firms' corporate governance system is unnecessary. This lack of reporting is, again, detrimental because the firms are assuming that all stakeholders' behaviour is homogeneous in that none of them are remotely interested in the way that the firms are directed and controlled.

Three firms did not disclose information on their management mission and leadership, making said domain the most complied with as ninety two percent of the firms reporting on their style of management; however, only seventy two percent made reference to their overall corporate strategy. Many firms may question the need to disclose their corporate strategy, though, as it is a core element in their business dynamics, it may be of interest to current and potential stakeholders. Moreover, eighty eight percent indicated their protocols and standards and seventy two percent mentioned policies and norms. These domains are very important to stakeholders as they indicate the delimitations of the firms' operations; in a sense, it gives stakeholders an idea of the boundaries that the firms consider when seeking to achieve their strategic objectives. Eighty percent of the firms complied with their performance evaluation, however, only nineteen firms (i.e. seventy six percent) stated to implement monitoring of the execution of their policies, processes and procedures. A lack of monitoring ultimately means that there is a lack of evaluation and/or internal auditing. This could indicate a couple of things, one, the firms are not assessing the intricacies of their system or, two, the firms do not consider reporting on their monitoring practices relevant to current and potential stakeholders.

Findings show that sixty percent of the firms complied with the section of risk management, but, only fifty two percent of the firms (i.e. thirteen), stated their key risks and opportunities. This depicts firms' position on risk, that is, they intend to have a strategic plan to address potential risk. Nonetheless, the firms either do not have any key risks and opportunities, which is extremely unlikely, or they consider that transparently sharing such information is not beneficial to the firms or stakeholders' decision making. Interestingly, the rights of stakeholders and relations with them accounted for the least compliance (i.e. forty percent), followed by fair remuneration or compensation accounting for sixty percent compliance. Hence, the practice of reporting on corporate governance continues to be somewhat incomplete, and some would say arbitrary. It is clear that there are, for the case of this study, no regulations that determine the specific elements that should be complied with, however, as was stated in the review of literature, there are many international organizations that provide sufficient information on the dos and don'ts of corporate governance disclosure.

In the majority of cases, eighteen, the compliance with corporate social responsibility domains was greater or equal to the compliance with corporate governance. However, results also indicate that the firms do not necessarily consider CSR compliance and disclosure to be equally as important as corporate governance. Table 3 illustrates the firms' individual compliance with corporate social responsibility and corporate governance reports. As may be appreciated, only eight firms complied equally with CSR domains and corporate governance domains; the lowest compliance rate, among such firms, was seventy eight percent. The latter indicates that the firms that consider that CSR is equally as important as corporate governance tend to be more active in their practice of disclosure.

Seven firms presented a higher compliance with corporate governance than with corporate social responsibility; the lowest compliance rate was twenty two percent with corporate governance and eleven

Table 3. Firms' corporate social responsibility (CSR) and corporate governance (CG) report compliance (figures in percent)

Firm	CSR compliance	CG compliance	Firm	CSR compliance	CG compliance
1	100	100	14	100	78
2	100	67	15	67	100
3	89	67	16	100	100
4	89	89	17	89	89
5	78	100	18	22	78
6	11	22	19	100	67
7	11	0	20	89	78
8	89	100	21	56	11
9	100	100	22	67	89
10	78	89	23	89	89
11	22	0	24	78	78
12	56	56	25	100	67
13	67	44			

percent with CSR domains. Ten firms demonstrated a higher compliance with CSR than with corporate governance; the lowest compliance rate, for said firms, was eleven percent for CSR and zero for corporate governance. The latter is consistent with the notion that neither corporate social responsibility nor corporate governance are significant or add value to the firms and their current and potential stakeholders' decision making.

The attributes of the firms' corporate governance seem to be well aligned with those of CSR. For instance, twenty three of the firms that state communication as an important element in their governance also demonstrated compliance with the communication domain in the CSR report. The twenty firms that disclose regulatory frameworks in their corporate governance report also communicate on regulations in their CSR report. And the twenty three firms that provide specifics on the board structure and management mission and leadership have incorporated the disclosure of governance in their CSR reports. Nevertheless, only one of the analysed firms included all aspects of corporate social responsibility and corporate governance into a formal annual report. This firm, then, optimizes its disclosure by eliminating redundancies and providing current and potential stakeholders with a transparent overview of the firm's dynamics. In such case, the organization's corporate governance is conducive to its engagement in CSR as its policies, norms, and standards are designed to incorporate social responsibility within its dynamics.

Finally, it was found that the firms' reports varied in compliance in accordance with the industries they belong to. In reference to the analysed firms' CSR reports, the beverage, construction, computing, retail, banking, mining, and pharmaceutical industries were most compliant with the transparent communication of their endeavours. In regards to corporate governance reports, the beverage, banking, electric, computing, and consumer goods industries presented greater compliance within their reports. Therefore, findings indicate that the industries of the companies analysed in this study that are more socially responsible and disclose their corporate governance are the beverage, banking, and computing industries; however, the firms that operate within the electric and construction industries are not far behind.

CONCLUSION

There is still no regulation in Mexico that requires firms to disclose their policies, actions, and results; that is, transparent communication on corporate social responsibility and corporate governance continues to be a voluntary practice. However, the fact that the firms are actively disclosing social information as well as governance information is important for current and potential stakeholders' decision making. Because stakeholders' interests to know and understand the dynamics of firms have increasingly grown, transparent disclosure may, ultimately, have a positive impact on stakeholders' perspectives of the organizations. Stakeholders respond positively to firms that not only act in a socially responsible manner, but also to organizations that are honest in their practices. Such response leads to trust in the firm, satisfaction, enhanced corporate image, positive stakeholder-to-stakeholder word-of-mouth, brand loyalty, and, in turn, business growth of the firm.

It seems as though firms still consider that corporate governance is of little or no importance to stakeholders or, at least, of less interest than corporate social responsibility. The latter would certainly explain why the analysed firms have not made enough efforts to transparently communicate their standards, bylaws, and structure with current and potential stakeholders. It is plausible that the analysed firms consider that CSR practices should be shared because of the social impact of their endeavours, or that the disclosure of corporate governance remains an internal issue and, thus, not worthy of being shared with potential stakeholders.

For all intents and purposes, and in accordance with the literature and organizational practices, corporate governance should be conducive to corporate social responsibility because it is the system that guides the operations of an organization; however, the analysed firms operating in Mexico are demonstrating the opposite. It would seem that the firms have succumb to the notion, or the understanding, that socially responsible practices sit well with stakeholders' perceptions that influence their decision making in a way that corporate governance does not. The fact of the matter is that firms considering that the disclosure of their information is inconsequential or that it does not add value, are absolutely missing out on the potential positive effects of communicating, that is, providing current and potential stakeholders with valuable information which, in turn, serves as determinants for their decision making.

STUDY LIMITATIONS AND FUTURE RESEARCH DIRECTIONS

The study's limitations include the sample size, as only twenty five multinational firms operating in Mexico were considered for analysis. That in mind, future research could analyse a greater sample of firms considering the differences in regulations and norms in the various countries in which they operate. Also, the implications of the engagement in corporate social responsibility and the disclosure of corporate governance and CSR on stakeholder perspectives of the firms may be analysed. Further, a cross-cultural analysis may be implemented as to determine the implications of the differences in corporate social responsibility and corporate governance engagement within industries, as well as their transparent and prompt disclosure.

REFERENCES

Adams, C. A., Hill, W. Y., & Roberts, C. B. (1998). Corporate social reporting practices in western Europe: Legitimating corporate behaviour? *The British Accounting Review*, *30*(1), 1–21. doi:10.1006/bare.1997.0060

ASX Corporate Governance Council. (2003). *Principles of good corporate governance and best practice recommendations*. Retrieved August 25, 2015, from http://www.shareholder.com/shared/dynamicdoc/ASX/364/ASXRecommendations.pdf

Baker, H. K., & Anderson, R. (2010). *Corporate governance: A synthesis of theory, research, and practice*. Hoboken, NJ: John Wiley & Sons, Inc. doi:10.1002/9781118258439

Baker, N. A., & Naser, K. (2000). Empirical evidence on corporate social disclosure practices on Jordan. *International Journal of Commerce and Management*, *10*(3/4), 18–34. doi:10.1108/eb047406

Belkaoui, A., & Karpik, P. G. (1989). Determinants of the corporate decision to disclose social information. *Accounting, Auditing & Accountability Journal*, *2*(1), 36–51. doi:10.1108/09513578910132240

Berglöf, E., & Claessens, S. (2006, March). Enforcement and good corporate governance in developing countries and transition economies. *The World Bank Research Observer*, *21*(1), 123–150. doi:10.1093/wbro/lkj005

Black, B. S., Jang, H., & Kim, W. (2006). Does corporate governance predict firms market values? Evidence from Korea. *Journal of Law Economics and Organization*, *22*(2), 366–413. doi:10.1093/jleo/ewj018

Bowman, E. H., & Haire, M. (1976). Social impact disclosure and corporate annual reports. *Accounting, Organizations and Society*, *1*(1), 11–21. doi:10.1016/0361-3682(76)90004-0

Brammer, S., & Pavelin, S. (2005). Corporate community contributions in the United Kingdom and the United States. *Journal of Business Ethics*, *56*(1), 15–26. doi:10.1007/s10551-004-3236-4

Capaul, M. (2003). *Corporate governance in Latin America*. Chief Economist Office Latin America and the Caribbean Region World Bank. Retrieved August 21, 2015, from http://web.worldbank.org/archive/website00894A/WEB/PDF/CORPOR-2.PDF

Carroll, A. B., & Buchholtz, A. K. (2008). Strategic management and corporate public affairs. In A. B. Carroll, & A. K. Buchholtz (Eds.), Business and Society. Ethics and stakeholder management (7th ed.; pp. 168-171). South-Western Cengage Learning.

Casanova, L., & Dumas, A. (2010). Corporate social responsibility and Latin American multinationals: Is poverty an issue? *Universia Business Review*, *25*, 132–145.

CCPA. (2000). *Corporate community involvement: Establishing a business case*. Melbourne: Centre for Corporate Public Affairs.

Cemefi. (2013, October). *Centro Mexicano para la Filantropía*. Retrieved October 23, 2013, from Información institucional: http://www.cemefi.org/nosotros/informacion-institucional.html

Chapple, W., & Moon, J. (2005a). Corporate social responsibility (CSR) in Asia: A seven-country study of CSR web site reporting. *Business & Society*, *44*(4), 415–439. doi:10.1177/0007650305281658

Chapple, W., & Moon, J. (2005b). CSR in Asia. *Business & Society*, *44*(4), 415–441. doi:10.1177/0007650305281658

Chatterjee, D. (2011, October). A content analysis study on corporate governance reporting by Indian companies. *Corporate Reputation Review*, *14*(3), 234–246. doi:10.1057/crr.2011.13

Chong, A., Izquierdo, A., Micco, A., & Panizza, U. (2003). *Corporate governance and private capital flows to Latin America*. Washington, DC: Inter-American Development Bank.

Core, J. E. (2001). A review of the empirical disclosure literature. *Journal of Accounting and Economics*, *31*(1-3), 441–456. doi:10.1016/S0165-4101(01)00036-2

Cormier, D., & Gordon, I. M. (2001). An examination of social and environmental reporting strategies. *Accounting, Auditing & Accountability Journal*, *14*(5), 587–616. doi:10.1108/EUM0000000006264

Correa, M. E., Flynn, S., & Amit, A. (2004). *Responsabilidad social corporativa en América Latina: Una visión empresarial. Série CEPAL Medio Ambiente y Desarrollo No. 85*. Santiago, Chile: UN CEPAL.

Crowther, D., & Rayman-Bacchus, L. (2004). *Perspectives on corporate social responsibility*. London: Ashgate.

Dahlsrud, A. (2008). How corporate social responsibility is defined: An analysis of 37 definitions. *Corporate Social Responsibility and Environmental Management, 15*(1), 1–13. doi:10.1002/csr.132

De Oliveira, J. A. (2006, Spring). Corporate citizenship in Latin America: New challenges for business. *Journal of Corporate Citizenship, 21*, 17–20. doi:10.9774/GLEAF.4700.2006.sp.00003

Deegan, C. (2002). The legitimising effect of social and environmental disclosures: A theoretical foundation. *Accounting, Auditing & Accountability Journal, 15*(3), 282–312. doi:10.1108/09513570210435852

Demb, A., & Neubauer, F. F. (1992). The corporate board: Confronting the paradoxes. *Long Range Planning, 25*(3), 9–20. doi:10.1016/0024-6301(92)90364-8 PMID:10120319

Dobers, P., & Halme, M. (2009). Corporate social responsibility and developing countries. *Corporate Social Responsibility and Environmental Management, 16*(5), 237–249. doi:10.1002/csr.212

Drew, S. A., Kelley, P. C., & Kendrick, T. (2006). CLASS: Five elements of corporate governance to manage strategic risk. *Business Horizons, 49*(2), 127–138. doi:10.1016/j.bushor.2005.07.001

Europe, C. S. R. (2000). *Communicating corporate social responsibility*. Brussels: CSR Europe.

European Commission. (2013, March 19). *A guide to communicating about CSR*. Retrieved October 2013, from http://ec.europa.eu/enterprise/policies/sustainable-business/files/csr/campaign/documentation/download/guide_en.pdf

Fernández, A. M., & Rajagopal, N. A. (2014). Convergence of corporate social responsibility and business growth: An analytical framework. *International Journal of Business Excellence, 7*(6), 791–806. doi:10.1504/IJBEX.2014.065508

Ferre, Z., Melgar, N., & Rossi, M. (2010). *Corporate social responsibility in Uruguay: What enterprises do and what people think about it*. United Nations. Retrieved October 20, 2015, from http://unctad.org/en/docs/dtlktcd20102_en.pdf

Fig, D. (2005). Manufacturing amnesia: Corporate social responsibility in South Africa. *International Affairs, 81*(3), 599–617. doi:10.1111/j.1468-2346.2005.00471.x

Forstater, M., Zadek, S., Guang, Y., Yu, K., Hong, C. X., & George, M. (2010). *Corporate responsibility in African development: Insights from an emerging dialogue*. Beijing: The Institute of West-Asian and African Studies of the Chinese Academy of Social Sciences. Retrieved October 21, 2015, from http://www.iisd.org/pdf/2011/corporate_responsiblity_in_african_development.pdf

FRC. (2014). *The UK corporate governance code*. London: The Financial Reporting Council Limited. Retrieved October 23, 2015, from https://www.frc.org.uk/Our-Work/Publications/Corporate-Governance/UK-Corporate-Governance-Code-2014.pdf

Gray, R., Javad, M., Power, D. M., & Sinclair, C. D. (2001). Social and environmental disclosure and corporate characteristics: A research note and extension. *Journal of Business Finance & Accounting, 28*(3/4), 327–356. doi:10.1111/1468-5957.00376

Gray, R., Owen, D., & Maunders, K. (1987). *Corporate social reporting: Accounting and accountability*. London: Prentice-Hall.

GRI. (2013). *About GRI*. Retrieved October 23, 2013, from The Global Reporting Initiative: https://www.globalreporting.org/information/about-gri/Pages/default.aspx

Haslam, P. A. (2004). *The corporate social responsibility system in Latin America and the Caribbean*. Ottawa: Canadian Foundation for the Americas. Retrieved October 20, 2015, from http://www.focal.ca/pdf/csr_04.pdf

Healy, P. M., Hutton, A. P., & Palepu, K. G. (1999). Stock performance and intermediation changes surrounding sustained increases in disclosure. *Contemporary Accounting Research*, *16*(3), 485–520. doi:10.1111/j.1911-3846.1999.tb00592.x

Herremaus, I. M., Akathaporn, P., & McInnes, M. (1993). An investigation of corporate social responsibility reputation and economic performance. *Accounting, Organizations and Society*, *18*(7-8), 587–604. doi:10.1016/0361-3682(93)90044-7

Hilb, M. (2012). *New corporate governance. Successful board management tools*. New York: Springer. doi:10.1007/978-3-642-23595-5

Hopkins, M. (1998). *The planetary bargain: Corporate social responsibility comes of age*. London: Macmillan.

ICGN. (2014). *ICGN global governance principles*. London: International Corporate Governance Network. Retrieved October 23, 2015, from http://www.fsa.go.jp/singi/corporategovernance/siryou/20140930/14.pdf

Kim, O., & Verrecchia, R. E. (1994). Market liquidity and volume around earnings announcements. *Journal of Accounting and Economics*, *17*(1-2), 41–67. doi:10.1016/0165-4101(94)90004-3

Kolk, A. (2005). Corporate social responsibility in the coffee sector: The dynamics of MNC responses and code development. *European Management Journal*, *23*(2), 228–236. doi:10.1016/j.emj.2005.02.003

Kotler, P., & Lee, N. (2005). *Corporate social responsibility. Doing the most good for your company and your cause*. Hoboken, NJ: John Wiley & Sons, Inc.

Logsdon, J. M., Thomas, D. E., & Van Buren, H. J. III. (2006, March). Corporate social responsibility in large Mexican firms. *Journal of Corporate Citizenship*, *2006*(21), 51–60. doi:10.9774/GLEAF.4700.2006.sp.00007

López-Fernández, A. M. (2013). Influence of corporate social responsibility on consumers shopping behavior and determining competitive posture of the firm. *Journal of Marketing Analytics*, *1*(4), 222–233. doi:10.1057/jma.2013.18

López-Fernández, A. M. (2015). Effect on stakeholders perception of CSR: Analysis of information dynamics through social media. *International Journal of Business Competition and Growth*, *4*(1/2), 24–43. doi:10.1504/IJBCG.2015.070662

Maguire, M. (2011, January). The future of corporate social responsibility reporting. *The Frederick S. Pardee center for the study of the longer-range future. Issues in Brief (Alan Guttmacher Institute)*, (19): 1–8.

Maignan, I., & Ralston, D. A. (2002). Corporate social responsibility in Europe and the U.S.: Insights from businesses self-presentations. *Journal of International Business Studies*, *33*(3), 497–514. doi:10.1057/palgrave.jibs.8491028

Matten, D., & Moon, J. (2008). Implicit and explicit CSR: A conceptual framework for a comparative understanding of corporate social responsibility. *Academy of Management Review*, *33*(2), 404–424. doi:10.5465/AMR.2008.31193458

MCA. (2009). *Corporate Governance voluntary guidelines*. New Delhi: Ministry of Corporate Affairs, Government of India. Retrieved October 22, 2015, from http://www.mca.gov.in/Ministry/latestnews/CG_Voluntary_Guidelines_2009_24dec2009.pdf

Moon, J. (2007). *The contribution of corporate social responsibility to sustainable development. Sustainable development*. John Wiley & Sons, Ltd and ERP Environment.

Nerantzidis, M., Filos, J., & Lazarides, T. G. (2012, May). The puzzle of corporate governance definition(s): A content analysis. *Corporate Board: Role. Duties & Composition*, *8*(2), 13–23.

Niello, J. V. (2006). *Responsabilidad social empresarial (RSE) desde la perspectiva de los consumidores*. Santiago, Chile: UN CEPAL.

OConnor, A., & Meister, M. (2008, March). Corporate social responsibility attribute rankings. *Public Relations Review*, *34*(1), 49–50. doi:10.1016/j.pubrev.2007.11.004

ODonovan, G. (2002). Environmental disclosures in the annual report: Extending the applicability and predictive power of legitimacy theory. *Accounting, Auditing & Accountability Journal*, *15*(3), 344–371. doi:10.1108/09513570210435870

OECD. (2005, July 13). *Corporate Governance*. Retrieved August 20, 2015, from Glossary of statistical terms: https://stats.oecd.org/glossary/detail.asp?ID=6778

OECD. (2008). *Russian Federation. Strengthening the policy framework for investment*. Paris: OECD Investment Policy Reviews.

OECD. (2011). *OECD Guidelines for Multinational Enterprises*. OECD Publishing. Retrieved November 13, 2013, from http://www.oecd-ilibrary.org/governance/oecd-guidelines-for-multinational-enterprises_9789264115415-en

Patten, D. (1991). Exposure, legitimacy, and social disclosure. *Journal of Accounting and Public Policy*, *10*(4), 297–308. doi:10.1016/0278-4254(91)90003-3

Peinado-Vara, E. (2006). Corporate social responsibility in Latin America. *Journal of Corporate Citizenship*, *2006*(21), 61–69. doi:10.9774/GLEAF.4700.2006.sp.00008

Porter, M. E., & Kramer, M. R. (2006, December). Strategy and society. The link between competitive advantage and corporate social responsibility. *Harvard Business Review*, *84*(12), 78–92. PMID:17183795

Pratt, L., & Fintel, E. (2002). Environmental management as an indicator of business responsibility in Central America. In P. Utting (Ed.), *The greening of business in developing countries: Rhetoric, reality and prospects* (pp. 41–57). London: Zed Books & UNRISD.

Rochlin, S., Witter, K., Monaghan, P., & Murray, V. (2005). *Putting the corporate into corporate responsibility (CR)*. Greenleaf Publishing Limited and Accountability.

Rogerson, S. (2004). Aspects of social responsibility in the information society. In G. Doukidis, N. Mylonopoulos, & N. Pouloudi (Eds.), *Social and economic transformation in the digital era* (pp. 31–46). Hershey, PA: Idea Group Publishing. doi:10.4018/978-1-59140-158-2.ch003

Rosas, A. J. (2010, June). Responsabilidad social empresarial: Hacia una agenda de investigación en México. *Administración y Organizaciones, 24*(12), 75–89.

Rossow, R. M. (2015). *Corporate social responsibility in India. How the Companies Act may augment regional disparities.* Washington, DC: CSIS. Retrieved October 21, 2015, from http://csis.org/files/publication/150330_corpresponsibility.pdf

Schmidheiny, S. (2006, Spring). Turning Point. A View of Corporate Citizenship in Latin America. *Journal of Corporate Citizenship, 21*(4), 21–24. doi:10.9774/GLEAF.4700.2006.sp.00004

Singh, D. R., & Ahuja, J. M. (1983). Corporate social reporting in India. *The International Journal of Accounting, 18*(8), 151–169.

Snider, J., Hill, R. P., & Martin, D. (2003). Corporate social responsibility in the 21st Century: A view from the worlds most successful firms. *Journal of Business Ethics, 48*(2), 175–187. doi:10.1023/B:BUSI.0000004606.29523.db

Solomon, J. (2007). *Corporate governance and accountability.* West Sussex, UK: John Wiley & Sons, Ltd.

Spence, L., & Schmidpeter, R. (2003, June). SMEs, social capital and the common good. *Journal of Business Ethics, 45*(1), 93–108. doi:10.1023/A:1024176613469

Stanwick, P. A., & Stanwick, S. D. (1998, January). The relationship between corporate social performance, and organizational size, financial performance, and environmental performance: An empirical examination. *Journal of Business Ethics, 17*(2), 195–204. doi:10.1023/A:1005784421547

TSX. (2006). *Corporate governance. A guide to good disclosure.* Toronto: Toronto Stock Exchange. Retrieved August 22, 2015, from http://www.ecgi.org/codes/documents/tsx_gtgd.pdf

UN. (2006). *Guidance on good practices in corporate governance disclosure.* Geneva: United Nations Conference on Trade and Development. Retrieved August 23, 2015, from http://unctad.org/en/docs/iteteb20063_en.pdf

UN. (2007). *CSR and Developing Countries. What scope for government action?* New York: Sustainable Development Innovation Briefs. Retrieved October 20, 2015, from https://sustainabledevelopment.un.org/content/documents/no1.pdf

UN Global Compact. (2013). *Participants and Stakeholders.* Retrieved November 13, 2013, from UN Global Compact Participants: http://www.unglobalcompact.org/ParticipantsAndStakeholders/index.html

UNCTAD. (2008). *Guidance on corporate responsibility indicators in annual reports*. New York: United Nations Publication.

Utting, P. (2005). Corporate responsibility and the movement of business. *Development in Practice*, *15*(3&4), 380–386.

WBCSD. (2013). *Membership*. Retrieved November 13, 2013, from World business council for sustainable development: http://www.wbcsd.org/about/members/members-list-region.aspx

Xueming, L., & Bhattacharya, C. B. (2006, October). Corporate social responsibility, customer satisfaction, and market value. *Journal of Marketing*, *70*(4), 1–18. doi:10.1509/jmkg.70.4.1

Zerban, A. (2013). The need for social and environmental accounting standard: Can Islamic countries have the lead? *Eurasian Journal of Business and Management*, *1*(2), 33–43.

Chapter 13
Building Brands in Emerging Economies:
A Consumer-Oriented Approach

Sandra Nunez
Tecnológico de Monterrey, Mexico

Raquel Castaño
Tecnológico de Monterrey, Mexico

ABSTRACT

One of the most important goals of brand managers is to build strong, long-lasting brands. The meaning consumers give to brands comes from a dynamic process of interpretation formed in terms of the context in which they are used, the socio-psychological nature of their consumers, and the cultures to which these costumers belong. By acknowledging the importance of understanding how brands can be built in emerging economies, this paper analyzes the case of three brands in three different emerging economies. We highlight how successful firms develop their marketing strategies based on their understanding of the local consumer market they are serving. Ultimately, this paper is intended to provide managerial guidance on the basis of the analysis of brands and consumers in emerging economies.

INTRODUCTION

One of the most important goals of brand managers is to build strong, long-lasting brands. However, to do so, brand managers must understand the needs that these brands cover for their consumers. These needs will undoubtedly be impacted by the culture of the market, as marketing is a discipline circumscribed to context (Sheth & Sisodia, 1999). Indeed, Burgess and Steenkamp (2006) called for more research on emerging markets in order to advance marketing science and propose guidelines to conduct such research. They placed a strong emphasis on understanding the new constructs (market particularities) that past research has not addressed.

Emerging markets bring particularities that are unknown or a rare practice to the industrialized or developed countries. For example, the concept of *guanxi* refers to the "durable social connections and

DOI: 10.4018/978-1-5225-0902-8.ch013

networks a firm uses to exchange favors for organizational purposes" (Gu, Hung, & Tse, 2008, p. 12). *Guanxi* positively impacts sales growth and market shares. Other researchers have acknowledged the concept of *ubuntu* as important for the African context, as it explains consumers' decisions and the power that word-of-mouth has in the market. *Ubuntu*, or humaneness, refers to "caring and community, harmony and hospitality, respect and responsiveness that individuals and groups display for one another" (Mangaliso, 2001, p. 24). Without an understanding of these concepts that govern certain cultures, brand managers might face difficulties communicating with their customers.

The meaning consumers give to brands comes from a dynamic process of interpretation that is formed in terms of the context in which they are used, the socio-psychological nature of their consumers, and the cultures to which these customers belong. The purpose of this paper is to understand how strong brands are built in emerging markets. First, we will review the existing literature on building brands in these markets. Then we will discuss the concepts of globalization, glocalization, and reverse innovation. Next, we will address culture and its effects on consumer behavior, following by an introduction of the methodology used in the present research and a discussion of the findings. Finally, we will present our conclusions and practical implications for brand managers.

BUILDING BRANDS IN EMERGING MARKETS

Scant research exists on building brands in emerging markets; in fact, the available research mostly discusses how global brands (from developed countries) enter emerging markets and how they are perceived. For example, Kapferer (2008) focused on brands of developed countries entering emerging markets. He noted how, in emerging markets, companies prefer to enter with new brands rather than using existing ones in order to avoid the risk of decreasing brand capital. He also cautioned about the naming of the brands, which may cause trouble based on connotations in another region or language; the translation might also be perceived as a counterfeit of the "real" product. In another study, Akram, Merunka, and Shakaib Akram (2011) found that, in emerging markets, perceived brand globalness positively affects both perceived brand quality and perceived brand prestige; these relationships are moderated by consumer ethnocentrism.

Sheth (2011) presented five key issues from emerging markets that are very different from industrialized markets: market heterogeneity, sociopolitical governance, chronic shortage of resources, unbranded competition, and inadequate infrastructure. Market heterogeneity refers to the fragmentation of the market. Sociopolitical governance is the dominance of institutions such as religion, government, nongovernmental organizations, business groups, and local communities. It also refers to the presence of mono- or oligopolies. A chronic shortage of resources could refer to power, raw materials, or skilled labor. In terms of unbranded competition, Sheth argued that the prevalence of unbranded products might be a result of poor infrastructure or because of self-produced goods. Finally, an inadequate infrastructure can refer not only to a lack of roads or a poor maintenance state, but also a lack of or inefficient communication technologies.

Despite all these constraints, Sheth (2011) defined three comparative advantages of emerging economies: policy, raw materials, and nongovernmental organizations (NGOs). In terms of policy, he noted how governments' large influence can move the economy by being a large customer to certain industries and promoting trade within the country and with other countries. Some governments even have state-owned companies, which are sometimes the market leaders that may even become global leaders. In terms of raw materials, emerging economies possess a large base of resources that industrialized countries do not have. For example, India has become a leader in IT skilled labor, while countries such as Mexico or Brazil have access to multiple sources of natural resources and countries like Russia can provide energy. In regard to NGOs, the needs of the emerging markets have moved toward social entrepreneurship. These social entrepreneurships have special marketing needs and also have a social impact that is not seen in more developed countries. In the next section, we will discuss the terms *globalization*, *glocalization*, and *reverse innovation* in order to understand their place and function in emerging economies.

Globalization, Glocalization, and Reverse Innovation

Globalization is the production and distribution of products and services of a homogenous type and quality around the world. Theodore Levitt (1983), in his famous *Harvard Business Review* article, argued that globalization is empowered by the mass production technologies. He also stated that the differences in tastes and products disappear because global companies impose the tastes of the industrialized economies. He acknowledged the existence of multinationals that cater to local tastes, but only as a matter of convenience because they have to in order to survive, albeit at high costs. He conceived both views as mutually exclusive. The perfect example is Coca-Cola and Pepsi, which have worldwide distribution with the same formula for every country.

Meanwhile, glocalization is the "tailoring and advertising of goods and services on a global or near-global basis to increasingly differentiated local and particular markets" (Robertson, 2012, p. 194). With glocalization, the brands market the products developed in industrialized countries but adapt them to local tastes. Yet not every product has been developed in industrialized markets, as globalization and glocalization assume. A good example is McDonald's menu, where they have a standard line of products, but offer custom options such as avocado burgers in Mexico, a teriyaki burger in Japan, and a chicken camembert burger in France.

In contrast, some innovations have been coined in developed markets due to their special needs—mostly, scarce resources. This process has been called reverse innovation, or the "ability to innovate specifically for emerging markets" (Govindarajan & Trimble, 2013, p. xiii). Reverse innovation can be seen as the opposite of glocalization according to Sheth (2011) because it refers to exporting innovations from the emerging markets to the industrialized ones. One example is GE India's development of a portable electrocardiogram machine. It was invented to serve the needs of the Indian market and has since been commercialized in developed countries. Next, we will discuss culture.

Culture

Culture is "a system of inherited conceptions expressed in symbolic forms by means of which men communicate, perpetuate, and develop their knowledge about and attitudes toward life" (Geertz, 1973, p. 89). Culture refers to everything that influences individuals' thought processes and behaviors, preferences, how they make decisions, and even how they perceive the world around them. Culture is acquired and learned rather than innate as a set of deep ordering principles (Hawkins & Mothersbaugh, 2012).

Culture can be seen more clearly when travelling from one country to another or even between social classes and ethnic groups within a single nation. In many cases, there are no ways to explain particular cultural practices because they are regularly due to historical reasons. It is also important to mention that, due to cultural influences, individuals behave, think, and feel in a consistent mode with that of other members of the same culture because it seems "normal" or "correct" to do so. Thus, culture affects the choice of, usage of, and resistance to products and even the particular brands we pick (Hawkins & Mothersbaugh, 2012; Mariampolski, 2006).

Culture is also based on cultural values and principles that affirm what is desirable. The norms are the boundaries set on behavior that specify behaviors for particular situations; the violation of these norms results in sanctions or penalties. Thus, cultural values lead to norms and the corresponding sanctions, which in turn influence consumption patterns. Consequently, culture provides the framework within which people and household lifestyles evolve (Hawkins & Mothersbaugh, 2012). It is important that marketers understand the nature of culture and the role it plays in human relations because elements of culture are interrelated; thus, changing one piece of culture has implications for the whole while a failure to understand cultural differences can produce negative consequences (Mariampolski, 2006).

A useful way to understand the differences in consumer behavior across cultures is to comprehend the values embraced by different cultures. Many of the values vary across cultures and affect consumption, but one of the cultural values that have the greatest impact on consumer behavior is the other-oriented values that reflect society's view of the appropriate relationship between individuals and groups within that society (Hawkins & Mothersbaugh, 2012). Hofstede's (1997) research on culture initially identified four dimensions—

1. Power distance,
2. Individualism versus collectivism,
3. Masculinity versus femininity, and
4. Uncertainty avoidance—and subsequently added two more dimensions—namely,
5. Long-term orientation versus short-term normative orientation and
6. Indulgence versus restraint (Hofstede, 2015).

Furthermore, culture has an impact on consumer behavior. Zhang, Beatty, and Walsh (2008) found that people from individualistic countries were harder to satisfy than individuals from collectivistic ones. Consumers from collectivistic countries tend to be more imitative whereas individualistic cultures have a higher tendency to try new brands, products, and services. They are more innovative in their purchases (Steenkamp, Hofstede, & Wedel, 1999). Individualistic cultures prefer advertising messages that emphasize individual benefits whereas collectivistic ones prefer messages with in-group content (Han & Shavitt, 1994). This phenomenon was more evident for products purchased and consumed socially than individually. In the same way, Choi, Lee, and Kim (2005) stated that advertising in collectivistic countries contains more celebrity appeals than those of the individualistic countries.

De Mooij and Hofstede (2002) found that expenditures on leisure and entertainment are negatively correlated with the power distance dimension of culture. For example, Koreans allocate a higher proportion of their income than their North American counterparts to apparel and education as these categories are relevant to communicate their social status, which is a characteristic of collectivism (Chung, 1998). In the following section, we will discuss the methodology for this research and the background of the brands under study.

Methodology

The qualitative method selected for this research was the case study. Specifically, we analyzed three cases: Natura from Brazil, Kingfisher from India, and Oxxo from Mexico. Data for this study were collected from a variety of secondary sources, such as Euromonitor, the brands' websites, and online news reports.

Natura from Brazil

Natura is a cosmetics company founded in Brazil in 1969 (Natura, 2015). This company differentiated itself from other companies by using natural active ingredients in their formulas. Today it is the leading brand in cosmetics and direct sales in Brazil and the largest cosmetics maker in Latin America (Antunes, 2014). It has operations in Brazil, Argentina, Chile, Mexico, Peru, Colombia, and France. Natura established itself as the cosmetics leader in Brazil by introducing natural ingredients. Natura is the largest corporation with the B Corporation distinction, which is awarded to companies that "use the power of business to solve social and environmental problems" (bcorporation, 2015).

Kingfisher from India

Kingfisher is the leading beer brand in the Indian market, with more than 50% of the market (Stock, 2015). The brand, which dates back to 1915, is owned by United Breweries Limited (UBL, 2015). Kingfisher currently maintains an alliance with Heineken Group, the largest beer brand globally, which owns 42.1% of United Breweries Limited (Dhody, 2015).

Oxxo from Mexico

Oxxo is a convenience store chain owned by FEMSA Comercio. The Mexican company was opened in 1890 and is now a leader in the beverage industry. The first Oxxo opened in 1978 (Oxxo, 2015). It currently owns 12,853 points of sale between Mexico and Colombia, all of which are owned by FEMSA as they do not have franchises. In 2014, Oxxo became the leading competitor in the fast food industry in the Mexican market, surpassing McDonald's, Burger King, Subway, and Domino's Pizza (Celis, 2015).

FINDINGS AND DISCUSSION

Context

Table 1. presents some statistics about the three countries for the case studies (World Bank, 2015). Although India has a lower gross domestic product (GDP) per capita, it has a very large population, which makes it an attractive market for any product. Mexico and Brazil have a lower population, but still they are some of the most populated countries on the planet. Another interesting point of fact is the percentage of the total population living in rural areas. Although many believe that Mexico is predominantly a rural country, almost 80% of its population lives in urban areas; the same could be said about Brazil, with nearly 85% of its population living in urban areas. Only India still has a predominantly rural market.

Table 1. Statistics from Brazil, India, and Mexico

Country	Population (millions)	GDP (growth %)	GDP (per capita, in US$)	GINI Index	Urban population (% of total)	Deforestation (average anual %)
Brazil	200.4	3.1	11,384.6	52.9	85	0.5
India	1252.1	6.9	1,595.7	36.8	32	-0.46
Mexico	122.3	3.6	10,230.2	48.1	79	0.3

The percentage of the population living in urban areas has a great impact on the products available for each market and the needs they must cover. People in urban areas are usually more related to the global market and exposed to foreign ideas, needs, and wants. This exposure helps globalization by allowing people to standardize the tastes of the "global culture"; it also helps glocalization because of the need for customization for the specific market. Meanwhile, the special needs of emerging economies favor reverse innovation. As the old adage says, need is the mother of invention.

One of the commonalities among the three economies studied was the GINI Index, which measures the inequality in the distribution of family income in a certain country. The larger the number, the more inequality exists. In the three countries studied, the largest inequality is in Brazil, followed by Mexico and finally India. This confirms Sheth's (2011) observation that there is a large heterogeneity of customers, at least in terms of their income.

Figure 1. shows the Internet penetration in each of the emerging markets under study. In Brazil and Mexico, the growth rate for Internet users has been almost the same for the last 10 years, at 174% and

Figure 1. Internet users as a measure of the people that gets access to the global internet network per every 100 inhabitants (WorldBank, 2015)

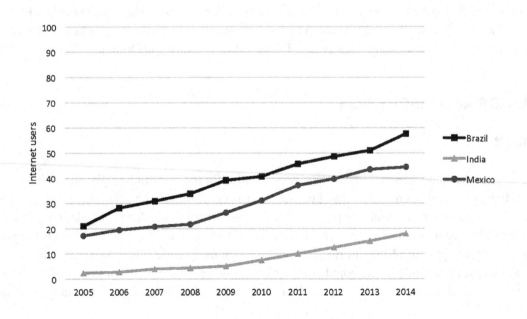

158%, respectively. Internet penetration has increased more than 6 times in India in the same period, from 2.4 to 18%. Despite the large increase for India, compared to Mexico and Brazil, it continues to be the country with the smallest penetration per every 100 inhabitants.

In Brazil, the beauty and personal care market size represents 101,751.1 million BRL (Euromonitor, 2015c). Natura Cosméticos was the leader until 2013, but in 2014 Unilever Brasil took the lead with 11.8% of market share against 11.3% from Natura. The favored channel of distribution for beauty and personal care products is store-based retailing, with a 72% value; however, non-store retailing is dominated by direct selling (beauty consultants) with a 26.3% value. Natura is widely distributed through the network of beauty consultants and has developed a great experience in the channel.

India favors local production because it has heavy taxes on imports, on-trade sale of alcohol, and a luxury tax (Euromonitor, 2015a). This complicates the entrance and growth of global competitors, added to the fact that there are different taxes in each region. The government has also prohibited the advertising of alcoholic drinks since 2000. Being a local brand with a long heritage, Kingfisher had a strong brand recall for those consumers active before 2000. What Kingfisher did for the newer generations was to add to the holding an airline company and paint its beer name on the planes; thus, any advertisement for the airline also worked for the beer. The airline is now in bankruptcy, but it served the purpose of boosting beer sales.

Mexico's convenience stores almost tripled in 10 years, growing from 3,433 in 2002 to 12,720 in 2012 (Euromonitor, 2013b). In the regulatory framework, the opening hours for establishments that sell alcoholic drinks can vary from state to state; however, convenience stores in large cities can sell these types of drinks without restriction, although there may be some municipalities that consider it illegal to sell alcohol after midnight (Euromonitor, 2015b). Oxxo is in a good position to be able to sell alcoholic beverages due to its 24-hour format in large cities.

Socio-Psychological Consumer Behavior

Brazil is known for the aggressive and illegal deforestation of the Amazon rainforest. This damage to the environment raises high levels of concern about ecology, leading to the trend of eco-worriers (Euromonitor, 2015f). Eco-worriers, specifically in Brazil, are very much concerned with sustainability and fair trade. The latter is also linked with favoring local producers. In addition, women are highly concerned about appearance and spend a considerable amount of their annual income on beauty products (Euromonitor, 2015d). In fact, Brazil became the largest plastic surgery market in the world in 2013 (Euromonitor, 2015d).

India has been showing economic progress as a rural society that is migrating to the metropolis and sending money back home (Euromonitor, 2015e). In India, rural consumers mirror the aspirations of urban consumers and look for branded, high-quality products. Although their economy is not soaring, they do not settle for lower-quality products just because they cost less. This trend has also positively affected the beer market for the producers, because they are now developing more premium brands (Euromonitor, 2015a). The majority of people in India belong to the Hindu or Muslim religions, which prohibit alcohol consumption. However, urbanization has led young consumers to travel abroad and use telecommunication technologies to learn about the Western world, incorporating part of the culture transmitted to their own. In turn, young Indians have tasted and consume beer and spirits.

Mexico has a large middle class that includes dual-income households; in major cities, the commutes are longer than they used to be in previous years. Thus, the need for convenience foods, such as frozen, canned, or prepared foods, has grown as consumers are constantly on the go (Euromonitor, 2013a). There is a very rooted tradition of eating on the street, including foods such as tamales, tacos, and pozole. Furthermore, Mexico is the largest consumer of carbonated soft drinks and bottled water. Despite the large water consumption, it has different objectives than soft drinks. In Mexico, bottled water is also used as a source of clean water when otherwise not available, such as for cooking or bathing babies. Moreover, consumers buy alcoholic beverages (mostly beer) from convenience stores. Although cash is the most common payment method, the use of both ATMs and debit cards has tripled in the last 10 years. However, Mexicans only use ATMs to withdraw money and prefer to make other transactions in person. Oxxo has leveraged these characteristics of the market by offering a convenient way to get the products and services the consumers want (prepared foods, carbonated beverages, and banking services) in the same place.

Culture

Emerging economies are sometimes said to be very similar in culture, especially those located in geographical proximity. However, this might not always be the case. Figure 2 shows the different cultural dimensions for the three economies examined in this paper: Mexico, Brazil, and India.

Although the three markets are very similar in various dimensions, in two dimensions, they differ greatly: Mexico has a very high score for indulgence, Brazil has a medium score, and India holds the lowest score for this dimension whereas Mexico and Brazil have high scores in uncertainty avoidance, while India has a medium-low score. In addition, for masculinity there is a visible difference as India and Brazil are more alike than Brazil and Mexico. Although all three countries are emerging economies, they do not have similar cultural dimensions. Moreover, Mexico and Brazil are both from the same region, but they do not coincide in every dimension. As a result, brand managers should be careful in assuming they can use the same strategy and the same offer for two markets, even when they are geographically close in proximity.

Figure 2. Cultural dimensions' scores for Brazil, Mexico and India (Hofstede, 2015)

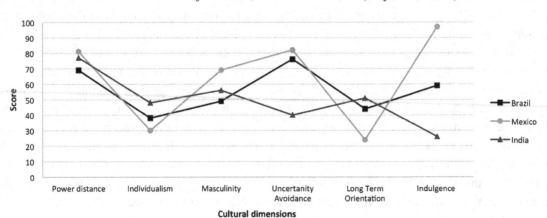

Globalization, Glocalization, and Reverse Innovation in Brands' Strategies

The three phenomena—globalization, glocalization, and reverse innovation—cannot be separated from each other in emerging economies. Globalization and the exposure that the younger demographics from India have from Western cultures have led to an increase in beer consumption in that country. Another form of globalization is present in their strategies, such as using bathing suit calendars to sell Kingfisher beer. That is an import from other economies in order to promote the products. Yet glocalization has also been present as the beer has been changing according to the tastes of the market, which is relatively new to its consumption. Political forces have pushed the local development of breweries. In this manner, reverse innovation is being put to work now because they will export the knowledge and formulas produced in India by opening a brewery to produce Kingfisher beer in London. They will thus be exporting a locally developed taste to a developed economy.

In the case of Brazil, the global trend was toward beauty and care for the environment. Natura followed the global trend and developed a line of products; however, the company catered to the Brazilian consumer, with natural active ingredients being provided by the local environment. Natura developed the knowledge to manage sales through beauty consultants and use stores in different countries for different purposes. In Brazil, the company opened stores to boost product sales. Meanwhile, in Mexico, these stores turned out to be more of a social club to meet other consultants and get training. Now, they also operate in France—one of the capitals of beauty and fashion.

In Mexico, Oxxo was created to serve as a distribution channel for the carbonated beverages and beers produced by FEMSA in order to boost sales (Euromonitor, 2014). Global trends indicated that convenience stores were a format worth exploring. Despite gaining experience in the retail industry, Oxxo found that consumers were looking for convenience not only to shop for beverages or last-minute necessities, but also to eat fast when not at home, complete bank transactions, buy cellphone credit, and even play lotto at the same place and time. With this experience, Oxxo developed a strong information system that allowed the company to gather information to increase efficiency and then decided to replicate the model in other markets, such as Colombia and—more recently—the US. In Colombia, Oxxo had to cater to the specific needs of the local consumers, who demanded a place to sit and eat their prepared food as well as more produce in their meals. In the following section, we will provide our conclusions.

CONCLUSION

Once brands are established in their local markets, they tend to look for opportunities in other countries and diversify their offer to suit the needs of their consumers. When finding another market to open operations, usually they also look for emerging economies, as in the case of Natura and Oxxo. However, as we demonstrated, not all emerging economies are the same. Product use, stores, and services differ from country to country, even between regions of the same country.

Globalization, glocalization, and reverse innovation go hand-in-hand in emerging economies. The urbanization of emerging economies has promoted the trend toward globalization. People in emerging countries also follow global trends. Such globalization is what makes people want to consume beer as they see it on TV and want to fit in with more global friends. In addition, they shop at convenience stores because both men and women have to work, follow a hectic schedule, and need fast retail outlets. They look for natural products because they care about their appearance and well-being.

However, not every detail can remain unchanged; companies must adapt to local markets. Beer needs to be adjusted for consumers experiencing its taste for the first time in generations. Convenience stores need to offer a place to sit in economies that have a hectic schedule but still like to eat seated. Natural cosmetics producers have to use local ingredients to favor local commerce and deliver on their promise of fair trade and sustainability.

In fact, this customization leads to reverse innovation by attending to the special needs of a market and then exporting it to others. Kingfisher beer is now being produced in the UK (Kingfisher, 2015), Oxxo recently opened a store in the US (El Financiero, 2014), and Natura has operations in France. Overall, knowledge of the market cannot be substituted by any theory or prior experience, even within emerging economies. Consumers need to be analyzed from a socio-demographic perspective, markets should be analyzed for opportunities and constraints, and consumers' cultural and socio-psychological characteristics need to be addressed.

IMPLICATIONS

The meaning consumers give to brands comes from a dynamic process of interpretation that is formed in terms of the context in which they are used, the socio-psychologic nature of their consumers, and the cultures to which these customers belong. Brand managers should look for opportunities to increase their business and brand equity by being attentive to consumers' changing needs, trends in consumption, and other markets, which can be either emerging or industrialized economies. When the company has developed a competitive advantage and a brand name, it might innovate elsewhere if this advantage is valuable for other markets.

REFERENCES

Akram, A., Merunka, D., & Shakaib Akram, M. (2011). Perceived brand globalness in emerging markets and the moderating role of consumer ethnocentrism. *International Journal of Emerging Markets*, *6*(4), 291–303. doi:10.1108/17468801111170329

Antunes, A. (2014). *Brazil's Natura, the largest cosmetics maker in Latin America, becomes a B Corp*. Retrieved from http://www.forbes.com/sites/andersonantunes/2014/12/16/brazils-natura-the-largest-cosmetics-maker-in-latin-america-becomes-a-b-corp/

bcorporation. (2015). *B Corporations*. Retrieved from https://www.bcorporation.net/

Burgess, S. M., & Steenkamp, J.-B. E. (2006). Marketing renaissance: How research in emerging markets advances marketing science and practice. *International Journal of Research in Marketing*, *23*(4), 337–356. doi:10.1016/j.ijresmar.2006.08.001

Celis, F. (2015). *Vikingo de Oxxo 'noquea' a Ronald McDonald*. Retrieved from http://www.elfinanciero.com.mx/empresas/vikingo-de-oxxo-noquea-a-ronald-mcdonald.html

Choi, S. M., Lee, W.-N., & Kim, H.-J. (2005). Lessons from the rich and famous: A cross-cultural comparison of celebrity endorsement in advertising. *Journal of Advertising, 34*(2), 85–98. doi:10.108 0/00913367.2005.10639190

Chung, Y. S. (1998). Culture and consumption expenditure patterns: Comparison between Korean and United States households. *Journal of Consumer Studies & Home Economics, 22*(1), 39–50. doi:10.1111/j.1470-6431.1998.tb00714.x

De Mooij, M., & Hofstede, G. (2002). Convergence and divergence in consumer behavior: Implications for international retailing. *Journal of Retailing, 78*(1), 61–69. doi:10.1016/S0022-4359(01)00067-7

Dhody, T. (2015). *Kingfisher just got sold to Heineken for Rs 872 Crore.* Retrieved from http://www. scoopwhoop.com/news/heineken-buys-kingfisher/

El Financiero. (2014). *Abre Oxxo en Estados Unidos.* Retrieved from http://www.elfinanciero.com.mx/ monterrey/abre-oxxo-en-estados-unidos.html

Euromonitor. (2013a). *Consumer Lifestyles in Mexico.* Euromonitor.

Euromonitor. (2013b). *FEMSA's latest acquisition shows potential for soft drinks and retail.* Euromonitor.

Euromonitor. (2014). *FEMSA Comercio SA de CV in retailing (Mexico).* Euromonitor.

Euromonitor. (2015a). *Alcoholic drinks in India.* Euromonitor.

Euromonitor. (2015b). *Alcoholic drinks in Mexico.* Euromonitor.

Euromonitor. (2015c). *Beauty and personal care in Brazil.* Euromonitor.

Euromonitor. (2015d). *Consumer lifestyles in Brazil.* Euromonitor.

Euromonitor. (2015e). *Consumer lifestyles in India.* Euromonitor.

Euromonitor. (2015f). *Eco worriers: Global green behaviour and market impact.* Euromonitor.

Geertz, C. (1973). *The interpretation of cultures.* New York: Basic Books.

Govindarajan, V., & Trimble, C. (2013). *Reverse innovation: Create far from home, win everywhere.* Harvard Business Press.

Gu, F. F., Hung, K., & Tse, D. K. (2008). When does guanxi matter? Issues of capitalization and its dark sides. *Journal of Marketing, 72*(4), 12–28. doi:10.1509/jmkg.72.4.12

Han, S.-P., & Shavitt, S. (1994). Persuasion and culture: Advertising appeals in individualistic and collectivistic societies. *Journal of Experimental Social Psychology, 30*(4), 326–350. doi:10.1006/jesp.1994.1016

Hawkins, D., & Mothersbaugh, D. (2012). *Consumer Behavior: Building Marketing Strategy* (12th ed.). McGraw-Hill Education.

Hofstede, G. (1997). *Cultures and Organizations: Software of the Mind.* New York: McGraw-Hill.

Hofstede, G. (2015). *Country comparison.* Retrieved from http://geert-hofstede.com/

Kapferer, J.-N. (2008). The new strategic brand management: creating and sustaining brand equity. Les editions d'Organization.

Kingfisher. (2015). Retrieved from http://www.kingfisherbeerusa.com/heritage.html

Levitt, T. (1983). The globalization of markets. *Harvard Business Review*, *61*(3), 92–102.

Mangaliso, M. P. (2001). Building competitive advantage from ubuntu: Management lessons from South Africa. *The Academy of Management Executive*, *15*(3), 23–33. doi:10.5465/AME.2001.5229453

Mariampolski, H. (2006). Ethnography for marketers: A guide to consumer immersion. *Sage (Atlanta, Ga.)*.

Natura. (2015). *Our history*. Retrieved from https://www.naturabrasil.fr/en/about-us/our-history

Oxxo. (2015). *Nuestra historia*. Retrieved from http://www.oxxo.com/quienes-somos/historia.php

Robertson, R. (2012). Globalisation or glocalisation? *Journal of International Communication*, *18*(2), 191–208. doi:10.1080/13216597.2012.709925

Sheth, J. N. (2011). Impact of emerging markets on marketing: Rethinking existing perspectives and practices. *Journal of Marketing*, *75*(4), 166–182. doi:10.1509/jmkg.75.4.166

Sheth, J. N., & Sisodia, R. S. (1999). Revisiting marketings lawlike generalizations. *Journal of the Academy of Marketing Science*, *27*(1), 71–87. doi:10.1177/0092070399271006

Steenkamp, J. E., Hofstede, F., & Wedel, M. (1999). A cross-national investigation into the individual and national cultural antecedents of consumer innovativeness. *Journal of Marketing*, *63*(2), 55–69. doi:10.2307/1251945

Stock, K. (2015). *Forget InBev. Here are the markets where local beers rule*. Retrieved from http://www.bloomberg.com/news/articles/2015-10-12/forget-inbev-and-sabmiller-here-are-the-markets-where-local-beers-rule

UBL. (2015). *About Us-UBL at a Glance*. Retrieved from http://124.153.77.59/ubl_glance.aspx

World Bank. (2015). Retrieved September 14, 2015, from World Bank http://data.worldbank.org/

Zhang, J., Beatty, S. E., & Walsh, G. (2008). Review and future directions of cross-cultural consumer services research. *Journal of Business Research*, *61*(3), 211–224. doi:10.1016/j.jbusres.2007.06.003

Chapter 14
Training Effectiveness:
A Perspective of Engaged vs. Disengaged Employees

Snigdha Mohapatra
BIMTECH, India

Pravat Kumar Mohanty
Utkal University, India

ABSTRACT

HR practitioners time and again busy in finding the worth of their training programs. Outputs of training/ Training Effectiveness/ROI of training programs are taking a huge attention of any HR department in any organization. Often attention was paid to the training program itself, the training environment, the trainer and the organizational climate and culture to apply the same into work. But many a times the very important part i.e. trainees were left aside. Present research is an attempt to address this gap. Trainees though found to be an important factor in success of any training program often this factor is limited to theoretical analysis. Rarely organizations and particularly the training department dare to ponder this. The type of trainee or in other way the characteristic of a trainee is found to be influential in many of the researches earlier. Here the attempt is to measure the link between the level of engagement and the perception of training effectiveness of the same trainees. This will help the training department to be more cautious while choosing their trainees to deliver an effective training program to fetch a dream achieved.

INTRODUCTION

Training is highly advocated by the practitioners of HR. It is often suggested as the best medicine available to any type of disease the organization is suffering from. But the question is if training is so beneficial then where the outputs as expected in the beginning of any training program. The crux lies at the heart of the training programs i.e. trainees. Saks' (2002) survey data, suggest about 40% of trainees fail at first level of transfer i.e. within 15 days of receiving training. 70% weakens the learning in transferring them to job in next 1 year after the program. Ultimately it is found that only 20% of training invest-

DOI: 10.4018/978-1-5225-0902-8.ch014

ments result in improving individual's or organization's performance. In another study attempts were made to do training effectiveness analysis. The results point toward distinct factors i.e. the very unique culture of the organization, a well-structured career planning with a clear indication of incentives and organizational support for the same. This signifies the importance of the organization irrespective of the type of training been conducted as a decision maker of training effectiveness. Hence others also put emphasis on the employees who receive these training programs. Training participants' cognitions i.e. training self-efficacy and instrumentality are expected to be the powerful motivational forces influencing important distal outcomes. Training self-efficacy and instrumentality is defined as 'can do' and 'will do' respectively. The survey was conducted on 254 employees. The study concludes that the 'can do' is a primary predictor that motivates to learn, the 'will do' is the primary predictor for motivation to transfer contents to job. A cross-sectional survey from a broad range of Norwegian service organizations was conducted taking 343 trainees into account. It was conducted to find the relationship between perceived training initiatives in an organization, and its consequences on both employee's job performance and citizenship behaviors. All the three variables were significantly mediating each other as per the analysis. In addition, self-motivation of employees was found to be an important moderate too.

These imply that training never a fact of independent dimension. This is been affected and mediated by several factors either related to organization or to the employees. As employees are found to be a crucial pin to play the tune of success the term "effective or in more technical term engaged employee" comes to the fore-front.

In the turbulent time the value of an employee comes to the picture. Thus we can say not all rather only the engaged employees are the ones to be termed as assets of any organization. Erickson and Gratton (2007) add a nomenclature called "signature experiences" propagated by the engaged employees in form of skills, stamina, and commitment i.e. visible and distinctive in the work environment help to succeed in any business. It is also noticed that innovative product or associated developments in the product makes a company visible in the product market only. A unique bundle of resources that are complex, intangible and dynamic can only create the difference worldwide. As Joo and Mclean (2006) state that engaged employees are strategic assets to strengthen the organizational assets for sustained competitive advantage.

In such scenario it's tough for practitioners, researchers and thinkers of HR discipline to take that bold step to understand the technicalities failure in training. The current study is an attempt to understand the thin line connection between training effectiveness and engagement level of employees in an organizational set up.

OBJECTIVES

1. To find out the employee's attitude towards effectiveness of training.
2. To find the linkage between level of engagement and effectiveness of training.

LITERATURE REVIEW

- **Training for Skilled Labor:** Increasing efficiency and effectiveness of an employee in particular job by a systematic process of assistance is known as training. According to Silberman and Phillips (2006), training and development has the ability to maintain the organization's goals and objectives. As it analyzes needs, designs and develops training programs; conducts training at each level and also evaluates them. This is how the HR department can take initiative for the organization to remain competitive in all times.

American Society of Training and Development found that in 2010 U.S. organizations spent about $171.5 billion on employee learning and development. Sixty percent ($103 billion) of total expenditures were spent on internal expenses (i.e. learning function's staff salaries, administrative learning costs, and non-salary delivery costs) and the remaining 40 percent ($68.5 billion) contributed to external expenses. Training and development is the priority of any human resource specialist in any business. To meet the needs of employees in different sector they use to put emphasis on variety of training program fit for their business and strategy. They also induce their managers to encourage the use of those training programs for a strategic development of the organization. Leading companies, such as Disney, Marriott, and Hewlett-Packard proved how training is important for their survival. They have a top management commitment to training and development, which they see as part of the corporate culture (Cascio, 2006). In another survey conducted in 2007 by Baldwin and Evans, concludes that a large number of those who were interviewed often commented that the success of their organizations relied on the continual skills development of their employees.

Research says in earlier days workers skill used to take 7-14 years to become obsolete, today it takes 3-5 years for 50% of skills to become archaic. According to American Society for Training and Development (ASTD), 42% of the total workforce needs training in different areas. Skills Gap poll conducted by ASTD also identified categories of skills most lacking among the responding companies. In first place was leadership. Executive-level skills, was reported lacking by 50 percent of respondents. Basic skills stood at 46 percent, professional or industry-specific skills at 41 percent, and managerial and supervisory skills at 31 percent.

- **Employee Engagement:** At present, there is no consistency in definition of the construct employee engagement. Engagement having been defined in several ways the measurement also took place in many distinct ways. Kahn (1990) defines employee engagement as "the harnessing of organization members' selves to their work roles; in engagement, people employ and express themselves physically, cognitively, and emotionally during role performances". The cognitive phase of employee engagement recount employees' thinking about the organization, about the employers or the leaders and about the working environment (both physical and social). The emotional aspect takes care of how employees feel about each of those three factors. Its basic desire is whether they have positive or negative attitudes toward all these three factors. The physical aspect of employee engagement looks after the physical energies put forth by the employee to accomplish their professional roles. Thus, according to Kahn (1990), engagement means to be psychologically as well as physically present when occupying and performing an organizational role. Schmidt et al.'s definition of engagement stands unique as he describes it as "An employee's involvement with, commitment to, and satisfaction with work". Employee engagement in literature was described by using data from Gallup's Q12 engagement survey (A well known study on employee engagement by Gallup consultancy). This integrates the very old classic constructs of job satisfaction (Smith et al., 1969), and organizational commitment (Meyer & Allen, 1991). An employee is expected to be completely involved in all the three aspects cognitively, emotionally and physically. This refer to active thinking about the organization and the work the employee working with, feeling happy about the work and putting all the effort to do his/her work effectively. All these three types of involvement should also follow the satisfaction level of the employee to be designated as employee engagement. These definitions often sound similar to the established constructs like 'organizational commitment' and 'organizational citizenship behavior' (OCB) (Robinson *et al* 2004). Thus Robinson *et al* (2004) defined engagement as 'one step up from commitment'. Truss *et al* (2006) define employee engagement as 'passion for work'. All these definitions include the three dimensions of engagement discussed by Kahn.

As the literature on this construct employee engagement suggests this is a multi-faceted construct, as previously suggested by Kahn (1990).

- **Role of Employee Engagement in Organizational Performance:** Kahn from his empirical research concludes that disengaged employees displayed incomplete role performances and were effortless, automatic or robotic and high levels of engagement lead to both positive outcomes for individuals, (e.g. quality of people's work and their own experiences of doing that work), as well as positive organizational-level outcomes (e.g. the growth and productivity of organizations).

The Gallup Organization (2004) found critical links between employee engagement, customer loyalty, business growth and profitability. The scores been compared on the variables like sales, customer complaints and turnover among the top 25 per cent on employee engagement in contrast to the bottom 25 per cent. Performance of stores in the bottom 25 per cent significantly found to be under-performing. Gallup cites numerous similar examples. Double digit growth companies have more engaged leaders working for the organization and they create a direct impact on their employees' level of engagement. The double digit growth of the company may be because they have a higher ratio of engaged employee while lower ratio of disengaged employee. Employee engagement, in fact, can make or break the bottom line (Lockwood, 2006). The performance data of the best companies in the USA show that in all the practice areas discussed previously, objectives are more easily met when employees are engaged and more likely to fall short when they are not. In order to maintain an employer brand, we see an emergence of a series of studies on employer of choice, which also measure engagement index and financial performance (Coleman, 2005). A recent SHRM Conference (2006) reported the dramatic difference in bottom-line results in organizations with highly engaged employees when compared to organizations whose employees had low engagement scores.

Hypothesis

On the basis of discussed literature in both the category the researcher formulated the hypothesis as followed.

H1: Attitude towards training effectiveness will vary on the basis of level of employee engagements.

Methodology

Given the exploratory nature of the research, a self-completed questionnaires method was followed in the current research. The research was conducted in 2011 and 2012, in one of the very important Government organizations dealing with transmission falling in the State Capital Region of Odisha. In the first phase of the research there were 200 employees who were approached to fill the questionnaires. All these approached employees were contacted at six different training programs conducted at the training centers (Power Training Centre i.e. technical and Management Training centre) of the organization. All the respondents were contacted at the closing ceremony of the respective training program. The respondents were approached personally for their responses. The researcher received 162 sets of completed questionnaires making a response rate of 81percent. The sample comprised 32 percent females and 68 percent males. The minimum qualification was diploma degree and minimum year of experience was 3years. The sample is comprised of 72% from technical and 28% from management training programs.

Measure

In this research, a self-made questionnaire was used to measure training effectiveness. The questionnaire was developed with reference to the existing literature to evaluate the attitude of trainees towards training effectiveness. The questionnaire was at first distributed to the experts (1 DGM, 3 AGMs and 10 executives of HRD department) of the training departments in the concerned organization. 10 questionnaires were distributed to the trainees of a technical training program too. The researcher took extra care to find the opinion of the experts and respondents of the pilot study to structure the questionnaire to the final format. Certain questions which were found confusing by the respondents or by the experts were dropped from the final list. 12 questions were finalized to measure attitude of trainees' towards training effectiveness (attached in appendix 1). Gallup q[12] was taken up as a measure of employee engagement, as it is established as a suitable instrument to measure employee engagement (Luthans and Peterson, 2002).

Result

On the basis of the scores of training effectiveness scale the respondents were categorized into three levels i.e. very effective (the score above 48), effective (the score above 36 to 47) and not-effective (36 or the score below 36). Table number 1 gives the picture of level of perceptual training effectiveness among the respondents.

To determine the employee engagement level Gallup q12 scale was used and the respondents were categorized into three levels i.e. actively engaged (the score above 48), engaged (the score above 36 to 47) and not-engaged (36 or the score below 36). Table number 2 gives the picture of level of employee engagement among the respondents.

Table 1. Levels of perceptual training effectiveness

Level of Training Effectiveness	Frequency	Percent
Ineffective	7	4.3
Effective	60	37.0
Very-effective	95	58.6
Total	162	100.0

Above table indicates that employees perceive the organizational training programs to be very effective. Only 7% of the employees perceive the training programs to be ineffective.

Table 2. Levels of employee engagement

Level of Employee Engagement	Frequency	Percent
Not-engaged	19	11.7
Engaged	84	51.9
Actively- engaged	59	36.4
Total	162	100.0

The sample indicates that the level of engagement in the organization is very satisfactory. 36% of respondents were found to be actively engaged and only 11.7% were disengaged in the organization.

To find the linkage between employee engagement and perceptual training effectiveness the correlation score were found out and it stands at 0.549. The correlation score indicates that both the constructs are related to each other and the score is also found to be statistically significant at 0.01 levels.

To predict the relationship between these two constructs regression analysis value is shown in table no-3.

The regression analysis is also found to be statistically significant at 0.01 levels. The model summary for this is shown in table no – 3. With trainees' level of engagement being the predictor to perceptual training effectiveness the predictor R value citing the simple co-relation is found to be 0.549. This is found to be acceptable to predict the model further. The R square indicates that perceptual training effectiveness can be predicted from the level of engagement. This stands 0.431 or 43% of the perceptual training effectiveness variable.

With the help of ANOVA measuring the difference in level of employee engagement and perceptual training effectiveness score were found out to be significant at 0.01 level too. Table no 4 gives the details about ANOVA analysis.

Further a post-hoc test as reflected in table- 5 indicates that the difference is more visible because of the significant difference between actively engaged and disengaged employees and engaged and disengaged, though there is no significant difference between disengaged and engaged group of employees.

This clearly accepts the hypothesis formulated in the beginning of the research. H1 states that there will be difference among the employees in regard to perceptual training effectiveness as a factor of level of employee engagement. The research data analysis also found a significant difference among the employee on the basis of their engagement level. The actively engaged employees are found different from the engaged and disengaged employees.

A further analysis of plotting the means of perceptual training effectiveness score on levels of employee engagement as shown in figure 1 indicates the clear-cut relationship between the two variables.

Table 3. Model description of levels of employee engagement on perceptual training effectiveness

Model	R	R Square	Adjusted R Square	Std. Error of the Estimate
1	.549	.431	.297	5.293
Predictors: (Constant), TOTALEE				
Dependent Variable: TOTALTE				

Table 4. ANOVA between levels of employee engagement and perceptual training effectiveness

		Sum of Squares	df	Mean Square	F	Sig.
Perceptual Training Effectiveness	Between Groups	1968.023	2	984.011	35.203	.000
	Within Groups	4444.471	159	27.953		
	Total	6412.494	161			

Table 5. Multiple Comparisons

Dependent Variable: Perceptual Training Effectiveness, LSD						
(I) LEVEL OF Employee Engagement	**(J) LEVEL OF Employee Engagement**	**Mean Difference (I-J)**	**Std. Error**	**Sig.**	**95% Confidence Interval**	
					Lower Bound	**Upper Bound**
Disengaged	Engaged	-1.547	1.343	.251	-4.20	1.11
	Actively engaged	-8.436*	1.395	.000	-11.19	-5.68
Engaged	Disengaged	1.547	1.343	.251	-1.11	4.20
	Actively engaged	-6.889*	.898	.000	-8.66	-5.12
Actively engaged	Disengaged	8.436*	1.395	.000	5.68	11.19
	Engaged	6.889*	.898	.000	5.12	8.66
*. The mean difference is significant at the 0.05 level.						

Figure 1 shows that at disengaged level of employee engagement (level 1 in the figure) the perceptual training effectiveness score is near to 45 and at engaged level (level 2 in the figure) it is just little below 47 but at actively-engaged (level 3 in the figure) the score is at 53. This gives a clear indication of the relationship between employee engagement levels and perceptual training effectiveness at the said organization.

Figure 1.

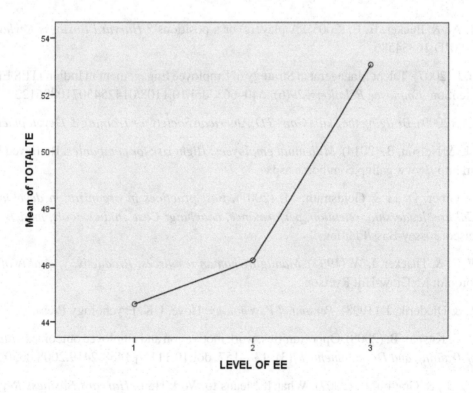

CONCLUSION

Keep hold of the key employees and developing them (75 percent of responses) is found to be the most critical activity to be catered by the HR professionals (HR Focus, 2006). A clear indication of how employee engagement and training are the crucial factors in organizational sustainability. Hence a vital question is does engaging employees is crucial for the organization or developing them. Holtgreve *et al.* (2002), is of opinion that training interventions can be the best ever solution towards the disease of disengagement. It will leverage the quality of the engagement index as a competitive advantage. This indicates training to be the antecedent to employee engagement. A recent study in manufacturing sector also adds the same point that training and development activities add value to employee engagement (Sarkar, 2011). On the other hand training effectiveness is always found dependent on the trainee characteristics and their level of motivation towards development. Trainees' motivation to use learned skills and knowledge in the work setting is highly dependent on the level of motivation of the employee to do so. Maximum behavioral changes among the trainees been mastered when they were highly motivated to use newly acquired skills on the job (Noe, 1986). On the basis of the literature and data collected in the current research this research question still stands tall whether the level of engagement is an antecedent towards training effectiveness or is a consequence to different training programs held in the organization. Being two indispensable practices in HR domain further research initiatives should clarify this. Better understanding of both the concepts can help the practitioners to reach the goal with proper interventions.

REFERENCES

Beatty, M. A., & Becker, B. E. (2005). A players' or a positions'? *Harvard Business Review*, *83*(12), 110–117. PMID:16334586

Bhatnagar, J. (2007). Talent Management Strategy of Employee Engagement in Indian ITES Employees: Key to Retention. *Employee Relations*, *29*(6), 640–663. doi:10.1108/01425450710826122

Bingham, T. (2009). *Bridging the Skills Gap - TD. American Society for Training & Development*. ASTD.

Brandon, J., & Nelson, B. (2014). *Millennial employees: flight risk for companies*. Retrieved March 30, 2014, from http://www.gallup.com/home.aspx

Carter, L., Giber, D. J., & Goldsmith, M. (2001). *Best practices in organization development and change: Culture, leadership, retention, performance, coaching: Case studies, tools, models, research*. San Francisco: Jossey-Bass/Pfeiffer.

Cascio, W. F., & Thacker, J. W. (1994). *Managing human resources: Productivity, quality of work life, profits*. Toronto: McGraw-Hill Ryerson.

Drenth, P., & Diederik, J. (1998). *Personnel Psychology*. Hove, UK: Psychology Press.

Dysvik, A., & Kuvaas, B. (2008). Opportunities, work motivation and employee outcomes. *International Journal of Training and Development*, *12*(3), 138–157. doi:10.1111/j.1468-2419.2008.00301.x

Erickson, T. J., & Gratton, L. (2007). What It Means to Work Here. *Harvard Business Review*, (Jan-Feb): 1–10. PMID:17348174

Harter, J. K., & Schmidt, F. L. (2002). *Well-Being in the Workplace and its Relationships to Business Outcomes: A review of the Gallup studies*. Retrieved Feb 28, 2014, from http://www.nhsemployers. org/~/media/Employers/Documents/Retain%20and%20improve/Harter%20et%20al%202002%20Well-beingReview.pdf

Harter, J. K., Schmidt, F. L., & Hayes, T. L. (2002). Business-Unit-Level Relationship between Employee Satisfaction, Employee Engagement, and Business Outcomes: A Meta-Analysis. *The Journal of Applied Psychology, 87*(2), 268–279. doi:10.1037/0021-9010.87.2.268 PMID:12002955

Holland, P., Sheehan, C., & De Cieri, H. (2007). Attracting and retaining talent: Exploring human resource development trends in Australia. *Human Resource Development International, 10*(3), 247–262. doi:10.1080/13678860701515158

Joo, B. (2006). Best Employer Studies: A Conceptual Model from a Literature Review and a Case Study. *Human Resource Development Review, 5*(2), 228–257. doi:10.1177/1534484306287515

Kahn, W. A. (1990). Psychological Conditions of Personal Engagement and Disengagement At Work. *Academy of Management Journal, 33*(4), 692–724. doi:10.2307/256287

Lewis, R. E., & Heckman, R. J. (2006). Talent Management: A critical review. *Human Resource Management Review, 16*(2), 139–154. doi:10.1016/j.hrmr.2006.03.001

Lockwood, N. R. (2006). Talent management: driver for organizational success. *SHRM Research Quarterly*. Retrieved Feb 19, 2015 from www.shrm.org

Luthans, F., & Peterson, S. J. (2005). Employee Engagement and Manager Self Efficacy: Implications for Managerial Effectiveness and Development. *Journal of Management Development, 21*(5), 376–387. doi:10.1108/02621710210426864

Robinson, I. (2006). *Human resource management in organisations: The theory and practice of high performance*. London: Chartered Institute of Personnel and Development.

Saks, A. M. (2002, June/July). *So what is a good transfer of training estimate? A reply to Fitzpatrick*. Retrieved Mar 2, 2014, from https://www.siop.org/tip/backissues/tipjan02/pdf/393_%20029to030.pdf

Sheehan, M. (2012). Developing managerial talent: Exploring the link between management talent and perceived performance in multinational corporations (MNCs). *European Journal of Training and Development, 36*(1), 66–85. doi:10.1108/03090591211192638

Singh, A., & Sharma, J. (2015, July). Strategies for talent management: A study of select organizations in the UAE. *The International Journal of Organizational Analysis, 23*(3), 337–347. doi:10.1108/IJOA-11-2014-0823

Truss, S. C., Edwards, E., Wisdom, C., Croll, K., & Burnett, J. (2006). *Working Life: Employee Attitudes and Engagement*. London: CIPD.

Chapter 15
Role of Consumer Knowledge in Developing Purchase Intentions and Driving Services Efficiency across Marketing Channels in Mexico

Rajagopal
EGADE Business School, Tecnologico de Monterrey, Mexico City, Mexico & Boston University, USA

ABSTRACT

This study is carried out in Mexico with an objective to analyse empirically the role of education in a transforming services marketing strategies of the firms. The study is carried on in Mexico through pragmatic investigation among the consumers subscribing to the communication and entertainment services. The analysis of primary data is developed around the theory of action that demonstrates the skills and confidence of individuals or groups towards making decision in acquiring or hiring services to improve their quality of life. The results of the study reveal that knowledge acquired on the services and value perceived by the consumers play key role in determining the intentions to purchases services. This study meticulously rows several arguments on how consumers with high level of education scrutinize the benefits offered by the firms marketing their communication and entertainment services, and build their value propositions on the services bought or contracted.

INTRODUCTION

Most firms are shifting their marketing philosophy to customer orientation by offering quality services in order to acquire and retain customers in increasing global competition. Through building personal relationships with the existing and potential customers, firms look towards inculcating the customer loyalty. However, developing relations appears to be challenging with educated customers as they are inquisitive, explorative, and meticulous in seeking information and solutions through services offered by

DOI: 10.4018/978-1-5225-0902-8.ch015

the firms. Customer centric firms focus on providing the customer services across the table giving access to comprehensive information that can satisfy the emerging issues of the customers. Such attention to detail requires well-trained and alert salespeople and efficient back office personnel. The competitive services marketing firms drive efforts to cultivate relationship competencies by ways of articulating their reasons for customer satisfaction, learn to build pro-customer rationale in resolving post-sales issues, build and retain alliances with more powerful customers, and excel in co-creating business culture within their customers (Isenberg, 2008).

In services marketing firms, loyalty is influenced by the existing knowledge of consumers and was found to be positively and significantly related to quality of information, right to information, and organizational competencies. Customer education was found to be positively associated with customer knowledge or expertise on the products or services. The customer education significantly affects customer loyalty and service quality delivered by the firms (Bell & Eisingerich, 2007). It has been observed that a service firm with customer orientation approach increases relationship quality while a low profile selling approach decreases relationship quality. The relationship quality significantly affects the possibilities of customers' future retention. Firms should emphasize on training employees on customer orientation, which would add additional value to a firm's service offering and influence acquisition and retention of the customers (Huang, 2008).

The expansion in retailing activities using new routes to markets and marketing technologies often demand higher education of consumers to develop compatibility in the selling and buying process. Such need generates increasing consumer knowledge on marketing tools in order to make optimum decisions. While focusing on consumer education, the services marketing issues are considered by the firms as market driven approach (Drummond, 2004). Service quality has attracted considerable attention among the global firms, and marketing services to consumers with high education profile has been considered as a value driven strategy by the firms to serve the premium and middle level consumer segments. It is argued that consumer education is a powerful quality that enables marketing strategy in variety of service contexts to stay competitive and derive higher customer values (Burton, 2002).

The purpose of this article is to analyze empirically the role of education in transforming services marketing strategies of the firms. The basic argument of this article is that the level of education among consumers empowers the consumers' behavior of acceptance or rejection to the services offered by the firms based on the knowledge, peer experience, brand value, competitive advantage, and operational efficiency of the services. The study is carried out in Mexico through pragmatic investigation among the consumers subscribing to the communication and entertainment services. The analysis of primary data is developed around the theory of action that demonstrates the skills and confidence of individuals or groups towards making decision in acquiring or hiring services to improve their quality of life. This study meticulously rows several arguments on how consumers with high level of education scrutinize the benefits offered by the firms marketing their communication and entertainment services, and build their value propositions on the services bought or contracted. This article concludes upon analyzing the data that the firms with indistinct information and unclear marketing strategies fail to create higher and sustainable customer value with the consumers having high educational profile than those having low educational background.

This article also considers the services marketing in reference to quality of services and customer education initiatives that are delivered by the firms. More specifically, the article explores the moderating effects of the increasing levels of customer expertise, which is seen as the outcome of customer education on the relative importance of service quality delivered in determining the customer value.

The article contributes to the existing literature as no substantial research has been contributed so far towards measuring the relationship between the level of education and effectiveness of marketing of services in Mexico.

REVIEW OF LITERATURE AND FRAMEWORK OF HYPOTHESES

Education, Knowledge, and Consumer Insights

The level of customer education is the key factor to measure the service quality delivered and the way it has been delivered (functional service quality). Customer education is also positively associated with customer expertise on the products and services, which are intended to be purchased. However, it has been observed that where there is a significant amount of research on customer knowledge and expertise, there is relatively less understanding of how the convergence of their knowledge with services quality determines the perceived value and satisfaction (Bell & Eisingerich, 2007). In marketing of services, the fairness that includes distributive fairness, procedural fairness and informational fairness is positively related to customer satisfaction. These factors are more critical to in-depth analysis by customers having high level of education as well as product specific knowledge. In the process of services delivery to adaptation, trust is identified as the key mediator of fairness leading to customer satisfaction and generating long-term value (Zhu and Chen, 2012). The knowledge of customers on services would help in differentiating services experiences in reference to the services quality and customer satisfaction (Rowley, 1997). In a competitive marketplace firms tend to develop customer oriented strategies and stay compatible to the customers' knowledge. Service-driven market orientation strategy consists of six components comprising customer orientation, competitor orientation, inter-functional orientation, performance orientation, long-term orientation, and employee orientation that have a significantly strong and positive relationship with service quality (Voon, 2006). Consumer education programs can provide significant benefits, including identification of market information, complaint and consumer redress procedures, and understanding a more technology-based consumer environment (Oumlil & Williams, 2000). Hence, in view of the above discussion, the hypothesis can be structured as:

H1: Consumers intend to acquire comprehensive knowledge on the contracted services to monitor efficiency of services delivery

The focus of consumer education in the global market environment has significant impact on the services industry. Firms involved in managing resources or designing options, from which consumers make choices, are in a much better position for influencing how social, cultural and environmental resources are used. In order to actualize this potential the firms position their services in congruence to the consumer education and develop self-efficacy, capacity for effective advocacy, and interdisciplinary collaboration. Firms also help in raising consumer awareness and the services quality of firms, and social and moral responsibilities associated with professional practice (Sibbel, 2009). Some studies discuss that though service quality has attracted considerable attention within the service marketing literature, high profile consumer education has not been considered a valuable strategy. It is argued that consumer education is a powerful quality strategy in a variety of service contexts and that it is already being used by an increasing number of service organizations. There exists relationship between consumer education and service quality prior to developing an information-education continuum that could help organizations recognize when consumer education might be a useful competitive strategy (Burton, 2002). Firms delivering services influence the degree of quality of services in references to the education of consumers, skills, and cognitive abilities toward reviewing the efficiency of services. Thus, services marketing firms try to build co-shopping and co-reviewing with customers of different levels of education (Sabrina, 2005). It has been observed that often consumers with high level of education develop negative perceptions on services marketing firms. These consumers resist the services firm's deceptive practices (perceived deception) on consumer's relational variables (satisfaction and loyalty intentions to the online retailer). Also, the level of education in consumers plays moderating role in determining consumer attitude toward the Internet (Sergio, 2010). An empirical research conducted for differentiating the various types of knowledge evidences that the relative effects of the self-assessed and objective knowledge depend on the type of information source. Therefore, the following hypothesis is posited:

H2 (a): Higher knowledge on the contracted services drives consumers to demand better quality of services

Consistent with prior research, this study shows that self-assessed knowledge is strongly linked to the consumer's use of personal sources of information including internal memory searches and word-of-mouth communication. Conversely, objective knowledge seems to have a positive impact on the consumer's motivation to seek external information (e.g. newspaper articles, mass media sources) about the service provider (Mattila & Wirtz, 2002). Another study reveals that most experiences of power occurred in high contact services, underlining the social nature of consumer power. While high power experiences occurred due to consumer knowledge, service failure accounted for low power experiences. High power consumers have greater self-oriented action thoughts while low power consumers have greater ruminative thoughts. High power consumers expect providers to focus on the core service while low power consumers have expectations regarding the interpersonal component of service delivery. High power consumers feel more positive emotions, less negative emotions and greater satisfaction than low power consumers, but there was no difference in the expressivity of emotions. Emotion expression mediated the relationship between emotions and satisfaction for high power consumers but not for low power consumers (Menon and Bansal, 2007). Therefore, based on the foregoing review of the literature and previous research, the following hypothesis is advanced:

H2 (b): Consumers tend to acquire information on services to empower consumers for assessing the quality of services to enhance satisfaction on services delivered.

Branding and Pricing Determinants

In the previous literature most research contributions about brand equity for services are based on theoretical or anecdotal evidence. In addition, the presumed differences in brand equity associated with search-dominant, experience-dominant, and credence-dominant services have yet to be empirically examined. Brand equity of services significantly affects the performance of services and is largely driven by the customer knowledge-trust levels. Such measures play key role in assessing whether consumer knowledge of a product category has an effect on the importance of brand equity across product types (Krishnan and Hartline, 2001). The value of commercial expertise is one of the most important determinants of both consumer satisfaction and identification of their services provider. Besides, corporate social responsibility contributes to building consumer identification with the company which is positively correlated to satisfaction too. Satisfaction thus is considered as both an affective and cognitive consumer response in the services industry which, along with identification, finally determines the attitudinal loyalty a consumer shows towards their provider (Perez et al, 2012).

The accuracy of consumer price knowledge is dependent on numerous factors. Consumers are more knowledgeable about the relationships between the prices of competitor brands than about the actual prices themselves. The accuracy of consumer knowledge of prices is dependent on how much importance they place on price, and it influences subjects' perceptions of themselves as shoppers (Rosa-Díaz, 2004). Buyers often communicate positive and negative purchasing experiences through word-of-mouth and social media, which creates special problems and opportunities to position products and services for marketers. Price mavenism that is associated with price-information searching and price-sharing behavior, is often considered a negative dimension of price (Byun & Sternquist, 2010). Some consumers have a tendency to be especially involved in the marketplace. They acquire information about many kinds of products, places to shop, and other facets of the market; and they engage in many product related conversations with other consumers to share their knowledge. These consumers 'market mavens' to denote their enthusiasm for shopping, buying, and talking to others (Goldsmith et al, 2006; Fieck & Price, 1987).

Pricing of services is a sensitive determinant in buying decision among consumers. Services should be priced in a way to reflect the customers' price sensitivity, the nature of the transaction and its cost, and the value of information. The pricing should also reflect the four characteristics of services: intangibility, perishability, lack of standardization, and inseparability of production and consumption. By analyzing the value of information, consumers' price sensitivity, and transaction costs other than search costs against the attributes of services offered, firms could make more profitable pricing decisions (Taher & Basha, 2006). It is very difficult for large-scale retailers to price thousands of items dynamically reflecting all constraints and policies. To solve this problem, a combined model approach may be adapted that contingently selects appropriate pricing models and integrates them. Consumers acquire knowledge through the competitor-referenced pricing and demand-driven pricing dynamics in the market. It has been observed in a study that consumers' store evaluations and product search behaviors are influenced by characteristics of the medium (retail versus e-tail) but this effect is moderated by both gender and price knowledge. Females prefer a brick and mortar environment and are likely to seek information at such retailers, even when similar products are available online. However, males evaluate online offers better than identical store offers, and are less inclined to engage in channel transition. The evaluations of online offers show positive relationship to price knowledge, whereas a reverse pattern of results is obtained for retail offers (Chandrashekeran & Suri, 2012). In reference to the above discussion, hypothesis may be framed as:

H3 (a): Consumers are sensitive to the price of services and express their perceptions among peers on purchase intentions

It is no longer enough to evaluate the price–quality relationship, but the whole life-cycle of commodities has to be traced. Bargain of commodities requires many skills, but the bargain of services requires new skills. The bargain of services requires consumer to be able to manage and evaluate skills bargained and increases administrative work. The educational system is challenged to teach these things more extensively and effectively to consumers. The consumption education in the context of growing information and communication technology may be understood as a pivot in transforming consumers' behavior and producing additional capabilities for the consumer to become a rational buyer of products and services (McGregor, 2007).

Although the individual price estimates of consumers differ significantly from the actual market prices, the price estimates of consumers make close to market prices based on their peer information and informal knowledge on price movements. In general, consumer price knowledge is continuously refreshed at point-of-purchase information sources disseminated either through kiosks or in-store promoters. However, the weakness in consumer price knowledge can be explained by differences in market price variation (Aalto-Setälä & Raijas, 2003). The taxonomy of product-price knowledge encompasses not just isomorphic prices, i.e. actually or formerly perceived and recalled prices bust also include inferential prices, such as the normal price, or the upper reservation price for a product. The price-setting conditions and confidence in prices memorized by consumers determine a consumer's product-price knowledge. There are several variables for measurement needed to qualify a person's product-price knowledge. It has been observed that the behavioral factors like price consciousness, the use of a shopping list, and shopping frequency, and brand confidence actively influence in one's product-price knowledge, even though the impact structure is not uniform (Pechtl, 2008). Buyers search differently on premium price products and simultaneously they compare also low price products. This behavior depends on the search costs of the purchase situation and the knowledge of the buyer involved (Smith, 2000). Considering the discussion on consumer behavior on pricing of services, the following hypothesis has been constituted in the study:

H3 (b): Consumers tend to acquire knowledge on product specific pricing from alternate source to determine decision on purchasing services

Consumers' Knowledge and Services Quality Perception

Consumers with good level of knowledge and education perceive that quality is the key to assessing whether or not the industry provides the desired service. Consumers hold the key to business survival and success. However, there is a gap between managers' perceptions of consumers' expectations and actual consumers' expectations. The main implication for the digital entertainment and communication industry is for managers to develop strategies which will meet consumers' expectations of service quality. However, there exists gap between firm's perceptions of consumers' expectations and actual consumers' expectations (Douglas and Connor, 2003). Effective service logistics can lower the cost and increase service value by improving customer satisfaction and loyalty. However, the conventional ways of the service logistics are information driven instead of knowledge-driven which are insufficient to meet the current needs. The knowledge-based service automation system incorporates various artificial intelligence technologies such as case-based reasoning, which is used for achieving four perspectives of knowledge acquisition, service logistics, and service automation and performance measurement, respectively (Cheung et al, 2006).

It has been observed that switching costs in the interrelationships between perceived value, perceived service quality, customer satisfaction, and customer retention relatively affect the customer loyalty and satisfactions with the services delivered. Service firms may benefit from pursuing a combined strategy of increasing customer satisfaction and switching costs both independently and in tandem, depending upon the product-market characteristics (Edward & Sahadev, 2011). Customers' knowledge and expectations on services quality are interrelated. Consumer expectations are positive predictors of perceived service quality (i.e. higher expectations lead to higher perceptions of quality) while relationship between expectations and perceived service quality is stronger in the competitive marketplace than the niche markets (Hamer, 2006). Consumers of services have expectations about what they will receive from the delivery system. These expectations are beliefs about future events which, when compared with the perceived actual service delivered, are presumed to influence satisfaction and assessments of overall service quality (Coye, 2004). In view of the discussion in the pre-text, hypothesis may be advanced as:

H4 (a): As consumers acquire higher knowledge on services contracted, they turn more conscious on the quality of services

H4 (b): Cognitive barrier of consumers for switching the services will increase as the perceived services quality and satisfaction increase

It has been observed in many research studies that consumers resist change in any buying or services system. Most consumers feels comfortable with the practices they have since long and do not respond to the innovations or changes in the services system despite the firms adequately transferring the knowledge on change attributes to the consumers. When consumers resist adopting an innovation because it requires them to alter established habits, the innovation is called a resistant innovation. However firms under certain circumstances may develop *coopetition* strategies, which involve some cooperation among competitive firms to make an effective strategy for marketing a resistant innovation. Managers should analyze the marketing problem, phases of services innovation, and the resources available to address it. Also it is important to consider the kind of specific resources and knowledge that might be exchanged during *coopetition* process and evaluate the industry climate including the role of consumers and all market players (Garcia et al, 2007). In emerging markets, most consumers who have technical knowledge in the specific services could help the firms in developing the services competitive, attractive, and potential in generating revenue as well as offer high value to the consumers. Firms must involve consumers in developing such co-creation. Firms should also aim at low-income segments and cater to consumers' tendency to buy a lot of the cheapest services. In order to stay ahead in the competition firms should develop their service stores into centers of learning, where shoppers can fill the gaps in their product knowledge (D'Andrea et al, 2010). Services quality is a sustainable source for the firms to gain competitive advantage in the services sector. Service quality drives differentiation and adds value to service offerings and is a tool to win strategic competitive advantage. Firms in competitive marketplace intend to impart consumer education as part of a package of service quality initiatives (Burton, 2002). Hence, the hypothesis may be framed as:

H5: Firms develop sustainable services packages co-creating with consumers and deliver higher satisfaction consumers

The role cycle of consumer begins as a chooser in the market at the initial stage. From the viewpoint of a consumer, buying is not the only way to obtain commodities as they can also be borrowed, fabricated individually or shared among the fellow consumers. Consumer's next role emerges as a user of the product and stands more critical to the products and services as compared to the initial stage. The third role of consumer in the marketing arena appears as a communicator. Consumers observe a strong hold of their power in this stage to share their views among the peers on the products and services that they have learnt, procured, and used. Social media has turned to be a powerful channel to disseminate the consumers' voice within the community through various informal and formal networks (Jarva, 2011).

STUDY DESIGN

Sampling

In order to measure the interrelationship between the knowledge of consumers and services quality in the telecommunication and entertainment firms, respondents including both men and women between the age group of 25-60 years were selected. The study was conducted among the customers of 2 major firms in each telecommunication and satellite entertainment service provider firms. The selected firms for the study were catering to consumers of the A/B, C+ and C demographic segments. The data was collected on 31 variables that were closely related towards influencing the information and knowledge building, services efficiency, and cognitive attributes of consumers. These variables include various perspectives of consumer knowledge, empowerment, brand value, services delivery, services efficiency, and consumer satisfaction in marketing of services to consumers for gaining optimal market share of firms. The data sets were categorized into the relational and economic variables selected for the study as illustrated in Table 1.

Data was collected from 247 respondents purposively selected, who were the customers of the selected services companies in Mexico City, administering a semi-structured questionnaire. Of the total sample respondents, men constituted 46.16 percent and women represented 53.84 percent. The data of 22 respondents (8.90 percent of total sample size) were omitted from the data analysis due to paucity of information. The respondents were involved in buying products and services from the telecommunication and satellite entertainment service provider firms in Mexico. In all, the data of 225 observations were analyzed in the study. It has been found that the overall response rate in the survey was 91.03 percent. The data collected from respondents were tested for its reliability applying the Cronbach Alfa test. Variables derived from test instruments are declared to be reliable only when they provide stable and reliable responses over a repeated administration of the test. The test results showed high reliability $(\alpha = 0.81)$ on an average for all observations included for analysis in reference to all variables pooled under different segments.

Table 1. Variables chosen for the study

Variables by Category	Information and Knowledge		Services Efficiency		Cognitive Attributes
Analytical Segments	Knowledge – Empowerment $(VS_1\text{-}8)$	Services Knowledge-Brand Value $(VS_2\text{-}5)$	Knowledge-Services Delivery $(VS_3\text{-}6)$	Services Delivery-Services Efficiency $(VS_4\text{-}7)$	Knowledge-Services Efficiency- Consumer Satisfaction $(VS_5\text{-}5)$
Hypotheses setting	$H_{1(a)}$, $H_{2(b)}$	$H_{2(a)}$, H_5	$H_{3(b)}$, $H_{4(a)}$	$H_{3(a)}$	$H_{(3a)}$, $H_{4(b)}$, H_5
Description of variables selected for data collection	Services information Trustworthiness Period of association Communicability Social value Knowledge acquisition Empowerment	Innovativeness Technology Value and lifestyle Corporate reputation Sustainability	Monitoring Services differentiation Services attributes Services delivery Services quality Services bundling	Services deliverables Service pricing Customer relations Competitive advantage Operational values Sincerity Value addition competence	Need Consumer Beliefs Consumer satisfaction Switching behavior Purchase intention

Data Collection Tools

Initially focus group discussion was carried out of a representative sample from selected industries in order to assess the responsibility of direct supervision of salespeople in industrial selling situations and the sales administration process in general. Based on the process flow in sales administration, major variable segments were identified keeping in view the objectives of the study. Accordingly pre-coded questionnaires were developed for the study and administered to the respondents. Besides questions with pre-coded options, some open ended questions were also administered separately for qualitative assessment of the responses. The content analysis was done to summarize the open ended questions using software QSR NVivo2. This software has powerful tools for combining subtle coding with qualitative linking, shaping and modeling qualitative information. The analysis of qualitative responses has largely benefited in deriving appropriate managerial implications of the study.

Questionnaires were initially drafted in English and later translated in Spanish for use in Mexico. Principal questions administered during the study have been listed in Appendix-A. Items were modified to fit the Spanish language, and to accommodate all customers and questionnaires were double back-translated (Churchill Jr., 1979). A pilot test showed that consumers understood the questions correctly. Questionnaires were administered by the undergraduate students of marketing program. In translating some questions the technique of equivalence or reformulation has been used to give a correct sense to the sentence.

Attributes of Instrument

Data was collected on the variables closely related towards influencing the buying behavior of products and services of telecommunication and satellite entertainment service provider firms in reference to overall customer satisfaction, consumer education, product information, applied knowledge, services reviews, competitive advantage, and marketing strategies. The results on the analysis of the selected variables refer to the customer values in correlation with the knowledge, economic, and behavioral variables in buying products and services from the telecommunication and satellite entertainment service provider firms.

Seven sources of influence included consumer education, fellow consumers, product knowledge, awareness on innovation and technology, product experience, competitive advantage (e.g. price, promotion, and post-sales services) and inter-personal experience with the salespeople. Six impersonal sources of influence included social network contents, product information brochures, Internet, do-it-yourself experience, and store displays. Respondents were asked to indicate on a four-point Likert scale (1-Totally agree; 4-Totally disagree) when they make a purchase decision on fashion apparel. Much research in academia uses a five-point scale because researchers believe that it may produce more reliable or valid results. However, the response format of this study used a four-point scale because the researchers believed that deleting the neutral point might result in more accurate responses.

Analyzing Non-Responsiveness

Questionnaires were administered to 247 respondents. However, the information of only 225 respondents qualified for the data analysis. The non-response bias has been measured applying two statistical techniques. Firstly, telephonic conversations were made with those respondents who either did not respond to the questions of survey or gave incomplete information of their preference to marketplace, store brands, lifestyle perceptions and logistics related issues (Gounaris et al, 2007). It was found that the main reason for the lack of response showing 59.09 percent respondents of the non-response cases was low confidence level of participation while 22.72 percent subjects failed to respond all questions of the survey due to paucity of time and 18.19 percent subjects depended on their accompanying persons to offer responses who could not do so. The customer response is considered as unit of analysis of this study. Secondly, *T-tests* were used to ascertain emerging differences between respondents and non-respondents concerning the issues pertaining to consumer education and customer services strategies. No statistically significant differences in pre-coded responses $(\alpha = 0.19)$ were found. A second test for non-response bias examined the differences between early and late respondents on the same set of factors (Armstrong and Overton, 1977, Rajagopal, 2011) and this assessment also yielded no significant differences between early and late respondents.

Construct of Measures and Data Validation

The constructs of the study were measured using reflective indicators showing effects on the core variables. The role of consumer education on service efficiency in reference to entertainment and telecommunication services is derived from 18-variables segment comprising consumer knowledge on services, empowerment, brand value, and consumer satisfaction related variables (VS_1, VS_2, and VS_5). The efficiency of services delivered was measured with 13-variables (services delivery-VS_3 and services efficiency led variables-VS_4) on a self-appraisal perceptual scale derived originally on the basis of focus group analysis as referred in the pretext. Motivation about this construct has been derived from an original scale developed by Jimenez and Cegarra-Navarro (2007) on market orientation, who conceptualized it as a multivariate construct comprising customer orientation, competitor orientation and inter-functional coordination as principal behavioral components. This scale also comprised triadic services performance paradigm among consumer education, services efficiency, and cognitive attributes (Verma and Rajagopal, 2013). The framework of hypotheses and spread of variables to test the hypotheses is exhibited in Figure 1.

Constructs related to the role of consumer education and cognitive factors determining the services performance (VS_1 and VS_2) were measured using 13-variable 'self-appraisal perceptual scale' comprising services information, trustworthiness, social value, empowerment, innovativeness, value and lifestyle, corporate reputation, and sustainability of services. Construct of services efficiency (VS_4) was measured in reference to 13-variable 'self-appraisal perceptual scale' consisting of services differentiation, delivery, services quality, services bundling, pricing and competitive advantage. The perceptional behavior of consumers that supports the value generation and helps in developing purchase intentions (VS_5) were measured using 5 variables including need, belief, satisfaction, switching behavior, and purchase intentions. Other variables were selected on the basis of focus group discussion.

All reflective constructs for all variable segments of the study were analyzed through the factor analysis model as a single confirmatory test. The goodness-of-fit statistics[1] comprising chi-square statistics (6.31), root mean square error of approximation (0.158), Tucker-Lewis fit index (0.725), comparative fit index (0.831) and incremental fit index (0.714) indicate that the model used for analysis in the study fits the data adequately. All variables were loaded significantly on their corresponding segments which revealed significant p-value at 0.01 to 0.05 levels.

The data collected from respondents was tested for its reliability applying the Cronbach Alfa test. Variables derived from test instruments are declared to be reliable only when they provide stable and reliable responses over a repeated administration of the test. The test results showed acceptable reliability level $\left(\alpha = 0.722\right)$ on an average for all observations included for analysis in reference to all variables pooled under different segments.

Model Specification

The methodology proposed to analyze the data on selected variables to reach the objectives of the study and test the constituted hypotheses comprises the estimation of services efficiency and analysis of the factors governing services efficiency. Let us assume that the services attractiveness at time t for j services in h market is A_{ser}^{tjh} and consumer knowledge on services contracted is $C_{kno}^{i_{(1,2,3...n)}}$ in reference to various products $\left(i_1, i_2, i_3 ... i_n\right)$ towards newness of products, price, guarantee, customer services, use value, and the like in h market at a given time t. Consumers expect quality of services $Q_{ser}^{i_{(1,2,3...n)}}$ in context to the knowledge acquired on the contracted products, which leads to consumer satisfaction C_{sat}^{ti} gained by effective delivery of services S_{del}^{ti}. Consumers search for information on various indicators prior to contracting entertainment and telecommunication services. Consumers acquire knowledge on price advantages B_{sp} and brand reputation R_{bs} particularly for the services contracted. Consumers acquire knowledge on prior to contract any entertainment and telecommunication services considering the various variables to develop purchase intentions. Accordingly, it may be expressed as:

$$C_{kno}^{i_{(1,2,3...n)}} = \prod_{jh}^{ti} \left(S_{del}, \ B_{sp}, \ R_{bs}, U_{val}, S_{it}, P_{vls}\right) \tag{1}$$

where, U_{val} indicates use value of services as perceived by the consumer, S_{it} denotes innovation and technology associated with the services, and P_{vls} refers to personal values and lifestyle. In the above equation $\prod$ shows the product function for the specified variables. Consumer knowledge determines the services attractiveness and purchase intentions. Hence, the services attractiveness for a contracted service by a consumer may be measured as:

$$A_{ser}^{jth} = \sum_{t}^{jh} \left[C_{kno}^{(i_{1,2,3...n})}\right] \left[Q_{ser}^{(i_{1,2,3...n})}, \ \ S_{del}^{ti}, \ B_{sp}, \ R_{bs}\right] \tag{2}$$

Hence,

$$A_{ser}^{tjh} = C_{kno}^{i_{(1,2,3...n)}} \left[C_{bi} \frac{\partial q}{\partial t}\right] = C_{bi} \left(\frac{\partial b'}{\partial k}\right)\left(\frac{\partial k}{\partial x}\right) = C_{bi} \frac{\partial q}{\partial k} \left[Q_{ser}^{(i_{1,2,3...n})}, S_{del}^{ti}, B_{sp}, R_{bs}\right] \tag{3}$$

where, C_{bi} denotes consumers' purchase intention of services for product $\left(i\right)$, (q) represents consistency in quality of services delivery and (k) indicates the knowledge gained by the consumer on particular contracted service. In the equation, b' expresses time taken in services delivery. The demand for the quality of services by the consumer to stay with the services $\left(\partial_t/\partial_k > 0\right)$, and customer services offered by the firm affecting the level of satisfaction $\left(\partial_{b'}/\partial_k > 0\right)$ increase simultaneously during the process of buying. In reference to the sales promises made at the time of services selling (x), knowledge acquired by the consumers on the services contracted (k) create lower values if the expectations of services are not complied $\left(\partial_k/\partial_x < 0\right)$ while the intention to purchase services is established if the firm complies promises made and delivers service on time $\left(\partial_{b'}/\partial_x > 0\right)$.

$$S_{eff}^{jti} = \alpha + kq + C_{bi} + b' \left(\rho \ C_{sat}^{ti} + \gamma C_{swt}^{ti}\right) + \varphi A_{ser}^{tjh} \tag{4}$$

In the above equation S_{eff}^{jti} denotes the efficiency of services for given products in a jth market at time t. In the same equation α is constant while ρ, γ, and φ are considered to the coefficients of variables pertaining to customer satisfaction on given services products C_{sat}^{ti} and probability of switching services/products C_{swt}^{ti} in a given time t.

In order to measure variations on the knowledge acquired by the consumers and intentions to purchase services as discussed in the pre-text, initial robust weighting matrix and optimal weighting matrix were employed using the equation:

$$C_{sat}^{ti} = \frac{\mu b'}{\mu k}\left(C_{bi}^{t}\right)\left[\tau\left(y_1 + y_2 + y_3 + \varepsilon_n\right)B_{sp}\right]^{ti}\left[\lim_{i \to \infty}\left(S_{eff}^{jti} + \frac{1}{i}\right)^{i}\right] \tag{5}$$

The above equation represents the response of consumers to services marketed in a given market j for product i, (μ) denotes the consumer preference for the services in reference to services delivery time (b') and knowledge acquired on services contracted (k), (γ_1) represents the trust on the firm, (γ_2) denotes inclination towards buying decision persuaded by innovation and technology associated with the services, (γ_3) shows the buying behavior derived by the operational efficiency of services, and (τ) refers to the structural parameter relating to the endogenous variables to one another.

Accordingly, considering the derivations of equations 2, 3, and 4 it may be defined that efficiency of services is the function of the factors as expressed in the following equation:

$$S_{eff}^{jti} = f\left[C_{kno}^{i(1,2,3...n)}, \ A_{ser}^{jth}, \ C_{sat}^{ti}\right] \tag{6}$$

Ordinary Least Square (OLS) method to measure the customer value for buying in shopping malls (dependent variable) in reference to the above discussed physical, cognitive and economic variable (independent variables) has been computed using the construct as below:

$$S_{eff}^{jti} = \alpha + \beta_1\left(C_{kno}^i\right) + \beta_2\left(Q_{ser}^i\right) + \beta_3\left(S_{del}^i\right) + \beta_4\left(B_{sp}\right) + \beta_5\left(R_{bs}\right) + \beta_6\left(C_{bi}\right) + \beta_7\left(C_{sat}\right) + \beta_8\left(C_{swt}\right) + \varepsilon$$

(7)

In the above the error term is denoted by ε in the above equation. The model explains that the service efficiency stimulate purchase intentions of consumers in reference to consumer knowledge, services attraction, and value for money. However, services efficiency generates brand reputation and consumer loyalty in the competition marketplace.

Results and Discussion

The data analysis has been carried on using AMOS 19 version. The descriptive statistics of the database is presented in Table 2.

It has been observed during the study that the firms offering entertainment and telecommunication services in the study region do not educate the consumers prior to selling the services. On the contrary inquisitive consumers get themselves educated on the services offed by the firms in acquiring knowledge from the available resources such as information available on the Internet, social media, and through peer interactions on buying experiences. The estimation of the constructs has been carried out using the equation 5 and the results of estimations are exhibited in Table 3.

Large number of consumers contract the entertainment services through telemarketing. Consumers are attracted towards the entertainment $\left(\gamma_1 = 0.731, p < 0.01\right)$ and telecommunication $\left(\gamma_1 = 0.742, p < 0.01\right)$ services contracted as customer services offered through telemarketing are trustworthy. The innovation and technology associated with the services stimulate purchase intentions of consumers and drive buying decision on entertainment $\left(\gamma_2 = 0.834, p < 0.01\right)$ and telecommunication $\left(\gamma_2 = 0.851, p < 0.01\right)$ services offered through telemarketing. It has been observed that marketing of

Table 2. Descriptive Statistics for the Selected Variable Groups for the Study

Variable Groups	Knowledge-Empowerment (VS$_1$-8)	Services Knowledge-Brand Value (VS$_2$-5)	Knowledge-Services Delivery (VS$_3$-6)	Services Delivery-Services Efficiency (VS$_4$- 7)	Knowledge-Services Efficiency - Consumer Satisfaction (VS$_5$-5)
Sample Size	225	225	225	225	225
Mean	5.379	6.631	7.583	5.291	5.836
Standard Deviation	0.874	0.649	0.627	0.882	0.614
Standard Error	0.082	0.073	0.051	0.066	0.068
Skewness	-0.846	-1.022	-0.739	-0.670	-0.843
Sample Variance	0.654	0.496	0.584	0.754	0.504
Factor Loading Communalities	4.317	3.728	4.294	5.039	4.521
Data reliability test-Cronbach (α) scores	0.82	0.73	0.87	0.81	0.77

VS=Variable Segment. Figures in parentheses indicate number of variables

Table 3. Estimations of Structural Equations

Services Segments		Parameters								
Shopping Clusters	Respondents	(γ_1)	(γ_2)	(γ_3)	(β)	$(\mu b')$	(μk)	SE	Chi-Square
ENT-TM	186	0.669*	0.731*	0.834*	0.633*	0.633*	0.724*	0.622*	2.914	84.06
ENT-VS	21	0.481**	0.249	0.392**	0.422**	0.522**	0.439**	0.535*	4.618	11.72
TELCO-TM	165	0.751*	0.742*	0.851*	0.737*	0.737*	0.712*	0.521**	2..487	76.20
TELCO-CSC	74	0.314+	0.331**	0.472**	0.191	0.391**	0.280+	0.591*	1.466	97.44

ENT-TM= Entertainment services purchased through telemarketing

ENT-VS= Entertainment services contracted through virtual shops

TELCO-TM = Telecommunication services purchased through telemarketing

TELCO-CSC= Telecommunication services contracted through customer services center

*p < 0.01, ** p <0.05, +p <0.10, SE= Standard Error

The sum of number of respondents in column 2 exceeds the total respondents as same respondents have contracted for more than one service

entertainment services through virtual shops is less preferred by the customers as time taken for delivering entertainment services $\left(\mu b' = 0.439, p < 0.05\right)$ through the virtual platform is longer and faulty while consumers do not prefer to stand on long queues $\left(\mu b' = 0.280, p < 0.10\right)$ in the customer services centers to contract telecommunication services. However, analyzing information through Internet on the services in order to build purchase intention by the consumers for entertainment $\left(\mu k = 0.535, p < 0.05\right)$ and from the customer service centers for telecommunication services $\left(\mu k = 0.591, p < 0.05\right)$ has significant impact on gaining knowledge on the services offered. The behavior of consumers towards buying entertainment $\left(\gamma_3 = 0.633, p < 0.01\right)$ and telecommunication $\left(\gamma_3 = 0.737, \ p < 0.01\right)$ services is highly influenced by the operational efficiency of services when contracted through telemarketing as compared to the other marketing outlets. It has been observed during the study that consumers under low-involvement conditions tend to reach deeper levels of information processing that develop lower levels of buying arousal among consumers. Involvement is a complex construct which encompasses many different dimensions such as value for money, competitive advantage, perceived risk and customer services (Rajagopal, 2011). Each of these dimensions lead to different effects, and comprehension of advertising message also determines the extent of information processing.

The results presented in Table 3 indicate that consumers with acquired knowledge on services intending to purchase, measure the level of satisfaction $\left(C_{sat}^{it}\right)$ by analyzing the trust in service provider, innovation and technology inputs in the services offered, and the degree of operational efficiency. The results indicate that the level of customer satisfaction of the services procured is higher in telemarketing channel for entertainment $\left(C_{Sat}^{it} = 0.669, p < 0.01\right)$ and telecommunication $\left(C_{Sat}^{it} = 0.751, p < 0.01\right)$ services as compared to the other marketing outlets. However consumers attempt to acquire information from alternate sources, most effectively through word of mouth for analyzing efficiency of services offered. Accordingly, consumers reach deeper levels of information processing under low involvement using their knowledge on sales promotions to determine the level of perceived risk (Van Raaij et al, 2001). Mexican services firms operate in restrained market competition and cannot afford losing a customer. Hence, orders for services are randomly accepted in order to keep serving the customers. As a result and as an effort to compensate for possible financial losses due to this volatility, Mexican retail services segment as a common practice takes on more work orders than they can normally complete on time causing dissatisfaction among consumers and trigger switching behavior (Elahee and Brooks, 2004). In view of the above analysis, the results have been found consistent with hypotheses H_1, $H_{2(a)}$ and $H_{2(b)}$.

The measures of core constructs are presented in the Table 4, which reveals that consumers acquire adequate information on the services to be contracted $\left(C^i_{kno} = 0.816, p < 0.01\right)$. The attraction of the services to the consumers $\left(A^{ti}_{ser} = 0.633, p < 0.01\right)$ depends on services efficiency and the extent of information available on the services. The results reveal that the higher the services efficiency $\left(S^i_{eff} = 0.738, p0 < 0.01\right)$ the higher the services attraction. It has been observed during the study and also supported by the results that efficiency of services leads to customer satisfaction $\left(C^i_{sat} = 0.794, p < 0.01\right)$ and reduces the possibilities of services switching $\left(C^i_{swt} = 0.275, p < 0.10\right)$ for the specific services $\left(i\right)$ in a given time $\left(t\right)$. Accordingly, the results presented above support the hypothesis $H_{4(b)}$.

The impact of consumer education on purchase intentions of services through different channels has been analyzed in reference to the data on various functional variables in Table 5. Consumers who have updated knowledge on the services, which they intend to contract, expect higher quality of services. However, the perceived quality of services among consumers differs across the services channels. The results exhibited in the Table 5 indicate that perceived services quality in all services marketing channels is statistically significant except on virtual channel for purchasing entertainment services $\left(Q^i_{ser} = 0.229\right)$. However delivery of telecommunication services were found significant through the telemarketing

Table 4. Measures of core constructs

Constructs	Statistical Measures	
	Robust Weight	**Optimal Weight**
Consumer Knowledge $\left(C^i_{kno}\right)$	0.816*	0.790
Services Attractiveness $\left(A^{ti}_{ser}\right)$	0.633**	0.512
Customer Satisfaction $\left(C^i_{sat}\right)$	0.794*	0.638
Services Switching $\left(C^i_{swt}\right)$	0.275+	0.481
Services Efficiency $\left(S^i_{eff}\right)$	0.783*	0.736
Coefficient of trend variable $\left(\beta\right)$	0.571**	0.558

*p < 0.01, ** p <0.05, +p <0.10

Table 5. Impact of Consumer Education on Services Purchase Intentions

Analytical variables[a]	Services shopping clusters			
	ENT-TM	ENT-VS	TELCO-TM	TELCO-CSC
Consumer knowledge on services $\left(C_{kno}^i \right)$	0.619*	0.358**	0.611*	0.736*
Perceived quality of services $\left(Q_{ser}^i \right)$	0.671*	0.229	0.717*	0.813*
Delivery of contracted services $\left(S_{del}^i \right)$	0.425**	0.342+	0.756*	0.722*
Knowledge on price advantages $\left(B_{sp} \right)$	0.623*	0.184	0.845*	0.616*
Awareness on brand reputation of services $\left(R_{bs} \right)$	0.615*	0.187	0.317+	0.554*
Purchase intention of consumers $\left(C_{bt} \right)$	0.630*	0.284+	0.561**	0.417*
Constant	0.1439	0.2215	0.3499	0.1079
$\bar{R}^2$	0.573**	0.193*	0.796*	0.513**

[a] =Variables are described in equation (5)
*p < 0.01, ** p <0.05, +p <0.10

$\left(S_{del}^i = 0.756, p < 0.01 \right)$ and customer services centers $\left(S_{del}^i = 0.722, p < 0.01 \right)$. Consumers acquire adequate knowledge on services pricing from all marketing channels to determine their purchase intention. The results presented in the above Table indicate that the higher the price advantages of services $\left[\text{ENT} - \text{TM} \left(B_{sp} = 0.623, p < 0.01 \right) \right]$ the stronger the purchase intentions $\left[\text{ENT} - \text{TM} \left(B_{sp} = 0.630, p < 0.01 \right) \right]$ in entertainment service product. Similar inference can be drawn to measure the purchase intentions of consumers towards telecommunication services through the tele-marketing $\left[\text{TELCO} - \text{CSC} \left(C_{bt} = 0.561, p < 0.05 \right) \right]$ channel and customer service center $\left[\text{TELCO} - \text{CSC} \left(C_{bt} = 0.617, p < 0.01 \right) \right]$. Consumers also gain awareness about the brand reputation on services offered to determine their purchase intentions. Hence, the results discussed above are consistent with the hypotheses $\mathbf{H}_{3(a)}$, $\mathbf{H}_{3(b)}$, and $\mathbf{H}_{4(b)}$.

The correlation matrix of peripheral variables of construct is exhibited in the Table 6 which reveals that the availability of information on services offered builds trust among consumers about the services intended to be purchased $\left(V_2, V_1 : r = 00.621, p < 0.01 \right)$ and trust on specific service products help consumers to perceive higher brand value $\left(V_1, V_5 : r = 00.742, p < 0.01 \right)$. Trustworthiness of services has positive implication on enhancing social value $\left(V_1, V_3 : r = 00.748, p < 0.01 \right)$ and strengthening the consumer intentions to purchase services $\left(V_3, V_7 : r = 0.675, p < 0.01 \right)$. Consumers reinforce their

Table 6. Pearson correlation matrix of principal variables of construct

Variables	Mean	SD	V_1	V_2	V_3	V_4	V_5	V_6	V_7
Trustworthiness (V_1)	3.29	0.816	**1.000**						
Information on services (V_2)	3.65	1.284	0.621*	**1.000**					
Social value (V_3)	4.62	1.193	0.748*	0.644*	**1.000**				
Innovation and Technology (V_4)	4.82	0.814	0.351+	0.512**	0.745*	**1.000**			
Brand value (V_5)	3.46	0.432	0.742*	0.324+	0.826*	0.612*	**1.000**		
Price advantage (V_6)	3.74	0.209	0.542**	0.251	0.628*	0.623*	0.575*	**1.000**	
Purchase intention (V_7)	2.96	0.145	0.473**	0.791*	0.675*	0.396+	0.622*	0.819*	**1.000**

(n=225)

*p < 0.01, ** p <0.05, + p <0.10, SD= Standard deviation

intentions towards buying services as they learn price advantages $\left(V_6, V_7 : r = 0.819, p < 0.01\right)$ and association of innovation and technology $\left(V_4, V_1 : r = 0.396, p < 0.10\right)$ with the services. Firms develop sustainable services packages integrating services information, innovation and technology, and price advantage over competing services. Integration of these variables in marketing of services helps the service providing firms in co-creating the social and brand value with consumers and deliver higher satisfaction to them. Accordingly, the results discussed above are found consistent with the hypotheses $H_{3(a)}$, $H_{3(b)}$, and H_5.

Managerial Implications

Consumer education can be used by the service delivery firms as an effective and viable tool to implement marketing strategies. However, some corporations use consumer education to motivate self-promotion, advertising and build self-reference criteria to help consumers in strengthening their purchase intentions. The consumer education programs have the potential to benefit consumers and enhance social and brand value of the services. Consumer education and counseling should be introduced by the services firms for specific services like health, education, telecommunication, finance etc. Such support on the consumer education would enhance information analysis and decision making abilities. Most of the services firms are of the view that there exists high demand for services like entertainment, telecommunication, transport, education, health, banking, and insurance and believe that services can be sold easily to the stressed consumers, which is not a correct notion in the growing market competition. However, marketing professionals have often oversimplified the problem of building successful services brands by educating the consumers on the services offered by the firm, the customer relations can play an important strategic role. Strong service brands can be built by co-creating with consumers and this process demands enormous awareness of services offered, corporate reputation, and competitive advantage.

The conventional wisdom on services marketing approaches indicate that firms should determine customers' needs and educate them about what can be offered by the firm to satisfy their needs but if firms do not have competency in disseminating appropriate information regarding operational efficiency of the firm, customer opinions, and expectations it would be difficult for the firm to retain existing customers or acquire new ones. For the services firms operating in global markets, it may be necessary to develop participatory awareness programs in collaboration with the consumers and social networks to achieve the required marketing results. During the study consumers suggested that they were influenced in making decisions to buy services provided the firms shared vital information on brand value, services attributes, price, consumer benefits, and periodical upgrade of services through customer interactive activities involving employees of the firm in educating the consumers. Such initiatives by the services marketing firms would make the consumer feel a greater sense of value for money and trust towards their employees to stay long the firm and narrow down the options of services switching.

Consumers' knowledge on services offered by the firm may be enhanced by strengthening the information dissemination through various Internet platforms. The most common and cost-effective approach to marketing on-line is search-term marketing, service, or related features of the services. This type of marketing involves low search costs and high information diffusion on search-oriented Web sites such as Yahoo!, Google, Lycos, MSN and many others. The idea is that there is no better time to try to drive a consumer to the relevant Web site than when the consumer has just searched for an alternate service. It is important for the services marketing firms to attain efficiency in services delivery with quality. Managers should ensure that the quality of decision making will generate tactical as well as long run relations with the consumers so the firm can gain competitive advantage over other firms. Firms should establish Face-to-face contacts to learn quickly and easily about the need, problems, and functional issues associated with the consumers for hiring the services. Such interactivity between the consumers and the firm would nurture trust among the consumers, enhance social value, and customer-centric face of the firm. This approach would enhance customer involvement to increase emotional response, which may be more desirable when personalized services are warranted.

CONCLUSION

This study discusses the role of consumer knowledge in developing intentions towards purchasing services of entertainment and telecommunication, which are essential in today's socio-economic lifestyle. The study reveals that consumers attempt to acquire information from various sources on the services offered by the firms. Consumers analyze the operational efficiency of the services and competitive advantages in reference to price, delivery of services, quality of services, and value for money upon purchase of services. The results of the study reveal that consumers intend to acquire comprehensive knowledge on the contracted services to monitor efficiency of services delivery and as consumers acquire higher knowledge on the contracted services they intend to demand better quality of services. The study observed that consumers are sensitive to the price of services and express their perceptions among peers on purchase intentions. However, consumers who are dissatisfied with the services offered are induced to switch the services from the present service provider.

Social media has emerged as one of the powerful resources portraying consumer experiences, which influence the consumer decision making towards buying services. Consumers also get involved in peer discussions to evaluate the brand value of services, corporate reputation of services firms and their operational efficiency in delivering services. The study reveals that most services marketing firms do not give priority to the consumer education on services and refrain from complying with the pre-sales promises that prompts switching behavior among the consumers. The study suggests that services firms should develop sustainable services packages by integrating public information on services, competitive advantages, and social values of services offered by the firm, co-creating with consumers for delivering higher satisfaction to consumers. The discussions in the study also divulge that purchase intentions on services are largely driven by services attractions, inter-personal influences, consumer-employee relations and comparative gains. Major factors that affect shopping purchase intentions include services innovation and technology, services upgrades, virtual support, brand value, and price.

Limitations of the Study

Like many other empirical studies this research might also have some limitations in reference to sampling, data collection and generalization of the findings. The samples drawn for the study may not be enough to generalize the study results. However, results of the study may indicate similar pattern of shopping behavior of urban consumers in shopping malls also in reference to other Latin American markets. The findings are limited to Mexican consumers and convenience sampling. Other limitations include the qualitative variables used in the study which might have reflected on making some causal statements. However, future studies could avoid these limitations by using data from several countries, representative samples, and additional variables.

Figure 1. Framework of Hypotheses and major variables of the study

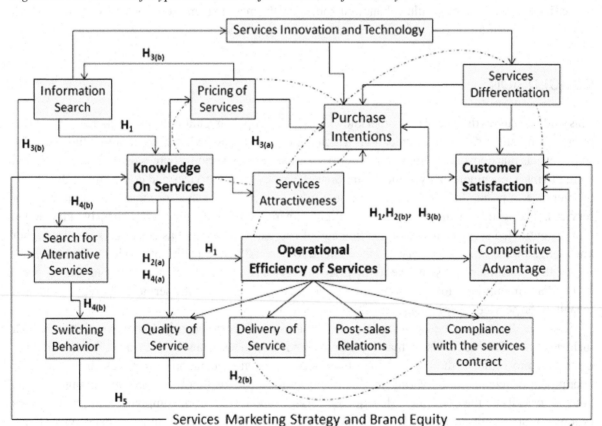

FUTURE RESEARCH PROSPECTS

The core idea of this study is to examine the cognitive factors comprising knowledge and consumer perceptions that influence shopping behavior of services through various channels of marketing. This study reviews the previous contributions on the subject and raises some interesting research questions in reference to the availability of services information, consumer knowledge, consumer interactivity, and operational efficiency in delivering the services. There are not many empirical studies that have addressed these questions either in isolation or considering the interrelationship of the above factors. The determinants of consumer behavior analyzed in this study can be further explored broadly with the lifestyle center management and consumer behavior research streams.

ACKNOWLEDGMENT

This paper has been developed out of the research project conducted by Rajagopal, Professor of Marketing (EGADE), ITSEM, Mexico City Campus on Consumer behavior towards services marketing under the aegis of Research Group on Consumer Behavior and Competitiveness, Monterrey Institute of Technology and Higher Education-ITESM, Campus Santa Fe, Mexico during 2011-13. Author expresses sincere thanks to Dean EGADE Business School and Dr Jorge Vera, Coordinator of the research group for extending administrative support to this project.

REFERENCES

Aalto-Setälä, V., & Raijas, A. (2003). Actual market prices and consumer price knowledge. *Journal of Product and Brand Management*, *12*(3), 180–192. doi:10.1108/10610420310476933

Bell, S. J., & Eisingerich, A. B. (2007). The paradox of customer education: Customer expertise and loyalty in the financial services industry. *European Journal of Marketing*, *41*(5), 466–486. doi:10.1108/03090560710737561

Burton, D. (2002). Consumer education and service quality: Conceptual issues and practical implications. *Journal of Services Marketing*, *16*(2), 125–142. doi:10.1108/08876040210422673

Byun, S. E., & Sternquist, B. (2010). Reconceptualization of price mavenism: Do Chinese consumers get a glow when they know? *Asia Pacific Journal of Marketing and Logistics*, *22*(3), 279–293. doi:10.1108/13555851011062232

Chandrashekaran, R., & Suri, R. (2012). Effects of gender and price knowledge on offer evaluation and channel transition in retail and e-tail environments. *Journal of Product and Brand Management*, *21*(3), 215–225. doi:10.1108/10610421211228838

Cheung, C. F., Chan, Y. L., Kwok, S. K., Lee, W. B., & Wang, W. M. (2006). A knowledge-based service automation system for service logistics. *Journal of Manufacturing Technology Management*, *17*(6), 750–771. doi:10.1108/17410380610678783

Coye, R. W. (2004). Managing customer expectations in the service encounter. *International Journal of Service Industry Management*, *15*(1), 54–71. doi:10.1108/09564230410523330

D'Andrea, G., Marcotte, D., & Morrison, G. D. (2010). Let emerging market customers be your teachers. *Harvard Business Review*, *88*(12), 115–120.

Douglas, L., & Connor, R. (2003). Attitudes to service quality- the expectation gap. *Nutrition & Food Science*, *33*(4), 165–172. doi:10.1108/00346650310488516

Drummond, G. (2004). Consumer confusion: Reduction strategies in higher education. *International Journal of Educational Management*, *18*(5), 317–323. doi:10.1108/09513540410543466

Edward, M., & Sahadev, S. (2011). Role of switching costs in the service quality, perceived value, customer satisfaction and customer retention linkage. *Asia Pacific Journal of Marketing and Logistics*, *23*(3), 327–345. doi:10.1108/13555851111143240

Elahee, M., & Brooks, C. M. (2004). Trust and negotiation tactics: Perceptions about business-to-business negotiations in Mexico. *Journal of Business and Industrial Marketing*, *19*(6), 397–404. doi:10.1108/08858620410556336

Feick, L. F., & Price, L. L. (1987). The market maven: A diffuser of marketplace information. *Journal of Marketing*, *51*(1), 83–97. doi:10.2307/1251146

Garcia, R., Bardhi, F., & Friedrich, C. (2007). Overcoming consumer resistance to innovation. *MIT Sloan Management Review*, *48*(4), 82–88.

Goldsmith, R. E., Clark, R. A., & Goldsmith, E. B. (2006). Extending the psychological profile of market mavenism. *Journal of Consumer Behaviour*, *5*(5), 411–419. doi:10.1002/cb.189

Hamer, L. O. (2006). A confirmation perspective on perceived service quality. *Journal of Services Marketing*, *20*(4), 219–232. doi:10.1108/08876040610674571

Huang, M. H. (2008). The influence of selling behaviors on customer relationships in financial services. *International Journal of Service Industry Management*, *19*(4), 458–473. doi:10.1108/09564230810891905

Isenberg, D. J. (2008). The global entrepreneur. *Harvard Business Review*, *86*(12), 107–111.

Jarva, V. (2011). Consumer education and everyday futures work. *Futures*, *43*(1), 99–111. doi:10.1016/j.futures.2010.10.016

Krishnan, B. C., & Hartline, M. D. (2001). Brand equity: Is it more important in services? *Journal of Services Marketing*, *15*(5), 328–342. doi:10.1108/EUM0000000005654

Mattila, A. S., & Wirtz, J. (2002). The impact of knowledge types on the consumer search process: An investigation in the context of credence services. *International Journal of Service Industry Management*, *13*(3), 214–230. doi:10.1108/09564230210431947

McGregor, S. L. T. (2007). Sustainable consumer empowerment through critical consumer education: A typology of consumer education approaches. *International Journal of Consumer Studies*, *29*(5), 437–447. doi:10.1111/j.1470-6431.2005.00467.x

Menon, K., & Bansal, H. S. (2007). Exploring consumer experience of social power during service consumption. *International Journal of Service Industry Management, 18*(1), 89–104. doi:10.1108/09564230710732911

Oumlil, A. B., & Williams, A. J. (2000). Consumer education programs for mature consumers. *Journal of Services Marketing, 14*(3), 232–243. doi:10.1108/08876040010327239

Pechtl, H. (2008). Price knowledge structures relating to grocery products. *Journal of Product and Brand Management, 17*(7), 485–496. doi:10.1108/10610420810916380

Perez, A., García de los Salmonesm, M., & Rodríguez del Bosque, I. (2013). (in press). The Effect of Corporate Associations on Consumer Behavior. *European Journal of Marketing, 47*(1).

Rajagopal. (2011). Impact of Radio Advertisements on Buying Behaviour of Urban Commuters. *International Journal of Retail and Distribution Management, 39*(7), 480-503.

Rosa-Díaz, I. M. (2004). Price knowledge: Effects of consumers attitudes towards prices, demographics, and socio-cultural characteristics. *Journal of Product and Brand Management, 13*(6), 406–428. doi:10.1108/10610420410560307

Rowley, J. (1997). Beyond service quality dimensions in higher education and towards a service contract. *Quality Assurance in Education, 5*(1), 7–14. doi:10.1108/09684889710156530

Sabrina, N. (2005). Influence on consumer socialization. *Young Consumers: Insight and Ideas for Responsible Marketers, 6*(2), 63–69. doi:10.1108/17473610510701115

Sergio, R. (2010). Relational Consequences of Perceived Deception in Online Shopping: The Moderating Roles of Type of Product, Consumers Attitude toward the Internet and Consumers Demographics. *Journal of Business Ethics, 95*(3), 373–391. doi:10.1007/s10551-010-0365-9

Sibbel, A. (2009). Pathways towards sustainability through higher education. *International Journal of Sustainability in Higher Education, 10*(1), 68–82. doi:10.1108/14676370910925262

Smith, G. E. (2000). Search at different price levels: The impact of knowledge and search cost. *Journal of Product and Brand Management, 19*(3), 164–178. doi:10.1108/10610420010332430

Taher, A., & Basha, H. E. (2006). Heterogeneity of consumer demand: Opportunities for pricing of services. *Journal of Product and Brand Management, 15*(5), 331–340. doi:10.1108/10610420610685884

Van Raaij, W. F., Strazzieri, A., & Woodside, A. (2001). New developments in marketing communications and consumer behavior. *Journal of Business Research, 53*(2), 59–61. doi:10.1016/S0148-2963(99)00075-2

Verma, R., & Rajagopal, . (2013). Conceptualizing service innovation architecture: A service – strategic framework. *Journal of Transnational Management, 18*(1), 3–22. doi:10.1080/15475778.2013.751869

Voon, B. H. (2006). Linking a service-driven market orientation to service quality. *Managing Service Quality, 16*(6), 595–619. doi:10.1108/09604520610711927

Zhu, Y. Q., & Chen, H. G. (2012). Service Fairness and Customer Satisfaction in Internet Banking: Exploring the Mediating Effects of Trust and Customer Value. *Internet Research, 22*(4), 482–498. doi:10.1108/10662241211251006

ENDNOTES

[1] The goodness-of-fit statistics that the Tucker-Lewis index (TLI) also known as the Bentler-Bonett non-normed fit index (NNFI), comparative fit index (CFI) and incremental fit index (IFI) tend to range between 0 and 1, with values close to 1 indicating a good fit. The TLI (NNFI) has the advantage of reflecting the model fit very well for all sample sizes. It is observed in past empirical studies these indices need to have values above 0.9 before the corresponding model can even be considered moderately adequate.

Section 5
Organizational Culture, Consumerism and Green Economics

Chapter 16

Moderating Role of Demands:
Abilities Fit in the Relationship between Work Role Stressors and Employee Outcomes

Bindu Chhabra
International Management Institute, India

ABSTRACT

The purpose of the present study was to explore the direct effect of work role stressors and Demands-Abilities (D-A) fit on the employee outcomes of job satisfaction, organizational citizenship behavior (OCB) and turnover intentions. The study further aimed to investigate the moderating role of D-A fit in the relationship between work role stressors and the above mentioned employee outcomes. The study was conducted using structured questionnaires for measuring the above mentioned variables. The sample of the study was 317 professionals from five sectors. Hierarchical multiple regression was used to analyze the data. Hierarchical multiple regression results showed that the work role stressors were negatively related to job satisfaction and OCB and positively related to turnover intentions. D-A fit was seen to be positively related to job satisfaction and OCB and negatively related to turnover intentions. The analysis also found some support for the stress buffering effect of high D-A fit in the prediction of job satisfaction, OCB and turnover intentions. This study contributes to the organizational behavior literature by focusing on the fact that the negative effects of work role stressors on employee outcomes can be mitigated by identifying the variables which act as a buffer to weaken this effect. The results of the study provide support for the fact that matching employees to their job can help in the mitigation of employees' stress resulting in positive employee outcomes, hence benefiting the organization in the long run.

INTRODUCTION

The menace of stress is taking its toll on working adults and has negative implications for both employees and organizations. Across a range of organizational contexts and cultures, research has consistently shown that experienced stress has deleterious effects on employees' mental and physical health, as well as on organizational outcomes such as job satisfaction, job performance and employee turnover (Ngo,

DOI: 10.4018/978-1-5225-0902-8.ch016

Foley & Loi, 2005; Kahn & Brosier, 1992; Newton & Jimmieson, 2009; O'Driscoll & Beehr, 1994). The detrimental effects of stress are building up in India as in United States and other developed countries. According to a survey by Associated Chambers of Commerce and Industry of India in 2015, increasingly demanding schedules and high stress levels in the private sector employees are leading to depression or general anxiety disorders and have wide range of effects like daytime fatigue, physical discomfort or low pain threshold leading to increased absenteeism and performance deterioration. The survey further points out that nearly 45% of the corporate employees in private sector sleep less than 6 hours a day, leading to severe sleep disorders. A large number of factors, ranging from technological changes, global competitive pressures, job insecurity and ever demanding customers to hazardous work environments and overbearing bosses, contribute to this stress. To promote employee physical and psychological health, positive job-related attitudes and performance, effective management of stress for employees has been a great challenge for the human resource practitioners.

Although the deleterious effects of work stress on employees' physical and mental health cannot be undermined, researchers have investigated a large number of factors that may moderate the negative effects of work role stressors on the organizational outcomes. This kind of research can be extremely beneficial to the human resource practitioners and other managers as it can help in designing the strategies which can reduce negative effect of work role stress. Researchers have investigated large number factors that may moderate the negative effects of stressors or job demands on the employee outcomes. These include Type A behavior (Kushnir & Melamed, 1991), locus of control (Daniels & Guppy, 1994; Vahtera, Pentti & Uutela, 1996), self-efficacy (Jimmieson, 2000), self-esteem (Makikangas & Kinnunen, 2003), proactivity (Parker & Sprigg, 1999), trust in management (Harvey, Kelloway & Duncan-Leiper, 2003), perceptions of the balance between effort and rewards (Siegrist, 2002) and subjective fit with organizational culture (Newton & Jimmieson, 2009). While many such task and individual variables have been identified, there is the need to identify additional variables that can buffer this negative effect. Identification of such variables can help in creating a healthy work environment without lowering the job demands. The present study aims to investigate the stress buffering effect of demands-abilities (D-A) fit.

The D–A fit has been defined as the extent to which a person's knowledge, skills, and abilities are congruent with the demands and requirements of their jobs (Edwards, 1996; Werbel & Johnson, 2001). This fit is complementary since the individual provides resources that respond to the demands of his/her environment (Muchinsky & Monahan, 1987).

The present study aims to contribute to the existing body of literature by examining the direct effect of work role stressors on employee outcomes of job satisfaction, organizational citizenship behavior and turnover intention in the Indian Organizations. The study further aims to investigate the moderating role of demands-abilities (D-A) fit in the relationship between work role stressors and the above mentioned employee outcomes.

Objectives of the Study

- To study the direct effect of work role stressors on the following employee outcomes
  - Job satisfaction
  - Organizational citizenship behavior
  - Turnover intention

- To study the direct effect of demands-abilities (D-A) fit on the above mentioned employee outcomes.
- To investigate the moderating effect of demands-abilities (D-A) fit in the relationship between work role stressors and employee outcomes.

Theoretical Framework and Hypotheses Development

For the purpose of meeting the above mentioned objectives, extensive review of literature was done and hypotheses were developed.

Work Role Stressors and Employee Outcomes

Research in the field of stress has mainly focused on the stimulus response paradigm suggesting that the employees in an organization have to work in stressful working conditions (stressors), which can result in a response characterized by negative attitudes and behaviors (Netemeyer, Maxham, & Pullig, 2005; Walker, Churchill & Ford, 1975). Research on organizational stressors has focused mainly on role stress, comprising of role ambiguity and role conflict (Kahn, Wolfe, Quinn, Snoek & Rosenthal, 1964). The excessive emphasis on role ambiguity and role conflict in the organizational stress research is undermining the importance of another critical stressor at workplace namely role overload. For this reason, the present study focuses on three types of work role stressors namely, role ambiguity, role conflict and role overload that have been identified as the common sources of the stress in the workplace (Boles, Wood & Johnson, 2003; Cooper, Dewe & O'Driscoll, 2001; Jackson & Scbuler, 1985).

Role ambiguity occurs when the employees do not have clear understanding about their role in the organization (Rizzo, House & Lirtzman, 1970). Role conflict is the result of incompatible expectations faced by the employees in their jobs, such that the compliance with one expectation makes it extremely difficult or impossible to comply with other expectation (Kahn et al, 1964). Role overload refers to the total amount of work and the time frame in which the work must be completed (Cooper et al., 2001). It occurs when the employees feel that there are too many responsibilities or activities expected of them in the light of time available, their abilities and other constraints (Rizzo et al., 1970).

Job satisfaction is one of the most researched attitudes and reflects how well people like or dislike various aspects of their jobs (Spector, 1985). Work role stress leads to emotional exhaustion in the employees leading to the feelings of helplessness, lowered self-esteem and lack of accomplishment (Cordes & Dougherty, 1993; Moore, 2000). The employees thus feel anxious and frustrated and develop negative attitudes towards their organizations, their work and towards themselves. This, in turn leads to job dissatisfaction. A large number of studies have shown a negative relationship between work role stressors and job satisfaction (Chang, Rosen, & Levy, 2009; Mulki, Jaramillo & Locander, 2008; Ngo, et al., 2005; Örtqvist & Wincent, 2006).

However, the impact of work role stress has not been as widely studied on another work outcome namely organizational citizenship behavior (OCB). Citizenship Behaviors are defined as the discretionary behaviors on the part of an individual, not formally recognized by the organizational reward system, yet they contribute to the effectiveness of the organization (Bateman & Organ, 1983; Smith, Organ & Near, 1983). These behaviors are often performed by the employees to support the interests of the organization even though they may not directly lead to individual benefits (Moorman & Blakely, 1995). Since OCBs are acts that typically go beyond an employee's roles and duties, it is likely that work role stress will discourage employees from indulging in such behaviors. When the stress at work becomes excessive and exceeds available resources, employees respond by reducing OCBs rather than compromising on their task performance. This is because of the fact that the negative consequences associated with lower OCBs are less than those associated with lower task performance (Organ, 1997). Further, social exchange theory (Cropanzano, Rupp & Byrne, 2003), effort-reward imbalance theory (Siegrist, 1996), and resource allocation theory (Kanfer & Ackerman, 1989) all propose that higher levels of work stress will lead to lower levels of OCBs. Recently, Jain and Cooper (2012) conducted a study on 402 operators working in business processing organizations (BPO) organization in northern India, to study the impact of stress on OCB. They found that stress was negatively related to most dimensions of OCB.

Working in a stressful work environment leads to lower job involvement and psychological withdrawal from the work group (Brief & Aldag, 1976) and hence increases the turnover intentions. Intentions to leave may be regarded as the last stage in the sequence of withdrawal cognitions, ranging from thinking of leaving to intending to search for alternative employment (Tett & Meyer, 1993). Work role stress is considered to be an important antecedent of withdrawal cognitions and turnover behavior (Hom & Griffeth, 1995). According to the theories of role stress, ambiguous or conflicting role demands evoke role strain (Kahn et al., 1964; Netemeyer, Johnston & Burton, 1990), which in turn leads to dissatisfaction and turnover behavior (Fisher & Gitelson, 1983; Jackson & Schuler, 1985; Ngo et al., 2005).

The review of literature for this section demonstrates that role ambiguity, role conflict and role overload will have a negative impact on employee outcomes. However, to further explore the relationship between work role stressors and the important employee outcomes of job satisfaction, OCB and turnover intentions, the following hypotheses are proposed:

H1: Work role stressors will have a negative effect on job satisfaction of the employees (H1a); organizational citizenship behaviors (OCB) exhibited by the employees (H1b) and will have a positive effect on the employees' turnover intentions (H1c).

Demands-Abilities Fit and Employee Outcomes

The concept of fit has been extensively studied in the organizational behavior literature (Cable & DeRue, 2002; Chang, Chi & Chuang, 2010; Gregory, Albritton & Osmonbekov, 2010; Guan, Deng, Risavy, Bond & Li, 2011; Kristof-Brown, Zimmerman & Johnson, 2005) and has been shown to influence job applicants' decision to choose certain organizations (Judge & Cable, 1997; Saks & Ashforth, 1997) and the recruiters decision to hire the participants (Cable & Judge, 1997; Kristof-Brown, 2000).

Fit can be evaluated subjectively or objectively (French, Rogers & Cobb, 1974). Subjective fit is defined as the match between the person and environment as they are perceived and reported by the person, and objective fit as the match between the person as he or she really is and the environment as it exists "independently" of the person's perception of it (French et al., 1974, p.316). Since objective reality must be filtered through individuals' perception, this kind of fit is a less proximal determinant of attitudes and behaviors compared to the subjective fit (Cable & DeRue, 2002; Kristof-Brown, et al., 2005). Thus, this study aims to study the effect of the perceptions of subjective D-A fit on employees' attitudes and behaviors.

There is a general recognition that Demands-Abilities fit has important implications for individual behaviors and work outcomes. Among job applicants in the United States, perceived D-A fit has been found to be related to career choice, perceived organizational attractiveness, and subsequent choices of organizations for employment (Holland, 1985; Saks & Ashforth, 1997; Schein, 1978). Among employees working in organizations, D–A fit was found to be related to job satisfaction (Boon et al., 2011; Cable & De Rue, 2002; Edwards, 1996), organizational commitment (Boon et al., 2011; Saks & Ashforth, 2002), the quality of work life (Edwards, 1996; Rice, Mc Farlin, Hunt, & Near, 1985), intent to leave (Boon et al., 2011; Chang et al., 2010; Saks & Ashforth, 2002), task performance (Chi & Pan, 2012), OCB (Boon et al., 2011) and positive adjustment in new organizations (Spokane, 1985). In sum, there exists extensive theoretical and empirical evidence supporting D –A fit as distinctive predictor for positive work-related attitudes. Kristof-Brown et al., (2005) concluded that D-A fit correlates positively with job satisfaction and organizational commitment, and negatively with intent to quit. It also has a moderate positive relationship with coworker satisfaction, supervisor satisfaction, and organizational identification.

The review of literature for this section demonstrates D-A fit will have a positive impact on employee outcomes. However, to further explore the relationship between the subjective D-A fit and the important employee outcomes of job satisfaction, OCB and turnover intentions, the following hypotheses are proposed:

H2: Demands-abilities fit will have a positive effect on job satisfaction of the employees (H2a), organizational citizenship behaviors (OCB) exhibited by the employees (H2b) and will have a negative effect on the employees' turnover intentions (H2c).

Moderating Role of D-A fit in the Relationship Between Work Role Stressors and Employee Outcomes

As shown in the previous section, there has been a lot of research showing the direct effect of subjective D-A fit on a large number of employee outcomes. However, very little work has been done with respect to the role of subjective fit in the stress coping process. The concept of fit is especially prominent in the organizational stress research (Hecht & Allen, 2005; Kreiner, 2006; Kristof-Brown et al., 2005). According to the person-environment approach (Lewin, 1935; Murray, 1938), person and environment work as joint determinants of employee well-being. How employees react to the work stressors or job demands might depend on how well the employees are matched with their organization and their jobs. Work stress will have minimal impact on negative employee outcomes when the employee works in a conducive environment. When the abilities of the person are in line with the demands of the job (high D-A fit), the person will have little difficulty performing the roles and responsibilities of the job. A sales executive is required to interact with a large number of people and if he has good social and persuasive skills to make these interactions fruitful, D-A fit is assumed to be there. For this person, excessive job demands like long working hours are less likely to lead to negative work outcomes than for a person who does not possess the ability to deal with people. The negative effect of work stressors on employee outcomes is thus attenuated because of the ability of the person to deal with the challenges of the job.

The review of literature for this section demonstrates that D-A fit will act as a buffer between work stressors and employee outcomes. However, to further explore the moderating role of subjective D-A fit in the relationship between work role stressors and important employee outcomes of job satisfaction, OCB and turnover intentions, the following hypotheses are proposed:

H3: Demands-abilities fit will moderate the relationship between work role stressors and job satisfaction (H3a), OCBs (H3b) and turnover intentions (H3c) such that the relationship will be stronger for the employees having low D-A fit than for employees having high D-A fit .

All the above mentioned hypotheses can be depicted with the help of the proposed model given in Figure 1.

Methodology

Sample

Purposeful (maximum variation) sampling was employed (see Patton, 1990). In order to enable investigations of patterns relating work role stressors, subjective D-A fit perceptions and employee outcomes, participants were contacted from a diverse range of organizations. In all 350 professionals were contacted but only 317 completed questionnaires were collected (response rate 91%). The sample consisted of the executives mainly from five sectors viz. education (39), service (100), information technology (105), manufacturing (41) and health care (12) working in Delhi and the National Capital region (NCR). However, 20 respondents were from the other sectors. Respondents ranged in age from 21 to 62 years (mean age 34.84 years and SD 9.94), 232 of them were males and 85 were female. 210 respondents were married and 107 of them were single. Maximum number of respondents fell in the age range of 31- 40 (104) and the majority of them (198) had the tenure ranging from 1-7 years in the organization.

Procedure

The employees of the various organizations were contacted and were asked to fill in the questionnaire. They were appraised regarding the academic purpose of the study and confidentiality of their responses was ensured.

Figure 1. Proposed model

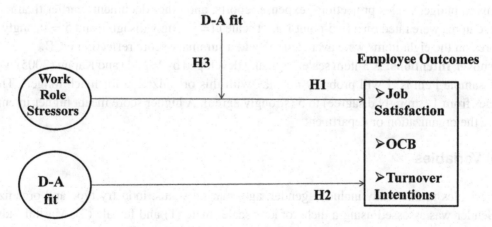

Research Instruments

1. **Demands-Abilities Fit:** The 3-item scale developed by Cable and DeRue (2002) was used to measure the Demands-Abilities fit. Responses to these items were on a 5-point scale (1= strongly disagree and 5 = strongly agree). High scores imply high demands-abilities fit and low scores imply low demands-abilities fit. The sample item of the scale is, "The match is very good between the demands of my job and my personal skills".
2. **Role Conflict:** The 3-item scale developed by Peterson et al. (1995) was used to measure the role conflict. Responses to these items were on a 5-point scale (1= strongly disagree and 5 = strongly agree). High scores imply high role conflict and low scores imply low role conflict. The sample item of the scale is, "I often get involved in situations in which there are conflicting demands".
3. **Role Ambiguity:** The 5-item scale developed by Peterson et al. (1995) was used to measure the role ambiguity. Responses to these items were on a 5-point scale (1= strongly disagree and 5 = strongly agree). However, the scores of all the 5 items were reversed. The sample item of the scale is, "I have clear planned goals and objectives for my job".
4. **Role Overload:** The 5-item scale developed by Peterson et al. (1995) was used to measure the role overload. Responses to these items were on a 5-point scale (1= strongly disagree and 5 = strongly agree). The sample item of the scale is, "There is a need to reduce some parts of my role".
5. **Job Satisfaction:** Facets of job satisfaction was measured using nine items chosen from Cellucci & DeVries (1978) questionnaire. There were two items for satisfaction with pay, three items for satisfaction with coworkers, two items for satisfaction with supervisor and two items for satisfaction with work itself. The sample items for measuring these four facets respectively are, "My organization pays better than competitors", "When I ask people to do things the job gets done", "The managers I work for back me up", and "My job is interesting". These nine items were rated on a five-point Likert scale (1= strongly disagree and 5 = strongly agree). High scores imply satisfaction with the facets of job satisfaction and low scores imply dissatisfaction with the facets of job satisfaction.
6. **Organizational Citizenship Behavior:** OCB was measured by adapting the Podsakoff, Mackenzie, Moorman & Fetter (1990) Organizational Citizenship Behavior Scale. The three OCB factors included were sportsmanship, conscientiousness, and civic virtue. Examples of these items are 'is willing to risk disapproval in order to express individual beliefs about what is best for the company' and 'turns in budgets, sales projections, expense reports, and other documents earlier than required'. These items were rated on a five-point Likert scale (1= strongly disagree and 5 = strongly agree). Scores on the eight items were averaged to yield a summary score reflecting OCB.
7. **Turnover Intentions:** A 3-item scale originally developed by Vigoda and Kapun (2005) was used. The sample item is 'I will probably not stay with this organization for much longer'. The scale ranges from 1 (strongly disagree) to 5 (strongly agree). A higher score meant higher intentions to leave the organization or department.

Control Variables

Control variables in this study included gender, age, marital status, industry type and organizational tenure. Gender was assessed using a dichotomous scale: male (1) and female (2). Marital Status was also assessed using a dichotomous scale: married (1) and single (2). Industry type was assessed using a nominal scale: education (1), service (2), IT (3), manufacturing (4), health care (5) and any other (6). Age and organizational tenure was measured in years using a continuous scale. Gender, age, marital status, industry type and organizational tenure were controlled for all regression analysis in order to minimize their influence on the focal variables in the study.

Data Analysis Overview

Hierarchical multiple regression analysis was used to examine the potential main effects of work role stressors and subjective D-A fit on employee outcomes. Each employee outcome indicator i.e. job satisfaction, OCB and turnover intentions, was regressed on the antecedent sets in four steps. Control variables were entered on Step 1, work role stressors on Step 2, subjective D-A fit on Step 3, and interaction term (i.e. work role stressors x subjective D-A fit) on Step 4. The magnitude of R^2 change at each step of hierarchical regression analysis was used to determine the variance explained by each set of antecedents. The beta values reported were used to determine the effect of each variable in the antecedent sets on employee outcomes.

Results

Preliminary Data Analyses and Overview of Analyses

Descriptive data (means and standard deviations), correlations, and Cronbach (1951) alpha coefficients are displayed in Table 1. As can be seen all scales demonstrated good internal consistency.

Main Effects

Work Role Stressors and Employee Outcomes

It was predicted that the work role stress will be negatively related to job satisfaction (H1a), OCB (H1b) and will be positively related to employees' turnover intentions (H1c). As can be seen from Table 2, entry of work role stressors in step 2 accounted for a significant increment in variance on job satisfaction, R^2

Table 1.

	Variables	Mean	SD	1	2	3	4	5	6	7	8	9
1.	Role Conflict	3.22	.78	(.71)								
2.	Role Ambiguity	2.20	.60	.067	(.78)							
3.	Role Overload	2.85	.82	.154**	.212**	(.86)						
4.	D-A Fit	3.69	.69	.04	-.430**	-.167**	(.70)					
5.	Job Satisfaction	3.37	.52	-.141*	-.460**	-.309**	.401**	(.74)				
6.	OCB	3.67	.42	-.004	-.388**	-.192**	.210**	.283**	(.72)			
7.	Turnover Intentions	2.74	1.02	.117*	.208**	.302**	-.198**	-.315**	-.205**	(.87)		
8.	Age	34.84	9.94	-.063	-.186**	.005	.288**	.140*	.152**	-.179**		
9.	Tenure	7.84	7.58	-.121*	-.199**	.007	.233**	.108	.139*	-.238**	.772**	

Table 2. Hierarchical multiple regression analyses employee outcomes (D-A fit as a moderator)

Independent Variables	Job Satisfaction β				Organizational Citizenship Behavior β				Turnover Intentions β			
Steps	I	II	III	IV	I	II	III	IV	I	II	III	IV
Step 1-Control Variables												
Gender	-.75	-.58	-.48	-.43	-.02	-.05	-.04	-.09	-.71*	-.93**	-.96**	-.87**
Age	.02	.005	-.02	-.03	.05	.04	.04	.04	.007	.01	.02	.02
Marital Status	-1.45**	-1.56**	-1.42**	-1.48**	.35	.32	.32	.28	.078	.19	.16	.21
Industry Type	-.47**	-.21	-.21	-.22	.14	.27	.27*	.28**	.07	-.007	-.007	-.03
Tenure with Organization	.003	-.04	-.04	-.02	.02	.005	.005	.00	-.10**	-.10**	-.10**	-.09**
Step 2-Job Stressors												
Role Conflict		-.13	-.18*	.63		.04	.04	.28		.07	.08	-.15
Role Ambiguity		-.61**	-.48**	-.48		-.40**	-.39**	-.13		.10*	.06	-.32
Role Overload		-.25**	-.22**	.55**		-.098**	-.097**	-.16		.22**	.21**	.47**
Step 3- Demands-Abilities fit												
Demands-Abilities fit			.52**	2.19**			.03	.43			-.13	-.39
Step 4- Interaction terms												
Role Conflict x D-A fit				-.07				-.02				.02
Role Ambiguity x D-A fit				.002				-.03				.04
Role Overload x D-A fit				-.07**				.006				-.03
Adjusted R²	.04	.28	.31	.33	.01	.16	.16	.16	.05	.16	.16	.16
R² change		.24**	.04**	.02**		.16**	.00	.003		.11**	.006	.01
F change (p-value)	3.74**	15.95**	16.94**	13.97**	1.84*	8.71**	7.73**	5.86**	4.54**	8.37**	7.70**	6.14**

*p<.05;**p<.01

ch. = .24, F = 15.95, p < .01(supporting H1a), organizational citizenship behavior, R^2 ch. = .16, F = 8.71, p < .01(supporting H1b) and turnover intentions, R^2 ch. = .11, F = 8.37, p < .01(supporting H1c). With respect to the work role stressors, the analyses revealed that role ambiguity and role overload were negatively related to job satisfaction (role ambiguity, β = -.61, p <.01 and role overload, β = -.25, p <.01) and OCB (role ambiguity β = -.40, p <.01and role overload β = -.098, p <.05). As expected, these two stressors were positively related to turnover intentions (role ambiguity, β = .10, p <.10 and role overload, β = .22, p <.01). However, role conflict was not significantly related to any employee outcome.

Subjective D-A fit and Employee Outcomes

The hierarchical multiple analyses were continued to assess the effect of D-A fit on job satisfaction (H2a), OCB (H2b) and turnover intentions (H2c). D-A fit was entered on Step 3 (see Table 2) after the control variables (Step 1) and work role stressors (Step 2). Entry of D-A fit on Step 3 accounted for the significant increment of explained variance in job satisfaction, R^2 ch. = .04, F = 16.94, p < .01(supporting H2a). The analyses revealed that D-A fit was positively related to job satisfaction, β = .52, p <.01. However, the entry of D-A fit in Step 3 did not account for a significant increment of explained variance in OCB, R^2 ch. = .00, F = 7.73, *ns* and turnover intentions, R^2 ch. = .006, F = 7.70, *ns.*, thus failing to support H2b and H2c.

Subjective D-A fit and Work Role Stressors-Employee Outcomes Relationship

The hierarchical regression analyses were continued to investigate the impact of subjective D-A fit on the work role stressors-employee outcomes relationship. As can be seen from Table 2, the work-role stressors X D-A fit interaction was entered on step 4. Entry of three interactions as a set in each regression analysis did not significantly explain further variance on the dependent variables. However, only the interaction of Role Overload X D-A fit on job satisfaction was also found to be significant, β = -.07, p <.001. In support of H3a, employees with high D-A fit were buffered from the negative effects of role overload on job satisfaction (β = -.146, t= -1.268, p=.106), so much so that the effect failed to reach statistical significance. However, as can be seen from Fig. 2, the negative effects of role overload on job satisfaction were aggravated for the employees reporting low D-A fit (β = -.445, t= -5.658, p <.001).

DISCUSSION

This study attempted to contribute to the existing research literature by studying the moderating role of D-A fit perceptions in the relationship between work role stressors and employee outcomes, apart from studying the main effects. Based on the extensive review of literature, it was hypothesized that work role stressors would be negatively related to the employee outcomes of job satisfaction, organizational citizenship behavior (OCB) and would be positively related to turnover intentions. Additionally, the employees' perception of D-A fit were predicted to impact job satisfaction and OCB positively and turnover intentions negatively. Further, D-A fit was expected to act as a buffer and weaken the relationship between work role stressors and employee outcomes.

Figure 2. Two-way interaction of role overload and D-A fit on job satisfaction

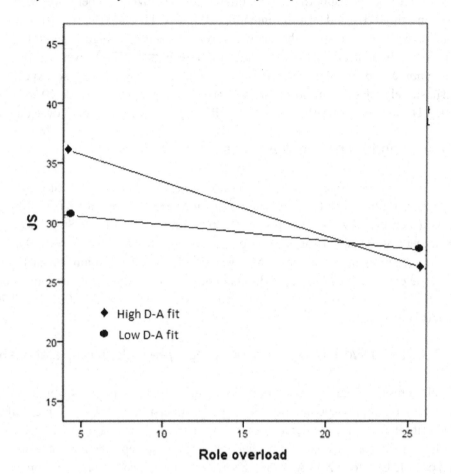

Work Role Stressors – Employee Outcomes

In line with the previous research (e.g. Chang et al., 2009; Fisher & Gitelson, 1983; Jackson & Schuler, 1985; Jain & Cooper, 2012; Mulki et al., 2008; Ortqvist & Wincent, 2006) and supporting H1 (a), H1(b) and H1(c), the results demonstrated that work role stressors, as a set, were significantly related to less favorable employee outcomes. Role ambiguity and role overload were significantly and negatively related to job satisfaction and OCB and positively related to turnover intentions. However, the results with respect to role conflict were not significant but in expected direction. These results are in line with the study by O'Driscoll & Beehr (1994) which showed the direct impact of role ambiguity on job satisfaction but no significant impact of role conflict was seen on job satisfaction.

Subjective Demands-Abilities Fit

The analysis revealed that D-A fit was positively and significantly related to job satisfaction, thus supporting H2 (a). However, no significant impact of D-A fit was seen on OCB and turnover intentions, thus rejecting H2 (b) and H2 (c).

While further research is needed in different contexts and organizations, the results of the study provide support for the possibility that high fit with the organizational culture and the job has the capability of reversing the attitudes and behaviors that are otherwise associated with work role stressors. It is interesting to note here that D-A fit is not significantly related to OCB and turnover intentions. This is because of the fact that OCBs are discretionary behaviors and people perform these acts if their values match with the values of the organization and if employees identify with the organization. However, high D-A fit does not necessarily arouse those kinds of positive emotions towards the organization, as the person identifies more with the job and not with the organization. Therefore, the person does not feel the need to perform the behaviors which are discretionary and not a part of roles and responsibilities.

With respect to the moderating role of D-A fit in the relation between work role stressors and employee outcomes, several discussion points arise. In all, only one interaction between work role stressors and D-A fit was found to be significant in the prediction of employee outcomes. D-A fit acted as a buffer to attenuate the negative effect of role overload on job satisfaction such that the employee perceiving high fit reported high job satisfaction in the face of these stressors, than employees perceiving low fit. This interaction provides some support for H3 (a) and is in line with the prediction that if a person perceives a fit between his abilities and the demands of the job, the negative effect of stressors is mitigated leading to higher job satisfaction.

IMPLICATIONS

Previous findings on the relations between work role stressors, subjective fit and employee outcomes have been established mainly among the employees from western cultures (e.g., United States, Europe); this study provides significant findings from Indian culture, which suggest universality of the impact of these variables on employee outcomes.

This study contributes to the organizational behavior literature by focusing on the fact that the negative effects of work role stressors on employee outcomes can be mitigated by identifying the variables which act as a buffer to weaken this effect. The results of the study highlight the importance of the concept of subjective D-A fit for the managers and the employees to help them in coping up with the demands of the job. The finding that the high perception of fit between the demands and abilities can mitigate the negative effect of the work role stressors on employee outcomes has strong positive implications for the organizations and the managers. Since it is not always possible to reduce stressors from the workplace, increasing the employees' perception of fit with the job can lead to a less strained workforce which is satisfied and willing to continue its membership with the organization. Additionally, providing employees with proper training can increase their perception of D-A fit and can improve their capability of handling various stressors, hence benefiting the organization in the long run.

Practical implications of the study include the importance of fit concept for both the employees and organizations. For employees, fit is crucial for improving job satisfaction, reducing work stress and enhancing personal growth. For organization, fit becomes essential for attracting and retaining talented workforce, utilizing their skills effectively, and in general leveraging human potential most critically. It will be useful for the organizations to develop fit scales and standards. During the process of recruitment and selection, these fit scales can be used to assess the fit of the candidates which can be matched with the organizational fit standards, resulting in high D-A fit. The concept of fit can be further applied after organizational entry i.e. during training and socialization.

LIMITATIONS AND SCOPE FOR FUTURE RESEARCH

As the design of the present study was cross-sectional, causal conclusions concerning the impact of work role stressors and subjective fit perceptions on employee outcomes cannot be drawn. A longitudinal study where the work role stressors and subjective D-A fit perceptions are related to employee outcomes at a later point in time would provide a more rigorous test of relationships.

This study uses self-report measures to asses work role stressors, subjective D-A fit perceptions and employee outcomes. Although the measures used were reliable, the very fact that the independent, dependent and moderating variables were assessed using self-report measures could lead to the problems of common method variance. Further, with self-report measures, social desirability biases become a cause of concern. Future studies can also employ qualitative techniques to identify emergent themes in this area.

Other organizational and dispositional factors (e.g. Personality) that were not included in the study may have been important and might account for some relationships that were found in the study. Future studies can focus on such variables to get more comprehensive explanation of the results.

The present study does not distinguish between the directions of employees' misfit. For example, low demands-abilities fit may be because of the fact that the employee does not have the skill and ability to perform the job or because he is over skilled to perform the job. The outcomes of the misfit might be different for the people who are over skilled versus those who are under skilled. Future research can delve into this area by maintain the direction of misfit.

The sample of the study was only limited to the Indian employees from Delhi and NCR. There might be some culture specific issues which were overlooked. Future studies may benefit from an exploration of a wider range of employees at different organizational levels, cultures, and sectors.

REFERENCES

Bateman, T., & Organ, D. (1983). Job satisfaction and the good soldier: The relationship between affect and employee citizenship. *Academy of Management Journal*, *26*(4), 586–595. doi:10.2307/255908

Boles, J. S., Wood, J. A., & Johnson, J. (2003). Interrelationships of role conflict, role ambiguity, and work-family conflict with different facets of job satisfaction and the moderating effects of gender. *Journal of Personal Selling & Sales Management*, *23*(2), 99–113.

Boon, C., Den Hartog, D. N., Boselie, P., & Paauwe, J. (2011). The relationship between perceptions of HR practices and employee outcomes: Examining the role of person-organization and person-job fit. *International Journal of Human Resource Management*, *22*(1), 138–163. doi:10.1080/09585192.2011 .538978

Brief, A. P., & Aldag, R. J. (1976). Correlates of role indices. *The Journal of Applied Psychology*, *61*(4), 468–472. doi:10.1037/0021-9010.61.4.468

Cable, D. M., & DeRue, D. S. (2002). The convergent and discriminant validity of subjective fit perceptions. *The Journal of Applied Psychology*, *87*(5), 875–884. doi:10.1037/0021-9010.87.5.875 PMID:12395812

Cable, D. M., & Judge, T. A. (1997). Interviewers perceptions of person–organization fit and organizational selection decisions. *The Journal of Applied Psychology*, *82*(4), 546–561. doi:10.1037/0021-9010.82.4.546 PMID:9378683

Cellucci, A. J., & DeVries, D. L. (1978). Measuring managerial satisfaction: A manual for the MJSQ. Technical Report II, Center for Creative Leadership.

Chang, C. H., Rosen, C. C., & Levy, P. E. (2009). The relationship between perceptions of organizational politics and employee attitudes, strain, and behavior: A meta-analytic examination. *Academy of Management Journal*, *52*(4), 779–801. doi:10.5465/AMJ.2009.43670894

Chang, H. T., Chi, N. W., & Chuang, A. (2010). Exploring the moderating roles of perceived person-job fit and person-organization fit on the relationship between training investment and knowledge workers turnover intentions. *Applied Psychology*, *59*(4), 566–593. doi:10.1111/j.1464-0597.2009.00412.x

Chi, N. W., & Pan, S. Y. (2012). A multilevel investigation of missing links between transformational leadership and task performance: The mediating roles of perceived person-job fit and person-organization fit. *Journal of Business and Psychology*, *27*(1), 43–56. doi:10.1007/s10869-011-9211-z

Cooper, C. L., Dewe, P. J., & O'Driscoll, M. P. (2001). *Organizational stress: A review and critique of theory, research and application*. London: Sage.

Cordes, C. L., & Dougherty, T. W. (1993). A review and integration of research on job burnout. *Academy of Management Review*, *18*(4), 621–656.

Cronbach, L. J. (1951). Coefficient alpha and the internal structure of tests. *Psychometrika*, *16*(3), 297–334. doi:10.1007/BF02310555

Cropanzano, R., Rupp, D. E., & Byrne, Z. S. (2003). The relationship of emotional exhaustion to work attitudes, job performance, and organizational citizenship behaviors. *The Journal of Applied Psychology*, *88*(1), 160–169. doi:10.1037/0021-9010.88.1.160 PMID:12675403

Daniels, K., & Guppy, A. (1994). Occupational stress, social support, job control, and psychological well-being. *Human Relations*, *47*(12), 1523–1544. doi:10.1177/001872679404701205

Edwards, J. R. (1996). An examination of competing versions of the person–environment fit approach to stress. *Academy of Management Journal*, *39*(2), 292–339. doi:10.2307/256782

Fisher, C. D., & Gitelson, R. (1983). A meta-analysis of the correlates of role conflict and ambiguity. *The Journal of Applied Psychology*, *68*(2), 320–333. doi:10.1037/0021-9010.68.2.320

French, J. R. P., Jr., Rodgers, W.L., & Cobb, S. (1974). Adjustment as person–environment fit. In G. Coelho, D. Hamburg, & J. Adams (Eds.), Coping and adaptation (pp. 316–333). New York: Basic Books.

Gregory, B. T., Albritton, M. D., & Osmonbekov, T. (2010). The mediating role of psychological empowerment on the relationships between P-O fit, job satisfaction, and in-role performance. *Journal of Business and Psychology*, *25*(4), 639–647. doi:10.1007/s10869-010-9156-7

Guan, Y., Deng, H., Risavy, S. D., Bond, M. H., & Li, F. (2011). Supplementary fit, complementary fit, and work-related outcomes: The role of self-construal. *Applied Psychology, 60*(2), 286–310. doi:10.1111/j.1464-0597.2010.00436.x

Harvey, S., Kelloway, E. K., & Duncan-Leiper, L. (2003). Trust in management as a buffer of the relationships between overload and strain. *Journal of Occupational Health Psychology, 8*(4), 306–315. doi:10.1037/1076-8998.8.4.306 PMID:14570525

Hecht, T. D., & Allen, N. J. (2005). Exploring links between polychronicity and well-being from the perspective of person-job fit: Does it matter if you prefer to do one thing at a time? *Organizational Behavior and Human Decision Processes, 98*(2), 155–178. doi:10.1016/j.obhdp.2005.07.004

Holland, J. L. (1985). *Making vocational choices: A theory of careers.* Englewood Cliffs, NJ: Prentice-Hall.

Hom, P.W. & Griffeth, R. W. (1995). *Employee turnover.* Cincinnati: South-Western College Publishing.

Jackson, S., & Schuler, R. (1985). A meta-analysis and conceptual critique of research on role ambiguity and role conflict in work settings. *Organizational Behavior and Human Decision Processes, 36*(1), 16–78. doi:10.1016/0749-5978(85)90020-2

Jain, A. K., & Cooper, C. L. (2012). Stress and organizational citizenship behaviors in Indian business process outsourcing organizations. *IIMB Management Review, 24*(3), 155–163. doi:10.1016/j.iimb.2012.06.004

Jimmieson, N. L. (2000). Employee reactions to behavioral control under conditions of stress: The moderating role of self-efficacy. *Work and Stress, 14*(3), 262–280. doi:10.1080/02678370010015343

Judge, T. A., & Cable, D. M. (1997). Applicant personality, organizational culture, and organization attraction. *Personnel Psychology, 50*(2), 359–393. doi:10.1111/j.1744-6570.1997.tb00912.x

Kahn, R., Wolfe, D., Quinn, R., Snoek, J., & Rosentbal, R. (1964). *Organizational stress: Studies in role conflict and ambiguity.* New York: Wiley.

Kahn, R. L., & Byosiere, P. (1992). Stress in organizations. In M. D. Dunnette & L. M. Hough (Eds.), *Handbook of industrial and organizational psychology* (Vol. 3, pp. 571–650). Palo Alto, CA: Consulting Psychologists Press.

Kanfer, R., & Ackerman, P. L. (1989). Motivation and cognitive abilities: An integrative / aptitude-treatment interaction approach to skill acquisition. *The Journal of Applied Psychology, 74*(4), 657–690. doi:10.1037/0021-9010.74.4.657

Kreiner, G. E. (2006). Consequences of work-home segmentation or integration: A person-environment fit perspective. *Journal of Organizational Behavior, 27*(4), 485–507. doi:10.1002/job.386

Kristof-Brown, A. L. (2000). Perceived applicant fit: Distinguishing between recruiters perceptions of person–job and person–organization fit. *Personnel Psychology, 53*(3), 643–671. doi:10.1111/j.1744-6570.2000.tb00217.x

Kristof-Brown, A. L., Zimmerman, R. D., & Johnson, E. C. (2005). Consequences of individuals fit at work: A meta-analysis of person-job, person-organization, person-group, and person supervisor fit. *Personnel Psychology*, *58*(2), 281–342. doi:10.1111/j.1744-6570.2005.00672.x

Kushnir, T., & Melamed, S. (1991). Work-load, perceived control and psychological distress in Type A/B industrial workers. *Journal of Organizational Behavior*, *12*(2), 155–168. doi:10.1002/job.4030120207

Lewin, K. (1935). *A dynamic theory of personality*. New York: McGraw-Hill.

Makikangas, A., & Kinnunen, U. (2003). Psychosocial work stressors and well-being: Self-esteem and optimism as moderators in a one-year longitudinal sample. *Personality and Individual Differences*, *35*(3), 537–557. doi:10.1016/S0191-8869(02)00217-9

Moore, J. E. (2000). One road to turnover: An examination of work exhaustion in technology professionals. *Management Information Systems Quarterly*, *24*(1), 141–168. doi:10.2307/3250982

Moorman, R. H., & Blakely, G. L. (1995). Individualism-collectivism as an individual difference predictor of organizational citizenship behavior. *Journal of Organizational Behavior*, *16*(2), 127–142. doi:10.1002/job.4030160204

Muchinsky, P. M., & Monahan, C. I. (1987). What is person-environment congruence? Supplementary versus complementary models of fit. *Journal of Vocational Behavior*, *31*(1), 268–277. doi:10.1016/0001-8791(87)90043-1

Mulki, J. P., Jaramillo, F., & Locander, W. B. (2008). Effect of ethical climate on turnover intention: Linking attitudinal- and stress theory. *Journal of Business Ethics*, *78*(12), 559–574. doi:10.1007/s10551-007-9368-6

Mulki, J. P., Lassk, F. G., & Fernando, J. (2008). The effect of self-efficacy on salesperson work overload and pay satisfaction. *Journal of Personal Selling & Sales Management*, *28*(3), 283–295. doi:10.2753/PSS0885-3134280305

Murray, H. A. (1938). *Explorations in Personality*. Boston: Houghton Mifflin.

Netemeyer, R. G., Johnston, M., & Burton, S. (1990). An analysis of role conflict and role ambiguity in a structural equations framework. *The Journal of Applied Psychology*, *75*(2), 148–157. doi:10.1037/0021-9010.75.2.148

Netemeyer, R. G., Maxham, J. G. III, & Pullig, C. (2005). Conflicts in the work-family interface: Links to job stress, customer service employee performance, and customer purchase intent. *Journal of Marketing*, *69*(2), 130–143. doi:10.1509/jmkg.69.2.130.60758

Newton, C. J., & Jimmieson, N. L. (2009). Subjective fit with organizational culture: An investigation of moderating effects in the work stressor-employee adjustment relationship. *International Journal of Human Resource Management*, *26*(8), 1770–1789. doi:10.1080/09585190903087198

Ngo, H. Y., Foley, S., & Loi, R. (2005). Work role stressors and turnover intentions: A study of professional clergy in Hong Kong. *International Journal of Human Resource Management*, *16*(11), 2133–2146. doi:10.1080/09585190500315141

ODriscoll, M. P., & Beehr, T. A. (1994). Supervisor behaviors, role stressors and uncertainty as predictors of personal outcomes for subordinates. *Journal of Organizational Behavior, 15*(2), 141–155. doi:10.1002/job.4030150204

Organ, D. W. (1997). Organizational citizenship behavior: Its construct clean-up time. *Human Performance, 10*(2), 85–97. doi:10.1207/s15327043hup1002_2

Örtqvist, D., & Wincent, J. (2006). Prominent consequences of role stress: A meta-analytic review. *International Journal of Stress Management, 13*(4), 399–422. doi:10.1037/1072-5245.13.4.399

Parker, S. K., & Sprigg, C. A. (1999). Minimizing strain and maximizing learning: The role of job demands, job control, and proactive personality. *The Journal of Applied Psychology, 84*(6), 925–939. doi:10.1037/0021-9010.84.6.925 PMID:10639910

Patton, M. Q. (1990). *Qualitative Evaluation and Research Methods*. Thousand Oaks, CA: Sage.

Peterson, M. F., Smith, P. B., Akande, A., Ayestaran, S., Bochner, S., Callan, V., & Viedge, C. et al. (1995). Role conflict, ambiguity, and overload: A 21-nation study. *Academy of Management Journal, 38*(2), 429–452. doi:10.2307/256687

Podsakoff, P. M., Mackenzie, S. B., Moorman, R. H., & Fetter, R. (1990). Transformational leader behaviors and their effects on followers trust in leader, satisfaction, and organizational citizenship behaviors. *The Leadership Quarterly, 1*(2), 107–142. doi:10.1016/1048-9843(90)90009-7

Rice, R. W., McFarlin, D. B., Hunt, R. G., & Near, J. P. (1985). Organizational work and the perceived quality of life: Toward a conceptual model. *Academy of Management Review, 10*(2), 296–310.

Rizzo, J., House, R. J., & Lirtzman, S. I. (1970). Role conflict and ambiguity in complex organizations. *Administrative Science Quarterly, 15*(2), 150–163. doi:10.2307/2391486

Saks, A. M., & Ashforth, B. E. (1997). A longitudinal investigation of the relationships between job information sources, applicant perceptions of fit and work outcomes. *Personnel Psychology, 50*(2), 395–425. doi:10.1111/j.1744-6570.1997.tb00913.x

Saks, A. M., & Ashforth, B. E. (2002). Is job search related to employment quality? It all depends on fit. *The Journal of Applied Psychology, 87*(4), 646–654. doi:10.1037/0021-9010.87.4.646 PMID:12184569

Schein, E. (1978). *Career dynamics: Matching individual and organizational needs*. Reading, MA: Addison-Wesley.

Siegrist, J. (1996). Adverse health effects of high-effort/low-reward conditions. *Journal of Occupational Health Psychology, 1*(1), 27–41. doi:10.1037/1076-8998.1.1.27 PMID:9547031

Smith, C. A., Organ, D. W., & Near, J. P. (1983). Organizational citizenship behavior: Its nature and antecedents. *The Journal of Applied Psychology, 68*(4), 653–663. doi:10.1037/0021-9010.68.4.653

Spector, P. E. (1985). Measurement of human service staff satisfaction: Development of the Job Satisfaction Survey. *American Journal of Community Psychology, 13*(6), 693–713. doi:10.1007/BF00929796 PMID:4083275

Spokane, A. R. (1985). A review of research on person–environment congruence in Hollands theory of careers. *Journal of Vocational Behavior*, *26*(3), 306–343. doi:10.1016/0001-8791(85)90009-0

Tett, R. P., & Meyer, J. P. (1993). Job satisfaction, organizational commitment, turnover intention, and turnover: Path analysis based on meta-analytic findings. *Personnel Psychology*, *46*(2), 259–293. doi:10.1111/j.1744-6570.1993.tb00874.x

Vahtera, J., Pentti, J., & Uutela, A. (1996). The effect of objective job demands on registered sickness absence spells: Do personal, social and job-related resources act as moderators? *Work and Stress*, *10*(4), 286–308. doi:10.1080/02678379608256809

Walker, O. C. Jr, Churchill, G. A. Jr, & Ford, N. M. (1975). Organizational determinants of the industrial salesmens role conflict and ambiguity. *Journal of Marketing*, *39*(1), 32–39. doi:10.2307/1250800

Werbel, J. D., & Johnson, D. J. (2001). The use of person–group fit for employment selection: A missing link in person–environment fit. *Human Resource Management*, *40*(3), 227–240. doi:10.1002/hrm.1013

Chapter 17
A Discussion on Indian Consumers' Hedonic and Non-Hedonic Values

Manit Mishra
International Management Institute, Bhubaneswar, India

ABSTRACT

The present study aims at attaining a better understanding of the hedonic consumer value of material-ism and non-hedonic values of happiness, life-satisfaction and religiosity. As a conceptual paper, the study refers to literature and prior empirical research with the objective of linking a significant body of literature on these apparently diverse constructs into a unifying theoretical framework. The study offers new research directions in the form of propositions for further empirical investigation.

GENESIS

The concept of the hedonic construct of materialism as an inherent constituent of lifestyle has been a profoundly dialectical construct. The issue has been of interest to a range of people – from the dilettante who have dabbled in its aura to the prophets whose homilies have castigated it as a source of retrogression towards spiritual bankruptcy.

The text book definition of materialism states that it is a personality – like trait which distinguishes between individuals who regard possessions as essential to their identities and their lives and those for whom possessions are secondary (Schiffman & Kanuk, 2005, p. 157 – 158). Over the last five decades, researchers have been paying increasing amount of attention to materialism (e.g. Belk 1983, 1984, 1985, 1987, 1988, 1990, 1991; Kasser 2002; Richins 1987, 1994a, 1994b; Richins and Dawson, 1992; Moschis & Churchill, 1978; Mukerji 1983; Pollay 1986; Ward & Wackman, 1971)

The two major studies on Materialism and its scale development have been carried out by Belk (1984, 1984) and Richins and Dawson (1992). Belk viewed materialism as an integration of personality traits – possessiveness, non-generosity and envy. He proposed an indirect measurement system of personality through empirical determination of these three traits by using three subscales measuring each of these

DOI: 10.4018/978-1-5225-0902-8.ch017

traits. On the other hand, Richins and Dawson (1992) conceptualised materialism as a value whose influence goes beyond mere consumption arenas. Their measurement scale for materialism in an individual is based on three dimensions or "orienting values" – acquisition centrality, acquisition as the pursuit of happiness and possession defined success. The development of these scales has given a very potent tool to the researchers since they can quantify a concept as intangible, abstract and subjective as materialism.

The primary purpose of this article is to bring together apparently disparate and yet interconnected strands of research and present an integrated model of hedonic and non-hedonic values of consumer behavior. Materialism has been profoundly explored through literature and prior empirical research to provide possible directions for future research. The article has a secondary objective of stimulating more research in areas underexplored in the context of Indian consumers.

THE HEDONIC CONSTRUCT MATERIALISM: AS DEFINED IN MARKETING

O Shaughnessy and O Shaughnessy (2002) believe that the tendency towards materialism is an inherent constituent of human condition and it was widespread prosperity which fuelled the emergence of both marketing activity and consumerist behaviour simultaneously. Materialism, as a field of study, gained greater attention over last two and a half decades (e.g. Belk, 1984; Burroughs & Rindfleisch, 2002; Richins & Dawson, 1992) and its causes and consequences (e.g. Larsen, Sirgy and Wright, 1999; Rindfleisch, Burroughs and Denton, 1997; Sirgy, *et. al.* 1998). The consumer researchers have studied materialism as a personality trait (Belk, 1984; 1985), as a consumer value (Richins 1987; Richins & Dawson, 1992), as a consumer attitude (Campbell, 1969), as an orientation towards money and possessions (Moschis & Churchill, 1978), as a way of life (Daun, 1983; Steiner, 1975), as an acquisitive ideology (Bishop, 1949) and Holt (1998) raised an important question as to whether materialism is more about "how" rather than "what" one consumes.

The evidence from Sociology shows that the desire to possess material things is present in most cultures (Mukerji, 1983) and it could be because such a desire is a basic human characteristic (Rubin, 1986). It raises a very important question as to how does one differentiate the "materialistic" from the "mundane". The available research indicates towards the following differentiating criteria: a strong belief that possessions give pleasure which leads to seeking pleasure through possession rather than through other means such as personal relationships, experiences and achievements (see Richins & Dawson, 1992).

MATERIALISM IN INDIAN CULTURE

In Indian culture, materialism has been a widely-debated issue with both proposing and opposing schools of thought. However, the oral tradition of passing on knowledge from one generation to another may have resulted in poor documentary evidence. Chatterjee and Datta (1984) explained that "though materialism in some form or other has always been present in India, and occasional references are found in the *Vedas*, the Buddhist literature, the epics as well as in the later philosophical works, we do not find any systematic work on materialism, nor any organized school of followers as the other philosophical schools possess. But almost every work of the other schools states, for refutation, the materialistic views. Our knowledge of Indian materialism is chiefly based on these."

The significance of materialism in Indian culture cannot be fully imbibed without paying attention to the ancient scripture of *Bhagvad Gita*, which is highly revered and adhered to within the Indian society. In course of his conversation with the mighty warrior Arjuna, Lord Krishna explains that, "by developing purity of intention, passions directed towards mundane objects die producing tranquility of mind which in turn gives rise to the inward silence in which the soul begins to establish contact with the Eternal from which it is surrendered, and experience the presence of the Indwelling God" (Radhakrishnan, 2006). The emphasis is on emancipation and assimilation with the Almighty through renunciation. Any form of predilection towards mundane objects is thought of as an obstacle in the path leading to the God. The reason for this absolute disdain towards fulfillment of desire has been conveyed in the following lines, "whatever pleasures are born of the contacts (with material objects) are only sources of sorrow, they have a beginning and an end, O son of Kunti (Arjuna), no wise man delights in them" (Radhakrishnan, 2006). Thus, the *Bhagvad Gita* advocates detachment from desires as proof of wisdom.

Further, the difficulty in attaining this end too has been widely acknowledged and means have been suggested. Lord Chaitanya, a highly revered 13th century Indian saint, believed that, "by chanting the holy name of the Lord one can directly associate with the supreme Lord by sound vibration. As one practices this sound vibration, he passes through three stages of development: the offensive stage, the clearing stage and the transcendental stage. In the offensive stage one may desire all kinds of material happiness, but in the second stage one becomes clear of all material contaminations. When one is situated in the transcendental stage, he attains the most coveted position – the stage of loving God" (Prabhupada, 1995, p. x). It is a representative statement of a majority of schools of thought who believed in the inferiority of material happiness vis-à-vis the attainment of spiritual enlightenment. AC Bhaktivedanta Swami Prabhupada (1995, p. xi) further goes on to propagate that, "being engaged in the superior activities of Krsna consciousness, superior men naturally retire from the inferior activities of material existence."

However, the Indian culture is not without its share of critiques of this meta-physical perspective of materialism. In ancient Indian philosophy, materialism developed around 600 BC with the works of Ajita Kesakambali, Payasi and the proponents of *Charvaka* School of philosophy. Payasi, a 6th century BC materialist philosopher has written in *Payasi – sutanta*, as quoted by Chattopadhyaya (1993), "Neither is there any other world, nor are there beings reborn otherwise than from parents, nor is there fruit or result of deed well-done or ill-done." The words may sound iconoclastic but the tone of these early materialists seem to be one of rebellion against anti-materialism rather than conviction in materialism.

However, the *Charvaka* system of Indian philosophy, also known as *Lokayata*, was more brazen in its advocacy of materialism. This branch of Indian philosophy is not considered to be part of the six orthodox schools of Hinduism – *Nyaya* and *Vaisheshika*, *Mimansa* and *Vedanta*, *Samkhya* and *Yoga* – which recognise the authority of the *Vedas* as divine revelation and function as pairs (Beck, 2003). An important contributor to the *Charvaka* philosophy was Brihaspati who enunciated the principle:

Yavvajivet sukham jivet; Rinam kritvaa ghritam pibet;

Bhasmibhutasya Dehasya; Punaraagamanam kutah.

This may be translated as:

As long as you live, live happily; Take a loan and drink ghee;

After a body is reduced to ashes; Where will it come back from?

The *Charvakas* adopted and disseminated the idea that good living, symbolised by *ghee,* was the route to self – fulfillment. The existence and development of contradictory beliefs only contributed towards the significance of materialism in Indian culture. In this context, the present research assumes greater degree of importance as it intended to empirically examine materialism among Indians, which has theoretically existed and has been a subject of much debate for last 2,500 years.

MEASUREMENT OF THE MATERIALISM CONSTRUCT

Academicians have been making an attempt to empirically measure materialism construct by operationalising it. The various approaches to measure materialism can be broadly categorised into two types. The researchers who have adopted the first approach believe that materialism is a multi-dimensional construct and therefore may be inferred by measuring the related constructs. It required construction of separate scales for each related construct or dimension. The materialistic tendencies of an individual respondent may be inferred by obtaining the summation of scores on each sub-scale representing respective dimensions. Some of the researchers who have adopted this methodology are Dickins and Ferguson (1957), Inglehart (1981) and Belk (1984).

The second approach to measure materialism is more direct and is accomplished through the use of attitude scales. It considers materialism to be a one-dimensional construct and uses a multi-item Likert-type scale to obtain the materialism score of a respondent. The instrument consists of a battery of statements that try to explore materialistic tendencies in an individual respondent through analysis of his beliefs e.g., "It is really true that money can buy happiness" (Wackman, Reale & Ward, 1972) or motives e.g. "It is important for me to have really nice things" (Richins, 1987). Richins and Dawson (1992) scale uses the latter approach.

Richins & Dawson (1992) suggested that "materialism represents a mindset or constellation of attitudes regarding the relative importance of acquisition and possession of objects in one's life." Even as they conceptualised materialism as a value, Richins and Dawson (1992) avoided measuring materialism through ranking method in which the individual respondent is required to rank a set of end states on the basis of their relative importance to him. Instead they operationalised materialism through measurement of three centrally held beliefs relevant to the materialistic value: acquisition centrality, the role of acquisition in happiness and the role of possessions in defining success. A factor analysis revealed the underlying dimensions as success, centrality and happiness. Here success represents, "use of possessions as an indicator of success in life," centrality concerns, "the importance of acquisition and possession generally," and happiness reflects "the perception that possessions are needed for happiness."

However, the aforementioned scales of materialism were developed in USA. A comparison between the cultures of USA and India on the five dimensions of culture – power distance, uncertainty avoidance, individuality, masculinity and long term orientation; revealed certain disparities (see Hofstede, 2001), as given in Table 1.

The pertinent issue, therefore, is - Is materialism a universal construct that can be measured through the same scale everywhere? Can a scale of materialism, germinated by evaluating responses from a western

Table 1. Culture comparison: India vs. USA

Sl. No.	Dimensions of culture	Index value		Range of index value	
		India	USA	Lowest (Country)	Highest (Country)
1.	Power distance	77	40	11 (Austria)	104 (Malaysia)
2.	Uncertainty avoidance	40	46	08 (Singapore)	112 (Greece)
3.	Individualism	48	91	06 (Guatemala)	91 (USA)
4.	Masculinity	56	62	05 (Sweden)	95 (Japan)
5.	Long term orientation	61	29	00 (Pakistan)	118 (China)

society, be equally valid and reliable when used on a sample of Indian consumers who are culturally on a diametrically opposite end from their western counterparts? This is a pertinent research questions the consumer researchers need to find an answer to.

MATERIALISM: RELATIONSHIPS WITH NON-HEDONIC CONSTRUCTS OF SIGNIFICANCE

Materialism cannot be thought of as an intrinsic and parochial value that does not influence and get influenced by some of the other variables which identify a consumer.

Materialism and Happiness

A major differentiating factor of materialistic people is that they intend to attain "happiness through acquisition rather than through other means such as personal relationships, experience or achievements (Richins and Dawson, 1992). That brings us to a very significant question- does materialism contribute to happiness? Belk (1984) made an attempt to arrive at a tentative answer by using two measures of feelings of well-being – Gurin, Veroff and Feld (1960) measure and, Bradburn and Caplovitz (1965) measure. Even though no causal relationship could be established, the study did throw up strong evidence indicating that "materialistic people do not tend to be happy people." This finding was substantiated by Richins (1987). She believed that for materialistic people, material possessions may be equated to an "addictive drug of which consumers need larger and larger doses to maintain happiness". This indeed could be a very plausible explanation for the negative relationship between materialism and happiness.

Some evidence in this regard has also been put forth by Kasser (2002), who contends that those who possess strong materialistic values have a greater risk of unhappiness, depression, low self – esteem and problems of intimacy regardless of culture. This brings us to the first proposition which needs to be investigated in the context of Indian culture:

Proposition 1: The more materialistic consumers in India are likely to be less happy compared to the less materialistic consumers.

Materialism and Life Satisfaction

Richins (1987) found that more materialistic people are more dissatisfied with their life as compared to people who are less materialistic. Richins and Dawson (1992) carried out a more profound and comprehensive survey and came to the conclusion that though life satisfaction of materialists is low but they are more likely to be dissatisfied with their circumstances than with themselves. This leads us to believe that materialism is more of an "effect" than a "cause". This inference is in keeping with the findings of Rindfleisch *et. al.* (1997) that materialists tend to rely on material possessions as substitutes for their lack of satisfying inter–personal relationships. Even as the causal relationship is debatable, there is substantial empirical evidence to support the idea that, "beyond a rather low threshold, material well being does not correlate with subjective well being" (Abela, 2006; citing Csikszentmihalyi, 2000; Diener, 2000; Myers, 2000).

Ahuvia and Wong (2002) have a different justification for this phenomenon. They argued that materialism prioritises lower order needs over higher order needs which results in lower levels of life satisfaction. Hence, there are innurable findings that people who are highly focused on materialistic values have lower personal well being and psychological health than those who believe that materialistic pursuits are relatively unimportant (Kasser, 2002, p. 22).

However, the bone of contention is the evidence that suggests that the differences in life satisfaction between the more materialistic and the less materialistic are relatively small (De Anggelis, 2004). Therefore, it was pertinent to find out if materialism and life satisfaction are positively or negatively correlated, when urban Indian consumers are taken into consideration. Given the weight of evidence against a positive relationship, the following proposition is formulated and put forth herewith for the research community to explore empirical evidence in Indian context.

Proposition 2: The more materialistic Indian consumers have lesser life satisfaction as compared to the less materialistic consumers.

Materialism and Religiosity

Belk (1984, 1985) compared the materialistic tendencies of students from a religious institution, in terms of the average materialism score, with four other groups – machine shop workers, business students, insurance secretaries and fraternity members. He found that the religious institution students had the lowest score. In another study conducted the other way round, it was found that YUPPIES exhibited lesser religiosity compared to the general population (Burnett and Bush, 1986). The reason could be explained by the fact that most mainstream religions and religious cults have advocated pursuit of higher goals compared to pursuit of worldly goods (see Belk, 1983). Therefore, an inclination towards religious teachings would result in apathy, if not antipathy, towards possessions and acquisitions.

However, without materialism the society may appear to be more puritan but unless there is opportunity to get spoilt (from the religious point of view), there would be no merit in virtue. This belief stems from the existence of many sub cults within Indian society who have propagated material values. The Indian consumer has been under the influence of *Charvakas* – who strongly recommended life of pleasure, as well as Jainism and Buddhism, who believed that the key to salvation lies in rejecting the material goods. The Indian consumer, thus, has been subjected to extreme ends of the spectrum on the issue of religiosity and materialism. Even though it is expected that more religious individuals are likely to be less materialistic compared to less religious individuals, it would be interesting to obtain empirical evidence for the same in Indian context, given the Indians exposure to diametrically opposite views on materialism. Based on the discussion, the following proposition was formulated.

Proposition 3: More religious consumers are expected to be less materialistic in comparison to less religious consumers.

DISCUSSION AND DIRECTIONS FOR FUTURE RESEARCH

The Indian consumer has the unique distinction of being subjected to 2500 years of proposing and opposing rhetoric with respect to materialism. In this regard, the present study may be considered a small step towards developing a deeper understanding of a dynamic and dialectic construct that materialism is.

The practice of using an instrument developed in one country to measure the same value in another cultural environment, under the assumption that it carries the same meaning, is questionable (Hofstede, 2001, p.07). The paper puts forth the necessity of scale development and validation using Indian respondents to capture the complex construct of materialism. Secondly, the propositions submitted in this paper bring to fore the scope for research in future in exploring the relationship of the hedonic value of materialism with the non-hedonic values of happiness, life-satisfaction, and religiosity. These states of existence can be very unique and region specific and therefore demand more research, both at a global as well as a local level.

In addition, materialism being an eclectic construct, needs further research to operationalise the abstract relationships it has with different aspects of consumer's behavior, demographics and psychographics. In particular reference to the Indian consumers, there are two prominent issues that require profound attention and examination by researchers. Firstly, materialism is not a static construct which remains stagnant over the life time of a consumer. Future research needs to address the dynamic nature of materialism by carrying out a longitudinal study. Secondly, the present research should encourage academicians to investigate the antecedents and consequences of materialism. The impact of a range of stimuli and cues (e.g. media, peer group, family values, marketing mix modification, discretionary income and even genes) on materialism can be taken into consideration. The present author sincerely hopes that this study would give an impetus to further research on materialism among Indian consumers.

REFERENCES

Abela, A. V. (2006). Marketing and Consumption: A Response to OShaughnessy and OShaughnessy. *European Journal of Marketing*, 40(1/2), 5–16. doi:10.1108/03090560610637284

Ahuvia, A. C., & Wong, N. Y. (2002). Personality and Values based Materialism: Their Relationship and Origins. *Journal of Consumer Psychology*, 12(4), 389–402. doi:10.1016/S1057-7408(16)30089-4

Beck, S. (2003). *India and Southeast Asia to 1875*. World Peace Communication Books.

Belk, R. W. (1983). Worldly Possessions: Issues and Criticisms. Advances in Consumer Research, 10, 514-519.

Belk, R. W. (1984). Three Scales to Measure Constructs Related to Materialism: Reliability, Validity, and Relationships to Measures of Happiness. Advances in Consumer Research, 11, 291-297.

Belk, R. W. (1985). Materialism: Trait Aspects of Living in a Material World. *The Journal of Consumer Research, 12*(December), 265–280. doi:10.1086/208515

Belk, R. W. (1987). Material Values in the Comics: A Content Analysis of Comic Books Featuring Themes of Wealth. *The Journal of Consumer Research, 14*(June), 26–42. doi:10.1086/209090

Belk, R. W. (1988). Possessions and the Extended Self. *The Journal of Consumer Research, 15*(September), 139–168. doi:10.1086/209154

Belk, R. W. (1990). The Role of Possessions in Constructing and Maintaining a Sense of Past. Advances in Consumer Research, 17, 669-676.

Belk, R. W. (1991). The Ineluctable Mysteries of Possessions. *Journal of Social Behavior and Personality, 6*(6), 17–55.

Bishop, F. P. (1949). *The Ethics of Advertising*. London, UK: Robert Hale.

Bradburn, N. M., & Caplovitz, D. (1965). *Report on Happiness*. Chicago: Aldine.

Burnett, J. J., & Bush, A. J. (1986). Profiling the Yuppies. *Journal of Advertising Research, 26*(April/May), 27–35.

Burroughs, J. E., & Rindfleisch, A. (2002). Materialism and Well-Being: A Conflicting Values Perspective. *The Journal of Consumer Research, 29*(December).

Campbell, D. T. (1969). Materialism. In J. P. Robinson & P. R. Ishliver (Eds.), *Measure of Social Altitudes* (pp. 651–652). Ann Arbor, MI: Institute for Social Research.

Chatterjee, S., & Datta, D. (1984). *An introduction to Indian philosophy* (8th ed.). University of Calcutta.

Chattopadhyaya, D. (1993). *Indian Philosophy* (7th ed.). New Delhi: People's Publishing House.

Csikszentmihalyi, M. (2000). The Costs and Benefits of Consuming. *The Journal of Consumer Research, 27*(September), 267–272. doi:10.1086/314324

Daun, A. (1983). The Materialistic Lifestyle: Some Socio-Psychological Aspects. In L. Uusitalo (Ed.), *Consumer Behavior and Environmental Quality* (pp. 6–16). New York: St. Martin's.

De Anggelis, T. (2004). Consumerism and its Discontents. *American Psychological Association Monitor, 35*(6), 52.

Dickins, D., and Ferguson, V. (1957). Practices and Attitudes of Rural White Children and Parents Concerning Money. *Mississippi Agricultural Experiment Station Technical Bulletin*, 43.

Diener, E. (2000). Subjective Well-Being: The Science of Happiness. *The American Psychologist, 55*(1), 34–43. doi:10.1037/0003-066X.55.1.34 PMID:11392863

Gurin, G., Veroff, J., & Feld, S. (1960). *Americans View Their Mental Health*. New York: Basic Books.

Hofstede, G. (2001). *Culture's Consequences: Comparing Values, Behaviors, Institutions, and Organizations Across Nations*. New Delhi: SAGE.

Holt, D. B. (1998). Does Cultural Capital Structure American Consumption? *The Journal of Consumer Research, 25*(1), 1–25. doi:10.1086/209523

Inglehart, R. (1981). Post-materialism in an Environment of Insecurity. *The American Political Science Review, 75*(04), 880–900. doi:10.2307/1962290

Kasser, T. (2002). *The High Price of Materialism*. Cambridge, MA: MIT Press.

Larsen, V., Sirgy, M. J., & Wright, N. D. (1999). Materialism: The Construct, Measures, Antecedents, and Consequences. *Academy of Marketing Studies Journal, 3*(2), 75–107.

Moschis, G. P., & Churchill, G. A. (1978). Consumer Socialization: A Theoretical and Empirical Analysis. *JMR, Journal of Marketing Research, 15*(4), 544–609. doi:10.2307/3150629

Mukerji, C. (1983). *From Graven Images: Patterns of Modern Materialism*. New York: Columbia University Press.

Myers, D. G. (2000). The Funds, Friends, and Faith of Happy People. *The American Psychologist, 55*(1), 56–67. doi:10.1037/0003-066X.55.1.56 PMID:11392866

OShaughnessy, J., & OShaughnessy, N. J. (2002). Marketing, the Consumer Society and Hedonism. *European Journal of Marketing, 36*(5/6), 524–547. doi:10.1108/03090560210422871

Pollay, R. W. (1986). The Distorted Mirror: Reflections on the Unintended Consequences of Advertising. *Journal of Marketing, 50*(2), 18. doi:10.2307/1251597

Prabhupada, A. C., & Swami, B. (1995). *Teachings of Lord Chaitanya: The Golden Avatar*. The Bhaktivedanta Book Trust.

Radhakrishnan, S. (2006). *The Bhagvadgita, 24*[th] *Impression*. Harper Collins Publishers.

Richins, M. (1987). Media, Materialism, and Human Happiness. *Advances in Consumer Research. Association for Consumer Research (U. S.), 14*, 352–356.

Richins, M. L. (1994a). Special Possessions and the Expression of Material Values. *The Journal of Consumer Research, 21*(3), 522–533. doi:10.1086/209415

Richins, M. L. (1994b). Valuing Things: The Public and Private Meanings of Possessions. *The Journal of Consumer Research, 21*(3), 504–521. doi:10.1086/209414

Richins, M. L., & Dawson, S. (1992). A Consumer Values Orientation for Materialism and its Measurement: Scale Development and Validation. *The Journal of Consumer Research, 19*(3), 303–316. doi:10.1086/209304

Rindfleisch, A., Burroughs, J. E., & Denton, F. (1997). Family Structure, Materialism, and Compulsive Consumption. *The Journal of Consumer Research, 23*(4), 312–325. doi:10.1086/209486

Rubin, N. (1986). It is the Season to be Greedy. *Parents, 61*, 134-137, 217, 222-226.

Schiffman, L. G., & Kanuk, L. L. (2005). *Consumer Behavior* (8th ed.). PHI.

Sirgy, J. M., Lee, D. J., Kosenko, R., Lee, H., & Rahtz, D. (1998). Does television Viewership Play a Role in The Perception of Quality of Life? *Journal of Advertising*, 27(1), 125–142. doi:10.1080/00913 367.1998.10673547

Steiner, G. A. (1975). *Business and Society*. New York: Random House.

Wackman, G. B., Reale, G., & Ward, S. (1972). Racial Differences in Responses to Advertising among Adolescents. In Television in Day-to-Day Life. Rockville, MD: U.S. Department of Health, Education and Welfare.

Ward, S., & Wackman, D. (1971). Family and Media Influences on Adolescent Consumer Learning. *American Behavioral Scientist*, 14, 415-427.

Chapter 18
Key Performance Indicators for the Organized Farm Products Retailing in India

Rajwinder Singh
International Management Institute, India

Ajit Pal Singh
Defense University, Ethiopia

Bhimaraya A. Metri
International Management Institute, India

ABSTRACT

The Non-livestock products include Horticulture products (flowers, fruits, nuts, vegetables and medicinal plants) and Agriculture products (Crops like; rice, cotton, wheat). These items share the maximum sale of the farm products. Unfortunately, the farm production in India has witnessed a huge wastage. It has attracted the attention of many practitioners and policy makers. Witnessing the opportunity many organized retail players have entered the arena to sell farm products. However, the supply chain (SC) performance measurement has remained the major challenge as "No measurement no improvement". Many organizations are searching for an efficient SC performance measurement system. Our study recommends that the SC performance shall be improved by developing a SC strategy based on a limited set of key performance indicators (KPI). Otherwise, managers shall waste time and resources on the undesirable performance indicators. We have identified and classified the KPI for non-livestock retailing SC management into five groups. These are 1) Customer Attraction Metrics (product quality, product personality, process quality); 2) Inventory Metrics (fill rate, customer response time, return adjustment, spoilage adjustment, and Vendor managed inventory); 3) Attractiveness Metrics (inventory cost, distribution cost, Return on investment, stakeholder value, sales profit and channel flexibility); 4) Transportation Metrics (shipping errors, and volume flexibility); and 5) Customer Metrics (lead time, delivery flexibility, and backorder flexibility). This grouping shall help the practitioners to focus on a limited set of KPI for better management of supply chains.

DOI: 10.4018/978-1-5225-0902-8.ch018

INTRODUCTION

Supply chain performance measurement (SCPM) is one of the key managerial tasks integrated planning, organizing, motivating the workforce and controlling events. In this context performance measurement is related to strategic intent, and the broad set of metrics taken as a reference to monitor and guide an organization. However, "performance" implies predetermined parameters and "measurement" imply an ability to monitor events and activities in a meaningful way. The need of SCPM has long been recognized and many attempts are made to develop a better performance measurement system.

To develop a SCPM, it is necessary to understand supply chain (SC) performance metric and performance indicators. A metric is a measurement, taken over time that communicates vital information about a process or activity. The major requirement for being a metric versus an indicator must derive appropriate action. In other words, if you are off target, the metric shows you that and, enables you to start action to get back on target. It is a meaningful measure on the other hand Indicators can be the counts. They come from processes and their inputs, outputs and outcomes. The Indicators come from outputs or their outcomes. The performance indicators and measures shall be the same and often used interchangeably for performance measurement SCPM.

Performance measurement is a very challenging task which has a great occurrence in the field of management as studies and reports. It is of great interest to managers and researchers. Brown and Laverick (1994) defined performance evaluation as a means to verify the effectiveness of their decisions for successful development of business. The Council of Logistic Management (1995) establishes that measurement is related to the level of performance of a company, and that an effective measurement calibrates the results of a company in terms of functional evaluation, process evaluation and benchmarking. McIntyre et al. (1998) defined the measurement of performance as a tool of management, which enables the further understanding of operations and processes and metrics are valued by the financial institutions and are a way in which to compare organizations.

India holds second position in the production of fruits and vegetables with production of 91.3 MT of fruits and 163.39 MT of vegetables during 2014-15. The production of 137.7MT of marine, meat and poultry products has put India in the second position worldwide. The food grain production in India has touched 251.12 MT in FY 2015. Despite good production the 20-40 percent of agriculture products go wasted (Paul Artiuch & Samuel Kornstein 2012, p2). This wastage has been witnessed in the rich farm belt of North India. According to TOI news, India wastes 21 million tonnes of wheat every year (TOI, 2013). These challenges in the farm production have attracted the attention of many researchers and policy makers to find a solution for the same. Expecting the great opportunity to harvest profits many big organized retailers have entered into the arena of retail business.

India holds the fifth-largest global retail destination with a 10 percent contribution to the GDP and 8 percent of the employment. According to the Boston Consulting Group and Retailers Association report, "Retail 2020: Restrospect, Reinvent, Rewrite" the retail market is forecasted to double from US$ 600 billion in 2015 US$ 1 trillion in 2020 with overall market growth of 12 percent per annum with 20 percent growth for the modern retail and 10 percent for the traditional retailers (IBFC, 2015).

Farm retailing has been divided into three categories. The *category one* includes the selling of Livestock products (meat, dairy, poultry, eggs). The category two includes the Non-livestock products (including Horticulture products (flowers, fruits, nuts, vegetables and medicinal plants) and Agriculture products (Crops like; rice, cotton, wheat and spices). The *category three* includes the processed products (fats, jams and oils etc.). Farm retailing is the business activity in the sale of farm products directly to final consumers for personal, non-business use. We have focused on the organized retailing of Non-livestock farm products due to the majority of the problems faced by this segment. In this paper an attempt has been made to know the Key Performance Indicators (KPI) for the better supply chain management (SCM) of the Non-livestock products.

The *introduction* part of the paper puts light on the farm product retailing sector as well as the need of study. The *second* section focuses on the necessity of performance measurement. The *third* part focuses on the literature survey. Here, an attempt has been made to produce the relevant studies to prepare a database of KPI. The *database and analysis* section helps to classify the KPI into manageable sets. *Finally,* we have focussed on the conclusion, recommendation and limitation of the study.

Is Performance Measurement Necessary?

Performance measurement is the ultimate necessity for all the organizations as it helps to understand the competitive position of the organizations. Today, the organized retail players are concerned about the market competition. The market competition has shifted from individual company performance to SC performance resulting into cut throat SC vs. SC competition. The SCPM has crossed the functional and company boundaries to discover the ways to achieve the ultimate SC goals.

A review of the literature identifies the need of performance measurement system. A strategic performance measurement system affects and influences the business performance (Blenkinsop and Burns, 1992). A management control system is categorized as interactive when top management uses it personally and regularly involve themselves in the decisions of subordinates. Neely (1998), Kaplan and Norton (2001) also quoted that a SCPM system is meant to be interactive since its main role is to facilitate the implementation of the business strategy and to question strategic assumptions. This type of system shall guide organizational learning, strategic control and therefore influences business results (Simon, 1999).

When systems are used for this purpose, four conditions are typically needed to be met:

1. Information generation;
2. Regular information processing;
3. Information interpretation;
4. and face-to-face meeting for improvement.

Information generated by the management control system is an important and recurring addenda addressed by the highest level of management; the process demands frequent and regular attention from operating managers at all levels of the organization; data are interpreted and discussed in face–to–face meetings of superiors, subordinates and peers; the process relies on the continual challenge and debate on underlying data, assumptions and action plans (Simon, 1999).

Weber and Schaeffer (2000) quoted that given the multitude of measures, managers who try to use BSC as an interactive system will be overloaded and they can't use the system interactively. However, Lipe and Salterio (2002) find that scorecard framework help manager's judgment to focus on what is important and do not overload managers. Mercer, William M &Co., (1999) find that BSC is an effective method to determine pay and rewards.

The literature shows that from the mid 90s, practitioners have concentrated on financial and non-financial measures (Ittner et al. 1997, 2002) or on the performance and behavioral effects of incorporating non-financial performance measures. They have investigated the measures included in the company's strategic performance.

Gate (1999) and Maisel (2001) in their survey studies focused on behavioral and performance effect of using the measures included in a company`s a Strategic Performance Measurement (SPM) system. Kald's (2002) found that SPM are used both diagnostically and interactively. So, all the researchers put light on the role of performance measurement. It is concluded that performance management help to take decision on the following areas:

1. Competitive strategy formulation to achieve organization objectives.
2. To predict failures before time for better managerial decision making.
3. Flow of information for better internal and external communication.
4. Development of evaluation and reward system for achieving.
5. Benchmarking the performance of different teams, individuals, firms and industries.
6. Using information for better managerial decision making.
7. Effective strategic implementation of process and its improvement.
8. Provide feedback to decisions made.
9. Discover better means to improve the industry.
10. Motivate the teams modify objectives to secure better competitive position.
11. Identify the stakeholder needs.
12. Maximizes profits.
13. Consistent delivery schedule.

Literature Survey on Key Performance Indicators

Measuring SC performance leads to informed decision making to track and tracking of efficacy and efficiency failure. It leads to more informed decision making with regard to SC flow. The aim of implementing a SCPM system is to improve the performance of an organization.

In order to assess the success of SC an adequate performance measurement system need to be developed. The basic requirement for the system is to have a feedback system, selected set of goals, to achieve the goals efficiently and effectively. Lee and Billington (1992) quoted that a SC should have an adequate performance metrics and firms only aim at achieving their own performance standards. Neely et al., (1995) defines performance measurement as the process of quantifying the effectiveness and efficiency of action. Effectiveness is the extent to which a customer's requirements are met and efficiency measures how economically a firm's resources are utilized when providing a pre-specified level of customer satisfaction. SCPM systems are described as the overall set of metrics used to quantify both efficiency and effectiveness of action.

There are many challenges in developing and adopting a SCPM system. Many times the participants of SC do not share the same views about the advantages of SCM. Also, the partners in the same chain do not have the same views and do not react equally to a group of KPI due to multi-dimensional nature of KPI (Spekman et al. 1998). Beamon (1999) suggested a system of three dimensional measurements: resources, output and flexibility. Vorst (2000), identified performance indicators on three levels: supply chain level, organizational level and process level. Gilmour (1999) quotes that performance measurement of the SC are traditionally marked by the emphasis on logistics activities and there is a need to focus on the study of logistic activities to generate value for the customers. The turning of this focus to another direction does not imply that there is no need to use operational measures linked to the logistic performance. It establishes the need to develop a new group of performance metrics which will enable to evaluate how much the processes of the SC contributes in giving the customer more value.

Bunte et al., (1998) advocated relating KPI to both effectiveness and efficiency. Van Hoek (1998), quoted that SCM is a characterized control based on web of relations and integration of processes among functional, geographic and organizational interfaces. The modification in the way SCs are controlled (which ceases to be based on property and vertical integration to become based on a web of relationships among interfaces), shows the importance of developing research about systems of evaluating performance in SC.

There is a need to adopt an efficient and effective set of KPI for evaluating SC performance. McIntyre et al., (1998) cited in the study of Caplice and Sheffi (1994) that a good metric has the qualities of compatibility, validation, utility, robustness, integration, sufficient level of details and behavioral soundness. Beamon et al., (1998) studies have shown that KPI to measure supply SC performance include the characteristics of inclusiveness, universality, measurability and consistency. Evaluation of organization is complicated in the presence of multiple inputs, outputs in the system. These aspects require a shift in the focus of performance evaluation and benchmarking from characterizing performance in terms of single measures to evaluating and benchmarking from characterizing performance in terms of single measures to evaluating performance as a multidimensional systems perspective.

Venkatraman and Ramanuja (1986) identified organizational performance as financial performance and operational+financial performance. Benita (1998) and Viswanadham (2000) viewed SC performance in terms of qualitative and quantitative measures. Under qualitative measures they covered customer satisfaction (pre-transaction satisfaction, transaction satisfaction and post-transaction satisfaction), flexibility (with respect to changing environment), information and material flow integration, effective risk management and supplier performance under quantitative measures are non-financial measures ((cycle time or lead time, customer service level(order fill rate, stock out rate, back order level and delivery probability), inventory levels, resource utilization)) and financial measures(fixed and variable cost). Luning et al., (2000) developed a framework for food quality. They divided food quality in product and process quality. Product quality is divided into food-safety and health, sensory properties and shelf life, product reliability and convenience. Quality is divided into production system characteristics, environmental aspects and marketing.

Krajewski and Ritzman (2002), in their study to evaluate SC performance of Beef industry identified: Lead Time, Cost (farm costs, abbation/processing costs, etc.), Capacity (truck or shipment delivery, machine capacity), Quality, Delivery (Delivery speed, production lead time and delivery reliability), Flexibility (customer service flexibility, order flexibility, location flexibility, delivery time flexibility) as determinants to evaluate supply chain performance. Aramyan et al., (2005) developed a conceptual framework of performance measurement for Agrifood SC. It contains financial and non-financial indicators.

SCOR model-The Supply Chain Operations Reference-model (SCOR) model has a large number of KPI based on basic SC activities These activities are; plan, source, make, deliver and return. Kaplan and Norton (1996) proposed a Balance Score Card (BSC). It translates an organization's overall mission and strategy into specific, measurable operational and performance metrics across four perspectives, i.e. Learning and Growth for Employees, Internal Business Processes, Customer Satisfaction and Financial Performance.

Jasbir Ali and Sanjeev Kapoor (2005) quoted that food processing is one of the emerging sectors of Indian economy and has been identified as a thrust area for socio-economic development. They advised the focus on consumer preference variation and environmental role in Agri-food SC performance assessment. The environmental component affects quality and quantity of farm products, i.e., freshness, food safety and environmental issues. Dr. Arpita Khare (2006), quoted that the focus of SCM is not only to create efficient, competitive organizations, but also to foster the relationships within the organization's various functional departments and inter-organizational relationships to fulfill the needs of customers. At the root of the changes is a dramatic fall in the cost of handling and transmitting information. Information can be handled and shared far more cheaply than before. Another important contribution of technology to organizations has been the visibility it has provided to managers and made decision-making easier.

The days when companies could survive and prosper by focusing on the wants and needs of one stakeholder-the shareholders-are long gone the days when organizations could survive and prosper by focusing on the wants and needs of two stockholders-the shareholders and the customers-are also numbered, if not yet already passed. Despite the fact that customer focus was rallying cry for many of the management revolutions that swept the business world during the 1980s and 1990s-such as Just in Time, Total Quality Management and Business Process Re-engineering. Other worthy initiatives have tried to place greater emphasis on other individual stakeholders, such as Human Resource Management, for example, but have tended to lose sight of the broader picture (Marc J. Epstein, 2000). Mohd Nishat Faisal (2007) discusses some of the innovative SCM practices which can be adapted by Indian companies to reduce the cost related to managing inventories and obsolescence, ultimately resulting in improved customer services. These are Vendor Managed Inventory (VMI), Radio Frequency Identification (RFID), Collaborative Planning and Forecasting (CPFR).

The literature survey revealed many researchers have focused on some of the aspects of food processing SC. However, no study has been conducted in the light of research objectives. Hence, an attempt has been made to study the SC related problems and find remedies for the same.

Research Questions

The major questions to conduct this research are as follows:

Q1: Are Key Performance Indicators are same for all the industries?
Q2: What are the Key Performance Indicators to measure supply chain performance of organized non-livestock retailing business?
Q3: Is it useful to adopt a selective set of Key Performance Indicators?
Q4: How can we classify the Key Performance Indicators?

Research Hypothesis

SCOR model recommends the KPIs as-Cycle time metrics (e.g., production cycle time and cash-to-cash cycle), Cost metrics (e.g., cost per shipment and cost per warehouse pick), Service/quality metrics (on-time shipments and defective products) and Asset metrics (e.g., inventories). TCS (2015) conducted a survey across five broad retail segments: Fashion, including apparel, footwear, and accessories, Department stores, Food and grocery, Consumer durables and information technology (CDIT), and Other retailers including books, gifts, pharmacy formats. The survey finds the KPIs and process in five functional areas: Inventory, Warehouse, Suppliers, Transportation, People. Neeraj Anand, Neha Grover, (2015) classified KPI for retail industry into four major categories: transport optimization, information technology optimization, inventory optimization and resource optimization. These key indicators are arranged precisely for retail industry. All these studies show that there is a need of a specific set of KPI for measuring SC performance of specific retail business because the different retail player face different problems and challenges. Also, the different studies mentioned in the reference propose different sets of KPI for different business, geographic location and maturity level of the industry. Hence, the set of KPI shall also need to be different for a different sector of retail business. Hence, we propose the hypotheses:

Ho1: The required KPI for Organized non-livestock retailing are different from other sectors as well as the industry as a whole.

The production attraction index plays an important role to sell a product resulting in better profitability of SC (Laigang Song, 2008, p. 79). This attraction information shall be analyzed using RFID data and frequency of product lifting from the shelf as well as product return data. However, the available information and function of RFID system shall impact the return decision making like; excess stock return, return transshipment, automatic return handling, and return tracking/tracing (Yoon Min Hwang, Jae Jeung Rho, 2008, p. 23). Inventory management is the major aspect of SCM. Many research scholars have mentioned inventory management as an important aspect of SCM (Aramyan, L. 2006; TCS, 2015). Logistics plays a crucial part in the SCM. It is an important component to add value to various activities (Chapman, R.; Soosay, C.; Kandampully, J., 2003). Also, the operations management and customer satisfaction play an important role in SCM (Gilmour, P., A. 1999; Ittner, CD., and Larcker DF. 1998). These studies are the basis to prove that:

Ho2: The Key Performance Indicators to measure supply chain performance of organized non-livestock retailing business shall include product attraction, inventory components, financial metrics logistics management, and customer satisfaction.

DATABASE AND METHODOLOGY

This research is based on the primary data collected from the organized retailing organizations engaged with non-livestock farm products with the help of a questionnaire. A list of respondents was prepared by collecting addresses from PROWESS, organizational web sites, yellow pages and information published in retail reports. The total 500 respondents were selected randomly and were sent the questionnaire. It was found that 111 respondents answer the complete questionnaire resulting the response rate of 22 percent. It was due to the highly busy schedule of the persons working at the level of manager and above.

The target population selected for this research consists of practitioners-Retail Store Managers, Supply Chain Managers, MIS Managers, Vice-President marketing, etc. operating in major cities of Punjab (Bathinda, Amritsar, Patiala, Kharar, Ropar, Mohali, Patiala, Ludhiana, Jallandhar, Gurdaspur, Rajpura, Faridkot, Muktsar), New Delhi and Gurgaon. They were also personally contacted to answer the questionnaire. The composition of surveyed respondents consists of 5% consultants with organized retail industry and 95% of the respondents are from an organized retail service sector (Vice Presidents Marketing/Supply Chain Managers/Store Managers/MIS Manager). Due to the descriptive nature of this study, a proportionate sample of respondents was selected from the persons directly engaged in this business in the top 10 organized retail players.

A 21-item/statement was used for measuring key performance indicators for the organized retailing. The statements were developed on a 5 point Likert scale ranging from "very low to very high (5)". The questionnaire developed based on literature survey was sent to leading researchers and practitioners for comments. Based on the comments it was found that some of the indicators were not suitable for Indian non-livestock retailing, and these were deleted from the list to set at 18. The scale so generated was refined and purified to obtain a reliable scale for this purpose.

The reliable scale so developed was tested for reliability: Scale reliability alpha$\geq$0.7, Kaiser-Meyer-Okline (KMO$\geq$ 0.7, item-to-total correlation$\geq$ 0.5, inter-item correlation $\geq$ 0.3and Communality $\geq$0.5) and Bartlett's Test of Sphericity (Approximate Chi-Square, Degree of freedom, Significance) before applying factor analysis. The scale so selected was taken as an indicator to proceed to the next step of factor analysis. Finally, the Factor Analysis was done to group the various KPI. The results are shown the succeeding sections.

Analysis of Results

Questionnaire Development

A questionnaire was developed to identify the KPI for Non-livestock retailing in North India. The statements were collected for this purpose from the literature survey as well as consultants and practitioners engaged with the SCM of organized Non-livestock retailing were discussed. During the discussion with experts, these statements were reduced to 21 from 26 based on Indian conditions.

Scale Development

A scale was developed to select the applicability of the KPI for this research ranging from very low (1) to very high (5) on the Likert scale. Initially, 26 variables/items were selected for KPI measuring SC performance of Non-livestock retail industry. Finally, the pilot survey analysis results for scale reliability, reduced the items to 21.

Scale Refinement

The scale so generated was tested for reliability using reliability analysis-scale (Alpha) for 26 refined statements. The scale reliability has reduced the statements to 21. The results of 111 samples collected indicated scale reliability (Cronbach's Alpha=0.7072) which is good enough for conducting factor analysis (Cronabach, 1990).

Factor Analysis

The Factor Analysis has reduced one more item due to discriminant validity using the technique of 'principal Component Analysis'. Finally, Factor Analysis was conducted again to classify the 19 statements. The factor analysis has classified the statements into 5 groups. The overall KMO value of this research is 0.701. The results are shown in Table 1. Here, it is worth mentioning that KMO value above 0.7 is good enough for research in social sciences. The statements are classified in 5 groups which explain

74.29% of the variance. The Communality is greater than 0.5. The results of the factor analysis using Principal Component Analysis are shown in Table 1 below:

The groups classified using factor analyses are explained as follows:

1. **Product Attraction Metrics:** This group has the loadings in the range of 0.949 to 0.956. The KPI covered here are-Product quality, Product personality, and Process quality. It has an Eigen Value of 2.957 and explains 14.784% of the variance. The scale reliability for this factor is 0.913.
2. **Inventory Metrics:** This group has the loadings in the range of 0.923 to 0.896. The KPI covered here are -Fill rate, Customer response time, Return adjustment, Spoilage adjustment, and VMI. It has an Eigen Value of 4.244 and explains 21.22% of the variance. The scale reliability for this factor is 0.905.

Table 1. Factor analysis results for key performance indicators

Metrics	Components					Communality
	Product Attraction Metrics (1)	Inventory metrics (2)	Financial metrics (3)	Transportation metrics (4)	Customer Response metrics (5)	
Product Quality	.949					.912
Product Personality	.967					.943
Process Quality	.956					.941
Fill Rate		.923				.854
Customer Response Time		.909				.827
Return Adjustment		.836				.709
Spoilage Adjustment		.929				.884
VMI		.896				.827
Inventory Cost			.868			.773
Distribution Cost			.958			.932
ROI			.910			.846
Stakeholder Value			.957			.925
Sales Profits			.938			.904
Channel Flexibility			.517			.392
Shipping Errors				.781		.656
Volume Flexibility				.719		.554
Lead Time					.557	.502
Delivery Flexibility					.780	.794
Backorder Flexibility					.613	.546
Eigen Values	2.957	4.244	4.967	1.549	1.143	
% Variance	14.784	21.222	24.83	7.743	5.714	
Cumulative % Variance	60.839	46.055	24.83	68.582	74.29	
Scale Reliability Alpha	0.913	0.905	0.967	0.752	0.706	

3. **Financial Metrics:** This group has the loadings in the range of 0.868 to 0.517. The KPI covered here are inventory cost, distribution cost, ROI, stakeholder value, sales profit and channel flexibility. It has an Eigen Value of 4.967 and explains 24.83% of the variance. The scale reliability for this factor is 0.967.

4. **Transportation Metrics:** This group has the loadings in the range of 0.781 to 0.719. The KPI covered here are shipping errors, and volume flexibility. It has Eigen Value of 1.549 and explains 7.743% of the variance. The scale reliability for this factor is 0.752.

5. **Customer Response Metrics:** This group has the loadings in the range of 0.557 to 0.780. The KPI covered here are Lead time, Delivery flexibility, and Backorder flexibility. It has an Eigen Value of 1.143 and explains 5.714% of the variance. The scale reliability for this factor is 0.706.

Discussion of Results

This paper has classified the KPI into five groups using Factor Analysis. These groups include Product Attraction Metrics, Inventory Metrics, Financial Metrics, Transportation Metrics and Customer Response Metrics. The results show that the majority of the individual KPIs are in consonance with the studies conducted in different industries. However, all the groups of KPI for the organized Non-livestock industry do not exactly match with the required group sets of KPI for other industries (SCOR model; Kaplan and Norton, 1992; TCS, 2015). Hence, the different industries need different groups of KPIs. So, the hypothesis: "Ho1: The required KPI for Organized non-livestock retailing are different from other sectors as well as the industry as a whole" is proved.

Also, the major KPI needed for the different industries resembles. The Product attraction metrics are important to attract and retain customers. Companies use production attraction index to sell a product resulting in better profitability of SC (Laigang Song, 2008, p. 79). The customer attraction needs sufficient inventory in wide variety for better SC execution (Joseph Y. Saab Jr.; Henrique L. Correa, Michael R. Bowers, 2008; A. Angulo, H. Nacthmann, M.A. Waller 2004; J.H. Bookbinder, M. Gumus, E.M. Jewkes, 2010). The ultimate objective of SCM is better, financial performance (Jacques Verville, Nazim Taskin, Sweety Law, 2011; Jun Wu, Jian Li, Jia Chen, Yingxue Zhao, Shouyang Wang, 2011). The transportation (Arash Shahin, Fatemeh Jaferi, 2015) helps to add value to the business activities resulting in customer satisfaction (Purushottam L. Meena, S.P. Sarmah, Santanu Sinha, 2012; Pramod Kumar Mishra, B. Raja Shekhar, 2013). Hence the hypothesis "Ho2: The Key Performance Indicators to measure supply chain performance of organized non-livestock retailing business shall include product attraction, inventory components, financial metrics logistics management, and customer satisfaction" is proved. The understanding of these groups shall help the organized retailers better manage their business.

CONCLUSION, RECOMMENDATION, AND LIMITATIONS

This study has proven that the different industries need different groups of KPIs. However, many of the KPIs appear across most of the industries, despite the variability of KPI in a group set of KPIs. The Organized Non-livestock retailing organizations need to do extensive study while selecting a set of KPI. It is due to the fact that the wrong selection of KPIs shall waste time and resources resulting in reduced profits. The future research is recommended to address the following questions:

1. What KPI set is suitable for a specific level of SC execution?
2. How the qualitative metrics shall be translated in quantitative output?
3. How shall the KPI trade-off decisions shall be made?
4. How shall we develop a business performance model?

Despite, the best efforts this study has many limitations. The major limitation is the failure to involve major sums of top level SC practitioners. It was due to their highly busy schedule as well as the privacy policies exercised by the companies. It is also required to study the organized and unorganized sector together better understanding of the gap between these two sectors. However, the purpose of this study is not to validate the results by statistical inference, but provides the insights to the practitioners and policy maker for betterment of the business.

REFERENCES

Abbas, F., Mitchell, L., & Mehmet, C. K. (2002). Streamlining Supply Chain Management with E-Business. *Proceedings:38th MBAA Annual Meeting*.

Anand, N., & Grover, N. (2015). Measuring retail supply chain performance: Theoretical model using key performance indicators (KPIs). *Benchmarking International Journal (Toronto, Ont.)*, *22*(1), 135–166.

Angulo, A., Nacthmann, H., & Waller, M. A. (2004). Supply chain information sharing in a vendor managed inventory partnership. *Journal of Business Logistics*, *25*(1), 101–120. doi:10.1002/j.2158-1592.2004.tb00171.x

Aramyan, L. (2006). Performance Indicators in Agri-Food Production Chains. Springer. doi:10.1007/1-4020-4693-6_5

Arpita, K. (2006). Supply Chain Management: Improving the efficiency. *Synergy Journal of ITS*.

Artiuch, P., & Kornstein, S. (2012). Sustainable approaches to reduce agriculture waste in India. MIT. Available at http://web.mit.edu/CoLab/pdf/papers/Reducing_Food_Waste_India.pdf

Beamon, B. M. (1998). Supply Chain Design and Analysis: Models and Methods. *International Journal of Production Economics*, *55*(3), 281–294. doi:10.1016/S0925-5273(98)00079-6

Beamon, B. M. (1999). Measuring Supply chain Performance. *International Journal of Operations & Production Management*, *19*(3), 275–292. doi:10.1108/01443579910249714

Beamon, B. M. (1999). Measuring Supply Chain Performance. *International Journal of Operations & Production Management*, *19*(3), 275–292. doi:10.1108/01443579910249714

Blenkinsop, S. A., & Burns, N. (1992). Performance measurement revisited. *International Journal of Operations & Production Management*, *12*(10), 16–25. doi:10.1108/01443579210017213

Bookbinder, J. H., Gumus, M., & Jewkes, E. M. (2010). Calculating the benefits of vendor managed inventory in a manufacturer-retailer system. *International Journal of Production Research*, *48*(19), 5549–5571. doi:10.1080/00207540903095434

Brown, N., & Laverick, S. (1994). Measuring Corporate Performance. *Long Range Planning, 27*(4), 89–98. doi:10.1016/0024-6301(94)90059-0

Bunte, F. M., Mulder, F., & van Tongerenen, J. J. (1998). Meting van de performance van agrarische produktiekolommen. Onderzoekverslag 163. LEI.

Caplice, C., & Sheffi, Y. (1994). A review and evaluation of logistic metrics. *The International Journal of Logistics Management, 5*(2), 11–28. doi:10.1108/09574099410805171

Chapman, R., Soosay, C., & Kandampully, J. (2003). Innovation in Logistics Services and the New Business Model: A Conceptual Framework. *International Journal of Physical Distribution & Logistics Management, 33*(7), 630–650. doi:10.1108/09600030310499295

Council of Logistic Management. (1995). *World class Logistics: The Challenge of Managing Continuous Change.* Oak Books, IL: CLM.

Cronabach, L. (1990). *Essentials of Psychological Testing.* New York: Harper and Row.

Gates, S. (1999). *Aligning Strategic Performance Measures and Results.* New York, NY: The Conference Board.

Gilmour, P. A. (1999). Strategic Audit Framework to Improve Supply Chain Performance. *Journal of Business & Industrial Marketing, 14*(5/6), 355-363.

Hwang, Y. M., & Rho, J. J. (2008). RFID system for centralized reverse supply chain in the apparel industry. In *Proceedings of the 22nd International Symposium and Workshop on Global Supply Chain, Intermodal Transportation and Logistics.* Available at https://www.utoledo.edu/research/ututc/docs/Proceedings_Busan_Symposium_20.pdf

IBFC India Brand Equity Foundation. (2015). Available at http://www.ibef.org/industry/food-industry-presentation

Ittner, C. D., & Larcker, D. F. (1997). Quality strategy, strategic control systems, and organizational performance. *Accounting, Organizations and Society, 22*(3-4), 293–314. doi:10.1016/S0361-3682(96)00035-9

Ittner, C. D., & Larcker, D. F. (1998). Are non-financial measures leading indicators of financial performance? An analysis of customer satisfaction. *Journal of Accounting Research, 36*(supplement), 1–35. doi:10.2307/2491304

Ittner, C. D., & Larcker, D. F. (2001). Assessing empirical research in managerial accounting: A value-based management perspective. *Journal of Accounting and Economics, 32*(1), 349–410. doi:10.1016/S0165-4101(01)00026-X

Ittner, C. D., & Larcker, D. F. (2002). Determinants of performance measure choices in worker incentive plans. *Journal of Labor Economics, 2*(S2), S58–S90. doi:10.1086/338674

Ittner, C. D., & Larcker, D. F. (1996). Measuring the impact of quality initiatives on firm financial performance. *Advances in the Management of Organizational Quality, 37.*

Ittner, C. D., Larcker, D. F., & Rajan, M. V. (1997). The choice of performance measures in annual 44 bonus contracts. *Accounting Review, 72,* 231–255.

Ittner, C. D., Larcker, D. F., & Randall, T. (2002). *Performance implications of strategic performance measurement in financial services firms*. Wharton School Working Paper.

Kaplan, R., & Norton, D. (1996). Using the Balance Scorecard as Strategic Management System. *Harvard Business Review*, (Jan-Feb), 75–85.

Kaplan, R., & Norton, D. (2001). *The Strategy-Focused Organisation*. Harvard Business School Press.

Kaplan, R. S., & Norton, D. P. (1992). The balanced scorecard—measures that drive performance. *Harvard Business Review, 70*(1), 71–79. PMID:10119714

Krajewski, L., & Ritzman, L. (2002). *Operations Management: Strategy and Analysis* (6th ed.). New York, NY: Prentice-Hall.

Lee, H., & Billington, C. (1992). Managing supply Chain Inventory: Pitfalls and Opportunities. *Sloan Management Review, 3*, 65–73.

Lipe, M., & Salterio, S. (2000). The balanced scorecard: Judgmental effects of common and unique performance measures. *Accounting Review, 75*(3), 283–298. doi:10.2308/accr.2000.75.3.283

Lipe, M., & Salterio, S. (2002). A note on the judgmental effects of the balanced scorecards information organization. *Accounting, Organizations and Society, 27*(6), 531–540. doi:10.1016/S0361-3682(01)00059-9

Luning, P. A., Marcelis, W. J., & Jongen, W. M. F. (2002). Food Quality Management: a techno-managerial approach. Wageningen: Wageningen Pers.

Mohd, N. F., Banwet, D. K., & Ravi, S. (2007). Information risks management in supply chains: An assessment and mitigation framework. *Journal of Enterprise Information Management, 20*(6), 677–699. doi:10.1108/17410390710830727

Neely, A. (1999). The performance measurement revolution: Why now and what next? *International Journal of Operations & Production Management, 19*(2), 205–228. doi:10.1108/01443579910247437

Pramod Kumar Mishra, B. (2013, January). Consumer behaviour, customer satisfaction vis-a-vis brand performance: An empirical study of dairy food supply chain in India. *International Journal of Indian Culture and Business Management, 7*(3), 399–412. doi:10.1504/IJICBM.2013.056216

Purushottam, L. (2012, January). Measuring satisfaction in buyer supplier relationship from suppliersperspective. *International Journal of Business Performance and Supply Chain Modelling, 4*(1), 60–74. doi:10.1504/IJBPSCM.2012.044974

Saab, Jr., Correa, & Bowers. (2008). Optimising performance with distributor managed inventory in a FMCG supply chain. *International Journal of Business Excellence, 1*(1/2), 121-38.

Shahin, A., & Jaferi, F. (2015, January). The shortest route for transportation in supply chain by minimum spanning tree. *International Journal of Logistics Systems and Management, 22*(1), 43–54. doi:10.1504/IJLSM.2015.070893

Simon, H. A. (1979). Information Processing Models of Cognition. *Annual Review of Psychology, 30*(1), 363–396. doi:10.1146/annurev.ps.30.020179.002051 PMID:18331186

Simons, R. (2000). *Performance Measurement & Control Systems for Implementing Strategy: Text & Cases*. Upper Saddle River, NJ: Prentice Hall.

Song, L. (2008). *Supply Chain Management with Demand Substitution* (PhD Thesis). University of Tennessee, Knoxville, TN.

Speakman, R. (1998). An Empirical investigation into Supply Chain Management: A perspective on partnerships. *International Journal of Physical Distribution & Logistics Management, 28*(8), 630–650.

Suhong, L. (2004). The impact of supply chain management practices on competitive advantage and organizational performance. *International Journal of Management Sciences, 11*, 112–119.

Tata Consultancy Services. (2015). *Retail Operations Benchmarking and Excellence Survey 2015, Measuring Supply Chain Performance*. Available at httpwww.tcs.com/SiteCollectionDocuments/White%20Papers/Retail-Operations-BenchmarkingExcellence-Survey-Measuring-Supply-Chain-Performance-0215-1.pdf

Times of India. (n.d.). *India wastes 21 million tonnes of wheat every year: Report*. Available at http://timesofindia.indiatimes.com/india/India-wastes-21-million-tonnes-of-wheat-every-year-Report/articleshow/17969340.cms

Van der Vorst, J. G. A. J. (2000). *Effective food supply chains: Generating, modeling and evaluating supply chain scenarios*. Proefschrift Wageningen.

Van Hoek, R. (1998). Measuring the measurable-measuring and improving performance in supply chain. *Supply Chain Management, 3*(4), 187–192. doi:10.1108/13598549810244232

Venkatraman, N., & Ramanuja, V. (1986, July/October). Measurement of business performance in strategy research: A comparison of approaches. *Academy of Management Review, 11*(4).

Verville, J., Taskin, N., & Law, S. (2011, January). Buyer-supplier relationships in supply chain management: Relationship, trust, supplier involvement, and performance. *International Journal of Agile Systems and Management, 4*(3), 203–221. doi:10.1504/IJASM.2011.040515

Wu, J., Li, J., Chen, J., Zhao, Y., & Wang, S. (2011, January). Risk management in supply chains. *International Journal of Revenue Management, 5*(2-3), 157–204. doi:10.1504/IJRM.2011.040307

Chapter 19

Incidence of Green Accounting on Competitiveness:
Empirical Evidences from Mining and Quarrying Sector

Ramakrushna Panigrahi
International Management Institute, Bhubaneswar, India

ABSTRACT

The traditional growth theories and neoclassical economic development models have dominated the economic policies in both developed and developing economies over last decades. As a result, the global output has increased manifold due to inherent cost competitiveness ingrained in neoclassical model that heavily relies on optimization of output and resources based on the marginality principle. However, income growth has resulted in environmental degradation and depletion of natural resources as the framework of SNA does not treat these resources as fixed capital and hence, the depreciation of such resources are not treated aptly in the framework of income accounting. The environmental degradation and the recent phenomenon in global warming and the debate of climate change have taken centre-stage in the political discourse. This prompts for an urgent need for an institutionalized market oriented framework to treat environmental costs and depletion of natural resources. This paper makes an attempt to provide a framework to estimate green income from Mining and Quarrying sector by incorporating depreciation factor and examines its implications for export competitiveness of the sectors which use the output of Mining sector as inputs.

INTRODUCTION

The traditional growth theories and neoclassical economic development models have dominated the economic policies in both developed and developing economies over last decades. As a result, the global output has increased manifold due to inherent cost competitiveness ingrained in neoclassical model that heavily relies on optimization of output and resources based on marginality principle. Such optimization delivers high levels of growth as witnessed in recent decades and the income growth is reflected in the

DOI: 10.4018/978-1-5225-0902-8.ch019

System of National Accounting. However, income growth has resulted in environmental degradation and depletion of natural resources as the framework of SNA does not treat these resources as fixed capital and hence, the depreciation of such resources are not deducted aptly from the income aggregates. However, the depreciation of man-made fixed capital is accounted for in the existing framework. Such zero-depreciation treatment to natural capital undermines the prices of output from the primary sector; specifically the Mining as well as Forestry sector. Since the inputs for the secondary sector and tertiary sector are output from the primary sector, such underestimation reflects on the prices of goods and services produced in an economy. In an increasingly globalised world economy, where all the countries aim at higher exports for their economic growth, cost-competitiveness determines the terms of trade, and hence the trade balance. The recent phenomenon in global warming and the debate of climate change have taken centre-stage in the political discourse. Many economists and advocates of sustainable development have long emphasized the need towards a green accounting system. In such scenario, the cost-competitiveness hitherto enjoyed by countries will decrease as accounting depreciation of natural capital would make production of output more expensive.

The environmental degradation and depletion of natural resources due to the process of industrialization and thereby achieving an export-led growth for the economy have warranted ample attention of academicians in the recent decades. Traditionally, both environmental aspects were neglected in the standard accounting system of an economy, since the objective has been to accomplish a higher rate of growth through maximum usage of available resources. With expansion and growth of an economy, the uses of environmental and natural resources become more intensive, and their excessive depletion posed a threat to the sustainability of the existing system of production.

Natural resources have been considered as *free goods* in economics. Such treatment in the System of National Accounts does not reflect the real cost of extracting natural resources. The underestimation of costs has resulted in over-exploitation of natural resources, specifically, the exhaustible resources in a competitive market economy, where firm maximizes profits by minimizing costs. However, in the wake of global environmental awareness, environmental repercussions resulting from the economic activities can no longer be neglected, especially in the estimations incomes aggregates, which represent development of an economy.

National income has been considered as one of the most important indicators of development. In the context of green accounting, on the definition of *income,* it is apt to quote J. R. Hicks (1946) here:

The purpose of income calculations in practical affairs is to give people an indication of the amount which they can consume without impoverishing themselves. Following out this idea it would seem that we ought to define a man's income as the maximum value which he can consume during a week, and still expects to be as well off at the end of the week as he was at the beginning. Thus when a person saves he plans to be better off in the future; when he lives beyond his income he plans to be worse off. Remembering that the practical purpose of income is to serve as a guide for present conduct, I think it is fairly clear that this is what the central meaning must be.

From this definition, it is amply clear the estimates of macroeconomic aggregates should represent true income figures for an economy. In SNA, national income measured in terms of *Value Added* is defined as a single measure of the value of goods and services produced in an economy during a particular period of time (one year), which ensures that none of the value of goods and services produced is counted more than once. If the income is overestimated, it provides a wrong guide, and subsequently distorts the estimates of growth, development and welfare. In SNA, *consumption of fixed capital (assets)* i.e., *depreciation* is estimated only for *man-made capital* while ignoring the *natural capital*. Environmental economists argue that the *depreciation factor* in SNA is grossly underestimated, since the depletion of environmental resources (such as land, air and water) and natural resources (such as forests and minerals) is not taken into account though they are used for all economic activities. The computations of *Net Value Additions* do not consider this *depreciation* in conventional SNA. These resources and their depreciation need to be considered as *fixed capital* (at par with *man-made capital*) in the production process, since any economic activity cannot be undertaken without having a bearing on such resources. However, a mere increase in national income cannot be considered as a true indicator of economic development particularly if it is attained at the cost of a degraded environment and depleted natural resource base. Thus, for sustainable growth, macroeconomic policies need figures of *sustainable income*. This paper makes an attempt to provide a framework to estimate green income from Mining and Quarrying sector by incorporating depreciation factor and examines its implications for export competitiveness of the sectors which use the output of Mining sector as inputs for their production.

REVIEW OF LITERATURE

Hotelling (1931), Brookshire et.al (1980), Mitra (1981), Nadkarni(1987), Lutz and Serafy (1988), Serafy (1989), Nogaard (1989), Gilbert et.al (1990), Rao(1991), Nadkarni (1993), Barbier and Markandya(1993) have addressed the importance of environmental degradation and implications of environmental concerns in national welfare. Among all these studies, Serafy (1989) pointed out the methods to calculate the environmental cost due to the depletion of natural resources. In poor countries, natural resources are not restored to same level as they are depleted. In such a case, national income should impute a capital consumption charge based on technically acceptable criteria against current receipts to obtain the true income from such activities. Serafy has outlined two approaches to estimate environmental costs: *depreciation* approach and *user cost* approach. The weakness of depreciation approach is that in case of countries, such as Saudi Arabia where the country derives almost 100 per cent of receipts from, say, petroleum extraction, it would give us a GDP of 100 and a NDP of zero. In this context, Serafy proposed an alternative of conversion to a permanent income stream, where *true* income can be obtained. The formula is: $(X/R) = 1 - [1/(1+r)^{n+1}]$, where X is true income, R is total receipts, 'r' is the rate of discount and 'n' is the number of years (periods) the resource is to be liquidated. R-X would be the user cost or depletion factor that should be set aside from Value-Additions. Once a discount rate is fixed, true income can be obtained by using the above-mentioned formula. According to him number of years (n) can also be decided on the basis of the rate at which the owner is extracting. However, both *n* and *r* can be changed periodically, say every five years, guided by changes in the long-term market prices.

Serafy argues that user cost approach is an effective way of persuading developing countries to extract natural resources in a limited and planned way that depend on them. This way consumption of natural resources could be protracted over a long period of time. Using user cost approach, depletion factor could be estimated and adjusted in income accounting, which shall give us true income figures. However, he considers depreciation approach as the second-best alternative to deduct a depletion factor from an inflated value-additions from the sector to make the contribution *green* so far as exhaustible natural resources are concerned.

Database and Methodology

The DES officially provides the estimates of sector wise income aggregates based on conventional SNA that does not take into account environmental concerns. The Value-additions adjusted for environmental costs can be obtained by two ways:

1. Estimating environmental costs sector wise *at source* and integrating them into sectoral income
2. Estimating environmental costs by taking into consideration the sectoral interdependence of an economy.

In the first method, the true income aggregates are obtained but the sectoral interdependence of environmental repercussions is not captured. In the second method, sectoral interdependence of environmental repercussions is captured. However, to capture the interdependence of sectoral income as well as environmental repercussions, it is essential to estimate sector wise environmental costs. For this reason, both the methods (1) and (2) should be considered in the estimation of green income of an economy.

As far as the first method is concerned, environmental costs can be estimated in two ways:

1. Estimating the environmental costs for the entire economy by taking into account total degradation in environment / depletion of natural resources.
2. Estimation of environmental costs at source of degradation.

In the first case, one can estimate total expenditure needed to restore the environment into original level before the accounting period and estimate the cost of depreciation of natural resources. However, it is difficult to estimate the extent of environmental degradation for an economy due to following reasons. First, pollutions are of different forms and leads to aggregation problems. Second, pollutions apart, depletion of exhaustible natural resources cannot be aggregated for the entire economy. Even if one is able to estimate the extent of degradation, it is impossible to segregate the damage caused to the environment / natural resources in the particular year under consideration. Hence, keeping in mind the methodological limitations, method (b) is considered more relevant and practical as far as estimation of environmental costs is concerned.

In the context of income accounting, the natural resources are divided into two parts i.e., exhaustible resources and renewable resources. For exhaustible natural resources the *user cost* approach is used. And for renewable natural resources the *depreciation* approach should be most appropriate. In the case of pollution and degradation of environmental resources the *defensive expenditures* approach should be used as that would provide most reasonable estimates of true income.

This paper has chosen the Mining and Quarrying sector of Odisha state in India to estimate the green income from this sector. The state of Odisha is chosen as the Mining and Quarrying sector is largest in the country accounting for 95 per cent of Chromite, 92 per cent of nickel ore, 55 per cent of Bauxite and 33 per cent of Iron ore deposits of the country. Apart from major minerals, Odisha also accounts for 20 per cent coal production in India with largest inventory of coal reserves. Odisha's mineral production in terms of value accounts for 11.89 per cent of total mineral production and is the highest among all the states. This has prompted to choose the Mining and Quarrying sector of Odisha to estimate green income and its implications for cost competitiveness in the present study.

The detailed disaggregated data on various minerals are taken from documents published by official sources in the state of Odisha and by Government of India. All the data related to estimating green contribution are collected from government sources namely, DES and Department of Mines and Geology, Government of Odisha. It may be noted that the reported figures of minerals extractions may be underestimation due to prevalent illegal mining in the state. Due to strict judiciary intervention, the extraction of minerals has gone down drastically in recent years. Also, the miners have a tendency of under-reporting the extent of extraction which may further undermine the green estimates aimed to be derived in this paper. It may be noted that, all the relevant and consistent data required to estimate green income form Mining and Quarrying sector are available for the year 2010-11, the latest data available from official sources. For this purpose, the state NVA figures from the Mining and Quarrying sector are adjusted for environmental costs only at constant prices for the same year.

Mining and Quarrying Sector in Odisha

The share of Mining sector in the state income has increased drastically over the period 2004-05 t0 2010-11. From a share of 7.54 per cent in 2004-05 it has gone up to 10.79 per cent in the year 2010-11 at constant prices. However, the NVA as reported by DES from this sector has gone up to huge extent during the period 200405 to 2010-11. In real terms, this sector has gone up from Rs. 58.61 billion to Rs. 244.31 billion at constant prices. Thus, the income as estimated through conventional SNA from this sector has gone up by more than four times in a span of just 6 years.

However, as discussed, this income generated from this sector is not green income as any extraction of mineral resources has to compromise with its availability in future. Further, the stock of these resources is depleted with extraction to a large extent with additional expansion of any economy. We may note that illegal mining in the state has further contributed hugely to over-exploitation of mineral resources in the state. In the accounting system, depreciation of such important resource base is not considered due to the prevalent distinction practised between man-made and natural capital. Also the process of extraction of mineral resources pollutes environment and need to be taken into account. However, in the present study such environmental costs due to pollution are not estimated due to non-availability of appropriate data and *only depreciation of natural capital* is accounted for.

In the context of estimating depreciation of mineral resources, Serafy's (1989) formula to determine the true income is quite relevant. As it was argued earlier, if depreciation approach is applied to value the depleted or degraded resources at current prices, the gross product would remain unchanged, but the net product would be adjusted to reflect the depreciation of environmental capital that has occurred during the accounting period.

But in practice, if depreciation approach is used, it would leave gross value of output unchanged and the net value would be zero as it wipes out the entire proceeds from natural resource sales. Hence, user cost approach would be most appropriate in case of mineral resources. The user cost approach avoids the difficulties of putting a value on the stock of resource, but it relies on the conscious assessment of current extraction rates in relation to the total available stock, measured in physical terms. The net extraction cost of mineral resources could be split into a capital element or user cost and a value added element that represents true income.

Estimation of Green Income Mining and Quarrying Sector

Since the stock of different mineral resources is different in physical terms and also their extraction rates are different, assuming a common *n* (it is the number of years over which the asset is being liquidated) for all the items of minerals is not appropriate. Therefore, appropriate *n* for different minerals are decided by dividing the total reserve of a particular mineral by its extraction in the year 2010-11. In some cases, the data on total reserve of a few minerals like Silica Sand, Stealite, Shale, Fuelsite Quartise are not available though the amount of extraction in the year 2010-11 is available. In such cases, *n* is assumed to be infinite and hence, the user costs are also assumed to be zero. Also in case of certain minerals, where *n* is very large (above 300), the user cost (depletion factor), is assumed to be zero (since with such large n the ratio $R / (1+r)^{n+1}$ tends to zero). As the data on total reserve in case of minor minerals are not available, *n* is assumed to be 30 and the user cost is calculated accordingly. The user costs for different minerals are finally added up and the aggregated amount is treated as the user cost from the GVA of Mining and Quarrying sector.

Next, though data[1] on different extraction rates of minerals and their total stocks are available in physical terms, the data on NVA from different minerals are not available either at current prices or at constant prices. The data on GVA from different minerals are available and the CFC for the entire sector is estimated by the DES. Thus, for estimation of green income, the estimated user cost for different minerals will have to be added to GVA. From this figure of GVA, the CFC is to be deducted to arrive at the corrected NVA from this sector.

Estimation of the User Cost in the Mining and Quarrying Sector

As per Serafy's formula, to split the net revenue into user costs and true income, a discount rate of 3 per cent is assumed in the case of Mining and Quarrying sector. As all the corrections of income figures are with reference to constant prices, this discount rate of 3 per cent is considered to be the most appropriate.

The numbers of years, over which different minerals are being liquidated, is determined separately for different minerals on the basis of their ratio of total reserve and the volume of extraction in the year 1994-95. Now applying the formula, the user cost and true income components from the total receipts from the Mining and Quarrying sector is estimated. The following table presents the estimation results of user cost and true income for different minerals.

From the table 1.1, it is evident that, the green value additions account for Rs.244,913.12 against the reported value of Rs. 282,871.3 million and the user cost accounts for Rs.37,958.18 million. But this green value addition from the Mining and Quarrying sector needs to be adjusted for other environmental degradation as well. For example, the transport of minerals from mines to the factory or port involves large scale transportation which pollutes the environment through vehicular pollution. Here the depletion fator is quite significant compared to the reported value of products from the Mining and Quarrying sector. It might be noted that the green value additions estimated in this study is only 86.5 per cent of the reported income and the remaining 13.5 per cent accounts for the user cost that represents depletion of mineral resources. If the environmental cost of vehicular pollution is further incorporated, the green income will further fall below the 86.5 per cent of reported income.

Table 1. Estimation of user cost and Green income for different (million INR at constant prices)

Sl Minerals	R	N	X	R-X
Bauxite	1893.8	372	1893.8	0
Chromite	40640.9	40	28545.03	12095.87
Iron Ore	171297.1	63	145464.5	25832.6
Manganese	8097.7	190	8069.0	28.7
Coal	58435.9	587	58435.9	0
China Clay	20	2415	20	0
Dolomite	464.9	222	464.2	0.5
Fire Clay	16	2700	16	0
Graphite	8.9	231	8.89	0.01
Lime Stone	1055.1	264	1054.6	0.5
Mineral Sand	873.7	870	873.7	0
Pyrophylite	0.9	1670	0.9	0
Minor Minterals	100.4	300	100.4	0
Total:	282871.3	-	244913.12	37958.18

Notes: X is true income; R is total receipts; n is the number of years (periods) the resource is to be liquidated; and R-X is the user cost;
Source: Computed by the author

Implications for the Market and Cost Competitiveness

Since the framework of SNA does not have any provision to account for depreciation of natural capital and the environmental capital, the value additions from various sectors of the economy do not represent the true (green) income. Subsequently, the equilibrium prices of sectoral output are highly undermined. To a large extent, developing countries like India have gained from such treatment of natural capital as undermined equilibrium prices result in enhanced cost competitiveness in the international markets. As a result, India has exported large quantities of mineral in the recent past and has gained from such trade. However, as estimated in this study, introduction of user cost for the natural capital in the SNA will raise the output prices from Mining sector by at least 13.5 per cent. Since the output of Mining and Quarrying sector are mainly used as inputs in Manufacturing and services sectors, the output prices would likely to go up accordingly. Further, if environmental cost due to vehicular pollution are incorporated, the cost of production and subsequently the prices should further o up; compromising the export competitiveness of the countries which have heavily depended on a market oriented neoclassical model of export led growth. However, as the environmental degradation assumes alarming proportions which reflect in global warming and other livelihood issues, it is the collective responsibility of all the countries to address them in a market oriented framework lest it go beyond the control of policy intervention. It may be noted that, despite urgent need to address these issues at local level, no country individually could act as such action would result in reduced export competitiveness. However, if these issues are addressed collectively, individual countries can retain cost competitiveness without harming environmental resources as done in the absence of an institutionalized framework.

CONCLUSION

From the estimation of user cost and subsequent green income from the Mining and Quarrying sector, it is evident that, the green income is only 86.5 per cent of the reported income through existing SNA, which is indeed a gross underestimation. Moreover, if we consider the extent of illegal mining and actual extraction of mineral resources, true income will be further less from this sector which is alarming as such extraction is not at all sustainable. Also, environmental costs in terms of vehicular pollution would reduce the green income figures and subsequently the equilibrium prices of inter-sectoral input-output of the economy, especially which use minerals as raw-materials for production. Given the recent trends in global warming and pollution levels of major global cities, time has come to deal with environmental issues collectively in an instituitilized market oriented framework to make the global production and economy sustainable.

REFERENCES

Alison, G., Onno, K., & Jaap, A. (1990). *Natural Resource Accounting: Issues related to classification and Valuation of Environmental Assets*. Amsterdam: Institute for Environmental Studies.

Atkinson, G., R. Dubourg, K. Hamilton, M. Munasinghe, D. Pearce & C. Young (1997). *Measuring Sustainable Development: Macroeconomics and Environment*. Edward Elgar.

Brookshire, D. S., Randal, A., & Stoll, R. J. (1980). Valuing Increments and Decrements in Natural Resource Service Flows. *American Journal of Agricultural Economics, 62*(3).

Daly, H. E. (1989). Toward a measure of Sustainable Social Net National Product. In Environmental Accounting for Sustainable Development. The World Bank.

Department of Mines and Geology. (n.d.). *Geology and Mineral Resources of Odisha*. Department of Mines and Geology, Government of Odisha, Bhubaneswar. Retrieved 21 November from: http://www. orissaminerals.gov.in/Download/GEOLOGY_MINERAL_RESOURCES_ORISSA.pdf

Dornbusch, R., Fischer, S., & Startz, R. (2012). *Macroeconomics* (7th ed.). Boston: Irwin McGraw-Hill.

Edward, B. B., & Anil, M. (1993). Environmentally Sustainable Development: Optimal Economic Condition. In B. B. Edward (Ed.), *Economics and Ecology: New Frontiers and Sustainable Development*. London: Chapman & Hall.

El Sahah, S. (1989). The Proper Calculation of Income from Depleteble Natural Resources. In Environmental Accounting for Sustainable Development. The World Bank.

EPW Research Foundation. (1997). *National Accounts Statistics in India: 1950-51 to 1995-96*. Mumbai, India: EPW Research Foundation.

Government of India. (2014). *Provisional Coal Statistics: 2013-14*. Coal Controllers Organization, Ministry of Coal, Government of India.

Hotelling, H. (1931). The Economics of Exhaustible Resources. *The Journal of Political Economy, 39*(2).

Lutz, E., & El Serafy. (1989). *Environmental and Resource Accounting: An Overview*. Environment Department Working Paper No 6. The World Bank.

Nadkarni, M. V., & Ravichandran, M. (1987). Economics of Preventing Industrial Pollution. In Economics of Environment. Lancer International.

Perrings, C., Gilbert, A., Pearce, D., & Harrison, A. (1989). *Natural Resource Accounts for Botswana - Environmental Accounting for a Natural Resource Based Economy*. London: Paper.

Planning and Coordination Department. (2012). *Economic Survey:2011-12*. Government of Odisha.

Rao, C. H. H. (1991). Agricultural Development and Ecological Degradation. In India: The Emerging Challenges. Sage Publications.

Richard, N. B. (1989). Three Dilemmas of Environmental Accounting. *Ecological Economics*, *40*(1).

Tapan, M. (1981). Some Results on the Optimal Depletion of Exhaustible Resources Under Negative Discounting. *The Review of Economic Studies*, *48*(4).

ENDNOTES

[1]   All the data on minerals used for this sub-sector are taken from Department of Mines and Geology and other official documents of Government of Odisha

Chapter 20
Moderating Role of Demographics on Attitude towards Organic Food Purchase Behavior:
A Study on Indian Consumers

Arpita Khare
Indian Institute of Management, India

ABSTRACT

The purpose of the current research is to examine moderating role of demographics on attitude towards organic food purchase behavior. Environmental attitude components were classified as actual, verbal, and affect commitment. Data was collected through survey technique in six cities across India. The findings revealed that consumers' attitude towards organic food purchase was influenced by attitude components of Actual and Verbal commitment and moderated by demographic factors of income, gender and age. The findings can be of use to firms marketing organic food brands in India. Environmental attitude factors and demographic factors like income, age, and gender can be used for profiling consumers. With increased growth of organic food market in the country, green marketing and organic food products are upcoming research areas. There is limited research on Indian consumers' attitude towards organic food products. The findings can provide valuable insights to companies marketing these products in the country.

INTRODUCTION

The concept of organic farming is not a novel concept as in the past many regions in India practiced organic farming. However, after independence there was food scarcity in the country. To tackle the food shortage, government invested on chemical fertilizers in order to boost agricultural productivity. In recent years, ancient concept of organic cultivation has again gained momentum due to awareness among consumers about deteriorating effects of pesticide residues on environment and human health

DOI: 10.4018/978-1-5225-0902-8.ch020

(Chandrashekhar, 2010). Organic food is defined as food item prepared or grown without using harmful pesticides, preservatives and other chemicals. As organic food consumption is becoming popular among health and environment conscious consumers (Technopak, 2012), it was assumed that understanding factors affecting Indian consumers' attitude towards organic food would be useful for companies marketing organic food. In recent years, there has been increased demand for organic food products among metropolitan consumers. The monthly expenditure on organic products was reported to be highest in Mumbai followed by Delhi, Bangalore, and Chennai. Recent press releases suggest that sixty two percent of metropolitan consumers buy organic food. Retailers state that health and environmental concern are major reasons for consumers preferring organic food (Sally, 2013).

Organic vegetable is most popular food product among Indian consumers and accounts for sixty eight percent followed by fruits, pulses, juices, grains and milk (Technopak, 2012). Organic packaged food and beverages are other product items popular with Indian consumers. Most Indian consumers felt that organic food is healthier than conventionally grown food. Scientific and health related factors influenced consumers' attitude towards organic food. Indian consumers' attitude towards organic food items was affected by availability, price, region where it was grown, processing, packaging and total time taken from farm to market (Sally, 2013).

Organic food market is expected to grow at Compound Annual Growth Rate of around nineteen percent during year 2012-2017 (PRWEB, 2013). The global organic food and beverages market is projected to grow at USD 104.5 billion by 2015. India ranks tenth in the world based on total cultivable land under organic certification and area under organic food certification is currently 5.21 million hectare (The Economic Times, 2012). India produced around 1.34 million certified organic products in last year. Organic food items like sugarcane, cotton, basmati rice, pulses, tea, spices, coffee, oil seeds, fruits, and other value added products are being cultivated across different states in the country. The increased production of organic food is driven by increased demand for organic food in domestic market. Province/state of Madhya Pradesh ranked first in organic food cultivation followed by Rajasthan and Uttar Pradesh (APEDA, 2013). The other Indian states involved in organic farming are Gujarat, Kerala, Karnataka, Uttaranchal, Sikkim, Maharashtra, Tamil Nadu, and Himachal Pradesh (Chandrashekar, 2010; The Economic Times, 2012). These reports clearly indicate that the organic food market in India has high untapped potential and thus provides a huge opportunity for researchers as well as practitioners.

RESEARCH OBJECTIVES

Research in western countries on organic products has discussed the influence of attitudes and past environmental buying behavior. Factors like environmental attitude, health concern, lifestyle, and peer influence affect pro-environment behaviour (Bigne´, 1997; Fraj & Martı´nez, 2002; Junaedi, 2007; Fraj & Martı´nez, 2007; Pickett-Baker and Ozaki, 2008; Smith and Paladino, 2010; Akehurst et al. 2012). This research primarily focuses on the moderating role of demographic factors on environmental attitude towards organic food buying behavior among Indian consumers. Given that organic food is a nascent market and likely to grow substantially in the coming years (PRWEB, 2013), it was assumed that understanding consumers' attitude towards organic food would help companies marketing these products to understand consumers better. Researchers in western countries have examined multiple dimensions like socio-demographics, food buying behaviour, and nutritional composition that influence awareness level and purchase of organic foods (Hill & Lynchehaun, 2002; Brugarolas Molla`-Bauza` et al., 2005; Krystallis & Chryssohoidis, 2005; First & Brozina, 2009). However, there is limited research in the Indian context on organic food buying behavior. Chakrabarti (2010) in his research on Indian consumers' purchase of organic food found health motivation as important factor affecting organic food. Attitudes like conviction about utility of organic food, consumer innovativeness, word-of-mouth activity for organic food, and commitment towards stores selling organic food were important predictors to consumers' preference for organic food. He had used expert panel to understand consumers' preference for organic food. Expanding on existing work on organic food attitudes, the current research extends Chakrabarti's work and attempts to understand consumer organic food attitude and its relationship with environmental attitude. There was limited discussion on role of demographics on organic food purchase. Drawing from earlier research on organic food, it was assumed that influence of demographics on organic food purchase cannot be ignored. Thus, focus of the current research is to investigate the role of demographics on environmental attitude dimensions on organic food purchase behavior. While there are several psychological and behavioural factors that influence buying patterns, attitude dimensions play a significant role in determining purchase behavior. Attitudinal dimensions like affect, verbal and actual commitment were considered for discussion. These dimensions were drawn from earlier researches on organic food products in Western countries.

LITERATURE REVIEW

Environmental Friendly Buying Behavior

Researchers have discussed influence of several factors like ecological concern, pro-environmental values, past green buying, lifestyles, and demographics on consumers environmental friendly purchase behaviour. Fraj and Martinez (2006) suggest that self-fulfillment values play an important role in predicting Spanish consumers' ecological behaviour. Thogersen and Olander (2003) examined relationship between Danish consumers' environment-friendly behaviour and its impact on other behavioural domains. They indicate that 'spillover' of environment-friendly behaviour occurs in case of consumers who place importance to universalistic values of environment consciousness. Jansson et al. (2010) found that values, beliefs, norms, and habits were positively related to Swedish consumers' curtailment behaviour and willingness to adopt green innovations. Zabkar and Hosta (2013) suggest influence of pro-social environment perceptions of Slovenian consumers' on willingness to buy green products. Environmental related information, attitudes, and beliefs affected consumers' self-perception and commitment towards green product purchase. Similarly, Harland et al. (2007) states that social norms, awareness about environment, conviction that environment is suffering generates sense of responsibility to exhibit pro-environmental attitudes. Personal and social norms were vital in creating consumers' commitment towards environment. These researchers discuss individual and social factors influencing green or environmental friendly buying. The current research focuses only on consumers' attitude towards organic food products. The following section examines factors affecting consumers' preference for organic food.

Attitude Towards Organic Food

With increased interest of consumers for organic products, firms are interested in understanding factors influencing consumers' attitudes towards organic food. Organic production combines best environmental practices, biodiversity, preservation of natural resources, and animal-welfare practices (de Magistris & Gracia, 2008). Organic food consumption decisions are driven by consumers' concern for environment, health, improved taste, and nutritional value (Misra et al., 1991; Davies et al., 1995; Kristensen, 1997; Brugarolas Molla`-Bauza` et al., 2005; Krystallis & Chryssohoidis, 2005).

Aertsens et al. (2009) applied Schwartz's Value theory and Theory of Planned Behaviour (TPB) to understand organic food consumption. Consumers associated organic food with values like security, hedonism, universalism, benevolence, stimulation, self-direction and conformity. Subjective, personal norms and perceived behavioural control affected organic food consumption. In case of TPB, other researchers have discussed role of subjective norms, personal values, and emotions in predicting individual's organic food consumption (Thøgersen & Olander, 2006; Dean et al., 2008; Park & Sohn, 2012; Kim & Chung, 2011). Johnston (2008) reported that egocentric values were stronger motivators than altruistic values. It enabled individuals to show their commitment towards environmental issues.

First and Brozina (2009) examined influence of cultural values on organic food consumption in Western European countries. The findings revealed "health protection (including health improvement and prevention), care for other society members (including child health care, local development contribution, care for farmers, retailers and local agriculture), hedonic pleasure (including taste), and environmental protection (including environmental protection and responsibility to the world" as important concerns for organic food consumption. Countries having lower scores on individualism and assertiveness were likely to consider environment protection as important motive for organic food purchase. de Magistris and Gracia (2008) found that health concern and attitude towards environment were important factors influencing for organic food purchase. Consumers having positive attitudes towards environment protection, pollution, and environmental damages are likely to be involved in pro-environmental activities. They are involved in environmental protection, recycling, and willing to buy organic food. Further, attitude towards organic food was important in predicting consumers' willingness to buy organic food (Padel & Foster, 2005; Durham & Andrade, 2005). Hill & Lynchehaun (2002) state that personal factors like personality, values and lifestyles, and attitudes, extrinsic and intrinsic factors related with organic food packaging, taste, quality, price, and safety, cultural values, and knowledge about organic food affects consumption decisions. Bartels and van den Berg (2011) categorized organic food consumers as 'non, light, and heavy'. The differences among consumers were on factors like innovativeness, social identification, and attitudes towards antioxidants in fresh fruits and vegetables. Heavy users were conscious about health issues about organic food. Whereas, non-users did not seek information about sustainable food products, antioxidants, and health issues related to consuming un-organic food items. A recent study highlighted that collectivistic values and environmental attitudes are strong determinants of Chinese consumers' attitudes towards green foods (Perrea et al., 2014). Another study pointed out that organic food consumption and an active lifestyle has a high correlation (Goetzke & Spiller, 2014). Tung et al. (2015) demonstrated that individual vegetarianism influence organic food attitude. Also individuals living with young children demonstrate more positive attitudes toward organic food.

Squires et al. (2001) examined the relationship between health, diet concern, environmental concern, confidence in conventional food industry, demographics, and nature of organic food industry in New Zealand and Denmark. Green self-perception and personal eco-identity were more important in predicting consumers' preference for organic food rather than environmental concern. New Zealanders concerned about health and diet placed importance to organic food. In more mature organic markets, environmental concerns were important in predicting consumers' preference for organic food. Makatouni (2002) posit that life values centered on human beings, animal well-being, and environment were important in predicting British consumers' decision to purchase organic food. Values related to human beings were health, responsibility for health and well-being for self and family, relaxed, satisfaction, long life, and happiness. These values focused on individual and family. The protection of animal and environment on health were other two important values.

H$_{1a}$: Consumers' environment friendly attitude like affect commitment would positively influence their organic food purchase behavior.

H$_{1b}$: Consumers' environment friendly attitude like verbal commitment would positively influence their organic food purchase behavior.

H$_{1c}$: Consumers' environment friendly attitude like actual commitment would positively influence their organic food purchase behavior.

Influence of Demographic factors on Organic Food Purchase

Tsakiridou et al. (2008) found that Greek consumers were informed about organic food products. Demographic factors like education and income affected attitudes and consumption of organic food. This was primarily driven by desire to protect the environment. Older consumers were more concerned about nutritional value of organic food than young consumers. Environmental and health related factors were motivating factors influencing consumers' perceptions, attitudes, and consumption of organic food. Padel and Foster (2005) state that consumers' associated organic food with fruits and vegetables. Motivations for purchasing organic food were primarily due to health and environmental concerns. Households with kids used complex criteria like health to motivate kids to eat organic food. Young working women and middle aged women were informed about organic vegetables. They were more likely to buy organic fruits and vegetables. Barriers to buying organic food were price, availability, visual presentation of product, eating habits, quality, and mistrust about organic food. Fotopoulos and Krystallis (2002) posit that education affected consumers' awareness about organic food. They clustered consumers' preference for organic food according to region, income levels, and diet habits. Lea and Worsley (2005) examined relationship between Australian consumers' beliefs about organic food, personal values, and socio-demographic factors. They posit consumers perceived organic food items to be healthier, tastier, and beneficial for environment. Women had more positive attitude towards organic food than men. Personal values like concern for environment and equality were important in predicting consumers' preference for organic food. Drawing from these studies, it was assumed that demographic factors would moderate the attitude components in influencing Indian consumers' preference for organic food products.

H$_2$: Demographic factors like age, income, gender, education and marital status would moderate consumers' attitude towards organic food purchase.

Organic Food Purchase Behavior

Organic food purchase behavior was considered as the dependent variable. Several dimensions of organic food purchase behavior have been discussed by researchers. They can be classified under non-chemical ingredients, recyclable and health related benefits. Aertsens et al. (2011) found that Belgian consumers' motivation for consuming organic vegetables was because it did not contain synthetic pesticides, was better for the environment, healthy, of superior quality and tasted better. Objective and subjective knowledge about organic food was positively related to a positive attitude towards organic food and greater experience with products. Consumers purchasing organic food felt that they were members of "ecological organization". Attitude towards organic food was influenced by subjective knowledge, ecological organization membership, norms, motivations and female gender. The consumption of organic vegetables was positively affected by ecological organization membership, subjective knowledge, attitudes, and presence of kids in the household.

Roddy et al. (1994) in their research on Irish consumers state that organic food was associated with superior taste, flavor, quality, and free from pesticides. Negative perceptions about organic food were related to unavailability, high price, and promotional issues. Krystallis and Chryssohoidis (2005) attempted to understand whether factors affecting Greek consumers' willingness to purchase conventional and organic food were similar and did their preference for organic food differ according to product type. Consumers' willingness to buy organic food was affected by food security, quality, trust on certificate, and brand name. Consumers were willing to pay more for organic food products because they believe that these products are of higher quality. However, consumers having concerns organic food were unwilling to pay for them. In another research, Zakowska-Biemans (2011) examined consumers' preference for organic food among Polish consumers. Consumers conceptualized organic food as healthy, safe, and having no chemical ingredients. Chen (2009) posits positive relationship between health consciousness and environmental attitudes on Taiwanese consumers' attitude towards organic foods. In another research on British consumers, Sirieix et al. (2013) compared consumers' perceptions and attitude towards sustainable and other label food brands. They were skeptical about unfamiliar brands and terminologies like 'climate friendly'. Trust and familiarity with brands were important criteria for buying organic food labels. An examination of literature on factors suggests influence of environmental friendly attitudes on consumers' organic food purchase behavior (Padel and Foster, 2005; Durham and Andrade, 2005; Tsakiridou et al. 2008; Johnston, 2008; Sirieix et al. 2013). An examination of literature provided interesting insights about organic food purchase.

The hypothesized model is depicted in Figure 1.

Summary of the major research conducted on consumers' attitude towards organic food is provided in Table 1.

Figure 1.

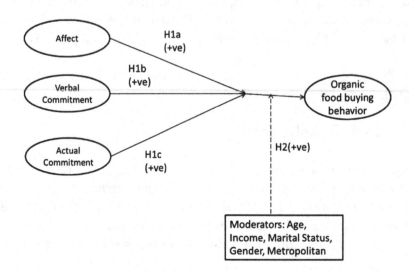

RESEARCH METHODOLOGY

Measures

Drawing from research on environmental attitudes and their influence on environmental friendly buying, Fraj and Martinez (2007) had conceptualized attitude under three components: affect commitment, verbal commitment, and actual commitment. The scales were adapted from their research. To measure environmental commitment, attitude model comprising of affect, cognitive, and behaviour components has been used by researchers (Chan, 2000; Fraj and Martinez, 2007). Fraj and Martinez (2007) in their research on Spanish consumers, had examined influence of affect and verbal commitment factors on actual commitment to purchase green products. Actual commitment factor had been used as dependent factor. However, in current research, these three factors were taken as three constructs measuring consumers' environment friendly attitude. The influence of these three factors on organic food purchase was

Table 1. Major studies in organic food purchase behavior

Author	Country	Contribution
Roddy et al. (1994)	Irish consumers	Organic food was associated with superior taste, flavour, quality, and free from pesticides. Negative perceptions about organic food were related to unavailability, high price, and promotional issues
Squires et al. (2001)	Denmark and New Zealand consumers	Green self-perception and personal eco-identity were more important in predicting consumers' preference for organic food rather than environmental concern
Makatouni (2002)	British consumers	Life values centred around human beings, animal well-being, and environment were important in predicting consumers' decision to purchase organic food
Krystallis and Chryssohoidis (2005)	Greek consumers	Consumers' willingness to buy organic food was affected by food security, quality, trust on certificate, and brand name
Lea and Worsley (2005)	Australian consumers	Women had more positive attitude towards organic food than men.
Tsakiridou et al. (2008)	Greek consumers	Demographic factors like education and income affected attitudes and consumption of organic food
First and Brozina (2009)	Western European consumers	Cultural values influence organic food consumption
Chen (2009)	Taiwanese consumers	Positive relationship between health consciousness and environmental attitudes on consumers' attitude towards organic foods
Aertsens et al. (2011)	Belgian consumers	Objective and subjective knowledge about organic food has a positive relationship to attitude towards organic food and greater experience with products
Zakowska-Biemans (2011)	Polish consumers	Consumers conceptualized organic food as healthy, safe, and having no chemical ingredients
Sirieix et al. (2013)	British consumers	Trust and familiarity with brands were important criteria for buying organic food labels
Perrea et al. (2014)	Chinese consumers	Collectivistic values and environmental attitudes are strong determinants of Chinese consumers' attitudes towards green foods
Goetzke & Spiller (2014)	German consumers	Organic food and an active lifestyle has a high correlation
Tung et al. (2015)	Taiwanese consumers	Individual vegetarianism influence organic food attitude. Individuals living with young children demonstrate more positive attitudes toward organic food

examined. The organic food purchase behaviour was measured using scale developed by Lee (2009). The items were modified to understand consumers' attitude towards organic food and purchase intention. Five point Likert scale was used to measure all factors.

Sample

Prior to selecting the sample, different organized retailers across five major cities were identified. The selection of the stores was based upon their readiness to stock and sell organic food items. Discussion with the store managers revealed that organic food was a popular category sold in their stores. Most consumers were interested in purchasing organic vegetables and fruits on a regular basis. However, the store managers could not provide the monthly sales data of organic food items due to confidential reasons. The stores selected were Subhiksha, Reliance Fresh, Easy Day, and Food Bazaar. These stores have chains across the country and stock similar organic food product categories. This ensured similarity across sample distribution and would reduce biasness.

Convenience sampling method was used. Data collection was done during months of November 2013-January 2014. Consumers were randomly approached in six major cities in India (Bangalore, Chennai, Delhi, Lucknow, Jaipur, & Kolkata). Selection of cities was based on convenience sampling with an objective to get representation from eastern, western, northern and southern regions of India. The store managers were approached and the objective of the research was communicated to them. Their help was sought for data collection. Respondents were contacted randomly at the stores identified (Subhiksha, Reliance Fresh, Easy Day, and Food Bazzar) while they were shopping for food items. Data was collected at different days of the week and both in morning and evening in order to reduce biasness. Sample inclusion was based on consumers' awareness about 'organic food'. Following the procedure of earlier studies (Chan, 2000; Fraj & Martinez, 2007), consumers were presented with three simplified definitions of organic food and asked to indicate which according to them explained organic food. The respondents providing the correct answer were presented with questionnaire on organic food (The socio-demographic details of respondents are presented in Table 2). Total respondents contacted were 1,500 people and 666 people qualified for sample inclusion.

FINDINGS AND DISCUSSIONS

Bhalla and Lin's (1987) methodology was followed for pretesting the scales. In the attitude scale, two items from each Affect and Actual commitment sub-scale, and three items from Organic purchase behavior scale were removed because they failed to meet the desired 0.5 factor loading and failed to fit. All items from Verbal commitment sub-scale were retained as they met Nunnally's (1978) recommended level of internal consistency for scale development. The scale validation methodology followed in other studies is used (Chan, 1999; Fraj & Martinez, 2006). Cronbach alpha values for the factors is above acceptable limit of 0.60 (Malhotra, 2008) and ranged between .674-.806.

For each of the constructs, the measurement model has been checked. The value for χ^2, degrees of freedom and fit indices for Actual Commitment sub-scale are χ^2 =50.460, df =14; CFI =0.926, GFI=0.978; AGFI=0.956; RMSEA = 0.063, for Verbal commitment sub-scale the values are χ^2 =29.305, df =14; CFI = 0.971, GFI=0.987; AGFI=0.975; RMSEA = 0.041, for organic food purchase behavior the values are χ^2 =21.164, df =9; CFI =0.976, GFI=0.990; AGFI=0.976; RMSEA = 0.045 and for

Table 2. Demographic Description of Respondents

	Variable	Frequency	Percentage
Gender	Male	376	75.0
	Female	125	25.0
Age (years)	18-21	74	14.8
	22-25	124	24.8
	26-30	130	25.9
	31-40	128	25.5
	41-50	40	8.0
	51 and above	5	1.0
Marital Status	Married	251	50.1
	Single	250	49.9
Education	Higher Secondary	103	20.6
	Graduation	290	57.9
	Post Graduation	108	21.6
Household Income (monthly)	Below INR 10,000 (below $153)	45	9.0
	INR 10,000- 20,000 ($153-307)	104	20.8
	INR 21,000- 30,000 ($307-461)	160	31.9
	INR 31,000- 40,000 ($461-615)	86	17.2
	INR 41,000 – 50,000 ($615-769)	43	8.6
	Above 50,000 ($ 769)	63	12.6
Total		501	

Affect sub-scale the values are $\chi2 = 14.272$, df =5; CFI = 0.959, GFI=0.991; AGFI=0.974; RMSEA = 0.053. The fit indices clearly indicate that the models are having good fit for the data (Hair et al. 1995).

CFA indicated that all factor loadings ranged from 0.628 to 0.859 and corresponding t-values are statistically significant ($p < 0.001$) providing support for convergent validity. In relation to goodness of fit scales, the residuals are inferior to .05 for all components, which suggests that the adjustment of the factor analysis was acceptable (Grande, 2000; Fraj & Martinez, 2006). Chi-square significance level (p) for all factors is .000. Goodness-of-fit indices were within acceptable range (Hair et al. 1995).

Organic food purchase behavior was taken as dependent factor. Step wise regression analysis was run to understand the moderating role of demographic factors on affect, actual and verbal commitment factors on organic food purchase behavior. The results are shown in Table 3.

Stepwise regression model revealed that demographic factors moderated consumers' attitude towards organic food purchase. In the first model, 'actual commitment' emerged as the predictor variable for organic food purchase behavior (R^2=.415, $p < 0.00$). The first model suggests that actual commitment towards environment accounts for 41.5 percent of Indian consumers' attitude towards organic food purchase behavior (see Table 3).

The results support earlier researches (Roddy et al. 1994; Aertsens et al. 2011; Zakowska-Biemans, 2011). In the second model, 'actual commitment and gender' factors emerge as predictors (R^2 =.431, p<0.00), and account for 43.1 percent of attitude towards organic food purchase behavior. In the third

Table 3. Step-wise Regression

Model	Variable	B	R²	Adjusted R²	Significance
1.	**First regression (Dependent Variable: Organic food buying behaviour)**		.415	.414	
	Actual Commitment	.644			.000*
	**N=665; d.f=1; F=471.171; significant F=.000**				
2.	**Second regression (Dependent Variable: Organic food buying behaviour)**		.431	.429	
	Actual Commitment	.626			.000*
	Gender	.128			.000*
	N=665; d.f=2; F=251.239; significant F=.000				
3.	**Third regression (Dependent Variable: Organic food buying behaviour)**		.446	.443	
	Actual Commitment	.518			.000*
	Gender	.128			.000*
	Verbal commitment	.163			.000*
	N=665; d.f=3; F=177.624; significant F=.000				
4.	Forth regression **(Dependent Variable: Organic food buying behaviour)**		.459	.456	
	Actual Commitment	.489			.000*
	Gender	.166			.000*
	Verbal commitment	.164			.000*
	Income	.123			.000*
	N=665; d.f=4; F=140.327; significant F=.000 ***significant at 0.05 level**				
5.	Fifth regression **(Dependent Variable: Organic food buying behaviour)**		.464	.460	
	Actual Commitment	.483			.000*
	Gender	.149			.000*
	Verbal commitment	.159			.000*
	Income	.116			.000*
	Age	-.074			.014*
	N=665; d.f=5; F=114.358; significant F=.000 ***significant at 0.05 level**				

model, 'verbal commitment' was introduced. Actual commitment, verbal commitment and gender emerged as predictors and account for 44.6 percent of (R^2=.446, p<0.00) attitude towards organic food purchase behavior. In the fourth model, 'income' was introduced. Actual commitment, verbal commitment, gender and income emerged as predictors and account for 45.9 percent of (R^2=.459, p<0.00) attitude towards organic food purchase behavior. In the fifth model, Actual commitment, verbal commitment, gender, income and age emerged as predictors (R^2=.464, p<0.00), and account for 46.4 percent of attitude towards organic food purchase behavior. Therefore H_{1b}, H_{1c} and H_2 are accepted. The β value for age variable is negative which suggest that there is a negative relationship between age of consumers and their attitude towards organic food. The younger consumers are more likely to purchase organic food. The findings are in tandem with findings of Padel and Foster (2005). They posit that younger consumers are likely to exhibit favourable attitude towards organic food. Similar conclusions can be drawn from the current research. The findings support other researches which suggest that women and income affects attitude towards organic food (Squires et al. 2001; Lea & Worsley, 2005; Tsakiridou et al. 2008).

The research findings suggest that attitude components like actual commitment, verbal commitment towards environment are moderated by demographic factors like income, age and gender. Individuals involved in environmental issues and concerned about environment protection are likely to have favorable attitude towards organic food products. The findings support earlier researches which suggest influence of pro-environmental values and attitudes on purchase decision (Makatouni, 2002; Harland et al. 2007; Fraj & Martinez, 2007; First & Brozina, 2009; Zabkar & Hosta, 2013). The results indicate that demographic variables play an important role in influencing consumers' choice towards organic food purchase.

The findings posit that companies marketing organic food products must use attitudinal and demographic profiling for targeting consumers. Marketing of organic food should focus on providing detailed information about ingredients and health related implications. Since consumers' interested in organic food belong to high income and younger generation segments, targeting them would involve focusing on product quality and its nutritional composition. They would be therefore interested in reading the labels in order to understand organic food product composition. Women are conscious about health of their family and are likely show more interest in organic food. The findings support earlier research where demographic and attitudinal factors are important in predicting organic food purchase behavior (Padel & Foster, 2005; Durham & Andrade, 2005; de Magistris & Gracia, 2008; Perrea et al., 2014; Tung et al. 2015).

MARKETING IMPLICATIONS

Researches on Indian consumers' attitude towards organic food have discussed importance of health and environmental concerns (Technopak, 2012; The Economic Times, 2012). Chakrabarti (2010) in his research on Indian consumers had suggested that choice for organic food products was influenced by utility, reputation of store, and certification. The findings of current research add to his work. This research attempts to understand the moderating role of demographic factors in influencing organic food purchase decision. Earlier research on Indian consumers has not examined the role of demographic and attitudinal factors on organic food purchase. The findings can help in understanding influence of both psychographic and demographic factors on purchase decisions.

The research findings posit that income levels determine consumers' perception about organic food items. They are aware about impact of consuming organic food items on health and environment and are therefore cautious about its content. Their preference for organic fruits, vegetables, and other food items is based on ingredients, quality, and authenticity. Companies marketing organic food should place information about composition and ingredients on packages. This would enable consumers to check ingredients, composition, and quality aspects of the product before purchasing them. Since organic food consumption has health related implications, consumers prefer to analyze information before purchasing. Information about ingredients on packages helps them in understanding the health benefits of those items. This enables consumers to take an informed decision.

The implications of current research for companies are two-fold. Organic food consumption is increasing (The Economic Times, 2012; Sally, 2013) and therefore marketing of organic food becomes important. Companies should pay special attention to labeling and packaging of the products as it enforces quality, authenticity, and freshness of food items. Packaging would enhance utilitarian and hedonic value of products. It would help companies build brand awareness for organic products. The socio-demographic factors like income, age and gender were found to be important factors influencing consumers' attitude towards organic food. Firms engaged in manufacturing or selling organic food products need to maintain and enhance health benefits, freshness and taste factors. Lifestyle and income related consumer profiling can be done in order to target consumers.

Family health and well-being can be used as popular themes to build awareness about organic food. In India, currently organic food marketing, promotions, and advertisements are limited. Companies are not using national or state level advertisements to promote organic food. Using promotions and advertisements to communicate health and environmental benefits of adopting organic food can generate greater awareness among non-users. The companies can offer more value to consumers by launching products in different packaging sizes, flavors, and providing information about where the product was grown, processing, and health related benefits associated with its consumption. Detailed information about ingredients and composition can enable consumers compare different product features and purchase items relevant for their family needs. Visual images on packages about freshness, quality, certification, and naturalness of organic food can help in improving consumers' perception about organic food brands.

The increased market share of organic food shows that consumers are aware of the ill-effects of non-organic food (The Economic Times, 2012; Sally, 2013). They are willing to pay a high price premium for organic food. Higher income groups are not willing to compromise on health and environment related issues. They are willing to spend on quality food items that do not have any side-effects and preservatives. Organic food costs about forty to sixty percent more than conventional food items. Gurtoo (2013) found that sixty two percent of high income households prefer organic food items. This suggests a clear need for companies to focus enforcing on quality and non-chemical ingredients while marketing organic food. Consumers associate organic food with good health and "health-halo effect" (Mielach, 2013). They believe that organic food are healthy and do not contain any harmful ingredients.

In India, many firms are trying to market their organic food categories. The major organized retail chains like Nilgiris, Godrej Nature's Basket, More, Spencers, Food Bazaar, and Fab India stock organic foods (Chatterjee, 2012). While designing marketing strategy, firms should understand that though organic food products are gaining popularity, it is still a niche market. The promotional campaigns should spread awareness about product attributes, its benefits, and non-chemical ingredients. There is a need to educate people about organic food because they often think natural and organic food is the same. They purchase fresh food from farms and equate them to organic. They lack awareness that fresh food items like vegetables and fruits can contain chemical/fertilizer residues if they are not cultivated with the help of organic farming techniques. Firms should provide information about organic food products on the labels. This will enable consumers to understand the actual composition of organic food items and its impact on health and environment.

LIMITATIONS AND FUTURE RESEARCH DIRECTIONS

Research in India on organic food product category is in nascent stages. Though the organic food market is predicted to grow in coming years, research on understanding consumers' attitude, lifestyle and values in predicting consumption of organic food is limited. Academic researches taken up in this area can help in providing valuable insights about consumers' predisposition towards organic food. The current research focused only on influence of three attitude components (affect, behaviour, and cognition) and demographics on Indian consumers' attitude towards organic food. It presents limited set of factors for understanding consumer attitudes. Factors like past environmental friendly behaviour, ecological concern, social influence, and psychographics can be taken up to provide a comprehensive understanding of consumer attitude. Study on products of organic food retailers can be conducted to understand product related dimensions affecting consumers' purchase decision. Future research can be conducted to understand difference between consumers' attitude towards organic and non-organic food. Consumers' perception and attitude towards specific organic food brands sold at the retail stores can be taken up for further study. This would help in understanding the brand related attributes and consumers' attitude towards them.

REFERENCES

Aertsens, J., Mondelaers, K., Verbeke, W., Buysse, J., & Van Huylenbroeck, G. (2011). The influence of subjective and objective knowledge on attitude, motivations and consumption of organic food. *British Food Journal*, *113*(11), 1353–1378. doi:10.1108/00070701111179988

Aertsens, J., Verbeke, W., Mondelaers, K., & Van Huylenbroeck, G. (2009). Personal determinants of organic food consumption: A review. *British Food Journal*, *111*(10), 1140–1167. doi:10.1108/00070700910992961

Akerhurst, G., Afonso, C., & Gonclaves, H. M. (2012). Re-examining green purchase behaviour and green consumer profiles: New evidences. *Management Decision*, *50*(5), 972–988. doi:10.1108/00251741211227726

APEDA. (2013). *National Programme for organic food production*. Retrieved on 22nd February 2014 from http://www.apeda.gov.in/apedawebsite/organic/Organic_Products.htm

Bartels, J., & van den Berg, I. (2011). Fresh fruit and vegetables and the added value of antioxidants: Attitudes of non-, light, and heavy organic food users. *British Food Journal*, *113*(11), 1339–1352. doi:10.1108/00070701111179979

Bigne´, J. E. (1997). *El consumidor verde: bases de un modelo de comportamiento*. Esic Market.

Brugarolas Molla-Bauza, M., Martinez-Carrasco Martinez, L., Martinez Poveda, A., & Rico Perez, M. (2005). Determination of the surplus that consumers are willing to pay for an organic wine. *Spanish Journal of Agricultural Research*, *3*(1), 43–51. doi:10.5424/sjar/2005031-123

Chakrabarti, S. (2010). Factors influencing organic food purchase in India- expert survey insights. *British Food Journal*, *112*(8), 902–915. doi:10.1108/00070701011067497

Chan, K. (2000). Market segmentation of green consumers in Hong Kong. *Journal of International Consumer Marketing*, *12*(2), 7–24. doi:10.1300/J046v12n02_02

Chandrashekar, H. M. (2010). Changing scenario of organic farming in India: an overview. *International NGO Journal*, *5*(1), 34-39. Retrieved on 22nd February 2014 from. uni-mysore.ac.in/14660/1/Changing Scenario of Organic Farming in India.pdf

Chatterjee, B. (2012). *Organic Foods enter India to a low-key welcome*. Retrieved on 19th March 2014 from http://www.businesseconomics.in/?q=node/1267

Chen, M.-F. (2009). Attitude toward organic foods among Taiwanese as related to health consciousness, environmental attitudes, and the mediating effects of a healthy lifestyle. *British Food Journal, 111*(2), 165–178. doi:10.1108/00070700910931986

Churchill, G. A., Iacobucci, D., & Israel, D. (2010). *Marketing research: A south Asian perspective*. New Delhi, India: Cengage Learning.

Davies, A., Titterington, A., & Cochrane, C. (1995). Who buys organic food? A profile of the purchasers of organic food in Northern Ireland. *British Food Journal, 97*(10), 17–23. doi:10.1108/00070709510104303

de Magistris, T., & Gracia, A. (2008). The decision to buy organic food products in Southern Italy. *British Food Journal, 110*(9), 929–947. doi:10.1108/00070700810900620

Dean, M., Raats, M. M., & Shepherd, R. (2008). Moral concerns and consumer choice of fresh and processed organic foods. *Journal of Applied Social Psychology, 38*(8), 2088–2107. doi:10.1111/j.1559-1816.2008.00382.x

Durham, C. A., & Andrade, D. (2005). *Health vs. environmental motivation in organic preferences and purchases*. paper presented at the American Agricultural Economics Association Annual Meeting, Providence, RI.

First, I., & Brozina, S. (2009). Cultural influences on motives for organic food consumption. *EuroMed Journal of Business, 4*(2), 185–19. doi:10.1108/14502190910976538

Fotopoulos, C., & Krystallis, A. (2002). Organic product avoidance: reasons for rejection and potential buyers' identification in a countrywide survey. *British Food Journal, 104*(3-5), 233-260.

Fraj, E., & Martı'nez, E. (2002). *Comportamiento del Consumidor Ecolo'gico*. Madrid: Esic Editorial.

Fraj, E., & Martinez, E. (2006). Environmental values and lifestyles as determining factors of ecological consumer behaviour: An empirical analysis. *Journal of Consumer Marketing, 23*(3), 133–144. doi:10.1108/07363760610663295

Fraj, E., & Martinez, E. (2007). Ecological consumer behaviour: An empirical analysis. *International Journal of Consumer Studies, 31*(1), 26–33. doi:10.1111/j.1470-6431.2006.00565.x

Goetzke, B. I., & Spiller, A. (2014). Health-improving lifestyles of organic and functional food consumers. *British Food Journal, 116*(3), 510–526. doi:10.1108/BFJ-03-2012-0073

Gurtoo, H. C. (2013). *Taste for organic foods*. Retrieved on 19th March 2014 from http://www.hindustantimes.com/lifestyle/food/taste-for-organic-foods/article1-1109620.aspx

Harland, P., Staats, H., & Wilke, H. A. M. (2007). Situational and Personality Factors as Direct or Personal Norm Mediated Predictors of Pro-environmental Behavior: Questions Derived from Norm-activation Theory. *Basic and Applied Social Psychology, 29*(4), 323–334. doi:10.1080/01973530701665058

Hill, H., & Lynchehaun, F. (2002). Organic milk: Attitudes and consumption patterns. *British Food Journal, 104*(7), 526–542. doi:10.1108/00070700210434570

Jansson, J., Marell, A., & Nordlund, A. (2010). Green consumer behavior: Determinants of curtailment and eco-innovation adoption. *Journal of Consumer Marketing, 27*, 358–370.

Johnston, J. (2008). The citizen-consumer hybrid: Ideological tensions and the case of whole foods market. *Theory and Society, 37*(3), 229–270. doi:10.1007/s11186-007-9058-5

Junaedi, M. F. S. (2007). The roles of Consumer's knowledge and emotion in ecological issues: An Empirical Study on Green Consumer Behavior. *Gadjah Mada International Journal of Business, 9*(1), 81–99.

Kim, H. Y., & Chung, J.-E. (2011). Consumer purchase intention for organic personal care products. *Journal of Consumer Marketing, 28*(1), 40–47. doi:10.1108/07363761111101930

Kristensen, L. (1997). *Implementation of organic food in the public sector in New Zealand* (MCom thesis). School of Horticulture, Christchurch Polytechnic, New Zealand.

Krystallis, A., & Chryssohoidis, G. (2005). Consumers willingness to pay for organic food: Factors that affect it and variation per organic product type. *British Food Journal, 107*(5), 320–343. doi:10.1108/00070700510596901

Lea, E., & Worsley, T. (2005). Australians organic food beliefs, demographics and values. *British Food Journal, 107*(11), 855–869. doi:10.1108/00070700510629797

Lee, K. (2009). Gender differences in Hong Kong adolescent consumers green purchasing behaviour. *Journal of Consumer Marketing, 26*(2), 87–96. doi:10.1108/07363760910940456

Makatouni, A. (2002). What motivates consumers to buy organic food in UK?British Food Journal, 104(3-5), 345-352.

Malhotra, N. K. (2008). *Marketing research: An applied orientation*. Pearson Education India. doi:10.1108/S1548-6435(2008)4

Mielach, D. (2013). *Consumers Overestimate benefits of organic food*. Retrieved on 19ᵗʰ March, 2014 from http://www.businessnewsdaily.com/4257-organic-food-labels.html

Misra, S. K., Huang, C. L., & Ott, S. L. (1991). Consumer willing to pay for pesticide-free fresh produce. *Western Journal of Agricultural Economics*, (16): 218–227.

Nunnally, J. C. (1967). *Psychometric Theory* (2nd ed.). New York, NY: McGraw-Hill.

Padel, S., & Foster, C. (2005). Exploring the gap between attitudes and behaviour. *British Food Journal, 107*(8), 606–625. doi:10.1108/00070700510611002

Park, S.-Y., & Sohn, S. H. (2012). Exploring the normative influences of social norms on individual environmental behavior. *Journal of Global Scholars of Marketing Science: Bridging Asia and the World, 22*(2), 183–194. doi:10.1080/12297119.2012.655142

Perrea, T. G., Grunert, K., Krystallis, A., Zhou, Y., Huang, G., & Hue, Y. (2014). Testing and validation of a hierarchical values-attitudes model in the context of green food in China. *Asia Pacific Journal of Marketing and Logistics, 26*(2), 296–314. doi:10.1108/APJML-09-2013-0106

Pickett-Baker, J., & Ozaki, R. (2008). Pro-environmental products: Marketing influence on consumer purchase decision. *Journal of Consumer Marketing, 25*(5), 281–293. doi:10.1108/07363760810890516

PRWEB. (2013). *Organic Food market in India set for incessant growth finds TechSci Research report.* Retrieved on 22nd February, 2014 from http://www.prweb.com/releases/2013/9/prweb11174562.htm

Roddy, G., Cowan, C., & Hutchinson, G. (1994). Organic food: A description of the Irish market. *British Food Journal, 96*(4), 3–10. doi:10.1108/00070709410060998

Sally, M. (2013). *Increase in consumption of organic food products: ASSOCHAM Survey.* Retrieved on 22nd February 2014 from http://articles.economictimes.indiatimes.com/2013-05-23/news/39475623_1_organic-food-organic-products-organic-sector

Sirieix, L., Delanchy, M., Remaud, H., Zepeda, L., & Gurviez, P. (2013). Consumers perceptions of individual and combined sustainable food labels: A UK pilot investigation. *International Journal of Consumer Studies, 37*(2), 143–151. doi:10.1111/j.1470-6431.2012.01109.x

Smith, S., & Paladino, A. (2010). Eating clean and green? Investigating consumer motivations towards the purchase of organic food. *Australasian Marketing Journal, 18*(2), 93–104. doi:10.1016/j.ausmj.2010.01.001

Squires, L., Juric, B., & Cornwell, T. B. (2001). Level of market development and intensity of organic food consumption: Cross cultural study of Danish and New Zealand Consumers. *Journal of Consumer Marketing, 18*(5), 392–409. doi:10.1108/07363760110398754

Technopak. (2012). *Organic Food Market in India.* Retrieved on 22nd February 2014 fromhttp://www.globalorganictrade.com/files/market_reports/OTA_India_Market_Report_2012.pdf

The Economic Times. (2012). *India's organic food market growing at over 20%.* Retrieved on 22nd February 2014 from http://articles.economictimes.indiatimes.com/2012-08-23/news/33342399_1_organic-food-organic-cotton-chemical-free-food

Thogersen, J., & Olander, F. (2003). Spillover of environment-friendly consumer behaviour. *Journal of Environmental Psychology, 23*(3), 225–236. doi:10.1016/S0272-4944(03)00018-5

Thøgersen, J., & Olander, F. (2006). The dynamic interaction of personal norms and environment-friendly buying behavior: A panel study. *Journal of Applied Social Psychology, 36*(7), 1758–1780. doi:10.1111/j.0021-9029.2006.00080.x

Tsakiridou, E., Boutsouki, C., Zotos, Y., & Mattas, K. (2008). Attitudes and behaviour towards organic products: An exploratory study. *International Journal of Retail & Distribution Management, 36*(2), 158–175. doi:10.1108/09590550810853093

Tung, S., Tsay, J. C., & Lin, M. (2015). Life course, diet-related identity and consumer choice of organic food in taiwan. *British Food Journal, 117*(2), 688–704. doi:10.1108/BFJ-11-2013-0334

Zabkar, V., & Hosta, M. (2013). Willingness to act and environmentally conscious consumer behaviour: Can pro-social status perceptions help overcome the gap? *International Journal of Consumer Studies, 37*(3), 257–264. doi:10.1111/j.1470-6431.2012.01134.x

Zakowska-Biemans, S. (2011). Polish consumer food choices and beliefs about organic food. *British Food Journal, 113*(1), 122–137. doi:10.1108/00070701111097385

APPENDIX

Affect: Fraj and Martinez (2007)	
It frightens me to think that much of the food I eat is contaminated with pesticides.(retained)	Retained
It genuinely infuriates me to think that the government doesn't do more to help control pollution of the environment.	Retained
I become incensed when I think about the harm being done to plant and animal life by pollution.	Retained
I get depressed on smoggy days.	Retained
I rarely ever worry about the effects of smog on myself and family	Retained
When I think of the ways industries are polluting, I get frustrated and angry.	Deleted
The whole pollution issue has never upset me too much since I feel it's somewhat overrated.	Deleted
Verbal commitment: Fraj and Martinez (2007)	
I'd be willing to ride a bicycle or take the bus to work in order to reduce air pollution.	Retained
I would be willing to use a rapid transit system to help to reduce air pollution	Retained
I would donate a day's pay to a foundation to help improve the environment.	Retained
I would be willing to stop buying products from companies guilty of polluting the environment, even though it might be inconvenient.	Retained
I'd be willing to write local authorities weekly concerning ecological problems.	Retained
I wouldn't go house to house to distribute literature on the environment.	Retained
I would not be willing to pay a pollution tax even if it would considerably decrease the smog	Retained
Actual Commitment: Fraj and Martinez (2007)	
I guess I've never actually bought a product because it had a lower polluting effect.	Retained
I keep track of my congressman and senator's voting records on environment issues.	Retained
I have contacted a community agency to find out what I can do about pollution.	Retained
I make a special effort to buy products in recyclable containers.	Retained
I have switched products for ecological reasons.	Retained
I have never joined a cleanup drive.	Retained
I subscribe to ecological publications.	Retained
I have attended a meeting of an organization specifically concerned with bettering the environment.	Deleted
I have never attended a meeting related to ecology.	Deleted
Organic food buying behavior: Adapted from Lee (2009)	
I often buy food products that are against animal-testing	Retained
I often buy food products that contain no or fewer chemical ingredients	Retained
When I consider buying a product, I will look for a certified environmentally-safe or organic stamp	Retained
I often buy food products that support fair community trades	Retained
I understand that chemicals are being used in food products that are harmful	Retained
I prefer to purchase food items that do not contain preservatives	Retained
I often buy food products that are labeled as environmentally safe	Deleted
I often buy products that use recycled/ recyclable packaging	Deleted
I am interested in buying food products that do not contain artificial chemicals	Deleted

Compilation of References

Aalto-Setälä, V., & Raijas, A. (2003). Actual market prices and consumer price knowledge. *Journal of Product and Brand Management*, *12*(3), 180–192. doi:10.1108/10610420310476933

Abbad, M. M. (2013). E-banking in Jordan. *Behaviour & Information Technology*, *32*(7), 618–694. doi:10.1080/0144 929X.2011.586725

Abbas, F., Mitchell, L., & Mehmet, C. K. (2002). Streamlining Supply Chain Management with E-Business. *Proceedings:38th MBAA Annual Meeting*.

Abela, A. V. (2006). Marketing and Consumption: A Response to OShaughnessy and OShaughnessy. *European Journal of Marketing*, *40*(1/2), 5–16. doi:10.1108/03090560610637284

Abrol, D., Prajapati, P., & Singh, N. (2011). Globalization of the Indian pharmaceutical industry: Implications for innovation. *Institutions, Etc.*, *3*(2), 327–365.

Adams, C. A., Hill, W. Y., & Roberts, C. B. (1998). Corporate social reporting practices in western Europe: Legitimating corporate behaviour? *The British Accounting Review*, *30*(1), 1–21. doi:10.1006/bare.1997.0060

Adelaar, T., Chang, S., Lancendorfer, K. M., Lee, B., & Morimoto, M. (2003). Effects of media formats on emotions and impulse buying intent. *Journal of Information Technology*, *18*(4), 247–266. doi:10.1080/0268396032000150799

Adewale, A. A., Ibidunni, A. S., Joke, B., & Tiwalade, O. (2014). Biometric Enabled E-Banking in Nigeria: Management and Customers' Perspectives. *Information and Knowledge Management*, *4*(11), 23–28.

Aertsens, J., Mondelaers, K., Verbeke, W., Buysse, J., & Van Huylenbroeck, G. (2011). The influence of subjective and objective knowledge on attitude, motivations and consumption of organic food. *British Food Journal*, *113*(11), 1353–1378. doi:10.1108/00070701111179988

Aertsens, J., Verbeke, W., Mondelaers, K., & Van Huylenbroeck, G. (2009). Personal determinants of organic food consumption: A review. *British Food Journal*, *111*(10), 1140–1167. doi:10.1108/00070700910992961

Agarwal, R., & Prasad, J. (1998). A conceptual and operational definition of personal innovativeness in the domain of information technology. *Information Systems Research*, *9*(2), 204–215. doi:10.1287/isre.9.2.204

Agarwal, R., & Prasad, J. (1998). The antecedents and consequents of user perceptions in information technology adoption. *Decision Support Systems*, *22*(1), 15–29. doi:10.1016/S0167-9236(97)00006-7

Agarwal, R., & Prasad, J. (1999). Are individual differences germane to the acceptance of new information technologies? *Decision Sciences*, *30*(2), 361–391. doi:10.1111/j.1540-5915.1999.tb01614.x

Agarwal, R., & Prasad, J. (2000). A field study of the adoption of software process innovations by information systems professionals. *IEEE Transactions on Engineering Management*, *47*(1), 295–308. doi:10.1109/17.865899

Ahuvia, A. C., & Wong, N. Y. (2002). Personality and Values based Materialism: Their Relationship and Origins. *Journal of Consumer Psychology*, *12*(4), 389–402. doi:10.1016/S1057-7408(16)30089-4

Akerhurst, G., Afonso, C., & Gonclaves, H. M. (2012). Re-examining green purchase behaviour and green consumer profiles: New evidences. *Management Decision*, *50*(5), 972–988. doi:10.1108/00251741211227726

Akram, A., Merunka, D., & Shakaib Akram, M. (2011). Perceived brand globalness in emerging markets and the moderating role of consumer ethnocentrism. *International Journal of Emerging Markets*, *6*(4), 291–303. doi:10.1108/17468801111170329

Aladwani, A. M. (2001). Online banking: A field study of drivers, development challenges, and expectations. *Internet J Informat Manag*, *21*(3), 213–225. doi:10.1016/S0268-4012(01)00011-1

Alharbi, S., & Drew, S. (2014). Using the Technology Acceptance Model in Understanding Academics Behavioural Intention to Use Learning Management Systems, (IJACSA). *International Journal of Advanced Computer Science and Applications*, *5*(1), 143–155. doi:10.14569/IJACSA.2014.050120

Alison, G., Onno, K., & Jaap, A. (1990). *Natural Resource Accounting: Issues related to classification and Valuation of Environmental Assets*. Amsterdam: Institute for Environmental Studies.

Althaus, D., & Boston, W. (2015, March 17). *Why Auto Makers Are Building New Factories in Mexico, not the U.S.* Retrieved from The Wall Street Journal: http://www.wsj.com/articles/why-auto-makers-are-building-new-factories-in-mexico-not-the-u-s-1426645802

Ambak, K., Ismail, R., Abdullah, R. A., Latiff, A. A., & Sanik, M. E. (2013). Application of Technology Acceptance Model in Predicting Behavioral Intention to Use Safety Helmet Reminder System, *Research Journal of Applied Sciences*. *Engineering and Technology*, *5*(3), 881–888.

Amin, H. (2007). Internet banking adoption among young intellectuals. *Journal of Internet Banking and Commerce*, *12*(3), 1–14.

Amin, H., Hamid, M. R. A., Lada, S., & Anis, Z. (2008). The adoption of mobile banking in Malaysia: The case of Bank Islam Malaysia Berhad. *International Journal of Business and Society*, *9*(2), 43–53.

Amit, R., & Schoemaker, P. (1993). Strategic assets and organizational rents. *Strategic Management Journal*, *4*(1), 33–46. doi:10.1002/smj.4250140105

Amity, M., & Wei, S.-J. (2009). Service Offshoring and Productivity: Evidence from the US. *World Economy*, *32*(2), 203–220. doi:10.1111/j.1467-9701.2008.01149.x

Amos, C., Holmes, G. R., & Keneson, W. C. (2014). A meta-analysis of consumer impulse buying. *Journal of Retailing and Consumer Services*, *21*(2), 86–97. doi:10.1016/j.jretconser.2013.11.004

Anand, N., & Grover, N. (2015). Measuring retail supply chain performance: Theoretical model using key performance indicators (KPIs). *Benchmarking International Journal (Toronto, Ont.)*, *22*(1), 135–166.

Angulo, A., Nacthmann, H., & Waller, M. A. (2004). Supply chain information sharing in a vendor managed inventory partnership. *Journal of Business Logistics*, *25*(1), 101–120. doi:10.1002/j.2158-1592.2004.tb00171.x

Antunes, A. (2014). *Brazil's Natura, the largest cosmetics maker in Latin America, becomes a B Corp*. Retrieved from http://www.forbes.com/sites/andersonantunes/2014/12/16/brazils-natura-the-largest-cosmetics-maker-in-latin-america-becomes-a-b-corp/

APEDA. (2013). *National Programme for organic food production.* Retrieved on 22nd February 2014 from http://www. apeda.gov.in/apedawebsite/organic/Organic_Products.htm

Applbaum, K. (2000). Crossing borders: Globalization as myth and charter in American transnational consumer marketing. *American Ethnologist, 27*(2), 257–282. doi:10.1525/ae.2000.27.2.257

Apte, U. M., & Karmarkar, U. S. (2007). Business Process Outsourcing (BPO) and Globalization of Information Intensive Services. In U. M. Apte & U. S. Karmarkar (Eds.), *Managing in the Information Economy: Current Research Issues* (pp. 59–81). doi:10.1007/978-0-387-36892-4_3

Apte, U. M., Karmarkar, U. S., & Nath, H. K. (2008). Information Services in the U.S. Economy: Value, Jobs, and Management Implications. *California Management Review, 50*(3), 12–30. doi:10.2307/41166443

Apte, U. M., & Nath, H. K. (2012). U.S. Trade in Information-Intensive Services. In U. S. Karmarkar & V. Mangal (Eds.), *The UCLA Anderson Business and Information Technologies (BIT) Project: A Global Study of Business Practice.* Singapore: World Scientific Books. doi:10.1142/9789814390880_0006

Aramyan, L. (2006). Performance Indicators in Agri-Food Production Chains. Springer. doi:10.1007/1-4020-4693-6_5

Arens, Z. G., & Rust, R. T. (2012). The duality of decisions and the case for impulsiveness metrics. *Journal of the Academy of Marketing Science, 40*(3), 468–479. doi:10.1007/s11747-011-0256-3

Arpita, K. (2006). Supply Chain Management: Improving the efficiency. *Synergy Journal of ITS.*

Artiuch, P., & Kornstein, S. (2012). Sustainable approaches to reduce agriculture waste in India. MIT. Available at http:// web.mit.edu/CoLab/pdf/papers/Reducing_Food_Waste_India.pdf

ASX Corporate Governance Council. (2003). *Principles of good corporate governance and best practice recommendations.* Retrieved August 25, 2015, from http://www.shareholder.com/shared/dynamicdoc/ASX/364/ASXRecommendations.pdf

Ataullah, A., & Le, H. (2006). Economic reforms and bank efficiency in developing countries: The case of the Indian banking industry. *Applied Financial Economics, 16*(9), 653–663. doi:10.1080/09603100500407440

Atkinson, G., R. Dubourg, K. Hamilton, M. Munasinghe, D. Pearce & C. Young (1997). *Measuring Sustainable Development: Macroeconomics and Environment.* Edward Elgar.

Baffour Awuah, G., & Amal, M. (2011). Impact of globalization: The ability of less developed countries(LDCs) firms to cope with opportunities and challenges. *European Business Review, 23*(1), 120–132. doi:10.1108/09555341111098026

Baker, H. K., & Anderson, R. (2010). *Corporate governance: A synthesis of theory, research, and practice.* Hoboken, NJ: John Wiley & Sons, Inc. doi:10.1002/9781118258439

Baker, N. A., & Naser, K. (2000). Empirical evidence on corporate social disclosure practices on Jordan. *International Journal of Commerce and Management, 10*(3/4), 18–34. doi:10.1108/eb047406

Balasubramanian, S., Peterson, R. A., & Jarvenpaa, S. L. (2002). Exploring the implications of m-commerce for markets and marketing. *Journal of the Academy of Marketing Science, 30*(4), 348–361. doi:10.1177/009207002236910

Barney, J. B., & Arikan, A. M. (2001). The resource-based view: origins and implications. In The Blackwell handbook of Strategic Management. Blackwell.

Barney, J. B. (1991). Firm resources and sustained competitive advantage. *Journal of Management, 17*(1), 99–120. doi:10.1177/014920639101700108

Barney, J. B., & Hesterly, W. S. (2012). *Strategic Management and Competitive Advantage.* New Jersey: Pearson.

Bartels, J., & van den Berg, I. (2011). Fresh fruit and vegetables and the added value of antioxidants: Attitudes of non-, light, and heavy organic food users. *British Food Journal, 113*(11), 1339–1352. doi:10.1108/00070701111179979

Bart, Y., Shankar, V., Sultan, F., & Urban, G. L. (2005). Are the drivers and role of online trust the same for all web sites and consumers? A large-scale exploratory empirical study. *Journal of Marketing, 69*(4), 133–152. doi:10.1509/jmkg.2005.69.4.133

Bashir, I., & Madhavaiah, C. (2014). Determinants of Young Consumers' Intention to Use Internet Banking Services in India. *Vision: The Journal of Business Perspective, 18*(3), 1–11.

Bateman, T., & Organ, D. (1983). Job satisfaction and the good soldier: The relationship between affect and employee citizenship. *Academy of Management Journal, 26*(4), 586–595. doi:10.2307/255908

Bauer, R. A. (1960). Consumer behaviour as risk taking. In D. F. Cox (Ed.), *Risk Taking and Information Handling in Consumer Behaviour* (pp. 22–23). Cambridge, MA: Harvard University Press.

bcorporation. (2015). *B Corporations*. Retrieved from https://www.bcorporation.net/

Beamon, B. M. (1998). Supply Chain Design and Analysis: Models and Methods. *International Journal of Production Economics, 55*(3), 281–294. doi:10.1016/S0925-5273(98)00079-6

Beamon, B. M. (1999). Measuring Supply chain Performance. *International Journal of Operations & Production Management, 19*(3), 275–292. doi:10.1108/01443579910249714

Beatty, M. A., & Becker, B. E. (2005). A players' or a positions'? *Harvard Business Review, 83*(12), 110–117. PMID:16334586

Beatty, S. E., & Ferrell, M. E. (1998). Impulse buying: Modeling its precursors. *Journal of Retailing, 74*(2), 169–191. doi:10.1016/S0022-4359(99)80092-X

Beck, S. (2003). *India and Southeast Asia to 1875*. World Peace Communication Books.

Belk, R. W. (1983). Worldly Possessions: Issues and Criticisms. Advances in Consumer Research, 10, 514-519.

Belk, R. W. (1984). Three Scales to Measure Constructs Related to Materialism: Reliability, Validity, and Relationships to Measures of Happiness. Advances in Consumer Research, 11, 291-297.

Belk, R. W. (1990). The Role of Possessions in Constructing and Maintaining a Sense of Past. Advances in Consumer Research, 17, 669-676.

Belkaoui, A., & Karpik, P. G. (1989). Determinants of the corporate decision to disclose social information. *Accounting, Auditing & Accountability Journal, 2*(1), 36–51. doi:10.1108/09513578910132240

Belk, R. W. (1985). Materialism: Trait Aspects of Living in a Material World. *The Journal of Consumer Research, 12*(December), 265–280. doi:10.1086/208515

Belk, R. W. (1987). Material Values in the Comics: A Content Analysis of Comic Books Featuring Themes of Wealth. *The Journal of Consumer Research, 14*(June), 26–42. doi:10.1086/209090

Belk, R. W. (1988). Possessions and the Extended Self. *The Journal of Consumer Research, 15*(September), 139–168. doi:10.1086/209154

Belk, R. W. (1991). The Ineluctable Mysteries of Possessions. *Journal of Social Behavior and Personality, 6*(6), 17–55.

Bell, S. J., & Eisingerich, A. B. (2007). The paradox of customer education: Customer expertise and loyalty in the financial services industry. *European Journal of Marketing, 41*(5), 466–486. doi:10.1108/03090560710737561

Bentler, P. M. (2007). Can scientifically useful hypotheses be tested with correlations? *The American Psychologist*, *62*(8), 772–782. doi:10.1037/0003-066X.62.8.772 PMID:18020745

Berger, A., & Mester, L. (2003). Explaining the Dramatic Changes of Performance of U.S. Banks: Technological Change, Deregulation and Dynamic Changes in Competition. *Journal of Financial Intermediation*, *12*(1), 57–95. doi:10.1016/S1042-9573(02)00006-2

Berglöf, E., & Claessens, S. (2006, March). Enforcement and good corporate governance in developing countries and transition economies. *The World Bank Research Observer*, *21*(1), 123–150. doi:10.1093/wbro/lkj005

Berkowitz, J. (2013, June). *Free-Trade Cars: Why a U.S.–Europe Free-Trade Agreement Is a Good Idea*. Retrieved from Car and Driver: http://www.caranddriver.com/features/free-trade-cars-why-a-useurope-free-trade-agreement-is-a-good-idea-feature

Berridge, K. C. (2004). Motivation concepts in behavioral neuroscience. *Physiology & Behavior*, *81*(2), 179–209. doi:10.1016/j.physbeh.2004.02.004 PMID:15159167

Berry, L. (1983). Relationship Marketing. In L. Berry, L. Shostack, & G. Upah (Eds.), *Emerging Perspectives on Services Marketing* (pp. 25–28). Chicago, IL: American Marketing Association.

Bettman, J. R. (1979). An information processing theory of consumer choice. *Journal of Marketing*, *43*(1), 37–53. doi:10.2307/1250740

Bhagwati, J. N. (1987). Trade in Services and the Multilateral Trade Negotiations. *The World Bank Economic Review*, *1*(4), 549–569. doi:10.1093/wber/1.4.549

Bhat, B., & Bowonder, B. (2001). Innovation as an enhancer of brand personality: Globalization experience of titan industries. *Creativity and Innovation Management*, *10*(1), 26–39. doi:10.1111/1467-8691.00188

Bhatnagar, J. (2007). Talent Management Strategy of Employee Engagement in Indian ITES Employees: Key to Retention. *Employee Relations*, *29*(6), 640–663. doi:10.1108/01425450710826122

Bhattacharya, A. (2015). New Paradigms in Business Strategies of Banks. *Bank Quest*, *86*(3), 10–16.

Bigne´, J. E. (1997). *El consumidor verde: bases de un modelo de comportamiento*. Esic Market.

Bingham, T. (2009). *Bridging the Skills Gap - TD. American Society for Training & Development*. ASTD.

Bishop, F. P. (1949). *The Ethics of Advertising*. London, UK: Robert Hale.

Black, B. S., Jang, H., & Kim, W. (2006). Does corporate governance predict firms market values? Evidence from Korea. *Journal of Law Economics and Organization*, *22*(2), 366–413. doi:10.1093/jleo/ewj018

Blenkinsop, S. A., & Burns, N. (1992). Performance measurement revisited. *International Journal of Operations & Production Management*, *12*(10), 16–25. doi:10.1108/01443579210017213

BMWi. (2013). *German Mittelstand: Engine of the German Economy*. Retrieved from Federal Ministry of Economics and Technology: https://www.bmwi.de/English/Redaktion/Pdf/factbook-german-mittelstand,property=pdf,bereich=bmwi2012,sprache=en,rwb=true.pdf

Boles, J. S., Wood, J. A., & Johnson, J. (2003). Interrelationships of role conflict, role ambiguity, and work-family conflict with different facets of job satisfaction and the moderating effects of gender. *Journal of Personal Selling & Sales Management*, *23*(2), 99–113.

Bookbinder, J. H., Gumus, M., & Jewkes, E. M. (2010). Calculating the benefits of vendor managed inventory in a manufacturer-retailer system. *International Journal of Production Research, 48*(19), 5549–5571. doi:10.1080/00207540903095434

Boon, C., Den Hartog, D. N., Boselie, P., & Paauwe, J. (2011). The relationship between perceptions of HR practices and employee outcomes: Examining the role of person-organization and person-job fit. *International Journal of Human Resource Management, 22*(1), 138–163. doi:10.1080/09585192.2011.538978

Bowman, E. H., & Haire, M. (1976). Social impact disclosure and corporate annual reports. *Accounting, Organizations and Society, 1*(1), 11–21. doi:10.1016/0361-3682(76)90004-0

Bradburn, N. M., & Caplovitz, D. (1965). *Report on Happiness*. Chicago: Aldine.

Brady, J., & Davis, I. (1993). Marketing's mid-life crisis. *The McKinsey Quarterly*, (2): 17.

Brammer, S., & Pavelin, S. (2005). Corporate community contributions in the United Kingdom and the United States. *Journal of Business Ethics, 56*(1), 15–26. doi:10.1007/s10551-004-3236-4

Brandon, J., & Nelson, B. (2014). *Millennial employees: flight risk for companies*. Retrieved March 30, 2014, from http://www.gallup.com/home.aspx

Breuer, P., Moulton, J., & Turtle, R. (2013). *Applying advanced analytics in consumer companies*. New York: McKinsey & Co.

Brief, A. P., & Aldag, R. J. (1976). Correlates of role indices. *The Journal of Applied Psychology, 61*(4), 468–472. doi:10.1037/0021-9010.61.4.468

Brookshire, D. S., Randal, A., & Stoll, R. J. (1980). Valuing Increments and Decrements in Natural Resource Service Flows. *American Journal of Agricultural Economics, 62*(3).

Brown, N., & Laverick, S. (1994). Measuring Corporate Performance. *Long Range Planning, 27*(4), 89–98. doi:10.1016/0024-6301(94)90059-0

Brugarolas Molla-Bauza, M., Martinez-Carrasco Martinez, L., Martinez Poveda, A., & Rico Perez, M. (2005). Determination of the surplus that consumers are willing to pay for an organic wine. *Spanish Journal of Agricultural Research, 3*(1), 43–51. doi:10.5424/sjar/2005031-123

Buchanan, L., & O'Connell, A. (2006). Brief History of Decision Making. *Harvard Business Review, 84*(1), 32–41. PMID:16447367

Buehler, R. (2010). Transport Policies, Automobile Use, and Sustainable Transport: A Comparison of Germany and the United States. *Journal of Planning Education and Research, 30*(1), 76–93. doi:10.1177/0739456X10366302

Bunte, F. M., Mulder, F., & van Tongerenen, J. J. (1998). Meting van de performance van agrarische produktiekolommen. Onderzoekverslag 163. LEI.

Burgess, S. M., & Steenkamp, J.-B. E. (2006). Marketing renaissance: How research in emerging markets advances marketing science and practice. *International Journal of Research in Marketing, 23*(4), 337–356. doi:10.1016/j.ijresmar.2006.08.001

Burnett, J. J., & Bush, A. J. (1986). Profiling the Yuppies. *Journal of Advertising Research, 26*(April/May), 27–35.

Burroughs, J. E. (1996). Product symbolism, self meaning, and holistic matching: The role of information processing in impulsive buying. *Advances in Consumer Research. Association for Consumer Research (U. S.), 23*, 463–469.

Burroughs, J. E., & Rindfleisch, A. (2002). Materialism and Well-Being: A Conflicting Values Perspective. *The Journal of Consumer Research, 29*(December).

Burton, D. (2002). Consumer education and service quality: Conceptual issues and practical implications. *Journal of Services Marketing, 16*(2), 125–142. doi:10.1108/08876040210422673

Byun, S. E., & Sternquist, B. (2010). Reconceptualization of price mavenism: Do Chinese consumers get a glow when they know? *Asia Pacific Journal of Marketing and Logistics, 22*(3), 279–293. doi:10.1108/13555851011062232

Cable, D. M., & DeRue, D. S. (2002). The convergent and discriminant validity of subjective fit perceptions. *The Journal of Applied Psychology, 87*(5), 875–884. doi:10.1037/0021-9010.87.5.875 PMID:12395812

Cable, D. M., & Judge, T. A. (1997). Interviewers perceptions of person–organization fit and organizational selection decisions. *The Journal of Applied Psychology, 82*(4), 546–561. doi:10.1037/0021-9010.82.4.546 PMID:9378683

Campbell, D. T. (1969). Materialism. In J. P. Robinson & P. R. Ishliver (Eds.), *Measure of Social Altitudes* (pp. 651–652). Ann Arbor, MI: Institute for Social Research.

Capaul, M. (2003). *Corporate governance in Latin America.* Chief Economist Office Latin America and the Caribbean Region World Bank. Retrieved August 21, 2015, from http://web.worldbank.org/archive/website00894A/WEB/PDF/CORPOR-2.PDF

Caplice, C., & Sheffi, Y. (1994). A review and evaluation of logistic metrics. *The International Journal of Logistics Management, 5*(2), 11–28. doi:10.1108/09574099410805171

Carroll, A. B., & Buchholtz, A. K. (2008). Strategic management and corporate public affairs. In A. B. Carroll, & A. K. Buchholtz (Eds.), Business and Society. Ethics and stakeholder management (7th ed.; pp. 168-171). South-Western Cengage Learning.

Carter, L., Giber, D. J., & Goldsmith, M. (2001). *Best practices in organization development and change: Culture, leadership, retention, performance, coaching: Case studies, tools, models, research.* San Francisco: Jossey-Bass/Pfeiffer.

Casaloˊ, L. V., Flavian, C., & Guinalıu, M. (2007). The role of security, privacy, usability and reputation in the development of online banking. *Online Information Review, 31*(5), 583–603. doi:10.1108/14684520710832315

Casanova, L., & Dumas, A. (2010). Corporate social responsibility and Latin American multinationals: Is poverty an issue? *Universia Business Review, 25*, 132–145.

Cascio, W. F., & Thacker, J. W. (1994). *Managing human resources: Productivity, quality of work life, profits.* Toronto: McGraw-Hill Ryerson.

CCPA. (2000). *Corporate community involvement: Establishing a business case.* Melbourne: Centre for Corporate Public Affairs.

Celis, F. (2015). *Vikingo de Oxxo 'noquea' a Ronald McDonald.* Retrieved from http://www.elfinanciero.com.mx/empresas/vikingo-de-oxxo-noquea-a-ronald-mcdonald.html

Cellucci, A. J., & DeVries, D. L. (1978). Measuring managerial satisfaction: A manual for the MJSQ. Technical Report II, Center for Creative Leadership.

Cemefi. (2013, October). *Centro Mexicano para la Filantropía.* Retrieved October 23, 2013, from Información institucional: http://www.cemefi.org/nosotros/informacion-institucional.html

Chakrabarti, S. (2010). Factors influencing organic food purchase in India- expert survey insights. *British Food Journal, 112*(8), 902–915. doi:10.1108/00070701011067497

Chandrashekar, H. M. (2010). Changing scenario of organic farming in India: an overview. *International NGO Journal,* *5*(1), 34-39. Retrieved on 22nd February 2014 from. uni-mysore.ac.in/14660/1/Changing Scenario of Organic Farming in India.pdf

Chandrashekaran, R., & Suri, R. (2012). Effects of gender and price knowledge on offer evaluation and channel transition in retail and e-tail environments. *Journal of Product and Brand Management, 21*(3), 215–225. doi:10.1108/10610421211228838

Chang, C. H., Rosen, C. C., & Levy, P. E. (2009). The relationship between perceptions of organizational politics and employee attitudes, strain, and behavior: A meta-analytic examination. *Academy of Management Journal, 52*(4), 779–801. doi:10.5465/AMJ.2009.43670894

Chang, H. T., Chi, N. W., & Chuang, A. (2010). Exploring the moderating roles of perceived person-job fit and person-organization fit on the relationship between training investment and knowledge workers turnover intentions. *Applied Psychology, 59*(4), 566–593. doi:10.1111/j.1464-0597.2009.00412.x

Chan, K. (2000). Market segmentation of green consumers in Hong Kong. *Journal of International Consumer Marketing, 12*(2), 7–24. doi:10.1300/J046v12n02_02

Chapman, R., Soosay, C., & Kandampully, J. (2003). Innovation in Logistics Services and the New Business Model: A Conceptual Framework. *International Journal of Physical Distribution & Logistics Management, 33*(7), 630–650. doi:10.1108/09600030310499295

Chapple, W., & Moon, J. (2005a). Corporate social responsibility (CSR) in Asia: A seven-country study of CSR web site reporting. *Business & Society, 44*(4), 415–439. doi:10.1177/0007650305281658

Chatterjee, B. (2012). *Organic Foods enter India to a low-key welcome.* Retrieved on 19th March 2014 from http://www. businesseconomics.in/?q=node/1267

Chatterjee, D. (2011, October). A content analysis study on corporate governance reporting by Indian companies. *Corporate Reputation Review, 14*(3), 234–246. doi:10.1057/crr.2011.13

Chatterjee, S., & Datta, D. (1984). *An introduction to Indian philosophy* (8th ed.). University of Calcutta.

Chattopadhyaya, D. (1993). *Indian Philosophy* (7th ed.). New Delhi: People's Publishing House.

Chell, E. (2001). *Entrepreneurship: Globalization, Innovation and Development.* Cengage Learning EMEA.

Chen, M.-F. (2009). Attitude toward organic foods among Taiwanese as related to health consciousness, environmental attitudes, and the mediating effects of a healthy lifestyle. *British Food Journal, 111*(2), 165–178. doi:10.1108/00070700910931986

Chesnais, F., & Simonetti, R. (2000). Globalization, Foreign Direct Investment and Innovation. *European Integration and Global Corporate Strategies, 17*, 1.

Chester, A., Clarke, A., & Libarikian, A. (2016). *Transforming into an analytics-driven insurance carrier.* New York: McKinsey & Co.

Cheung, C. F., Chan, Y. L., Kwok, S. K., Lee, W. B., & Wang, W. M. (2006). A knowledge-based service automation system for service logistics. *Journal of Manufacturing Technology Management, 17*(6), 750–771. doi:10.1108/17410380610678783

Cheyipai. (2015, July 30). *China's Used-Car E-commerce is Rising Rapidly.* Retrieved from Financial Content: http://markets.financialcontent.com/stocks/news/read?GUID=30362668

Chiappini, R. (2012, October). Offshoring and Export Performance in the European Automotive Industry. *Competition & Change, 16*(4), 323–342. doi:10.1179/1024529412Z.00000000020

Chi, N. W., & Pan, S. Y. (2012). A multilevel investigation of missing links between transformational leadership and task performance: The mediating roles of perceived person-job fit and person-organization fit. *Journal of Business and Psychology*, *27*(1), 43–56. doi:10.1007/s10869-011-9211-z

Chircu, A. M., & Kauffman, R. J. (2000). Limits to value in electronic commerce-related IT investments. *Journal of Management Information Systems*, *17*(2), 59–80.

Choi, S. M., Lee, W.-N., & Kim, H.-J. (2005). Lessons from the rich and famous: A cross-cultural comparison of celebrity endorsement in advertising. *Journal of Advertising*, *34*(2), 85–98. doi:10.1080/00913367.2005.10639190

Chong, A., Izquierdo, A., Micco, A., & Panizza, U. (2003). *Corporate governance and private capital flows to Latin America*. Washington, DC: Inter-American Development Bank.

Christensen, C. (2013). *The innovator's dilemma: when new technologies cause great firms to fail*. Harvard Business Review Press.

Chung, Y. S. (1998). Culture and consumption expenditure patterns: Comparison between Korean and United States households. *Journal of Consumer Studies & Home Economics*, *22*(1), 39–50. doi:10.1111/j.1470-6431.1998.tb00714.x

Churchill, G. A., Iacobucci, D., & Israel, D. (2010). *Marketing research: A south Asian perspective*. New Delhi, India: Cengage Learning.

Churchill, H. (1942). How To Measure Brand Loyalty. *Advertising and Selling*, *35*, 24.

Clarke, G. R. G., & Wallsten, S. J. (2006). Has the Internet increased trade? Developed and developing country evidence. *Economic Inquiry*, *44*(3), 465–484. doi:10.1093/ei/cbj026

Co, C. Y. (2007). US Exports of Knowledge-intensive Services and Importing-country Characteristics. *Review of International Economics*, *15*(5), 890–904. doi:10.1111/j.1467-9396.2007.00703.x

Coley, A. L. (2002). Affective and cognitive processes involved in impulse buying. *MSc Study*, 1-91.

Computerworld. (2009). *Defining Business Analytics and Its Impact on Organizational Decision-Making*. Author.

Conlon, J. (2015). *The Brand Brief Behind Nike's Just Do It Campaign*. Branding Strategy Insider Website. Retrieved from: http://www.brandingstrategyinsider.com/2015/08/behind-nikes-campaign.html

Cooper, C. L., Dewe, P. J., & O'Driscoll, M. P. (2001). *Organizational stress: A review and critique of theory, research and application*. London: Sage.

Corbitt, B. J., Thanasankit, T., & Yi, H. (2003). Trust and e-commerce: A study of consumer perceptions. *Electronic Commerce Research and Applications*, *2*(3), 203–215. doi:10.1016/S1567-4223(03)00024-3

Cordes, C. L., & Dougherty, T. W. (1993). A review and integration of research on job burnout. *Academy of Management Review*, *18*(4), 621–656.

Core, J. E. (2001). A review of the empirical disclosure literature. *Journal of Accounting and Economics*, *31*(1-3), 441–456. doi:10.1016/S0165-4101(01)00036-2

Cormier, D., & Gordon, I. M. (2001). An examination of social and environmental reporting strategies. *Accounting, Auditing & Accountability Journal*, *14*(5), 587–616. doi:10.1108/EUM0000000006264

Correa, M. E., Flynn, S., & Amit, A. (2004). *Responsabilidad social corporativa en América Latina: Una visión empresarial. Série CEPAL Medio Ambiente y Desarrollo No. 85*. Santiago, Chile: UN CEPAL.

Council of Logistic Management. (1995). *World class Logistics: The Challenge of Managing Continuous Change*. Oak Books, IL: CLM.

Courchane, M., Nickerson, D., & Sullivan, R. J. (2002). Investment in Internet Banking as a Real Option: Theory and Tests. *Journal of Multinational Financial Management, 12*(4-5), 347–363. doi:10.1016/S1042-444X(02)00015-4

Coye, R. W. (2004). Managing customer expectations in the service encounter. *International Journal of Service Industry Management, 15*(1), 54–71. doi:10.1108/09564230410523330

Crawford, G., & Melewar, T. C. (2003). The importance of impulse purchasing behavior in the international airport environment. *Journal of Consumer Behaviour, 3*(1), 85–98. doi:10.1002/cb.124

Crime in India. 2011-Compendium. (2012). National Crime Records Bureau, Ministry of Home Affairs, Government of India, New Delhi, India. Retrieved from reportwww.ncrb.gov

Cronabach, L. (1990). *Essentials of Psychological Testing*. New York: Harper and Row.

Cronbach, L. J. (1951). Coefficient alpha and the internal structure of tests. *Psychometrika, 16*(3), 297–334. doi:10.1007/BF02310555

Cropanzano, R., Rupp, D. E., & Byrne, Z. S. (2003). The relationship of emotional exhaustion to work attitudes, job performance, and organizational citizenship behaviors. *The Journal of Applied Psychology, 88*(1), 160–169. doi:10.1037/0021-9010.88.1.160 PMID:12675403

Crowther, D., & Rayman-Bacchus, L. (2004). *Perspectives on corporate social responsibility*. London: Ashgate.

Csikszentmihalyi, M. (2000). The Costs and Benefits of Consuming. *The Journal of Consumer Research, 27*(September), 267–272. doi:10.1086/314324

Cunningham, R. M. (1956). Brand Loyalty - What, Where, How Much? *Harvard Business Review, 34*, 116–128.

Cunningham, R. M. (1961). Customer Loyalty to Store and Brand. *Harvard Business Review*, (November-December), 127–137.

Curran James, M., & Meuter Matthew, L. (2005). Self-service technology adoption: Comparing three technologies. *Journal of Services Marketing, 19*(2), 103–113. doi:10.1108/08876040510591411

D'Andrea, G., Marcotte, D., & Morrison, G. D. (2010). Let emerging market customers be your teachers. *Harvard Business Review, 88*(12), 115–120.

Dahlsrud, A. (2008). How corporate social responsibility is defined: An analysis of 37 definitions. *Corporate Social Responsibility and Environmental Management, 15*(1), 1–13. doi:10.1002/csr.132

Daly, H. E. (1989). Toward a measure of Sustainable Social Net National Product. In Environmental Accounting for Sustainable Development. The World Bank.

Daniels, K., & Guppy, A. (1994). Occupational stress, social support, job control, and psychological well-being. *Human Relations, 47*(12), 1523–1544. doi:10.1177/001872679404701205

Das, S., & Jhunu, D. (2011). Designing a Biometric Strategy (Fingerprint) Measure for Enhancing ATM Security in Indian E-Banking System. *International Journal of Information and Communication Technology Research, 1*(5), 197–203.

Daun, A. (1983). The Materialistic Lifestyle: Some Socio-Psychological Aspects. In L. Uusitalo (Ed.), *Consumer Behavior and Environmental Quality* (pp. 6–16). New York: St. Martin's.

Davenport, T. H. (2006). Competing on Analytics. *Harvard Business Review, 84*(1), 98–107. PMID:16447373

Davenport, T. H., Barth, P., & Bean, R. (2012). How Big Data Is Different, *MIT*. *Sloan Management Review*, *54*(1), 22–24.

Davies, A., Titterington, A., & Cochrane, C. (1995). Who buys organic food? A profile of the purchasers of organic food in Northern Ireland. *British Food Journal*, *97*(10), 17–23. doi:10.1108/00070709510104303

Davis, F. D. (1989). Perceived usefulness, perceived ease of use, and user acceptance of information technology. *Management Information Systems Quarterly*, *13*(3), 319–340. doi:10.2307/249008

Davis, F. D., Bagozzi, R. P., & Warshaw, P. R. (1989). User acceptance of computer technology: A comparison of two theoretical models. *Management Science*, *35*(8), 982–1003. doi:10.1287/mnsc.35.8.982

Davis, F. D., Bagozzi, R. P., & Warshaw, P. R. (1992). Extrinsic and intrinsic motivation to use computers in the workplace. *Journal of Applied Social Psychology*, *22*(14), 1111–1132. doi:10.1111/j.1559-1816.1992.tb00945.x

Day, G. S. (1994). The capabilities of market-driven organizations. *Journal of Marketing*, *58*(4), 37–52. doi:10.2307/1251915

Day, G. S. (2011). Closing the marketing capabilities gap. *Journal of Marketing*, *75*(4), 183–195. doi:10.1509/jmkg.75.4.183

De Anggelis, T. (2004). Consumerism and its Discontents. *American Psychological Association Monitor*, *35*(6), 52.

de Magistris, T., & Gracia, A. (2008). The decision to buy organic food products in Southern Italy. *British Food Journal*, *110*(9), 929–947. doi:10.1108/00070700810900620

De Mooij, M., & Hofstede, G. (2002). Convergence and divergence in consumer behavior: Implications for international retailing. *Journal of Retailing*, *78*(1), 61–69. doi:10.1016/S0022-4359(01)00067-7

De Oliveira, J. A. (2006, Spring). Corporate citizenship in Latin America: New challenges for business. *Journal of Corporate Citizenship*, *21*, 17–20. doi:10.9774/GLEAF.4700.2006.sp.00003

de Young, R. (2001). *The financial progress of pure-play internet banks*. BIS Papers, No. 7.

Dean, M., Raats, M. M., & Shepherd, R. (2008). Moral concerns and consumer choice of fresh and processed organic foods. *Journal of Applied Social Psychology*, *38*(8), 2088–2107. doi:10.1111/j.1559-1816.2008.00382.x

Deardorff, A. V. (2001). International Provision of Trade Services, Trade, and Fragmentation. *Review of International Economics*, *9*(2), 233–248. doi:10.1111/1467-9396.00276

Deardorff, A. V., & Stern, R. M. (2008). Empirical Analysis of Barriers to International Services Transactions and the Consequences of Liberalization. In A. Mattoo, R. M. Stern, & G. Zanini (Eds.), *A Handbook of International Trade in Services*. Oxford, UK: Oxford University Press.

Dedrick, J., & Kraemer, K. L. (2008, April). Globalization of innovation: the personal computing industry. In *2008 Industry Studies Conference Paper*. doi:10.2139/ssrn.1125025

Deegan, C. (2002). The legitimising effect of social and environmental disclosures: A theoretical foundation. *Accounting, Auditing & Accountability Journal*, *15*(3), 282–312. doi:10.1108/09513570210435852

Dekimpe, M. G., Parker, P. M., & Sarvary, M. (2000). Globalization: Modeling technology adoption timing across countries. *Technological Forecasting and Social Change*, *63*(1), 25–42. doi:10.1016/S0040-1625(99)00086-4

Deloitte India Fraud Survey Edition. (2014). Retrieved from http://www2.deloitte.com/content/dam/Deloitte/in/Documents/finance/in-finance-annual-fraud-survey-noexp.pdf

Demb, A., & Neubauer, F. F. (1992). The corporate board: Confronting the paradoxes. *Long Range Planning*, *25*(3), 9–20. doi:10.1016/0024-6301(92)90364-8 PMID:10120319

Department of Mines and Geology. (n.d.). *Geology and Mineral Resources of Odisha*. Department of Mines and Geology, Government of Odisha, Bhubaneswar. Retrieved 21 November from: http://www.orissaminerals.gov.in/Download/GEOLOGY_MINERAL_RESOURCES_ORISSA.pdf

Depner, H., & Bathelt, H. (2005). Exporting the German Model: The Establishment of a New Automobile Industry Cluster in Shanghai. *Economic Geography*, *81*(1), 53–81. doi:10.1111/j.1944-8287.2005.tb00255.x

Depue, R. A., & Collins, P. F. (1999). Neurobiology of the Structure of Personality: Dopamine Facilitation of Incentive Motivation and Extraversion. *Behavioral and Brain Sciences*, *22*(3), 491–569. doi:10.1017/S0140525X99002046 PMID:11301519

Dhody, T. (2015). *Kingfisher just got sold to Heineken for Rs 872 Crore*. Retrieved from http://www.scoopwhoop.com/news/heineken-buys-kingfisher/

Dholakia, U. M. (2000). Temptation and resistance: An integrated model of consumption impulse formation and enactment. *Psychology and Marketing*, *17*(11), 955–982. doi:10.1002/1520-6793(200011)17:11<955::AID-MAR3>3.0.CO;2-J

Dickins, D., and Ferguson, V. (1957). Practices and Attitudes of Rural White Children and Parents Concerning Money. *Mississippi Agricultural Experiment Station Technical Bulletin*, 43.

Diener, E. (2000). Subjective Well-Being: The Science of Happiness. *The American Psychologist*, *55*(1), 34–43. doi:10.1037/0003-066X.55.1.34 PMID:11392863

Dinis, A. (2006). Marketing and innovation: Useful tools for competitiveness in rural and peripheral areas. *European Planning Studies*, *14*(1), 9–22. doi:10.1080/09654310500339083

Dittmar, H. (2001). Impulse buying in ordinary and "compulsive" consumers. In E. U. Weber, J. Baron, & G. Loomes (Eds.), *Conflicts and Tradeoffs in Decision Making* (pp. 110–135). Cambridge, UK: University of Cambridge.

Dittmar, H., Beattie, J., & Friese, S. (1995). Gender identity and material symbols: Objects and decision considerations in impulse purchases. *Journal of Economic Psychology*, *16*(3), 491–511. doi:10.1016/0167-4870(95)00023-H

Dittmar, H., & Drury, J. (2000). Self-image–is it in the bag? A qualitative comparison between ordinary and excessive consumers. *Journal of Economic Psychology*, *21*(2), 109–142. doi:10.1016/S0167-4870(99)00039-2

Dobers, P., & Halme, M. (2009). Corporate social responsibility and developing countries. *Corporate Social Responsibility and Environmental Management*, *16*(5), 237–249. doi:10.1002/csr.212

Dornbusch, R., Fischer, S., & Startz, R. (2012). *Macroeconomics* (7th ed.). Boston: Irwin McGraw-Hill.

Dougherty, C. (2009, August 7). *Driving Out of Germany, to Pollute Another Day*. Retrieved from The New York Times: http://www.nytimes.com/2009/08/08/world/europe/08germany.html?hpw&_r=0

Douglas, L., & Connor, R. (2003). Attitudes to service quality- the expectation gap. *Nutrition & Food Science*, *33*(4), 165–172. doi:10.1108/00346650310488516

Drenth, P., & Diederik, J. (1998). *Personnel Psychology*. Hove, UK: Psychology Press.

Drew, S. A., Kelley, P. C., & Kendrick, T. (2006). CLASS: Five elements of corporate governance to manage strategic risk. *Business Horizons*, *49*(2), 127–138. doi:10.1016/j.bushor.2005.07.001

Drori, G. S., Meyer, J. W., & Hwang, H. (2006). *Globalization and organization: World society and organizational change*. Oxford University Press.

Drummond, G. (2004). Consumer confusion: Reduction strategies in higher education. *International Journal of Educational Management*, *18*(5), 317–323. doi:10.1108/09513540410543466

Dunning, J. H. (2002). *Regions, Globalization, and the Knowledge-based Economy*. Oxford University Press. doi:10.1093/0199250014.001.0001

Durham, C. A., & Andrade, D. (2005). *Health vs. environmental motivation in organic preferences and purchases*. paper presented at the American Agricultural Economics Association Annual Meeting, Providence, RI.

Dysvik, A., & Kuvaas, B. (2008). Opportunities, work motivation and employee outcomes. *International Journal of Training and Development*, *12*(3), 138–157. doi:10.1111/j.1468-2419.2008.00301.x

Economist. (2012). *The Deciding Factor: Big Data and Decision Making*. The Economist Intelligence Unit.

Edward, B. B., & Anil, M. (1993). Environmentally Sustainable Development: Optimal Economic Condition. In B. B. Edward (Ed.), *Economics and Ecology: New Frontiers and Sustainable Development*. London: Chapman & Hall.

Edward, M., & Sahadev, S. (2011). Role of switching costs in the service quality, perceived value, customer satisfaction and customer retention linkage. *Asia Pacific Journal of Marketing and Logistics*, *23*(3), 327–345. doi:10.1108/13555851111143240

Edwards, J. R. (1996). An examination of competing versions of the person–environment fit approach to stress. *Academy of Management Journal*, *39*(2), 292–339. doi:10.2307/256782

El Financiero. (2014). *Abre Oxxo en Estados Unidos*. Retrieved from http://www.elfinanciero.com.mx/monterrey/abre-oxxo-en-estados-unidos.html

El Sahah, S. (1989). The Proper Calculation of Income from Depleteble Natural Resources. In Environmental Accounting for Sustainable Development. The World Bank.

Elahee, M., & Brooks, C. M. (2004). Trust and negotiation tactics: Perceptions about business-to-business negotiations in Mexico. *Journal of Business and Industrial Marketing*, *19*(6), 397–404. doi:10.1108/08858620410556336

EPW Research Foundation. (1997). *National Accounts Statistics in India: 1950-51 to 1995-96*. Mumbai, India: EPW Research Foundation.

Erickson, T. J., & Gratton, L. (2007). What It Means to Work Here. *Harvard Business Review*, (Jan-Feb): 1–10. PMID:17348174

Eroglu, S. A., Machleit, K. A., & Davis, L. M. (2001). Atmospheric qualities of online retailing: A conceptual model and implications. *Journal of Business Research*, *54*(2), 177–184. doi:10.1016/S0148-2963(99)00087-9

Euromonitor. (2013a). *Consumer Lifestyles in Mexico*. Euromonitor.

Euromonitor. (2013b). *FEMSA's latest acquisition shows potential for soft drinks and retail*. Euromonitor.

Euromonitor. (2014). *FEMSA Comercio SA de CV in retailing (Mexico)*. Euromonitor.

Euromonitor. (2015a). *Alcoholic drinks in India*. Euromonitor.

Euromonitor. (2015b). *Alcoholic drinks in Mexico*. Euromonitor.

Euromonitor. (2015c). *Beauty and personal care in Brazil*. Euromonitor.

Euromonitor. (2015d). *Consumer lifestyles in Brazil*. Euromonitor.

Euromonitor. (2015e). *Consumer lifestyles in India*. Euromonitor.

Euromonitor. (2015f). *Eco worriers: Global green behaviour and market impact*. Euromonitor.

European Commission. (2012a, November 8). *Action plan for the EU automotive industry in 2020*. Retrieved from European Commission: http://europa.eu/rapid/press-release_MEMO-12-845_en.htm

European Commission. (2012b, November 8). *CARS 2020: Action Plan for a competitive and sustainable automotive industry in Europe*. Retrieved from European Commission: http://eur-lex.europa.eu/legal-content/EN/TXT/PDF/?uri= CELEX:52012DC0636&from=EN

European Commission. (2013, March 19). *A guide to communicating about CSR*. Retrieved October 2013, from http:// ec.europa.eu/enterprise/policies/sustainable-business/files/csr/campaign/documentation/download/guide_en.pdf

Europe, C. S. R. (2000). *Communicating corporate social responsibility*. Brussels: CSR Europe.

Fan, P. (2011). Innovation, Globalization, and Catch-up of Latecomers: Cases of Chinese telecom firms. *Environment and Planning-Part A*, *43*(4), 830–849. doi:10.1068/a43152

Fatima, A. (2011). E-Banking Security Issues – Is There A Solution in Biometrics? *Journal of Internet Banking and Commerce*, *16*(2), 1–9.

Federal Bureau of Investigation. (2014). Annual Report, Internet Crime Compliant Center (IC3). New York: Author.

Feick, L. F., & Price, L. L. (1987). The market maven: A diffuser of marketplace information. *Journal of Marketing*, *51*(1), 83–97. doi:10.2307/1251146

Fernández, A. M., & Rajagopal, N. A. (2014). Convergence of corporate social responsibility and business growth: An analytical framework. *International Journal of Business Excellence*, *7*(6), 791–806. doi:10.1504/IJBEX.2014.065508

Ferre, Z., Melgar, N., & Rossi, M. (2010). *Corporate social responsibility in Uruguay: What enterprises do and what people think about it*. United Nations. Retrieved October 20, 2015, from http://unctad.org/en/docs/dtlktcd20102_en.pdf

Fig, D. (2005). Manufacturing amnesia: Corporate social responsibility in South Africa. *International Affairs*, *81*(3), 599–617. doi:10.1111/j.1468-2346.2005.00471.x

Fiore, A. M., & Kim, J. (2007). An integrative framework capturing experiential and utilitarian shopping experience. *International Journal of Retail & Distribution Management*, *35*(6), 421–442. doi:10.1108/09590550710750313

First, I., & Brozina, S. (2009). Cultural influences on motives for organic food consumption. *EuroMed Journal of Business*, *4*(2), 185–19. doi:10.1108/14502190910976538

Fisher, C. D., & Gitelson, R. (1983). A meta-analysis of the correlates of role conflict and ambiguity. *The Journal of Applied Psychology*, *68*(2), 320–333. doi:10.1037/0021-9010.68.2.320

Focus. (2009, January 25). *Abwrackprämie - 2500 Euro Kaufanreiz*. Retrieved from Focus Online: http://www.focus.de/ auto/news/abwrackpraemie-2500-euro-kaufanreiz_aid_364939.html

Forstater, M., Zadek, S., Guang, Y., Yu, K., Hong, C. X., & George, M. (2010). *Corporate responsibility in African development: Insights from an emerging dialogue*. Beijing: The Institute of West-Asian and African Studies of the Chinese Academy of Social Sciences. Retrieved October 21, 2015, from http://www.iisd.org/pdf/2011/corporate_responsiblity_in_african_development.pdf

Fotopoulos, C., & Krystallis, A. (2002). Organic product avoidance: reasons for rejection and potential buyers' identification in a countrywide survey. *British Food Journal*, *104*(3-5), 233-260.

Fraj, E., & Martı'nez, E. (2002). *Comportamiento del Consumidor Ecolo'gico*. Madrid: Esic Editorial.

Fraj, E., & Martinez, E. (2006). Environmental values and lifestyles as determining factors of ecological consumer behaviour: An empirical analysis. *Journal of Consumer Marketing, 23*(3), 133–144. doi:10.1108/07363760610663295

Fraj, E., & Martinez, E. (2007). Ecological consumer behaviour: An empirical analysis. *International Journal of Consumer Studies, 31*(1), 26–33. doi:10.1111/j.1470-6431.2006.00565.x

Francois, J., & Hoekman, B. (2010). Services Trade and Policy. *Journal of Economic Literature, 48*(3), 642–692. doi:10.1257/jel.48.3.642

Frank, R. E. (1967). Is Brand Loyalty a Useful Basis for Market Segmentation? *Journal of Advertising Research, 7*(2), 27–33.

FRC. (2014). *The UK corporate governance code*. London: The Financial Reporting Council Limited. Retrieved October 23, 2015, from https://www.frc.org.uk/Our-Work/Publications/Corporate-Governance/UK-Corporate-Governance-Code-2014.pdf

French, J. R. P., Jr., Rodgers, W.L., & Cobb, S. (1974). Adjustment as person–environment fit. In G. Coelho, D. Hamburg, & J. Adams (Eds.), Coping and adaptation (pp. 316–333). New York: Basic Books.

Freund, C., & Weinhold, D. (2002). The Internet and International Trade in Services. *The American Economic Review, 92*(2), 236–240. doi:10.1257/000282802320189320

Freund, C., & Weinhold, D. (2004). The effect of the Internet on international trade. *Journal of International Economics, 62*(1), 171–189. doi:10.1016/S0022-1996(03)00059-X

Furst, K., Lang, W., & Nolle, D. (2001). Internet Banking in the U.S.: Landscape, Prospects, and Industry Implications. *Journal of Financial Transformation, 2*, 45–52.

Gamrowski, B., & Rachev, S. (1999). A Testable Version of the Pareto-Stable CAPM. *Mathematical and Computer Modelling, 29*(10-12), 61–81. doi:10.1016/S0895-7177(99)00093-X

Ganesh, J., Arnold, M. J., & Reynolds, K. E. (2000). Understanding the Customer Base of Service Providers: An Examination of the Difference between Switchers and Stayers. *Journal of Marketing, 64*(July), 65–87. doi:10.1509/jmkg.64.3.65.18028

Garcia, R., Bardhi, F., & Friedrich, C. (2007). Overcoming consumer resistance to innovation. *MIT Sloan Management Review, 48*(4), 82–88.

Gardner, M. P., & Rook, D. W. (1988). Effects of impulse purchases on consumers' affective states. *Advances in Consumer Research. Association for Consumer Research (U. S.), 15*, 127–130.

Gates, S. (1999). *Aligning Strategic Performance Measures and Results*. New York, NY: The Conference Board.

Geertz, C. (1973). *The Interpretation of cultures*. New York: Basic Books.

Gerybadze, A., & Reger, G. (1999). Globalization of R&D: Recent Changes in the Management of Innovation in Transnational Corporations. *Research Policy, 28*(2), 251–274. doi:10.1016/S0048-7333(98)00111-5

Geuss, M. (2014, October 25). *Porsche, Mercedes building electric cars to challenge Tesla*. Retrieved from Ars Technica: http://arstechnica.com/cars/2014/10/porsche-mercedes-building-electric-cars-to-challenge-tesla/

Ghezzi, A., Renga, F., Balocco, R., & Pescetto, P. (2010). Mobile payment applications: Offer state of the art in the Italian market. *Info, 12*(5), 3–22. doi:10.1108/14636691011071130

Gilmour, P. A. (1999). Strategic Audit Framework to Improve Supply Chain Performance. *Journal of Business & Industrial Marketing, 14*(5/6), 355-363.

Gliem, J. A., & Gliem, R. R. (2003). *Calculating, interpreting, and reporting Cronbach's alpha reliability coefficient for Likert-type scales*. Midwest Research-to-Practice Conference in Adult, Continuing, and Community Education.

Goetzke, B. I., & Spiller, A. (2014). Health-improving lifestyles of organic and functional food consumers. *British Food Journal, 116*(3), 510–526. doi:10.1108/BFJ-03-2012-0073

Goldsmith, R. E., Clark, R. A., & Goldsmith, E. B. (2006). Extending the psychological profile of market mavenism. *Journal of Consumer Behaviour, 5*(5), 411–419. doi:10.1002/cb.189

Google. (2012). *The New multi-screen world: Understanding cross-platform consumer behavior*. Retrieved from https://think.withgoogle.com/databoard/media/pdfs/the-new-multi-screen-world-study_research-studies.pdf

Gorodnichenko, Y., Svejnar, J., & Terrell, K. (2008). *Globalization and Innovation in Emerging Markets (No. w14481)*. National Bureau of Economic Research. doi:10.3386/w14481

Gorodnichenko, Y., Svejnar, J., & Terrell, K. (2010). Globalization and Innovation in Emerging Markets. *American Economic Journal. Macroeconomics, 2*(2), 194–226. doi:10.1257/mac.2.2.194

Gounaris, S., & Koritos, C. (2008). Investigating the drivers of internet banking adoption decision: A comparison of three alternative frameworks. *International Journal of Bank Marketing, 26*(5), 282–304. doi:10.1108/02652320810894370

Government of India. (2014). *Provisional Coal Statistics: 2013-14*. Coal Controllers Organization, Ministry of Coal, Government of India.

Govindarajan, V., & Trimble, C. (2013). *Reverse innovation: Create far from home, win everywhere*. Harvard Business Press.

Gray, R., Javad, M., Power, D. M., & Sinclair, C. D. (2001). Social and environmental disclosure and corporate characteristics: A research note and extension. *Journal of Business Finance & Accounting, 28*(3/4), 327–356. doi:10.1111/1468-5957.00376

Gray, R., Owen, D., & Maunders, K. (1987). *Corporate social reporting: Accounting and accountability*. London: Prentice-Hall.

Gregory, B. T., Albritton, M. D., & Osmonbekov, T. (2010). The mediating role of psychological empowerment on the relationships between P-O fit, job satisfaction, and in-role performance. *Journal of Business and Psychology, 25*(4), 639–647. doi:10.1007/s10869-010-9156-7

GRI. (2013). *About GRI*. Retrieved October 23, 2013, from The Global Reporting Initiative: https://www.globalreporting.org/information/about-gri/Pages/default.aspx

Griffiths, P., Sedefov, R., Gallegos, A. N. A., & Lopez, D. (2010). How Globalization and Market innovation Challenge,How We Think about and Respond to Drug Use: 'SpiceaCase Study. *Addiction (Abingdon, England), 105*(6), 951–953. doi:10.1111/j.1360-0443.2009.02874.x PMID:20659053

Grunfeld, L. A., & Moxnes, A. (2003). *The Intangible Globalization: Explaining the Patterns of International Trade in Services*. Norwegian Institute of International Affairs Working Paper 657.

GTAI. (2015). *Industry Overview - The Automotive Industry in Germany*. Retrieved from Germany Trade & Invest: http://www.gtai.de/GTAI/Content/EN/Invest/_SharedDocs/Downloads/GTAI/Industry-overviews/industry-overview-automotive-industry-en.pdf

Guan, Y., Deng, H., Risavy, S. D., Bond, M. H., & Li, F. (2011). Supplementary fit, complementary fit, and work-related outcomes: The role of self-construal. *Applied Psychology*, *60*(2), 286–310. doi:10.1111/j.1464-0597.2010.00436.x

Gu, F. F., Hung, K., & Tse, D. K. (2008). When does guanxi matter? Issues of capitalization and its dark sides. *Journal of Marketing*, *72*(4), 12–28. doi:10.1509/jmkg.72.4.12

Gupta, S., Lehmann, D. R., & Stuart, J. A. (2003). *Valuing Customer*. HBS Marketing Research Paper, No. 03-08.

Gurin, G., Veroff, J., & Feld, S. (1960). *Americans View Their Mental Health*. New York: Basic Books.

Gurtoo, H. C. (2013). *Taste for organic foods*. Retrieved on 19th March 2014 from http://www.hindustantimes.com/lifestyle/food/taste-for-organic-foods/article1-1109620.aspx

Hair, J. F., Black, W. C., Babin, B. J., & Anderson, R. E. (2013). *Multivariate data analysis: a global perspective* (7th ed.). New Delhi: Pearson Education.

Hamer, L. O. (2006). A confirmation perspective on perceived service quality. *Journal of Services Marketing*, *20*(4), 219–232. doi:10.1108/08876040610674571

Han, S.-P., & Shavitt, S. (1994). Persuasion and culture: Advertising appeals in individualistic and collectivistic societies. *Journal of Experimental Social Psychology*, *30*(4), 326–350. doi:10.1006/jesp.1994.1016

Harland, P., Staats, H., & Wilke, H. A. M. (2007). Situational and Personality Factors as Direct or Personal Norm Mediated Predictors of Pro-environmental Behavior: Questions Derived from Norm-activation Theory. *Basic and Applied Social Psychology*, *29*(4), 323–334. doi:10.1080/01973530701665058

Harmancioglu, N., Zachary Finney, R., & Joseph, M. (2009). Impulse purchases of new products: An empirical analysis. *Journal of Product and Brand Management*, *18*(1), 27–37. doi:10.1108/10610420910933344

Harter, J. K., & Schmidt, F. L. (2002). *Well-Being in the Workplace and its Relationships to Business Outcomes: A review of the Gallup studies*. Retrieved Feb 28, 2014, from http://www.nhsemployers.org/~/media/Employers/Documents/Retain%20and%20improve/Harter%20et%20al%202002%20WellbeingReview.pdf

Harter, J. K., Schmidt, F. L., & Hayes, T. L. (2002). Business-Unit-Level Relationship between Employee Satisfaction, Employee Engagement, and Business Outcomes: A Meta-Analysis. *The Journal of Applied Psychology*, *87*(2), 268–279. doi:10.1037/0021-9010.87.2.268 PMID:12002955

Harvey, S., Kelloway, E. K., & Duncan-Leiper, L. (2003). Trust in management as a buffer of the relationships between overload and strain. *Journal of Occupational Health Psychology*, *8*(4), 306–315. doi:10.1037/1076-8998.8.4.306 PMID:14570525

Haslam, P. A. (2004). *The corporate social responsibility system in Latin America and the Caribbean*. Ottawa: Canadian Foundation for the Americas. Retrieved October 20, 2015, from http://www.focal.ca/pdf/csr_04.pdf

Hawkins, D., & Mothershaugh, D. (2012). *Consumer Behavior: Building Marketing Strategy* (12th ed.). McGraw-Hill Education.

Healy, P. M., Hutton, A. P., & Palepu, K. G. (1999). Stock performance and intermediation changes surrounding sustained increases in disclosure. *Contemporary Accounting Research*, *16*(3), 485–520. doi:10.1111/j.1911-3846.1999.tb00592.x

Hecht, T. D., & Allen, N. J. (2005). Exploring links between polychronicity and well-being from the perspective of person-job fit: Does it matter if you prefer to do one thing at a time? *Organizational Behavior and Human Decision Processes*, *98*(2), 155–178. doi:10.1016/j.obhdp.2005.07.004

Heinemann, A. W., Linacre, J. M., Wright, B. D., Hamilton, B. B., & Granger, C. (1994). Prediction of rehabilitation outcomes with disability measures. *Archives of Physical Medicine and Rehabilitation, 75*(2), 133–143. PMID:8311668

Herremaus, I. M., Akathaporn, P., & McInnes, M. (1993). An investigation of corporate social responsibility reputation and economic performance. *Accounting, Organizations and Society, 18*(7-8), 587–604. doi:10.1016/0361-3682(93)90044-7

Heymann, E. (2014, May 26). *The future of Germany as an automaking location.* Retrieved from Deutsche Bank Research: https://www.dbresearch.com/PROD/DBR_INTERNET_EN-PROD/PROD0000000000335484/The+future+of+Germany+as+an+automaking+location.pdf

Hilb, M. (2012). *New corporate governance. Successful board management tools.* New York: Springer. doi:10.1007/978-3-642-23595-5

Hill, H., & Lynchehaun, F. (2002). Organic milk: Attitudes and consumption patterns. *British Food Journal, 104*(7), 526–542. doi:10.1108/00070700210434570

Hirschman, E. C. (1985). Cognitive processes in experimental consumer behavior. *Research on Consumer Behavior, 1*, 67–102.

Hoch, S. J., & Loewenstein, G. F. (1991). Time-inconsistent preferences and consumer self-control. *The Journal of Consumer Research, 17*(4), 492–508. doi:10.1086/208573

Hoekman, B. (1996). Asssessing the General Agreement on Trade in Services. In The Uruguay Round and the Developing Countries. Cambridge, UK: Cambridge University Press.

Hoekman, B., & Mattoo, A. (2008). Services Trade and Growth. In J. A. Marchetti & M. Roy (Eds.), *Opening Markets for Trade in Services: Countries and Sectors in Bilateral and WTO Negotiations.* Cambridge, UK: Cambridge University Press. doi:10.1596/1813-9450-4461

Hoekman, B., Mattoo, A., & Sapir, A. (2007). The Political Economy of Services Trade Liberalization: A Case for International Regulatory Cooperation? *Oxford Review of Economic Policy, 23*(3), 367–391. doi:10.1093/oxrep/grm024

Hofstede, G. (2015). *Country comparison.* Retrieved from http://geert-hofstede.com/

Hofstede, G. (1997). *Cultures and Organizations: Software of the Mind.* New York: McGraw-Hill.

Hofstede, G. (2001). *Culture's Consequences: Comparing Values, Behaviors, Institutions, and Organizations Across Nations.* New Delhi: SAGE.

Holbrook, M. B., & Hirschman, E. C. (1982). The experiential aspects of consumption: Consumer fantasies, feelings, and fun. *The Journal of Consumer Research, 9*(2), 132–140. doi:10.1086/208906

Holland, J. L. (1985). *Making vocational choices: A theory of careers.* Englewood Cliffs, NJ: Prentice-Hall.

Holland, P., Sheehan, C., & De Cieri, H. (2007). Attracting and retaining talent: Exploring human resource development trends in Australia. *Human Resource Development International, 10*(3), 247–262. doi:10.1080/13678860701515158

Holt, D. B. (1998). Does Cultural Capital Structure American Consumption? *The Journal of Consumer Research, 25*(1), 1–25. doi:10.1086/209523

Hom, P.W. & Griffeth, R. W. (1995). *Employee turnover.* Cincinnati: South-Western College Publishing.

Hopkins, M. (1998). *The planetary bargain: Corporate social responsibility comes of age.* London: Macmillan.

Hosseini, & Mohammadi. (2012). Review Banking on Biometric in the World's Banks and Introducing a Biometric Model for Iran's Banking System. *Journal of Basic and Applied Scientific Research, 2*(9), 9152–9160.

Hotelling, H. (1931). The Economics of Exhaustible Resources. *The Journal of Political Economy, 39*(2).

Hotz-Hart, B. (2000). Innovation Networks, Regions, and Globalization. The Oxford Handbook of Economic Geography, 432-450.

Howard, J. A., & Sheth, J. N. (1969). *The theory of buyer behavior* (Vol. 14). New York: Wiley.

Huang, M. H. (2008). The influence of selling behaviors on customer relationships in financial services. *International Journal of Service Industry Management, 19*(4), 458–473. doi:10.1108/09564230810891905

Hunt, S. D., & Morgan, R. M. (1995). The Comparative Advantage Theory of Competition. *Journal of Marketing, 59*(April), 1–15. doi:10.2307/1252069

Hwang, Y. M., & Rho, J. J. (2008). RFID system for centralized reverse supply chain in the apparel industry. In *Proceedings of the 22nd International Symposium and Workshop on Global Supply Chain, Intermodal Transportation and Logistics*. Available at https://www.utoledo.edu/research/ututc/docs/Proceedings_Busan_Symposium_20.pdf

IBFC India Brand Equity Foundation. (2015). Available at http://www.ibef.org/industry/food-industry-presentation

IBM. (2008, August). *Automotive 2020 - Clarity beyond the chaos*. Retrieved from IBM Global Business Services: http://www-07.ibm.com/shared_downloads/6/IBM_Automotive_2020_Study_Clarity_beyond_the_Chaos.pdf

ICGN. (2014). *ICGN global governance principles*. London: International Corporate Governance Network. Retrieved October 23, 2015, from http://www.fsa.go.jp/singi/corporategovernance/siryou/20140930/14.pdf

Inglehart, R. (1981). Post-materialism in an Environment of Insecurity. *The American Political Science Review, 75*(04), 880–900. doi:10.2307/1962290

International Data Corporation's (IDC)'s Business Strategy: 2014 U.S. Consumer Channel Preference Survey Results - Online and Internet Banking Is a Key Component of Omni-Channel Strategy. (n.d.). Retrieved from https://www.idc.com/getdoc.jsp?containerId=FI252651

Internet Society. (2015). *Global Internet Report 2015. Mobile evolution and development of the Internet*. Internet Society Website. Retrieved from: http://www.internetsociety.org/globalinternetreport/section/2

Iribarren, M. M., Jiménez-Giménez, M., García-de Cecilia, J. M., & Rubio-Valladolid, G. (2011). Validación y propiedades psicométricas de la escala de impulsividad estado (EIE). *Actas Españolas de Psiquiatría, 39*(1), 49–60. PMID:21274822

Isenberg, D. J. (2008). The global entrepreneur. *Harvard Business Review, 86*(12), 107–111.

Ittner, C. D., & Larcker, D. F. (1996). Measuring the impact of quality initiatives on firm financial performance. *Advances in the Management of Organizational Quality, 37*.

Ittner, C. D., Larcker, D. F., & Randall, T. (2002). *Performance implications of strategic performance measurement in financial services firms*. Wharton School Working Paper.

Ittner, C. D., & Larcker, D. F. (1997). Quality strategy, strategic control systems, and organizational performance. *Accounting, Organizations and Society, 22*(3-4), 293–314. doi:10.1016/S0361-3682(96)00035-9

Ittner, C. D., & Larcker, D. F. (1998). Are non-financial measures leading indicators of financial performance? An analysis of customer satisfaction. *Journal of Accounting Research, 36*(supplement), 1–35. doi:10.2307/2491304

Ittner, C. D., & Larcker, D. F. (2001). Assessing empirical research in managerial accounting: A value-based management perspective. *Journal of Accounting and Economics, 32*(1), 349–410. doi:10.1016/S0165-4101(01)00026-X

Ittner, C. D., & Larcker, D. F. (2002). Determinants of performance measure choices in worker incentive plans. *Journal of Labor Economics*, 2(S2), S58–S90. doi:10.1086/338674

Ittner, C. D., Larcker, D. F., & Rajan, M. V. (1997). The choice of performance measures in annual 44 bonus contracts. *Accounting Review*, 72, 231–255.

Iyer, E. S. (1989). Unplanned purchases: Knowledge of shopping environment and time pressure. *Journal of Retailing*, 65(1), 40–57.

Jackson, S., & Schuler, R. (1985). A meta-analysis and conceptual critique of research on role ambiguity and role conflict in work settings. *Organizational Behavior and Human Decision Processes*, 36(1), 16–78. doi:10.1016/0749-5978(85)90020-2

Jain, A. K., & Cooper, C. L. (2012). Stress and organizational citizenship behaviors in Indian business process outsourcing organizations. *IIMB Management Review*, 24(3), 155–163. doi:10.1016/j.iimb.2012.06.004

Jansson, J., Marell, A., & Nordlund, A. (2010). Green consumer behavior: Determinants of curtailment and eco-innovation adoption. *Journal of Consumer Marketing*, 27, 358–370.

Jarva, V. (2011). Consumer education and everyday futures work. *Futures*, 43(1), 99–111. doi:10.1016/j.futures.2010.10.016

Jayawardhena, C., Wright, L. T., & Dennis, C. (2007). —Consumers Online: Intentions, Orientations and Segmentation. *International Journal of Retail & Distribution Management*, 35(6), 515–526. doi:10.1108/09590550710750377

Jeyaraj, A., Rottman, J. W., & Lacity, M. C. (2006). A Review of the Predictors, Linkages, and Biases in IT Innovation Adoption Research. *Journal of Information Technology*, 21(1), 1–23. doi:10.1057/palgrave.jit.2000056

Jimmieson, N. L. (2000). Employee reactions to behavioral control under conditions of stress: The moderating role of self-efficacy. *Work and Stress*, 14(3), 262–280. doi:10.1080/02678370010015343

Johnston, J. (2008). The citizen-consumer hybrid: Ideological tensions and the case of whole foods market. *Theory and Society*, 37(3), 229–270. doi:10.1007/s11186-007-9058-5

Jones, M. A., Reynolds, K. E., Weun, S., & Beatty, S. E. (2003). The product-specific nature of impulse buying tendency. *Journal of Business Research*, 56(7), 505–511. doi:10.1016/S0148-2963(01)00250-8

Joo, B. (2006). Best Employer Studies: A Conceptual Model from a Literature Review and a Case Study. *Human Resource Development Review*, 5(2), 228–257. doi:10.1177/1534484306287515

Judge, T. A., & Cable, D. M. (1997). Applicant personality, organizational culture, and organization attraction. *Personnel Psychology*, 50(2), 359–393. doi:10.1111/j.1744-6570.1997.tb00912.x

Junaedi, M. F. S. (2007). The roles of Consumer's knowledge and emotion in ecological issues: An Empirical Study on Green Consumer Behavior. *Gadjah Mada International Journal of Business*, 9(1), 81–99.

Kahan, R. (1998). Using database marketing techniques to enhance your one-to-one marketing initiatives. *Journal of Consumer Marketing*, 15(5), 491–493. doi:10.1108/07363769810235965

Kahn, R. L., & Byosiere, P. (1992). Stress in organizations. In M. D. Dunnette & L. M. Hough (Eds.), *Handbook of industrial and organizational psychology* (Vol. 3, pp. 571–650). Palo Alto, CA: Consulting Psychologists Press.

Kahn, R., Wolfe, D., Quinn, R., Snoek, J., & Rosentbal, R. (1964). *Organizational stress: Studies in role conflict and ambiguity*. New York: Wiley.

Kahn, W. A. (1990). Psychological Conditions of Personal Engagement and Disengagement At Work. *Academy of Management Journal*, 33(4), 692–724. doi:10.2307/256287

Kaiser, T., & Steiner, E. (2013, September 6). *Absurde russische Zölle nerven deutsche Exporteure*. Retrieved from Die Welt: http://www.welt.de/wirtschaft/article119765151/Absurde-russische-Zoelle-nerven-deutsche-Exporteure.html

Kamarulzaman, Y. (2007). Adoption of travel e-shopping in the UK. *International Journal of Retail & Distribution Management*, *35*(9), 703–719. doi:10.1108/09590550710773255

Kanfer, R., & Ackerman, P. L. (1989). Motivation and cognitive abilities: An integrative / aptitude-treatment interaction approach to skill acquisition. *The Journal of Applied Psychology*, *74*(4), 657–690. doi:10.1037/0021-9010.74.4.657

Kapferer, J.-N. (2008). The new strategic brand management: creating and sustaining brand equity. Les editions d'Organization.

Kaplan, R. S., & Norton, D. P. (1992). The balanced scorecard—measures that drive performance. *Harvard Business Review*, *70*(1), 71–79. PMID:10119714

Kaplan, R., & Norton, D. (1996). Using the Balance Scorecard as Strategic Management System. *Harvard Business Review*, (Jan-Feb), 75–85.

Kaplan, R., & Norton, D. (2001). *The Strategy-Focused Organisation*. Harvard Business School Press.

Karmarkar, U. S. (2010). The Industrialization of Information Services. In *Handbook of Service Science*. Springer. doi:10.1007/978-1-4419-1628-0_18

Kasman, A., & Kasman, S. K. (2006). Technical Change in Banking: Evidence from Transition Countries. *International Journal of the Economics of Business*, *13*(1), 129–144. doi:10.1080/13571510500520044

Kasser, T. (2002). *The High Price of Materialism*. Cambridge, MA: MIT Press.

Kaushik, R. K. (2015). Smart Cities Cyber Security in India: The Problems and Solutions. *Cyber Security in India Blogspot*. Retrieved on November 10, 2015, from http://cybersecurityforindia.blogspot.mx/2015/11/smart-cities-cyber-security-in-india.html

Kerlinger, F. N., & Lee, H. B. (2002). *Investigación del comportamiento*. México City, Mexico: McGraw-Hill.

Kim, G., Shin, B., & Lee, H. G. (2009). Understanding dynamics between initial trust and usage intentions of mobile banking. *Information Systems Journal*, *19*(3), 283–311. doi:10.1111/j.1365-2575.2007.00269.x

Kim, H. Y., & Chung, J.-E. (2011). Consumer purchase intention for organic personal care products. *Journal of Consumer Marketing*, *28*(1), 40–47. doi:10.1108/07363761111101930

Kim, O., & Verrecchia, R. E. (1994). Market liquidity and volume around earnings announcements. *Journal of Accounting and Economics*, *17*(1-2), 41–67. doi:10.1016/0165-4101(94)90004-3

Kimura, F., & Lee, H. (n.d.). The Gravity Equation in International Trade in Services. *Review of World Economics*, *142*(1), 92-121.

Kingfisher. (2015). Retrieved from http://www.kingfisherbeerusa.com/heritage.html

Knox, S. (1998). Loyalty Brand Segmentation and the Customer Development Process. *European Management Journal*, *16*(6), 729–737. doi:10.1016/S0263-2373(98)00049-8

Koenig-Lewis, N., Palmer, A., & Moll, A. (2010). Predicting young consumers take up of mobile banking services. *International Journal of Bank Marketing*, *28*(5), 410–432. doi:10.1108/02652321011064917

Kohli, A. K., & Jaworski, B. J. (1990). Market orientation: The construct, research propositions, and managerial implications. *Journal of Marketing*, *54*(2), 1–18. doi:10.2307/1251866

Kolk, A. (2005). Corporate social responsibility in the coffee sector: The dynamics of MNC responses and code development. *European Management Journal*, 23(2), 228–236. doi:10.1016/j.emj.2005.02.003

Kollat, D. T., & Willett, R. P. (1967). Customer impulse purchasing behavior. *JMR, Journal of Marketing Research*, 6(1), 21–31. doi:10.2307/3150160

Koncz-Bruner, J., & Flatness. (2010, October). U.S. International Services Cross-Border Trade in 2009 and Services Supplied Through Affiliates in 2008. *Survey of Current Business*, 18-35.

Kotler, P., & Lee, N. (2005). *Corporate social responsibility. Doing the most good for your company and your cause.* Hoboken, NJ: John Wiley & Sons, Inc.

Koufaris, Kambil, & LaBarbera. (2001). Consumer Behavior in Web-Based Commerce: An Empirical Study. *International Journal of Electronic Commerce*, 6(2).

Koufaris, M. (2002). Applying the technology acceptance model and flow theory to online consumer behavior. *Information Systems Research*, 13(2), 205–223. doi:10.1287/isre.13.2.205.83

Kozlenkova, I. V., Samaha, S. A., & Palmatier, R. W. (2014). Resource-based theory in marketing. *Journal of the Academy of Marketing Science*, 42(1), 1–21. doi:10.1007/s11747-013-0336-7

Krajewski, L., & Ritzman, L. (2002). *Operations Management: Strategy and Analysis* (6th ed.). New York, NY: Prentice-Hall.

Kreiner, G. E. (2006). Consequences of work-home segmentation or integration: A person-environment fit perspective. *Journal of Organizational Behavior*, 27(4), 485–507. doi:10.1002/job.386

Krishnan, B. C., & Hartline, M. D. (2001). Brand equity: Is it more important in services? *Journal of Services Marketing*, 15(5), 328–342. doi:10.1108/EUM0000000005654

Kristensen, L. (1997). *Implementation of organic food in the public sector in New Zealand* (MCom thesis). School of Horticulture, Christchurch Polytechnic, New Zealand.

Kristof-Brown, A. L. (2000). Perceived applicant fit: Distinguishing between recruiters perceptions of person–job and person–organization fit. *Personnel Psychology*, 53(3), 643–671. doi:10.1111/j.1744-6570.2000.tb00217.x

Kristof-Brown, A. L., Zimmerman, R. D., & Johnson, E. C. (2005). Consequences of individuals fit at work: A meta-analysis of person-job, person-organization, person-group, and person supervisor fit. *Personnel Psychology*, 58(2), 281–342. doi:10.1111/j.1744-6570.2005.00672.x

Krystallis, A., & Chryssohoidis, G. (2005). Consumers willingness to pay for organic food: Factors that affect it and variation per organic product type. *British Food Journal*, 107(5), 320–343. doi:10.1108/00070700510596901

Kuhnimhof, T., Buehler, R., Wirtz, M., & Kalinowska, D. (2012, September). Travel trends among young adults in Germany: Increasing multimodality and declining car use for men. *Journal of Transport Geography*, 24, 443–450. doi:10.1016/j.jtrangeo.2012.04.018

Kushnir, T., & Melamed, S. (1991). Work-load, perceived control and psychological distress in Type A/B industrial workers. *Journal of Organizational Behavior*, 12(2), 155–168. doi:10.1002/job.4030120207

Kwon, H.-K. (2004, February). Markets, Institutions, and Politics under Globalization. Industrial Adjustments in the United States and in Germany in the 1990s. *Comparative Political Studies*, 37(1), 88–113. doi:10.1177/0010414003260128

Larsen, V., Sirgy, M. J., & Wright, N. D. (1999). Materialism: The Construct, Measures, Antecedents, and Consequences. *Academy of Marketing Studies Journal*, 3(2), 75–107.

Lascu, D. N., & Yip, G. S. (1994). Total Global Strategy: Managing for Worldwide Competitive Advantage. *Journal of Marketing*, *58*(3), 121. doi:10.2307/1252318

Lassar, W. M., Chris, M., & Lassar, S. S. (2005). The relationship between consumer innovativeness, personal characteristics, and online banking adoption. *International Journal of Bank Marketing*, *23*(2), 176–199. doi:10.1108/02652320510584403

Laukkanen, T., & Kiviniemi, V. (2010). The role of information in mobile banking resistance. *International Journal of Bank Marketing*, *28*(5), 372–388. doi:10.1108/02652321011064890

Laukkanen, T., & Pasanen, M. (2009). Mobile banking innovators and early adopters: How they differ from other online users. *Journal of Direct, Data and Digital Marketing Practice*, *10*(3), 294–261.

LaValle, S., Lesser, E., Shockley, R., Hopkins, M. S., & Kruschwitz, N. (2011). Big Data, Analytics and the Path from Insights to Value. *MIT Sloan Management Review*, *52*(2), 21–31.

Lea, E., & Worsley, T. (2005). Australians organic food beliefs, demographics and values. *British Food Journal*, *107*(11), 855–869. doi:10.1108/00070700510629797

Lee, H., & Billington, C. (1992). Managing supply Chain Inventory: Pitfalls and Opportunities. *Sloan Management Review*, *3*, 65–73.

Lee, K. (2009). Gender differences in Hong Kong adolescent consumers green purchasing behaviour. *Journal of Consumer Marketing*, *26*(2), 87–96. doi:10.1108/07363760910940456

Lee, T. Y., & Bradlow, E. T. (2011). Automated marketing research using online customer reviews. *JMR, Journal of Marketing Research*, *4*(5), 881–894. doi:10.1509/jmkr.48.5.881

Lee, Y.-H., Hsieb, Y.-C., & Chen, Y.-H. (2013). An investigation of employees use of e-learning systems: Applying the technology acceptance model. *Behaviour & Information Technology*, *32*(2), 173–189. doi:10.1080/0144929X.2011.577190

Lennon, C. (2009). *Trade in Services and Trade in Goods: Differences and Complementarities*. The Vienna Institute for International Economic Studies Working Papers 53.

Levitt, T. (1983). The globalization of markets. *Harvard Business Review*, *61*(3), 92–102.

Lewin, K. (1935). *A dynamic theory of personality*. New York: McGraw-Hill.

Lewis, R. E., & Heckman, R. J. (2006). Talent Management: A critical review. *Human Resource Management Review*, *16*(2), 139–154. doi:10.1016/j.hrmr.2006.03.001

Liao, C., Chen, J. L., & Yen, D. (2007). Theory of planning behavior (TPB) and customer satisfaction in the continued use of e-service: An integrated model. *Computers in Human Behavior*, *23*(6), 2804–2822. doi:10.1016/j.chb.2006.05.006

Lim, N. (2003). Consumers perceived risk: Sources versus consequences. *Electronic Commerce Research and Applications*, *2*(3), 216–228. doi:10.1016/S1567-4223(03)00025-5

Lin, J. S., & Chang, H. C. (2011). The role of technology readiness in self-service technology acceptance. *Managing Service Quality*, *21*(4), 424–444. doi:10.1108/09604521111146289

Lipe, M., & Salterio, S. (2000). The balanced scorecard: Judgmental effects of common and unique performance measures. *Accounting Review*, *75*(3), 283–298. doi:10.2308/accr.2000.75.3.283

Lipe, M., & Salterio, S. (2002). A note on the judgmental effects of the balanced scorecards information organization. *Accounting, Organizations and Society*, *27*(6), 531–540. doi:10.1016/S0361-3682(01)00059-9

Liu, L., & Nath, H. (2016). *Information and Communications Technology (ICT) and Services Trade.* SHSU Economics and International Business Working Paper No. 1601.

Liu, L., & Nath, H. (2013). Information and Communications Technology (ICT) and Trade in Emerging Market Economies. *Emerging Markets Finance and Trade, 49*(6), 67–87. doi:10.2753/REE1540-496X490605

Liu, L., Nath, H., & Tochkov, K. (2015). Comparative Advantages in U.S. Bilateral Services Trade with China and India. *Journal of Asian Economics, 38,* 79–92. doi:10.1016/j.asieco.2015.04.002

Lockwood, N. R. (2006). Talent management: driver for organizational success. *SHRM Research Quarterly.* Retrieved Feb 19, 2015 from www.shrm.org

Logsdon, J. M., Thomas, D. E., & Van Buren, H. J. III. (2006, March). Corporate social responsibility in large Mexican firms. *Journal of Corporate Citizenship, 2006*(21), 51–60. doi:10.9774/GLEAF.4700.2006.sp.00007

López-Fernández, A. M. (2013). Influence of corporate social responsibility on consumers shopping behavior and determining competitive posture of the firm. *Journal of Marketing Analytics, 1*(4), 222–233. doi:10.1057/jma.2013.18

López-Fernández, A. M. (2015). Effect on stakeholders perception of CSR: Analysis of information dynamics through social media. *International Journal of Business Competition and Growth, 4*(1/2), 24–43. doi:10.1504/IJBCG.2015.070662

Luarn, P., & Lin, H. H. (2005). Toward an understanding of the behavioural intention to use mobile banking. *Computers in Human Behavior, 21*(6), 873–891. doi:10.1016/j.chb.2004.03.003

Luning, P. A., Marcelis, W. J., & Jongen, W. M. F. (2002). *Food Quality Management: a techno-managerial approach.* Wageningen: Wageningen Pers.

Luo, X., Sivakumar, K., & Liu, S. S. (2005). Globalization, Marketing Resources, and Performance: Evidence from China. *Journal of the Academy of Marketing Science, 33*(1), 50–65. doi:10.1177/0092070304265050

Luthans, F., & Peterson, S. J. (2005). Employee Engagement and Manager Self Efficacy: Implications for Managerial Effectiveness and Development. *Journal of Management Development, 21*(5), 376–387. doi:10.1108/02621710210426864

Lutz, E., & El Serafy. (1989). *Environmental and Resource Accounting: An Overview.* Environment Department Working Paper No 6. The World Bank.

Maguire, M. (2011, January). The future of corporate social responsibility reporting. *The Frederick S. Pardee center for the study of the longer-range future. Issues in Brief (Alan Guttmacher Institute),* (19): 1–8.

Maignan, I., & Ralston, D. A. (2002). Corporate social responsibility in Europe and the U.S.: Insights from businesses self-presentations. *Journal of International Business Studies, 33*(3), 497–514. doi:10.1057/palgrave.jibs.8491028

Mai, N. T. T., Jung, K., Lantz, G., & Loeb, S. G. (2003). An exploratory investigation into impulse buying behavior in a transitional economy: A study of urban consumers in Vietnam. *Journal of International Marketing, 11*(2), 13–35. doi:10.1509/jimk.11.2.13.20162

Makatouni, A. (2002). What motivates consumers to buy organic food in UK?British Food Journal, 104(3-5), 345-352.

Makikangas, A., & Kinnunen, U. (2003). Psychosocial work stressors and well-being: Self-esteem and optimism as moderators in a one-year longitudinal sample. *Personality and Individual Differences, 35*(3), 537–557. doi:10.1016/S0191-8869(02)00217-9

Malhotra, N. K. (2008). *Marketing research: An applied orientation.* Pearson Education India. doi:10.1108/S1548-6435(2008)4

Mangaliso, M. P. (2001). Building competitive advantage from ubuntu: Management lessons from South Africa. *The Academy of Management Executive*, *15*(3), 23–33. doi:10.5465/AME.2001.5229453

Mann, C. L., & Civril, D. (2008). *U.S. International Trade in Other Private Services: Do Arm's Length and Intra-Company Trade Differ?*. Brandeis Business School, Brandeis University.

Marchand, D. A., & Peppard, J. (2013). Why IT Fumbles Analytics. *Harvard Business Review*, *91*(1), 104–112.

Mariampolski, H. (2006). Ethnography for marketers: A guide to consumer immersion. *Sage (Atlanta, Ga.)*.

Martin, A., Jekel, R., & Simons, E. (2011). *Better Decision Making with Proper Business Intelligence*. Chicago, IL: A.T. Kearney.

Matten, D., & Moon, J. (2008). Implicit and explicit CSR: A conceptual framework for a comparative understanding of corporate social responsibility. *Academy of Management Review*, *33*(2), 404–424. doi:10.5465/AMR.2008.31193458

Mattila, A. S., & Wirtz, J. (2002). The impact of knowledge types on the consumer search process: An investigation in the context of credence services. *International Journal of Service Industry Management*, *13*(3), 214–230. doi:10.1108/09564230210431947

Mattoo, A., Rathindran, R., & Subramanian, A. (2006). Measuring Services Trade Liberalization and Its Impact on Economic Growth: An Illustration. *Journal of Economic Integration*, *21*(1), 64–98. doi:10.11130/jei.2006.21.1.64

Mattoo, A., Stern, R. M., & Zanini, G. (2008). *A Handbook of International Trade in Services*. Oxford, UK: Oxford University Press.

MCA. (2009). *Corporate Governance voluntary guidelines*. New Delhi: Ministry of Corporate Affairs, Government of India. Retrieved October 22, 2015, from http://www.mca.gov.in/Ministry/latestnews/CG_Voluntary_Guidelines_2009_24dec2009.pdf

McAfee, A., & Brynjolfsson, E. (2012). Big Data: The Management Revolution. *Harvard Business Review*, *90*(10), 60–68. PMID:23074865

McCarthy, N. (2013, September 13). *Germany is the World's No. 1 Automobile Exporter By Far*. Retrieved from Statista: http://www.statista.com/chart/1451/germany-is-the-worlds-no-one-automobile-exporter-by-far/

McGregor, S. L. T. (2007). Sustainable consumer empowerment through critical consumer education: A typology of consumer education approaches. *International Journal of Consumer Studies*, *29*(5), 437–447. doi:10.1111/j.1470-6431.2005.00467.x

Menon, K., & Bansal, H. S. (2007). Exploring consumer experience of social power during service consumption. *International Journal of Service Industry Management*, *18*(1), 89–104. doi:10.1108/09564230710732911

Merrie, B. (2000). Price and Brand Name as Indicators of Quality Dimensions of Customer Durables. *Journal of the Academy of Marketing Science*, *28*(3), 359–374. doi:10.1177/0092070300283005

Miao, C. H., Wei, Y. D., & Ma, H. (2007). Technological Learning and Innovation in China in the Context of Globalization. *Eurasian Geography and Economics*, *48*(6), 713–732. doi:10.2747/1539-7216.48.6.713

Michael, D. (2014). Consumer's intentions to use e-readers. *Journal of Computer Information Systems*, (Winter), 66–76.

Mielach, D. (2013). *Consumers Overestimate benefits of organic food*. Retrieved on 19th March, 2014 from http://www.businessnewsdaily.com/4257-organic-food-labels.html

Misra, S. K., Huang, C. L., & Ott, S. L. (1991). Consumer willing to pay for pesticide-free fresh produce. *Western Journal of Agricultural Economics*, (16): 218–227.

Mohd, N. F., Banwet, D. K., & Ravi, S. (2007). Information risks management in supply chains: An assessment and mitigation framework. *Journal of Enterprise Information Management, 20*(6), 677–699. doi:10.1108/17410390710830727

Mohr, D., Müller, N., Krieg, A., Gao, P., Kaas, H.-W., Krieger, A., & Hensley, R. (2013, August). *The road to 2020 and beyond: What's driving the global automotive industry?* Retrieved from McKinsey & Company: http://www.mckinsey.com/~/media/mckinsey/dotcom/client_service/automotive%20and%20assembly/pdfs/mck_the_road_to_2020_and_beyond.ashx

Moon, J. (2007). *The contribution of corporate social responsibility to sustainable development. Sustainable development.* John Wiley & Sons, Ltd and ERP Environment.

Moon, J. W., & Kim, Y. G. (2001). Extending the TAM for a world-wide-web context. *Information & Management, 38*(4), 217–230. doi:10.1016/S0378-7206(00)00061-6

Moore, J. E. (2000). One road to turnover: An examination of work exhaustion in technology professionals. *Management Information Systems Quarterly, 24*(1), 141–168. doi:10.2307/3250982

Moorman, R. H., & Blakely, G. L. (1995). Individualism-collectivism as an individual difference predictor of organizational citizenship behavior. *Journal of Organizational Behavior, 16*(2), 127–142. doi:10.1002/job.4030160204

Morey, T., Forbath, T., & Schoop, A. (2015). Customer Data: Designing for Transparency and Trust. *Harvard Business Review, 93*(5), 97–105.

Morgan Lewis. (2014). *IT Governance blog, List of Data Breaches and Cyber Attacks.* Retrieved on November 15, 2015, from http://www.itgovernance.co.uk/blog/list-of-data-breaches-and-cyber-attacks-in-july/

Morgan Lewis. (2016). *Privacy and Cyber Security, Corporate information available publicly on Internet.* Retrieved from www.morganlewis.com

Moschis, G. P., & Churchill, G. A. (1978). Consumer Socialization: A Theoretical and Empirical Analysis. *JMR, Journal of Marketing Research, 15*(4), 544–609. doi:10.2307/3150629

Muchinsky, P. M., & Monahan, C. I. (1987). What is person-environment congruence? Supplementary versus complementary models of fit. *Journal of Vocational Behavior, 31*(1), 268–277. doi:10.1016/0001-8791(87)90043-1

Mukerji, C. (1983). *From Graven Images: Patterns of Modern Materialism.* New York: Columbia University Press.

Mulki, J. P., Jaramillo, F., & Locander, W. B. (2008). Effect of ethical climate on turnover intention: Linking attitudinal- and stress theory. *Journal of Business Ethics, 78*(12), 559–574. doi:10.1007/s10551-007-9368-6

Mulki, J. P., Lassk, F. G., & Fernando, J. (2008). The effect of self-efficacy on salesperson work overload and pay satisfaction. *Journal of Personal Selling & Sales Management, 28*(3), 283–295. doi:10.2753/PSS0885-3134280305

Murray, H. A. (1938). *Explorations in Personality.* Boston: Houghton Mifflin.

Myers, D. G. (2000). The Funds, Friends, and Faith of Happy People. *The American Psychologist, 55*(1), 56–67. doi:10.1037/0003-066X.55.1.56 PMID:11392866

Nadkarni, M. V., & Ravichandran, M. (1987). Economics of Preventing Industrial Pollution. In Economics of Environment. Lancer International.

Nair, I., & Mukunda Das, V. (2012). Using Technology Acceptance Model to assess teachers attitude towards use of technology as teaching tool: A SEM Approach. *International Journal of Computers and Applications*, *42*(2), 1–6. doi:10.5120/5661-7691

Nakahara, T. (1997). Innovation in a Borderless World Economy. *Research Technology Management*, *40*(3), 7.

Narula, R. (2014). *Globalization and Technology: Interdependence, Innovation Systems and Industrial Policy*. John Wiley & Sons.

Narver, J. C. & Slater, S. F. (1990). The effect of a market orientation on business profitability. *Journal of Marketing*, *54*, 20-35.

Nassbaum, B. (2016). *Smart Cities – The Cyber Security and Privacy Implications of Ubiquitous Urban Computing*. The Center for Internet and Society. Retrieved on March 20, 2016, from http://cyberlaw.stanford.edu/blog/2016/02/smart-cities

Natura. (2015). *Our history*. Retrieved from https://www.naturabrasil.fr/en/about-us/our-history

Neely, A. (1999). The performance measurement revolution: Why now and what next? *International Journal of Operations & Production Management*, *19*(2), 205–228. doi:10.1108/01443579910247437

Nerantzidis, M., Filos, J., & Lazarides, T. G. (2012, May). The puzzle of corporate governance definition(s): A content analysis. *Corporate Board: Role. Duties & Composition*, *8*(2), 13–23.

Netemeyer, R. G., Johnston, M., & Burton, S. (1990). An analysis of role conflict and role ambiguity in a structural equations framework. *The Journal of Applied Psychology*, *75*(2), 148–157. doi:10.1037/0021-9010.75.2.148

Netemeyer, R. G., Maxham, J. G. III, & Pullig, C. (2005). Conflicts in the work-family interface: Links to job stress, customer service employee performance, and customer purchase intent. *Journal of Marketing*, *69*(2), 130–143. doi:10.1509/jmkg.69.2.130.60758

Newton, C. J., & Jimmieson, N. L. (2009). Subjective fit with organizational culture: An investigation of moderating effects in the work stressor-employee adjustment relationship. *International Journal of Human Resource Management*, *26*(8), 1770–1789. doi:10.1080/09585190903087198

Ngai, E. W. T., & Gunasekaran, A. (2007). A review for mobile commerce research and applications. *Decision Support Systems*, *43*(1), 3–15. doi:10.1016/j.dss.2005.05.003

Ngo, H. Y., Foley, S., & Loi, R. (2005). Work role stressors and turnover intentions: A study of professional clergy in Hong Kong. *International Journal of Human Resource Management*, *16*(11), 2133–2146. doi:10.1080/09585190500315141

Niello, J. V. (2006). *Responsabilidad social empresarial (RSE) desde la perspectiva de los consumidores*. Santiago, Chile: UN CEPAL.

Normalini, M. K., & Ramayah, T. (2012), Biometrics Technologies Implementation in Internet Banking Reduce Security Issues? *Procedia- Social and Behavioral Sciences*, *65*, 364-369.

Nunnally, J. C. (1967). *Psychometric Theory* (2nd ed.). New York, NY: McGraw-Hill.

Oakey, R. P., & Cooper, S. Y. (1989). High technology industry, agglomeration and the potential for peripherally sited small firms. *Regional Studies*, *23*(4), 347–360. doi:10.1080/00343408912331345542

OCass, A., & Ngo, L. V. (2011). Winning through Innovation and Marketing: Lessons from Australia and Vietnam. *Industrial Marketing Management*, *40*(8), 1319–1329. doi:10.1016/j.indmarman.2011.10.004

OConnor, A., & Meister, M. (2008, March). Corporate social responsibility attribute rankings. *Public Relations Review*, *34*(1), 49–50. doi:10.1016/j.pubrev.2007.11.004

ODonovan, G. (2002). Environmental disclosures in the annual report: Extending the applicability and predictive power of legitimacy theory. *Accounting, Auditing & Accountability Journal*, *15*(3), 344–371. doi:10.1108/09513570210435870

ODriscoll, M. P., & Beehr, T. A. (1994). Supervisor behaviors, role stressors and uncertainty as predictors of personal outcomes for subordinates. *Journal of Organizational Behavior*, *15*(2), 141–155. doi:10.1002/job.4030150204

OECD. (2005, July 13). *Corporate Governance*. Retrieved August 20, 2015, from Glossary of statistical terms: https://stats.oecd.org/glossary/detail.asp?ID=6778

OECD. (2008). *Russian Federation. Strengthening the policy framework for investment*. Paris: OECD Investment Policy Reviews.

OECD. (2011). *OECD Guidelines for Multinational Enterprises*. OECD Publishing. Retrieved November 13, 2013, from http://www.oecd-ilibrary.org/governance/oecd-guidelines-for-multinational-enterprises_9789264115415-en

OECD. (2014). The digital economy today. In *Measuring the Digital Economy: A New Perspective*. Paris: OECD Publishing; doi:10.1787/9789264221796-5-en

Ofek, E. (2002). *Customer Profitability and Lifetime Value*. Harvard Business School (Publication reference 9-503-019).

Okechukwu, O. M., & Majesty, E. I. (2012). ATM Security Using Fingerprint Biometric Identifer: An Investigative Study. *International Journal of Advanced Computer Science and Applications*, *3*(4), 68–72. doi:10.14569/IJACSA.2012.030412

Olshavsky, R. W., & Granbois, D. H. (1979). Consumer decision making-fact or fiction? *The Journal of Consumer Research*, *6*(2), 93–100. doi:10.1086/208753

Ondrus, J., & Pigneur, Y. (2006). Towards A Holistic Analysis of Mobile Payments: A Multiple Perspectives Approach. *Electronic Commerce Research and Applications*, *5*(3), 246–257. doi:10.1016/j.elerap.2005.09.003

Organ, D. W. (1997). Organizational citizenship behavior: Its construct clean-up time. *Human Performance*, *10*(2), 85–97. doi:10.1207/s15327043hup1002_2

Örtqvist, D., & Wincent, J. (2006). Prominent consequences of role stress: A meta-analytic review. *International Journal of Stress Management*, *13*(4), 399–422. doi:10.1037/1072-5245.13.4.399

OShaughnessy, J., & OShaughnessy, N. J. (2002). Marketing, the Consumer Society and Hedonism. *European Journal of Marketing*, *36*(5/6), 524–547. doi:10.1108/03090560210422871

Oumlil, A. B., & Williams, A. J. (2000). Consumer education programs for mature consumers. *Journal of Services Marketing*, *14*(3), 232–243. doi:10.1108/08876040010327239

Oxxo. (2015). *Nuestra historia*. Retrieved from http://www.oxxo.com/quienes-somos/historia.php

Ozer, M., & Cebeci, U. (2010). The Role of Globalization in New Product Development. *Engineering Management. IEEE Transactions on*, *57*(2), 168–180.

Padel, S., & Foster, C. (2005). Exploring the gap between attitudes and behaviour. *British Food Journal*, *107*(8), 606–625. doi:10.1108/00070700510611002

Parker, S. K., & Sprigg, C. A. (1999). Minimizing strain and maximizing learning: The role of job demands, job control, and proactive personality. *The Journal of Applied Psychology*, *84*(6), 925–939. doi:10.1037/0021-9010.84.6.925 PMID:10639910

Park, S. Y. (2009). An Analysis of the Technology Acceptance Model in Understanding University Students' Behavioral Intention to Use e-Learning. *Journal of Educational Technology & Society*, *12*(3), 150–162.

Park, S.-Y., & Sohn, S. H. (2012). Exploring the normative influences of social norms on individual environmental behavior. *Journal of Global Scholars of Marketing Science: Bridging Asia and the World*, *22*(2), 183–194. doi:10.108 0/12297119.2012.655142

Passaris, C. E. (2006). The Business of Globalization and the Globalization of Business. *Journal of Comparative International Management*, *9*(1).

Patten, D. (1991). Exposure, legitimacy, and social disclosure. *Journal of Accounting and Public Policy*, *10*(4), 297–308. doi:10.1016/0278-4254(91)90003-3

Patton, J. H., Stanford, M. S., & Barratt, E. S. (1995). Factor structure of the barratt impulsiveness scale. *Journal of Clinical Psychology*, *51*(6), 768–774. doi:10.1002/1097-4679(199511)51:6<768::AID-JCLP2270510607>3.0.CO;2-1 PMID:8778124

Patton, M. Q. (1990). *Qualitative Evaluation and Research Methods*. Thousand Oaks, CA: Sage.

Paul, I., & Marion, D. (2003). Successful New Product Pricing Practices: A Contingency Approach. *Marketing Letters*, *14*(4), 289–305. doi:10.1023/B:MARK.0000012473.92160.3d

Pavlou, P. A. (2003). Consumer acceptance of electronic commerce: Integrating trust and risk with the technology acceptance model. *International Journal of Electronic Commerce*, *7*(3), 101–134.

Pechtl, H. (2008). Price knowledge structures relating to grocery products. *Journal of Product and Brand Management*, *17*(7), 485–496. doi:10.1108/10610420810916380

Pederson Christian, S. (2000). Sparsing Risk and Return in CAPM: A General Utility Based Model. *European Journal of Operational Research*, *123*(3), 628–639. doi:10.1016/S0377-2217(99)00114-9

Peinado-Vara, E. (2006). Corporate social responsibility in Latin America. *Journal of Corporate Citizenship*, *2006*(21), 61–69. doi:10.9774/GLEAF.4700.2006.sp.00008

Perea y Monsuwé, T., Dellaert, B. G. C., & de Ruyter, K. (2004). What drives consumers to shop online? A literature review. *International Journal of Service Industry Management*, *15*(1), 102–121. doi:10.1108/09564230410523358

Perez, A., García de los Salmonesm, M., & Rodríguez del Bosque, I. (2013). (in press). The Effect of Corporate Associations on Consumer Behavior. *European Journal of Marketing*, *47*(1).

Perraudin William, R. M., & Sorensen, B. E. (2000). The Demand of Risky Assets: Sample Selection and Household Portfolios. *Journal of Econometrics*, *97*(1), 117–144. doi:10.1016/S0304-4076(99)00069-X

Perrea, T. G., Grunert, K., Krystallis, A., Zhou, Y., Huang, G., & Hue, Y. (2014). Testing and validation of a hierarchical values-attitudes model in the context of green food in China. *Asia Pacific Journal of Marketing and Logistics*, *26*(2), 296–314. doi:10.1108/APJML-09-2013-0106

Perrings, C., Gilbert, A., Pearce, D., & Harrison, A. (1989). *Natural Resource Accounts for Botswana - Environmental Accounting for a Natural Resource Based Economy*. London: Paper.

Pescher, C., Reichhart, P., & Spann, M. (2014). Consumer decision-making processes in mobile viral marketing campaigns. *Journal of Interactive Marketing*, *28*(1), 43–54. doi:10.1016/j.intmar.2013.08.001

Peter, P., & Krishnakumar, S. (2010). Emotional Intelligence, Impulse Buying and Self-Esteem: The Predictive Validity of Two Ability Measures of Emotional Intelligence. *Advances in Consumer Research. Association for Consumer Research (U. S.)*, 37877–37878.

Peterson, M. F., Smith, P. B., Akande, A., Ayestaran, S., Bochner, S., Callan, V., & Viedge, C. et al. (1995). Role conflict, ambiguity, and overload: A 21-nation study. *Academy of Management Journal*, *38*(2), 429–452. doi:10.2307/256687

Peterson, R. A. (1994). A meta-analysis of Cronbachs coefficient alpha. *The Journal of Consumer Research*, *21*(2), 381–391. doi:10.1086/209405

Pickett-Baker, J., & Ozaki, R. (2008). Pro-environmental products: Marketing influence on consumer purchase decision. *Journal of Consumer Marketing*, *25*(5), 281–293. doi:10.1108/07363760810890516

Pikkarainen, T., Pikkarainen, K., Karjaluoto, H., & Pahnila, S. (2004). Consumer acceptance of online banking: An extension of the technology acceptance model. *Internet Research: Electronic Networking Applications and Policy*, *14*(3), 224–235. doi:10.1108/10662240410542652

Piron, F. (1991). Defining impulse purchasing. *Advances in Consumer Research. Association for Consumer Research (U. S.)*, *18*, 509–514.

Piron, F. (1993). A comparison of emotional reactions experienced by planned, unplanned and impulse purchasers. *Advances in Consumer Research. Association for Consumer Research (U. S.)*, *20*, 341–344.

Planning and Coordination Department. (2012). *Economic Survey:2011-12*. Government of Odisha.

Podsakoff, P. M., Mackenzie, S. B., Moorman, R. H., & Fetter, R. (1990). Transformational leader behaviors and their effects on followers trust in leader, satisfaction, and organizational citizenship behaviors. *The Leadership Quarterly*, *1*(2), 107–142. doi:10.1016/1048-9843(90)90009-7

Polese, M., & Verreault, R. (1989). Trade in Information-Intensive Services: How and Why Regions Develop Export Advantages. *Canadian Public Policy*, *XV*, 4, 376–386.

Pollay, R. W. (1986). The Distorted Mirror: Reflections on the Unintended Consequences of Advertising. *Journal of Marketing*, *50*(2), 18. doi:10.2307/1251597

Porter, M. E., & Kramer, M. R. (2006, December). Strategy and society. The link between competitive advantage and corporate social responsibility. *Harvard Business Review*, *84*(12), 78–92. PMID:17183795

Powell, T. C., & Dent-Micallef, A. (1997). Information technology as competitive advantage: The role of human, business, and technology resources. *Strategic Management Journal*, *18*(5), 375-405.

Prabhupada, A. C., & Swami, B. (1995). *Teachings of Lord Chaitanya: The Golden Avatar*. The Bhaktivedanta Book Trust.

Pramod Kumar Mishra, B. (2013, January). Consumer behaviour, customer satisfaction vis-a-vis brand performance: An empirical study of dairy food supply chain in India. *International Journal of Indian Culture and Business Management*, *7*(3), 399–412. doi:10.1504/IJICBM.2013.056216

Pratt, L., & Fintel, E. (2002). Environmental management as an indicator of business responsibility in Central America. In P. Utting (Ed.), *The greening of business in developing countries: Rhetoric, reality and prospects* (pp. 41–57). London: Zed Books & UNRISD.

PricewaterhouseCoopers. (2016). Turnaround and Transformation in Cyber Security. In The Global State of Information Security. PwC.

PRWEB. (2013). *Organic Food market in India set for incessant growth finds TechSci Research report.* Retrieved on 22nd February, 2014 from http://www.prweb.com/releases/2013/9/prweb11174562.htm

Punnoose, A. C. (2012). Determinants of Intention to Use eLearning Based on the Technology Acceptance Model. *Journal of Information Technology Education: Research, 11*, 301–337.

Purushottam, L. (2012, January). Measuring satisfaction in buyer supplier relationship from suppliers perspective. *International Journal of Business Performance and Supply Chain Modelling, 4*(1), 60–74. doi:10.1504/IJBPSCM.2012.044974

Quest Trend Magazine. (2015a, June 11). *How the 10 largest automakers have internationalized their production.* Retrieved from Quest Trend Magazine: http://www.quest-trendmagazine.com/en/automobile-industry/economic-trends/internationalization/internationalization-of-production-by-the-automobile-manufacturers.html

Quest Trend Magazine. (2015b, June 15). *The dramatic internationalization of the locations of worldwide automobile production.* Retrieved from Quest Trend Magazine: http://www.quest-trendmagazine.com/en/automobile-industry/economic-trends/internationalization/internationalization-of-automobile-production.html

Quinn, J. B. (1992). *Intelligent Enterprise: A Knowledge and Service Based Paradigm for Industry.* The Free Press.

Radhakrishnan, S. (2006). *The Bhagvadgita, 24th Impression.* Harper Collins Publishers.

Rajagopal. (2005). Measuring Variability Factors in Consumer Values for Profit Optimization in a Firm – A Framework for Analysis. *Journal of Economics and Management, 1*(1), 85-103.

Rajagopal. (2006a). Measuring Customer Value Gaps: An Empirical Analysis in the Mexican Retail Market. *Economic Issue, 10*(1), 19-40.

Rajagopal. (2006b). Measuring Customer Value and Market Dynamics for New Products of a Firm: An Analytical Construct for Gaining Competitive Advantage. *Global Business and Economics Review, 8*(3-4), 187-205.

Rajagopal. (2011). Impact of Radio Advertisements on Buying Behaviour of Urban Commuters. *International Journal of Retail and Distribution Management, 39*(7), 480-503.

Rajagopal, , & Sanchez, R. (2004). Conceptual Analysis of Brand Architecture and Relations within Product Categories. *The Journal of Brand Management, 11*(3), 233–247. doi:10.1057/palgrave.bm.2540169

Ramanathan, S., & Menon, G. (2006). Time-varying effects of chronic hedonic goals on impulsive behavior. *JMR, Journal of Marketing Research, 43*(4), 628–641. doi:10.1509/jmkr.43.4.628

Rana, T., & Kamala, M. A. (2012). Evaluating biometrics for online banking: The case for usability. *International Journal of Information Management, 32*(5), 489–494. doi:10.1016/j.ijinfomgt.2012.07.001

Rao, C. H. H. (1991). Agricultural Development and Ecological Degradation. In India: The Emerging Challenges. Sage Publications.

Rattner, S. (2011). The Secrets of Germany's Success: What Europe's Manufacturing Powerhouse Can Teach America. *Foreign Affairs, 90*(4), 7–11.

Reddy, P. (2002). *The Globalization of Corporate R & D: Implications for Innovation Systems in Host Countries.* Routledge.

Reichheld, F. F., & Sasser, W. E. (1990). Zero Defections: Quality Comes to Services. *Harvard Business Review, 68*, 105–111. PMID:10107082

Reinartz, W. J., & Kumar, V. (2000). On the Profitability of Long-Life Customers in a Non-contractual Setting: An Empirical investigation and implementation for Marketing. *Journal of Marketing, 64*(4), 17–35. doi:10.1509/jmkg.64.4.17.18077

Reinartz, W. J., & Kumar, V. (2002). The Mismanagement of Customer Loyalty. *Harvard Business Review*, (July), 4–12. PMID:12140857

Reuters. (2014, August 20). *Stress für Exporteure nach Russland*. Retrieved from Handelsblatt: http://www.handelsblatt.com/politik/konjunktur/nachrichten/export-einbrueche-stress-fuer-exporteure-nach-russland/10358412.html

Rezaei Dolatabadi, H., & Ebrahimi, H. (2010). —Factors Influencing Iranian Consumers' Trust in Internet Shopping‖. *European Journal of Soil Science*, *16*(2).

Rice, R. W., McFarlin, D. B., Hunt, R. G., & Near, J. P. (1985). Organizational work and the perceived quality of life: Toward a conceptual model. *Academy of Management Review*, *10*(2), 296–310.

Richard, N. B. (1989). Three Dilemmas of Environmental Accounting. *Ecological Economics*, *40*(1).

Richins, M. (1987). Media, Materialism, and Human Happiness. *Advances in Consumer Research. Association for Consumer Research (U. S.)*, *14*, 352–356.

Richins, M. L. (1994a). Special Possessions and the Expression of Material Values. *The Journal of Consumer Research*, *21*(3), 522–533. doi:10.1086/209415

Richins, M. L. (1994b). Valuing Things: The Public and Private Meanings of Possessions. *The Journal of Consumer Research*, *21*(3), 504–521. doi:10.1086/209414

Richins, M. L., & Dawson, S. (1992). A Consumer Values Orientation for Materialism and its Measurement: Scale Development and Validation. *The Journal of Consumer Research*, *19*(3), 303–316. doi:10.1086/209304

Rindfleisch, A., Burroughs, J. E., & Denton, F. (1997). Family Structure, Materialism, and Compulsive Consumption. *The Journal of Consumer Research*, *23*(4), 312–325. doi:10.1086/209486

Riquelme, H. E., & Rios, R. E. (2010). The moderating effect of gender in the adoption of mobile banking. *International Journal of Bank Marketing*, *28*(5), 328–341. doi:10.1108/02652321011064872

Rizzo, J., House, R. J., & Lirtzman, S. I. (1970). Role conflict and ambiguity in complex organizations. *Administrative Science Quarterly*, *15*(2), 150–163. doi:10.2307/2391486

Robertson, R. (2012). Globalisation or glocalisation? *Journal of International Communication*, *18*(2), 191–208. doi:10.1080/13216597.2012.709925

Robinson, I. (2006). *Human resource management in organisations: The theory and practice of high performance*. London: Chartered Institute of Personnel and Development.

Rochlin, S., Witter, K., Monaghan, P., & Murray, V. (2005). *Putting the corporate into corporate responsibility (CR)*. Greenleaf Publishing Limited and Accountability.

Roddy, G., Cowan, C., & Hutchinson, G. (1994). Organic food: A description of the Irish market. *British Food Journal*, *96*(4), 3–10. doi:10.1108/00070709410060998

Rogerson, S. (2004). Aspects of social responsibility in the information society. In G. Doukidis, N. Mylonopoulos, & N. Pouloudi (Eds.), *Social and economic transformation in the digital era* (pp. 31–46). Hershey, PA: Idea Group Publishing. doi:10.4018/978-1-59140-158-2.ch003

Rook, D. W., & Gardner, M. P. (1993). In the mood: Impulse buying's affective antecedents. *Research in Consumer Behavior*, *6*(7), 1-28.

Rook, D. W. (1987). The buying impulse. *The Journal of Consumer Research*, *14*(2), 189–199. doi:10.1086/209105

Rook, D. W., & Fisher, R. J. (1995). Normative influences on impulsive buying behavior. *The Journal of Consumer Research, 22*(3), 305–313. doi:10.1086/209452

Rook, D. W., & Gardner, M. P. (1993). In the mood: Impulse buying's affective antecedents. *Research in Consumer Behavior, 6*, 1–28.

Rook, D. W., & Hoch, S. J. (1985). Consuming impulse. *Advances in Consumer Research. Association for Consumer Research (U. S.), 12*, 23–27.

Rosa-Díaz, I. M. (2004). Price knowledge: Effects of consumers attitudes towards prices, demographics, and socio-cultural characteristics. *Journal of Product and Brand Management, 13*(6), 406–428. doi:10.1108/10610420410560307

Rosas, A. J. (2010, June). Responsabilidad social empresarial: Hacia una agenda de investigación en México. *Administración y Organizaciones, 24*(12), 75–89.

Rossbach, H. (2013, August 2). *Exporteure stoßen zunehmend auf Hindernisse.* Retrieved from Frankfurter Allgemeine: http://www.faz.net/aktuell/wirtschaft/wirtschaftspolitik/aussenhandel-exporteure-stossen-zunehmend-auf-hindernisse-12315836.html

Rossow, R. M. (2015). *Corporate social responsibility in India. How the Companies Act may augment regional disparities.* Washington, DC: CSIS. Retrieved October 21, 2015, from http://csis.org/files/publication/150330_corpresponsibility.pdf

Rowley, J. (1997). Beyond service quality dimensions in higher education and towards a service contract. *Quality Assurance in Education, 5*(1), 7–14. doi:10.1108/09684889710156530

Rubin, N. (1986). It is the Season to be Greedy. *Parents, 61*, 134-137, 217, 222-226.

Rycroft, R. W. (2003). Technology-based Globalization Indicators: The Centrality of Innovation Network Data. *Technology in Society, 25*(3), 299–317. doi:10.1016/S0160-791X(03)00047-2

Saab, Jr., Correa, & Bowers. (2008). Optimising performance with distributor managed inventory in a FMCG supply chain. *International Journal of Business Excellence, 1*(1/2), 121-38.

Sabrina, N. (2005). Influence on consumer socialization. *Young Consumers: Insight and Ideas for Responsible Marketers, 6*(2), 63–69. doi:10.1108/17473610510701115

Saks, A. M. (2002, June/July). *So what is a good transfer of training estimate? A reply to Fitzpatrick.* Retrieved Mar 2, 2014, from https://www.siop.org/tip/backissues/tipjan02/pdf/393_%20029to030.pdf

Saks, A. M., & Ashforth, B. E. (1997). A longitudinal investigation of the relationships between job information sources, applicant perceptions of fit and work outcomes. *Personnel Psychology, 50*(2), 395–425. doi:10.1111/j.1744-6570.1997.tb00913.x

Saks, A. M., & Ashforth, B. E. (2002). Is job search related to employment quality? It all depends on fit. *The Journal of Applied Psychology, 87*(4), 646–654. doi:10.1037/0021-9010.87.4.646 PMID:12184569

Sally, M. (2013). *Increase in consumption of organic food products: ASSOCHAM Survey.* Retrieved on 22nd February 2014 from http://articles.economictimes.indiatimes.com/2013-05-23/news/39475623_1_organic-food-organic-products-organic-sector

Schein, E. (1978). *Career dynamics: Matching individual and organizational needs.* Reading, MA: Addison-Wesley.

Schiffman, L. G., & Kanuk, L. L. (2005). *Consumer Behavior* (8th ed.). PHI.

Schmidheiny, S. (2006, Spring). Turning Point. A View of Corporate Citizenship in Latin America. *Journal of Corporate Citizenship*, *21*(4), 21–24. doi:10.9774/GLEAF.4700.2006.sp.00004

Schniederjans, M. J., Schniederjans, D. G., & Starkey, C. M. (2014). *Business Analytics Principles, Concepts, and Applications: What, Why, and How?* Upper Saddle River, NJ: Pearson Education.

Sergio, R. (2010). Relational Consequences of Perceived Deception in Online Shopping: The Moderating Roles of Type of Product, Consumers Attitude toward the Internet and Consumers Demographics. *Journal of Business Ethics*, *95*(3), 373–391. doi:10.1007/s10551-010-0365-9

Shahin, A., & Jaferi, F. (2015, January). The shortest route for transportation in supply chain by minimum spanning tree. *International Journal of Logistics Systems and Management*, *22*(1), 43–54. doi:10.1504/IJLSM.2015.070893

Sheehan, M. (2012). Developing managerial talent: Exploring the link between management talent and perceived performance in multinational corporations (MNCs). *European Journal of Training and Development*, *36*(1), 66–85. doi:10.1108/03090591211192638

Sheth, J. N. (1979). The surpluses and shortages in consumer behavior theory and research. *Journal of the Academy of Marketing Science*, *7*(4), 414–427. doi:10.1007/BF02729689

Sheth, J. N. (2011). Impact of emerging markets on marketing: Rethinking existing perspectives and practices. *Journal of Marketing*, *75*(4), 166–182. doi:10.1509/jmkg.75.4.166

Sheth, J. N., & Sisodia, R. S. (1999). Revisiting marketings lawlike generalizations. *Journal of the Academy of Marketing Science*, *27*(1), 71–87. doi:10.1177/0092070399271006

Sibbel, A. (2009). Pathways towards sustainability through higher education. *International Journal of Sustainability in Higher Education*, *10*(1), 68–82. doi:10.1108/14676370910925262

Siegrist, J. (1996). Adverse health effects of high-effort/low-reward conditions. *Journal of Occupational Health Psychology*, *1*(1), 27–41. doi:10.1037/1076-8998.1.1.27 PMID:9547031

Simon, H. A. (1979). Information Processing Models of Cognition. *Annual Review of Psychology*, *30*(1), 363–396. doi:10.1146/annurev.ps.30.020179.002051 PMID:18331186

Simons, R. (2000). *Performance Measurement & Control Systems for Implementing Strategy: Text & Cases*. Upper Saddle River, NJ: Prentice Hall.

Singh, M. (2014). *10 biggest cyber-attacks of 2014*. BGR India. Retrieved on November 15, 2015, from http://www.bgr.in/news/10-biggest-cyber-attacks-of-2014/

Singh, A., & Sharma, J. (2015, July). Strategies for talent management: A study of select organizations in the UAE. *The International Journal of Organizational Analysis*, *23*(3), 337–347. doi:10.1108/IJOA-11-2014-0823

Singh, D. R., & Ahuja, J. M. (1983). Corporate social reporting in India. *The International Journal of Accounting*, *18*(8), 151–169.

Sirgy, J. M., Lee, D. J., Kosenko, R., Lee, H., & Rahtz, D. (1998). Does television Viewership Play a Role in The Perception of Quality of Life? *Journal of Advertising*, *27*(1), 125–142. doi:10.1080/00913367.1998.10673547

Sirieix, L., Delanchy, M., Remaud, H., Zepeda, L., & Gurviez, P. (2013). Consumers perceptions of individual and combined sustainable food labels: A UK pilot investigation. *International Journal of Consumer Studies*, *37*(2), 143–151. doi:10.1111/j.1470-6431.2012.01109.x

Sitalakshmi, V., & Indika, D. (2008). Biometrics in banking security: A case study. *Information Management & Computer Security, 16*(4), 415–430. doi:10.1108/09685220810908813

Smith, C. A., Organ, D. W., & Near, J. P. (1983). Organizational citizenship behavior: Its nature and antecedents. *The Journal of Applied Psychology, 68*(4), 653–663. doi:10.1037/0021-9010.68.4.653

Smith, G. E. (2000). Search at different price levels: The impact of knowledge and search cost. *Journal of Product and Brand Management, 19*(3), 164–178. doi:10.1108/10610420010332430

Smith, S., & Paladino, A. (2010). Eating clean and green? Investigating consumer motivations towards the purchase of organic food. *Australasian Marketing Journal, 18*(2), 93–104. doi:10.1016/j.ausmj.2010.01.001

Snider, J., Hill, R. P., & Martin, D. (2003). Corporate social responsibility in the 21st Century: A view from the worlds most successful firms. *Journal of Business Ethics, 48*(2), 175–187. doi:10.1023/B:BUSI.0000004606.29523.db

Solomon, J. (2007). *Corporate governance and accountability*. West Sussex, UK: John Wiley & Sons, Ltd.

Song, L. (2008). *Supply Chain Management with Demand Substitution* (PhD Thesis). University of Tennessee, Knoxville, TN.

Speakman, R. (1998). An Empirical investigation into Supply Chain Management: A perspective on partnerships. *International Journal of Physical Distribution & Logistics Management, 28*(8), 630–650.

Spector, P. E. (1985). Measurement of human service staff satisfaction: Development of the Job Satisfaction Survey. *American Journal of Community Psychology, 13*(6), 693–713. doi:10.1007/BF00929796 PMID:4083275

Spence, L., & Schmidpeter, R. (2003, June). SMEs, social capital and the common good. *Journal of Business Ethics, 45*(1), 93–108. doi:10.1023/A:1024176613469

Spokane, A. R. (1985). A review of research on person–environment congruence in Hollands theory of careers. *Journal of Vocational Behavior, 26*(3), 306–343. doi:10.1016/0001-8791(85)90009-0

Squires, L., Juric, B., & Cornwell, T. B. (2001). Level of market development and intensity of organic food consumption: Cross cultural study of Danish and New Zealand Consumers. *Journal of Consumer Marketing, 18*(5), 392–409. doi:10.1108/07363760110398754

Stanwick, P. A., & Stanwick, S. D. (1998, January). The relationship between corporate social performance, and organizational size, financial performance, and environmental performance: An empirical examination. *Journal of Business Ethics, 17*(2), 195–204. doi:10.1023/A:1005784421547

Steenkamp, J. E., Hofstede, F., & Wedel, M. (1999). A cross-national investigation into the individual and national cultural antecedents of consumer innovativeness. *Journal of Marketing, 63*(2), 55–69. doi:10.2307/1251945

Steiner, G. A. (1975). *Business and Society*. New York: Random House.

Stern, H. (1962). The significance of impulse buying today. *Journal of Marketing, 26*(2), 59–62. doi:10.2307/1248439

Stock, K. (2015). *Forget InBev. Here are the markets where local beers rule*. Retrieved from http://www.bloomberg.com/news/articles/2015-10-12/forget-inbev-and-sabmiller-here-are-the-markets-where-local-beers-rule

Strack, F., & Deutsch, R. (2006). Reflective and impulsive determinants of consumer behavior. *Journal of Consumer Psychology, 16*(3), 205–216. doi:10.1207/s15327663jcp1603_2

Suh, B., & Han, I. (2002). Effect of trust on customer acceptance of Internet banking. *Electronic Commerce Research and Applications, 1*(3-4), 247–263. doi:10.1016/S1567-4223(02)00017-0

Suhong, L. (2004). The impact of supply chain management practices on competitive advantage and organizational performance. *International Journal of Management Sciences, 11*, 112–119.

Sullivan, R. J. (2000). *How Has the Adoption of Internet Banking Affected Performance and Risk in Banks? A Look at Internet Banking in the Tenth Federal Reserve District*. Financial Industry Perspective, Federal Reserve Bank of Kansas City, Occasional Papers.

Sullivan, R. J., & Zhu, W. (2005). *Internet Banking: An Exploration in Technology Diffusion and Impact*. Federal Reserve Bank of Kansas City, Payments System Research Working Paper # PSR-WP-05-05.

Sun, L. Y., & Pan, W. (2011). Market Orientation, Intrapreneurship Behavior, and Organizational Performance: Test of a Structural Contingency Model. *Journal of Leadership & Organizational Studies, 18*(2), 274–285. doi:10.1177/1548051809334189

Suresh, M., & Shashikala, R. (2011). Identifying Factors of consumer Perceived Risk towards Online Shopping in India. *3rd International Conference on Information and Financial Engineering*. IPEDR.

Svensson, G. (2002). Beyond Global Marketing and the Globalization of Marketing Activities. *Management Decision, 40*(6), 574–583. doi:10.1108/00251740210433963

Swenson, D. L. (2012). The influence of Chinese trade policy on automobile assembly and parts. *CESifo Economic Studies, 58*(4), 703-730.

Tabachnick, B. G., & Fidell, L. S. (2001). *Using multivariate statistics*. Academic Press.

Taher, A., & Basha, H. E. (2006). Heterogeneity of consumer demand: Opportunities for pricing of services. *Journal of Product and Brand Management, 15*(5), 331–340. doi:10.1108/10610420610685884

Tang, R. (2009, November 16). *The Rise of China's Auto Industry and Its Impact on the U.S. Motor Vehicle Industry*. Retrieved from Federation Of American Scientists: http://fas.org/sgp/crs/row/R40924.pdf

Tapan, M. (1981). Some Results on the Optimal Depletion of Exhaustible Resources Under Negative Discounting. *The Review of Economic Studies, 48*(4).

Tata Consultancy Services. (2015). *Retail Operations Benchmarking and Excellence Survey 2015, Measuring Supply Chain Performance*. Available at httpwww.tcs.com/SiteCollectionDocuments/White%20Papers/Retail-Operations-BenchmarkingExcellence-Survey-Measuring-Supply-Chain-Performance-0215-1.pdf

Taylor, S., & Todd, P. A. (1995). Assessing IT usage: The role of prior experience. *Management Information Systems Quarterly, 19*(4), 561–570. doi:10.2307/249633

Technopak. (2012). *Organic Food Market in India*. Retrieved on 22nd February 2014 fromhttp://www.globalorganictrade.com/files/market_reports/OTA_India_Market_Report_2012.pdf

Tett, R. P., & Meyer, J. P. (1993). Job satisfaction, organizational commitment, turnover intention, and turnover: Path analysis based on meta-analytic findings. *Personnel Psychology, 46*(2), 259–293. doi:10.1111/j.1744-6570.1993.tb00874.x

Thakur, R., & Srivastava, M. (2013). Customer usage intention of mobile commerce in India: An empirical study. *Journal of Indian Business Research, 5*(1), 52–72. doi:10.1108/17554191311303385

The Economic Times. (2012). *India's organic food market growing at over 20%*. Retrieved on 22nd February 2014 from http://articles.economictimes.indiatimes.com/2012-08-23/news/33342399_1_organic-food-organic-cotton-chemical-free-food

The Economist. (2007, February 22). *The big-car problem*. Retrieved from The Economist: http://www.economist.com/node/8738865

The World Bank. (2015, March 25). *Overview*. Retrieved from The World Bank: http://www.worldbank.org/en/country/china/overview

Thogersen, J., & Olander, F. (2003). Spillover of environment-friendly consumer behaviour. *Journal of Environmental Psychology, 23*(3), 225–236. doi:10.1016/S0272-4944(03)00018-5

Thøgersen, J., & Olander, F. (2006). The dynamic interaction of personal norms and environment-friendly buying behavior: A panel study. *Journal of Applied Social Psychology, 36*(7), 1758–1780. doi:10.1111/j.0021-9029.2006.00080.x

Times of India. (n.d.). *India wastes 21 million tonnes of wheat every year: Report*. Available at http://timesofindia.indiatimes.com/india/India-wastes-21-million-tonnes-of-wheat-every-year-Report/articleshow/17969340.cms

Truss, S. C., Edwards, E., Wisdom, C., Croll, K., & Burnett, J. (2006). *Working Life: Employee Attitudes and Engagement*. London: CIPD.

Tsakiridou, E., Boutsouki, C., Zotos, Y., & Mattas, K. (2008). Attitudes and behaviour towards organic products: An exploratory study. *International Journal of Retail & Distribution Management, 36*(2), 158–175. doi:10.1108/09590550810853093

TSX. (2006). *Corporate governance. A guide to good disclosure*. Toronto: Toronto Stock Exchange. Retrieved August 22, 2015, from http://www.ecgi.org/codes/documents/tsx_gtgd.pdf

Tucker, W. T. (1964). The Development of Brand Loyalty. *JMR, Journal of Marketing Research, 1*(3), 32–35. doi:10.2307/3150053

Tung, S., Tsay, J. C., & Lin, M. (2015). Life course, diet-related identity and consumer choice of organic food in taiwan. *British Food Journal, 117*(2), 688–704. doi:10.1108/BFJ-11-2013-0334

UBL. (2015). *About Us-UBL at a Glance*. Retrieved from http://124.153.77.59/ubl_glance.aspx

Ulf, J., Maria, M., & Matti, S. (2001). Measuring to Understand intangible Performance Drivers. *European Accounting Review, 10*(3), 407–437. doi:10.1080/09638180126791

UN Global Compact. (2013). *Participants and Stakeholders*. Retrieved November 13, 2013, from UN Global Compact Participants: http://www.unglobalcompact.org/ParticipantsAndStakeholders/index.html

UN. (2006). *Guidance on good practices in corporate governance disclosure*. Geneva: United Nations Conference on Trade and Development. Retrieved August 23, 2015, from http://unctad.org/en/docs/iteteb20063_en.pdf

UN. (2007). *CSR and Developing Countries. What scope for government action?* New York: Sustainable Development Innovation Briefs. Retrieved October 20, 2015, from https://sustainabledevelopment.un.org/content/documents/no1.pdf

UNCTAD. (2008). *Guidance on corporate responsibility indicators in annual reports*. New York: United Nations Publication.

Utting, P. (2005). Corporate responsibility and the movement of business. *Development in Practice, 15*(3&4), 380–386.

Vahtera, J., Pentti, J., & Uutela, A. (1996). The effect of objective job demands on registered sickness absence spells: Do personal, social and job-related resources act as moderators? *Work and Stress, 10*(4), 286–308. doi:10.1080/02678379608256809

Van der Vorst, J. G. A. J. (2000). *Effective food supply chains: Generating, modeling and evaluating supply chain scenarios*. Proefschrift Wageningen.

Van Hoek, R. (1998). Measuring the measurable-measuring and improving performance in supply chain. *Supply Chain Management, 3*(4), 187–192. doi:10.1108/13598549810244232

Van Raaij, W. F., Strazzieri, A., & Woodside, A. (2001). New developments in marketing communications and consumer behavior. *Journal of Business Research, 53*(2), 59–61. doi:10.1016/S0148-2963(99)00075-2

VDA. (n.d.). *Importance of trade policy for industry and for Germany as an industrial location*. Retrieved from Verband der Automobilindustrie: https://www.vda.de/en/topics/economic-policy-and-infrastructure/trade/importance-of-trade-policy-for-industry-and-for-germany-as-an-industrial-location

Venkatesh, M., Morris, G., & Davis, F. D. (2003). User acceptance of information technology: Toward a unified view. *Management Information Systems Quarterly, 27*(3), 425–478.

Venkatesh, V. (2000). Determinants of perceived ease of use: Integrating control, intrinsic motivation, and emotion into the technology acceptance model. *Information Systems Research, 11*(4), 342–365. doi:10.1287/isre.11.4.342.11872

Venkatesh, V., & Davis, F. D. (1996). A model of antecedents of perceived ease of use: Development and test. *Decision Sciences, 27*(3), 451–481. doi:10.1111/j.1540-5915.1996.tb01822.x

Venkatesh, V., & Davis, F. D. (2000). A theoretical extension of the technology acceptance model: Four longitudinal field studies. *Management Science, 46*(2), 186–204. doi:10.1287/mnsc.46.2.186.11926

Venkatesh, V., & Morris, M. G. (2000). Why Dont Men Ever Stop to Ask for Directions? Gender, Social Influence, and Their Role in Technology Accptance and Usage Behavior. *Management Information Systems Quarterly, 24*(1), 115–139. doi:10.2307/3250981

Venkatraman, N., & Ramanuja, V. (1986, July/October). Measurement of business performance in strategy research: A comparison of approaches. *Academy of Management Review, 11*(4).

Verghees, B. J. (2014). *Cyber Security, A Growing CIO Priority*. Bangaluru, India: Wipro Ltd.

Verma, R., & Rajagopal, . (2013). Conceptualizing service innovation architecture: A service – strategic framework. *Journal of Transnational Management, 18*(1), 3–22. doi:10.1080/15475778.2013.751869

Verplanken, B., & Herabadi, A. (2001). Individual differences in impulse buying tendency: Feeling and no thinking. *European Journal of Personality, 15*(1), 71–83. doi:10.1002/per.423

Verville, J., Taskin, N., & Law, S. (2011, January). Buyer-supplier relationships in supply chain management: Relationship, trust, supplier involvement, and performance. *International Journal of Agile Systems and Management, 4*(3), 203–221. doi:10.1504/IJASM.2011.040515

Viaene, S., & Van den Bunder, A. (2011). The Secrets to Managing Business Analytics Projects, *MIT. Sloan Management Review, 53*(1), 64–70.

Virgin. (2011). *The psychology of impulse purchase*. Retrieved from http://www.virgin.com/entrepreneur/psychology-impulse-purchase

Vohs, K. D., & Faber, R. J. (2007). Spent resources: Self-regulatory resource availability affects impulse buying. *The Journal of Consumer Research, 33*(4), 537–547. doi:10.1086/510228

Voon, B. H. (2006). Linking a service-driven market orientation to service quality. *Managing Service Quality, 16*(6), 595–619. doi:10.1108/09604520610711927

Wackman, G. B., Reale, G., & Ward, S. (1972). Racial Differences in Responses to Advertising among Adolescents. In *Television in Day-to-Day Life*. Rockville, MD: U.S. Department of Health, Education and Welfare.

Walker, O. C. Jr, Churchill, G. A. Jr, & Ford, N. M. (1975). Organizational determinants of the industrial salesmens role conflict and ambiguity. *Journal of Marketing, 39*(1), 32–39. doi:10.2307/1250800

Wangpipatwong, S., Chutimaskul, W., & Papasratorn, B. (2008). Understanding Citizen's Continuance Intention to Use e-Government Website: A Composite View of Technology Acceptance Model and Computer Self-Efficacy. *The Electronic Journal of E-Government*, *6*(1), 55–64.

Ward, S., & Wackman, D. (1971). Family and Media Influences on Adolescent Consumer Learning. *American Behavioral Scientist*, *14*, 415-427.

Ward, M. J., Marsolo, K. A., & Froehle, C. M. (2014). Applications of business analytics in healthcare. *Business Horizons*, *57*(5), 571–582. doi:10.1016/j.bushor.2014.06.003 PMID:25429161

WBCSD. (2013). *Membership*. Retrieved November 13, 2013, from World business council for sustainable development: http://www.wbcsd.org/about/members/members-list-region.aspx

Weinberg, P., & Gottwald, W. (1982). Impulsive consumer buying as a result of emotions. *Journal of Business Research*, *10*(1), 43–57. doi:10.1016/0148-2963(82)90016-9

Wei, T., Marthandan, G., Chong, A., Ooi, K., & Arumugam, S. (2009). What drives Malaysian m-commerce adoption? An empirical analysis. *Industrial Management & Data Systems*, *109*(3), 370–388. doi:10.1108/02635570910939399

Wen-Chia, T. (2012). A study of consumer behavioral intention to use e-books: The Technology Acceptance Model perspective. *Innovative Marketing*, *8*(4), 55–66.

Werbel, J. D., & Johnson, D. J. (2001). The use of person–group fit for employment selection: A missing link in person–environment fit. *Human Resource Management*, *40*(3), 227–240. doi:10.1002/hrm.1013

Wernerfelt, B. (1984). A resource-based view of the firm. *Strategic Management Journal*, *5*(2), 171–180. doi:10.1002/smj.4250050207

Wernerfelt, B. (2014). On the role of the RBV in marketing. *Journal of the Academy of Marketing Science*, *42*(1), 22–23. doi:10.1007/s11747-013-0335-8

Weun, S., Jones, M. A., & Beatty, S. E. (1998). Development and validation of the impulse buying tendency scale. *Psychological Reports*, *82*(3c), 1123–1133. doi:10.2466/pr0.1998.82.3c.1123 PMID:9709520

Wind, Y. (1986). The Myth of Globalization. *Journal of Consumer Marketing*, *3*(2), 23–26. doi:10.1108/eb008160

Wolfe, D. A. (2000). Globalization, Information and Communication Technologies and Local and Regional Systems of Innovation. In Transition to the knowledge society: Public policies and private strategies. Vancouver: UBC Press.

Wood, M. (1998). Socio-economic status, delay of gratification, and impulse buying. *Journal of Economic Psychology*, *19*(3), 295–320. doi:10.1016/S0167-4870(98)00009-9

World Bank (WB). (n.d.). *World Development Indicators*. Retrieved from http://data.worldbank.org/data-catalog/world-development-indicators

World Bank. (2015). Retrieved September 14, 2015, from World Bank http://data.worldbank.org/

World Trade Organization (WTO). (2011). *Composition, definitions & methodology*. Available at: https://www.wto.org/english/res_e/statis_e/its2011_e/its11_metadata_e.pdf

World Trade Organization (WTO). (n.d.). *Trade in Commercial Services Trade*. Retrieved from http://www.wto.org/

Wu, J., Li, J., Chen, J., Zhao, Y., & Wang, S. (2011, January). Risk management in supply chains. *International Journal of Revenue Management*, *5*(2-3), 157–204. doi:10.1504/IJRM.2011.040307

Xiaoni, Z., Prybutok, V. R., & Strutton, D. (2007). Modelling influences on impulse purchasing behaviours during the online marketing transactions. *Journal of Marketing Theory and Practice, 15*(1), 79–89. doi:10.2753/MTP1069-6679150106

Xiao, S. H., & Nicholson, M. (2011). Mapping impulse buying: A behaviour analysis framework for services marketing and consumer research. *Service Industries Journal, 31*(15), 2515–2528. doi:10.1080/02642069.2011.531123

Xueming, L., & Bhattacharya, C. B. (2006, October). Corporate social responsibility, customer satisfaction, and market value. *Journal of Marketing, 70*(4), 1–18. doi:10.1509/jmkg.70.4.1

Yaghoubi & Bahmani. (2010). Factors Affecting the Adoption of Online Banking An Integration of Technology Acceptance Model and Theory of Planned Behavior. *International Journal of Business and Management, 5*(9), 159–165.

Yao, H., & Zhong, C. (2011). The analysis of influencing factors and promotion strategy for the use of mobile banking. *Canadian Social Science, 7*(2), 60–63.

Youn, S. H. (2000). *The Dimensional Structure of Consumer Buying Impulsivity: Measurement and Validation* (Doctoral Dissertation). The Graduate School of The University of Minnesota.

Yu, J., Ha, I., Choi, M., & Rho, J. (2005). Extending the TAM for a t-commerce. *Information & Management, 42*(77), 965–976. doi:10.1016/j.im.2004.11.001

Zabkar, V., & Hosta, M. (2013). Willingness to act and environmentally conscious consumer behaviour: Can pro-social status perceptions help overcome the gap? *International Journal of Consumer Studies, 37*(3), 257–264. doi:10.1111/j.1470-6431.2012.01134.x

Zakowska-Biemans, S. (2011). Polish consumer food choices and beliefs about organic food. *British Food Journal, 113*(1), 122–137. doi:10.1108/00070701111097385

Zeithaml, V., Berry, L., & Parasuraman, A. (1988). Communication and Control Process the Delivery of Services Quality. *Journal of Marketing, 52*(2), 35–48. doi:10.2307/1251263

Zerban, A. (2013). The need for social and environmental accounting standard: Can Islamic countries have the lead? *Eurasian Journal of Business and Management, 1*(2), 33–43.

Zhang, J., Beatty, S. E., & Walsh, G. (2008). Review and future directions of cross-cultural consumer services research. *Journal of Business Research, 61*(3), 211–224. doi:10.1016/j.jbusres.2007.06.003

Zhiwei, Z., & Larry, S. (2004). Information network technology in the banking industry. *Industrial Management & Data Systems, 104*(5), 409–417. doi:10.1108/02635570410537499

Zhou, L., & Wong, A. (2003). Consumer impulse buying and in-store stimuli in Chinese supermarkets. *Journal of International Consumer Marketing, 16*(2), 37–53. doi:10.1300/J046v16n02_03

Zhu, W. (2005). *Technology Innovation and Market Turbulence: A Dot com Example*. Federal Reserve Bank of Kansas City, Payments System Research Working Paper # PSR-WP-05-02.

Zhu, D.-S., Lin, T. C.-T., & Hsu, Y.-C. (2012). Using the technology acceptance model to evaluate user attitude and intention of use for online games. *Total Quality Management, 23*(8), 965–980. doi:10.1080/14783363.2012.704269

Zhu, Y. Q., & Chen, H. G. (2012). Service Fairness and Customer Satisfaction in Internet Banking: Exploring the Mediating Effects of Trust and Customer Value. *Internet Research, 22*(4), 482–498. doi:10.1108/10662241211251006

About the Contributors

Rajagopal is Professor of Marketing at EGADE Business School of Tecnologico de Monterrey, Mexico City Campus and Life Fellow of the Royal Society for Encouragement of Arts, Manufacture and Commerce, London. He is also Fellow of the Chartered Management Institute, and Fellow of Institute of Operations Management, United Kingdom. He is also Visiting Professor at Boston University, Boston, Massachusetts. He has been listed with biography in various international directories. He offers courses on Competitor Analysis, Marketing Strategy, Advance Selling Systems, International Marketing, Services Marketing, New Product Development, and other subjects of contemporary interest to the students of undergraduate, graduate, and doctoral programs. Dr. Rajagopal holds Post-graduate and doctoral degrees in Economics and Marketing respectively from Ravishankar University in India. His specialization is in the fields of Marketing Management. He has to his credit 50 books on marketing management and rural development themes and over 400 research contributions that include published research papers in national and international refereed journals. He is Editor-in-Chief of International Journal of Leisure and Tourism Marketing, International Journal of Business Competition and Growth, and International Journal of Built Environment and Asset Management. Dr. Rajagopal is also Regional Editor of Emerald Emerging Markets Case Studies, published by Emerald Publishers, United Kingdom. He is on the editorial board of various journals of international repute. His research contributions have been recognized by the National Council of Science and Technology (CONACyT), Government of Mexico by awarding him the highest level of National Researcher-SNI Level- III in 2013.

Ramesh Behl is the Director and Professor of Information Systems at International Management Institute. His teaching expertise includes Information Technology based Decision Making, E-Business, Information Systems Management, Business Intelligence, Enterprise Systems, and Customer Relationship Management. In addition to teaching, Ramesh is an active researcher in the area of e-Business and Information Systems Management. He has also designed and developed number of software for various industry applications. Ramesh is a United Nations fellow on Information Systems & International Operations and SAP Certified Consultant. He is an international accredited professor of International Accreditation Organization (IAO), USA. Professor Behl has over twenty-nine years of teaching, research and consulting experience in the area of Information Technology and E-Business. He has worked with Indian Institute of Foreign Trade, New Delhi, and Indian Institute of Management, Lucknow and Statesman New Delhi, and has worked on various research and consulting assignments for government and private organizations. Professor Behl has authored eighteen books, fifteen case studies and more than 45 research papers of National and International Repute. He has conducted training and delivered lectures to the faculty and students of various International universities in Singapore, Indonesia, Hong Kong,

Australia, China, Germany and Thailand. He has been awarded "Outstanding Academic Award 2010" from SAP, and South East Asia, Japan and "Best Professor in Information Technology" as part of Asia's Best B-School Awards presented at Singapore in July, 2011.

* * *

Siddhartha Bhattacharyya is currently Professor and Head of Information Technology of RCC Institute of Information Technology, Kolkata, India. He is also the Dean (Research & Development) of the institute from November 2013. Dr. Bhattacharyya has two Bachelor's degrees in Physics, and Optics and Optoelectronics. He obtained Master's degree in Optics and Optoelectronics from University of Calcutta, India. He completed PhD in Computer Science and Engineering from Jadavpur University, India in 2008. He is the co-author of 3 books and co-editor of 5 books and published more than 135 research papers.

Natasha Patricia Bojorges Moctezuma is a Doctoral Scholar of Management Science at EGADE Business School, Tecnológico de Monterrey. She is also a member of the research group of Consumer Behaviour of the school. She has published a few research papers and participated in international conferences by contributing papers.

Raquel Castaño is professor of Marketing and Consumer Behavior at EGADE Business School, Tecnologico de Monterrey. She received her Ph.D degree and a master´s degree in Management from Tulane University. She also obtained a master´s degree in Marketing from EGADE Business School. Professor Castaño's research focuses on the roles of emotion and cognition in decision making. Examples of this research include the role of temporal distance and mental simulation in the adoption of new products. Dr. Castaño´s research has been published in the Journal of Marketing Research; Journal of Consumer Psychology and Marketing Letters among others.

Bindu Chhabra is working as an Associate Professor at International Management Institute, Bhubaneswar. She holds a PhD in Psychology from Guru Nanak Dev University, India. She has an academic experience of over 18 years. Her areas of research interest include personality, work attitudes, stress management, emotional intelligence and leadership. She has published various research papers in national and international journals. She has undertaken various Management Development Programs with the organizations Indian Public Sector and government organization including Ministry of Social Defense, Government of India. She is the recipient of National Education Leadership Award for Best Teacher in Human Resource Management.

Ajitabh Dash is an Assistant Professor at the Regional college of Management, Bhubaneswar, Odisha, India. He has received his Master degree in Business Administration from the Fakir Mohan University in 2008 and his PhD in Management from the same university in 2012. His areas of specialization are consumer behavior, bottom of pyramid marketing, marketing research and international marketing. His research interests include electronic commerce, marketing, quantitative analysis, and managerial issues of emerging technologies. He has published several articles in many reputed journals.

Ruchika Gupta is Associate Professor at Amity Business School, Amity University, Greater Noida, India. She holds MSc in Computer Science and a PhD in Management Information Systems. In her career of over 12 years she has held multiple responsibilities as a teacher, trainer, mentor, and administrator. She has organized conferences, seminars, and workshops and is serving as Reviewer, Advisory Board member and Editor of several Journals. She has published business cases and research papers in national and international journals and has 26 copyrights to her credit. Her research areas include Information System, Information Technology and Cyber Security.

Pierre Haddad holds a Master's degree in Innovation and Technology from Boston University and a Master's degree in International Business from the Paris School of Business. Pierre also studied as an exchange student at the University of Mississippi and James Cook University Singapore. He has experienced several internships, in different countries (United Arab Emirates, Senegal, Mexico, France), in the hotel industry and banking industry in the fields of communication, marketing, finance and business development.

Saerom Jang holds a Bachelor of Arts in Theology, Christian Culture, from Anyang University in South Korea. She worked at two Korean fashion companies as a sales associate and a sales division manager, as well as with a Korean trading company, Jinsung Eurotec Co., LTD., as an operations manager before pursuing an M.S. in Multinational Commerce at Boston University. Currently, she is completing her last semester at Boston University and will graduate in May of 2016.

Arpita Khare is a Faculty at Indian Institute of Management- Rohtak, Haryana. She has a MBA degree in Marketing and D. Phil in International Management from University of Allahabad. With over eighteen years of academic and research experience, her research interests span over consumer behaviour, retailing, services marketing and supply chain management. She has authored quite a few research papers in international and national journals.

Andrée Marie López-Fernández is currently a full-time Professor and Researcher at the School of Economics and Business (ECEE) at the Universidad Panamericana. She has received a Bachelor's degree in Business Management from the Tecnologico de Monterrey, Mexico City Campus, and obtained the Doctoral Degree in Administrative Sciences from the EGADE Business School Mexico City. Her research areas of interest include corporate social responsibility, marketing strategy, strategic marketing and consumer behaviour.

Raju Mandal is Assistant Professor of Economics at Assam University, Silchar, India. His research interests include economics of natural resources and environment, climate change and agricultural issues, climate change and crime, and economics of social sector. He has published research papers in refereed journals like Economic Analysis and Policy, Economic and Political Weekly, Indian Journal of Human Development, and Indian Journal of Agricultural Economics. He earned his PhD in Economics from Gauhati University, Assam, India. He was awarded the Raman Fellowship by the University Grants Commission, Government of India, to conduct his post-doctoral research at Sam Houston State University, Texas, USA.

Bhimaraya Metri is Dean (Academic) and Professor of operations management at International Management Institute (IMI) New Delhi, India. Prior to this, he has held positions of Dean (Academic), Dean (Graduate Program), Program Chairs at Management Development Institute, Gurugram, India, and Coordinator of Doctoral Program at Birla Institute of Technology and Science, Pilani, India. He has extensively published in national, international journals, edited books and proceedings. He has edited two books and written various book chapters. He has obtained PhD from Indian Institute of Technology (IIT), Bombay, Mumbai, India. Currently, he is the President, Indian Subcontinent, Decision Sciences Institute (DSI), Atlanta, USA. He teaches and conducts research in supply chain management, quality management and project management.

Manit Mishra, PhD, is Associate Professor (Marketing & Quantitative Techniques) at International Management Institute (IMI), Bhubaneswar, India. His teaching expertise includes Marketing Research, Business Analytics, Consumer Behavior, and Retail Management. His areas of research interest are hedonic consumption behavior modeling and methodological research. He has co-authored a book entitled "Retail Marketing" and published research papers in Journal of Retailing and Consumer Services, Asian Case Research Journal, Indian Journal of Marketing, IUP Journal of Marketing Management and IUP Journal of Management Research. He is actively involved in conducting training sessions in multivariate data analysis and structural equation modeling.

Pravat Kumar Mohanty is a Retd. Professor, Department of Business Management, Utkal University, Bhubaneswar, India.

Sandeep Kumar Mohanty is an assistant professor of marketing in Birla Global University, Odisha, India. He has done MA English and MBA in marketing specialization from the prestigious Utkal University and he has completed his PhD from Vinod Gupta School of Management, IIT Kharagpur. He has more than nine years of teaching and research experience in the field of marketing. His area of interests cover social marketing, cross cultural communication, advertisement and branding. He has taught students of both under graduation level and post-graduation level while working with four prestigious organizations in his life time.

Snigdha Mohapatra is currently working as Asst. Professor, Birla Institute of Management and Technology, in the area of Psychology and Organizational Behavior. Her areas of research interest are Employee engagement, training effectiveness and emotional intelligence. She holds PhD degree in Business Administration in the area of training and development. She holds M. Phil and Master's Degree in Psychology from Utkal University, Odisha. She has over 10 years of teaching experience and 4 years research experience. She has published several research papers in refereed peer-reviewed Journals such as Indian Journal of research, ISTD, International Journal of Development and Social Research and HRM Review. She has also presented several research papers at International and National seminars.

Hiranya K. Nath is Professor of Economics at Sam Houston State University, Huntsville, Texas (USA). His research interests include inflation and relative price behavior, information economy, and various issues related to developing and transition economies. Dr. Nath has published in highly regarded peer-reviewed journals like Applied Economics, California Management Review, Comparative Economic Studies, Economic Analysis and Policy, Economic Record, Economics Letters, Empirical Economics, Emerging Markets Finance & Trade, Journal of Asian Economics, Journal of International Trade & Economic Development, Journal of Macroeconomics, Journal of Money, Credit and Banking, and Review of Development Economics. He earned his Ph.D. in Economics from Southern Methodist University, Dallas (USA).

Sandra Nuñez is a doctoral scholar at EGADE Business School, Tecnológico de Monterrey in Mexico. Her research interests are focused on consumer behavior and branding, especially topics related to consumer-brand relationships, counterfeits and innovation. She has obtained Master's degree in Marketing Communications (2006) from the Illinois Institute of Technology and MBA in 2007 as well as a B.S. in Chemical Engineering (2003) from Tecnológico de Monterrey, Mexico.

Ramakrushna Panigrahi is Associate Professor in the area of Economics at International Management Institute, Bhubaneswar, India. He obtained Ph. D in the area of Environmental Economics and M. Phil in Agricultural Economics. His research is primarily in the area of development economics. He has published a number of research papers in the journals like 'Journal of International Development' and 'Journal of Human Development'. He has authored business cases including 'Maruti India Suzuki Limited: Sustaining Profitability', published by IVEY is widely used to teach managerial economics course. His teaching interests include Managerial Economics, Macroeconomics, International Business and Geopolitics.

Gazal Punyani is a Full-time Research Scholar at College of Business Management, Economics and Commerce, Mody University, Lakshmangarh, Rajasthan (2013-Present). Her research title is: "An Analysis of Information Technology Adoption and Evaluation of E-service Quality with special reference to Public, Private and Foreign banks in Rajasthan". Her main research interests are Banking Technology, E-service Quality and Marketing. Before entering in field of research, she studied Master of Business Administration (MBA) from Sikkim Manipal University and Bachelors of Business Administration (BBA) from JVWU, Jaipur.

Ananya Rajagopal is an Industrial and Systems Engineering from Tecnologico de Monterrey, Mexico City Campus. She has been working with commercial banking division at HSBC Corporate Office, Mexico City since 2006. She has published several papers in international journals of repute and contributed research works in international conferences and edited books.

Jhuma Ray is currently working as an Assistant Professor in the Department of Engineering Science and Management and is the former Head of the Department of Basic Science & Humanities of RCC Institute of Information Technology, Kolkata, India. She In addition, she is acting as a Nodal Officer of Equity Assurance Plan Committee under TEQIP-II (Technical Education Quality Improvement Program), World Bank funded Project She did her Bachelors from University of Calcutta, and MBA in Finance from F.M. University, India. She has several research publications in international journals and conference proceedings to her credit. She has also authored chapters in books published by reputed publishers. Her research interests include Portfolio management and Risk Optimization procedures.

Melissa Renneckendorf holds a MSc in Administrative Studies with a concentration in Innovation & Technology from Boston University, USA and a MA in International Business from Munich Business School, Germany with a focus in International Entrepreneurship and Marketing. She has completed multiple internships in the automotive, transportation and travel industry, before and during her studies. These positions allowed her to gain practical experience in purchasing, marketing, logistics, and controlling.

Pável Reyes-Mercado obtained PhD in Management Science from EGADE Business School, Tecnologico de Monterrey, Mexico City in 2015. His professional experience includes holding positions at Alcatel, Coca Cola Femsa Company and HSBC Bank. Currently, he is serving as professor in Anáhuac University, Mexico City and teaches in courses on marketing topics at graduate and undergraduate level. His research interests include adoption of innovations, technology-enabled marketing, and online consumer behavior.

Alexander Schuelke holds a MSc in Administrative Studies with a concentration in Innovation & Technology from Boston University, USA and a MA in International Business from Munich Business School, Germany. During his studies, Alexander gained practical experience in telco, insurance, and B2B industries and worked at multinational corporations in the fields of strategy, marketing, and business development. He currently lives in Munich and works as a Junior Consultant at UNITY AG, a management consultancy for future-oriented corporate management.

Sourabh Sharma is an Associate Professor for Information Systems at International Management Institute (IMI), Bhubaneshwar. He is an eminent Management Consultant, outstanding Professional Practitioner, Trainer, Academician and Educationist Counselor in Management, has been associated with Management Education and Industrial practitioner for over a decade now. He is expertise in the areas of Management Information System, Database Management System, Software Project Management, Data warehousing & Mining and many different Programming languages. He has also given his consultancy to Union Bank, Ujjain to convert their pension management software from Foxpro to Visual Basic. He started his career with Reliance Communications as a database consultant and served there for four years. Since last 11 years he is in management consultancy and teaching.

Ajit Pal Singh is an Assistant Professor at College of Engineering, Defence University, Bishoftu, Ethiopia. He is B.Tech. (Industrial Engineering) from NIT, Jalandhar and M.Tech from IIT, Delhi. He is pursuing Ph.D. on Project Management. He has more than 15 years of teaching experience with contribution of many papers to the international conferences, seminars and journals of national and international repute. His area of specializations includes Operations Management, Project Management and Production Management.

Rajwinder Singh is a graduate (Mech. Engg.) from Thapar University, Patiala, Masters in Business Administration from Punjabi University, Patiala and Ph.D. from Guru Nanak Dev University, Amritsar. He has also qualified Six-Sigma Green Belt from KPMG, Certificate in Project Management and Master Teachers Program from Indian School of Business, Hyderabad. He has completed 4 research projects and contributed 21 research papers in the leading international journals and 41 papers in various conferences/seminars at the national and international levels and contributed many chapters in books. He held the several academic and administrative responsibilities so far his career and served as Member Board of Studies. He is member of various academic societies. His area of research is Operations, projects and Quantitative Management.

Siddharth Varma is Professor at IMI, Delhi in the area of Operations & Quantitative Methods. A Mechanical Engineer from the erstwhile University of Roorkee and M. Tech from IIT, Delhi he holds an MBA from AIT, Bangkok and a Ph.D from IIT, Delhi. After working 13 years in the industry he shifted to academics in the year 2000. He was Associate Professor at IMT, Ghaziabad and subsequently became Director (NCR Centre) at University of Petroleum & Energy Studies (UPES). He has presented papers in conferences and published papers in national as well as international journals. His areas of interest are Operations Management, Supply Chain Management and Project Management.

Index

Recommended Reference Books

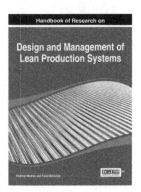

ISBN: 978-1-4666-5039-8
© 2014; 487 pp.
List Price: $260

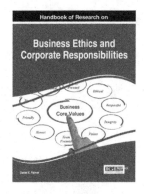

ISBN: 978-1-4666-7476-9
© 2015; 508 pp.
List Price: $212

ISBN: 978-1-4666-6182-0
© 2014; 325 pp.
List Price: $180

ISBN: 978-1-4666-4474-8
© 2014; 735 pp.
List Price: $276

ISBN: 978-1-4666-5950-6
© 2014; 290 pp.
List Price: $156

ISBN: 978-1-4666-6595-8
© 2015; 406 pp.
List Price: $156

Publishing Information Science and Technology Research Since 1988

Support Your Colleagues and Stay Current on the Latest Research Developments
Become a Reviewer

In this competitive age of scholarly publishing, constructive and timely feedback significantly decreases the turn-around time of manuscripts from submission to acceptance, allowing the publication and discovery of progressive research at a much more expeditious rate.

The overall success of a refereed journal is dependent on quality and timely reviews.

Several IGI Global journals are currently seeking highly qualified experts in the field to fill vacancies on their respective editorial review boards. Reviewing manuscripts allows you to stay current on the latest developments in your field of research, while at the same time providing constructive feedback to your peers.

Reviewers are expected to write reviews in a timely, collegial, and constructive manner. All reviewers will begin their role on an ad-hoc basis for a period of one year, and upon successful completion of this term can be considered for full editorial review board status, with the potential for a subsequent promotion to Associate Editor.

Join this elite group by visiting the IGI Global journal webpage, and clicking on "**Become a Reviewer**".

Applications may also be submitted online at:
www.igi-global.com/journals/become-a-reviewer/.

Applicants must have a doctorate (or an equivalent degree) as well as publishing and reviewing experience.

If you have a colleague that may be interested in this opportunity, we encourage you to share this information with them.

Any questions regarding this opportunity can be sent to:
journaleditor@igi-global.com.

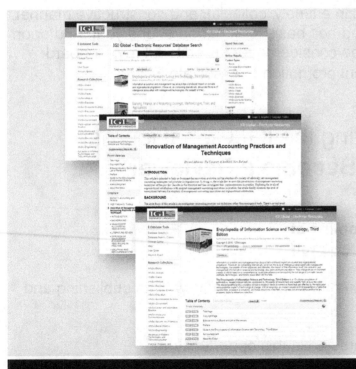